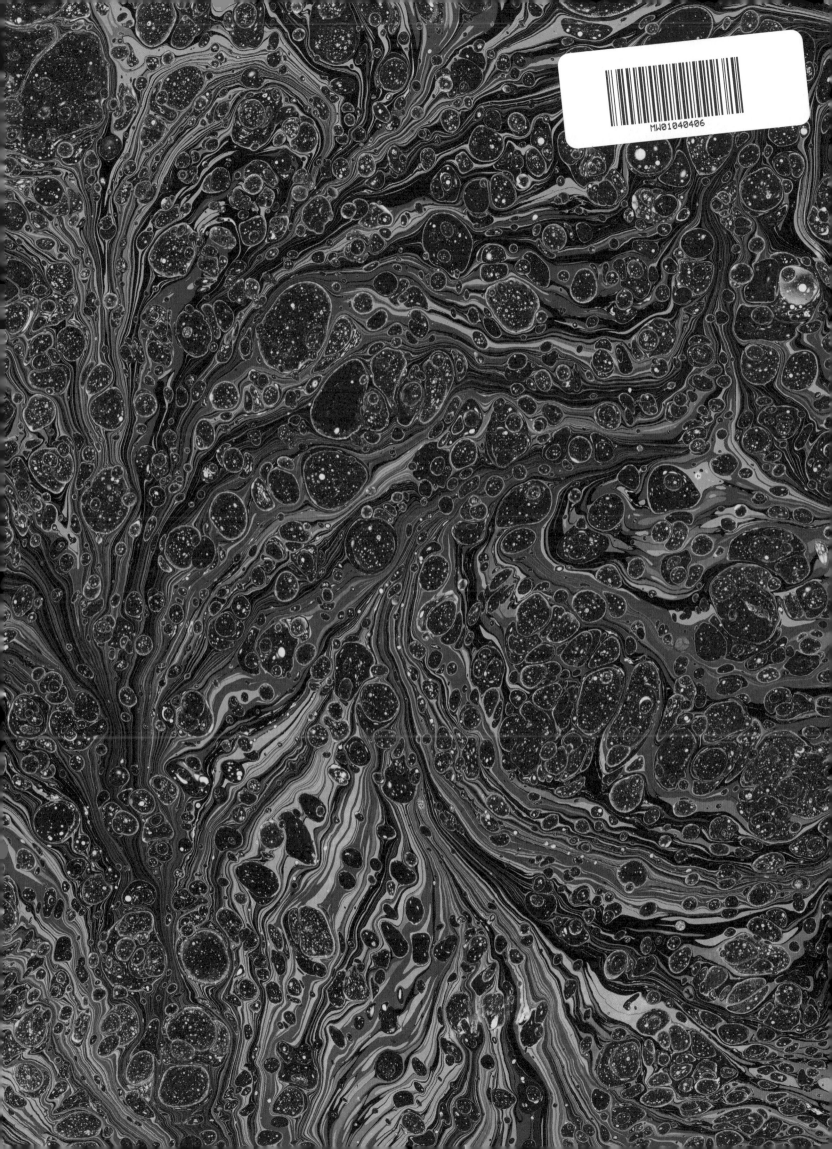

German
Armored Trains
1904-1945

Wolfgang Sawodny

Schiffer Military History
Atglen, PA

Book translation by Dr. Edward Force

Book Design by Ian Robertson.

Copyright © 2010 by Schiffer Publishing.
Library of Congress Control Number: 2010924943

Printed in China.
ISBN: 978-0-7643-3523-5

This book was originally published in German under the title
Die Panzerzüge des Deutschen Reiches by Eisenbahn Kurier-Verlag

We are interested in hearing from authors with book ideas on related topics.

Published by Schiffer Publishing Ltd.
4880 Lower Valley Road
Atglen, PA 19310
Phone: (610) 593-1777
FAX: (610) 593-2002
E-mail: Info@schifferbooks.com.
Visit our web site at: www.schifferbooks.com
Please write for a free catalog.
This book may be purchased from the publisher.
Please include $5.00 postage.
Try your bookstore first.

In Europe, Schiffer books are distributed by:
Bushwood Books
6 Marksbury Avenue
Kew Gardens
Surrey TW9 4JF, England
Phone: 44 (0) 20 8392-8585
FAX: 44 (0) 20 8392-9876
E-mail: Info@bushwoodbooks.co.uk.
Visit our website at: www.bushwoodbooks.co.uk

Contents

Foreword

The fact cannot be denied that in bygone days war was seen as an acceptable and legitimate means of settling political disagreements. That the military made use of technical progress for it, and even took the lead in such developments, was unavoidable with this attitude, and inevitably led to our present-day position, where, in view of the tremendous possibilities that technology has given us in this respect, and that are a threat to humanity, and even to humankind itself, we must basically consider this question and, hopefully, act accordingly.

It is obvious that an invention like the steam railroad could not be omitted from a thoroughgoing test of its utility in this sense. While its advantages as a means of military transport were recognized quickly, it took an amazingly long time before its vehicles were used for combat purposes. Despite a series of tests in the 19th century, of which the American Civil War of 1861-1865 in particular showed a broad spectrum of uses that anticipated future developments, but that were scarcely noticed by the European general staffs, it was only their use in the Boer War (South Africa, 1899-1902) that heightened notice and inspired many of the great powers of the time to make corresponding plans, which more or less survived until they were put into practice in the ensuing warlike events. In the Boer War, though, a clear differentiation also developed, which was taken over later — especially in World War I — by most countries: on the one hand, the railroad artillery, which utilized guns — generally of large calibers — from firing positions behind the front; on the other, armored trains, which — with very varied manpower and armament — were themselves suited for direct combat action on the fronts because of their armor protection. While the western Entente powers used only the railroad artillery (armored trains, when present at all, played only a marginal role), the eastern states, at first Russia and Austria-Hungary, and later all the successor states in that area, were the domain of the armored train. In Russia, heavy railroad batteries were built only for coastal protection and remained subordinate to the navy, while those with smaller-caliber guns were designated "heavy armored trains" and integrated into several armored-train units as support weapons. This can be seen in the evaluation of eastern literature, in which everything that fired from rails — including the railroad anti-aircraft guns of World War II — is called an "armored train." The German Reich, in its central location, developed both types, both the railroad artillery and the armored-train weapon.

While the railroad artillery continued to draw attention, especially through its impressive gun designs, and thus gained numerous detailed descriptions in the literature, armored trains had very seldom been dealt with at the time, although they appeared especially interesting on account of their varied rolling stock and differing sizes and equipment, but also since their small crews were assigned to various service arms, so that their independent supply basis and direct subordination to higher command offices gave them a special position as self-contained and relatively independent units

in the armies, rather more like a warship than any other part of the land army. Of the two publicized attempts to provide a worldwide overview, not limited by time, one was completely insufficient and confusing, while the other — which appeared recently — is also not without gaps and errors. Even serious nationally and temporally limited studies have to date been very few — for example, for Britain, Poland, and the USA in the Civil War.

In view of the flood of other military-technical and historical, and railroad-historical literature, this is astonishing, especially for Germany, after research had shown that the country had been building armored trains since the end of 1899, and had had such army units from 1912 through 1945. In the years just after World War I there were more than 40, in World War II no fewer than 58 regular armored trains, quite apart from makeshift railroad protection trains, 19 armored engines, and a whole series of smaller armored railroad vehicles (railcars, etc.). A point that divides this period into two frankly unbalanced periods came in 1921. Since the Reichswehr had to give up, once and for all, the armored trains that had survived World War I, or had been built according to similar principles on orders from the victorious powers, the German Reichsbahn was able, just a few weeks later, to get permission from those same powers to maintain railroad protection trains that were armored and became the progenitors of the armored trains used by the German Wehrmacht in World War II.

One reason for the neglect of this subject until then is surely the remarkable difficulty of documenting them. In the army structure, they were often not introduced at company strength, and so they are scarcely traceable. Original information for the World War I period is scarcely available anymore, and evidence had to be pieced together from a few very meager and widely scattered sources, mostly secondary in nature. A complete picture was not to be formed, yet I hope I can provide at least an approximate impression of those times. For the period between 1918 and 1938 the sources are much more favorable, although some gaps must remain here too.

Even for the World War II period documentation is not simple. The documents of the central command positions, the Commander of the Armored Trains at the Army High Command, and the Railroad Armored Train Replacement Unit have generally been lost, as have the records of production facilities in eastern Germany and the occupied lands. Researching the action history from the mountains of documents dealing with army groups, armies, corps, and divisions to which armored trains were assigned appeared to be an insurmountable labor of Sisyphus at first, what with the spatially scattered areas of action and the often-changing subordination conditions. Locating former members of the armored trains would also seem hopeless, with an estimated number of at most 10,000 troops out of some 12 million Wehrmacht members — and this 40 years after the war ended, but here luck opened a door, although only a very narrow one at first. Persistent further questions, but particularly later systematic research with the active assistance of the search services of the German Red

Cross in Munich and the Deutsche Dienststelle (WASt) in Berlin, to whom my heartiest thanks go out for their patient and constant acceptance of my endless and urgent questions, finally resulted in finding and interviewing former members of almost all the armored train units of World War II. Their information of the times and places of action made it possible to do specific research in the files of the Military Archives in Freiburg and document so much. Also of incalculable value were the private photo albums of these former armored-train crewmen. Although the pictures taken by amateurs were often of mediocre quality, they were, in the prevailing absence of technical data, often the only means of being able to identify the armored trains in their varying structures, for some changed their appearance completely through rebuilding, sometimes more than once. In selecting pictures for this book many of these photos had to be included, because of the uniqueness of many motifs, despite sometimes serious deficiencies in clarity and contrast, and often a small format had to be chosen for their reproduction. I ask the reader to be understanding here.

Unfortunately, space does not allow these many helpers to be named here, but I send them all my heartiest thanks. Without their cooperation, it would have been impossible to write this thorough historical account of the building and service of the German armored trains. Naturally, I also wish to thank numerous other institutions and their staffs (of whom I may mention in particular, as a representative Mr. Werner Loos of the Military Archives in Freiburg, because of his involvement, which went far beyond the usual extent), plus other persons from all over the world who willingly and helpfully provided information and photographs to support my work: the Federal Archives in Koblenz, Freiburg, Aachen-Kornelimuenster, and Potsdam, the war or military departments of the Main State Archives in Munich and Stuttgart, the Military History Research Office in Freiburg, now in Potsdam, the Military History Museum in Dresden, the archives in the Museum of the Engineer School of the Bundeswehr in Munich, the Austrian Federal and War Archives and the Museum of Military History in Vienna, the Imperial War Museum in London and the Royal Armored Corps Tank Museum in Bovington, the Service historique de l'arme/e de terre and the Etablissement de conception et de production audiovisuelle des armées in Paris, the archives of the journal "La vie du rail" in Paris, the Military History section of the Royal Netherlands Army in The Hague, the Vojensky historicky archives and the Statni ustredni archives in Prague, the museum of Traffic and Technology in Berlin, the Railroad Museum in Nuernberg, the Bundesbahn-Ausbesserungswerke in Munich-Neuaubing and Nuernberg, the historical archives of the Friedrich Krupp AG in Essen, the Steyr-Damler-Puch AG in Steyr, Austria, Frau Helga Mueller in Roesrath-Hoffnungsthal, Mesrs. Carlotto Asmus of Weilheim, Rudolf Balzert of Bebra, Norbert Bartel of Cologne, Joachim Deppmeyer of Uelzen, Reinhard Dober of Munich, Hans von Donat of Stuttgart, Hans-Joachim Ellissen of Hamburg, Wolfgang Fleischer of Freital, Vladimir Francev of Prague, Johann Christian Gembe of Vaterstetten, Horst Gleiss of Holm,, Helmut Griebl of Laaben, Austria, Axel Gutmann of Schwabbruck, Fritz Hahn of Oberkochen, Albert Hellrung of Schwelm, Ernst Hochberger of Sinn, Alfred Klein-Wisenberg of Vienna, Werner Koehler of Paderborn, Dr. Alan R. Koenig of Lincoln NE, USA, Thomas Kolley of The Hague, Netherlands, Wilfried Kopenhagen of Berlin, Guenter Krause of Werl, Dr. Nikolaus Krivinyi of Vienna, Wolfgang Laudien of Bodenstein, Stefan Lauscher of Duesseldorf, Dierk Lawrenz of Handeloh, Dr. Rolf Loettgers of Siegen, John Loop of Bothell, USA, Janusz Magnuski of Warsaw, Paul Malmassari of Mourmelon-le-Grand, France, Friedrich Masch of Munich, Juerg Meister of Bonny Hills, Australia, Karlheinz Muench of Schwetzingen, Dr. Nicola Pignato of Tarento, Italy, Dr. Hermann Rahne of Dresden, Dr. Werner Regenberg of Nussloch, Raphael Rues of Baden, Switzerland, Bernd Ruesch of Langenau, Dr. Thomas Samek of Hamburg, Kurt Sarrazin of Iserlohn, Georg Schlaug of Gronau, Ernst Schnug of Neuss, Ulrich Schwarze of Erlangen, Walter J. Spielberger of Poertschach, Karl Heinz Stahmann of Bokel, Hofrat Dr. Erwin Steinboeck of Vienna, Jiri Tintera of Prague, Waldemar Trojca of Speyer, Gyoergi Villanyi of Budapest, Ulrich Walluhn of Erfurt, Hansjuergen Wenzel of Koblenz, Juergen Wilhelm of Margetshoechheim, Adolf Wuensche of Ulm, and Wilhelm Zimmermann of Hamburg. Very special thanks to Paul Malmassari and the Editions Heimdal of Bayeux for permission to reproduce (here reduced to 1/87 scale) the drawings from his book which was published there, Mr. Ulrich Schwarze for the preparation of further drawings, and to my wife, who bore with extraordinary patience the fact that I dedicated ten years of my spare time to working on this subject.

It may seem inopportune at a time when a change in the originally expressed outlook seems to be building more and more, when so much is said about disarmament and, especially in my country, military subjects are already held in noticeably low esteem, to publish a book on such a subject. Yet every aspect of history— be it positive or negative—deserves to be preserved as material for observation and study by coming generations. This publication may also have an effect in such a sense. I have limited myself to a portrayal of the facts, presenting them in accordance with my present state of knowledge, and avoided any political evaluation. This will surely strike the readers in very different ways, according to their standpoints, and such an expression of opinion should, if possible, not be shaped in advance by the author's views.

The value of the armored trains as means of combat was, of course, to be evaluated. They were to be judged individually according to the demands that had been determined in the guidelines and requirements for their service. Here too, I have tried to provide the verdict as coolly and well-balanced as possible, even though I am aware of the impossibility of absolute objectivity. Former commanders of armored trains, who answered applicable questions willingly and, as I could tell, completely without prejudice, have been very helpful to me. Thus, I hope that I have been able to create a fairly authentic picture of the events of those times.

The German names of the time were used when naming localities; the appropriate names in the language of the country— when determinable—can be found in a list at the end of the book. I have avoided footnotes on items in the text, the great majority of which would have referred to archives and statements from former armored-train members.

The information on the history of the German armored trains more than forty years ago is remarkable enough. The full extent of the existence of this unique type of weapon with its variety of constructions and equipment was as little known to date as their frequency of use, which culminated in the years from after World War I through World War II. Thus, the gathering of these facts seems to me to be a necessary contribution to military history. The use and adaptation of this rolling stock is naturally of special interest from the railroad's point of view, but in this context the attention is focused on a hitherto very unknown chapter of the German Reichsbahn, the rail protection service, which certainly deserves much more thorough study. Thus, I hope that my work has been able to fill a gap in the literature on military and railroading history.

Elchingen, Summer 1996
Prof. Dr. Wolfgang Sawodny

Foreword to the Second Edition

I am extremely thankful to the publishers for giving me the opportunity to correct errors from the first edition in a new one. In the ten years that have passed, further information on the subject has naturally been submitted to me or come to light through my own research. A new formation of large areas of the first part (prewar times, World War I, free corps era), thus seemed appropriate. On the other hand, corrections and completions in the second part (rail protection and World War II) could be worked into the original version. Naturally, interesting photographic material has also been found. While this could be placed in the vicinity of the appropriate texts in the first part, it would have meant an incalculable amount of work on a complete change in the layout of the second part. For this part, the additional photographic material has been gathered in an addendum, with references to the pages of the appropriate chapters. Naturally, it is again appropriate to express thanks, especially to those who have loyally provided me with information in the ten years that have passed since the first edition appeared: Helmut Griebl of Laaben, Axel Gutmann of Schwabbruck, Stefan Lauscher of Korschenbroich, the unfortunately too early deceased Janusz Magnuski of Warsaw, Karlheinz Muench of Schwetzingen, Dr. Werner Regenberg of Nussloch, Herbert Schirmboeck of Vienna, Jiri Tintera of Prague, and Hansjuergen Wenzel of Koblenz, but particularly Paul Malmassari of Paris, who always stood by me and helped by unselfishly making the results of his research and his extensive photo collection available to me. Others, who helped even with special studies, were able to contribute important completing data, such as Stefano diGiusto of Vienna-Bruessel, Arthur Przeczek of Chicago, and Friedrich-Wilhelm Stroucken of Brueggen. Thanks are also due to the Etablissement de Communication et de Production Audiovisuelle de la Défense in Ivry, the Library of History of the Times in Stuttgart, and the German Historical Museum in Berlin for providing pictorial material, and to the Universal Library in Ulm for providing literature.

Nersingen, May 2006
Prof. Dr. Wolfgang Sawodny

Prefaces

As a railroad engineer and commander of several armored trains, I took part in numerous actions of these trains during the Russian campaign of World War II. Here I learned of the effectiveness of these generally little-known weapons. The armored trains stood out in action then through their mobility and firepower, even though sometimes in very difficult conditions.

I would like particularly to emphasize the feeling of unity and comradeship of the soldiers in an armored train. In World War II they were a mixed unit, usually consisting of infantrymen, artillerymen, tank soldiers, engineers, A/A gunners, communications men, medics, and railroad men.

The author deserves special thanks for taking up this hitherto unknown subject of war history and, first in 1986 and 1989, reporting on their development and action in two booklets, which gained much attention. Not least on account of this attention, but particularly through his tireless and inclusive research, he can now provide a thorough and precise presentation of this material, validly portraying the entire historical development from 1904 to the end of World War II and documenting the significance of the use of this weapon both at the beginning of the Weimar Republic and in World War II, in which it was part of the armored troops.

This book thus fills a significant gap in the literature of railroad and military history.

Helmut Walter
Brigadier General, retired

At the beginning of 1939, I was a young railroad engineer ordered to Armored Train No. 3 in Munich. In those days of doing one's military duty unquestioningly, the position of a technical leader which, despite the low military rank, offered a great deal of authority and responsibility with a so unusual and little-known weapon seemed to be an interesting assignment.

The very first combat service in the bloody battle at Konitz clearly showed the weaknesses and strengths of the armored train. Later transferred to Krakow to take the same position in a captured Polish armored train, I could study the clearly different outlook of our enemy on this weapon—in technical terms as well.

At the end of 1941 I came as a technical officer to the central office of the staff officer of the armored trains under the General of the Fast Troops, later the Commander of the Armored Trains under the Army High Commander, where I remained until the war ended. My tasks there included not only keeping records of the German and captured armored trains, but in particular the turning of gained experience into improvements and new features that were evaluated for use according to the most agreed-on viewpoints in cooperation with Inspection 6 of the General Army Office and the Chief of Army Equipment in the OKH. Thus, as of the beginning of 1942 I was involved in the essential developments in this realm.

While the railroad artillery, thanks to its impressive gun calibers, always drew attention to itself, the armored trains, carefully differentiated from the artillery, were largely unnoticed, although in terms of numbers and equipment they should have been viewed as significant means of warfare. Thus, I am thankful to the author for having taken up this material and not only trying to document their technical details and their action in World War II as completely as possible, but also to shed light on their historical development that led up to it.

May this book honor the memory of all those who had to lose their lives in the course of their military duty with the armored trains in a senseless, even criminal war.

Franz Englberger
Technical Bundesbahn Oberamtsrat, retired
(BZA Munich)

A characteristic, unmistakable feature of the armored trains—armed and armored railroad vehicles—is their union with the rail lines, and thus also with the particulars of rail traffic. It is thus obvious that the majority of their crews were recruited from railroad men. When they were first drafted, railroad men from the most varied service arms were assigned to the armored trains. After all, such a train was only capable of functioning and action when specialists like engine drivers, firemen, wagon masters, switchers, and radiomen were available to take charge of the trains and the technical facilities.

Not only in the realm of the Reichsbahn, but also on the rail network in the occupied areas—from Narvik in the north to Athens in the south, from the Atlantic coast in the west to the Caucasus in the east—the requirements and safety measures of railroad operation applied, and were to be followed by armored trains as well as all other rail vehicles. Many planned actions came to grief because of axle and meter loads, load dimensions, and borderlines. The most important requirements, still known today as the concept of "railroad building and operating order," was also the rule for the "rolling" action of the armored trains and saved many a crewman's life if an all too ambitious and overly eager commander wanted to give orders that could not be carried out in terms of railroad technology.

In addition, in view of the high cost of material for the railroad cars that were rebuilt or built new for this purpose, their technical service and maintenance were of the greatest importance. What was more practical than to entrust well-trained railroaders with all of these tasks?

A railroad engineer was assigned to each armored train as a "special leader" (technical leader). He not only had the task of constantly checking the technical setup, the servicing, and the maintenance of the costly vehicle, namely the locomotive, but he also had to check whether bodies and chassis, bridges, switches, and curves were able to handle the high axle pressures of the armored vehicles. Since almost all the armored trains were drawn by steam locomotives, even in World War II, the role of the technical leader was vital. A steam locomotive, robust as it may look beside a modern electric type, was very much in need of servicing and reacted sensitively if its maintenance was neglected. After a certain number of kilometers, "washing out" was a necessity: the firebox and steam pipes had to be rid of slag and scale, for which a railroad service center behind the front had to be visited. In addition, coal and water supplies were soon used up and had to be replenished. Thus, many a successful action had to be broken off or threatening battle halted to carry out these restorative measures at the right time. When the return trip was announced for these reasons, an audible sigh of relief could often be heard through the whole train's intercom. The special leader's appeal to the commander to visit a service center

for locomotive servicing took one to two weeks (depending on the kilometers covered), a rest stop two or three days with the baggage train, which usually awaited its train at the site of the service center. With the supply train too, there was much for the railroad men to do. Numerous devices and machines, as well as the locomotive, often had to be serviced and repaired to be ready for action.

To be sure, this rest stop was very short sometimes, when an unarmored so-called "black" spare locomotive was ordered by radio. Then the radiomen quickly cobbled up a makeshift connection for lights and the intercom, and after a few hours the combat train was ready for action again. The radiomen were also taken from the peacetime railroad because of their knowledge of Morse code, which was then customary for reporting the trains in and out. Since the radio symbols were identical, the railroaders could be trained as radiomen much faster than other people. In view of its mobility, and thus often-changing locations, the radio communication with the command posts and the units in the vicinity of the train was vitally important. Railroaders often filled these key positions as well.

Often enough, too, the armored train encountered destroyed stretches of track, or was itself flung from the tracks by mines or other explosives. Then the train's engineers were called for. They too were usually ex-railroaders, who had useful experience in repairing rails and roadbeds and had learned in their profession to work with "German" equipment. In short, railroaders of the most varied service arms were essential for a functioning armored train.

Looking back, I thank fate for having been called to this service arm as a railroader. I am firmly convinced that I survived my more than two years of service as a radioman in an armored train almost unscathed until its destruction in July 1944 only because I felt relatively safe—or so it seemed—in the "rolling fortress." The comradeship among the crewmen must also be called exemplary in hindsight. The lack of space, especially in the 2x2-meter radio cabin, and the cramped togetherness—almost like a U-boat—surely contributed to friendships that lasted beyond the war and still exist today.

Thanks and recognition go to the author of this book for portraying the history of the German armored trains in exhausting and time-consuming detailed work and thus preserving it for the future. He does not try to glorify the actions of the armored trains, but to close a gap in our military history dispassionately and factually. He was also the man who motivated me to organize two meetings of former armored-train soldiers in Frankfurt am Main. The fact that in 1986 more than 80 and in 1989 even over 100 "formers" took part—for many it was a first reunion in more than 40 years—and listened tensely to the author's words, shows that a real need for these gatherings is at hand, as well as for the gathering and presentation of the history of the German armored trains.

Hans Beckmann
Bundesbahn-Oberamtsrat, retired
(Hauptverwaltung der DB, Frankfurt/Main)

From the Beginning to 1921

Pre-history

After Stephenson's steam locomotive had pulled the first railroad train from Stockton to Darlington on September 27, 1825, and thus introduced a new epoch in transportation, it was obvious that it would not be long before the military would also recognize the great value of this invention for their purposes. In fact, just a year later the French naval officer Montgéry—although his country did not yet have this means of transit—recommended the establishment of a complete armored train made of three armored cars, each with two howitzers, with a locomotive running in the middle. Naturally this suggestion came much too early, for a more or less connected rail network had to develop first before the railroad could attain a real military significance. The German Friedrich Wilhelm Harkort had recognized this early, and had suggested the building of a rail line (between Weser and Lippe, later one along the Rhine valley) in 1833, solely for strategic reasons.

In the beginning, the railroad was used most often as a means of transportation. Since 1830, small detachments—under 100 men—are known to have been moved short distances by rail. In 1839, 8000 men were brought back to Berlin on ten trains after finishing maneuvers at Potsdam. The first large, non-peacetime troop transport took place in 1846, when the Prussian VI. Army Corps (over 12,000 men) was transferred by the new means of transit to the border of the city-republic of Krakow to prevent a spread of unrest there into Prussian territory. The 1848-49 revolutionary wars not only brought extensive troop transports into the lands of the Austro-Hungarian monarchy, but with the blowing up of an arch of the bridge from the mainland to Venice, it also saw the first attempt to prevent traffic by damaging the rails. For the next 15 years, Austria-Hungary remained the leader in the realm of military transport—later along with France, which could gain useful experience in the 1854-1856 Crimean War. This war also saw the first building of a field rail line for purely military purposes. Although the first major troop transport had taken place in Prussia, that country at first remained somewhat in the background. Only in 1857, when Helmuth von Moltke, Sr., who had already been closely connected with military transport since the thirties and had recognized its extraordinary possibilities, became Chief of the Prussian General Staff did this change. His organizational plans for advance by rail were an essential prerequisite for the striking success that Prussia gained in the wars of 1864, 1866, and 1870-71.

Yet it is necessary to go back again to the revolution years of 1848-49. Not only did the first large-scale transport for military purposes take place then, but so did the first documented uses of railroad trains as a means of warfare. When the Austrian army corps advanced from Bohemia to besiege Vienna, the railroad personnel, who had allied with the rebels, objected, so the troop-transport "security" locomotives were sent ahead, each with a flatcar attached, manned with soldiers, for whose protection rails had been lain on their sides, one over another, to protect them. Such cars, which obviously were effective, were apparently used by the Austrians later in the same conflict in Hungary and Italy.

If the forerunner of the infantry car of an armored train was thus created, the first gun mount was set on a railroad car in the American civil War, which was indeed a "railroad war," with numerous troop and supply transports, frequent attempts by both sides to destroy rails and their rebuildings and detours. At first Confederate General Robert E. Lee had a 32-pound naval gun mounted behind an angled armor shield on a seven-axle flatcar. This "railroad monitor" saw action on June 29, 1862, at Savage Station, east of Richmond, VA. For the Union side, the Baldwin Locomotive Works in Pittsburgh built an armored 15.2 cm gun in a swivel mount on a flatcar, but this railroad gun at first awakened no interest and was removed, but later several similar designs were created at the Atlantic & North Carolina Railroad works in Newberne. An armored train with six such gun cars and an armored locomotive was stopped by the Confederates in August 1864 by a shot through the boiler, and was then burned. For the siege of Petersburg in October 1864, the union army even mounted a 32 cm mortar on a railroad car.

In Europe, Austria-Hungary even planned the building and use, in the war with Prussia in 1866, of two armored trains armed with rocket batteries on the Danube line, but the war ended so quickly that these trains were never built. In 1869, before the Franco-Prussian war began, Emperor Napoleon III attempted to build an armored train comprised of three railroad cars armed with mitrailleuses (forerunners of machine guns). The production dragged on into 1871. While the train never saw action in beleaguered Paris, it later fell into the hands of the Communards, who used it on the ring line. After the enclosing of Paris by the Prussians, though, Naval Chief Engineer M. Dupuy du Lóme had four armored gun cars with 14- and 16-cm naval guns built at the Paris-Orleans railroad workshops in the city, plus two armored locomotives and an armored repair-shop train. These units were used repeatedly against the Prussians, including in the last attempt to break free on January 19, 1871, at the Rueil depot. After the armistice they remained in Paris, and were later also captured by the Parisian Communards and used on the Seine bridges and between Batignolles and Asniéres. Though these armored railroad batteries could show no spectacular success, several direct shell hits, in which the cars actually tipped over without suffering serious damage, at least showed the benefits of the armor protection. Along with the Parisian armored trains, others were built and used during the Franco-Prussian War and the fighting against the Commune in Brittany and Perigord. All were disarmed by the beginning of 1972. In the eighties, two prototypes of heavily armed armored trains were built in France, but they quickly disappeared into the depots or were dismantled.

While the American and most of the French designs can be seen from a present-day standpoint as forerunners of the railroad artillery, it was the British who assembled the first actual armored train—characterized by the combination of various service arms, especially the infantry and artillery. In 1882, in the Egyptian campaign against

Arabi Pasha, the royal Marines started with two cars and gradually built up a train that finally consisted of the following units: 1. Contact car made of rail-building materials, 2. Car with a 40-pound cannon in front, 3. Car with Nordenfelt machine cannon, 4. Car with 9-pound gun, 5. Locomotive protected with rails and sandbags, and 6-8. Infantry cars, each with two Gatling machine guns. This was a combination that was to remain valid to the end of World War II. In 1885 a small British armored train was used as a rail-protection train when the line from the Red Sea to the Nile was built. A year later a similar one was built in India, and finally, in 1894, one—but with an unarmored locomotive—in Mother England, which carried out coast guard tasks during the Fashoda conflict with France in 1898.

The actual breakthrough for the armored train came in the South African Boer War of 1899-1902, which the British began with twelve small trains (usually with one infantry car, armed with a machine gun, in front and in back of the locomotive; later a gun car with a small-caliber (usually 6-pound) gun was added. After two such trains were lost in action because of unsound tactics, the others—their numbers were raised to 19 during the war, and their weapons improved—were used mainly for rail protection and repairs, and to escort troop and supply trains against the guerilla-fighting Boers and caused them significant losses.

In the final phase of the Russo-Japanese War of 1904-05, armored trains appear to have been used by the Russians to cover their withdrawals in Manchuria. Japanese armored trains are also said to have existed. At the beginning of the Mexican Revolution (1911) the dictator Porfirio Diaz—creator of the Mexican rail network—had several armored trains built and equipped with machine guns. Some of them fell into the hands of the revolutionaries and were used by them.

The First German Armored Trains

The first mention of an armored rail vehicle in the literature of the German Reich seems to be the mention in the British plan for such a battery for use against fortifications in 1866. It could be pushed along rails at the top of a wall, was open on top, and had only frontal armor. In 1871 the Prussians were confronted by French armored train batteries on the city's rail lines during the siege of Paris. At the end of 1899, at the suggestion and costs of military officials (presumably the General staff), the prototype of an armored train was built at the Gruson works in Magdeburg and tested on the Berlin-Kunersdorf (actually Kummersdorf) military line. The cars were fitted with armor plates hung on moveable beams and could be penetrated only by explosive shells from howitzers. Their bodies had shooting loopholes. On the armored car in front of the locomotive, a Maxim machine gun was mounted on a pivot with a traverse of 270 degrees. The train was manned by members of the Saxon and Wuerttemberg companies of Railroad Regiment No. 2. The Kaiser himself showed interest in the results of the tests. It was decided, though, that such trains, even if they were armored by small-caliber (3.7 cm) rapid-fire cannons instead of machine guns, were useful only on the ring rails around fortifications. Test runs in Metz and Strassburg proved positive, and the train was stationed there. It is interesting that a mention in the "Deutsche Heeres-Zeitung" of January 30, 1900, continued two issues later (February 3)—probably for security reasons—had to be denied with the significant words: "In No. 3, page 45, we reported on test runs on the Berlin-Kunersdorf line of an armored train made with light Gruson armor plates. As we have been informed by responsible sources, these test runs never took place, and our reporter had been wrongly informed about the matter." It was not the existence of the train itself that was disputed but only its test runs, and precisely speaking, those on the Berlin-Kunersdorf line, where they certainly did not take place, what with the false location. The existence of the train is supported by a French Secret Service report of December 12, 1899, which included additional details beyond those in the cited newspaper report.

A change in outlook is seen in the use of armored trains in the Boer War (1899-1902), which was followed by Germany with intense interest and empathy for the Boers. Soon there was also an opportunity for their own practical experience.

On January 12, 1904, the Hereros in the colony of German Southwest Africa rebelled against their colonial masters. Their main attack was aimed at the town of Okahandja, located some 300 kilometers inland on a 60-cm narrow-gauge line from the port of Swakopmund, where the line curved to the south and ran another 70 km to the capital of Windhoek, then the end of the line. The residents of Okahandja withdrew into the fortress, defended by 71 men. When this news became known in Swakopmund, a relief troop of 60 men under 1st Lt. von Zuelow was sent by train. The train included a passenger car as a staff car, three crew cars, three baggage cars, and three freight cars, in which horses were loaded. It was pulled by one of the usual double field locomotives with 0-6-0 + 0-6-0 axle order for the 60-cm gauge. The numbers 104 A and B visible on this locomotive do not correspond to the numbering system of the Swakopmund-Windhoek line, but are probably an

The only picture that could be found showing the improvised armored train of the German Reich that was used in 1904 during the Herero uprising in Southwest Africa to relieve the besieged Okahandja shows the double field locomotive, No. 104, with its cab very unsatisfactorily protected from the front with sandbags. At the right edge of the picture is a similarly "protected" car. Source: W. Sawodny collection.

old field-train designation, which allows no clear identification, such as of a manufacturing firm, what with the double records common at the time. The fighting power of von Zuelow's troop grew to over 100 men on the way, some of whom had to be left to secure the depots on the line. On the evening of 13 January they reached Waldau, the last station before Okahandja. On the final 20 kilometers of the line the tracks were badly damaged, and great numbers of Hereros waited on the heights on either side. 1st Lt. von Zuelow thus had the train armored with rolled sheet steel plates and bags of sand and rice. On 15 January, at 5:30 AM they set out. Under the protection of the train, the track damage could be repaired despite sometimes-heavy fire by the Hereros. At 11:30 AM they reached Okahandja. Some of the newly arrived men were a welcome reinforcement for the fortress, while the rest established the depot and the train as a second support point.

To be sure not very much was won, though the Hereros drew back from the place into the surrounding highlands. Just as the destruction of the Osona bridge over the Swakop River had broken the line to Windhoek temporarily, now a 20-meter railroad bridge west of Okahandja had been destroyed, so that the armored train and the people were stranded. An attempt to use the train to reopen the line toward Swakopmund on 20 January failed with losses. Only the advance of the 2nd Field Company under Captain Franke, summoned from the southern part of the colony and advancing from Windhoek, broke the siege and relieved Okahanja on 27 January. In the subsequent opening of the line to Swakopmund via Waldau and Karibib (1/31-2/2/1904), the armored train, now armed with machine guns, provided valuable service. When it met the detachment of the gunboat "Habicht" in Karibib, it was even armed with 3.7 cm guns and used for further securing of the entire Swakopmund-Windhoek line. Soon the Hereros were driven off to the north and east of the rail line, so it had fulfilled its task.

These events gave the final impetus to have serious discussions on the building of armored trains for the German Army. By early July 1904, the Chief of the General Staff, Count von Schlieffen, sent a message to the Ministry of War in which he noted the favorable experiences that had been had with armored trains protected from gunfire and armed with rapid-firing guns, and suggested that for the German Reich, under certain conditions, the use of such units could be advantageous for securing the railroads on the borders and in etappe areas of enemy lands, as well as for reconnaissance. Thereupon a commission of the Ministry of War and the General staff was set up to clear up the following questions:

1.) How can armored trains be used:
    a.) during mobilizations and advances,
    b.) during operations (in withdrawal combat for railroad objects, scouting, fighting for fortifications),
    c.) in etappe areas?
2.) What are their disadvantages, for example, their sensitivity to artillery fire and by resulting derailing?
3.) How should the armor be planned and the train armored?

Planning began with a train of high-side cars with a locomotive and tender in the middle. Both the locomotive and the car walls should be protected against infantry fire with armor plates. The cars should have one or two rows of loopholes, and their equipping with rapid-fire guns was foreseen. To be tested were such questions as:

    a.) How thick must the armor plates be?
    b.) Are tender locomotives easier to protect against gunfire?
    c.) Is it sufficient to armor only the middle zone of a locomotive's boiler?

4.) What peacetime preparations are necessary to secure the suitable rolling stock, the armor, and the equipment? How does one conceive the technical development? Experiences with the armoring of locomotives and cars were to be acquired from the transit troops.

At the Kummersdorf firing range, firing tests with various armors were begun. The Commission gave an interim report on them early in March 1906. It was noted very particularly that the armor was effective even against the French copper shot (balle D). It was determined that this could be attained with high-side cars with iron walls, if:

1.) at a 5-cm interval, behind it another 5-cm sheet-iron wall set up, and the space in between filled with gravel:
2.) at a 16-cm interval behind it a 3-cm wooden wall set up, and the space in between filled with gravel,
3.) behind the iron wall of the car a sandbag covering of at least 20 cm will be attached.

On locomotives, cylinders, boilers, pipes, and the water box of the tender, and particularly the cab, need armor protection, though for reasons of space, it may not be applicable everywhere in the portrayed form. Plates of 8-mm steel or 10-mm rolled iron must be applied, to provide protection from gunfire. Firing on a car roof with nailed-on sheet iron gave favorable results and suggested that on the locomotive boiler structures too, angled armor plates can provide protection. Ways to equip a tender locomotive with an added tender and six cars quickly should be found; for this, only places with large railroad shops can be considered. Practical tests by the railroad brigade are regarded as necessary.

The Commission issued a further report at the end of February 1907. It had come up with the following results:

1.) Armored railroad trains can be used: in border protection, in etappe areas threatened by enemy forces or populations, in colonial warfare.
2.) According to the conclusion of tests, effective protection against infantry fire (S shots and French balle D) is attained most simply:
    a.) through the use of 5-mm iron and rippled iron plates available in all railroad workshops, when one applies two iron plates one after the other, and either fills the space between them of at least 2 cm with gravel or sand, or leaves a space of at least 6 cm empty. For locomotives, iron armor is to be used on the boiler and the driver's position.
    b.) For all railroad cars suitable for personnel transport (only those with iron walls come into consideration, since they simplify armoring), protection against infantry fire is attained by installing wooden boxes inside the cars, 16 cm away from the wall, and filling the space with gravel or sand. Atop the box, a wide board is attached, with sandbags on it for head protection. If only wooden cars should be available, then a 5-mm sheet-metal wall is to be attached first.

The Inspection of the Transport Troops was commissioned to prepare directions for the armoring and protection of railroad trains. It is noteworthy that nothing more is said in the Commission's reports of arming the trains with guns.

The development initiated by the chief of the General Staff, Count von Schlieffen, was continued promptly by his successor, Helmuth von Moltke the younger, who followed him in office in 1905.

In 1906, while the Commission was still at work, the establishment of 32 armored trains, built according to the basic concepts set up by it, but because of financial considerations the program had to be reduced to 14 trains, of which 13 were actually built.

The Service Instructions for Armored Trains of 1910

To activate this program the Minister of Public Works, along with the Minister of War, published the aforementioned service instructions for the equipping. Mobilization and use of armored trains, for which quickly attached armor for locomotives and cars was intended, so that in case of mobilization the equipping of the relevant trains would be possible within 24 hours. The locomotives used were to be exclusively those of Series T 9.3 (later DR-Series 91.3).

A protective hood made of 5- and 10-mm thick cast iron plates, to be set on the runways, was planned for these locomotives. It was double-walled on the sides with an 8-cm gap, open at the front, and covered only the steam dome and the cab on top; to the front of the steam dome was another vertical armor plate. The cab was accessible via double-walled doors running on rollers. There was a loading flap on each side above the coal box; if an armor plate extended ahead of the water tank it was also to be fitted with a flap, with the zinc pipe for taking on water to be stuck through it. Depending on the lifting cranes at the workshops that prepared the armored trains, the hood could consist of one piece or of parts assembled over the locomotive. To protect the cylinders, pushrods, and steam pipes, 10-mm iron skirts, attached to the protective hood and linked with tension rods, were planned.

A Prussian T 9.3 fitted with armor according to 1910 service regulations. The armor aprons over the drive wheels are missing. Behind is a tender, unarmored but fitted with ash protection. Photo: P. Scheffler collection

An armored train according to 1910 service regulations. Of the six cars in the front half, the first (a rebuilt brake van with observation post armored and roofed over, but open at sight level) and the fourth are of the 20-ton; the others are of the 15-ton Omk(u) type with iron walls (reinforced with inside double walls). The same series may be presumed for the rear half. The crew of infantrymen fires over the sandbag breastworks; the open cars can be covered with tent canvas. Photo: J. Magnuski collection

For the twelve cars of each armored train, at least four of which, including the first and last, with the brake van, had to have a braking system, Omk(u) open coal cars with 5-mm thick iron walls were used, either those of the Koenigshuette type (20-ton capacity, overall length 7.5 m without, 8 mm with brake van, axle base 3.6 meters, sidewall height 150 cm), or those built to Standard II d1 or generalized A 6 design (15-ton capacity, overall length 6.6 or 7.3 m, axle base 3 or 3.3 meters, without or with brakes, sidewall height 125 cm). Behind the iron walls, with a gap of 16 cm, a wooden wall of 3-cm thick boards was to be installed and the space between filled with gravel. Here the doors, which were protected by 10-mm cast iron sheets, were cut out. Sandbags were placed on the sidewalls as head protection and mountings for the guns. Folding military benches were carried for the crews. Armor of 10-cm cast iron plate was also planned for the brake vans and axle bearings of the cars.

Finally, a round observation turret made of 4-mm Krupp steel with a cast iron top was provided for the commander. Its three legs could be screwed onto the floor of a car, and had eight loopholes (120 mm long, 25 mm high) two meters up. The means of communication were meager, to be sure. A tube connection was planned as a link between the commander and the engine driver, but the track observer in the brake van could communicate with the driver only by a signal line. All these parts had to be stored at the workshop designated for their fitting so that the locomotive and car could be armored in the time span (24 hours) provided.

The cold, shut-down train could be ready to roll within three hours, while a locomotive under steam could be ready in half an hour. The designated speeds were: marching (locomotive at the head of the train) 60 kph on main lines, 30 kph on sidelines, in action (locomotive in the middle of the train) usually 25 kph, but these standards could naturally be increased in action up to the limits of technical safety, depending on the conditions. The water supply guaranteed a range of 100 km, and coal for 250 km was carried. After 1500 km, the locomotive had to undergo maintenance, the so-called "washing out," at a railroad workshop.

The establishment of the armored trains was based on the approval of the War Ministry; the right of application was held by the Railroad Department of the Grand General Staff (Eisb.Abt.Gr.Gen.St.), and in case of war, by the Chief of Field Railroad Affairs (Chef FEW). For technical matters, the production of the armor, its installation, and the equipping of the trains for action readiness, but also for the formation of the technical staff, the military pendant of the Railroad Direction, the Line Command (Lin.komm.), was responsible. The rolling stock that was used for the armored trains remained the property of the responsible Railroad Direction. The War Ministry had to pay rent to it for the duration of use of the armored trains. The technical crews who were assigned permanently to the armored trains were to be provided by the appropriate railroad administration. They consisted of the technical travel leader, two locomotive drivers, two stokers, two conductors, and six (for six rather than four brake vans, ten) brakemen, including the relief personnel. The technical leader was to be a reserve officer or officer's aide, the conductors and drivers at least corporals, but preferably non-commissioned officers of the reserve. In cases of mobilization, the entire technical crew was assigned to the Army.

In case of war, the armored trains were directly subordinate to the Grand General Staff and were assigned by it to various armies or corps commands to carry out special tasks, with the latter then having the power to issue military commands. The military crews of company strength (mostly infantry armed with machine guns) were assigned by this command office for the tasks assigned to them, though it was naturally recommended that frequent changes be avoided. The company leader was in charge, as the commander of the armored train, of both the military and the technical crews; the technical leader was responsible for operations, and was to cooperate effectively with the commander.

A train's trips were to be reported to the railroad service officers by the commander or technical leader, and took place on lines with regular service under full consideration of all general action requirements as telegraphically reported special trains (but the expression "armored train" was not to be used, as all travel preparations of these units were under the strictest secrecy), and in given circumstances, the appropriate precedence was to be granted. When entering lines with limited or halted traffic or under enemy fire, the applicable requirements for the mission could be set aside, depending on the situation and urgency, although only to the smallest possible degree. At least one official of the technical personnel (technical leader, engine driver) was to be acquainted with the line; the official in the brake van at the front of the train was to observe the tracks and signals, and could—if necessary—give the engine driver a direct signal to stop.

As tactical possibilities of use of the armored trains, it was stated in the service instructions: During mobilization, marching and advancing, protection of important rail lines, their structures and junctions, restoration of rail lines or cover for such work, support of weak troop units and taking of important objects on rail lines in enemy country; during withdrawal, the moving of remaining troops; in etappe regions, protection of the operating rail lines; and in fortification combat, unspecified tasks.

The armored trains described in the service instructions already showed several characteristics that were specific for German railroad vehicles of this type and remained so until the end of World War II, as opposed to those of most other countries. One was the strong (for these first German armored trains, even exclusive) emphasis of the infantry components; the other was the large number of cars, which was otherwise avoided, so as not to offer the enemy a large target, and to maintain the greatest possible mobility.

Even before the appearance of these service instructions—in November 1907, thus shortly after the work of the appropriate commission was finished—the line commands near the western and western borders were instructed to prepare and store the materials for a total of 13 armored trains according to the already provided guidelines. Most of the trains appear to have been finished during 1912, but the specified time limit of 24 hours for their readiness after mobilization could be met by only nine of them. For the others, periods of 10 to 14 days were calculated.

Unfortunately, only incomplete information is available on the distribution of the 13 armored trains. In 1912 the Krupp firm was to have built two each for the Lin.komm B (Muenster) and H (Cologne); Lin.komm P (Ludwigshafen) reported the completion of the material for PZ IX on May 1, 1912, with its readiness set at noon of the second mobilization day. The material for the two armored trains (No. X and XI) of Lin.komm. O (Mainz) was available in the main workshop at Darmstadt as of November 13, 1912, but the two trains could be made ready for action only on the 11th mobilization day. Of PZ IV and VI it is known that they were set up by the Lin. komm. Z in Alsace-Lorraine (No. IV in Muehlhausen)—surely on schedule as of the second mobilization day. PZ III—presumably

based in Trier (Lin.komm. S, Saarbruecken)—was even ready on the mobilization day. As for the other three armored trains, one can very probably assume that they were stationed in the eastern Lin.komm. G (Posen), L (Breslau), N (Koenigsberg), and R (Bromberg) near the border.

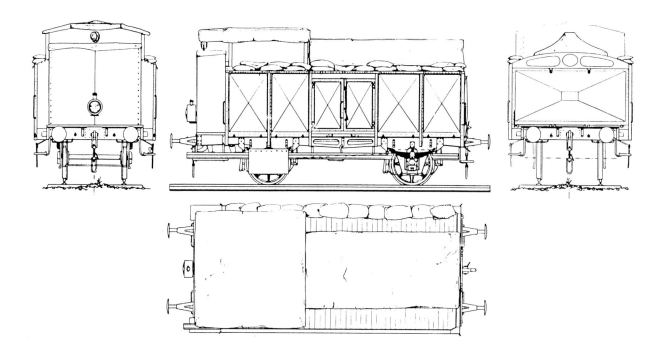

Above: Drawing of an armored train car on the basis of the Omk(u) Koenigshuette design type for 20-ton load weight with brakes. Length 8.00 meters, wheelbase 3.60 meters, load length 6.00 meters, load width 2.85 meters, load height 1.50 meters, weight of the car (unarmored) 8.4 tons. Drawing: P. Malmassari

Left: Another 1910 type armored train. The cars seem to have folding roof panels; the observation place has not been covered here.

The specialty of this armored train, which otherwise uses the usual 20-ton coal cars, is the G-wagon placed behind the locomotive. Photo: C. Asmus collection

World War I

The German Reich

When the German Reich ordered mobilization at 5:00 PM on August 1, 1914, the Army High command (OHL) was able to utilize nine armored trains within 24 hours. At least one was ready for action even more quickly, for PZ III moved from Trier and took part in the first action of the beginning First World War, the occupation of the Grand Duchy of Luxembourg, on the night of August 1-2, 1914.

The command conditions corresponded to those printed in the Service Instructions of 1910. The armored trains were subordinate to the Railroad Department of the Grand General Staff, the leader of which, Lt.Col. (later Major General) Wilhelm Groener, became the chief of the Field Railroad Service (Chef FEW) when the war began (in 1916 Colonel von Oldershausen took his place). Tactically, they were assigned—as noted—by the OHL to individual armies or (more rarely) to corps high commands for certain tasks, which the military command powers then utilized to their fullest extent, while their technical operation was left to the responsible Lin.komm. or M.E.D. In other ways, too, the requirements in the service instructions of 1910 appear to have remained valid, at least as long as no other concept—suiting the circumstances of the war—was made known.

Unfortunately, information about the action of German armored trains in World War I is sparse and disconnected, so that a complete picture can no longer be gained. The official historical writings in the Reich archives are almost completely silent about them, as is the single published volume on the field railroads; only in a few manuscript chapters on this last subject can a few hints be found. In individual reports from the time of World War I armored trains turn up here and there, usually without designation or specific information on their composition and armament. This lack of precise information was already lamented in the literature of the twenties and thirties, but not overcome. Original sources no longer seem to be available. Thus, we must be satisfied with these few fragments today.

On the advance through Belgium, the armored trains were used with good results on reconnaissance runs along the outpost lines and for mobile support of the open right flank of the advancing German army. Supplying the cavalry troops marching in the lead, through the largely unpacified hinterlands, was conducted by armored trains. Further important tasks developed for them in securing the connecting lines to the rear, which were threatened by Belgian guerillas, and where they protected the disembarking of troops, covered troop and material movement on endangered roads, as well as repairs and other work on rail lines. To fight the guerillas, an armored train operated within a large detachment for several weeks in September 1914 in the Braine-le-Comte—Soignies—Enghien—Ath—Tournai area. The action of an armored train in securing the rail junction at Tergnier (south of Laon) in mid-September 1914 is also known. In Alsace, the successful counterattack on August 10, 1914, against the French, who had advanced from Belfort through the Burgundian Gates and had occupied Muehlhausen, was supported by at least two armored trains. An armored train also accompanied the advance of the 6th Army to Luneville. On February 20, 1915, an armored train advancing from Muenster fired on the French positions at Sattel, in the Vosges, near Stossweier and Ampfersbach, and vanished again. Once more the action of such units on the western front was noted in the bloodily collapsed attack near Langemarck at the end of October 1914, one of the last attempts to keep the front in motion before it finally solidified into years of trench warfare.

On the eastern front, the German armored trains scouted the positions and strengths of Russian troop concentrations after the war began and covered the destruction troops that were to stop them in their advance over the East Prussian border. During the battle of Tannenberg at the end of August 1914, the armored train from the fortress of Thorn (Lin.komm R) covered from Strasburg out of the open right flank, and repeatedly took part in driving back Russian cavalry forces near Lauenburg and Radosk. At other positions on the eastern front armored trains were also successful in securing tasks. From November 1914 to March 1915 PZ IX was in Tilsit; during the 1915 summer offensive, after the line was converted to standard gauge, it advanced to Lesnaya, near Baranovici. In 1915 the action of armored trains in the combat in the Lodz—Warsaw area was noted.

In the first battles, several disadvantages became apparent in the armored trains built according to the service instructions of 1910. The armor and the armament were too weak, and the lack of an intercom system and headlights became unpleasantly notable. The five armored trains that did not go into service at the mobilization time and were therefore held back and redesigned as of November 1914, so as to eliminate their shortcomings. Of Armored Trains X and XI of Lin.komm O (Mainz), which were among this group, it is known that they were assigned for their first service to Lin.komm Z (Strasbourg) only on April 24, 1915. The trains that went into

An armored train of the mobilization type in action in Alsace in August 1914. The view of the likewise open command car shows the built-in armored observation turret with observation slits. Photo: W. Sawodny collection

A rebuilt armored train of the mobilization type (presumably PZ XII, in Romania in 1916). At the front (right side of the picture) and the rear are cars in which an armored turret with a 5.3 cm cannon was installed; the infantry cars (three in the front half, five in the rear) are now fitted with fixed roofs; in the front half there are also two flat cars with house-like bodies for guns on wheeled mounts. Photo: War Archives, Vienna

Part of the same train, with the roof design of the infantry cars and the installation of the armored turret on the flat roof of the Omk car can be seen better. Photo: Federal Archives, Koblenz

Close-up of the flat car with swiveling house-like body, here housing a captured Russian 7.62-cm Putilov 02 gun on a wheeled mount. The big front window is covered by the shield of the gun. Photo: Federal Archives, Koblenz

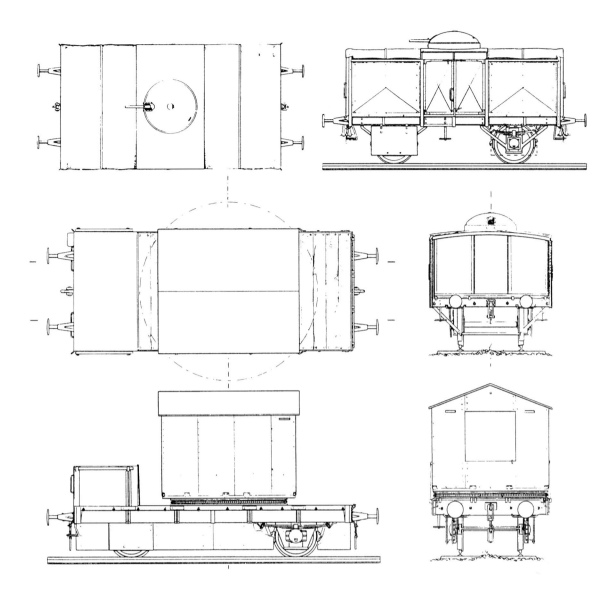

Omk(u) car, according to Standard II d1 or Generalized A6, with 5.3 cm gun in Gruson turret. *Below:* Unloaded Omk cars acording to Standard II d3 or Generalized A1, with swiveling armored cabin (length 3.18 m, width 2,80 m, height to peak 2.59 m from car bed, inside height 2.25 m) for a field gun on a wheeled mount. Drawings: P. Malmassari

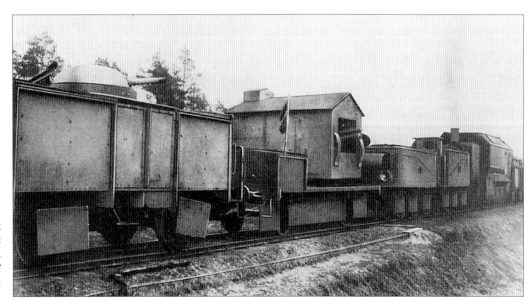

The late PZ V. Note the observation turret on the gun cabin and the bulges in front for the gun's wheels (here a 7.7-cm FK 96 new type), allowing it to be set closer to the front window. Photo: J. Magnuski collection

Equipped at first with only optical or acoustic communications, the armored trains were equipped with telephones later. Here a look through the open door at the built-in observation turret for the commander, in which the telephone was located. Photo: J. Magnuski collection

the mobilization type in the number and appearance of the cars, but the infantry cars now have roof structures, and probably strengthened armor. Between the upper edges of the car walls and the roof are a row of loopholes in the lightly armored body, which is still protected additionally by sandbags. But the most notable features are the gun cars, which replace some of the infantry cars (so that the total number of cars remains twelve). The one type, of which there are two, is based on the same iron 15-ton Omk(u) coal car as the infantry car, which now has a flat roof. In the middle of the car, an armored turning turret (by Gruson) with a 5.3-cm gun is installed. The other type, of which there are also two, is a flat car—presumably a bodiless Omk car according to Standard II d3 or Generalized type A 1 (wheelbase 4 meters, length with buffers 8.80 meters)—with a turning cabin-like armored structure with a large front window, which is covered by the shield of the gun that stands behind it. The gun, on a typical wheeled field artillery mount, is clearly a captured Russian 7.62-cm Putilov M 02 cannon in the picture (the German 7.7 cm new-type F.K. 96 field gun was probably used as well, and on the western front also the French 7.5 cm M 97 or 12 field gun). A basically more primitive reequipping is seen in PZ III. The infantry cars, all of the 20-ton type, still have open tops (covered with tent canvas), but only a wooden (though probably covered with sheet iron) structure to protect the shooters' heads. Two of the infantry cars were modified into gun cars (with cabin-like fixed roofs), and the front of the car was replaced by a round armored structure with a sliding opening, through which the gun, a 3.7-cm Masch.K, could fire. An A/A machine gun was mounted on the flat roof of this new body later. All of these rebuildings were so simple that they could be done at field workshops.

Another photo, though, shows an armored train with two locomotives in double traction and six cars (another photo shows the structure of two of them, but lacks notations of time and place). Here too, the high-wall freight cars with iron walls were probably the basis, but the added roof structures with armored observation posts on the infantry cars and well-integrated armored cupolas on the Gruson turrets with their 5.3-cm guns on the gun cars appear to be designed purposefully, as would be expected of solid workshop work without time pressure. In front there is also a mine-launcher car; its primary weapon fired from the open-topped back of the car. We can assume that this is one of the armored trains that were rebuilt before going into service. In these pre-planned measures, the number of cars was also decreased considerably. Not only does the photo give evidence of this (though it could show only part of the train), but

service at mobilization were rebuilt correspondingly. The installation of a phone system and headlights naturally caused few problems. Unfortunately, no precise information about the modifications is available, but the surviving pictorial material allows conclusions—though probably not far-reaching ones—to be drawn. An armored train in Romania in 1916-17 (presumably No. XII) corresponds to

The construction of an improved infantry and gun car is seen at an unidentified workshop. The cars obviously belong to the armored train shown in the third picture from the top of page 19. Photo: Bibl. fuer Zeitgeschichte, Stuttgart

Above and right: The rebuilt Armored Train III. The infantry cars (all of the 20-ton type) still have open tops but were fitted with wooden breastworks for the shooters. In the first car (with a roof), a semicircular armored gun position for a 3.7 cm machine cannon was installed, with a wide front window closed by a sliding armor plate (visible in the lower photo). Later an AA machine gun was mounted on the flat roof of the gun position (bottom photo). Photo: M. Hohmann collection and Archives of the Munich Engineer School

An armored train of the improved type (1915). At the far left, presumably a mine-launcher car (open on top at the rear). Behind it are two cars with armored Gruson turrets (note the more solid roof design, also found on the infantry car behind the two armored T 9 locomotives and an observation turret in the center. At the end of the train (far right) is probably another mine-launcher car. All cars are the 20-ton type. Photo: W. Sawodny collection

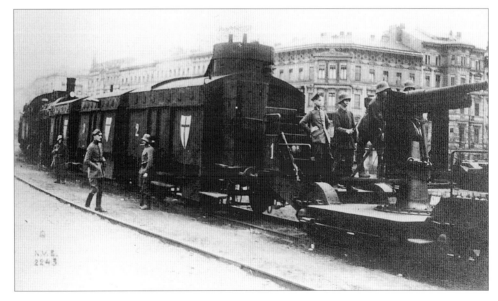

The postwar Armored Train No. IV; its infantry cars came from the World War Armored Train No. X (1915 type). These also show a solid roof design, plus some turning turrets with machine guns. At right is a car with a Russian Type 02 7.62-cm gun rebuilt for A/A use (all cars are the 15-ton type). Photo: W. Sawodny collection

surviving data on the Mainz PZ X, in particular, show that along with the Mainz locomotive 7325 (T 9.3)—like that of PZ XI—had a total of seven cars (Coeln 66252, Muenster 60302, Breslau 33509, 34457, 39003, 54012 and 83159). Since some of these cars were used in the postwar PZ IV and have been documented as such in photos, the same signs of careful designing can be seen in them: firmly attached and well-armored—though differently (arched)—roofs with more purposeful structures (turning turrets with heavy machine guns, command posts). Whether a railroad car used on this PZ IV shortly after the war (six of which were built by Rheinmetall by mounting a Russian 7.62-cm F.K. 02 rebuilt as an A/A gun with a socket mount on special cars also captured in Russia, on which naval guns had been mounted previously) were already in service before November 1918 (and whether such cars were also used in other armored trains) is not known.

To equip the trains with guns, the equipment of the fortress artillery was used at first, since they were already made for mounting on fixed mounts. Here the armored turret developed in the mid-1880s

by the Gruson works in Magdeburg for use in field fortifications was used. It consisted of an armored cupola of 40-mm hard-cast steel, in which a specially developed mount for a rapid-fire gun was installed. Although the firm also offered larger calibers, after 1900 the German Army seems to have used only the 5.3-cm S.K. L/24 (the gun's caliber is always stated briefly in documents and books as 5 cm), which was thus used in the armored trains. The armored cupola was atop a cast iron cylinder that was 5 mm thick in front (where it was protected by earth in field fortifications); in the readily reachable door area to the rear it was 14 mm thick. The armored cupola, including the gun, was turned (360 degrees in 15 seconds) by a handwheel with a setting brake. The turret could hold two men (gunner and loader); the gun was aimed via a notch and sight. For the entire armored turret there was a horsedrawn two-wheeled transport cart; it could be moved into position on rollers of field-railroad gauge (60 cm). For use in armored trains, these rollers were removed and the turret was firmly attached to the car floor by angle irons or on a pedestal of appropriate height, so that only the armored cupola stuck out; the lower part was

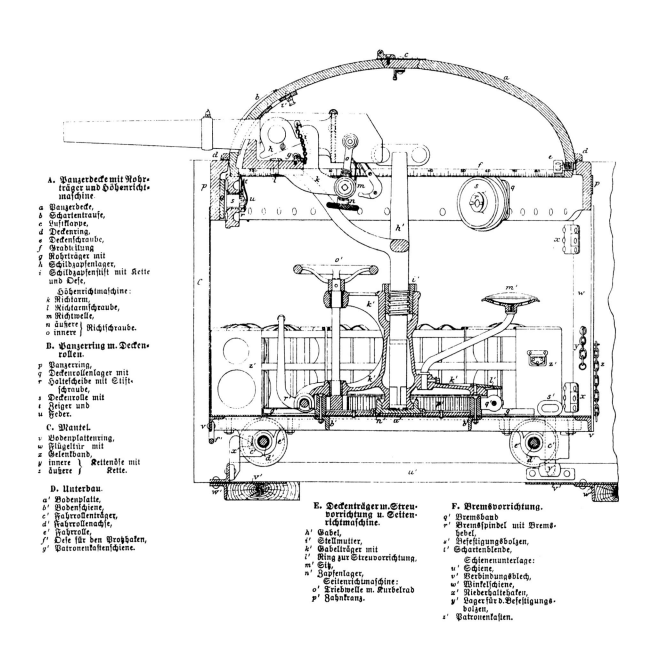

Design of the Gruson armored turret with 5.3-cm cannon, from Berlin, Waffenlehre (1907).

The Gruson turret, on the transport cart at left, in position at right. Only the cupola was armored and easily turned; the lower part was protected by a breastwork in fortifications. On the car, the rollers (removed for installation in armored train cars) on which the turret could be unloaded onto field railroad tracks and brought into position, can be seen. Photos: J. Magnuski collection and Imperial War Museum, London

Guns used in armored trains in World War I: *above:* Five-barreled, hand-operated 3.7-cm revolver cannon, Hotchkiss system, here on a makeshift AA mount. *upper right:* 3.7-cm naval machine cannon on a socket mount, here installed on a wheeled mount. From Muther, Das Geraet der leichten Artillerie, Vol. IV (1929)

Right: Russian 7.62-cm F.K. 02 as a railroad A/A gun on a special car, as it was used—possibly at the end of World War I—by armored trains. Photo: W. Sawodny collection

behind the protection of the armored car walls. From the supplies of the fortress artillery, the obsolete, hand-operated five-barreled 3.7-cm revolver cannon of the Hotchkiss system was still used. Its more effective successor, developed by the Navy in the early 1890s, was also used; this was the single-barreled water-cooled 3.7-cm machine cannon, which had been mustered out at the beginning of the war because of its no longer satisfactory ballistic performance (except its rate of fire, raised from 40 to 250 shots per minute, it corresponded to the 3.7-cm revolver cannon). It was important that the light space was not exceeded in the placement of the gun vertically to the direction of the train; this limited the barrel length. All in all, small-caliber, rapid-fire guns mounted on socket mounts were used for installation in armored trains.

Barrel lengths and mounts at first prevented the use of larger-caliber guns. Among the troops, the provision for an armored cabin on a flat car was created, in which any German or captured light field guns with their wheeled mounts could be housed. The gun inside the cabin already had a certain limited traverse field, but the whole armored cabin could be turned 360 degrees by using two handwheels and a gear mechanism. The target was aimed at directly. Only when enough light field guns (German 7.7-cm F.K.96 new type and Russian 7.62-cm F.K.02) had been fitted to socket mounts as A/A guns and the need of the anti-aircraft defense (behind which the armored trains certainly ranked) had been supplied—thus toward the end of the war—was the use of such guns on armored trains considered. Whether, and to what extent, they were used before the war ended is unclear, but such a gun was mounted on a special car for PZ IV before March 1919. A table of technical data of the guns used on armored trains in World War I will be found in the next chapter.

Besides the armored locomotives of the T 9.3 series, which were used most often, and sometimes in tandem, there were others. PZ IX, set up at Ludwigshafen, is shown in a photo with a Palatine T 3 (No. 204) and tender. For use on the eastern front, where long-distance runs required greater supplies of coal and water, the T 9.3 was used with two extra tenders in front. But they were also replaced by the towed tenders of freight locomotives. The Erfurt Machine 4642 (Prussian G 7.2) was already armored when the war began, and reached the western front. In 1915 it was reported as badly damaged by the M.E.D.1 (Brussels). From 1916 to the war's end it was with M.E.D. 7 (Nisch) in the Balkans, although whether it was still armored is questionable (possibly also with PZ IV?) The following later armorings can be documented: In 1915, Bs1 3229, 3260, 3310

The standard locomotive for German armored trains in World War I was, according to the 1910 service instructions, the Prussian T 9.3. Photo: EK Archives

A provisionally armored (cab, cylinder with steam pipe to smoke chamber, skirts for the wheels) Prussian G 3 Kattowitz 3144 in 1917. Photo: U. Walluhn collection

Two Prussian T 9.3 armored locomotives in tandem. The armor shows minor differences. Photo: W. Sawodny collection

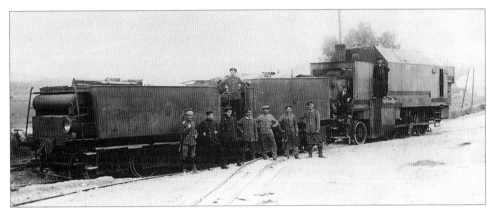

An armored T 9.3 with two (unarmored) extra tenders in front, increasing its radius of action. Photo: U./ Schwarze collection

The armored Bavarian-Palatine T 3 No. 204 (with an extra tender behind it) of the PZ IX, assembled in Ludwigshafen. Photo: Imperial War Museum, London

The Prussian G 7.1 used as an armored locomotive for long-distance trips in the east (originally published in the Great Pictorial Atlas of the War and wrongly identified as a captured Russian armored train!). Photo: W. Sawodny collection

Front view of the armored G 7.1, showing very clearly the similarity of the armor to that of the T 9.3 according to the 1910 service instructions. Photo: II. Wenzel collection

(all G 3), Erf 4726 (G 7.2); in 1917: Bsl 3343, Erf 3165, Ktz 3144, 3181, 3182 (all G 3), Erf 4417 (G 7.1), Erf 5162 (G 8.1); in 1918: Bsl 3386—on October 29, 1918!—and Ktz 3159 (G 3).

All of these locomotives—including those from Erfurt—were later found in the east. The figures for the last two years seem somewhat surprising in view of the fact that in the winter of 1916-17 the total number of armored trains had been much decreased. One must draw the conclusion that after the reduction of "official" armored trains, the available supplies in the east led to the formation of makeshift units, for which the G 3 was generally used (the photographed Kattowitz loco 3144 also has only temporary armor on the cab and running gear!). After the war, these trains may have been used by Border Patrol East, making up the majority of numbers 8 to 19, some of which can be traced to Lithuania and particularly in the industrial area of Upper Silesia early in 1919. Of the four armored Kattowitz G 3s, three were mustered out by the Germans early in the twenties; the fourth (Ktz 3181) was used in the Polish "Kaniow" armored train. For the other German armored trains of postwar times, no G 3 can be documented as its locomotive. Pictures of the aforementioned Palatine T 3s and one G 7.1 show that the armoring of other types was done primarily according to the 1910 service instructions for the T 9.3; they all show the armored hood set on the side boards over the boiler and cab, and skirts linked with rods in front of the wheels. All the G 7 and 8 of the regular armored trains were probably equipped like that.

After these rebuildings and improvements, the armored-train weapon in 1915, despite being limited to the rail lines, is shown to have had a variety of uses; a contemporary source states: The services that armored trains have accomplished in the present war can in fact not be valued highly enough." With the transition to trench warfare in the west and the pacification of the backline areas there, though, the armored trains lost their realm of activity. After the occupation of Russian Poland and the adjoining eastern border regions, movement ended for a long time in the northern part of the eastern front occupied by German troops as well by the end of September 1915. So here too, only the tasks of securing tracks or troop and material transport in the backline areas remained for the armored trains. In the early summer of 1916, PZ III was stationed in Nisch; it had probably accompanied the advance of the German troops in Serbia since October 1915. Later it was replaced by PZ IV.

In view of the static fronts in the West and East, and the resulting limited possibilities of using armored trains, it was decided in the summer of 1916 to reduce them from thirteen to seven, but the worsening war situation did not allow this at first. Cutting down had been influenced by, among other things, the entry of Romania in the war on August 27, 1916, which made support of the Austro-Hungarian troops there by German troops necessary. On September 9, PZ II and XII were transferred from the western front to Romania. While no data on the action of PZ II is available, PZ XII supported the retaking of the Petroszeny Basin from Puj on September 14. On November 9-10, 1916 it supported the German troop breakthrough at the Red Tower Pass by repeatedly breaking through the Romanian positions near Robesti. The two armored trains are known to have been in the Romanian theater of war until the beginning of 1917, and at that time a third one—No. IV—saw action in Dobrudja, and it may have supported the advance of the Bulgarian Army, coming from Serbia, into that area the previous autumn.

In a listing of the railroad troops from late September 1916, the stationings of the 13 armored trains are stated as follows: On the western front, PZ I and III with the M.E.D. 1 (Lille), PZ VIII with M.E.D. 2 (Sedan), PZ VII with M.E.D. 3 (Hirson), PZ V, VI, X, XI and XIII with the Lin.komm. Z (Strasbourg); in the East, PZ IX in the Kovel area, PZ II and XII in Transylvania, PZ IV with M.E.D. 7 (Serbia). During the winter half-year of 1916-17, the number of armored trains was in fact decreased to seven. The two armored trains from Mainz can serve again as examples: PZ X was left in Altona on October 24, 1916, PZ XI returned to the manufacturers in Darmstadt on April 13, 1917 and was dismantled. The remaining armored trains were given new numbers. PZ V was now PZ I, PZ X now PZ II, PZ XII now PZ V, and PZ XIII now PZ VII; PZ III, IV and VI retained their numbers.

In mid-February 1917, the 204th Infantry Division held maneuvers in the region north and east of Ghent, in which three armored trains (probably PZ I, III and V) took part; they stood ready with only their technical crews at Terdonck (Ghent-Selzaete line), Loochristi (Ghent-Lokeren line) and Wetteren (Ghent-Alost line). PZ V was surely among them, as it had been inspected by the Chef FEW in that area in August 1917 and went to the workshop at Mechelen in November 1917.

For the beginning of 1918, the distribution of the armored trains was listed as follows: PZ I with M.E.D. 1 (Lille), PZ III with Lin.komm. Brussels, PZ IV with M.E.D. 7 (Serbia), PZ VI with Lin.komm. Z (Strasbourg), PZ II, V and VII were deactivated in the North Sea coastal area of Germany. PZ IV was sent to Gradsko during the Allied 1918 summer offensive. On September 2, 1918 it took part in the defense of that city and in the evacuation runs during the withdrawal from it on September 24. On September 26 it undertook the destruction of the line from Veles toward Skoplje, on September 29 it helped to defend the latter city, covered the retreat of numerous transport and hospital trains, and finally set off to the north after destroying the railroad bridge over the Vardar. Although it is not cited further, it may also have been involved in the hasty

A German armored train (presumably PZ X or XI of the Lin.komm Mainz) is seen on the Metz-Verdun line in the summer of 1916. Photo: C. Asmus collection

withdrawal battles that led via Vranje and Nisch to the Belgrade area after the fall of Bulgaria on September 30. In the conquest of Riga and creation of a bridgehead north of the Duena in September 1917, a broad-gauge Russian armored train fell into German hands and was used by them.

When the peace negotiations with the Soviet Republic in Brest-Litovsk broke down in February 1918, the Central Powers occupied Estonia, large areas of White Russia and all of the Ukraine to Rostov at the mouth of the Don. Armored trains were activated for this: PZ II (ex-X), which was transferred from Altona to Courland on February 16, 1918, and PZ V and VII. These armored trains could only operate behind the front line established by the end of 1917 (north of Riga—along the Duena to Duenaburg—east of Vilna and Lida—west of Slonim and Baranovici—Punsk—east of Kovel—west of Dubno), where the rail lines had been rebuilt to the Central European gauge.

In the advance into Russia, which was made essentially by rail, the transport trains were preceded by 'patrol trains' (manned only by infantry) and makeshift armored trains assembled from captured Russian wide-gauge stock (with added gun cars, probably armed with field guns on open mounts)—the locomotives, protected only by sandbags, always ran in the middle of the train. Trains of the latter type are known to have operated on the Holoby—Perespa—Kivercy—Rovno line, on the line from Alexandria (where it took part in combat) to Yekaterinoslav (where it was held up by bridge

destruction on April 5, 1918), and in the Pripyet area between Luniniec and Gomel, where Russian armored trains, which it fought successfully, were active. Although it cannot be documented, it can be assumed that the captured armored train on hand in the bridgehead north of Riga took part in the advance in the Baltic area toward Valk and beyond.

The German troops under General von der Goltz, who were transferred to Finland early in April 1918 to support the Finns in their fight against the Soviet troops, were much delayed in their advance by the actions of two Russian armored trains. Thus toward the end of that month, the Germans also improvised an armored train, which was ready for action in three days, but was later improved on the basis of experience: Four X-cars loaded with gravel were at the front as control cars; a four-axle SS-car was used as a gun car \ (with forward-sloping walls of 18-mm cast sheet iron and an opening at the front with a sheet-iron door for the 7.5-cm mountain gun, its wheeled mount set on a swinging (max. 30 degrees) platform, in its back housing with gable roof a front MG 08 that fired over the big gun, and several loopholes on the sides); a Gm car for the commander (with an observation post of 18-mm sheet metal on the roof of the front half of the car, and three heavy MG 08, one in the front hatch just under the roof, firing over the gun car, the other two in side hatches); a Gm car as a light machine-gun car (two MG 08/15 in side hatches); a fully armored Finnish freight locomotive (probably Series

An armored train of the mobilization type, with added gun cars. The T 9.3 bears armor skirts over the wheels. Note also the fixed but unprotected pipe for boiler water running from the extra tender to the locomotive. Photo: EK Archives

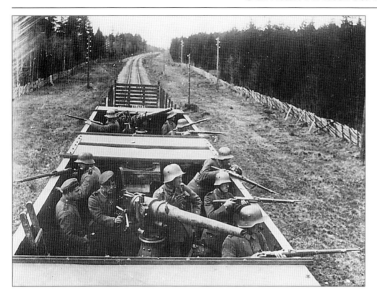

This picture is attributed to an armored train in Finland in 1918. But it must be noted that neither the car itself nor its armament (two small-caliber—ca. 5 cm?—(naval) guns on socket mounts—on the front one, the notch and sight for direct aiming are clearly visible) agrees with the detailed description of the train by its commander (see text). Whether another—otherwise undocumented—armored train was used in Finland, or whether the location was in error (Baltic states, 1919, where improvised armored trains—as this one obviously is—were used?) must remain unanswered. Photo: Federal Archives, Koblenz

Tk 2) pulling a tender; an equipment car (Gm, for engineering gear and spare weapon parts, plus medical materials and a cooking pot with food supplies); a four-axle SS-car with track-building material; an ammunition car (Gm); an O-car on which two light hand-operated railcars and a heavy one were loaded; later this car was fitted with an A/A MG on a turning mount in ring-shaped armor; a rear car (Gm, later-SS car with a body like that of the gun car, with two side MG ports and two more in the rear wall, armed with two captured Russian machine guns); two gravel-loaded control cars (Type X). All the Gm-cars had a sheet-iron covering screwed on behind the wooden walls, the gap being filled with gravel. On the roof were two 5-mm sheets with sand or felt between them. While the command, gun and rear cars could be entered only through bottom hatches, the equipment and ammunition cars had side doors. The cars loaded track-building material, and railcars as well as the control cars only had their axle ends protected with armor plate. There were telephone and speaking-

tube connections linking all the cars, plus a mechanical bell signal linking the locomotive, commander's and rear cars, and emergency signal flags in the commander's and rear cars. Special emphasis was placed on protecting the communication and air-brake lines under the cars. In case of damage to the air-brake lines, frozen brakes could be released by using internal safety valves. Also of note is the water intake with a 7-meter hose, mounted behind an armor plate under the locomotive's cab, which allowed taking on water from rivers, lakes, etc.

The crew consisted of two officers, 10 NCOs, and 48 to 50 men (6 gunners, 18-20 machine gunners, the rest engineers). There was also an interpreter who could communicate with the Finnish locomotive crew. If need be, up to a company of infantry could also be carried.

The just-finished armored train was able, along with a cycle company, to capture the railroad junction of Riihimaeki in a half-hour fight and drive a Soviet armored train stationed there to flight. After that, it successfully secured track repair work and troop arrivals on the Riihimaeki-Lahti line, driving off several enemy attacks. The capture of a station guarded by one of the two enemy armored trains, along with a platoon of riflemen, is noteworthy. These Soviet armored trains, which had withdrawn to behind a destroyed bridge, could even be captured by men from the crews, who were sent forward on railcars, after they had been surrounded and cut off by other German troops. Later the armored train covered the flank of these German troops and carried out mopping-up activities along the line.

Armored trains were also used outside Europe. In the colony of Togo, an armored train was active on the line north of Lome on August 14, 1914; in Cameroun an armored car armed with machine guns was used to defend the bridge over the Dibamba at Yapoma by Reserve Detachment No. 2 on October 6, 1914.—It is noteworthy that the Railroad Double Company No. 34-38, which was transferred to the Hedschas line in the Near East in the spring of 1918, put two specially built armored railcars, equipped with four machine guns and strong lights, into service in June. They gave good service in securing the otherwise poorly guarded Dera—Amman—Katrane line, but had to be blown up in September 1918 in their withdrawal north of Amman after their backlne connections had been broken by an English offensive.

As escorts to defend transport trains from air attacks, a number of cars were temporarily armored and armed with A/A machine guns from 1916 on. Ten O- and twenty C-cars were rebuilt in this way at the Mons workshop in 1916, as were ten of each type at the branch

An A/A car built and used on the western front to protect transports. The right picture shows the machine-gun position. Photos: Museum fuer Verkehr und Technik, Berlin, and P. Malmassari collection

workshop in Schaerbeek. A photo of two of these cars in Hirson shows three-axle cars covered externally with wood, half of each fitted with a breastwork surrounding a platform, on which the A/A MG was mounted.—A photo documents an armored rail auto. Known only as a drawing, it is obviously an armored transporter for road and rail use. It has a gasoline-electric powerplant. The vehicle could be lifted by two auto jacks and the rail wheels lowered. Whether it ever went into production is questionable.

Although it does not really belong among the armored rail vehicles, it might be mentioned as a curiosity that in Palestine a German railroad engineer unit stationed in Afule mounted an aircraft engine at first on a flatcar, and later, because of the unpleasant prop-wash, on an automobile fitted with locomotive wheels, and used this forerunner of the Kruckenberg rail Zeppelin, which is said to have reached quite a speed, for patrol runs.

Despite this very incomplete information, it can be seen that during World War I, along with the armored trains, a remarkably broad spectrum of military rail vehicles were used, and in fact, wherever German troops served—even in faraway theaters of war, especially when the fronts were moving. Of course, they did not all achieve remarkable results.

In their freight-car-like appearance and with their weak armament, most German armored trains were not spectacular. Thus it is no wonder that in wartime illustrations of them, imagination often ruled, and in the captions of armored-train photos from those days, mystifications were numerous. The more impressive-looking Austro-Hungarian armored trains were often called German; even Oefele describes only one of them in his small booklet "Panzerautos und Panzerzuege" of 1915.

Of the seven regular armored trains of 1917-18, six definitely survived beyond the war's end (see below); only PZ I cannot be documented. It was probably lost during the withdrawal from the West.

A captured German rail-protection armored truck is carried away by the Russians on a wide-gauge flatcar. Photo: J. Magnuski collection

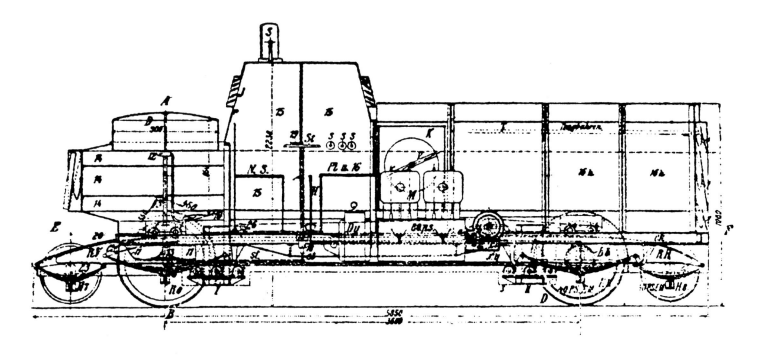

Drawing of an armored German transport vehicle for road and rail, from a Russian source, Whether it was ever built is unknown. Picture: J. Magnuski collection

"French sentries in combat with a German armored train" says this picture postcard of World War I, showing an Austro-Hungarian train, not one of which saw service on the western front! Picture: Museum fuer Verkehr und Technik, Berlin

Austria-Hungary

For a portrayal of the German armored trains, though, those of the Dual Monarchy are of interest in other ways. For one thing, such locomotives and cars came to the German Army via the successor states and were sometimes still used to the end of the war in 1945; for another, the Dual Monarchy's railroad troops were very innovative when it came to armored trains and developed several forward-looking concepts with long-term effects.

When the war broke out, the Dual Monarchy had no armored trains, but railroad companies located in Galicia and Wolhynia improvised several on their own initiative in a few weeks; they were used with great success in the withdrawal fighting.

This experience inspired the Austrian War Ministry as of October 1914 to contract with the Budapest-North factory of the Royal Hungarian State Railways (MAV) for the building of six armored trains (No. I-VI). Each train included an armored locomotive of the Hungarian 377 series and two cars. The armor at first consisted of 12-mm steel plates, which turned out to be insufficient. After some experimenting, armor of two-layer Martin cast-steel plates was developed, which also held off the pointed Russian artillery shells. Between the 12-mm outer and 8-9-mm inner steel wall, 40 mm apart, was a layer of wood. Of the cars, which had axle protection, one (Series 140) was hand-braked, the other was from Series 148-150. Each car had five ports for machine guns (two on each side and one in front). Supply containers and probably also recondensation equipment for the water-cooled Schwartzlose M 7/12 machine guns were installed above the ports. There were also fifteen (Type 140 cars) or eleven (Type S 148-150) loopholes for rifles, closed with armor plates. In the rear wagon (Type S 148-150) was a water tank with a capacity of four cubic meters, which was linked with the locomotive by an armored tube. Some 500 kilograms of coal could also be carried in this car. Along with the 4.3 cubic meters of water and 1.5 cubic meters of space for coal in the locomotive itself, the train's action radius was increased to 100 km. Both cars had round armored observation turrets with vision slits on their roofs. The front car had a rail clearer, plus a carrier rack under the floor, which allowed material for repairing track damage to be carried.

As 1914 turned to 1915, it was recognized—much as in the German Reich—that machine guns alone were not sufficient, and two more armored trains (No. VII and VIII) with the following composition were contracted for: the MG car (with a round observation turret moved to the side on the roof and a larger water tank inside) was now in the center of the train, flanked by two armored locomotives of the MAV 377 series; at the ends of the train were Type 140 or 141 gun cars, the rear half of their bodies having an enclosed body similar to that of the machine gun car (with one machine gun port on each side); on top was a large fixed turret with another MG port to the front, crowned with the usual round observation turret and vision slits. The front half of the car bore a round armor shield, inside which a 7- (6.6-) cm L/30 torpedo-boat gun was mounted at first; before delivery, it was fitted with an armored turning turret. These gun cars were also fitted with hand brakes, carriers for track-building material and rail clearers. These two armored trains went to the front in March 1915. Another gun car of this type was made to reequip PZ V, while PZ I and II were given improvised gun cars built on tender chassis, on which the 7-cm gun was mounted not inside a turret, but behind a sliding round shield, thus having only a limited traverse field. In PZ II, another gun port was provided on each side, through which a 4.7-cm L/33 naval gun could be fired. Some of these armored trains (definitely No. V and VII) received additional gun cars with larger-caliber (8- or 10-cm) guns.

After Italy entered the war, two more armored trains (No. IX and X) were built in Carinthia; they included armored locomotives and two infantry cars armed with machine guns, though their design did not correspond with those of the first MAV armored trains (No. I-VIII).

Captain Schober of the 15th Railroad Company, which had done the first armored-train improvisation when the war began, had an improved armored train, with various innovations, built in the first half of 1915. He used a Type 97 locomotive with smoke ducting and an added tender, two flat machine gun cars rounded on the outside, and an almost streamlined gun car with a turning turret in the middle (built on State Railway car 303.343), with its own motor, so it could run independently of the train as an individual vehicle.

Austro-Hungarian Armored Train No. III. This pattern was used for all the trains built in 1914 (PZ I-VI); later some were equipped with improvised gun cars. Photo: War Archives, Vienna

Armored Trains VII and VIII, built in the spring of 1915, had gun cars, but just one, between the infantry wagons coupled to the two locomotives (MAV Series 377). Photo: Vojensky Historicky Archiv Prag

Thus the concept of a self-propelled armored car was realized. This train—at first named after its inventor—was later numbered XI. Finally, Armored Train XII was formed of an already existing Series 29 armored locomotive (with extra tender) and two infantry cars armed with machine guns, but besides these "official" ones, improvised armored trains were made up later, including a narrow-gauge example for the Bosnian-Herzegovinian State Railway.

The crews of the Austro-Hungarian armored trains toward the end of the war were listed as an officer and 48 men, but were surely smaller at the beginning (PZ II had one officer and 30 men in 1915).

Another development of the Austro-Hungarian armored trains that pointed to the future was the use of pairs of two trains for mutual protection (improvisations of the 5th Railroad company under Captain

As of mid-1917, only five armored trains remained in service, all consisting of the material from PZ I-VIII, but uniformly consisting of one gun car, one infantry car and the locomotive. Photo: War Archives, Vienna

Especially interesting was Captain Schober's armored train, built in the summer of 1915, for it included a motorized car (at left, with the gun turret) that could operate on its own. A similar infantry car to the one in front of the loco was located behind it. Photo: W. Sawodny collection

Kossowicz in November 1914), a means of operation that showed its effectiveness particularly in the Russian Civil War of 1917-1920 and led to the formation of corresponding "armored train divisions) in the Red Army, which existed even throughout World War II. They were established in the German Wehrmacht only in 1944, although they had been promoted much earlier (in 1919!).

The Austro-Hungarian armored trains saw service on all fronts, and frequent and long transfer runs were often necessary to bring the few available units to all the scenes of action at which troops of the Habsburg Monarchy were fighting.

But for the Austro-Hungarian armored trains too, the "freezing" of the fronts lessened their uses. Thus of the twelve armored trains, No. I, II, VI, X, XI and XII were taken out of service in September 1917, while the others were modified, so that along with the armored locomotive they had only one gun car and one machine-gun car (all of the Hungarian MAV type). No. IX had been destroyed by Romanian artillery fire on August 29, 1916. So from that time until the war's end, only five armored trains (III, IV, V, VII and VIII) were active. But the Austrians—just like the Germans—put provisional broad-gauge armored trains into service during the occupation of southwestern Russia in the spring of 1918 for the "railroad advance". Their later history is unknown.

All the active armored trains, plus most of the retired ones, were taken over by the successor states of the Habsburg Monarchy. They were divided as follows:

Yugoslavia:	No. V
Poland:	No. III and VIII
Hungary:	No. IV and VII, plus retired No. XI and material from No. I, VI, VII and VIII (old); of them, No. VII and a car from the old No. VII were captured by the Czechs in 1919.
Czechoslovakia:	Retired No. II plus cars from No. VI and VII, plus the units captured from Hungary later.

There that all remained in service—except three cars that were scrapped—until World War II, in which Hungary used its trains, while those of Yugoslavia, Poland and Czechoslovakia fell into German hands in 1939 or 1941.

Further Austro-Hungarian armored trains (No. X, XII?) were said to be at the Vienna Arsenal at the war's end in 1918 and had to be disarmed there later according to the Treaty of St. Germain.

During the Austro-Hungarian border combat in Carinthia, the Austrians used an improvised armored train from April 29 to June 13, 1919; it was numbered XIII and had to be broken up at Spittal on the Drau on June 14, 1919.

In 1933 the Austrian Army built six provisional armored trains (locomotives of Series 30, each with two open freight cars with stone armor and gun shields, one heavy machine gun as their main weapon, and two control cars). They saw action in the fighting around Vienna in February 1934 and were taken out of service later. In 1939 the Austrians planned to build an interesting armored train. It was to consist essentially of an armored four-axle railcar with one observation turret and two turning turrets (for AA machine cannons), two gun cars and two control cars. A very similar assemblage was seen in 1942 with the Diesel locomotive of the German "SP 42" armored train project. It later became Armored Railcar No. 16, and it is likely that the 1939 Austrian plan served as its model.

Other Countries

For the western Entente powers, armored trains played only a meager role. This was mainly because of what quickly became an almost immobile, heavily fortified front line in a positional war. On the other hand, this strongly favored the development of heavy railroad artillery.

The French made very little use of armored trains. An improvised train, consisting of 15 cars protected by railroad ties, three closed cars and two flat ones, was set up by the Marine Brigade in September 1914. At first it protected the rail line along the Oise from Pontoise to Creil; later it saw service in the Montdidier-Roye area, where it was damaged on September 20, and shortly afterward it was withdrawn, no further traces being found. A second armored train was assembled in Le Havre in September-October 1914. On October 3 it was transferred to the Antwerp area. It appears to have turned up at Verdun in March 1916. A third French armored train was used by the 10th Army in the St. Pol-Arras-Bethune area in December 1914; later it was transferred to the 2nd Army, and no later traces have been found.

Two armored trains were put into service near Antwerp by the Belgians early in September 1914. They consisted of a turntable car with 18-mm armor and a 5.7-cm rapid-fire gun at the front (with loopholes for machine guns and rifles on the sides); the armored locomotive was originally a 4-4-2 tender type 15, later to be replaced by a 0-6-0 Type 32 loco with pulled three-axle tender (Type 32), followed by a two-axle armored car with a machine gun and several loopholes. Each train was assigned a second armored locomotive for reconnaissance and communication. The crew consisted of one officer, 5 NCOs and 49 men, two engine drivers and one fireman. Both trains operated in the Ghent-Antwerp-Termonde-Netherlands border area until early October, when Antwerp was taken by the Germans. A third armored train being built there could be sent to Ostend in time, and Train No. 2 also went there. Train No. 1 was

Drawing of the planned Austrian M 39 armored train

I Railcar with Diesel-electric drive
  1 Observation turret with built-in range finder
  2 Turret for Landsverk L 62 A/A with 4 cm Bofors gun
  3 Balcony for M 7/12 heavy machine gun

  4 Loopholes for rifles or light machine guns
II Artillery car with 10-cm M 38 howitzer in armored turret, 3 and 4 as above
III Flatcar for train security and transport of track-building material.

Drawing: War Archives, Vienna

The light Belgian Armored Train No. 1 fell into German hands early in October 1914. Photo: W. Zimmermann collection

A heavy Belgian armored train of 1914; in present-day terms it is more like railroad artillery. Photo: W. Sawodny collection

to go to Ghent, but was derailed near Boom and fell into German hands. Its crew later took over Armored Train No. 3 in Ostend. Trains 2 and 3 were then moved to Dunkerque, from which they carried out tasks in the Nieuport-Dixmude area. In addition to these "light" trains, three "heavy" armored trains were also built with British help (four flatcars, each with a British 10.5-cm gun), but these should, by present-day standards, be assigned to the railroad artillery.

The British themselves built two armored trains for coastal protection; the first was stationed in Norfolk since December 1914, the second in Scotland since April 1915. They also consisted of a gun car, a 0-6-2 tender locomotive (Class N 1 of the GNR) and an infantry car. They remained in service until 1923 to guard against communistic uprisings.—The Irish rebellion of 1916 caused the British to build two armored trains and one railcar; they remained there for a time after the uprising. In the renewed Irish tension of 1918, two more armored trains were put into service.—In the British colonies, armored patrols were used on the Uganda railways on the border of German East Africa, and in the occupation of German Southwest Africa, the South African troops used armored trains with

10.5- and 15-cm guns on the line running inland from Luederitz Bay.

Russia is said to have sent an armored train to China during the Boxer Rebellion of 1900, and some are said to have covered the retreat from Manchuria in the last phase of the Russo-Japanese War (1905). Railroad artillery was used in the defense of Port Arthur. Whether the armored trains were retained after 1905 in view of the Russian unrest is not known. In any case, between 1912 and 1914 four new armored trains, each with an armored locomotive and two armored cars, each armed with a small-caliber gun (3.7-, 5.7- or 7.62-cm) and several 7-mm machine guns, and two control cars, were put into service. Thus Russia and the German Reich were the only nations that entered World War I with such trains. During the war, other armored trains were built (at least 15) with varying equipment, and captured cars and weapons were also utilized, the former naturally in the captured parts of the German Reich and Austria-Hungary, in which standard gauge was used, so that the Russian broad-gauge trains could not be used. Also worthy of special note is an armored railcar built in 1916. The four-axle vehicle was driven by a 120-HP motor, had armor 15 mm thick and two 7.62-cm guns in turning turrets.

Very little has become known of the use of Russian armored trains in World War I. In 1914, one took part in the fighting around Tarnopol, another drove back a German attack on Skierniewice on November 19 of that year and took part in the pursuit of the beaten enemy at Koluszki on November 23. When the Russian forces were surrounded by the German counterattack the next day, the armored train was able to break through and take the Russian staff to safety. In this first war year, a Russian armored train was already captured by the Germans. In May 1915 a Russian armored train covered the withdrawal from Przemysl; another operated in the Brest-Litovsk area in August. On September 24, 1915 an armored train broke through the Austrian front line at Rudoczka (Rovno-Kovel line) and allowed the Russians to capture it. During the later advance, though, it was immobilized by a direct hit on the locomotive and remained lying between the lines, badly damaged, until the summer of 1916 (!). In April 1916, Russian armored trains were still active in that area; one was in Klevan (on the aforementioned line) and another in Mirogoszcze (Rovno-Dubno line). In the spring of 1916 a Russian armored train had to be given up in Kopyczynce, as its way back had been cut off, and in July 1917 another (made of captured German and Austrian material) fell into German hands in the breakthrough in Zloczov. The Austro-Hungarian troops also captured other Russian armored trains; there were seven on hand when the October Revolution of 1917 began.

An imperial Russian armored train of World War I. Photo: M. Ilohmann collection

A Russian armored railcar of 1916, with two 7.62-cm F.K.-M-02 guns in armored turrets. Similar vehicles were used by the Soviets in World War II and captured by the Germans.

Early in the Revolution, the Soviets agreed on a uniform design: Two two-turreted gun cars plus the locomotive (in front here). Details differed depending on the factory; the "Krasnoye Sormovo" type shown here, made in Nizhni Novgorod, still ran in German armored trains in World War II. Photo: J. Magnuski collection

But the armored trains attained their greatest significance in the fighting that followed this event in Russia. All the involved parties made much use of them, the Soviets as well as all the White armies from the successor states from parts of the Russian Empire: Finland, Estonia, Latvia, Lithuania and Poland, and even the Allied intervention troops, just as—before the armistice—the Central Powers had done. Sometimes they were assembled in "armored train divisions", with heavy (stronger artillery weapons) and light (infantry with small-caliber guns) working together. In southern Russia in particular, almost only such packs of armored trains were involved in the battles along with the cavalry units. The best-known was the command train in which the Soviet War Commissar Leon Trotsky hurried from front to front. It consisted—drawn by two armored locomotives—of not only a strong radio and telegraph station, but also a library, a print shop, and its own power station, and it carried cars with which towns off the rail lines could be reached. In the fighting around Petrograd

in the autumn of 1919, his military escort command was directly involved.—In the Russo-Polish War of 1920 too, the armored trains played a major role. Several of them were captured by the Poles, who also had a goodly number of their own constructions (in all, between 1918 and 1921, no fewer than 85 Polish armored trains are said to have existed. The following figures have been stated for the Red Army: In November 1918, 23; at the end of 1919, 59; and in 1921 as many as 103 armored trains. They generally consisted of an armored locomotive, a control car, and just two large four-axle gun cars, each with two turning turrets armed with guns, so they were quite powerful in battle, yet very compact and mobile. Many of these trains remained in service, after being overhauled and modernized, into World War II, where the concept of the armored train division was maintained (two armored trains with escort vehicles—living and supply trains, armored railcars, etc.). Later the Poles took up this pattern for their armored trains, adding just one infantry car ("storm-car") to the two gun cars.

Postwar Fighting of German Armored Trains

The Results of the Armistice

Just as in the area of the former Russian Empire, armored trains reached their true significance in Germany only after the end of World War I. After signing the armistice on November 11, 1918, the main task was bringing back the million-man German Army, which was still across the borders almost everywhere. This succeeded, quickly and smoothly, thanks to the still-intact command structure in the west. Of course the soldiers who returned to their homeland went their way quickly and almost completely under the influence of the troops trained in the reserve army during the revolution, and because of their weariness of war. Things were different in the east. Here the Central powers had occupied a large area in the spring of 1918, including the Baltic states, western White Russia, and all of the Ukraine to the Narwa—Pleskau–Polozk-Borissow—Dniepr line from south of Mogilew to Rogatschew—Gomel–Klintzy–Makowo—Gluchow—Miropolje–Belgorod—Waluiki—Kantemirowka–Millerowo—Lichaja–Gornaja-Rostow, with Podolia and the southern Ukraine, had fallen to the Austro-Hungarian army, with the exception of the Crimea and the area on the mainland in front of it, which was granted to the Germans. In Trans-Caucasia (Poti-Tiflis) too, there were German troops. In all, there were some 500,000 men stationed in that area (plus some 250,000 Austrian troops. But after almost all the capable units had been transferred to the western front for the 1918 offensives—outnumbered by far by reserve and home-guard troops, these being older or less experienced personnel whose fighting value was not to be valued very highly.

In the occupied areas (Ukraine, White Ruthenia, Poland, Lithuania, Latvia and Estonia), national regimes that cooperated with the Central powers had been set up which strove to become free of Russia. After the collapse of the Central powers, they oriented themselves—in every case toward independence from the Soviet Union, which was determined to haul them back—naturally toward the victorious Allies, though to varying degrees. The Poles did this most vigorously: The Lublin (Austrian) and Warsaw (German) governments declared themselves independent on November 7 and 11, 1918, and joined on the 14th to form the new state of Poland, which quickly showed a desire to expand on all sides. The railroad network of this newly created state was not open for the return of the German troops. The units that stretched far to the east in southern Russia thus had to take a long route to the northwest over the single, heavily overburdened rail line, which ran from Kowel via Brest-Litovsk and Bialystok to Prostken in East Prussia, to get home, and shortly before Kowel (Holoby from Rowno and Povursk from Sarny) or on the Pripjet line in Pinsk, they had to change from broad to standard gauge. The return of the units over such great distances and under these conditions, and in the Russian winter at that, promised difficult problems. In addition, Austro-Hungarian troops in the Ukraine had disbanded before the German armistice, and the German-friendly regime of the Hetman Skoropadski had had to give way very quickly to the national Ukrainian Directorate of Petlyura and Vinichenko, which met the Germans much less amiably.

To be sure, the transport back, which was planned to bring the most distant units back first, ran according to plan, so that the troops stationed in the Caucasus and Turkey—brought to the southern Ukraine by ship—reached home by the end of November. But soon these plans went to pieces, because the units stationed farther back, who were responsible for protecting the rail lines, did not want to wait until it was their turn, but took, and sometimes forced, their early transport. The rail lines became the property of the national Ukrainian forces, for whom—as for all the other opposition in the east—had every intention of arming and equipping themselves at the cost of the vanquished. The German transports were thus stopped, and the war-weary soldiers, who wanted to get home at any price, generally did not oppose being disarmed, not realizing that they were thus fully in the hands of the national Ukrainians in terms of their further travel and added plundering. Even agreements with the Directorate itself accomplished little, since its central power was meager and the local leaders ran things as they saw fit. To keep the lines open, makeshift broad-gauge armored trains used for the advance in the spring could have been very useful, but most of them—if they were still in existence at all—seemed to have fallen victim to the general relaxing of order. Only a single action of theirs has been recorded: On December 7 and 8, 1918, an armored train from Novograd-Wolynsk cleared the line to Iskorost.—On January 17, 1919 the staff of Army Group Kiev left the Ukrainian capital in two trains that were armed with guns, mine-throwers and machine guns, and reached Brest-Litovsk on January 21.

Keeping the rail link from Kowel to Prostken open, on the other hand, succeeded after the unreliable units stationed there were replaced by recruited volunteers. It was also protected by two armored trains until mid-February 1919: PZ VII, manned by members of Volunteer Battalion 40 in Goloby (hence its designation of VII/40), and PZ V, which returned from Brest-Litovsk to Lyck in East Prussia on February 23 as the last unit to return after the end of the transport. Despite the noted difficulties, the entire withdrawal from the Ukraine, including the cross-country march of the cavalry units, went remarkably smoothly. Although a time period of four months had been planned on, beginning with the armistice on November 11, 1918, the last troops reached the Kowel area at the end of January 1919, and the area between that city and the East Prussian border was turned over to Poland during February. Only at the edges of the formerly occupied zone did parts of the I. Army Corps get sent back from the Kharkov area, after agreement, across Soviet Russian territory. Parts of the 7th Home Guard Division were still in Odessa when the French occupied the city on December 18, 1918 (the Allies had landed at several Black Sea ports soon after the armistice), and the 15th Lw. Div., moved from Crimea to the mainland, was surrounded by national Ukrainian forces at Nikolayev early in January. They set up four armored trains, which operated successfully on the lines to Odessa, Dolinskaja, Snigirewka and Cherson. On March 2, 1919 an attack on Cherson by the Bolsheviks, who had meanwhile advanced into the Ukraine, was repelled with the help of one of these armored trains; on March 5 an attack on Nikolayev itself was driven off. The German troops in Nikolayev and Odessa were transported by sea on Allied ships between March 9 and 23, but some were interned in Saloniki and reached home only in June and July 1919.

In the area north of the Pripjet Marshes, the 10th Army moved fairly neatly out of White Ruthenia, the regime there disappeared without a trace, the Red Army followed and occupied Vilna on January 4. In mid-January the Germans were at a line east of Wolkowysk–east of Grodno–along the Memel to east of Kowno–Koszdary–Janow–Kiejdany. In mid-February 1919, Russian attacks at Kiejdany–Janow and Olita–Merecz could be held off or mopped up in counterattacks. For that in the last-named area, the Bug Protection

Troop was called in from the Brest area with PZ VII.—Clear signs of disorder (unwillingness to fight, leaving positions, forcing transport, disarmament without resistance) were shown, though, by the 8th Army in the north. The situation was equally serious. Bolshevik bands advanced from Pleskau in December, where the 5th Reserve Division fell apart, to the Gulf of Riga near Haynasch, so that the German troops still in Estonia—the Estonians were in a hostile mood too–had to fight their way laboriously toward Lemsal. In the Riga area they had already formed the Baltic Home Guard in November, and by the end of the month it had attained a strength of 1750 men (1000 of them Germans). German volunteer battalions formed the "Iron Brigade" (later upgraded to a division) there on December 21. Both units ran a broad-gauge armored train north of the Duena, (it is not known whether it was left over from the spring's railroad advance or built new), with which they made advances from Segewold in the direction of Ramozki, where strong enemy forces were found, and from Riga to the east, where they were able to drive Russian units that had advanced as far as the Oger bridge east of Uexkuell back to beyond Stockmannshof. On December 29, the Soviet attack from the north began and pushed the Baltic Home Guard and Iron Brigade back to the Duena. When uprisings took place in Riga, the city had to be evacuated on January 3, 1919 (the broad-gauge armored trains, which were unable to move back, were either blown up or fell into Bolshevik hands). The Soviets pushed across the Duena to the southwest, so that the Germans had to fall back to the Aa sector. On January 8, Mitau and Schaulen fell, and at the latter, the German PZ II stationed there was lost to the Russians, who put it to use. In mid-January the Germans had withdrawn to the Windau. The following six weeks brought more and more fighting along this front, but it remained essentially stable. Southeast of the Windau sector, which ended at Wekschni, somewhat east of the Memel-Prekuln line, as well as south of the Dubissa on the Tilsit-Schaulen line, very near the East Prussian border, there were only security troops of the 10th Army at Kiejdany. While the Estonians, with the help of the Finns, were able to drive the Soviet troops out of their territory on January-February 1919, They saw Latvia and Lithuania, which had scarcely any troops, were reduced to their western areas; the governments had had to flee from Riga to Libau and from Vilna to Kowno. In December 1918, the Allies (especially the British, who had sent a navy squadron to the Baltic coast)—fearing the complete victory of the Bolsheviks—along with the national governments, had encouraged the German troops to stay in this area temporarily to defend them, and this was even authorized in the Treaty of Versailles (Article 433). From the start, this was attainable only through intensive recruitment of volunteers, for whom the German offices offered bonuses and the Latvian

government made vague promises about eventual citizenship and land apportionment (which was taken much more concretely by the Germans than it was meant) and in fact it attracted very many—as well as many adventurers.

Besides the Baltic area, another trouble spot had developed on the eastern border of the Reich. In the province of Posen, the majority of whose inhabitants were Polish, a Polish congress had formed in November 1918 and called for the formation of national defense troops. After long negotiations, relations between the German Reich and Poland were broken off on December 15. On December 27, a Polish uprising broke out in Posen itself, spread like wildfire over the whole province, and could only be brought to a stop by quickly established German defenses in its border areas. The Poles' desire to expand soon spread along the entire eastern border of the Reich—from the southeast corner of East Prussia to Upper Silesia.

On the German side, the threats to the Reich emanating from the east caused the formation on November 19 of an AOK "Homeland Protection East", which was soon changed into the Central Office for Border Protection East in the Ministry of War, but was not a command office, but only an organization site. In January and February 1919, a fully new organization came about, under the OHL, which moved from Kassel to Kolberg for this purpose on February 14, the Oberkommando Grenzschutz Nord (Bartenstein), responsible for the troops in Courland,. Lithuania, East and West Prussia, and the Oberkommando Grenzschutz Sued (Breslau), responsible for the troops in eastern Posen Province, Lower and Upper Silesia, were set up after the dissolution of the Dienststelle Oberost and the eastern AOKs. The General Commands (I Koenigsberg, XX Allenstein, XVII Danzig, II Stettin, V Posen, moved to Glogau, VI Breslau) that had returned from the field remained in the hinterlands with their homeland divisions, in most cases consisting only of a cadre of officers, as the men had been released or disbanded. The 35th Infantry Division, returning from France to Gosslershausen (Recruiting District XVII) in January 1919, reported the presence of 300 officers but only 150 men (only company strength!). The personnel had to be added to slowly through recruitment of volunteers, so that these "divisions" gradually, at varying speeds—if at all—could approach their unit strengths. Across the border, in the Suwalki—Grodno—Olita area, the Home Guard Corps, with the 4th Home Guard Division—amplified by volunteers, of whom also other formations of the corps consisted—remained in existence. The 46th Home Guard Division, also a part of this army, had settled down to the north, in the Kowno area adjoining the assembled Reserve Corps South of Schaulen, the General Command x.b.V.52 had been pushed in, to which the 45th Reserve Division had been sent from the Reich, and the

A Reichswehr armored train, not identified to date. The fully armored loco may be a Prussian G 5.4. Note the unusual camouflage paint and the observation post on the command car (Omk with superstructures). The front car is presumably a mine-thrower car. Photo: H. Wenzel collection

Baltic Home Guards such as the "Iron Division" were subordinated to the VI. Reserve Corps, which was sent there from Breslau after the active VI. General Command had arrived in Germany. This unit was also strengthened with the 1st Guard Reserve Division from Berlin. The M.E.D.5 (moved from Wilna to Kowno) and 8 (from Schaulen to Tilsit and later to Libau) also remained in existence.

The Results of the Collapse Inside the Reich

The dynamic of the Kiel sailors' revolt, which spread over the land like wildfire, knocked the Kaiser and state rulers off their thrones and even compelled the parliamentary government of Prince Max of Baden, established at the last moment, to retreat. On the afternoon of November 9, 1918 the republic was proclaimed, formed of soldiers, workers and farmers. At first all the socialistic forces shared the power, the moderate socialist majority (SPD), which strove for a democracy on the basis of free and general elections including also bourgeois groups, and the USPD, which had split off from them in 1917, which wanted to establish a soviet republic and rejected early elections. The governing board, the council of the people's representatives, was parity-based, with three members of each party, and the chairman was the Social Democrat Friedrich Ebert. But by the end of December the divergent political viewpoints caused a split, the USPD members left the council of representatives, in which the Social Democrats were now in power alone. Then the Communist Party split from the USPD and at first remained a weak group, but the USPD itself now showed more radical tendencies.

As for armed forces, so-called People's Naval Divisions (Berlin, Koenigsberg, etc.) had been formed from the revolutionary seamen's guards. There were also many people's home guards and militias that recruited mustered-out or deserted soldiers and civilians, armed from military depots fallen into the hands of the revolutionaries or deserted by the security forces. These groups, responsible only to the local councils, the majorities of which inclined to the USPD if not the Communists, often agitated—all too often under unqualified leaders—beside or even against each other, so that chaos and free will resulted. The SPD had little to oppose them with, since only small numbers of Social Democrats were willing to take weapons in hand. Their leaders, with the Soviet Russian example in mind, inspired much fear that a soviet republic would become a soviet dictatorship. Ebert had already made contact with the OHL to be sure of defense against such dangers and the restoration of order, plus the establishment of his concepts to restrain the army, assistance that was promised him under the condition that democratization of the troops would not happen and the officers' power to command would remain. This agreement, the retention of an officer corps that was largely still monarchical and in any case anti-democratic, and that did not want to accept the military defeat, but rather pushed the guilt for the unlucky outcome of the war onto the socialist forces in every way, was a highly problematic step. The war-weary front troops, after their orderly return to Germany, had soon dispersed—under the influence of propaganda from the workers' and soldiers' councils—but agitated officers, in view of the chaotic conditions that grew more and more gripping and the economic problems, were able to collect volunteers in growing numbers, ready for economic and political reasons to take up weapons again. Thus the Free Corps arose, definitely a gathering of right-wing national circles (many Free Corps fighters later became National Socialist big shots). They saw the Communists and other militant left-wing socialists as their greatest enemy; the ruling moderate socialists despised them although they served them. Under the united command of the director of the country's defense and later Reich Defense Minister Gustav Noske and the still-existing OHL under Field Marshal von Hindenburg and their orderly command offices, the Free Corps gradually became a more and more powerful troop under united command, which in June 1919 reached a total strength of 400,000 men. The Reich government used them to oppose the forces of the extreme left, in which they saw their chief danger. In January 1919 the Free Corps in Berlin had already beaten the Spartacist People's Militia and the Red People's Naval Division; as of February 1919, they protected the national congress that met in Weimar. On March 6, 1919 the congress passed a law to create a temporary Reichswehr, which was to absorb the Free Corps. The first paragraph of the law defined the tasks:

1. Protection of the Reich's borders,
2. Carrying out the regulations of the Reich government,
3. Maintaining peace and order inside the country.

For all these tasks, armored trains were seen as very useful. Along with the few taken over from wartime and the makeshift products of a few Free Corps, a whole armada of such units arose quickly and in rapid succession. The conditions for their formation and subordination corresponded to those from the empire and the war: They were established by the Lin.Komm., they were subordinated first to the Chief of the FEW (Major General von Oldershausen), as of March 20, 1919 to the newly revived Railroad Unit of the Grand General Staff (Colonel von Velsen), whose Group V was responsible for them. After the General Staff was disbanded, the Railroad Unit was subordinated to the Troop Department of the Ministry of War on February 5, 1920, Later it became the Transport Section (T 7). The armored trains were still assigned by these command offices to individual units for certain uses; the rolling stock remained the property of the railroad authorities and was leased by the Army (Reich Defense) Ministry.

There do not seem to have been any uniform regulations at first. Thus many units that were assigned armored trains worked out their own standards, of which the author has found the following:

– Tactical and technical experience with armored trains (about their uses in Finland), by Lt. von Ahlfen (commander of the armored train used there; later he took over Reichswehr Armored Train No. 44 and showed his preference for these units even as a general of engineers in World War II; as commander of the surrounded city of Breslau, he had one built in March 1945), of February 25, 1919.
– (Tactical and technical) experiences with armored trains in the V.A.K. of March 7, 1919.
– Basic points for the building, formation and use of makeshift armored trains of the Lin.komm.R. of March 16, 1919.
– Corps command for formation and use of the armored train and patrol runs of the assembled Res.K. of March 23, 1919.
– Basic points for equipping and use of armored trains by the Eisb.Abt. of the Gr.Gen.St. of March 28, 1919.
– Service instructions for armored trains of the M.E.D.5 of May 1919.
– Experiences in the realm of using armored trains...in the undertaking against Munich by the Eisb.Abt. of the Gr.Gen.St., June 7, 1919.
– Brief instructions for armored trains of Wkr.Kdo.IV of December 10, 1919.

In July 1919 the Testing Department of the Railroad Troops (Vadeis) had been empowered by the Ministry of War with the composition of uniform service instructions for the equipping, mobilization and use of armored trains, but because of the disbanding of this office shortly thereafter, and the other effects of the treaty of Versailles, this was not done.

In terms of the technical requirements, all of these papers drew closely on the service instructions of 1910, to which they added only a few modifications and additions. For marching travel on main lines (with the locomotive in front), speeds were to be reduced to 40-50 kph. The assigned technical crew was to be a gang of railroad workers (6 to 8 men) with a leader for repair work, since obviously no railroad engineers were available for such work. The tasks of the technical leader were stated precisely. He was responsible for maintenance and repair of the rolling stock, directed the service as the conductor during a trip and during stops at stations (if they were vacant, he also took over the tasks of the railroad representative and transport leader), for repair and damage work on the lines he was the railroad-technical leader. The home depots of the armored train were to be chosen so that not only water and fuel supply would be assured, but there also would be a machine shop in the vicinity for maintenance of the locomotive; at the same time, they should also be in the neighborhood of the staff of the superior military troop unit. Repairs to the armored train had to be carried out at once and most quickly by the appropriate workshops, and they and the machine and operation offices had to see that the armored train was always ready to roll. The greatest value was placed on the means of information. Within the train were several systems like telephones (with which, what with the loud travel and battle noise, understanding was said to be difficult), speaking tubes, machine telegraph, bell systems, other acoustic and optical signals were side by side. For communication with command posts, a radio station was set up later. The technical and tactical directions in these instructions will be treated in the next applicable chapter.

A command of February 12, 1919 indicates that at that time, in addition to the M.E.D.5 (Kowno) and 8 (Tilsit), the Lin.komm.N (Koenigsberg), R (Bromberg), G (formerly Posen, then Frankfurt on the Oder), M (Berlin), L I (Breslau) and L II (Kattowitz), all on the eastern border, had armored trains. The first surviving list of Reichswehr armored trains, unfortunately, dates from only September 1, 1919, and another from June 19, 1920 indicate which line commands had set up the trains that existed at that time. Establishment dates are also known from some documents.

In all, the following picture results for 1919: Of the armored trains that survived the World War. II, V and VII were in the Brest-Litovsk or Courland area, early in March PZ IV, which had returned from the Balkan front at the war's end, joined them there, III was in Berlin and VI at the front between the Oder and Obra. The data on Armored Trains VIII-XIX are very meager, but most, if not all of them still existed. PZ VIII was divided into four patrol trains by the M.E.D.5 in March 1919. PZ XI, XVII and XIX (?, written as XX, but this one noted again at the right place) are still on the list as of September 1, 1919 for the General command VI (Breslau or Upper Silesia); it may be suspected that the G 3 locomotives armored there in 1917-18 were intended for those trains. There is no further evidence of their active service, and they are not included in later lists.

In the manner of designation, the numbering used in World War I was kept at first, with Roman numerals (although even before 1918, Arabic numerals were used at times). But for numbering up to LV, this proved to be too unhandy, so that in September 1919 a general change to Arabic numerals was made. Although this also applied to the World War I armored trains (No. III-VII), their numbers were still written in the old way in practice. This difference is followed here.

As of January 1919, Armored Trains 20 to 42 were built and put into service in quick succession in the eastern provinces bordering on Poland. One can assume that this building activity started suddenly and surface-covering, one can assume that it was done on command from the OHL, though this order has not survived. Armored Train PZ 20 appeared at the Lin.comm.L II (Ktz) in January 1919, PZ 21 before January 11, 22 on January 25 and 23 at Lin.comm R (Bbg) at the end of January 1919, PZ 24 and 25 (Jan.-Feb. 1919) at Lin.comm.L I (Bsl), PZ 27 and 28 (Jan.-Feb. 1919) at Lin.comm.N (Kbg), PZ 29 and 30 in the latter half of February at Lin.comm.R (Bbg), PZ 31 at Lin.comm.L I (Bsl), PZ 32 before April 1919 at Lin.comm.L II (Ktz), PZ 33 before May 1919, its Lin.comm. unknown, PZ 35 and 36 at the end of February 1919 at Lin.comm.V (Dzg), PZ 37 at Lin.comm.R (Bbg), PZ 38-40 (38 late January, the others in February 1919), and 42 at the Lin.comm.G (Psn/Ffo). Then the building activity moved to the interior of the Reich, though a few higher numbers (PZ 50, 52 and 55) were built at Lin.comm. on the eastern boundary (the first two at Lin.comm.G, PZ 55 at Lin.comm.R). PZ 44 and 45 in April 1919 at Lin.comm.X (Stn), PZ 46 before July 1919 at Lin.comm.T (Hal), PZ 47 at Lin.comm.U (Mag), and PZ 48 and 49 at Lin.comm.E (Dsd). This also took place in early summer at the latest, for the trains that were not finished by the signing of the Treaty of Versailles at the end of July 1919 could no longer be finished. This obviously applied to PZ 41 and 53, which were noted as "being built" in the list of September 1, 1919. There are gaps in the list for numbers 26, 34 and 51. The last is mentioned in secondary sources as being with the Volunteer Landesjaeger Corps in Torgau in July 1919. This is very probably a writing error, though. PZ 31 may have been meant, as it is documented for the named unit in November-December 1919, while a PZ 51 does not appear in any of the numerous documented listings. A special feature is found for PZ 54; this new number was given to World War PZ III on April 10, 1919. For two armored trains (No. 23 and 43) there is a note in the September 1, 1919 list: "Vadeis (Testing Department of the Railroad Troops)—unmanned." Since PZ 23 was very probably lost on February 17, 1919 (see page 45), one can assume the same for PZ 43, although concrete data for it cannot be found. It is striking that the building was done in pairs at the Lin. comm. It may be that cooperation of two armored trains was intended from the start. In the 10th Infantry Division, the two armored trains in Lissa (PZ 38 and 39) and Rawitsch (PZ 40 and 52) were actually united in a unit later. In documented actions, the paired use of two armored trains is very rare (PZ IV and VII in Lithuania, PZ 24 and 25 in an attack on Munich), and may be regarded as coincidental.

In any case, the number of armored trains in April-May 1919 may have reached a total of 40, which—in total—is also documented for July 1919. By September 1919 it was then—mainly by taking No. 8-19 out of service—already reduced to 33, and was to be reduced further in the future.

The World War Armored Train III in March 1919 with the Free Corps of Huelsen. For camouflage, the steel sidewalls of the O-cars had windows painted on to look like passenger cars. The Roman numeral of the armored train (intended to mean a third-class car; see also page 19, second picture from top) indicates this. The wooden head protection for the gunners above the upper edge of the car is also easy to see. Photo: W. Sawodny collection

Assembly, Armament, and Manning of the Reichswehr Armored Trains

Although not for all, more or less detailed data on the assembly, armament and manning of a whole series of armored trains of that time can be found. These range from the most detailed descriptions to summary vehicle listings, and will be presented below despite the variety.

For PZ III (later 54), we depend completely on the pictorial material. This at first shows, in two symmetrical halves, the World War I cars (20-ton type). Each half includes three infantry cars, still covered only with canvas, and at each end of the train a gun car armed with a 3.7-cm machine cannon but without an A/A machine gun. When it was changed to PZ 54, three more cars were added to these eight: another covered combat car behind the front gun car, details of which are not known, a G-car and a baggage car, which probably carried equipment, supplies or kitchen facilities. When it was disbanded in 1921, the following cars were listed for this train: Breslau 58976, 59242, 59502, 59990; Essen 32690, 107655; Kattowitz 23425, 24046, 24500; plus Brussels 5307, 82193, 151038 and Warsaw 30886, which probably belonged to the supply train.

For PZ IV there are only very brief data from early March 1919. According to them, the crew was intended to comprise a commander, an artillery officer (simultaneously deputy commander), a sergeant-major as technical leader, a sergeant, two secretaries, one medical NCO, two NCOs and eight men as gun crews, for four heavy machine guns four NCOs and 16 men, as infantry four sergeants and 60 men, in all 3 officers, 12 NCOs and 86 men, plus the railroad personnel from M.E.D.5. On March 10, the crew actually included only two officers, 10 NCOs and 65 men. The armament consisted of one light howitzer (l.F.H.) and one 7.62-cm Russian-built flak gun on socket mounts, and four heavy machine guns were on hand (increase to 6 heavy and 6 light machine guns planned). In April the armored train received four or five cars of PZ II, recaptured at Schaulen, probably

At this time the train still had a gun car with a 3.7-cm machine cannon, but the flak gun had been removed. Photo: W. Sawodny collection

in exchange for fewer good ones of its own. The light howitzer was eliminated, but in July 1919 two more cars were built for PZ IV at the Kovno workshop: one gun car (Alsace 5211, without walls) with an openly mounted Gruson turret with a 5-cm cannon over the front axle (over the rear were ammunition bunkers of 14-mm iron plates) and an Omk car (Breslau 67463), in the open half of which a 3.7-cm revolving gun was mounted, while two heavy machine guns were located in the closed half. In all, Armored Train No. IV, from June 1919 until its disbanding at the end of 1920, had the following cars:

The same train had been renumbered PZ 54 in April 1919. It was given additional cars (visible behind the infantry car): A G-car and a baggage car. Photo: Military Archives, Freiburg

The rear half of PZ IV in March 1920 (for the front half, see the picture on page 19). Behind the command and machine-gun cars, both from World War Armored Train X (later II), the Omk-car Breslau 67463 with 3.7-cm Rev.K. in the open part, and the Alsace 5211 car without body walls, with the Gruson turret (5.3-cm gun). Note the radio antenna with the flag on the command car. Photo: Federal Archives, Cologne

Brussels 48351 (Sml) as contact car loaded with track-building equipment), a special car (No. 1, previously railroad flak) with an openly mounted 7.62-cm A/A gun (Russian M 02 with only a shield, replaced in July 1920 with 7.7-cm Flak Ehrhardt in cylindrical steel armor one meter high) on a socket mount; Breslau 54012 (Omk) with closed armored body and armored heavy machine-gun turret (320-degree traverse) in front (two more heavy machine guns in side ports); Breslau 33509 (Omk) with closed armored body (2 heavy machine guns in side ports), which also carried the shock troop; Breslau 83195 (Omk, same equipment as Breslau 33509), which also served as the weapon-smith's and equipment car; Breslau 34457 (Omk), a command car with leader's position at one end, at the other a platform with two heavy machine guns (or optionally, a light mine-thrower could be mounted there); Breslau 39003 (Omk, same equipment as Breslau 54012); then came the two aforementioned gun cars, Breslau 67463 and Alsace 5211; at the end was the contact and track-building equipment car, Essen 103894 (Rw). All Omk cars were the 15-ton type II d1 or A 6. The closed cars, with arched roofs instead of the otherwise usual pointed type) had iron walls 6 mm thick, and behind them, with the space between partly filled with wooden planks, 12-mm steel armor. The same 12-mm steel plates were used as axle armor. Only the command car had an air brake, but there were four hand brakes. Telephone and speaking-tube connections ran from the command car to all the other cars and the locomotive, and the command car and loco were also connected by a machine telegraph and a signal line coupled to the steam pipe. There were four spotlights. Besides the heavy machine guns built into the cars, the shock troop had five light ones. The crew officially consisted of 3 officers, 9 NCOs and 49 men, plus 16 technical personnel, but for June 1920, only one officer, 3 NCOs and 32 men, plus a 4-man technical crew, were listed. Considered necessary were 16 NCOs and 62 men, but at least 11 NCOs and 44 men (not counting technical personnel). The supply train consisted until the end of 1919 of the Gm-cars Magdeburg 19701 as the kitchen car and Brussels 152396 as the supply car, with Brussels 12015 (C), Brussels 12590, Elberfeld 2797, Danzig 2163, Halle 2447, Koenigsberg 2913 and 2927 (all Type D).

What with the shortage of car material for normal traffic, it was ordered on October 21, 1919 that the supply trains of the armored trains should generally consist of only five captured cars, one of which was to be made into a kitchen car, one a supply car and one perhaps as a gunsmith's car (the rest as living quarters). PZ IV thus was given Brussels 152396 and 12590, plus Belgium 200110 (G) as a kitchen car and the four-axle Brussels 16245 and 16282 as living quarters. These five captured cars (mostly Belgian, sometimes also Russian, Polish or others) can be documented for all other armored trains as well.

For PZ V, the following composition was recorded in April 1919: R-car with rails and ties, covered O-car with 5-cm gun in Gruson turret and heavy machine gun in a front port, R-car, gun car with 7.7-cm F.K. 96 new type in a swiveling armored cabin, two machine-gun cars (covered O-cars), two living-quarter cars for the men, a writing-room car, an officers' car (command car with observation turret), locomotive T 9.3 with two tenders, R-car with building material, gun car with 7.62-cm Putilov 02 gun in swiveling armored cabin, R-car with 3.7-cm revolver cannon on socket mount, equipment car, kitchen car, living car for technical crew, covered O-car with 5-cm gun in Gruson turret and heavy machine gun in the front, R-car with track-building material. The integration of the living-quarter train in the combat train is interesting, presumably because there was no sure way of dropping the former. It was noted, though, that only the combat cars or even just the gun cars be taken along for action. For PZ VI no data are available; for PZ VII, which had T 9.3 E.-L. 7138 as its locomotive, only a summary of the weapons with four field guns and two MG.

When Armored Train No. VIII was divided into four patrol trains by the M.E.D.5 in March 1919, each was to be composed of a baggage car, a third-class (C) personnel car and an armored car with a heavy machine gun in a turning turret; thus Armored Train No. VIII must have consisted of four of each type of car. For the armored trains built for the Lin.komm.R (Bromberg) (No. 21-23, 29, 30, 37 and 55), the following composition was stated in the "Basic Points for the building and Use of Makeshift Armored Trains" issued by that office on March 16, 1919: One T 9.3 locomotive, the important parts of which, especially the cab, were protected with 16-20-mm armor plate. Three MG-cars, each with 4 heavy machine guns; Omk-car with 10-mm sheet iron in a gap 100 mm from the car wall, filled with fine gravel, covered inside with 25-mm thick wooden boards;

PZ 22, built by the Lin.komm..R (Bromberg). In front of the armored T 9.3 locomotive is a command car (recognized by the observation turret on the roof). After the loco is an MG car of similar type, behind that a G-car (supplies and kitchen). Then a car with slanted armored walls (mine launcher or gun car), built by the Lin.komm.R. Photo: J. Magnuski collection

roof made of two 40-mm wooden panels with 70-mm gravel layer between them; 5-mm iron plates outside; the space between the walls and roof either provisionally filled with sandbags or preferably with 16-mm iron plates, in it a port on either side for a machine gun and several loopholes for rifles (closable by flaps), another machine gun port in the front wall of the car; sliding doors and a floor hatch for exit; it was recommended that two of these cars be built as command cars with a round observation turret of 16-mm sheet iron with vision slits in the middle of the car. A mine-launcher car: An O-car without its walls, with an armored body made of double 10-mm steel plates, vertical front walls (with MG ports). Angled sidewalls: two light mine-throwers set on a platform. Room for the crew at the ends of the car, covered with armor plates. If needed, an additional A/A machine gun could be mounted in this car. A gun car: built like either the MG car or the launcher car; Gruson turret with 5-cm gun in the middle; one machine gun port in the front wall, optional fire openings for a mortar. One shock-troop car: G-car with armor like the MG car; several gun ports; flap doors and floor hatches for exiting. An equipment car: X- or O-car loaded with track-building material, plus a track-master's car or railcar for scouting trips. At the head of the train there should be one or two control cars loaded with gravel. The

supply car (G-car) with kitchen section and auxiliary tender should, if possible, not be taken into combat. — Foreseen as further equipment: 4 mortars, 6 light machine guns and 2 flame throwers for the shock troop, 2 spotlights. Means of communication were: Telephone connections among all cars; audible signals in all cars; signal horns and flags for all cars. The intended crew: one lieutenant or captain as train leader, 2 lieutenants, 2 sergeants, 10 NCOs, one weapon-master, 85 men, plus 15-man technical personnel (one technical travel leader, 3 locomotive drivers and firemen, 1 conductor, 2 brakemen, 5 workers). Later most of these armored trains — as were those in other areas — were equipped with additional gun cars, which had an 8.8-cm U-boat gun on a socket mount in an armored turret.

The following cars are documented for the armored trains of the Lin.komm.R in the disarmament early in 1921:

PZ 2: Breslau 44964, 81570, 103137; Coeln 2923, 28375; Essen 104601, Frankfurt 14043; Hannover 55856; Magdeburg 52469; Muenster 2257; auxiliary tender 1603; plus Brussels 383, 79576, 79654 and 155358.

PZ 29: Breslau 34156; Bromberg 78087; Essen 87496, 130219; Hannover 1219, 57276; Posen 12622.

Somewhat easier to recognize are these modern cars, in a picture of PZ 30, also built by Lin.komm.R. Behind the usual MG car are the gun car with Gruson turret, then the mine-thrower car and a stakeside car as a control car. Right: A look at the mine-thrower car of PZ 30. Photos (2): W. Huenemoerder; W. Sawodny collection

PZ 30: Breslau 52831, 84795, 89695; Coeln 57132; Elberfeld 20907; Alsace 17307; Halle 47793; Posen 11219; a Belgian tender; Brussels 60554, 62710, 62969, 67892.

PZ 55: Breslau 68544, 103465; Coeln 5026; Essen 104058, 283683; Halle 48624; Hannover 67797; Magdeburg 53576; Saarbruecken 12018; Tender 7280; Brussels 57608, 64089, 80837, 163560, 165671; Nisch 1203.

From this list it can be seen that the numbers represent the cars (7-8 combat cars, 1-2 contact cars—these could be either German or foreign types—5 baggage cars) match the rules given.

Also, the V.A.K., which saw action in the western part of Posen Province between Wartha and Bartsch, reported on March 7, 1919 on "tactical experiences with armored trains," from which the following data can be taken:

Armored trains of the 5th Infantry Division (Birnbaum—Bentschen—Wollstein sector): MG cars (4 machine guns, one firing through a hatch in the front wall; one mine-thrower, one spotlight); locomotive; two gun cars, each with a Gruson turret (5-cm gun); one infantry car (shock troop); one light car (contained a generator for the spotlight and train lights); one observation car (with armored brakeman's cabin as command post); auxiliary tender; tender locomotive; MG car (same setup as the one in front); plus a kitchen and a material car, which could be left behind with the baggage train. All—covered—cars had armor of steel plates on their walls and roof; the two (!) locomotives were armored with boiler plate on the cab, cylinders, and drive wheels; all vehicles were linked by telephone. The crews were listed as one officer and 60 men.

Armored trains of the 10th Infantry Division (Rawitsch-Krotoschin-Ostrovo sector): three empty flatcars as control cars; one gun car (two diagonally located Gruson turrets with 5-cm guns, one light machine gun, one spotlight); a medium launcher car (one medium mine-thrower, one light machine gun); one light launcher car (two light mine-throwers, one on a flat mount, one light machine gun); one MG car (4 heavy machine guns); one command car (radio station, one light machine gun, one spotlight); locomotive (one heavy machine gun). All cars were open boxcars; behind the walls were 12-cm gaps to a second plank wall, the space between filled with crushed stone, the machine guns fire through ports or over a bench. In the mine-thrower cars are ammunition and crew spaces, separated by walls up to 1.50 meters thick. The pusher locomotive (!) was to be armored carefully on its cab, tender and drive system. The crew was listed as 5 officers, 33 NCOs and men, plus three railroaders.

Specific data for some of the armored trains built by the Lin. komm.G are known (though from a later time—early 1920):

PZ 38 (Lissa): Contact car Sachsen 26758; MG car Alsace 102349 (Omk) with two heavy machine guns, U-boat car Essen 34339 (SSml) with two 8.8 cm U-boat guns, two machine guns and ammunition bunker; medium launcher car Essen 252740 with one medium mine-thrower and one light machine gun; light launcher car Essen 266109 with two light mine-throwers, one mounted high for flat fire; command car Essen 319079 (Ommk) with two heavy machine guns; locomotive Posen 5185 (G 8.1); depot car Breslau (D) 3489 for ammunition and spare parts; kitchen car Brussels 154688; gun car Augsburg 64260 (Omk) with two Gruson turrets (5 cm guns), MG car Saxony 45642 with one heavy MG; control car Essen 105108.

For PZ 39 (Lissa) as of July 1919, the following data for armament are given: three 5-cm guns in Gruson turrets, one medium and 5 light mine-throwers, six heavy machine guns. Detailed data are found for the beginning of 1920, as for PZ 38: Control car Coeln 81264 (Omk); U-boat car Essen 119466 (SSml) with two 8.8-cm U-boat guns, two machine guns and ammunition bunker; MG-car Hannover 34853 with two heavy machine guns; light launcher car Sachsen 55081 (Ommk(u) with two light mine-throwers, one for flat fire, one light machine gun; command car Essen 221502 (Ommk(u) with two heavy machine guns; locomotive Glogau 1927 (P 4); depot car Hannover 3386 (D) for ammunition and spare parts; kitchen car Brussels 22466; gun car Essen 292710 (Ommk) with two Gruson turrets and 5-cm guns; MG-car Essen 105057 with one heavy MG; control car Warsaw 178068.

For both trains, an additional description is given, mainly about the armor: the locomotives merely had good cab armor, the tenders were badly armored, the control cars were open two-axle freight cars without any armor, loaded with stone; the MG cars were open two-axle freight cars, their MG positions (on turning sockets) protected by double plank walls a meter high, with crushed stone between them; the U-boat cars had four axles and two 8.8 cm guns mounted diagonally at the ends, open with only gun shields, ammunition bunker in the middle, double plank walls, 1.5 m high on all sides, the ammunition bunker was also protected with 10-mm armor plate; the gun cars with two diagonally placed Gruson turrets, a poorly protected ammunition area between them; all two-axle launcher cars had double plank walls with crushed stone filling, the mine-throwers in open mountings, ammunition space covered, set up for two light machine guns firing over board; the command cars were covered, double board sidewalls with stone between, the roof strengthened with wooden walls and covered with sheet metal, on which was an open double-walled observation post, side ports for heavy MGs; depot and kitchen cars were unarmored. Floor hatches in all cars for entry. Communication by telephone and speaking tube.

For PZ 40 an incomplete description exists, dated in the spring of 1919, from which the following can be learned: At the head of the train were three control cars, the locomotive was armored, the combat cars (launcher, MG, gun and engineer cars) were O-cars with outer wooden and inner steel walls, the space between filled with small coal. At that time the train already had a car with two 8.8-cm U-boat guns. The 10th Infantry Division, in command at Lissa and Rawitsch (V.A.K.), recommended using pairs of armored trains. This also applied to PZ 38 and 39. PZ 40 was teamed with PZ 52 in the early summer of 1919, and even divided by exchanging cars into a lightly armed combat train (PZ 40) and a supporting artillery train (PZ 52); here the Soviet pattern becomes visible. The armor was now listed as some 30 cm of iron concrete and 1-cm steel plate; otherwise there is no description extant, but it can be assumed that in these trains too, the MG and launcher cars were open (covered with canvas), the depot, shock-troop and observation cars were G-cars.

PZ 40: 4 control cars (Coeln 73923, Augsburg 58412, Bromberg 47335, Magdeburg 27397); gun car with Gruson turret, 5-cm gun and a light machine gun; spotlight car with 60-cm spotlight; medium launcher car (Essen 107107) with a medium mine-thrower and a heavy machine gun; light launcher car (Essen 319805) with two light mine-throwers; shock-troop car; MG car with one heavy machine gun; armored locomotive Type S 3; gun car (Essen 107266) with Gruson turret (5 cm gun) and one light machine gun.

PZ 52: U-boat car (four-axle N 82714) with one (formerly probably two) 8.8-cm Krupp L/30 U-boat gun in an armored turret and ammunition bunker in the middle; U-boat car (four-axle) with two diagonally mounted 8.8-cm U-boat guns of the projecting type in armored turrets, with ammunition bunker in the middle; depot car with ammunition and spare supplies; locomotive Posen 7306 (T 9.3); flat-firing launcher car with mine-thrower and one heavy machine gun; gun cars Nuernberg 63747 and Hannover 69741. One observation car (Essen 322159) was eliminated in 1920. One of the not precisely identified cars was Essen 48555.

Only this photo of the 8.8-cm U-boat gun installed in armored trains exists, from PZ 30, showing only the upper part, with the gun installed in an armored hood. Photo: W. Huenemoerder; W. Sawodny collection

There were also, serving both of the trains, the baggage cars Brussels E 10303, 64912, 66763, 68969, 71536; A 79165, 82343, 115580, A 151635 and Warsaw 51899.

These four armored trains essentially correspond to the prescriptions of the 10th Infantry Division as of early March 1919, but the locomotives—as was customary everywhere—were now placed in the middle and the trains were equipped with 8.8-cm U-boat guns. This rearming was apparently done for many armored trains in the second quarter of 1919 (for the rearming of the armored trains of Lin.komm.N (Koenigsberg) and X (Stettin), such guns were made available on June 26, 1919' PZ 40 seems to be one of the first to receive them. The data on armor are interesting. While PZ 38 and 39 kept the original double walls with gravel filling, PZ 40 (and 52) first had the inner wooden wall replaced by one made of steel, and in a further step, the space between them was much enlarged and filled with concrete.

A car list exists only for PZ 50 of the lin.komm.G: Essen 210299, 290953, 291089, 291220, 292098, Kattowitz 4671, Posen 3804, Brussels 1645, 3584, 5547, 7345, 8701 and 25480.

For the armored trains of Lin.komm. L I (Breslau) and L II (Kattowitz), only the following car lists could be found:

PZ 24 (L I): Breslau 9202, 68399, 89934, 100116, 100169, Essen 51862, 58791, 126885, Hannover 60466, Brussels 5284.

PZ 25 (L I): Breslau 37760, 66820, 69041, 72477, 103873, Hannover 57348, Magdeburg 54328, Muenster 13141, Brussels 63564, 64151, 67847, 72893, 94814, 201100.

PZ 31 (L I): Breslau 10527, 90116, 101558, Coeln 66574, Essen 128684, 130394, Hannover 37134, Kattowitz 40160, Brussels 945, 3734.

PZ 33 (L II): Breslau 103416, 104681, Essen 209976, 28783, 245496, 246068, 249254, 252421, 258136, Brussels 2362, 80807, 82276, 154937, 162821, flak-dwelling car 532.

On March 26, 1919 the Lin.komm.X (Stettin) was ordered to set up two armored trains (PZ 44 and 45). Each was to include, besides the locomotive, one X, one SS, one G, one O or Om and four Omk cars. A detailed description of PZ 45 exists: Two-axle X-car Berlin 50034 as contact car (only axle armor, 70 x 70 cm, 17 mm thick, also in the same manner on all other cars of the train); gun car Essen 126585 (Omk), side armor 10 mm thick with 25-mm plank wall inside (doors 20-mm armor), front armor 12-mm plates with 60-mm plank wall in back, round open armored turret in the middle, 2.9 m diameter and 80 cm high, of 15-mm sheet steel, with an 8.8-cm Krupp L/30 U-boat gun on C/16 socket mount, at the ends ammunition bunkers 11.47 m high, covered by 17-mm steel plates, port in front wall for heavy machine gun; MG car Breslau 55292 (Omk), sidewalls (1.30 m high) with 10-mm steel plates and 25-mm plank wall in back, armored, front wall 12 mm with 25-mm planks, above to beginning of roof (50 cm high on sides) double steel wall of 2 x 10-mm at sides and 2 x 16 mm in front, car roof with 30-mm planking and 5-mm plates, round observation turret in the middle) height 69 cm, diameter 95 cm, of 17-mm sheet steel, with 8 closable vision slits (120 x 25 mm), two ports on each side for light machine guns, two ports in a front wall (different heights) for heavy machine guns, on each side three gun ports, and on the front two loopholes for rifles, side doors and floor hatch for exit; MG car Coeln 62455 (Omk), built like Breslau 55292. but only one heavy machine gun in the front wall, but with brake cabin armored with 17-mm sheet steel, spindle brake; locomotive Stettin 7308 (T 9.3), side armor (cab and

PZ 45, established by the Lin.Komm.X (Stettin). The loco (T 9.3), Stettin 7308) shows World War I armor. In front is the MG car, Breslau 55292 (Omk), behind it the Gm car, Cassel 14680, as a shock-troop car. Photo: Archives of the Engineer School, Munich

boiler) of 17-mm plates, rear wall (set back so far that the coal box is enlarged to 5-ton capacity) and cab roof with 12-mm plates, arched, folding 12-mm cylinder plates, 9-mm pushrod plates, folding 12-mm coupling plates; shock-troop car Cassel 14680 (Gm), 15- and 10-mm double armor on the sides, 45-mm wooden planks in between, front wall of 15-mm armor plates with 25-mm plank wall behind it, car roof with 25-mm planks and 5-mm sheet iron, one door on either side, two floor hatches, four loopholes in each sidewall, two in each end wall, shock troop armed with two light machine guns and two machine pistols; radio car Brussels 69199 (G) unarmored with 0.95 cm roof antenna and folding 6-meter mast could be installed, motor aggregate to operate the radio station; launcher car Berlin 28630 (Omk), walls removed and replaced by angled (tapering from 2.75-meter bottom width to 1.35-meter opening above) double armor walls (2 x 12 mm), vertical end walls of 2 x 16-mm steel plates, space for crew in the middle with 17-mm steel plates, at both ends light mine-throwers mounted on angled wood base; MG car Coeln 64303 (Omk) like Breslau 55292, but brake cabin with spindle brake and 17-mm armor; equipment car Altona 4527 (Sml), loaded with track-building material; communication by telephone, speaking tube and bell system; in the supply train kitchen and provision car Brussels 80901 (Gm), living-quarter cars Brussels 151387, 156636 (Gm), 160328 (G), sometimes baggage car 4761.

This composition corresponds to the establishment directive of March 26, 1919, and the same can probably be assumed for PZ 44, for which the following list of cars survives: Breslau 43197; Coeln 64336, 66597, 79610; Essen 5425, 129472; Frankfurt 46617; Magdeburg 50361; Saarbruecken 7517; Brussels 62697, 151095, 152571, 152577, Italian 156984.

PZ 48, set up by the Lin.komm.E (Dresden), was described as follows: Equipment car I (open freight car with axle armor, loaded with track-building equipment, barbed wire, sandbags and mines; gun car I (5.7-cm gun on socket mount in turret open at front, fully armored, two built-in heavy machine guns, another heavy machine gun and a light one, a medium spotlight, crew 9-10 men); observation car I (staff car, fully armored, two built-in heavy MGs, one light MG, a medium spotlight, an alarm siren, crew 12-17 men); MG car I (fully armored, four built-in heavy machine guns, one heavy machine gun with sled, one light one, 12-man crew); Saxony 754 locomotive and 735 tender (fully armored, 3-man crew); MG car II (like MG car I); observation car II (like observation car I plus telephone switchboard); launcher car I (O-car with armored sidewalls, covered ammunition and crew space, one light mine-thrower, one heavy A/A machine gun, another heavy machine gun, later also one light one, 7-man crew); launcher car II (like I); equipment car II (like I); the observation and MG cars had brakes, all cars were equipped with telephones, most also with a blinking device. Supply train: two personnel cars (unarmored, for 24 men each, 2 light machine guns each); kitchen car (unarmored, 3 men); ammunition car (makeshift armor, unarmored roof). In November 1919 the Railroad Flak Spotlight Train 527 was incorporated into the armored train, which consisted of the following unarmored cars: Command car (three light machine guns, a medium spotlight, 19-man crew, this car had the phone switchboard); motor car (radio station); spotlight car (open car with big spotlight); personnel car (used by the weapon-master, two light machine guns, three men); all these cars were later armored in a makeshift manner. The 5.7-cm guns were to be replaced by 7.7-cm F.K. 96 n.A., but it is doubtful whether this ever was done. These car numbers of this armored train are known (other than the flak-spotlight train): Berlin 44010; Breslau

72672, 73371, 89377, 90783, 101441, 104253; Coeln 62729, 66372; Nuernberg 79695 and Brussels 155012.—In November 1919 the crew numbered in all 5 officers, 21 NCOs and 91 men, plus 25 men of the flak-spotlight train.

For the second Saxon armored train, No. 49, eight combat cars and two flatcars (as protection cars) were listed in September 1920, along with the loco and tender: car numbers Baden 70097, 70338; Breslau 69795, 73421, 104254; Saxony 35245; Wuerttemberg 48040; Brussels 78756, 160333, 160760, 162309; Bulgaria 30005 (the last five belonged to the supply train). The equipment may have corresponded to that of PZ 48. In the autumn of 1919 the crew consisted of 3 or 4 officers, one officer's deputy, 10 to 12 sergeants of different ranks, 5 or 6 NCOs, 14 to 16 corporals and 54 to 75 men.

The great majority of the German cars found in all of these lists without more details were probably—as the surviving pictures show—iron Omk(u) coal cars of the 15-ton and (more rarely) 20-ton types with the roof designs known from World War I. But there were also (with or without inside armor) G-cars with flat roofs (Types II b1 and b3 and their successors II d8 and generalized type A 2, perhaps also three-axle II c13), Pg-cars, exitable O-cars (Type II b2 or d3 and generalized Type A 1), SS II d7 or A3, and perhaps earlier series for the 8.8-cm U-boat cannons, and as contact and equipment cars, Sml-types (II d5/A4, maybe also A11).

It should be noted that all these armored trains also correspond more or less to the recommendation that the Railroad Department of the Grand General Staff issued in their "Essentials for Equipping and Using Armored Trains" on March 28, 1919: an armored locomotive of the T 9 or G 7 series (the latter if larger radii of action were expected), equipped with a sucking apparatus for water; three MG cars with three or four heavy machine guns each; two gun cars, each with a small-caliber gun (up to 7.7 cm) protected by armor, or one gun car with two guns diagonally mounted; one or two launcher cars with two light or two light and two medium mine-throwers; a command car with an armored observation post and up to three heavy machine guns; an equipment car with three heavy machine guns, spare parts and ammunition; depending on the situation, also one to three control cars (X-cars loaded with sand or gravel); one armored shock-troop car with up to three heavy machine guns; a provision car (kitchen and food supplies). The total number of the combat cars—as far as is known for individual trains—actually varied in this realm between six and nine, usually adding up to seven or eight. The fittings in detail, though, especially the armor, was naturally very different, depending on the local conditions. Notwithstanding, an armor train was created that still had numerous cars but was well-balanced and very varied in armament. At the end of 1919 a uniform type of armored train was to be set up, modeled on PZ 46, which was then under construction in the Plaue workshop (later RAW Brandenburg-West). Because of the changing political conditions, this intention was never carried out.

When the number of armored trains per recruiting district was reduced to two (14 in all) in June 1920, the technically best and best-performing ones were to be kept, though in a way limited as follows: armored locomotive with tender, two gun cars, which simultaneously served as machine-gun cars (only when this was not possible could two additional cars be added as MG cars), one mine-launcher car, one survey section car (simultaneously command car?), one lazarette and kitchen car, two contact cars; there were also the five captured G-cars as personnel and office cars in the supply train. The mobilization plan from the same time gives statements about armament and personnel (which was to be set up besides the technical personnel in the chain of command):

Makeshift Fahrmbacher armor (Bavaria, May 1919). The front gun car, probably a modernized 10-ton type according to Standard II d 2 (note the sidewalls), with the 7.7-cm Field Gun 96 n.A., is armored somewhat "adventurously" with steel plates and sandbags. Behind it is the MG car (G-car). Photo: War Archives, Main City Archives, Munich

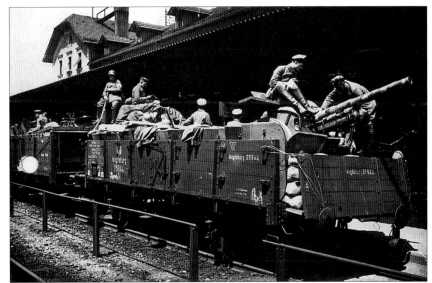

The rear gun car (Ok based on II b 2) of the same armored train, with the 7.7-cm Field Gun 16, is protected with the same material, but in a more regular arrangement. The mine-launcher car runs ahead of it. (Omk, generalized type A 1). Photo: War Archives, Main City Archives, Munich

The Guns of the German Armored Trains until 1921

Type	Rev.K. (5-barrel)	Masch.K.	S.K. in Pz.Laf.	Belgian Kas.-K. Maxim-Nordenfeldt
Caliber (cm)	3.7	3.7	5.3	5.7
Barrel length caliber/(m)	L.32.2(1.19)	L/30(1.105)	L/24(1.441)	L/26(1.499)
Barrel weight +breech (kg)	211	143	193	
Weight in firing position (kg)	468	790	2383*	–
Shot weight (kg) 0.45	0.465	1.75	2.7	
Muzzle velocity (m/sec)	400	540	495	487
Rate of fire (shots/minute)	40	250	30-35	–
Max. range (km) 4.3	6.0	ca. 5.0	6.4	

Type	Russian F.K.02	F.K.96 n.A.	F.K.16	U-boat K.
Caliber (cm)	7.62	7.7	7.7	8.8
Barrel length caliber/(m)	L/30(2.286)	L/27(2.08)	L/35(2.695)	L/30 (2.61)
Barrel weight +breech (kg)	400	335	644	
Weight in firing position (kg)	1040	1020	1325	1225
Shot weight (kg)	6.58	6.85	7.2	13.75
Muzzle velocity (m/sec)	588	465	545	590
Rate of fire (shots/minute)	15	6-10	10	
Max. range (km)	6.6	7.8	9.1	12.8

* Weight of the entire armored turret.
The data on the traverse and elevation angles were not given, because they can be influenced considerably by installation in the armored train.

2	guns;
3	light and medium mine-throwers;
11	heavy machine guns (each with 3750 Ss-,600 S.m.K.- and 150 S.m.K."L" shots
72	carbines (with 45 rounds each)
47	pistols (with 16 rounds each)
6	machine pistols (with 450 rounds each)
103	side arms
200	stick grenades
120	gas masks
1	telephone switchboard with 4 connections
1	cabinet with door
1	small radio set
1	first aid kit for a doctor and a medic NCO
15	handcarts
6	carrier pigeons

The crew, numbering 108 in all, was composed of 5 officers, 5 railroad officials (technical personnel), 26 NCOs and 72 men. This planning—as will be shown—remained in effect even after the decommissioning of the armored trains.

Technical data were occasionally also found for non-"official" makeshift armored trains:

Broad-gauge train (Baltic area, May 1919): two combat cars (armor: iron double walls, space filled with gravel, covered by iron ties), in the front one a 7.7-cm M 16 field gun and two heavy machine guns, in the rear one a five-barrel 3.7-cm revolving gun, a light mine-thrower, two heavy and one light machine guns.

Two armored trains (Lower Bavaria, April 1919): each with one howitzer protected with sandbags on a flatcar, two 3rd class cars also protected by sandbags and armed with machine guns, one pusher locomotive.

Fahrmbacher armored train (Augsburg, May 1919): Essen 97621 Omk(u) car with 7.7-cm M 96 field gun; MG car (G), locomotive of the Bavarian D XII series; coal car; command car (G with observation post); personnel car (G); kitchen car (G); personnel car (G); MG car (G); launcher car (Om) with one light mine-thrower; Omk car Magdeburg 25944 with 7.7-cm M 16 field gun; the combat cars were all provisionally armored with iron plates and sandbags; further arms: two tank guns, 100-man crew.

Lichtschlag Free Corps armored car (Ruhr area, 1920): Locomotive 7427 (no locality, probably T 9.3), four cars armed with mine-throwers and machine guns.

The two makeshift armored trains from Saxony, 1919-20, included one G and two or three O cars.

The guns used in the Reichswehr armored trains are the same as those of the World War I armored trains. The only addition was the 8.8-cm U-boat gun, greater numbers of which were available due to the immediate disarmament of the Navy than the 7.62- or 7.7-cm flak guns that they replaced. It is notable that here too, to avoid exceeding the train's clearance by the gun in a rectangular position, the short-barreled variations (L/30) were preferred. Also installed in the fixed armored turrets of the Dresden PZ 48 (and probably also PZ 49) were the Belgian 5.7-cm Maxim-Nordenfeldt casemate cannons used in the A7V tanks of World War I. mounted on socket mounts including cylindrical shields which allowed a traverse of up to 45 degrees on either side, and the barrel mount that allowed an elevation or lowering of 20 degrees.

A whole series of armored-train locomotives is also known. By far the most were from the T 9.3 series used for that purpose in World War I, but other types were also used, especially the G 7.

Series T 3	204	Bavarian Palatinate	WW I PZ IX
Series T 9.3	7055, probably Alsace-Lorraine		WWI PZ? PZ 24
	7138 Alsace-Lorraine		WWI PZ VII
	7228 Bromberg		PZ 30
	7247, no data		Lichtschlag armored train
	7267, no data		WWI PZ
	7268 Magdeburg		PZ 54
	7278 Bromberg		PZ 22
	7280 Koenigsberg		PZ 55
	7301 Kattowitz		PZ 32
	7306 Posen		PZ 52
	7308 Stettin		PZ 44
	7325 Mainz		WWI PZ X
	7333 Danzig		PZ 35, then IV
	7345 Altona		PZ 47
	7364 Danzig		PZ 36, then 22
	7372 Saarbruecken		PZ 44
Series G 7.1	4403 Breslau		PZ 31
	4470 Breslau		PZ 25
Series G 7.2	4618 Bromberg		?
	4726 Erfurt		WWI PZ V?
Series G 8.1	5185 Posen		PZ 38
Series P4.2	1927 Posen		PZ 39
	1931 Kattowitz?		PZ 20 or 32
Series IX V	1754 Saxony		PZ 48

Double listings result from locomotive changes. Without numbers, a Prussian S 3 of the Posen district is documented for PZ 40, and a Bavarian D XII for the Fahrmbacher armored train. There were also locomotives of types G 3, G 7.1 and G 8.1 mentioned on pages 22 and 24, which could not be documented after the war.

Fighting in the East

The occupation of Posen Province by the Poles at the turn of 1918 to 1919 could be held up only by locally formed units in the northern and western border areas, about on the Hohensalza—Argenau—Nakel—Kolmar—Czarnikau—Birnbaum—Tirschtiegel—Bentschen—Unruhstadt—Lissa—Rawitsch—Zduny line. Only gradually were the existing command structures filled out with recruits and spontaneous volunteers, who offered resistance to the further advances of the Poles and sometimes drove them backward.

A failed attack by the Poles on the rail junction at Bentschen on January 5, 1919 brought PZ VI there, and it could intervene successfully in the next Polish attempt, likewise in vain, on January 11. On the next day it mopped up the area west of Bentschen Lake as far as the Bomst railroad station. On January 25, though, this town and the nearby Unruhstadt were occupied by the Poles; only on February 12 could they be driven out again, as PZ VI took the Bomst station in a surprise attack.—Otherwise, very little is known of the action of the numerous newly built armored trains in the border area. We have the most information on the activities of the armored trains south of Bromberg. On January 11 the first armored train built there, PZ 21, brought the last German defenders back from the Schubin railroad station under heavy fire. This had a good moral effect, encouraging the German troops and terrifying the enemies, who evacuated the station hastily. Toward the end of the month, it operated on the line from Bromberg to Hohensalza. On January 21 it mopped up and secured the Hopfengarten depot, and on the next day it supported the attack from there on Gross-Neudorf. It arrived late for a second attack on this town on January 30, but—after capturing it—moved right on to Tannhofen. Two reports name PZ 22: It was used on the line from Bromberg to Schubin, where the Poles had advanced around Netzwalde toward the upper Netze Canal early in February 1919 . On February 10 it undertook a scouting advance toward the Netzwalde depot, during which it was derailed. The attacking Poles could be driven off, though, so that it could be brought back onto the rails and pulled back. On February 18 it fell victim to an electrically ignited mine on the same line, with the rear end of the train and the track destroyed, making retreat impossible. After using up their ammunition, the crew, who lost four dead and seven wounded, had to give up the train, which was taken over by the Poles and transported toward Schubin. But armored train No. 22 can be documented well after that date–until its disbanding early in 1921—but no trace of PZ 23, also built in Bromberg, can be found, other than a note in the list of September 1, 1919" "Vadeis—unoccupied!" Since an official renumbering is very unlikely, there remains only the suspicion that in both (!) reports the number of the armored train is wrong, and they concern PZ 23. The reports themselves give such a hint, as they refer to the last completed armored train of the PZ 21-23 series, and this—likewise documented—was PZ 23. The real PZ 22 must have seen action in the Nakel area, according to these reports, but nothing is known of its activities. Of the other armored trains built by Lin. komm.R (PZ 29, 30, 37 and 55), it is known only that PZ 30 secured the rail junction at Kreuz (west of Schneidemuehl) and also undertook an advance south of the Netze. From this it may be assumed that the lines around Schneidemuehl had also been secured by at least one armored train (PZ 29?), but this is not mentioned in the reports of the combat in that area. In the northern area there is only one further action of an armored train recorded. In the defense against Polish attacks on Argenau from April 8 to 11, 1919, an armored train that came from Thorn (PZ 35 or 36) provided help.

The following activities of armored trains in the southern sector have been described. On January 20, 1919, PZ 38 broke through from Lissa, in a salient of the front, as far as Luschwitz on the line leading to Wollstein and caused the Poles heavy losses, but also lost one armored car to rail explosions. On February 4 the Poles advanced to the rail lines north and south of Rawitsch and set out to destroy them. PZ 38, coming up from Lissa, prevented this by firing on them, so that the Poles finally retreated, even from Izbice, which lay near the line. The train also took part in mopping up the area south of Rawitsch. On February 7, with the help of this train, which had stayed at Rawicz at first, the Sarne area east of there was also won back. On February 18, one of the armored trains at Lissa (PZ 38 or 39) supported an attack on the station at Kankel (east of Lissa). Of the trains (No. 24, 25 and 31) set up by Lin.komm.L I (Breslau), one was with the Lierau Free Corps in the Kempen area in January 1919. Nothing else is known of their actions at that time, nor of PZ 32 (Lin. komm.L II, Kattowitz).

At the beginning of February 1919, the OHL planned to win back Posen Province by a large-scale pincer attack from the north and south. Even before the attack began, this led to intervention by the French, who set up a demarcation line, following the course of the front, which was not to be crossed by either side. Even so, there were armed incidents along this line again and again, in which armored trains were also involved, until January 10, 1920, when the Treaty of Versailles brought a final regulation of the border, and armored trains took part. All in all, though, the situation calmed down, making the concentration of armored trains no longer necessary. Thus more and more of them were transferred to other scenes of combat.

In Courland and Lithuania, after the Soviet advance in January 1919, the front remained stable in the following month. A new German command structure had been introduced, the decimated units were much strengthened by volunteers and by the transfer of new divisions from Germany. Among the reinforcements were two armored trains. PZ IV was transferred to the assembled Res.K. in Kovno on March

10, PZ V reached the "Iron Division" in Prekuln (east of Libau) on March 4, and PZ 21 was sent from the Bromberg area to Courland and stayed in the area east of Libau to secure rail lines. PZ VII was already with the Lw.K. in Olita. Meanwhile the German offensive had begun. PZ V immediately joined in the combat and was able to drive back Red attacks, also using an armored train, on the Windau bridge near Wenta and take Moscheiken on the morning of March 5 after pursuing the enemy along with other units. PZ V immediately scouted as far as Papile in the direction of Schaulen. On the next day it surprised an unloading battalion in Kurschani, was able to capture the transport train and put the covering armored train to flight. On March 10 PZ V got into a vigorous fight with a Red armored train on the other track near Schaulen and pursued it through Schaulen, which was hastily deserted by the Soviet troops, in the direction of Radziwilliski, but it was able to escape thanks to its higher speed. PZ V held Schaulen for a day with two companies that it brought in until reinforcements arrived; then it set out on the line toward Mitau.

Meanwhile, parts of the Res.K. stationed in Lithuania had moved northward from Kiejdany along with PZ IV and VII, in order to open the rail line from there to Schaulen. They reached Beisagola on March 12, then Radziwilliski. On March 14 a Red armored train was captured east of there at the depot in Laba; it was the former German PZ II, lost to the Reds in January. Its cars were divided between PZ IV and VII. The two trains then moved back to the southern Lithuanian area.

On March 16, PZ V moved forward to Janiski, but after a derailment it moved back; only on the next day was Janiski taken by the armored train with troops riding on it. Several days later, along with a company of the Brandis unit, it attacked Meiten and captured a Red armored train there. Meanwhile the Baltic Home Guard, moving from the west, had taken Tukkum on March 15 and moved forward from there to Mitau, which was taken on March 18. The Soviets made vigorous counterattacks, in which several armored trains took part,

PZ 30 is seen during its service at Kreuz (east of Schneidemuehl). At left is its commander, Lt. W. Huenemoerder. Photo: W. Huenemoerder, W. Sawodny collection

but the Baltic Home Guard could hold on until additional troops had arrived. PZ V remained stationed in Mitau in the following weeks, fighting especially on the Ekau north of the city, where it often dueled with a Russian armored train. On April 5, it drove off a Russian attack near Tittelmuende (east of Mitau). — It is said to have beaten back an attack by Lithuanian workers at the Libau railroad station, but it was obviously confused with PZ 21, which was in the area of that city. This armored train was withdrawn to East Prussia in May.

Meanwhile, the German Free Corps in Latvia had developed into a significant political force. They took the side of the German-Baltic minority, composed of the residents of the large landowners' estates and the prosperous city merchants, and hoped to strengthen them by settlements in those areas after the end of the military conflict. Along with the Baltic Home Guard, they had deposed the legal Latvian government of Ulmanis, recognized by the Allies, and set up an opposition government. With this action they turned not only the Allies but also the national governments of Estonia and Lithuania against them.

On May 19, 1919, PZ V had supported the capture of the railroad station at Garrosen on the Ekau east of Mitau; after that it took part in the Iron Division's advance on Riga and was to take the railroad bridge over the Duena before the city. This was done on May 2, but Red armored trains made such a disturbance that the bridge had to be blown up to prevent their advance. They were not content with the taking of Riga, and they advanced farther to the northeast. For this purpose, a makeshift armored train was prepared at the Riga workshops for the broad-gauge lines; it was armed with a field gun, a 5-cm cannon in a Gruson turret and four machine guns. Soon a conflict developed with the Estonians, who had taken the side of Ulmanis and his Letts. On June 4, 1919 an Estonian armored train opened fire on the Baltic troops at Ramozki. They were still able to take Wenden, but then negotiations were begun. Since the Bolsheviks were driven out of Courland and thus the purpose of the German troops in the Baltic area was finished in the eyes of the Allies, the Allied commander ordered the evacuation of northern Livonia and of half the troops in the rest of the Baltic area. But on June 21 another attempt was still made to restart the offensive and

reach the Lemsal-Wolmar line. The makeshift broad-gauge armored train got into combat with two Estonian armored trains near Lode, and all the armored trains were damaged. In their withdrawal, the German train covered the evacuation of Wenden. On June 29 it used barrage fire and gas grenades east of Riga. After Riga was evacuated early in July, the train was sent to Fichtenwald on the line to Tukkum, and in mid-August it was turned over to the Letts.

Under pressure from the Allies, the Reich government ordered the withdrawal of all German troops. A goodly number of the volunteer bands in Latvia objected, to be sure, and subordinated themselves to the White Russian command as a "German Legion". Among them was PZ V, but the "German Legion" also set up a makeshift armored train that bore the name of the unit's leader, Siewert. Nothing is known of its activities. In October 1919 an attempted White Russian/ German troop offensive in the direction of the Duena failed, to be followed by tough withdrawal fighting. On October 29, PZ V got into combat on the line from Mitau to Tukkum. Early in November it took part in the advance of the Plehwe Group to its last vain attack on Libau, which came to grief under fire from British ships' guns. On November 20 it appeared again before Tukkum. On the way back, it was derailed near Schlampen, was attacked and then set afire. The crew reached Mitau, but on the next day they set out back to the scene with a locomotive to blow up the rest of the train; then, along with all German troops that were still there, they left the Baltic area and headed for home.

Lithuania was also evacuated gradually. PZ VII was left behind at the beginning of November and became the Lithuanian armored train "Gedyminas". PZ IV had been sent to the Grodno area. This was turned over to the Poles at the end of April 1919. PZ IV covered the departure of the German transports and, on April 27, was the last to leave Grodno, withdrawing to Augustovo. In the next four months it remained in the Kovno area, repeatedly secured the demarcation line on the Bobr ahead of Augustovo, and was replaced by PZ 33, which had also been sent there; in July it accompanied transports from Radziwilliski. On August 30, PZ IV was sent back to Danzig. Little is known of PZ 33, which remained with AOK North until early October and was then to be assigned to the Rw.Gr.Kdo. II, but

PZ V is seen with the "Iron Division" in the Baltics in 1919. In the armored structure is the 7.7-cm F.K. 96 gun. Photo: W. Sawodny collection

An armored train (PZ 32?) is seen in the Upper Silesian industrial area during the first Polish revolt (August 1919). Photo: W. Sawodny collection

was crossed off on October 18 and thus disbanded. — On November 22 a German armored train (from East Prussia?) is said to have been brought an Allied commission to Radziwilliski for negotiations with Lithuania about the halting of German transports.

The Treaty of Versailles called for almost all of West Prussia west of the Vistula to be turned over to Poland, while Danzig with its surroundings was declared a free city under the protection of the League of Nations. The turnover took place on February 1, 1920. While the two Danzig armored trains (PZ 35 and 36) had already been moved back to the Reich in the summer of 1919, PZ IV was now brought back to Pomerania. For the southern part of East Prussia and the parts of West Prussia east of the Vistula, a plebiscite was planned. On February 12, 1920, the area was turned over to an inter-allied commission that met in Allenstein and had authority over occupation troops. The two East Prussian armored trains were moved to the free northern portion and located at Preussisch-Holland (PZ 27) and Wehlau (PZ 28). The plebiscite took place on July 11, 1920, and resulted in an overwhelming vote for remaining in the German Reich. The return took place on August 16, 1920; the two armored trains were immediately moved forward to secure the new Polish border, with the Wehlau train (PZ 28) going via Allenstein to the Gilgenburg-Soldau area.

It angered the Poles very much that the whole region of Upper Silesia, rich in natural resources and significant industries, in parts of which—especially in the south and east—great numbers of their landsmen lived, and which they therefore claimed as a part of their state, was also to have a plebiscite according to the Treaty of Versailles. Shortly after this fact was made known, and even before Allied troops entered the plebiscite area, the Poles sensed a chance in the summer of 1919 to gain the entire area through a revolt, which broke out on August 17 in the southern counties of Pless and Rybnik, and one day later in the industrial area itself. Unrest among the workers, though, had resulted in German troops (especially the 117th Infantry Division) and Free Corps already being stationed there, and even Armored Trains 20 and 32 were set up already. After initial Polish success, these troops soon gained the upper hand, and the revolt collapsed on August 24. At first the only armored train in this area was PZ 32, stationed in Gleiwitz. As early as August 17 it took the Tichau railroad station, which the Poles had occupied. On the night of August 19 it assisted in the rescue of Poppelau, and on the night of August 20 four other armored trains arrived as reinforcements: PZ 24, 38, 39, and 50. On that day an armored train (presumably PZ 32) accompanied the advance of a battalion via Zawodzie and Wilhelminenhuette to Myslowitz; in the next night PZ 32 drove the Poles out of Godow. On August 22 it came from Myslowitz to support the attack on Slupna, while PZ 24 covered the rear guard on the line southeast of Myslowitz. Further actions of the armored

trains are not known; on September 4, PZ 24, 38, and 50 had already returned to their homeland bases, while PZ 39 remained in the Upper Silesian industrial area for security until November 20, 1919.

At the end of January 1920, the German troops had to vacate Upper Silesia; an international commission with over 15,000 occupation troops—mainly French, but also small contingents of British and Italians—took over proceedings in Oppeln. The French taking of the Polish side in their fight with the Soviet Union, which inspired German demonstrations which also affected Polish inhabitants, and the very poor results of the plebiscites in East and West Prussia led to another attempted uprising by the Poles on August 18, 1920, which was disposed of through negotiations ten days later. The plebiscite on March 21, 1921, showed 60.3% for staying in the German Reich, 39.7% for union with Poland. The Allies thereupon discussed plans for division. Again the Poles wanted to create a *fait accompli*, and their troops, well organized this time and armed with, among other things, 16 armored trains, attacked on May 3. At first they were opposed only by weak self-protection units of German Upper Silesians. Thus, the Poles were able to take possession, in a short time, of nearly all the land to the right of the Oder, except for a few cities. To the annoyance of the British, who strengthened their own troop contingent (and built their own armored train), and the Italians, who entered the fray themselves, the very pro-Polish French did nothing to halt the uprising or protect the German population. But their cries for help struck a chord in the German Reich. A large number

A makeshift armored train (that of the Rossbach Free Corps?) is seen in the northern sector during the 1921 Polish uprising. After an iron coal car with an armored body comes a G-car with an observation turret. The type of the tender locomotive cannot be identified. Photo: W. Sawodny collection

The improvised "Brunner" armored train, used during the third Polish uprising in Upper Silesia (May-June 1921), consisted of three iron chalk cars (after II d 4 or A 7) with folding roof panels and an unarmored locomotive (T 9.3). Photo: DGEG Archives

After British troops arrived in Upper Silesia, they even built their own armored train at Oppeln in June 1921. The depicted Prussian T 14 locomotive was used. Photo: P. Malmassari collection

A Prussian T 14 was also used by the Germans as an armored locomotive in Upper Silesia in 1921. Photo: W. Sawodny collection

of Free Corps—although officially disbanded, they had remained in rural areas as "work cooperatives"—entered Upper Silesia illegally and, despite interference with their transports by left-wing forces, strengthened the home guards there so well that from Landsberg on the border via Rosenberg, Malapane, and Gogolin to the Oder south of Krappitz and then along the river, they formed a closed front. On May 21, 1921, the German units even went on the offensive and won a decisive victory over the Poles by storming the Annaberg. On June 3 the captured area was extended to the Kandrzin–Slawentzitz line. After tedious negotiations with the Allies, the entire plebiscite area was vacated by both the German and Polish troops early in July 1921. Upper Silesia was later divided in accordance with a decision of the League of Nations. For this conflict, several armored trains were set up by the Germans (remember that by the London Ultimatum of May 5, 1921, the Germans were forbidden to have armored trains!). Such makeshift jobs were mentioned in the northern sector with the Rossbach Free Corps in the Kreuzburg area (its participation in driving the Poles out of the border town of Kostau on May 19, 1919, is its only known action) and the Nollau Free Corps in the Carlsruhe area, plus one known as "Abt" in Gogolin in June 1919. Documented in a picture is the "Brunner" armored train from Ratibor, consisting of three Omk cars. The locomotive was probably a T 9.3 fitted with a pre-heater. After the fighting ended, the Inter-Allied Military Control Commission (IMKK) listed the German armored cars (the locomotives had obviously been un-armored already and assigned to normal railroad traffic). Furthermore, in Leobschütz they found five chalk cars according to II d4 or A 7 with an inner covering (probably a double wall) of iron plates (Essen 30551, Frankfurt 17458, Münster 17462 and 20338, Kattowitz 13751; three of them, including the last, came from the "Brunner" armored train); another similar chalk car (Erfurt 40072, with 10-mm iron plates added to the car's sides) was found in Ratibor. In Leobschütz the Hannover 11946 G-car was found with inner armor, plus the Halle 23436 limber car, armored with iron plates. In Oppeln there were three open cars (Breslau 56052, 100073, and 107548), which were protected provisionally with railroad ties and sandbags (only the axle ends were protected by iron plates); in the Gleiwitz AW were Posen 8732, Kattowitz 27310, and Saxony 47732. Their type is not noted, but their armoring with an iron double wall and the space between filled with sand suggests the usual Omk(u) according to II d1 or A 6. This number of cars is compatible with the formation of four armored trains.

PZ III (T 9.3 loco) is seen during its use by the von Hülsen Free Corps in March 1919. Photo: G. Krause collection

Fighting Within the German Reich

After the attempt to tame the unofficial People's Naval Division in Berlin on December 24, 1918, has failed miserably and the left wing socialist forces have been unable to take power for themselves through their delays and disunity at the beginning of January 1919, the political scene was dominated for years by the opposition of the majority-socialist government under Ebert, which stressed order and general elections, and the extreme left, at first represented by the USPD, later in growing numbers by the communists as well, which constantly caused strikes and uprisings, and even set up regional opposition governments. The former made use of the hastily assembled Free Corps, and later the Reichswehr, to fight them. Although this was ultimately a fight between extreme right- and left-wing forces, one must keep in mind that the troops generally acted under orders from the government, which used them to prevent the establishment of soviet-republican or Spartacist rules, even by so-called "Reich executions."

In the Berlin area there was just one WWI armored train, PZ III. When the Free Corps subdued the leftists in mid-January 1919, it tried to capture the Silesian railroad station, held by the Reds for six days, but failed. Otherwise, only one action of an armored train in this period is known. On February 7, an armored train with the 2nd Railroad Brigade in Hanau made the evacuation of the depot there to Seligenstadt possible. Since all the other existing armored trains can be located elsewhere, it must have been PZ IV, which had returned from the Balkans at the war's end and then was sent to Lithuania early in March. But when the demarcation line was set up along the front in Posen Province on February 16, 1919, this brought a strong limitation of possible action for the armored trains that had been set up for the Border Patrol East, which freed them for activities within the Reich. At first these armored trains remained subordinate to their original Lin.Komm., and were thus commanded off only temporarily. Only later were regular relocations undertaken little by little, and actual construction began in the Reich only as of March 1919.

The armored train from Berlin, PZ III, had been assigned to the Huelsen Free Corps, which was subordinated to the Volunteer Landesjäger Corps under General Maercker.

When three battalions of the Landesjäger Corps got into a serious situation on March 1, 1919, in Halle, where a revolutionary council had been established and a general strike had broken out, it was this armored train that contributed significantly to their relief. Because of this event another armored train, No. 29 from Bromberg, was made available to the Volunteer Landesjäger Corps. The two armored trains contributed to the successful reestablishment of the state order in the Halle-Merseburg-Corbetha-Markranstaedt-Leipzig area.

At the beginning of April 1919, the radical soldiers' council had overthrown the moderate socialist government at Magdeburg and taken a Reich minister, who was passing through, hostage, along with several high officers. Again, the Volunteer Landesjäger Corps of General Maercker was charged to eliminate these conditions, and again he called for PZ III (renumbered 54 since April 10) from Group Command I (General von Lüttwitz) in Berlin (to which it apparently had meanwhile returned). On April 9, 1919, this train took part in the occupation of the main station and southern part of Magdeburg. On April 11, 1919, PZ 54 (ex-III), along with the Goslar Riflemen, defended the station in Börssum against attacking Spartacists. In the night of April 16-17, 1919, it moved with a battalion of Landesjäger from Helmstedt toward Braunschweig as far as Riddagshausen, and on that day, along with other armored trains (others besides No. 29?), Braunschweig was occupied. On April 19, 1919, 13 persons were arrested in Schoeppenstedt and a cache of arms seized; on May 3 it supported an action against Holzminden, where workers and seamen had halted rail traffic since April 11.

In Bavaria, several leftist and moderate governments had replaced each other since the revolution in November 1918. But all of them showed separatist tendencies (the farther left, the more). It was known that since the founding of the German Reich in 1871, Bavaria had held out for special rights. Bavaria had also not signed the Reichswehr law passed by the National Assembly (March 6, 1919). On the night of April 6-7, 1919, the majority socialistic government of Hoffmann had been brought down and a soviet republic declared in Munich. Hoffmann and his colleagues moved to Bamberg, and the regaining of rule by their own power failed on April 16, 1919, in a fight near Dachau. There was nothing left for Hoffmann to do but appeal to the Reich government, which—not without withdrawing certain Bavarian special rights, such as its exception from setting up Reichswehr units—declared a "Reich execution" against Munich. It is noteworthy that this was conducted mainly by Prussian, Hessian, and Württembergish contingents; the strongest Bavarian formation, the von Epp Rifle Brigade, had to be set up in Thuringia. Only in Lower Bavaria did a few small corps arise and, later, move against Munich from the east. One of them, the Hutschenreuther Battalion founded in Straubing, had two makeshift armored trains. On April 24, 1919, merely by appearing, they prevented the occupation of Landshut by Red army men sent by train from Munich. Later they operated out of Mühldorf; on 29 April one of these armored trains cleaned out Dorfen. The Hutschenreuther Battalion did not take part in the fighting around Munich; instead, they fought the strong soviet-republican forces in the Rosenheim area. This city was occupied on 1 May, and Kolbermoor, which offered strong resistance, could be taken on May 3-4, 1919, with support from the armored trains.

Four armored trains were subordinated to the Reichswehr troops coming from Thuringia to occupy Munich. PZ 22 (from Bromberg) was assigned to the Görlitz Free Corps within the Friedeburg group. It advanced from Ingolstadt to Rohrmoos (8 km from Dachau) on April 29, 1919. Its advance on Dachau the next day was blocked at first, but in the afternoon, Dachau could be occupied after heavy fighting; the railroad station was the last bastion of the defenders. On 1 May PZ 22 set out from Allach in the direction of Munich, having heard that the main station there was unoccupied, and moved a short way behind the Hacker bridge unharmed. There it came to grief; one source says it hit a mine, another cites a direct hit on the locomotive as the reason. Before the following heavy attacks, the crew moved back to the nearby Deroy barracks, where they were taken prisoner the next morning.

The Deetjen group advanced from Regensburg via Freising to Schleissheim with three armored trains (No. 24 and 25 from Breslau and PZ 40 from Rawitsch), reaching it on the evening of April 29, 1919. The Lützow Free Corps, with PZ 40, was transferred from Landshut via Mühldorf to Markt Schwaben and approached Munich from the east, reaching Berg am Laim and Ramersdorf via Riem on the evening of 30 April almost without a fight. The train may have advanced to the eastern railroad station (but nothing is known of its actions then or later).

The other two armored trains of the Deetjen group advanced on Munich from Schleissheim on May 1, 1919. While PZ 24 secured the advance of the Haas group from Laim toward the southern railroad station, PZ 25 tried to move forward to the damaged PZ 22 beyond the Hacker bridge. Although it was able to defeat the strong force at the Donnersberg bridge, only a scouting troop reached the now-deserted armored train. A renewed advance of the united PZ 24 and 25 on parallel lines, covering each other, broke down under heavy mine-thrower fire right in front of the Hacker bridge, where their field of fire was limited by the many freight cars left in front of the main station. A renewed attack on the night of 1-2 May was also stopped in front of the Hacker bridge. Thus, it was not until midday on 2 May that PZ 25, now working alone, drove off the troops at the Hacker bridge and advanced to the now-plundered PZ 22 and on to the main station. Then the armored train went back to Schleissheim.—PZ 24, armed with revolver cannons, took part in the heavy fighting for the Giesing district on 2 May. After securing the movement of the Probstmayr Battalion from Pasing to the south station area, it went on to the east to support the von Epp group, but encountered a trap at Columbus Place and had to turn back with three dead and one wounded after the locomotive took a direct hit.—After the successful occupation of Munich early in May, the operation of a makeshift armored train under the command of Captain Fahrmbacher (the later World War II general) from Augsburg toward Kempten was mentioned. This armored train took part in the mopping up of Blaichach, Immenstadt, and Sonthofen on 14 May and reached Lindau on 17 May.

After the extinguishing of the Bavarian Soviet Republic in Munich, the Reich government decided to clean out the separatist movement in Saxony as well. The Volunteer Landesjäger Corps was given the job. General Maercker succeeded in occupying Leipzig without a fight on the night of May 10-11, 1919, in a lightning-fast move in which he had several marching columns enter the city concentrically. Three of them were using armored trains. One unit of the Landesjäger Corps, along with the corps staff and followed by the von Oven regiment, rode behind PZ 21 from Bitterfeld through Delitzsch directly into the main station of Leipzig; from Halle-Schkeuditz the 1st Landesjäger Regiment moved into the districts of Möckern and Gohlis with PZ 54, and the 2nd Landesjäger Regiment with PZ 24 advanced from Markranstädt to Lindenau and Leutzsch and from there via Elster and Pleisse into the center of the city. The

Armored Train 22 in Munich. The armor plate on the T 9.3 locomotive (see picture on page 39) has been removed so that the number (Bromberg 7258) can be read. Behind it is a rebuilt 15-ton coal car (A 6) with a built-in armored turret and a 5.3-cm gun. Photo: Munich City Archives.

Armored Train III, already renumbered as PZ 54, is seen after the attack on the Eisenach railroad station on May 19-20, 1919. The buildings, as can be seen in the picture, suffered much in the action. Photo: W. Sawodny collection

armored trains performed good service in taking and cleaning out the numerous tracks at the different depots of Leipzig.

While PZ 21 and 24 were withdrawn, PZ 54 (the former PZ III) remained with the Landesjäger Corps. After the action at Halle it was used in Thuringia. At midnight on 18-19 May it arrived in Eisenach and took prisoners. On the next night it was attacked at the station there, and not only one car of the train, but also a nearby freight train and freight halls were burned out. On 22 May it was fired on again at the depot with rifles, machine guns, and mine throwers. During the railroad strike in June it was sent from Weimar to Erfurt on June 18, 1919. From July 1919 on the Landesjäger Corps, now part of the Reichswehr Brigade No. 16, was assigned three more armored trains, stationed as followed: PZ 25 in Weimar, PZ 29 in Naumburg, PZ 46 with 54 in Halle, and PZ 51 in Torgau (probably a typographical error; maybe PZ 31 was meant, which was in September, along with PZ 25, under the command of the 9th Army Corps in Kassel). Further actions in which armored trains took part are documented: The occupation of Stettin by the Reichswehr on May 16, 1919, presumably involving armored trains 44 and 45, and that of Hamburg by the Lettow-Vorbeck Corps (PZ 39) on July 1, 1919. On 29-30 July a battalion formerly in Salzwedel, with two makeshift armored trains, each having two cars armed with machine guns and mine throwers, was transported via Güsten to Bernburg. On 19 August Chemnitz was occupied from all four sides, involving the use of four armored trains, surely including the Saxon PZ 48 and 49. On October 17, 1919, PZ 54, coming from Gräfenheinichen, ended a strike in the Zschornewitz power station, and on the 25th it occupied the "Leopold" mine in Bitterfeld and stayed there until 27 October, while PZ 29 was used in Delitzsch at that time. On October 27-28, 1919, an operation against Suhl took place, in which PZ 22 and 25 were involved. On November 19-20, 1919, armored trains No. 25, 31, and 54 were in action again in the Bitterfeld-Wolfen area. On January 30, 1920, PZ 49 covered troop unloadings at Oelsnitz and Lugau southwest of Chemnitz, and on 9 February those for the occupation of Plauen in Jocketa and Herlasgruen. Afterwards PZ 49 remained in Plauen.

Meanwhile, after long and difficult discussions the Treaty of Versailles had been signed, setting extraordinarily hard conditions for the German Reich. Among many others the OHL, the General Staff, was to be dissolved, and the total strength of the Army was to be reduced to 100,000 men, which was one quarter of its strength at that time. The troop reduction in particular—especially in view of the worsening economic situation—annoyed the Army and its leaders. The situation was even aggravated by the return of the rigorously-minded Free Corps troops from the Baltic area in December 1919, as all free corps were to be disbanded. At the head of the officers' opposition, which the government made responsible for signing the treaty, was the commander of the RW-Gr.Kdo.I, General von Lüttwitz. The uprising was finally ignited by the coming disbanding of the 2nd Naval Brigade of Captain Ehrhardt, then stationed in Döberitz, which was denied by von Lüttwitz. He was relieved of his command and fled to Ehrhardt, whose Navy Brigade marched to Berlin on the night of March 13, 1920, and there established a right-wing regime under Oberlandschaftsdirektor Kapp. Since the Reichswehr did not act against the rebels (as General von Seeckt said, "The Reichswehr does not fire on the Reichswehr."), the Ebert regime fled via Dresden (where General Maercker took at least an equivocal attitude) to Stuttgart and proclaimed a general strike, which was followed almost everywhere and completely crippled life in the Reich. So it was no wonder that the revolt collapsed within five days despite the inactivity of the Reichswehr. Many of the influential Reichswehr officers doubtless agreed with the goals of the rebels; almost all those in northern and eastern Germany joined them, while others took a waiting position and made sure, when the collapse of the revolt was obvious, to assure the government of their loyalty again, which for few others, such as General Bergmann in Stuttgart (which is why the government had gone there), had never been in question. On the other hand, the USPD and KPD not only joined in the general strike fully, but remained armed after the strike had collapsed, since they saw in the righteous indignation of the public a possibility of getting rid of not only the compromised Reichswehr, but also the socialist-majority government, the pro-Reichswehr attitude of which was blamed for causing the revolt (Reich Defense Minister Noske had to resign later), and thus to realize their goals. Thus, despite everything, there was nothing left for the government to do but utilize the cooperation of the Reichswehr again, which appeared loyal after the revolt, and which—as inactive as they had been about the rebels from their own ranks—had proceeded promptly and vigorously against the left wing forces, wherein armored trains were put to great use again.

It is not clear whether PZ IV, at Kummersdorf for shooting drills, was ordered to Berlin by the rebels. The surviving report by the armored train's commander gives no date for the transfer to the Anhalt depot to protect the extensive quantities of freight stored there. And the activities described in it begin only after the collapse of the revolt. PZ IV made a scouting trip in the direction of Küstrin on 20 March and was able to convoy a cattle transport to Berlin. At noon on March 20, 1920, it became known that Communist units had occupied the gasoline works at Adlersdorf. PZ IV drove them from there and from the bridge over the Teltow Canal to the southeast. On 23 March it mopped up the line to Jüterbog, after which it stayed at the Anhalt station.—On 17 March a Reichswehr detachment that had advanced from Halle in the direction of Eisleben along with an armored train (PZ 54?) escaped after a ten-hour battle with Spartacist bands that almost surrounded it, and had to return to Halle. On 20 March PZ 54 again fought off attacks from the south on the depot at Halle. In Cottbus, too, the leftists had taken power. The Reichswehr detachment there called for reinforcements on 19 March; they were sent on the march from Küstrin, protected by PZ 50. The transport was stopped by sabotage by railroad men and finally halted by exploded tracks near Cottbus. Storming of the train failed under fire from it. On 20 March the armored train got into the city by roundabout routes and drove off the rebels. On 22 March PZ 50 disarmed workers in Forst, and on 24 March in Senftenberg.—In Saxony, where the two regular armored trains (No. 48 and 49) were joined by three makeshift ones (in Dresden-Neustadt, Meissen, and Bautzen) since the beginning of 1920, unrest in Meissen and Grossenhain was nipped in the bud by the appearance of an armored train, and an armored train (No. 49?) was also active in the Vogtland at that time.—In Stettin, armed workers fought off the attack of an armored train on 18 March; two days later two crewmen of PZ 44 were killed, but in the end the Reichswehr kept the upper hand there too.—On 22 March PZ VI, stationed in Schwerin, was assigned to the Ribbentrop Detachment

for an action against Rostock, and on March 27, 1920, PZ 47 took part in mopping-up action in the Bernau-Eberswalde-Oderberg area. For the Reichswehr's actions against strong Red forces that arose in Thuringia, the Group South was assigned PZ 22 from Hannoversch-Münden on 17 March. It operated in the Hildburghausen-Meiningen area until the end of the month. On 7 and 8 April PZ 29 carried out pacifications in the Tangermünde-Stendal area; on 11 April it joined again with PZ 48 and 49 to cover the advance of the Reichswehr to occupy the region between Plauen and Chemnitz in western Saxony.

The heaviest fighting developed in the Ruhr area with its large numbers of industrial workers, who agreed with the leftist socialist and Communist tendencies, a region where, since the revolution, the course of moderate Reich government struck against disagreement and even opposition. After the Kapp revolt the Spartacists were able to activate and arm the masses, thus forming a large Red army that brought the entire Ruhr area into their possession by March 21, 1920. A counter-offensive by the Lichtschlag Free Corps, which had advanced from Osnabrück to Dortmund on 16 March, was halted. Large numbers were surrounded at the Dortmund-South freight depot and had to surrender the next day, along with the makeshift armored train, armed with mine throwers and machine guns that workers from Hagen took away with them. When the Red Army crossed the Lippe northward near Haltern an armored train was used against them, but torn-up rails prevented it from reaching the railroad station, and it could only fire on the city. In the next days combat developed, particularly south of Wesel, a city held by the Reichswehr. On 23 March a makeshift Red armored train made up of freight cars tried to move over the Lippe bridge toward Wesel, but had to turn back under defensive fire. Two days later, Reichswehr troops with their makeshift armored train, armed only with two light machine guns and one light mine thrower, pushed southward across the Lippe bridge. Two hundred meters beyond the bridge it was stopped when the locomotive was hit; a Red attempt to storm the stopped train failed, and it could be towed back by a spare loco sent from Wesel. Meanwhile, strong reinforcements to the Reichswehr had arrived north of the Lippe under cover of armored trains so that they

PZ IV is seen during the Kapp revolt in Berlin. The Russian 7.62-cm F.K.-02 flak gun is easy to recognize; behind it in the turret of the machine-gun car is a heavy MG-08. The train was then pulled by an unarmored Prussian G 8.1 locomotive, after having given up its original armored loco to the M.E.D. 5 on being transferred out of its area in July 1919. Only in May 1920, after the Ruhr fighting, was it supplied again with an armored loco. Photo: Agency for Pictures of History of the Times, Berlin

could go on the offensive. Also on 25 March, a company of Infantry Regiment No. 10, with the help of PZ 31, captured a camp southwest of Dülmen. On the next day PZ 20 set out from Rhade to Deuten and reached the destroyed Lippe bridge near Hervest-Dorsten the next day. From there it supplied covering fire to the forces attacking across the river, until on 29 March the bridge could be rebuilt provisionally and Dorsten taken. Farther to the east, PZ 31 took part in the taking of Haltern on 30 March, after the city had been briefly occupied the previous day but had had to be given up again. On 28 March 28 the Commander of Recruitment District VI, Lt.Gen. von Watter, who commanded the forces sent to the Ruhr area, moved from Münster to Wesel on PZ 25 to lead the attack from closer to the front. On 29 March a makeshift Red armored train had tried again to advance via Voerde toward Wesel but had been driven back. On 1 April PZ 32 carried an assault company in an attack on the Kirchhellen railroad station. Although the Red occupiers of the entrance signal box could be fought down, the depot itself could not be taken and the armored train had to withdraw. By tearing up the rails, the Reds prevented a repeat of the attack the next day. The group moving southward from Haltern had reached Recklinghausen that day, from which PZ 31 took captured Red guards away. Meanwhile, Reichswehr forces approaching the eastern Ruhr area (Haas Group) were in motion. On 31 March PZ IV liberated the "Sachsen" and "Radbod" mines near Hamm and led the infantry advance as it pushed into the city. On the next day Pelkum was captured, though the armored train could

not enter the city because of a blown-up bridge. On 2 April PZ IV operated near Nordbögge and advanced through Kamen to Kurl, which was cleaned out the next day. On 5 April it reached Dortmund and then secured its main station. On 3 April the 3rd Naval Brigade with PZ 32 occupied Gladbeck, after which the armored train supplied flank cover for the attack on Buer and later took part in the taking of Bottrop against heavy resistance. In the area of the Münster Division, an advance from Lünen to Derne (in the direction of Dortmund) took place with PZ 31 that day. On 5 April the Kabisch Group was assigned PZ 25 for an attack on Essen. It advanced from Mülheim on 7 April. Essen was taken without a fight—the Red Army finally had to give up. On 10 April the Hagen workers, who had captured the Lichtschlag Free Corps' armored train in Dortmund on 17 March, surrendered it in Schwerte—thus marking the beginning and the end of the Ruhr fighting.

One other event must be remembered, which is the Communist uprising in the central German industrial area in March 1921. It was the police's job to put it down; the Reichswehr only supplied heavy weapons (mine throwers, guns). Only after the end of the uprising (on 30 March) did regular troops occupy the area. PZ 55 was with the unit that moved into Bitterfeld. It is not clear whether it had not yet been delivered to the disarmament site in Kummersdorf or had been fetched back from it, as can be documented for additional cars of the protected train "Uhland" of the Württemberg Transport Defense (their actions in central Germany in March-April 1921 are reported

At the end of March, workers at the Leuna works built a makeshift armored train. *Right:* The armored cars in the assembly hall. *Below:* The armored train after it was turned over to the police troops. Photos: German Historical Museum, Berlin, and Military Historical Museum, Dresden

on pp. 62f). It is definite that it was the last of the Reichswehr armored trains to be disarmed in Kummersdorf in May-June 1921. The central German uprising is also of importance in that—otherwise only in the Ruhr area fighting in March-April 1920—an armored train was also used there by the leftists. It was built by the workers at the Leuna works on the night of 27-28 March and consisted of the locomotive and two cars armored with 15-mm steel plates, which had rifle ports and two machine-gun positions per car. It operated on the line from the Leuna factory to Grosskorbetha. On 28 March it was able to fight off an advance near Spergau. In the storming of the Leuna works on 29 March it fell into the hands of the police troops.

To conclude the action reports of all the armored trains, here is a brief overview of their stations and areas of action, as far as they are known. For WWI armored trains II-VII, the scant data from the time before the 1918 armistice are included.

PZ II: On August 21, 1914, in Darmstadt, Lin.Komm.C (Mainz); set up as PZ X; on April 24, 1915, went to Lin.Komm. Z in Alsace, and was also there in September 1916; on October 24, 1916, it left for Altona, where it was put out of commission; on February 16, 1918, reactivated as PZ II and sent to the eastern front; on January 8, 1919, it fell into Soviet hands in Schaulen and was used by them; on March 14, 1919, taken back at Laba; its material was divided between PZ IV and VII.

PZ III: Ready for action on August 1, 1914, (set up by Lin. Komm.S?); took part in the occupation of Luxembourg the next night; went to Serbia in 1915; in the early summer of 1916 it was in Nisch, was replaced by PZ IV, went to Belgium until 1918, and was in Berlin January 1919; given to the Volunteer Landesjäger Corps in Halle in March 1919; renamed PZ 54 (see there) on April 10, 1919.

PZ IV: Set up by the Lin.Komm.Z in Muehlhausen in 1914; replaced PZ III in Serbia, was shifted to northeastern Bulgaria for an assault on Dobrudja, and remained there until 1917; was in Macedonia since the summer of 1918; joined in withdrawal through Serbia; probably in Hanau early in February 1919; assigned to the M.E.D. 5 in Kovno early in March; as of 11 March advanced toward Schaulen, took on several cars from recaptured PZ II; in the Grodno-Augustowo-Suwalki area in April 1919 (border patrol); as of 30 June secured transports back from the Baltics from Radziwillischki to Kowno; transferred to Danzig area on July 14, 1919 (Langfuhr and Putzig); during the evacuation of West Prussia Danzig border patrol; stationed at Bütow, Further Pomerania, from February 3, 1920, onward; sent to the troop training center of Kummersdorf for firing drills on 5 March; in Berlin during the Kapp revolt (Anhalt Depot, fighting in Adlershof); to the Haas Group in the Ahlen-Soest area on 28 March; action between Hamm and Dortmund during the Ruhr fighting (31 March-6 April); cleaning-up action along the Ruhr line, Neheim-Hüsten—Arnsberg—Brilon, until mid-May, then back in Dortmund; subordinated to Engineer Battalion 13 in Ulm on 24 May; secured the Dornstadt airfield on June 25-29, 1920; turned in at the Neu-Ulm–Offenhausen ammunition depot on 8 November; released until 12/31/1920, dismantled in Kummersdorf.

PZ V: Set up 1914 as PZ XII, place unknown; in Romania in the summer and autumn of 1916; later in Belgium, renumbered PZ V in 1917 (updated at the Mecheln railroad shops in the autumn of 1917; later removed to a depot on the North Sea coast (Altona?); then to Lyck, East Prussia, on 23 February; to Prekuln, Latvia, on March 4, 1919; remained on the Courland front, taking part in many fights; destroyed near Schlampen on November 20, 1919.

PZ VI: Set up by Lin.Komm.Z (Alsace-Lorraine) in 1914; was there in the summer of 1916 and still there in 1918; went to Grenzschutz-Ost; on the Obra near Bentschen in January 1919; transferred to Mecklenburg September-October 1919; in Schwerin

March 1920; in Deutsch-Krone (Reichswehr Brigade 9) June 1920; disbanded at end of 1920.

PZ VII: Set up in 1914 as PZ XIII; was with Lin.komm. Z in the summer of 1916; renumbered PZ VII in 1917; later removed to a depot on the North Sea coast (Altona?); transferred to the eastern front; at Kowel in January 1919, later Brest-Litovsk; sent to southern Lithuania (Olita) in mid-February 1919; as of 11 March advanced from Kiejdany toward Schaulen; received material from recaptured PZ II; remained in Lithuania at the withdrawal on 9 November; became Lithuanian armored train "Gedyminas."

PZ VIII: Divided into four patrol trains with the M.E.D. 8 (Libau) in March 1919.

PZ XI, XVII, and XIX: were still run by Lin.Komm.L II in the summer of 1919; no longer documented after that.

PZ 20: Set up by Lin.Komm.L II (Kattowitz) in January 1919; in Upper Silesia until February 1920; action in Ruhr area in March 1920; then back in Silesia; in Rothsürben or Liegnitz with Reichswehr Brigade 6 in June 1920; disbanded at end of 1920.

PZ 21: Set up by Lin.Komm.R (Bromberg) before January 11, 1919; action south of that city; transferred to Courland (Libau area) in March 1919; to Lin.Komm.N in East Prussia in May, but also saw action in Leipzig; then back to East Prussia; with Reichswehr Brigade 20 in Heilsberg in June 1920; disbanded in autumn of 1920.

PZ 22: Set up by Lin.Komm.R on January 25, 1919; action south of Nakel (?); took part in operations against the Munich Soviet Republic in April-May 1919; to Hannoversch-Münden in September 1919 (still with Reichswehr Brigade 11 there in June 1920); action in Thuringia in October 1919 and March 1920; disbanded at end of 1920.

PZ 23: Set up by Lin.Komm.R January-February 1919; captured by the Poles at Netzwalde on 17 February after an explosion prevented its return; became Polish armored train "Rzepicha."

PZ 24: Set up by Lin.Komm.L I (Breslau) in January-February 1919; remained in Reich area; action in Munich April-May 1919; then in Leipzig in May; back to Upper Silesia in August-September 1919; with Reichswehr Brigade 6 in Lauban in June 1920; disbanded at end of 1920.

PZ 25: Set up by Lin.Komm.L I in January-February 1919; action in Munich in April-May 1919; remained inside the Reich; assigned to XI. Army Corps in Kassel in September 1919 (action at Weimar in July, Suhl in October, Bitterfeld in November); transferred to Wkr.VI (Hildesheim) on December 17, 1919; took part in fighting in Ruhr area in March-April 1920; still with Reichswehr Brigade 10 in Hildesheim in June 1920; disbanded at end of 1920.

PZ 27: Set up by Lin.Komm.N (Koenigsberg) in January-February 1919; remained in East Prussia for its entire existence; disbanded with Reichswehr Brigade 20 in Preussisch-Holland in the summer of 1920.

PZ 28: Set up by Lin.Komm.N in January-February 1919; remained in East Prussia; stationed with Reichswehr Brigade 1 at Wehlau in June 1920; disbanded at end of 1920.

PZ 29: Set up by Lin.Komm.R (Bromberg) in latter half of February 1919; already transferred to central Germany in March 1919; action and stationing in Halle in March, Naumburg in July, as of December 1919 in Magdeburg (with Reichswehr Brigade 4 there in June 1920); action in Delitzsch in March 1920; Chemnitz in April 1920; disbanded at end of 1920.

PZ 30: Set up by Lin.Komm.R in latter half of February 1919; action near Kreuz; assigned to Wkr.II (Stettin) in October 1919; with Reichswehr Brigade 2 in Stralsund in June 1920; disbanded at end of 1920.

PZ 31: Set up by Lin.Komm.L I (Breslau), exact date of transfer to Germany unknown; in July 1919 with the Volunteer Landesjäger

Corps in Torgau; assigned to XI. Army Corps in Kassel in October 1919 (action at Bitterfeld in November); assigned to Wkr.VI (Münster) in December 1919; took part in fighting in Ruhr area in March 1920; stationed at Münster in June 1920; disbanded at end of 1920.

PZ 32: Set up by Lin.Komm.L II (Kattowitz) before April 1919; sent to Ruhr combat in March 1920; then returned to Upper Silesia; with Reichswehr Brigade 8 in Breslau-Carlowitz in June 1920; disbanded at end of 1920.

PZ 33: When and where it was set up are unknown; with M.E.D.5 in Augustowo on border patrol from April to October 1919; disbanded in October 1919.

PZ 35: Set up by Lin.Komm.V (Danzig) at end of February 1919; time of transfer to Germany not exactly known; assigned to VII. Army Corps in Münster early in September 1919; disbanded in spring of 1920.

PZ 36: Set up by Lin.Komm.V at end of February 1919; time of transfer to Germany not exactly known; assigned to Reichswehr Brigade 4 in Magdeburg in September 1919; disbanded in spring of 1920.

PZ 37: Set up by Lin.Komm.R (Bromberg) to XVII, Army Corps in Thorn in October 1919; disbanded in spring of 1920.

PZ 38: Set up in Lissa by Lin.Komm.G (Posen/Frankfurt on the Oder) in latter half of January 1919 and saw action there; in the Upper Silesian industrial area in August-September 1919; made into a unit with PZ 39 early in January 1920 and transferred to Würzburg; assigned to Reichswehr Brigade 23 there; disbanded in autumn of 1920.

PZ 39: Set up by Lin.Komm.G in Lissa in February 1919; saw action in Hamburg in July; in the Upper Silesian industrial area from late August to November 20, 1919; combined with PZ 38 early in January 1920, see there.

PZ 40: Set up by Lin.Komm,G in Rawitsch in February 1919; action in Munich in April-May; then back to Rawitsch; formed a unit with PZ 52 in July 1919; the pair went to Reichswehr Brigade 24 in Nürnberg-Schweinau in January 1920; disbanded at end of 1920.

PZ 41: Under construction in September 1919, but not finished.

PZ 42: Set up by Lin.Komm.G (Posen/Frankfurt on the Oder); already disbanded at end of September 1919.

PZ 43: Time and place of origin not known; bears same comment as the lost PZ 23 in list of September 1919; thus, the loss of this train may be presumed (conditions not known).

PZ 44: Set up by Lin.Komm.X (Stettin) in April 1919, obviously remained in that area the whole time; stationed with Reichswehr Brigade 2 in Altdamm in June 1920; disbanded at end of 1920.

PZ 45: Set up by Lin.Komm.X in April 1919; transferred to Munich on July 29, 1919; still there with Reichswehr Brigade 21 in Oberwiesenfeld in June 1920.

PZ 46: Set up by Lin.Komm.T (Halle) in July 1919; transferred to Berlin area on December 17, 1919, rebuilt before that in RAW Plaue (Brandenburg-West), was to be "model armored train," which did not happen; with Reichswehr Brigade 15 in Jüterbog in June 1920; disbanded the same month.

PZ 47: Set up by Lin.Komm.U (Magdeburg); listed as being built early in September 1919; transferred to the Oder on December 17, 1919; in the Bernau—Oderberg—Eberswalde area in March 1920; with Reichswehr Brigade 5 in Küstrin in June 1920; disbanded in autumn of 1920.

PZ 48: Set up by Lin.Komm.E (Dresden); saw action in Chemnitz in August 1919; seems to have been stationed with Reichswehr Brigade 12 in Dresden the whole time; disbanded at end of 1920.

PZ 49: Set up by Lin.Komm.E; action near Chemnitz in August 1919, in Bautzen in the autumn, in Riesa in November, stationed in Plauen as of January 1920; to Reichswehr Brigade 19 at Leipzig-Gohlis in spring and Reichswehr Brigade 4 in Magdeburg in October 1920; disbanded at end of 1920.

PZ 50: Set up by Lin.Komm.G (Posen/Frankfurt on the Oder); to Upper Silesian industrial area in August-September 1919; went to Küstrin later; from there to action in Cottbus in March 1920; with Rechswehr Brigade 5 in Schwerin on the Warthe in June 1920; disbanded at end of 1920.

PZ 52: Set up by Lin.Komm.G and stationed in Rawitsch; made into a unit with PZ 40 in July 1919 (see there).

PZ 53: under construction in September 1919, but never finished.

PZ 54: PZ III (see there) was renumbered in April 1919; remained with Volunteer Landesjäger Corps in Halle; with Reichswehr Brigade 16 there in spring of 1920; temporarily (April-May 1920 and September 1920) also in Naumburg; disbanded at end of 1920.

PZ 55: Set up by Lin.Komm.R (Bromberg); transferred to the Halle—Magdeburg area in summer of 1919; later to the Berlin area; with Reichswehr Brigade 3 in Döberitz in June 1920; disbanded in spring of 1921.

The Saxon PZ 48. The 5.7-cm Maxim-Nordenfeldt guns were mounted in the fixed turrets in the same way, and with the same traverse and elevation, as in the A7V tank of World War I. Photo: A. Przeczek collection

General Experience in Actions of Armored Trains

Against poorly equipped and not strictly run opponents, the armored trains obviously proved to be an outstanding means of warfare and a very effective reinforcement of weak German forces. This initiated the hasty building of the first postwar armored trains to protect the eastern border against Poland, where rebel groups had formed, which then joined to form more or less regular fighting forces and, in their actions against the German Free Corps and Reichswehr troops, used armored trains in particular numbers, just like the Soviet forces in the Baltic area.

In the fighting inside the Reich, it was seen very soon that the armored trains, still appearing very martial and imposing, that could bring not only machine guns and mine throwers but also guns, heavy weapons with them, and with their crews (between 40 and over 100 men, often reinforced by added troop transports) formed an important combat force and had a strong effect against strikers or rebels, who were usually insufficiently armed. Often enough, their mere appearance was enough to scatter such gatherings and thus have a peaceful effect, or this goal was achieved quickly by the effect of their weapons. Especially when, which happened often enough for reasons of solidarity, during troop transportation to areas of unrest— railroaders crippled traffic, advancing armored trains served to open the lines. This demoralizing effect on the opponents, whether in battle against the Soviets in the Baltic area, the Poles on the eastern border, or within the Reich, was stressed again and again.

But when the enemy stood against them in larger groups under unified command, armored trains could also be put out of action easily (rail line damage or immobilization of the locomotive) or even be captured. This even happened within the Reich, as examples in the attack on Munich (May 1919) and the Ruhr fighting (March 1920) show. But it was rare enough that they had to fight against such a strong opponent; usually they could keep the upper hand. Thus, it is not surprising that the military command assigned a certain value to them, and that the small numbers of surviving World War I trains were soon joined by a number of newly built ones.

As already noted, a series of instructions for the use of armored trains from that era could be found. A difference must be made between combat activity against an enemy, as in the Baltic area, or on the Polish border and against rebels within the Reich.

In the first case, the conditions of a typical war almost prevail. Here the armored trains were assigned more numerous tasks than in World War I. Those listed were:

– Rail line scouting and general reconnaissance;
– Attacks on objects on the lines;
– Connection with and supplying of advance units (over lines threatened by the enemy);
– Transport and support for flying combat groups;
– Supporting weak forces and advancing to relieve them;
– Opening transport routes;
– Repair and maintenance of rail lines;
– Covering of retreats;
– Breaking and destroying of rail lines in this process;
– Border patrols;
– Rail line protection;
– Surveillance of railroad objects;
– Securing of troop transports and unloadings;
– Cleaning out areas near the tracks;
General points for making war with armored trains were also stated:
– Clear assignments (no planless runs);
– Assignment of an experienced NCO as the leader of every single combat car of the train;
– Strict firing discipline;

– A shock troop coming from the train and armed with machine guns is of great use. It can be used for scouting to the sides, patrolling the tracks, removing of barriers, occupying operational facilities, counterattacks from the train, and help in rebuilding work and securing building sites. The members must have experience in laying, locating, and removing mines of all kinds. Whistle signals from the locomotive to give information from the train are to be agreed on.
– Careful and constant observation to front and back (intact line) and to sides.
Securing to the rear (patrols, railcars, or second armored train) to avoid having the return route cut off.
– In enemy-threatened areas, travel or stopping at night or in fog is dangerous.
– In forests and low visibility areas, the train is almost defenseless against attacks and needs infantry protection.
– Stopping in good visibility places, especially on railroad embankments and bridges, is to be avoided.
– In defense against close combat, the train must always remain in motion (move back and forth).
– If the train comes under artillery fire, it must back up several hundred meters at once to make homing in on it difficult and avoid destruction of the line behind the train. Whether a quick advance through the area of fire may appear possible must be decided in the individual case; in any case, a greater risk for the train is to be avoided.
– If an unknown rail line is to be scouted, the armored train advances slowly. By scattering its own fire through the area, the enemy is encouraged to return fire and thus betray his position, and then to be fought down and driven away. The use of gas mines against enemies hidden in forests is recommended. Freedom from enemies is then assured by scouting troops, whom the train follows, moving forward and back. By pushing with the contact cars and sent-out patrols, it is to be determined whether the line is mined. These mines are to be removed. If the line is then free, operations can be taken up provisionally by the railroad men on the train.
– If the line is blocked, obstructions are to be moved aside. If there is a break (such as by explosion), it should first be repaired provisionally by the train's own building troop. Such work must be done as quickly as possible; the material brought along must be chosen accordingly (only wooden ties and rail spikes, cutting torches, easily manageable pieces of rail). The building site is to be secured by sentries.
– If larger destruction (such as blown-up bridges) is to be expected, which cannot be repaired with the materials on board, construction platoons with suitable equipment must be readied quickly. Their (and any long-term) work can be secured by the armored train, but the use of normal infantry forces is more to be recommended.
– When the train is near the enemy, a thorough examination of the surroundings is imperative. The front and flanks are to be secured appropriately.
– For advances in enemy territory, close coordination with one's own infantry and artillery is recommended.
Their commanders must be familiar with the specialties of the armored train and its conduct in action. Close contact with the infantry is always important; their leaders are always to be informed of the train's intentions, especially intended advances. The artillery must be informed of the position and all intended movements of the train, so that

if necessary, protection by barrage fire can be called for and guaranteed.

– In attacks on fixed enemy positions, such as in towns, cooperation with infantry proceeding behind the train is urgently advised. It repeatedly makes quick advances and stays as little as possible in the enemy's area of effect. Here too, enemy fire should be provoked by scattered fire and the enemy then fought down in his known positions. For this, the heavy weapons, especially the mine launchers, can be used. If the returned fire weakens, then the armored train moves energetically against the shaken enemy as far as the line is open (this is to be checked by using the control cars). If the armored train should be stopped before the enemy position by blockage of the track, then it should give cover to the attacking infantry. The artillery observer on the train goes forward with them; the train itself is to be placed in a covered position, such as a cut. The advancing infantry is followed by the engineers on railcars (and under cover) to remove the blockage as soon as possible.

– If an attack by enemy armored trains threatens, the line is to be broken so far forward that your own position cannot be seen from there. This blockade is to be observed and your own artillery is to home in on it. Remote-control mine traps can also be prepared.

– For your own withdrawal, fog-laying is a very useful possibility.

– When traveling through partisan-endangered territory, all stopping is to be avoided.

– The cooperation of two armored trains is recommended, whereby one provides cover for the other.

Also of interest are the experiences that were gathered by the Railroad Detachment of the Grand General Staff after the use of armored trains against the Soviet Republic in Munich on June 7, 1919. They follow here word-for-word, for they give insight into the mistakes that were obviously made then.

1. Long trips should be made only with a powerful auxiliary machine to spare the armored locomotive for the purpose of maintaining its full readiness for use at the moment of action.

2. Auxiliary trains, with personnel car, kitchen car, provision car, etc., should not be taken into battle; leave it at the last secured depot, have it follow with the auxiliary machine, or fetch it with the armored loco after the battle ends.

3. Maintain close and lasting contact with the command post to which the armored train is assigned. Request ongoing information on the situation in general, goals, tasks, one's own and neighboring units; be clear on all possible movements in the advance area and on the battlefield, in order to recognize one's own and hostile bodies of troops for sure always.

4. Report to the command post–even by convincing inspection– of the fighting value and strength of the train, since trains differ in fighting strength. A train whose fighting value is unknown will usually be regarded by the leadership as too weak and will not be given tasks that are suitable and fully utilize its armament. A train whose fighting strength is overvalued by the leadership is given tasks that it is not capable of fulfilling. Consider the results of both cases on the total situation.

5. Request terrain and railroad maps at the command post, take line profiles and depot plans from railroad stations, operational offices, inspections and administrations or line commands along.

6. Carry plenty of food, drinking water, and bandages in the auxiliary train.

7. Have a doctor ride in the train before going into battle, or arrange to meet at dressing stations, places and times of first aid treatment.

8. Fire control through command or telephone in the noise of battle is hopeless. Use good clear signals with a loud alarm bell: one, two, three strikes, etc., for opening fire, individual fire, sustained fire, etc. The same can be attained by building in a signal bell system, not with a weak-power bell, but an alternating current alarm device and sound.

9. Distribute as many officers as possible, at best for every gun, mine thrower, combat car; 1 or 2 extra officers for casualties, shock-troop undertakings, etc.

10. Create armored tenders, in order not to have to stop fighting to add water or coal in the face of advantageous combat moments.

11. Build floor hatches into all cars.

12. Strive for uniform armaments. 5- or 5.5-cm guns appear insufficient, 7.7- or 7.62-cm socket A/A guns or 8.8-cm U-boat cannons, but mounted on special cars with low centers of gravity, appear to be most promising.

13. Equip trains with spotlights on both ends.

14. Install a radio station when possible. Agree on wavelength with the intelligence commander at the advance command post.

15. Use every opportunity for joint training with combat troops. Carry out drills with two trains moving on two-track lines either in parallel formation or a train's length apart. Both procedures are appropriate for advance on two-track lines and very promising for entry to extensive railroad installations.

16. Do not move into enemy territory over bridges for the run out or back that are not secured by your own sentries or scouted by shock troops and opened if necessary.

At another place it is determined for this action in Munich that armored trains are limited strictly to the rail lines and thus are exposed to planned attacks and ambushes.

Intended especially for fighting unrest and revolts is the "Brief Instructions for Armored Trains" that Recruiting District Command IV issued on December 10, 1919. It recommends that along with the actual armored train crew, additional technical personnel (signal box repairmen, switchmen, shunters, and telephone crews) be taken along, so that for following troop transports the lines can be held open without outside help (e.g., in railroadmen's strikes), and also a number of added infantrymen (depending on the capacity of the train for such personnel), so that it can handle by itself such tasks as securing a large railroad depot, protection for troop unloadings, or the arrest of mob leaders (depending on the capacity of the train for such personnel). The strength of the train depends on its machine guns. Thus, the MG cars are its most effective means of fighting. In general, mine-thrower cars are useful only for special tasks (not suited as single units), and the gun cars are essentially only of value for morale, since guns are seldom of use in street fighting (this evaluation is interesting in view of the later rail-protection trains, which were armed only with machine guns). In order to increase the fighting strength of these cars, they too should essentially be armed with machine guns. As for tactics, it was said: "Action of the entire train is not always called for; it is, for example, necessary in the use of an armored train against a large factory with many workers from a small station which allows an overlook. In many cases, though, it will be necessary to divide the train and set up the cars individually. Only thus will the great fighting power of each car—namely that of the MG cars—be fully utilized; every car forms a fort on its own, a small center of power and a support point for its shock troop. The still-common hesitance of train commanders to divide their trains must be overcome. With separate setups, the leaders of the individual cars must be linked with the command post of the train commander. They are responsible for having the car crew immediately check and free the firing field, and that the train be secured by guards and patrols in darkness or smoke screens. (The train should be assembled so that it is easy to separate the individual cars—MG car at the end of a train)."

Several examples were given later for combat tasks that also—to characterize the speech of the times—were given word-for-word:

a. Reconnoiter a rail line and a station: The situation may require stopping a few kilometers before the station and sending a patrol in civilian clothes to make contact with the railroad employees.

b. Arresting rebellious workers located in a depot or workshop: Drive into the station; inconspicuously unload a shock troop that hides in the depot building, and agree on signals, but move the train back to a position where it is not visible from the depot building but can be called on for help by light signals.

c. Securing a troop unloading: (Armored train goes first). Find out (not by telephone) from where the unloading threatens danger. Set up the train in agreement with the depot super-visor so that the points from which the unloading can be fired on can be taken under fire. Under certain conditions, divide the train, also to prepare for crossfire. (Consider where the individual cars should be positioned in order to secure unloading, from front and back, and if possible also from the sides. Make sure the train can depart unhindered: block the track on which the train stands with wedges at a certain distance, so that wild locomotives or cars cannot approach the armored train.

d. Support the troops by putting down a rebellious locality, a factory, a mine, or the like: separated setup of the train in several groups, so that every group dominates a street, square, or factory yard. Agree with the troops on a code word or signal. Send out a shock troop that actively advances (securing the depot and important buildings near the tracks).

e. Apprehend rabble-rousers before the troops enter: Before departure, see to arrest orders and necessary identifications. Locate dwellings of those to be arrested definitely on the city map. Place reliable leaders at the depot under some pretext. Caution on the telephone. Determine arrival time in agreement with Lin.komm., so that the arrested persons can be brought to the armored train before dawn. Stop before the depot and send out the patrol that is to make the arrests. (Turning over the arrested parties to the appropriate court after brief questioning).

Additional information can be taken from a preliminary sheet of these instructions (if foregoing items are concerned and they are not included in the instructions themselves, they are added to the items in parentheses): Demonstration runs into areas of unrest: Ostensible appearance of the entire train (set up at well-visible places) but concealing the crew and weapons. Armor usually looks strong—whether it is exciting or calming, do not yield when workers want the train to leave during a strike.

Securing a large depot: Exact study of the site plans, enhanced by inquiry on the spot. Consider how one must set up individual "forts" in the form of armored cars. Every separated car must be linked to the commander (information central there) by telephone. Also with the commander is the shock troop, strengthened by civilian messengers (these are to be requested from the local guard). The shock troop takes action by going from the individual "forts" that serve it as a haven.

Armored trains were used only very sporadically by the leftists, since their building and use requires a certain forward-looking planning, which seldom was done in the often-spontaneous actions of that side. Only during the Ruhr fighting in March-April 1920 were they used—with little success—and in March 1921 an armored train built by Leuna workers made a brief appearance.

The Treaty of Versailles and the Disbanding of the Armored Trains

The Treaty of Versailles had been signed at the end of June 1919. Armored trains were not expressly mentioned in it. but even in the Reich government it seems to have been assumed that they fell under the general ban on armored vehicles (Article 171). Thus, the Reich Defense Minister called on August 26, 1919, for the disbanding of the existing armored trains. On 3 September he made known to the Reichswehr offices that in the future 100,000-man army there would be no armored trains as military formations; to be sure, the view was expressed at the same time that each of the seven infantry divisions to be formed would be issued material for the equipping of a number of armored trains (uniform design—the modified PZ 46 was to serve as the model) that were to be set up if needed and manned through command channels. In view of the many possible uses of armored trains already noted and the generally positive experiences with them, the Reichswehr was highly interested in being able to use this weapon, in view of the highly insecure situation in the country. Protests were expressed by the commanding offices against the disbanment of the available armored trains, and thus it was stated in September 1919 that it was supposed to remain in addition to plans.

To be sure, the subordination situation changed. After all the troop units, including the Free Corps, were gradually turned into Reichswehr brigades starting in June 1919, in September 1919, because of the Treaty of Versailles, the Grand General Staff and all subordinated structures that remained from Imperial Germany had to be dissolved. With that, the Railroad Department, to which the armored trains had been subordinated until then, disappeared along with the Inspection and Testing Department of the railroad troops, which had been responsible for technical development. Now the armored trains were assigned to the four newly formed Reichswehr Group Commands (I Berlin, including Silesia, Brandenburg, and Saxony; II Kassel, all of western Germany, including Thuringia, though the border area to 50 km east of the Rhine was demilitarized; III Kolberg, consisting of the Baltic area, East and West Prussia, Pomerania, and Mecklenburg, what remained after evacuating the Baltics and West Prussia being added to Command I; and IV Munich, all of Bavaria, later placed in Command II). In place of the Testing Department of the railroad troops, the Inspection of Weapons and Equipment, Department 6, Group IV was now responsible for evaluating experience and technical development. In charge of armored train matters in the Reichswehr Ministry was now the Engineer and Fortress Department W 5 (later J 5). The Line commands (later renamed Line Commissions) remained to handle business until about the middle of 1920 and were still responsible for transit and operational-technical matters, until this task passed to the railroad administration. The technical personnel (1 officer, 5

NCOs, 11 men) of the armored trains could at first be taken from the Railroad Building Company, which was made available to every Reichswehr group command. According to the dissolution already planned for the summer of 1920, it—like the tactical crew—had to be formed by the responsible recruiting district command by order. This reorganization took the rest of 1919, which scarcely resulted in the dismantling of armored trains at first. Thus, in the new distribution plan of December 2, 1919, there were still 31 units in existence:

Group Command I: 11 armored trains (No. 20, 24, 29, 32, 46, 47, 48, 49, 50, 54, 55)

Group Command II: 7 armored trains (No. IV, 2, 25, 31, 35, 36, 53; IV was to be assigned there only after the evacuation of Danzig and West Prussia)

Group Command III: 9 armored trains (No. V, VI, VII, 21, 27, 28, 30, 37, 44, and at first still IV)

Group Command IV: 4 armored trains (No. 38, 39, 40/52, 45)

Only with the complete evacuation of the Baltic area (December 1919), the separation of Danzig and West Prussia (February 1920), and the validity of the Treaty of Versailles (April 10, 1920) were their numbers reduced to 26. This was also called for because of the sharply reduced military budget. Thus, a request by Recruiting District IV on December 8, 1919, for permission to create additional makeshift armored trains for use against internal unrest had to be rejected for financial reasons (in spite of which three such trains were set up temporarily in Saxony), as was a similar request from Engineer Battalion 13 in Ulm in September 1920. All travel except that required by unusual conditions had to be approved by Department J 5 of the Reichswehr Ministry. There were always great difficulties with repair work and fuel supplying, not only for lack of finances, but also because those who worked at the railroad workshops refused more and more to carry out work on armored trains.

In the course of reducing the Army to 200,000 men as of May 1920, the dismantling of the existing armored trains was also to take place, but it was thought that the internal political situation did not allow the complete carrying out of this measure. They were supposed to cease to exist as planned formations, but each of the newly formed recruiting districts (I Koenigsberg, II Stettin, III Berlin, IV Dresden, V Stuttgart, VI Münster, and VII Munich) was to keep two armored trains ready for action (the technically best and best-performing of the existing ones, even though reduced in extent to five or at most seven combat cars), which if needed could be manned by the recruiting districts. Material from the excess trains that were to be dismantled could also be stored by each recruiting district for the armoring and equipping of another armored train (without rolling stock). The opinion—with the wish as father to the thought—also developed that, since the Treaty of Versailles did not expressly ban armored trains, keeping such units was not forbidden, and it was hoped that the Allies would understand.

The following trains were to remain in existence:

Recruiting District I	No. 21 and 28;
Recruiting District II	No. 30 and 44;
Recruiting District III	No. 55 and one other (PZ 50?);
Recruiting District IV	No. 48 and 49;
Recruiting District V	No. IV and 22;
Recruiting District VI	No. 25 and 31;
Recruiting District VII	No. 40/52 and 45.

This reduction to 14 armored trains was carried out in the summer and early autumn of 1920; the originally planned storage of material for a third armored train by the recruiting districts was not done; the excess units were sent to Kummersdorf, disarmed there, and the rolling stock was then given back to the railroad administrations.

The Allies, though, were absolutely not in agreement with the extensive stretching of the Treaty of Versailles that manifested in the Reichswehr's and government's desire to keep armored trains. They took an extremely strict opposite position. On November 8, 1920, their emissary conference rejected in very general form any request that was intended to allow the German Army weapons that were not named in the peace treaty or the protocols of the Armistice Commission. Several months of correspondence between the government and the Allied offices ensued, in which both sides insisted on their standpoints, but the Reich government had to vacate their position step by step.

At first, all existing armored trains that still existed had to be dismantled by December 31, 1920; all requests for limited further existence beyond this date were refused. Thus, the fourteen remaining armored trains were sent to Kummersdorf, dismantled there, and the rolling stock made available for civilian use. These measures were completed by June 30, 1921.

Although keeping complete armored trains was banned, the Reichswehr returned to the conception of the summer of 1919 and at least wanted to keep the material, at first for two trains—early in 1921 the request was reduced to one train—in storage. The armored trains were not to be a planned and independent formation, but to be set up temporarily for definite purposes and dismantled after fulfilling their tasks. Accordingly, the rolling stock (one locomotive and up to 14 cars) would be requested from the railroad administration only in case of need, armored, and armed with available weapons allowed by the peace treaty. The crews too would consist only of assigned personnel, but they wanted to try to include at least the technical personnel for one armored train per recruiting district in the budget of the 100,000-man Army.

The IMKK, though, insisted on getting rid of all materials that could be used to make armored trains. Even the request that such material be stored under Allied supervision, requested in case of need and then released, came to nothing. The question was finally decided by the London Ultimatum of May 5, 1921, in which the Allies completely imposed their view. The Reich government had to agree to these conditions without exception on 20 May. Thus, the further retention of material for armored trains by the Reichswehr was finally ended.

The Württemberg Traffic Guard

Now—as an addendum, so to speak—one of the countless home guards and militias of the time is treated especially because it was the only one that owned armored trains; it was one of the few (similar procedures in Augsburg, Elberfeld, and Karlsruhe did not last long) in which railroad men constituted the majority of the personnel, but also because it functioned as a model for the later country-wide railroad protection guard, under whose wings armored railroad trains could exist on German rail lines even after the Treaty of Versailles and the London Ultimatum, until the beginning of World War II.

On April 18, 1919, the administrative advisor and retired Captain Karl Heiges, responsible for the reclamation service in the general administration of the Württemberg State Railways in Stuttgart, assembled 30 railroad men, marched to the main station in Stuttgart, and drove out the official "Security Company," which did its job only

At right is the "armored car" of the Württemberg Traffic Guard, an iron coal car with wooden breastworks and a provisional roof. At left is a civilian car added (during action against Heidenheim) for transport purposes (a two-axle Type BCi?). Photo: Federal Archives, Koblenz

The second (Ulm) protected train of the Württemberg Traffic Guard. The combat cars were high-sided (1.55-meter) Omkk(u) cars of Type A 10, the locomotive of the Württemberg Series AD. Photo: Federal Archives, Koblenz

This picture of the same loco shows the number plate (No. 484). Photo: Federal Archives, Koblenz

imperfectly. As a result Heiges received strong support; at the end of the month his "Reserve Security Company" already numbered some 200 men. They remained under arms in the main Stuttgart station until July 18, 1919; repeatedly the Württemberg state government met under their protection in the fortress-like tower of the new station building. In the latter half of April 1919 another railroad protection company was formed in Ulm, which carried out strict checking on the Bavarian border in order to prevent inroads by the extreme leftists (the Soviet Republic then ruled in Bavaria). Later a statewide volunteer company was created, including the postal service (thus "transport" defense). By October 1919 the Württemberg Traffic Guard had already reached a strength of 10,000 men, about a third of whom belonged to Guard I; the rest formed the Guard II, a reserve that turned out only on special call. Karl Heiges, the initiator, was the state leader of the defense; subordinate to him were the district leaders at the individual railroad offices, and to them the local groups at the railroad stations. The state leader directed a main reserve, the district leaders an additional district reserve.

On April 27, 1919, the first "protected train" (makeshift armored train) of the Traffic Guard was set up in Stuttgart. It consisted, besides the locomotive, of two provisionally armored open freight cars and was manned by 30 volunteers from the Stuttgart Technical College, under the command of Reserve First Lieutenant Oskar Dirlewanger (a twilight figure who had difficulties even with the National Socialists, whom he joined in 1923; later he rose to be the commander of that SS brigade which bore his name, consisted of convicts, and was particularly despised for their cruel deeds). On March 19, 1920, the train, now with a 45-man crew, took over the securing of troop transports of Württemberg Reichswehr contingents between Untertürkheim and Kornwestheim, as they were being transported to the Ruhr area. On March 31, 1920, a second such protected train, composed in the same manner, was set up. The locomotive came from Stuttgart, the two armored cars from Ulm.

On June 25, 1920, an uprising of striking workers, who had seized weapons, broke out in Heidenheim. The Württemberg state government immediately took police action against them, in which both of the Traffic Guard's protected trains took part. The first (Series F loco, two armored open freight cars, one Type A passenger car, later a Type R stakeside car, but without stakes, was added) moved with the Stuttgart contingent through the Rems valley via Schwäbisch Gmünd and Aalen; the second, which was previously stationed in Tübingen (Type AD loco, two armored open freight cars, one Type A passenger car) with men from Göppingen moved via Ulm and Herbrechtingen. Both trains—the Stuttgart one first—arrived in Heidenheim between 3:32 and 4:00 AM on 26 June. The workers let themselves be disarmed without resistance, so that the trains could head out that afternoon; the locomotive of the Ulm train went there,

while the other loco pulled the cars of both trains to Stuttgart.

The next actions of the Württemberg Traffic Guard took place just two months later in the so-called Tax Strike. On the morning of August 28, 1920, one of these trains (57-man crew) went from Stuttgart to Kornwestheim and cleaned out the depot there without having to use weapons. The second reserve train, which first had to be mobilized, remained in Stuttgart. On 29 August a third such train was set up in Plochingen and saw action later in the Unterboihingen—Nürtingen—Tübingen area, while the train from Kornwestheim carried out pacification actions in Ludwigsburg and Backnang. The activities of these protected trains was particularly praised by the government after the strike was ended on September 5, 1920.

The leader of the Württemberg Traffic Guard, Karl Heiges, was called to Berlin on September 17, 1920, to build up a nationwide railroad protection in the Reich Transport Ministry; his successor was Regierungsrat Domisch.—At first the view was held that the citizen guards and militias were not under the regulations of the Treaty of Versailles, and even saw in their strengthening a means of getting around the required troop reduction. Thus, the Württemberg Traffic Guard and their three protected trains were still kept under arms.

When in March 1921 another Communist uprising broke out in central Germany, the Reichswehr armored trains were disarmed except for, at most, one (PZ 55). Thus, on 24 March the Württemberg Traffic Guard was asked by the Reich Transport Minister to intervene. While the Plochingen train was transferred to Stuttgart for security, a

These pictures show the third (Plochingen) train of the Württemberg Traffic Guard. The combat car is like that of the Ulm train, but has a provisional roof with ports and shields provided for MG 08 machine guns. Before and behind the loco (Württemberg T 5 from the 1217-1296 number series) are three Württemberg A-type compartment cars. On an added Omk-car (Type A 1), a field kitchen (goulash cannon) is loaded. The gun car at the end of the train is a 15-type coal car known from World War I (II d1 or A 6). Photos: Federal Archives, Koblenz

A close-up of the gun car of the third train. Note the special armor on the upper edge of the car (with sight slits, rifle and machine-gun ports). The rear wall has been removed; the barrel of the 7.7-cm F.K. 96 is easy to see. Photo: Federal Archives, Koblenz

The Württemberg T 5 of the "Uhland" already had all-around armor on the cab and sheet armor on the side water tanks. Photo: Federal Archives, Koblenz

train was assembled from the cars of the two other trains, consisting of a makeshift armored locomotive of the Württemberg T 5 series, five armored cars (armed with one light howitzer—probably F.K.—two medium mine- throwers and twelve machine guns), six second-class passenger cars, one kitchen, one workshop, and one other car with track building equipment (in all, 42 axles with 238 tons). The whole detachment of 150 Württemberg Traffic Guard men was under the command of Railroad Head-secretary (retired Captain) Gaugenmeier; the armored train itself was led by Oskar Dirlewanger. In order to avoid countermeasures from railroaders in sympathy with the rebels, the train was announced as the special excursion train "Uhland," and the train also ran under this name in its further actions. For this one it was subordinated to the Halle Railroad Direction, to which Railroad head secretary Rudolf Behne was sent from Stuttgart as a contact person. The train left Stuttgart late in the evening of 25 March and traveled via Würzburg—Fulda (several axle overheatings had to

be dealt with at Retzbach)—Bebra—Nordhausen to Sangerhausen, where it arrived at 3:40 PM on 26 March. It was not known that a leader of the Communist uprising, Max Hoelz, chanced to be in that city with an appropriately strong group of his followers. The train, arriving at the Sangerhausen railroad station not in fighting trim but in transport formation, was immediately surrounded by those forces and enclosed by track explosions at both entrances to the depot, but the Traffic Guard men were able to occupy the station building. The attempt to switch the train at the depot had to be given up because of the heavy fire from all around; it stayed there divided into three groups of cars, and the foremost one (locomotive and one machine-gun car) suffered heavy losses. When night fell the Traffic Guard men took all their weapons into the station building. Until 2:00 AM there were a few fire fights; then it became quiet. Patrols were sent out and found that Max Hoelz and his followers had left. The Traffic Guard had one dead (an engine driver) and 2 wounded to report,

The "Uhland" train, assembled from two trains of the Württemberg Traffic Guard, in action in Thuringia (March 1921). At the front are two Ommk(u) Type A 10 infantry cars, as in the Ulm and Plochingen trains, but now with fixed roofs. The second car is shown to be a command car by its observation cupola. Behind the armored T 5 are a transit car, a G-car (probably workshop or kitchen car), and a 15-ton coal car with a World War I-type roof. Photo: Federal Archives, Koblenz

while the Communists lost 25 dead and 70 wounded.—On 28 March the "Uhland" armored train, operating from Sangerhausen, took on the securing of the line from Sandersleben to Oberröblingen; on 1 April it went from there to Halle. On the way back, Max Hoelz was arrested in Könnern and brought to Sangerhausen, but they let him go, as they were not aware of his false papers.

After it had been seen in the fighting at Sangerhausen that the train's armor was insufficient, Reichsbahn head secretary Behne asked from Halle for help. He was able to get hold of some cars from Reichswehr armored trains that were at Kummersdorf for dismantling (responsible for these was Engineer Reimann of the Reichswehr Ministry), and on April 2, 1921, 20 armored train cars and additional armor plate for armoring locomotives were taken illegally from there to Sandersleben. From them two armored trains were set up: one (100 men) under Gaugenmaier, the other (105 men) under Dirlewanger. At first they remained in Sangerhausen to clean up the surrounding area. On April 13, 1921, the Gaugenmaier train was transferred to the Stendal—Rathenow line; the Dirlewanger train committed the provocative act (already committed time after

time by the Free Corps) of flying the old Imperial flag (black-white-red) instead of the Republican flag (black-red-gold). Because of this incident he and the train were sent back to Stuttgart, where he and his train arrived on the evening of 15 April. The Gaugenmaier train was now divided again, with the second half under the command of Railroad Operations Secretary Hofmann. On 16 and 17 April the two trains took over the protection of the Elbe bridge at Hämmerten and the Havel bridge at Rathenow; on 18 April the Gaugenmaier train was at Burg, near Magdeburg, the Hofmann train in Helmstedt, and on 19 April both were back at Sangerhausen, from where they set out that evening to return (reunited as one train at Würzburg) to Stuttgart, where they arrived at 1:20 AM on April 20, 1921.

Soon after that the Allies banned the use of armed citizen guards, which they rightfully saw as opposing the Treaty of Versailles. Because of the London Ultimatum, the Württemberg Traffic Guard had to be disbanded in July 1921, but this took place only pro forma, for meanwhile, with the approval of the Allies, the countrywide Railroad Guard had been set up, into which they could be transferred with their protected trains; but the material acquired from Kummersdorf surely must have been returned there.

The former Reichswehr armored train cars "organized" from Kummersdorf for trains of the Württemberg Traffic Guard in Thuringia (April 1921). In the upper photo the crew poses before their new train, the front car—with an MG port in the front—comes, as the legible car number (Cöln 62455) shows, from PZ 45. The large side openings in the middle car of the lower photo lets one assume that removing the armor had already begun at Kummersdorf. Photos: Federal Archives, Koblenz

From 1921 to the End of World War II

From the Disbanding of the Reichswehr Armored Trains to the Establishment of the German Wehrmacht (1921-1938)

The German Reichsbahn Guard

Since the decrease in the Reichswehr required by the Treaty of Versailles and the insufficient numbers of policemen no longer allowed sufficient securing of the railroad lines, the Reich Transport Ministry discussed the establishment of its own guard troop in 1920. This certainly was inspired in part by the fact that since July 25, 1920 (and until August 12, 1932), retired Lieutenant General Wilhelm Groener (leader of the Railroad Department of the Grand General Staff in 1912 and Chief of the Field Railroad Service in 1914-16) was the Reich Transport Minister. State Secretary von Stieler, who had previously been the President of the Railroad Administration in Stuttgart and thus knew the Württemberg Traffic Guard and its initiator and founder, Karl Heiges, well, had him come to Berlin to speak in September 1920. In the same month, Heiges was assigned to the Reich Transport Ministry and charged with setting up a countrywide railroad guard. Just six months later he had worked out an appropriate concept. The events of March 1921 in Thuringia and the action of the Württemberg Traffic Guard with their armored train also contributed to the Ministry's publication of their first "Guidelines for Railroad Protection and Security of Railroad Operation in Internal Unrest and Strikes" on April 5, 1921.

For the organization and leadership of the railroad guard activity, a department of supervision was established in the individual railroad offices; for the regulation of the various involved forces a permanent railroad guard commission, which consisted of a representative of the railroad management and the order police, and was to work with the management presidents and the commander of the police. Of course, the main task of rail security was given to the police, which was to make clear to the management which forces they were able to delegate and where they were located, but it was assumed that they could protect only the most important operational facilities and means (rolling stock needed for emergency use, heating buildings, supply depots, signal boxes, security sites, telephone and telegraph offices, management offices, freight and luggage halls, material dumps, and electric, gas, and water works essential for operation, as well as important artificial structures), which were chiefly concentrated in the depots. The connection between these depot crews was to be maintained by an easily mobile reserve of the railroad's own personnel. For this, those who were primarily in the railroad guarding system (railroad police) were to be used, but in cases of need they were to be strengthened by volunteers. Efforts were to be made to create a reliable core of such personnel. This reserve, to be called together at

Lieutenant General (retired) Wilhelm Groener, Reich Transport Minister from July 25, 1920, to August 12, 1923. Photo: W. Sawodny collection

Karl Heiges, who created the Württemberg Traffic Guard at Stuttgart in 1919. He also organized the countrywide Railroad Guard at the request of the Reich Transport Minister in the spring of 1921.

certain points and armed with long-range weapons (carbines were to be provided in limited quantities by the Reichswehr; otherwise only short-range weapons up to a caliber of 7.65 mm were allowed), was to be easily moved in makeshift-armed "railroad protection trains." In case of work stoppages in the realm of the railways themselves or their necessary supply facilities (electricity, gas and water works) with situations that could not be handled by the specified forces, the technical emergency service—above all when an emergency was proclaimed—could also be called in. Special value was given to the securing of means of communication, for which cooperation with offices of the postal system and providing of its own personnel, appropriate equipment, and transportation to restore broken connections or destroyed facilities, were foreseen.

In a tense situation the Railroad Guard Commission was to be called to meet; the leaders and deputies involved in railroad protection were to make mutual contact; and the places to be protected were to be inspected by them inconspicuously. The railroad personnel were to be called on to do their most extreme duty and urged to offer help in protecting the railroad. When needed, reinforced or permanent service was to be declared. The railroad surveillance personnel, including the volunteers (who were to serve with the railroad police as watchmen) were to be assembled and equipped with long-range weapons (carbines). The rail protection trains were to be brought to readiness; in case of action, they had priority over all other trains except help trains. For the messengers, reinforced or permanent service was to be called for, and the repair troops were to be assembled and equipped, and secured connections with the postal service and the Reichswehr were to be prepared. At an appropriate code word, the railroad protection service had priority in communication as well. For all railroad protection forces housing and provisions were to be prepared. In strikes, the protection of those willing to work was to be assured. The public was to be informed regularly, but also to be warned against unauthorized intervention in railroad operations, and the intervention of the guards was to be announced and appropriate threats of punishment were to be made known.

When unrest broke out, the railroad guards were to be summoned at the right time by the presidents of railroad operations in concert with the government leadership. Their actions were to take place quickly and according to agreed-on plans under strict leadership by the Railroad Protection Commission, whereby the representatives of the police were to decide on the tactical measures and the railroad leadership on the technical measures. If necessary, service was to be limited on vital lines by carrying out appropriate personnel movements and in certain cases according to a certain schedule.

The railroad management had the greatest leeway in carrying out railroad protection measures, so as to guarantee the necessary possibilities of suiting the situation and affording flexibility, but was to keep constant contact with neighboring administrations and the regular railroad protection commission of the Reich Transport Ministry, which was responsible for uniform regulation of railroad matters and, if necessary, support measures that went beyond the limits of the management. One of these boundary-crossing tasks was the securing of necessary north-south and east-west connections under all conditions. These lines were later defined as follows:

North-South: Hamburg — Harburg — Uelzen — Lehrte — Hannover — Nordstemmen — Kreiensen — Göttingen — Eichenberg — Bebra — Elm — Würzburg — Osterburken — Heilbronn — Mühlacker (Bruchsal–Karlsruhe) — Stuttgart — Ulm — Augsburg — Munich.

Reserve line: Göttingen — Kassel — Marburg — Giessen — Friedberg — Frankfurt on the Main — Darmstadt — Heidelberg — Bruchsal, as well as Duisburg — Düsseldorf — Cologne — Bonn — Koblenz — Mainz — Ludwigshafen — Germersheim — Bruchsal; between Augsburg and Würzburg the line through Treuchtlingen — Nürnberg was foreseen as another reserve line.

East-West: Gleiwitz — Kandrzin — Oppeln — Breslau — Liegnitz — Arnsdorf — Sagan — Guben — Frankfurt on the Oder — Berlin (Lehrter Depot) — Stendal — Lehrte — Hannover — Minden — Löhne (Osnabrück) — Bielefeld — Hamm (Münster) — Dortmund — Lamgendreer — Bochum — Essen — Mülheim — Duisburg — Düsseldorf — Cologne.

Reserve line: Breslau — Glogau — Rothenburg — Reppen — Küstrin — Berlin (Silesian Depot) — Berlin (Potsdam Depot) — Brandenburg — Magdeburg — Oschersleben — Halberstadt — Goslar — Seesen — Kreiensen — Holzminden — Scherfede — Arnsberg — Schwerte — Hagen — Witten — Langendreer.

The railroad managements had to connect their branch lines to these lines.

In setting goals for protecting the railroad traffic, not only from intervention from the unauthorized, but also to maintain it during work stoppages and strikes, these guidelines were bound to find opposition not only from the left wing, but naturally also from the workers' unions, which kept trying to take steps against the rail protection throughout the years until 1933, without being able to bring them to a stop. On the other hand, this setting of tasks also prejudiced the composition of the rail protection personnel. The officials outweighed the workers considerably (whereby the latter were scarcely to be found in the workshop employees, who were well organized by the unions); the main group in terms of age were the front fighters of World War I, who had maintained a proper attitude. From the railroad protection leadership the choice of such a group of people was also requested, since a weakening of the concept by unions, socialists, or even Communists was to be avoided. It is scarcely surprising under these conditions that in 1933 a proportion of some 80% National Socialists appeared among the railroad protection members.

Especially to be noted in this respect is, of course, the establishment of railroad protection trains, makeshift armored trains, just at the point in time when the Allies had insisted on the complete disarmament of the Reichswehr armored trains. The process is so interesting that the relevant excerpt from Karl Heiges' book *The Rail Guard Calls* should be quoted word-for-word: "So I decided, in view of the pressing need to have such trains for rail protection, to display an auxiliary train to the IMKK. We referred specifically to the fact that the Reichsbahn could not carry the protection of the railroad without such trains, as shown by experience in the central German uprising (of March 1921), that it thus had to halt service in case of explosions and other breaking of lines in such cases, because it could not encourage railroad men to risk their lives to repair destroyed lines in threatened areas. Halting of service would also affect the reparation transports. At the Erkner depot near Berlin, I therefore displayed one of my rail protection and repair trains to the IMKK. The locomotive and cars made such a makeshift impression on the IMKK, which was led in the viewing by a British colonel, that they did not make the prescribed objections, nor proclaim any contravention of the peace treaty. The Reichsbahn even received a written assurance from the IMKK that 'under certain technical conditions, such as the lack of armored turrets, double walls, etc., there would be no objection to the use of such protective arrangements.' We did not need to be told this twice. We now built bullet-secure railroad cars that fitted these conditions, which let the signs of makeshift origin fade into the background, yet always looked like other covered freight cars ... Even Oberrat Spalding of Frankfurt (Oder), calmly and perceptively, supported me in the assignment and promotion of our first supplies of such cars; on the night of June 6, 1921, they rolled to their assigned places all over Germany. As if fallen from heaven, there were suddenly rail protection trains near the regions where they presumably could be used, and only a few involved people knew of them. Very quietly the most suitable crews were chosen and trained in protection and repair tasks, which, like the possible means of using such trains, are very manifold. With the help of instructions to the leaders of such trains as to the conduct of the trains and an overview of the repair equipment and materials to be carried in the trains, the trains were equipped uniformly and the leaders and crews set to their tasks."

This shows that by keeping the harmless appearance of a freight car, which was deliberately chosen to disguise the actions of these trains from railroad men who were hostile to the rail guard and thus avoid hindrances if possible, the inner armor was strengthened from that of the car shown to the IMKK. How far they diverged from the accepted standards—the more so, the more time passed—is shown by the fact that in the early thirties two armored gun cars were even built for the Munich rail protection train! On the other hand, Heiges' words show that he wanted from the start to introduce a countrywide standard type of rail protection train, which can be documented from 1923 on.

The building up of the Reich rail guard proceeded smoothly, with the exception of the demilitarized zone in the Rhineland (the completely or preferably left-bank offices in Cologne, Trier, and Ludwigshafen, presumably also Mainz) and the group administration of Bavaria, which still retained special rights after the founding of the German Reichsbahn in 1920. After the experiences in Sangerhausen in March 1921, the introduction of a railroad guard with armored trains—even two per direction—was discussed in Bavaria too, and an official of the Augsburg office was sent to Stuttgart to observe and gain information. The railroad guard in Bavaria was set up at the beginning of 1922, at first independently of the rest of the Reichsbahn, but whether armored rail protection trains were already set up at that time cannot be determined. The building up of the rail guard was especially promoted by a series of railroad strikes between December 27, 1921, and February 8, 1922; that of early February 1922, which included all of northern Germany, was especially serious and brought almost all rail traffic in that area to a stop for a week. In May 1923 the railroad guard was activated in the administrative areas of Breslau and Oppeln, as attacks from the Poles were feared; in August 1923, on the occasion of a railroad men's strike, even two companies of Württemberg Railroad Guards were called to Berlin.

A larger action of the rail protection trains took place in October and November 1923. After the end of passive resistance in the occupied Ruhr area by the Stresemann government on September 26, 1923, the government had given the exclusive, complete power to avoid unrest in the Reich to the Reichswehr. In Saxony and Thuringia this was answered by the formation of a left wing regime of the SPD and Communists, which opposed the regulations of the Reichswehr. Thereupon the central government called for one of the already known "Reich executions." This was carried out by Reichswehr units, but the Railroad Guard protected their transports. On October 18, 1923, the Reich Transport Minister had already alerted the Railroad Guards and made 12 rail protection trains ready to secure depots and their own weapon stores. On 19 October six of these trains (two from Oppeln and one each from Berlin, Breslau, Frankfurt on the Oder, and Stettin) took over the securing of the Görlitz—Bautzen—Dresden transport route. On 20 October one train each from this group was in Görlitz, Röderau, and Leipzig-Wiederitzsch; the Görlitz

train advanced against communistic workers in Greiffenberg on 25 October. On 18 October a rail protection train from Stuttgart had been alerted. It ran via Nürnberg in the direction of Hof, where damage to the locomotive occurred, which could be repaired in Hof and Reichenbach in Vogtland. In Mehltheuer it was attacked by workers, but cleaned out the depot and its surroundings in a short time. From 22 October on it took over the securing of the Plauen—Oelsnitz line; on the 26th of that month it was in Herlesgruen. Meanwhile, a second Stuttgart rail protection train had been summoned; it was transferred to Jüterbog. The Elbe bridge near Riesa was also secured by a rail protection train. The trains of Halle, Kassel, and Magdeburg stood ready as reserves. On November 1, 1923, the actions in Saxony were finished; some of the trains returned to their home bases, but in Hamburg and Oppeln they remained armed because of continuing unrest. Just four days later they were alerted for a new, similar action in Thuringia. This time they were to secure the transport route from Hannover via Kassel to Thuringia. On 5 November one train each was in Kreiensen and Kassel, and two in Nordhausen (including the one from Stuttgart, which had gotten there via Eichenberg). Later they were advanced to the Eisenach—Erfurt—Artern line (the leadership of the rail protection was located in Neudietendorf). In all, six rail protection trains from Berlin, Halle, Kassel, Magdeburg (2), and Stuttgart were used in Thuringia. After the three Communist ministers of the Thuringian state government had resigned on 12 November, the six rail protection trains went on maneuvers at the Ohrdruf troop training camp (the Stuttgart reserve train did the same at Münsingen). On November 17, 1923, they finally returned to their home bases. In the whole operation their actions were limited solely to securing the tracks and depots; they took no part in the Reichswehr actions.

The structure of the Railroad Guard had meanwhile solidified so much that on December 31, 1923, the Reich Transport Ministry issued the "Guidelines for Railroad Protection and Security of Railroad Operation in Internal Unrest" anew in a revised form. Four essential changes from the earlier guidelines of April 5, 1921, may be noted:

1. In both the title and the text, the word "strike" and the passages referring to it have been removed, so as to offer the unions no direct target, but the setting of the goal of maintaining railroad operations, even with such hindrances, remained without doubt.
2. Calling in the Technical Emergency Service to afford help is no longer foreseen.
3. An emergency schedule is to be posted in every Reichsbahn office and updated regularly; the Railroad guard has as its first task the maintenance of service as so posted.
4. The structure of the Railroad Guard has meanwhile progressed so far that a concrete organizational plan can be set up.

The Reich Railroad Guard appeared as a non-permanent security service along with the actual Railroad Police, which had a strength of some 2000 men since 1924. It was called in at times of emergency or threatening danger, in agreement with the Reich government, in order to secure the facilities of the Reichsbahn and their operation, and to protect their employees against all attacks, namely from outside organizations or persons. It was to be applied only within the railroad realm. Only active railroad men who reported voluntarily could belong to the Railroad guard. In selecting them, emphasis was placed on weapon-trained and politically reliable (meaning right-inclined) people, and naturally this applied especially to leadership positions. The members of the Railroad Guard were called from their regular service for the duration of the need for protection in emergency cases.

The rail protection train of the Regensburg Reichsbahn Direction corresponded to the standard type of rail protection train, and was equipped with a Prussian G 10 armored tender-locomotive. Photo: Federal Archives, Koblenz

The structure foresaw local groups at all larger points of operation and junctions, especially on the lines classified as especially important and necessary for operation. These local groups were combined in district groups at the seats of operations offices, and a sufficient reserve was to be maintained there to strengthen the local guard in cases of need. At the Reichsbahn Direction level, an administration for rail protection was created that was to be in charge of suitable spaces, assistance staffs, and means of communication so as to guarantee a prompt application of means of protecting the railroad. Also at the seat of the Reichsbahn Direction a sufficient reserve was foreseen, formed of specially trained personnel and under reliable leaders, which could be utilized within the administrative district. In every Reichsbahn Direction district a so-called "Rail Protection and Repair Train" (Bzw), actually an armored train, was to be established. These were regarded as essential to maintain connections between the district and local groups, in order to bring guard personnel to dangerous places and repair crews to damaged rail sites promptly and safely and protect them there at their work, while also checking the usability of lines and to protect transport, especially of police and Reichswehr, in endangered areas, and to give the railroad personnel remaining on duty the feeling of being protected and thus keep them at their work. The crews of the trains were to be formed of especially reliable, disciplined people who were obligated to serve all over the Reich. If such a train were used in a different Reichsbahn district, it was subordinate to the railroad protection administration there. If several trains were used in one district, a special rail protection command would be set up, to which a higher official of the relevant rail protection office belonged as a liaison person to the applicable railroad protection commission.

While the organization and leadership of the rail protection forces was up to the Railroad Guard administrations, the cooperation of the Railroad Guard with the State Police, which still had the main responsibility for protecting the railroad facilities, was arranged especially in case of intervention through the permanent Railroad Protection Commission, which included members of the RBD and the police. These Railroad Protection Commissions also were to maintain permanent contact with those of their neighbor offices, as well as with the permanent Railroad Protection Commission of the RVM, which was responsible for general questions dealing with railroad protection and the support of protective measures of the RBD administrations. In the RVM there was also a board consisting of members of the administration and personnel organizations chiefly involved in rail protection to oversee the proper use of the

Railroad Guard. This board was to be heard before all actions of the Railroad Guard; in cases of pressing danger that required immediate action it was to be informed at once. During the action it was to be informed regularly of all actions; if necessary, it had the right to get information on the spot.

There is no detailed documentation of the strength of this non-permanent Railroad Guard that worked beside the Railroad Police, except that in the spring of 1933 its total strength was stated as some 50,000 men, many times more than the Railroad Police itself (some 2000 men). The crews of the available rail protection trains and railcars may have consisted of some 3500 men.

As the building of cars for the railroad protection trains by the RVM itself and their distribution to the administrations in June 1921 shows, a uniform composition of these units was striven for, although the offices surely must have suggested their own design features at first. This was especially true of the Stuttgart office, where the armored trains of the former Württemberg Traffic Guard continued to be used as rail protection trains. After the events of March and April 1921 in Thuringia, the number of trains at the RBD in Stuttgart was even increased, so that in September of that year there were no fewer than five railroad protection trains on hand (each consisting of the locomotive and four cars). In the actions in October and November 1923, rail protection trains of the Berlin, Breslau, Frankfort on the Oder, Halle, Hamburg-Altona, Kassel, Magdeburg, Oppeln, Stettin, and Stuttgart offices took part, with two trains each listed for Magdeburg, Oppeln, and Stuttgart. This gives a total of 13 rail protection trains, but it cannot be ruled out that other RBD offices also had such trains then, but they were not activated, though there could not have been many more.

With the new guidelines of December 1923, a uniform composition of the rail protection trains had finally been achieved. They consisted of flat cars at both ends, on which building material for track improvement and repair and restoration equipment were loaded. Then came, from each end to the central locomotive, three closed freight cars with inside armor and gun ports. In each half of the train there was a commander's car equipped with an armored observation post (specially mounted on a G-car, brake cabin, or roof structure of a baggage car). In the cars running inward (to the locomotive) there were usually a kitchen and a dressing station; the others were combat cars armed with heavy 08 machine guns and manned by infantry, and the crew could be used partly as a shock troop outside the train; there was also always a track-building troop included. In the rear half of the train there was a radio station, with

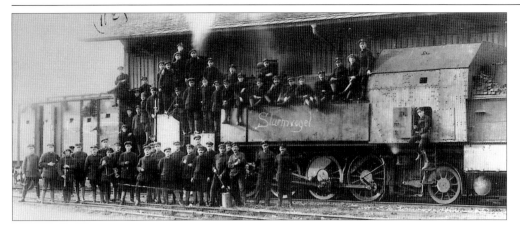

In 1925 the rail protection train of the Stuttgart RBD had obtained a Prussian T 14 locomotive. Like the earlier T 5 of the Württemberg Traffic Guard, it has a cab armored on all sides, but otherwise only steel plates along the sides of the water tank and in front of the cylinders. Photo: Federal Archives, Koblenz

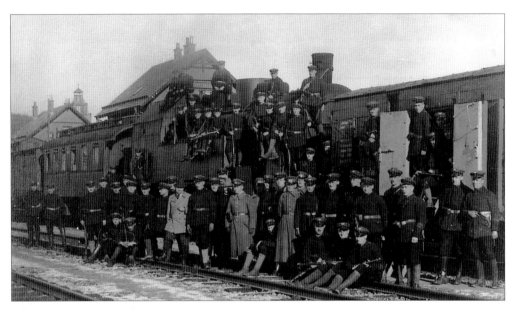

The Stuttgart RBD train in 1931 on maneuvers at the Muensingen troop training camp. The opened doors of the car before the loco clearly show the thick steel plates with which the wooden walls of the freight cars were armored. Photo: Federal Archives, Koblenz

The Breslau RBD rail protection train corresponded to the standard plan for these trains. The fully armored Prussian T 14 loco shows the photo dates from after 1930. For the observation posts the bodies of the three-axle freight cars were used. Note also the spotlight attached to this car. The cars were labeled "restoration cars." Photo: Federal Archives, Koblenz

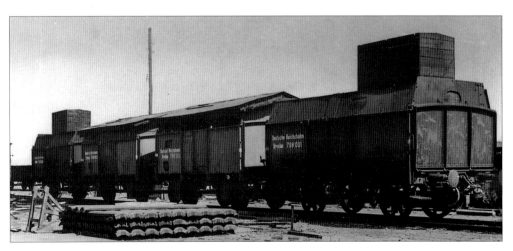

The Breslau RBD still used rail protection material of World War I and the Reichswehr, as this picture shows (central cars with roof structure). The front and rear wagons have steel armor plate. Behind the wooden exterior there may have been a weapon system. Photo: Federal Archives, Koblenz

its roof antenna usually running over several cars. The inner armor of the cars seems to have been of very different quality in the various trains, from armor plates of chrome-nickel steel (for the Munich rail protection train, such an inner armor was listed as 26 mm thick in the cars and 15 mm on the locomotive), to double walls filled with gravel or concrete and not secure from S.m.K. fire, although this was actually urged. The order of the cars within one half of a train varied in the individual rail protection trains, as a memo of 1933 shows the command cars at the ends of the train, in photos it is often the middle one of the three cars, and it is stated that in the Stuttgart train it was inside (right before and behind the locomotive). The final version of this Stuttgart train also had a total length of 108.7 meters and a total weight including the locomotive of 432 tons; the crew numbered 120 men (in 1933 the manpower of the rail protection trains was generally listed at 150 men). At first the locomotives were fitted for action with provisional cab armor, so as to make the train look like a normal freight train for camouflage purposes. In 1929-30 rail protection was included in the Reichswehr's mobilization planning. It was to relieve them in the area of railroad protection and was appropriately strengthened (apparently from 30,000 to 50,000 men). The number of 19 available rail protection trains was raised to 22, and now they were all equipped with fully armored locomotives, particularly of the 57 (G 10) and 93 (T 14) series.

Between 1930 and 1934 five armored high-performance rail cars (Bzt) were added to the rail protection and repair trains (Bzw). These were two-axle Diesel powered rail cars VT 807-811, delivered by Wegmann and MAN from 1926 to 1929 and producing twice 75 HP (84 kW), with a top speed of 70 kph.

The Karlsruhe RDB rail protection train had the same number of cars, but they were built of unusual materials. The loco is probably an armored Baden VI b or c. In the front half, after two G-cars, is a passenger car armored with outside steel plates. During the maneuvers shown here the crewmen left the first car through the floor hatch.

In the rear half of the Karlsruhe train, the middle one of the three cars was a Baden P 3 (Group 133e) baggage car. While the rail protection men at left practice rail repairs, the group at right gets the 75 1001 locomotive onto the track. Photos (2): Federal Archives, Koblenz

The Munich rail protection train of 1932-33 at the Oberwiesenfeld. The train does not yet have the 1938 gun cars, but already has an armored Series 57 (Prussian G 10) locomotive. Photo: BPM Schwandorf

The Munich rail protection men practice, with the shooters in a lying position. Photo: BPM Schwandorf

The cars used in regular traffic could be equipped in a few hours with the help of prepared armor plates; the crews were to number 40 men.

One could suspect that the requirements of 1923, that every RDB should maintain a rail protection train, would thus be fulfilled, for the sum of 22 protection trains and 5 railcars precisely equals the 27 administrations that existed at the beginning of the thirties. But the situation was not so simple, for the eastern offices in Oppeln and Breslau had three and the Königsberg office had two protection trains, and all three also had a railcar, so that there were eight administrations, even at this late date, that were still without an armored rail protection train. Besides the railcars, whose stationing is known completely, 19 rail protection trains can be located exactly. One can probably assume that the administrations that had protection trains in 1923 still had them in later years. Naturally, no such trains existed in the demilitarized Rhineland, in the offices of Ludwigshafen (dissolved 1936), Trier (Saarbrücken as of 1935), Mainz, and Cologne. Even after the troops entered this region in March 1936 no such trains—at least in the next two years—can be documented there. It is rather surprising that in the potentially explosive Ruhr area and its surroundings (the Essen and Wuppertal offices, as well as Münster and Frankfurt) there were no such units in existence, save for the Wuppertal railcar. The Augsburg and Schwerin offices also apparently had no armored rail protection trains.

Reichsbahn District (RBD)	Bzw	Bzt
Oppeln	3	VT 810
Breslau	3	VT 807
Koenigsberg	2	VT 811
Frankfurt on the Oder	1	
Stettin	1	
Dresden	1	VT 808
Halle	1*	
Berlin	1	
Erfurt	1*	
Kassel	1*	
Hannover/Magdeburg	1*	
Hamburg/Altona	1*	
Wuppertal		VT 809
Karlsruhe	1	
Stuttgart	1	
Nürnberg/Würzburg	1	
Regensburg	1	
Munich	1	

(Statements of 1923 marked with *)

The five railcars were mustered out between 1935 and 1937; only VT 811 was still in service in 1938, and was taken over by the German Wehrmacht as Armored Railcar No. 15.

Not much is known of actions of the rail protection trains after 1923. The year 1925 brought a series of railroad strikes, in which they were surely active on a local level. In 1931 there was a fear of invasions on the Polish border, and ten trains were prepared just in case. After the Reichstag fire on February 27, 1933, the National Socialists, who had come to power, accused the Communists of it and undertook an extensive program of arresting them; countermeasures were feared and the rail protection system was activated countrywide, with a total of 27,000 men assigned to surveillance measures. The use of the rail protection trains then was noticed keenly in France and considered a clear infraction of the Treaty of Versailles, which naturally did not frighten the National Socialists in power, but rather made them aware of this instrument. Thus, on March 18, 1933, at the Dallgow-Döberitz railroad station a great display of the Reichsbahn's protective measures took place before the then Prussian Reich Prime Minister Hermann Göring, who showed himself to be very impressed. From then on, the railroad guard was utilized for surveillance measures against hostile persons on railroad property and in trains. In 1934 the veteran members were replaced by younger forces, and in 1936 the railroad guard was considerably strengthened again. The Railroad Protection Leader Karl Heiges had been discharged in 1933 and replaced by NSDAP member Kleinmann (simultaneously State Secretary in the RVM).

In the summer of 1938, seven railroad protection trains (from the RBD of Königsberg (2), East, Breslau, Stettin, Nürnberg, and Munich) and one railcar (for Königsberg) were taken over by the German Wehrmacht as armored trains or railcars. Individual cars from another Oppeln rail protection train turned up in Armored Trains 22 and 23 in 1940. The other fourteen found use with the strengthened Railroad Guard—according to instructions of May 12, 1936, for it—after a special decision by the Chief of Transportation.

This was to be formed from the cadre personnel of the peacetime railroad guard through completion teams of older men (over age 35, later even older) whom the military draft offices had to make available, and went to the Wehrmacht, where it was subordinated to the commander of the railroad Units under the Chief of Transportation. In the RVM the rail and air protection specialist belonged to Group L (defense of the country); at the level of the administrations, the rail protection administrator (Dez 36) was subordinate to the Railroad Authority (Bbv; simultaneously operations manager of the administration), who, as in the military railroad management since 1899, was now, in the Wehrmacht railroad management of 1942, responsible for the railroad-technical side of all military questions that affected the railroad, and thus functioned as discussion partner for the transport service offices of the Army. Such Bbv with their subordinate offices (including the rail protection administrators) were active not only in the administrations in the Reich area, but also in the Ostbahn in the General Government (remaining Poland), the main railroad management (later Reich Traffic Direction) in the captured part of the Soviet Union, North (Riga), Center (Minsk),

In 1930 the Railroad Guard also took over five railcars, VT 807-811; here VT 809 is shown serving the Wuppertal district. Note the armored blinds on the windows, with rifle or machine-gun ports (in the middle windows of each half of the car). Photo: Federal Archives, Koblenz

A group of Breslau Rail Guard personnel before their railcar, VT 807. Photo: Federal Archives, Koblenz.

South (Poltawa or Kiev) and East (Dnjepropetrowsk or Poltawa), the railroad management in France and Belgium, plus the Netherlands and Danish railroads. Particularly in the regions in which the activities of partisans and resistance fighters increased and were directed against the transport routes as the war progressed, especially since 1943, thus in the east and in France the rail protection may have been of increasing significance, and in these regions the remaining rail protection trains may have been used. Some were apparently turned over to the RBD of Villach in the last phase of the war as they were in northern Slovenia, which was absorbed in the German Reich in May 1941 (the eastern part to the RBD of Vienna, the western part to that of Villach) as partisan activity spread more and more strongly. Besides armored rail vehicles of the Wehrmacht, a "rail armored car" and an "armored security train" of the railroad police in Cilli and a track-securing train named "Diesel" in Carinthia can be documented. Note the very different terminology, which does not allow closer identification—or the solution of the question of whether and how far it was a matter of rail protection trains. It is also known that the Bbv of the railroad administration in Lyon added two freight cars, armored inside and armed with machine guns, to its repair trains (called "Anna" and "Caesar" to protect its men who tried to repair blown-up tracks and were attacked by Maquis), thus turning them into rail protection trains, and one is probably right to assume that this was not an isolated case. These few documentations are the only known indications of the use of armored and armed vehicles by the Reichsbahn in World War II, and the role of the Reichsbahn Guard at that time remains a matter which is still to be elucidated.

Reichswehr and Other Plans

Although the rigorous application of the Treaty of Versailles to the German Reich by the Allies in the London Ultimatum of May 5, 1921, forbade the possession of armored trains, the Reichswehr continued to include them in its considerations for serious cases. Thus, the mobilization plan of 1920, which reckoned on 14 armored trains (two per recruiting district), went out of power only in August 1924. But the new mobilization plan of 1926, which was intended to expand the 100,000-man Army to 21 divisions, also called for such trains, and even two more than in the earlier plans, making 16 in all. For the 108 men of the crew, the following listing was made:

1	officer as commander of the armored train
1	sergeant (Feldwebel)
2	NCOs as group leaders
13	NCOs as machine-gun leaders
5	NCOs as mine-thrower leaders
3	artillery NCOs
2	NCOs for special tasks
40	machine-gunners
12	mine-thrower crewmen
10	artillerymen
6	radio and intelligence men
6	men without special tasks
1	medical officer (doctor)
1	medical NCO
5	railroad officials (technical personnel)

totals: 2 officers, 5 railroad men, 27 NCOs and 74 men

It is notable that, compared to 1920, the number of officers is reduced, because the limited cadre of the 100,000-man army allowed no better apportionment. No entries were made as to the equipment of

these armored trains, but one can assume that in view of the identical total crew strength it probably agreed in the earlier planning, as aside from the increased number of men and the better ammunition supply, similar equipping with heavy weapons (guns, grenade launchers, heavy machine guns) can be found for the first armored trains of the German Wehrmacht (1938).

That the Reichswehr planned on its own armored trains despite the Allied ban is also shown in H.Dv. 487, "Command and Combat of Combined Weapons," published in 1923, which deals with these units in Section XIII. The introduction says: "Armored trains are a quickly movable means of combat. They have great fighting power and strong moral effect, especially on inferior opponents. Their possible uses are limited by the fact that they are bound to easily destroyed rails, and that the locomotive can easily be put out of action by fire.

"Armored trains are not suitable for long fire fights or against enemies with artillery. Surprise attacks promise the most success. It must always be ascertained whether the more easily movable armored road vehicle can carry out the task more surely."

In a later section, the experiences of the fighting after the Russian Revolution bear fruit: "In extensive battle zones with few roads and against an inferior opponent, armored trains under enterprising commanders have a broad range of activity, as long as the waging of war is bound to the great rail lines. Under such conditions it can take the form of a railroad war. The troops operate in mixed groups on trains assembled for the purpose under the protection of armored trains."

The use of armored trains is formulated at similar length to the corresponding statements from right after the war:
– Securing of railroad transport movements,
– Protection of troop detraining,
– Disturbing enemy detraining,
– Railroad technical scouting and powerful track scouting, sometimes linked with tasks of interruption and destruction,
– Cooperation in powerful opening of important railroad lines and junctions,
– Securing of tracks, depots, and other structures, as well as reconstruction tasks,
– Cooperation in protection of non-attached flanks,
– In defense and border guarding for support and restraint, especially of weakly occupied fronts and weak reserves, as well as securing supplying and withdrawal,
– In pursuit,
– When withdrawing, to bring back defense forces left behind, secure loading depots and destroy lines and structures to be abandoned to the enemy,
– In backline areas, to mop up unsecured regions.

It is stressed that armored trains should be as short as possible for uniform command. Their composition is handled only summarily, from an included scheme the following sequence of cars may be derived: contact car loaded with sand; gun car (gun in turning turret, observation post for the train's commander); shock troop car (armored and armed with machine guns); locomotive with tender; medium launcher car (one mine-thrower); light launcher car (two mine-throwers); gun car, same composition as before; and equipment car (railroad building material) as rear contact car. It is based strongly on the realities of 1919-20. Armor giving protection against infantry fire and grenade splinters is regarded as sufficient for the locomotive and combat cars. Within the train, communication via several independent systems, to the outside via radio. Among the crew were, besides a combat crew (gun crews and shock troop to company strength) and the technical personnel—as before—a railroad construction troop was to be carried. The given technical details correspond to earlier statements as to readiness, speed (the 20-30 kph stated here is presumably only the combat speed), and radius of action (coal supply now stated as sufficient for 300 km). When properly armored trains are lacking, protected trains can be set up in makeshift manner instead, though when they are in action, lesser resistance is to be expected. In the choice of unloading depots, not only the security of supply, especially for the locomotive is stressed, but rather, for technical reasons, and for security from air raids, larger depots are inherently not regarded as favorable, but rather smaller depots in the vicinity of junctions are preferred. For camouflage from enemy air surveillance leaving cars on several tracks is recommended, although this delays readiness to move.

The chain of command is stated very briefly (command office at the top, assigning them to troops for specific tasks, operational supervision by the responsible command office, along with railroad service offices). A new idea is that frequent changes are recommended, since the enemy will otherwise notice and limit the train's use through rail disturbances, etc. Prerequisites for successful armored train action are a clear, definite task, knowledge of the total situation, strict secrecy for preparations, and as thorough a knowledge of the rail lines as possible, advantageously to be gained by air reconnaissance. Action in darkness or in wooded or poor visibility areas is to be avoided. In carrying out the task, but also in action, it must be considered that the ammunition supply of an armored train is limited; supplying at the right time is to be assured.

For extremely important rear protection during action against enemies, and for communication to the rear, machine-gun armed patrols on locomotives, railcars, or rail-equipped motor vehicles (taking along repair equipment for slight damage is a good idea) are recommended. Rear protection can also be afforded by a second armored train, which runs either behind the first one (if possible, in turns) or one train behind the other in case of double lines. If two or even more armored trains are at hand, a division into close- and long-range combat trains can be practical; their cooperation must be regulated carefully.

Unsecured structures and stations are to be searched carefully by patrols before running through them. If the train stops in enemy endangered country, it is to be secured by advance scouts and kept in constant readiness to fire in case of surprise attacks. Protection against wild trains or unmanned locomotives can be done by mining the line, by obstacles such as derailing or halting devices, etc., and by pushing the control car ahead.

Against local opposition, one lets the unloaded shock troop proceed outflanking, supported by bursts of fire from all the train's weapons; If the attack continues successfully or in case of own superior fire, the train advances ruthlessly. Under heavy opposition it is not good to involve the train in a lengthy fire fight. Heavy, well aimed artillery fire is escaped from behind a fog screen.

From the air, armored trains offer bombs no favorable target, as they are too narrow. On the other hand, they are very exposed to attack by low-flying fighter planes, which should be fought with planned return fire in a circle of 1000 meters. A/A machine guns must be ready to fire for air defense if the train is running.

The last part concerns fighting armored trains. If such occurs, the line is to be broken or blocked with mines. Good observation and quick reporting of the approaching train is important. In places where the train must move slowly (curves, upgrades, underpasses, wooded, poor visibility terrain), defensive traps using artillery and mine-throwers are to be set up. One can also let the train proceed through openly laid obstacles at which the heavy weapons are aimed. If enough forces are available an attack is recommended. This can be done either as a surprise attack from all sides and under as heavy fire on all cars as possible (so that the enemy cannot bring his firepower to bear), or by concentrating all firepower at first on the locomotive, so as to destroy it and thus immobilize the train. After that the train is fought down. In any case it is good to make a quick advance on the line behind the train and there prevent its retreat by destroying the rails. Against its support by following armored trains or other forces, one lays further obstacles (such as mines) on the enemy's side of the break in the line and places forces—when possible—for defense. Similar procedures apply to battles between armored trains. The most important goal is the destruction of the enemy locomotive. The enemy armored train will come under heavy fire at first. If possible, the shock troop is to be used to surround the enemy armored train and cut it off by breaking the rails. One's own train then moves forward to the attack under constant fire.—If an armored train wants to avoid an attack by an enemy train it lays a fog screen, pushes cars toward it or drops line blocking obstacles.—The essential change from the earlier instructions is the inclusion of the air force, as both a helper and opponent of armored trains.

The chapter "Armored Trains" in H.Dv. 487 of 1923 was included with terse wording and partly abridged as Section XXI of H.Dv. 300 "Leadership of Troops" of 1934. It now simply states the possible uses: "Armored trains can be used to secure railroad transport movements, troop loadings and unloadings, destruction work on railroads, repair work, supplying and withdrawing, in retreat as well as to clean out insecure areas and as a fast reserve (this was newly added)." The section about railroad combat with armored trains—like much else of minor importance—is completely omitted. The composition of the trail is described more precisely: "An armored train consists, besides the locomotive, usually of 8 to 10 cars, armed ones, control cars (with equipment), personnel and service cars. The locomotive with tender is usually placed in the middle of the train. At the front and rear ends there is one control (equipment or sandbag) car." In the listing of the crew, engineers with explosives are added if necessary, and it also reads: "Armored trains can temporarily be subordinated to army corps or corps commands. The operations supervision is conducted by the transport officer with the railroad operations offices." The "Temporary service instructions for armored railroad trains" of 1938 was based on H.Dv. 300, so that in terms of the instructions, a continuing transition from the earlier Reichswehr era to the German Wehrmacht of the Third Reich is noticeable.

In the period around 1930, several suggestions for improving and developing armored trains were made in the literature, but they had no practical results for lack of appropriate units. Retired Captain Hans Wagner, commander of the makeshift broad-gauge armored train set up in the Baltic area in the summer of 1919 and commander of the two-train Armored Train Division of the White Army of General Wrangel, which operated in southern Russia and Crimea, proposed in a series of articles published between 1929 and 1935 the taking over of the Russian system of cooperation of several armored trains, differentiated into heavy (gun calibers over 8 cm, lightly armored, functioning as artillery reserves from backline areas, thus lightly armored railroad artillery) and light (gun calibers under 8 cm, heavily armored, for actual combat tasks) types, and suggests several improvements. For the light armored train, which is of the most interest here, Wagner recommends two-axle car chassis throughout (if derailed, they can easily be returned to the rails), a small locomotive (small target) with a large tender (to give as great a range as possible), and the following car types:

1. Artillery lead car (at both ends behind the contact car): 7.5-cm mountain or naval gun in front, high rate of fire, on low mount with 270-degree traversing turret; in the lower body, one light machine gun in a balcony on each side, allowing weapon effect also along the train; in the rear part of the car a heavy machine gun in a gun port on each side.
2. Artillery Car 2: 7.5-cm mountain or naval gun in front, high rate of fire, in a turret with 360-degree traverse, mounted so high that it can fire over the gun on the lead car; two light machine guns in back, in diagonally mounted small turning turrets, which allow action against air and ground targets; on each side a heavy machine gun in a gun port.
    In the corresponding car in the second half of the train, a howitzer or mine thrower may be installed in a turret instead of a cannon, which can fire over the entire first half of the train.
    The Artillery Car 2 of the first half of the train can also be built as a command car. Then the radio station can be installed in the rear half of the car, an armored observation turret with vision slits on the roof, and over it a turning range finder, but this observation turret limits the traverse of the turret gun; it is therefore recommended that the command post is to be installed on the tender of the locomotive, which also allows direct communication of the train commander with the engine-driver.
3. Infantry Car: to be set up according to need; the cars are closed on all sides, heavily armored with an observation turret on the roof and two ports on either side for machine guns. On top of the car, openings and makeshift mounts for A/A machine guns are provided.

As armor that was (then) even conditionally secure against grenade hits (except at a vertical striking angle), Wagner recommends a double wall of 8- to 12-mm thick iron plate, with its interim space of 10 to 30 mm filled with concrete or a mixture of fine gravel and tar. Equipment that he considers indispensable: various and effective means of communication (radio set with azimuth device, telephone equipment with field cables, telephones or speaking tubes inside the train, machine telegraph to engine driver's position, signal flags, signal lamps and spotlights, flare pistols, smoke signals), a central electric fire control, movable shear telescopes and range finders, an electric generator as an independent source of electricity, steam heating and quick braking throughout, protected passages between all the cars, equipment to repair rail damage, to deal with derailments and carry out minor repairs, hand operated pump to secure the water supply, fog laying equipment and other means of camouflage. He lists the crew strength of such a train without added infantry cars as 4 officers, 25 NCOs, and 31 men. The good training of the crew appears more important to him than a higher number of men.

The entire armored train battle group (armored train division) should consist, besides two such combat trains and one heavy armored train (armored train artillery: two guns of 10 to 21-cm caliber, four heavy and eight light machine guns) of four lightly armored and armed motor driven armored railcars for reconnaissance and communication, two or three spare cars (one armored and armed one with a strong radio station as a command car for the group commander, if needed, also to be included in the combat train; otherwise, cars with special

equipment: special guns such as A/A guns, strong spotlights, etc.) with an armored spare locomotive, a recovery train (lightly armored and armed, to repair large damage to railroad premises and assist derailed vehicles; appropriately equipped with crane car, special tools and workshops, and with specially trained personnel) and personnel trains (housing for the crew, supply and provision car, equipment car, writing room, etc.).

A work published by retired Major Pirner in 1933 depends strongly on the German armored trains of World War I and the immediate postwar era, especially in the large number of cars, the use of O-cars, the armored cupolas of Gun Cars 2 and 3 and the type of armor. Pirner establishes as the main requirement of the armored train the combination of the highest firepower in the tightest space and its division to all sides as equally as possible. To be sure, he shows himself—as the proposed train length shows—to be not always consistent in the practical application of his requirements. He also prefers two-axle cars. The heavy machine guns with their high firepower are the main weapons of the armored train; they are also to be aimed forward beside the guns, and in general with the greatest possible sweep angle and overlapping. For artillery guns he recommends rapid-fire guns not under 5 cm caliber, and flat-trajectory guns up to 7.5 cm (high calibers require special cars because of their greater recoil), at best with two per car—the lighter caliber firing over the forward one. In the included drawing, to be sure, 8.8-cm cannons on four-axle cars as well as turrets mounted on separate cars with 5-cm guns are depicted. In all, Pirner's armored train consists of the following cars:

1. Control car
2. Gun Car 1 (four axles, 8.8-cm gun in turning shield mount on back part of car, front part closed with balconies for heavy machine guns at the corners and spotlight in the middle).
3. Gun Car 2 (two-axle O-car with armored roof and 5-cm cannon in armored cupola; two balconies with heavy machine guns at front).
4. Launcher Car 1 (two-axle O-car with one medium mine-thrower on road-metal bed).
5. Launcher Car 2 (two-axle O-car with two light mine-throwers on road-metal beds).
Cars 4 and 5 are only optional if needed.
6. Command Car 1 with observation turret, radio station, and spotlight.
7. Ammunition car (armored G-car with two heavy machine-gun balconies).
8. Kitchen car (armored G-car).
Cars 6 to 8 are spanned by a frame antenna for the radio station in the command car.
9. Armored locomotive (powerful freight loco with trailed tender).
10. Command Car 2 (for deputy commander, like 6), but without radio station, instead with two balconies with heavy machine guns.
11. Launcher Car 3 (like 5).
12. Launcher Car 4 (like 4).
Cars 11 and 12 are only optional if needed.
13. Gun Car 3 (like 3).
14. Gun Car 4 (like 2).
15. Contact car (like 1).

The locomotive should have the strongest pulling power. It is to be coupled in the middle; the armored train should be set up as symmetrically as possible (in Pirner's plan this is not completely carried out because of the frame antenna spanning three cars). A fast and effectively working brake is required; the best is an air-brake

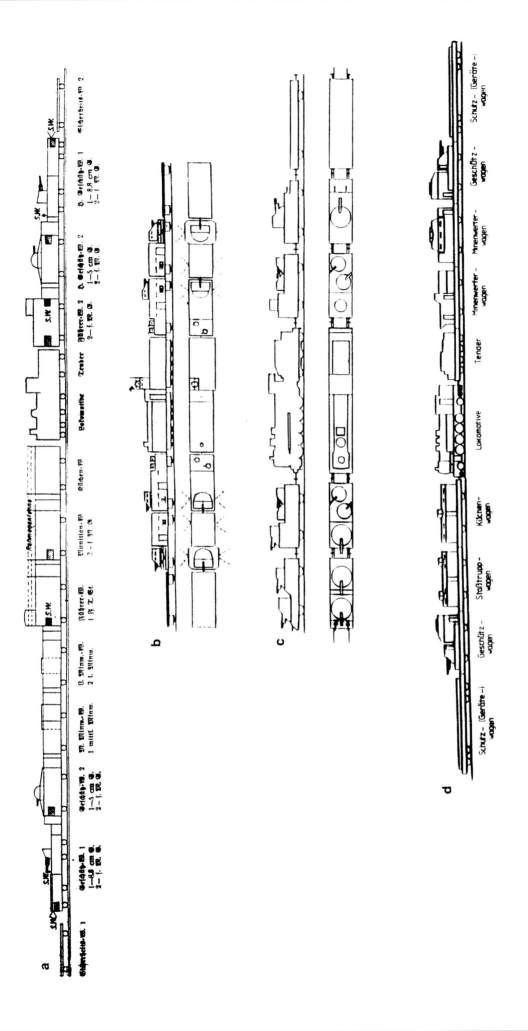

Armored train designs of the between-wars era.
a. Pirner (1933) orients himself completely to the Reichswehr armored trains of 1919-20 and proposes no fewer than ten combat cars.
b. In Wagner (1933), the low number of cars and the strong artillery indicate the Russian model.
c. Heigl (1930) advocates strong artillery fire concentration to the front (gun placement on three increasing levels!) and few cars. The machine guns are mounted in balconies and turrets to increase their sweep angles.
d. The H.Dv. 487 of 1923 has only two guns (one in front, one in back). The strong mine-launcher armament is still reminiscent of the immediate postwar era (1919-20). The number of combat cars (6) is a compromise and allows sufficient manning by infantry.

system for all the cars, activated from the locomotive. For the control car, which must be easy to uncouple, the removal of a buffer on the outside is recommended, so that with the asymmetrical forces during the impact, the enemy car will be made easier to derail.

For armor (presumably with iron outer walls), a plank wall at a distance of 15 cm and a space filled with gravel are cited, which should be safe from pointed bullets, including those with cores. The roofs consist of nickel-steel plates 15 cm thick. There are armored passages between the cars. Entering and exiting the cars are done exclusively through floor hatches (two per car).

The highest value is placed on smooth and effective communication within the train and with staffs and units outside. In the train, uniform command for all weapons and the locomotive is an absolute necessity; in this respect, the armored train is compared with a warship. A passage through all the cars would be desirable, but is broken by the locomotive in the middle. To equalize this disadvantage, the rear part of the train is commanded by a deputy commander in a second command car. For communication within the train, the speaking tube is recommended as the most reliable means; with the telephone, breaking of cables, overheating of isolators from the hot locomotive boiler, and unclear understanding due to battle noise are feared. The following connections exist:

– Command Car 1 to Command Car 2,
– Locomotive to Command Cars 1 and 2.
– Command Car 1 to all other cars in the front part of the train.
– Command Car 2 to all other cars in the rear part of the train.

Additional considered means of communication besides the radio station are the locomotive's whistle, light signals with lamps (also colored light) and headlights, the locomotive's smoke (white and black), and flare balls. — The fire control goes out from the commander in Command Car 1; for the rear part of the train, commands are conveyed through Command Car 2. All observation means and weapons are to be aligned uniformly and must have the same calibration.

The ammunition supply (per weapon) is cited:

Weapon	Combat Car	Ammo Car (combat train)	Ammo Car (personnel train)
7.5-8.8 cannon	150 ignition, 50 impact fuses		150-200 rounds
5 cm cannon	300 shells, 50 cartridges		200 shells, 100 cartridges
Heavy MG	5000 pointed, 500 with core	5000 pointed, 500 with core	10 canisters per gun
Hand grenades	2 cases per car	12 cases	24 cases

The control cars serve to carry track building material; tools and explosives are stored in the ammunition car of the combat train.

The crew is composed as follows:

Car	Officers	Non-coms	Men
Gun Car 1-4, each	1	2	14
Launcher Car 1 & 4 each	1	6	
2 & 3, each	1	1	7
Command Car 1	2	2	2
Command Car 2	1	2	10
Ammunition Car		2	8
Kitchen Car		1	3
Locomotive*		1	3
Combat Train total	9	20	108
Personnel Train	1	2	10
Person. Train Loco*		1	3
Total Armored Train	10	23	121

* Locomotives: 1 driver, 2 firemen, 1 communication man

The commander of an armored train must be a particularly capable officer with knowledge and understanding of all the various weapons and technical features of the train, as well as its unique means of fighting. The greatest value is to be placed on a careful training of the heterogeneously gathered crew. Their cooperation must be friction-free, and the loss of individual men must not put any weapon out of action, so that the training must always allow several possible actions of the individual. Quickness is the first requirement for the high combat power of an armored train. This concerns the reactions to commands in general as well as taking targets and opening fire—also while rolling—just as does exiting through the floor hatches, whereby cover must be found immediately.

The personnel train includes six fourth-class compartment cars (four bunks per compartment) for the crew, one for the locomotive personnel, and one with service space (writing room, paymaster, dispensary, etc.), a sleeping car for officers, two G-cars for supplies and provisions, one G-car as a workshop car (field smithy, armory) and an armored locomotive (as a spare in case the combat train's loco is disabled); the ammunition and workshop cars are also armored and equipped with light weapons, in order to be capable of self-defense in case of unrest in the hinterlands.

The possible uses and action recommendations listed by Pirner largely correspond to those in H.Dv. 487. Mobility and high fighting power as well as strong moral effect are attributed to the armored train. The thinner the front and the fewer roads are in the operating area, the more significant is the action of armored trains, especially in cooperation with simultaneously advancing or closely following troop units. Armored railcars are used for reconnaissance ahead of the armored train.

A base of operations (place to leave the personnel train) should be chosen, a not too large (otherwise endangered by air raids) railroad junction beyond the range of enemy artillery fire, lying if possible in the middle of the area of action, and having a railroad workshop. In case of internal unrest, placing the armored train in a railroad station also needs a free firing field. The separation of the combat and personnel trains allows only one-day runs to the scene of action.

Pirner also recommends the cooperation of at least two armored trains under the command of a staff officer. In case of separate action, they are to be provided with armored railcars armed with machine guns as reconnaissance vehicles.

These suggestions, to be sure, came at a point in time when the value of the armored train was more and more doubted, for since World War I both the Air Force, which could not only destroy armored trains with a direct hit, but could also immobilize them by destroying the tracks, as well as the development of armored wheeled and tracked vehicles, with which the same effect could be attained much more inclusively (not being bound to rail lines), with more mobility and less expense, had experienced an extraordinary increase and made the armored trains look like obsolete means of battle. Countries like Czechoslovakia and Poland, which previously gave much importance to this weapon, halted their development or reduced the number of their trains. Poland, in fact, also sought new ways to perform tasks with trains formed from armored rail cars which could also be used as individual vehicles, or tanks loaded on cars, which could be dropped, and trains made up of armored railcars were also seen outside Poland, including in the German Reich, as a futuristic possibility for the further development of this weapon. Both ideas were realized by the German Wehrmacht during World War II, with tanks unloaded from railroad cars already used at the beginning of the Russian campaign in June 1941, though that of light and heavy reconnaissance trains of motor-driven single vehicles only in 1944. — The Soviet Union, though, seems to have had full confidence in the further use of conventional armored trains the whole time.

German Armored Trains 1904-1945

Since 1924, the German Reich had also—in training and testing facilities that the Soviet Union made available—begun the development of air and armored weapons that, in the later wartime, were the most important means of the "Blitzkrieg" that spread out to a great many of the European countries. Their increasing promotion and significance also made the value of armored trains look more and more doubtful.

This manifested itself in the various editions of Fritz Heigl's "Pocket Book of tanks," a standard work of the time on all kinds of armored vehicles. In the 1930 edition a good deal of space is devoted to armored trains. These possible uses are listed:

- Covering troop transports and their unloading;
- Scouting and advancing into enemy country;
- Taking possession of important railroad objects, bridges, and tunnels;
- Carrying out fast repair work on destroyed railroad objects;
- Offensive and decisive intervention into a battle itself;
- Lateral protection of columns marching parallel to the tracks;
- Covering of withdrawals and making getting away from the enemy easier;
- Leading artillery combat from an indirect position;
- Defense against enemy armored trains;
- Coastal defense.

Heigl describes this as "in the European war, an astounding wealth of tasks fully worthy of fulfillment, which are in no way limited to one-sided situations" and deplores that "the armored trains, in a thankless way, still do not find the recognition that they should hold in the armament of the enemy." As a design principle, Heigl formulates the use of as few and as light cars as possible; the first must be a control car, the next a gun car, for the firepower to the front must be as great as possible; the guns are to be mounted in turrets with 360-degree traverse; the machine guns are to be arranged so that all dead angles can be fired on.

In the new edition of Heigl's pocket book for 1935, the text on armored trains has shrunk to a mere two pages; the first two paragraphs run: "The essential difference between armored railroad vehicles and other armored combat vehicles is their limitation to the railway network. To the same extent to which the motor vehicle took over traffic generally from the railroad, the motor vehicle also took over from the railroad the applicability for combat in motion. If one reflects that the tank is basically nothing else but a wheeled vehicle that lays its own 'rail line' through the terrain in the form of its tracks, one instantly understand the reason for the military devaluation of the armored railroad vehicles.

"But where the railroad is the only means of transit and thus becomes the lifeline of a war area, the armored train and railcar will still dominate the field, especially when long distances are to be covered. In the same way, the armored railroad train remains of importance for the protection of rail lines in endangered districts and for limited offensive undertakings along the tracks. Thus, one can cite only border protection and railroad protection as narrowly delineated realms of tasks for European conditions."

The beginning of the second section predicts in prophetic words the unexpected increase that the German armored train weapon was to take on in World War II in battle against the Soviet Union. At first the skeptical voices prevailed by far, giving the armored train no future any more.

Thus, it is not surprising that—when after the introduction of universal military service in 1935, the equipping of the German military forces was carried on with all power, and in 1939 the question: Armored trains or not? was also discussed—the 8th Section (technical) of the Army General Staff, after consulting the 5th Section (Transportation), it was recommended in a notice from Major Dr. Guderian (the uncle of the later tank general, Inspector-General of the Armored Troops and finally Chief of the Army General Staff): "Requirements for the development of new armored trains are set up, but in the list of the Weapons Office in agreement with the 5th Section, are not designated as urgent. In the view of the 5th Section, rails are primarily to serve transport and not combat. The enemy fire might be drawn directly onto the transport routes by armored trains with machine guns or cannons. The tank gives the possibility of fighting with armored vehicles sideward of the transport line. In withdrawals, armored trains could be used as a rear guard that is sacrificed (!). The same thing, though, can also be attained with an ordinary freight train that one allows to derail. A less costly sacrifice. All in all: Armored trains have little sense, little advantage. Armored railcars with machine guns or big guns might perhaps be better." But the notice simultaneously gives encouragement as to how one can attain armored trains with modest means. It cites the 22 rail protection trains of the German Reichsbahn, which are, of course, not secure from bullets with cores and are classified as ready to be scrapped. Some of them, though, are "barely usable," so that two such (the Munich and Breslau rail protection trains, later Armored Trains No. 3 and 4) are available if needed to the chief of Transportation, and two others (those of the Königsberg RBD, later Armored Trains No. 6 and 7) to the General command of the I.A.K. (East Prussia). Following this suggestion—even in somewhat expanded form, as will be shown later—the rail protection trains became the nucleus of the German Wehrmacht's armored train weapon.

77

The Armored Trains of the German Wehrmacht

The Command Structure

On February 22, 1938, the 5th Section of the Army General Staff (Gen. St. d. H.) issued preliminary instructions for the war organization of the transport system, which finally went into power later. The armored railroad trains were then placed in charge of the Commander of the Railroad Units (later Railroad Troops: Bedeis; Colonel, later Major General Will) under the Chief of Transportation (Colonel, later Major General Rudolf Gercke). Will was the Weapon Commander (Weapon General) of all railroad units for building, operation, and railroad protection, besides the armored trains, also the railroad engineers, building staffs and columns, and guard companies. This subordination, though, was based only on the troop services, insofar as they were not constituted without combat crews (then they took their orders from Bedeis via the appropriate transport command). The combat crew was to be taken from the Wehrmacht; only the technical crew was provided by the Reichsbahn. In case of mobilization, the armored trains were assigned as army troops by the Army High Command (OKH) to units of the Army for special combat tasks and were subordinate to the appropriate command offices. Only in the sense of railroad operations were they linked to the structures of the appropriate transport commands.

According to the urgings of the Army General Staff (see previous section), the rail protection trains were checked for their suitability as armored trains. The decision was made to set up seven such units. The general commands of the appropriate recruiting districts (I Königsberg, III Berlin, IV Dresden, VII Munich, VIII Breslau, IX Kassel) were charged by the OKH with putting them into service. They were to give advice for their armament and other equipment. After that, their establishment was finally ordered by the OKH in a command July 23, 1938. The crew, at company strength, was to be set up by the units of the individual recruiting districts, and included infantrymen, artillerymen (if needed), communication and medical personnel, and later on A/A artillerymen were added. For the technical crews, personnel of the German Reichsbahn were taken over. Responsible for the equipping of the armored trains was Inspection 2 (Infantry), plus the Field Equipment Inspection of the General Army Office (AHA) for the railroad-technical side, the Engineer Inspection (In 5), as of 1939 the separated In 10 (Railroad engineers). Replacements were handled by the deputy general command of the recruiting district that had set up the train, and as of 1940 by the division command for special use established there. This manifold responsibility was not favorable for a positive development, the replacement situation through the various involved units was not simple, nor was the blending of the crews of various origins into a unified troop body, as combat action required. In particular, though, the troop commanders to whom the armored trains were subordinated for action were not familiar with the special features of this weapon, which led again and again to impractical uses with inevitable results: ineffectiveness, even losses of men and materials. Despite this, the situation remained not only in the last peacetime year, but also in the first year and a half of the war, in which the only expansion, the takeover of five armored trains made from material captured in Czechoslovakia and Poland in 1939, took place. In any case, In 10 established considerations for further development of armored trains

and, in December 1940, gave appropriate assignments for a 1941 armored train and an SP 42 armored train, wherein it is interesting that the main characteristic from this side involved the decrease of being bound to the rails (by carrying unloadable tanks on special carrier cars and by armored vehicles that ran on both rails and roads and could be changed from one to the other as quickly as possible). In a memo of April 2, 1941, though, armored trains were not mentioned, aside from the material lists included as addenda (with the never-realized plan for an armored Diesel locomotive of 1260 HP or 925 kW), although they appeared in the organizational schemes (with the notation "number and equipment not yet determined").

The Chief of the Army General Staff, Franz Halder, dedicated a special section to armored trains in his comment of June 14, 1941, bringing out three points in the memo in which he took up the first two suggestions of In 10 from December 1940:

a. "I see the timely further development of armored railroad trains in equipping them with railroad cars suitable for carrying tanks, which along with their effect from the train, must have the possibility of leaving the railroad cars quickly at any time and attacking enemies, even at great distances from the tracks. Assignment of armored shock-troop cars is wanted." (This corresponds to requests of In 10 for the Armored Train 1941 and the easy loading and unloading ability for the SP 42, and at the time of this memo it was already accomplished in the form of an immediate solution for the six broad-gauge armored trains set up in the spring of 1941 for the Russian campaign.)

b. "I also request that the development of an armored railcar be introduced that can run on rails and roads and can quickly be put on or taken off the rails. It is conceived as a reconnaissance car of the railroad engineers, as railroad protection in areas of unrest, and as a leading advance vehicle for an armored train. (This demand also had been taken from the In 10 request for Armored Train 1941; later captured French armored scout cars, of Type 204 or 38(f), were modified, a makeshift solution that became a lasting one.)

c. Organizationally, I consider the creation of the position of a staff officer of the armored railroad trains to be necessary in wartime and already required now. He will have the task of taking care of the often-moving armored trains in terms of weapons and personnel, and of making suggestions for their use and further technical development.

As for the definite number of armored railroad trains necessary, a decision will be possible only later on."

The third request of the Chief of the General Staff was also realized quickly. In his diary we find under July 27, 1941, the entry "Staff officer of the armored railroad trains must be established," along with the Chief of the Organizational Department of the Army general Staff, the assigning of this service position to the General of the Fast Troops was decided. The reason for this momentous decision to remove the armored railroad trains from being subordinated to the Commander of the Railroad Troops and assigned to the Fast Troops is not known. With the approval of the OKH on August 9, 1941, this new office was installed, at the head of which the staff officer of the armored railroad trains entered. The service instructions for him were issued by the OKH on October 24, 1941. The assignment to the Fast Troops meant that the armored trains—and their further development—came under the responsibility of Inspection 6, which was responsible for this service arm; only the railroad-technical service remained as before under Wa Prüf 5 for the development of railroad-technical equipment and WuG 5 for their procurement (in this office there was no special branch for the railroad engineers), the areas of "armored combat vehicles" and "armored trains," though, were now handled by Wa Prüf 6 (Development) and WuG 6 (Procurement).

While the General of the Fast Troops in the Army Command had the duties of a division commander toward the armored trains, the staff officer of the armored railroad trains subordinate to him was their service commander with the duties of a regimental commander (the rights of command offices, to which the armored trains were subordinated for action, remained undisturbed by these regulations). The staff officer was to direct the actions of the armored trains in close cooperation with the chief of Transportation, via whom not only all the things that affected the work of the RVM in a personal or material way were to be directed (such as those concerning railroad personnel, locomotive and car material), but was also responsible, with the offices subordinate to him, for the use of the tracks by the armored trains, for the transit requirements and the work of transportation.

Lt. Col. (as of April 1, 1942, Colonel) Egon von Olszewski became the staff officer of the armored railroad trains, under the General of the Fast Troops, on September 20, 1941, as of April 1, 1943, commander of the armored railroad trains under the army command of the Chief of the Army General Staff, and remained the leader of the office until March 31, 1945. Photo: F. Englberger/W. Sawodny collection

Named to be the staff officer of the armored railroad trains by the Army Personnel Office was Lieutenant Colonel (Colonel as of April 1, 1942) Egon von Olszewski, born in Schwerin in 1898 and a teacher at the War School in Dresden before the war began. He entered his new post on September 20, 1941. His adjutant was First Lieutenant (later Captain) Walter Nietzsch, the technical worker was Lieutenant (later First Lieutenant) Franz Engelberger, and the staff included a secretary at NCO rank and four men (writer, messenger, telephoner, and chauffeur). Later the office was expanded further. In September, First Lieutenant Gerhard Riewendt took the additionally created position of an ordnance officer (simultaneously artillery officer). The staff was located in the Von-der-Goltz Barracks in Lötzen, East Prussia, a few kilometers eastward of the region between Rastenburg and Angerburg in which the Führer's "Wolf's Den" headquarters and the OKH "Mauerwald" headquarters were located. Just for the period from July 16 to November 1, 1942, these highest command posts were transferred to Winniza in the Ukraine to direct the offensive in the Don and Caucasus areas.

The creation of this position of the staff officer for armored railroad trains with the General of the Fast Troops showed its first visible effects in the spring of 1942. On April 1, 1942, the Armored Trains' own replacement unit was set up in Rembertow on the eastern edge of Warsaw; after six months a training unit joined it, which was later united with the replacement unit. In terms of war structure, both were subordinated to the Commander of the Fast Troops of Recruiting District I in Insterburg. Thus, a structure was created that allowed the replacement and later also the training in a uniform way and specific for the weapon.

On March 16, 1942, Lt. Col. von Olszewski informed General Staff Chief Halder of the composition and activity of the armored trains. On May 24, 1942, the General of the Fast Troops could already issue the "Temporary Guidelines for Structure and Action of Armored Railroad Trains" prepared by the staff officer of the armored railroad trains; we shall come back to it in detail. In 1943 a final edition of these guidelines was worked on, but it is not clear whether they were issued before the end of the war. No representative copy has been found anywhere, nor do any of the interviewed armored train commanders remember such guidelines.

Above all, though, in cooperation with In 6 of the AHA, which was responsible for the fast troops (the Group VI, responsible for the armored trains, was commanded by Lt. Col. Hans Albertz; his deputy was 1st Lt. Paul Obst), the plan for a standard armored train (Type BP 42) was drawn up. The In 6 proved therein to be considerably more conservative than the In 10. Not only was steam drive retained, but attempts were also made to take over various aspects (strong infantry crews from the earlier trains, unloadable tanks on carrier cars from the "Panzerzug 1941" concept of In 10, strengthened artillery weapons after Polish and Russian models) to create an all-purpose weapon that should be able to handle all imaginable demands (as so often, with the effect that this was in no way really emphatically the case). After the necessary steel for the production of armored trains could be obtained from a Ukrainian steel mill near Krivoy Rog (as can be learned from the application for the granting of a medal, this was accomplished by the staff officer of the armored trains), the OKH could order the manufacture of the first six armored trains of this uniform type on July 17, 1942, of which by the war's end a total of 24 (the second half of them of the improved Type BP 44) were contracted for. The later development of further armored rail vehicles (light and heavy scout trains, armored railcars) was also to be done in cooperation with the office of the Staff Officer of the Armored Trains with the General of the Fast Troops (later Commander of the Armored Railroad trains in the Ob.d.H.) with In 6 of the AHA, but this did not always work smoothly, since it appears that Lt. Col. Albertz was inclined to work alone, which made Colonel von Olszewski and his colleagues feel passed over, so that considerable friction often resulted.

Taking effect on January 25, 1943, the staff officer of the Armored Railroad Trains was promoted to Commander of the Armored Railroad Trains with the General of the Fast Troops. Only two months later (April 1, 1943), though, the "Fast Troops" service arm was dissolved and the "Armored Troops" created in its place, headed by the

Inspector General of the Armored Troops (Gen.Insp.d.Pz.Tr.), who was no longer—like the other service-arm generals—subordinate to the OKH, but directly to Hitler (Senior General Heinz Guderian, the legendary Panzergeneral, took over this office). The armored trains were assigned to the armored troops, to be sure, but their commander was not subordinate to their inspector general, but rather (formally) to the Supreme Commander of the Army (Hitler himself), meaning that he remained in an independent office under the Chief of the Army General Staff in the OKH (later they bore the correct designation, Commander of the Armored Railroad Trains with the Chief of the

The officer with the fur collar is Col. Ernest Bolbrinker, Chief of In 6; far left: Lt. Col. Hans Albertz, leader of Group VI (armored trains) in In 6; with monocle: Col. Hubertus Kewisch (staff officer to Commander of Armored Railroad Trains; in front of him: Major Ernst Naumann (Commander of Armored Train Replacement Battalion). Photo: H. Becker/W. Sawodny collection

The staff of the General of the Fast Troops (then Col. Cramer, seated in the middle) in the autumn of 1942 in Winniza; at right beside him is Col. von Olszewski; standing second from left Capt. Walter Nietzsch, Adjutant; third from right Lt. Franz Englberger, Technical Officer, both with the staff officer of the Armored Railroad Trains. Photo: F. Englberger/W. Sawodny collection

The staff of the commander of the Armored Railroad Trains with the Chief of the Army General Staff in September 1943 in front of the office building in Lötzen. From left to right: Lt. Dr. Oskar Stelzhammer (ordnance officer), Capt. Frank Drexler (former commander of PZ 62, later deputy commander and leader of training in the Armored Train Replacement Battalion), 1st Lt. Franz Englberger (technical officer), Col. Egon von Olszewski (commander), Col. Friedrich Becker (staff officer), and Capt. Bernd Oestermann (adjutant). Photo: W. Geipel/W. Sawodny collection

The staff officers with the Commander of the Armored Trains. From left to right: Lt.Col. Georg Dickhaeuser (March 20 to May 20, 1943), Col. Friedrich Becker (May 20, 1943, to November 30, 1943), Col. Hubertus Kewisch (December 1, 1943, to the closing of the office on March 31, 1945). Photos: Military Archives, Freiburg; H. Becker and W. Sawodny collection

Army General Staff). This meant a considerable rise to the level of an independent service-arm general, who manifested himself in the new service instructions as well as the personal expansion.

To the already existing officers' positions:

- Commander (unchanged, and for the whole period Col. von Olszewski)
- Adjutant (until January 1943 Capt. Nietzsch, then until June 1943 Capt. Herwig Schultze-Petzold, June 1943 to March 1944 Capt. Bernd Oestermann, March to May 1944 Capt. Helmut Walter, from June 1944 on Maj. Ludwig Ernst von Wedel)
- Technical Officer (unchanged and for the whole period 1st Lt. Franz Englberger)
- Ordnance (and Artillery) Officer (until March 1943 Lt. Gerhard Riewendt, March 1943 to June 1944 Lt. Dr. Oskar Stelzhammer, June 1944 to March 1945 1st Lt. Heinz Kranefuss)

there were now added:

- the Staff Officer (April to July 1943 Lt.Col. Georg Dickhäuser, September to November 1943 Col. Friedrich Becker, December 1943 to March 1945 Lt.Col, then Col. Hubertus Kewisch)
- as of June 1944 (to March 1945) Signal Officer 1st Lt. Hans-Joachim Heyden.

In April 1943 the office also included two NCOs, four men (including a chauffeur) and a woman staff helper; the personnel were much increased afterward.

According to service instructions, the Commander of the Armored Railroad Trains with the Army High Command (later the Chief of the Army General Staff) was the commander of all such units at the rank of a division commander (his staff officer held the rank of a regimental commander) and was to handle questions about the armored trains in the framework of the service instructions for weapon generals. At the same time, he was also at the disposal of the Inspector-General of the Armored Troops in these matters. In view of the specialties of this weapon (use of rails, quick change of location conditions, special action conditions), he had close contact with the command offices of the field army, to which the armored trains were tactically subordinated (their rights were not otherwise disturbed by their service subordination to the Commander of the Armored Railroad Trains) with the Army High Command (with whose agreement he was also to examine equipment, condition, and action of all other rail-securing vehicles, such as the line protection trains). These duties of the Commander of the Armored Railroad Trains with the Army High Command also extended to the units that were in the homeland war zone for refreshment or reorganization. This was unusual, for the units located there usually were subordinate to the Commander of the Replacement Army (BdE); only for the Inspector-General of the Armored Troops did the same exceptional regulation exist. For means of organization in the homeland war zone the following special agreements applied:

For personnel changes (such as the occupation of positions), the Commander of the Armored Railroad Trains was to send his proposals directly to In 6; they were examined by the AHA in mutual understanding.

Wishes for organizational revision, for use of finished products from captured supplies, etc., were to be expressed by the Commander via the Army General Staff to the Inspector General of the Armored Troops, who would pass them on, after checking them, to the Chief of Army Equipping and Commander of the Replacement Army.

The preparation and distribution of equipment for the armored trains was carried out by the AHA along with their commander, and equipment already prepared by the Armored Train Replacement Unit could be distributed by the Commander on his own responsibility.

The preparation of instructions, memos, and guidelines for the armored trains was done according to directives from the Inspector-General of the Armored Troops through the Commander's office.

Carrying out training for the armored trains was also done according to directives from the inspector General, but he was advised by the Commander.

This special position indicates the significance that was now given to the small special weapon (in the listing of the strength of the field army on October 1, 1943, with the armored trains having a total of 3740 men, and even later the total strength of these units could scarcely have gone much over this figure) that was considered obsolete and scarcely usable at the beginning of the war.

Active planning and development activity quickly arose in cooperation with In 6. In the spring of 1943 there was already work for armored rail cars armed with cannons—based on captured Russian vehicles, which in the first instance were themselves put into use for this purpose. For action in the Balkan area—involving the idea of In 10's "Panzerzug 1941" plans—light and heavy scout trains made up of motor-driven individual vehicles were designed, for which the OKH gave contracts for four of the first and ten of the second category in August and September 1943. Also in September 1943, twelve regular armored trains (BP 42, later developed further into Type BP 44) were ordered new. For 1944 such an astonishingly ambitious program developed that despite stretching, it could not by any means be accomplished before the war ended. Many developments (such as the tank-destroyer railcar, also the heavy scout trains in their full effectiveness) could not be built at all during the war.

The year 1944 also brought organizational changes. The frequent ignorance of the qualities of armored trains in subordinate command officers to whom the trains were assigned for action, which brought about problems and even losses, has already been mentioned above. This led to the fact that the armored trains in general remained subordinated to the armies. If their action took place within a level of a corps or division (a lower level was very exceptional), this ranking, as the war moved faster, consisted more and more of an assignment than a real subordination, meaning that the armored train commander achieved an ever-greater right to take part in planning the action and could turn directly to the superior offices when an arrangement did not seem purposeful to him. On the other hand, this high level of independence (consider that an armored train with its combination of infantry, artillery, armored removable parts, engineers, signal, medical, and railroad personnel and its supply train, which assured its supplying and made small overhauling and repair jobs possible, was an autonomous unit not exceeding a company's strength), in view of the relatively low rank of the leader (depending on the strength, usually a first lieutenant or captain; seldom did long-time commanders in this service reach the level of major, and a few lieutenants are even found at these positions) also concealed dangers. Less firm characters could easily be led to irregularities, even massive breaches of requirements, and in fact there were times when armored train commanders had to be replaced for such reasons, a few even being court-martialed.

To deal with these problems, armored train regimental staffs were set up for the tactical leadership of the trains at the beginning of 1944, with control over one commanded armored train and one armored command railcar equipped with radios. Belonging to the regimental staff, besides the regimental commander himself, the officers were an adjutant, plus the commander and technical leader of the command train. There was a radio troop, which—according to the task—operated high-performance equipment, tank-destroyer and A/A crews (for the planned equipment of two 7.5-cm antitank guns in armored turrets and two 2-cm A/A quads) and railroad technical personnel. It can be seen from a handwritten note that the armored train regiment was to have three battalions, each consisting of a BP 44 armored train, an armored heavy scout train, and an armored railcar. Assigned to the staff were, besides the command train, another train (light scout train) and a workshop train. The battalion's armored trains were to operate together, and here the pairwise action of two trains, urged since the end of World War I, for mutual cover and assistance was adopted. For its command, an appropriate number of armored train command positions were upgraded from K. (company leader) to B (battalion leader = captain or major), the material provided by the 1943-44 building program should have been enough for four such armored train regiments. They were to be assigned to army groups. The regimental commander thus also bore the title of "Commander of the Armored Trains with the Army Group (and its name)."

But the war's events led to a notable delay in the establishment of the armored train regiments, which had been planned for the

beginning of 1944, so the plan's numbers were not attained (the units were thus usually set up as armored train regimental battle groups) and the composition of the armored train types showed great variations. For example, all light and heavy scout trains were used in the Balkans. Pairwise use in battalions, though, was done regardless of the types. At first three armored train regiments were established:

- Armored Train Regiment No. 1 (Commander of the Armored Trains with Army Group F, Col. Friedrich Becker, Adjutant 1st Lt. Paul Roeser, as of November 1944 Capt. Ernst Seidel)
- Armored Train Regiment no. 2 (Lt.Col. Hans Georg von Türckheim zu Altdorf, Adjutant 1st Lt. Hans Berthold Lotze)
- Armored Train Regiment No. 3 (Lt.Col. Dr. Gerhard Günther, Adjutant 1st Lt. Günter Wydra).

But only Regimental Staff No. 1 (Command Train No. 1, under its commander, 1st Lt. Baron Grote, reached the staff only at the end of December 1944) could go into action at the right time in Croatia on February 1, 1944, and remained active there until the war ended (as of the end of March 1945 in Army Group E, which replaced Army Group F in that area). It was also the only one to which the workshop train (No. 1), as envisioned in the plans, could be delivered.— Regiment Staffs No. 2 and 3, whose commanders were called in March and April 1944, were planned for the eastern front. In April and May they undertook inspection trips, Lt.Col. von Türckheim with Armored Train 72B, in the Riga—Dünaburg–Polozk area (Army Group North and Wehrmacht Commander White Ruthenia), Lt.Col. Dr. Günther with Armored Train No. 72A to Army Group Center. At the beginning of June 1944 there was already an armored train battle group formed there under his command, which saw action in the Molodechno—Polozk area and later southeast of Minsk, but the staff was withdrawn already in the middle of the month.

Through the Russian summer offensive, the armored trains suffered such high losses that the final installation of the armored train regiments on the eastern front was delayed again. Regimental Staff No. 2 (Lt.Col. von Türckheim, now with Command Train No. 72A)

Colonel Friedrich Becker (center), Commander of Armored Trains with Army Group F (Armored Train Regiment 1) in February 1944; at left, Captain Heinz Becker (Cdr. PZ 65), at right Capt. Rudolf Jungke (Cdr. PZ 23; the train is in the background) Photo: H. Becker/W. Sawodny collection

Lt.Col. Hans Georg Baron von Türckheim zu Altdorf (Armored Train Regiment No. 2, second from right) on an inspection trip in the Polozk area in May 1944. Right: Capt. Hermann Hoppe, Cdr. PZ 67; center, in profile, with peaked cap and pistol holster, Capt. Richard Fischer, Cdr. PZ 26; far left, Lt. Wilhelm Sitzius, Cdr. Command Train 72B. Photo: W. Sitzius/W. Sawodny collection

Lt.Col. Dr. Gerhard Günther, Commannder of Armored Trains in Army Group Center (later North; Armored Train Regiment 3). He fell in combat with his armored train group in the Gotenhafen area on March 21, 1945. Photo: Military Archives, Freiburg

took up his position with Army Group A only at the end of November 1944, after the armored trains, formerly stationed in France, had been transferred into this area. When in January 1945, during the Russian offensive, almost all of this regiment's armored trains had been lost, he was transferred at the beginning of February 1945 to the Army Group Vistula to command the armored trains on the Oder front and in Pomerania (now with makeshift Command Train No. II, commanded by Lt. Georg Zartmann). Here he was able to move back through Nearer Pomerania and Mecklenburg with a battle group that still included four armored trains and several railcars in the second half of April 1945, and on May 2, 1945, he met American troops, to whom he surrendered.

In the Army Group Center, enough armored trains had assembled only at the end of October so that the Regimental Staff No. 3 (Lt. Col. Dr. Günther with Command train No. 72B) could go into action. At first an action area west and north of Warsaw was planned, but—following the pressure of events—he had to be transferred to East Prussia at once. Although they could largely avoid the Russian advances in January 1945 and reach Far Pomerania safely, the staff, with the four remaining armored trains (including the command train), was cut off from the ordered transfer trip to the Army Group Center in the Bautzen area by the Russian breakthrough to the Baltic Sea between Köslin and Schlawe in March; they were thrown back to the east, and the entire group collapsed in the Gotenhafen area toward the end of the month.

Shortly before the war ended, Regimental Staff No. 3 was reestablished (under Major Ernst Naumann, formerly the commander of the Armored Train Replacement and Training Battalion) for the remaining armored trains (makeshift Command Train No. III, 1st Lt. Messer) in what remained of Army Group Center's area (parts of the Sudetenland and the Protectorate of Bohemia and Moravia), but in view of the prevailing chaotic conditions it could not have achieved rational activity.

With Army Group South in Hungary, the number of armored trains remained far below the number needed for such a command

position, so that setting up a unit was never taken into consideration. The same was true in all other theaters of war in which armored trains were present—usually just one, if any at all (France, Italy).

Although attempts were obviously made until the war's end to improve the tactical command of the armored trains in such ways, the central office of the Commander of the Armored Trains with the Chief of the Army General Staff was apparently seen as less and less important. The strongly increasing losses of armored trains in 1944 (until the end of 1943, there had been scarcely any to report), which had nourished the doubt in the value of these weapons, had surely been the major factor. In August 1944, still rated at the second-highest level of urgency (equal to the Panther and Tiger tanks), the further growth of the weapon was strongly limited after an overview of their meager effectiveness and heavy losses during the summer months. Only in the last three months of the war could a new, almost hectic expansion be made, probably because, in view of the shortage of fuel, armored trains offered a last possibility of making weapon systems mobile.

It appears, though, that the Commander, Colonel von Olszewski, was regarded with growing mistrust. An indication of this is that, despite appropriate service positions, he never was promoted to the rank of general, and the request to grant him the German Cross in silver was held back from the end of 1944 to his departure from service in April 1945. This mistrust by those in power also may have been caused by the dubious role he played in the revolt of July 20, 1944. He was well acquainted with its central figure, Colonel Count von Stauffenberg, and probably knew about the plans. Although the position of the Commander of the Armored Trains itself had been moved back to Potsdam shortly before (significantly, it remained there when the new Chief of the General Staff, Guderian, assembled the OKH in Mauerwald again, after it had been made known that Hitler would never leave his Wolf's Den headquarters), both parts of PZ 72 were left near the Führer's headquarters. In the planned plot he was supposed to neutralize the command trains of Himmler and Göring that were there. After the failed assassination he was immediately ordered to guard the Wolf's Den. After this failure Col. von Olszewski was also arrested by the Gestapo and tried, but one could obviously prove nothing concrete against him, for he was released and could return to his position. But doubts as to his reliability may have remained.

So on December 7, 1944, the office of the Commander of the Armored Trains was subordinated to the Inspector General of the Armored Trains and its staff was reduced (among others, the position of staff officer was cut, along with the four remaining officers: Commander Colonel von Olszewski, Adjutant Major von Wedel, Ordnance 1st Lt. Kranefuss, and Technical Officer 1st Lt. Englberger, there were five writers and sketchers, one ordnance helper, and six staff helpers present). In the war diary of the organization department of the Army General Staff it says: "The conduct of armored trains in action and the experience thus gained, that the armored train is only capable of limited use and therefore will no longer be built because of the high consumption of material indicates that the armored trains as such will shortly die out."

The new service instructions granted the Commander of the Armored Trains the authority of a division commander as the commanding officer of all armored trains, including those in the homeland war zone (only those undergoing repairs or refreshing were under the Inspector of the Armored Troops or In 6). He was to supervise the action, condition, and training of the armored train crews by inspection trips or other personal contact, as well as by asking the command offices whose armored trains were subordinated, and the responsible offices of the Army General Staff. He was also to evaluate the war experiences in view of improving combat activity, armament, organization, and training of the armored trains. He was to advise the Inspector General of the Armored troops on all matters of action, organization, and training that concerned the armored trains, and on the latter's instruction, to work on such problems and those of their equipment, structure, and armament, and to prepare all applicable instructions, memos, etc. With the Inspector of the

Armored Troops (to whom the Replacement and Training Battalion was subordinate) and the In 6 he was, within the guidelines set by the Inspector General, to issue directives for carrying out the training, formation of fully capable replacements, new establishments, and refreshing of armored trains and the distribution of already prepared new equipment.

On April 1, 1945, the office of Commander of the Armored Trains with the Inspector General of the Armored Troops was completely dissolved and replaced by a small "Armored Trains" advisory board that included only the following personnel:

– Advisor: Major von Wedel
– Ordnance Officer: 1st Lt. Kranefuss
– Technical Officer: 1st Lt. Englberger
– 3 secretaries (one a first sergeant, one a sketcher)
– 2 female staff helpers

Its extent was cut back more or less to those who were on hand at the appointment of the Staff Officer of the Armored Railroad Trains with the General of the Fast Troops in August 1941. Colonel von Olszewski, who had functioned as the staff officer and then the Commander of the Armored Trains, was released from this office.

In addition, the office had been moved southward from Potsdam at the end of January 1945 and had been given quarters at the Strub near Berchtesgaden. As April turned to May 1945, they moved to Kufstein, in the direction of the Tyrol, and Major von Wedel became the combat commander there. On 4 May they surrendered to the Americans there after they had destroyed all the possessions of the office.

The Armored Train Replacement and Training Battalion

As one of the first measures taken after the office of Staff Officer of the Armored Trains with the General of the Fast Troops was created, the establishment of its own Replacement Battalion for Armored Railroad Trains took place on April 1, 1942. It was located on the grounds of the former Polish artillery shooting range at Rembertow, some 6 km from Praga, the eastern suburb of Warsaw, in a triangle of main railroad lines stretching from Warsaw via Malkinia to Bialystok and via Siedlce to Brest-Litovsk at a distance of some 6.5 km from the Zielonka—Rembertow line extending some 8.5 km eastward (total area ca. 55 sq,km). The Armored Train Replacement Battalion was settled in the barracks area of Rembertow at the southwest corner of the firing range, where the Garrison Administration and the Field NCO School of the Fast Troops were also located. The armored trains could be placed on several spur lines, which had probably been laid in Polish days in the space between the two tracks of the Rembertow—Zielonka line, which branched off from the two-track main line to Siedlce at the eastern end of the Rembertow depot without a crossing. Another track that led directly to the firing range just a little to the east served as the firing track for the armored trains. The extensive troop firing range also had all the other facilities, such as rifle ranges and a hand-grenade practice range for infantry training; a training area for engineers and a driving school for armored vehicles were also laid out near the Rembertow base. Supplies of shells came from a large ammunition store very close by—at the southwest edge of the town of Rembertow.

The Armored Train Replacement Battalion consisted at first of the staff (the commander, Ernst Naumann, was being promoted to Major; he was formerly commander of PZ 10; the adjutant was 1st Lt. Hermann Imm, the paymaster Eberhard Steinweg) and two companies under the command of 1st Lt. Max Warda (who was already replaced in the summer of 1942 by Captain Eduard Seele) and Captain Rudolf Winterberg (Seele and Winterberg had also formerly

Major Ludwig Ernst von Wedel, last Adjutant to the commander of the Armored Trains by the chief of the Army General Staff or Inspector general of the Armored Troops, took over the office on April 1, 1945, for the last five weeks of the year, after it had been cut down to an advisory board by the named Inspector General. Photo: F. Englberger/W. Sawodny collection

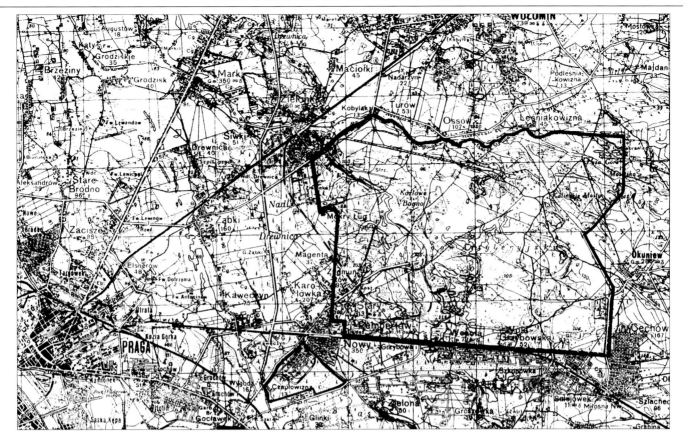

Above: Map of the troop training camp east of Warsaw (at the left edge of the map is Praga, the suburb on the east bank of the Vistula) between the Praga—Wolomin—Malkina and Praga—Rembertow—Siedlce lines. Southwest of Nowy Rembertow, the large ammunition factory is indicated.

Below: Southwestern quarter of the Rembertow training camp with the barracks area. The lines stretching northeastward from Rembertow into the firing range are the shooting tracks for the armored trains, of which the curved southern line was built only in 1943. The parking area for the armored trains, the so-called Naumann Depot, was between the two branches which, leading along the northeastern edge of the camp, joined to form the line to Zielonka. As of autumn 1943 the Wesola camp was also used by the enlarged Armored Train Replacement Battalion. Facsimiles: W. Sawodny collection

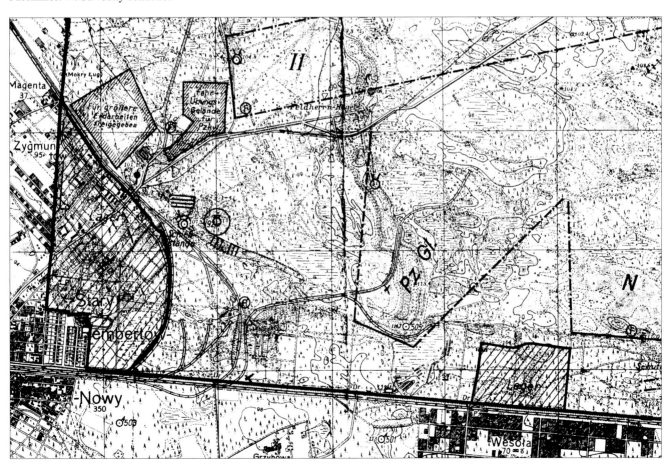

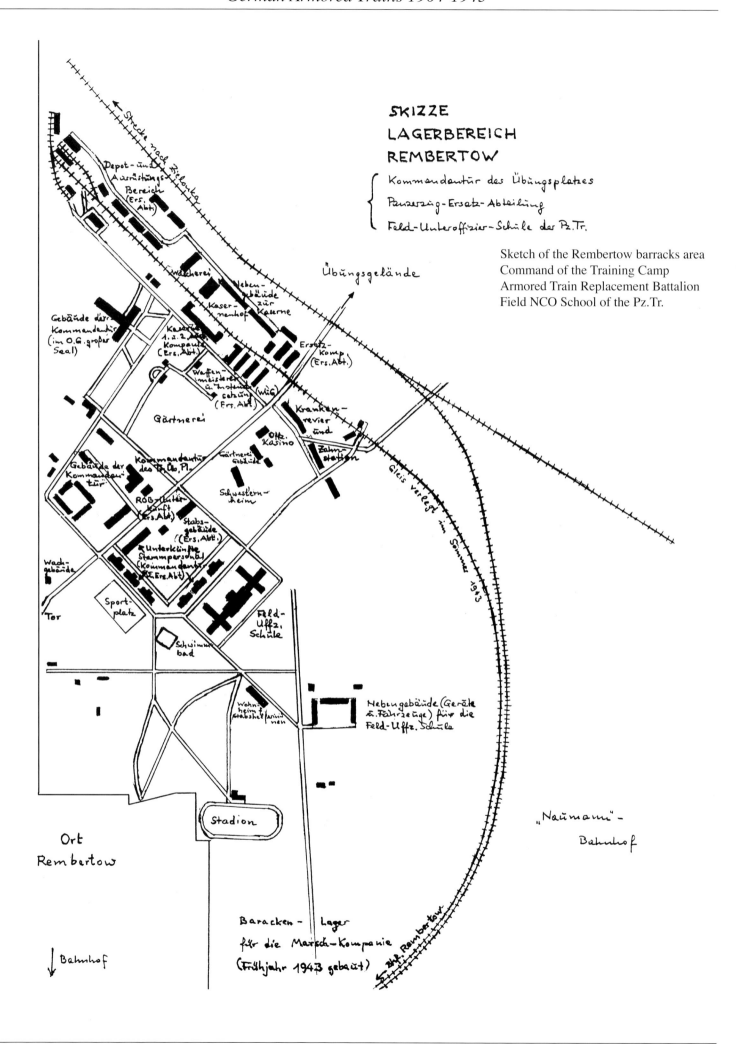

SKIZZE
LAGERBEREICH
REMBERTOW

Kommandantur des Übungsplatzes
Panzerzug-Ersatz-Abteilung
Feld-Unteroffizier-Schule der Pz.Tr.

Sketch of the Rembertow barracks area
Command of the Training Camp
Armored Train Replacement Battalion
Field NCO School of the Pz.Tr.

Strecke nach Beloka

Depot- und Ausrüstungs- Bereich (Ers. Abt.)

Übungsgelände

Wäscherei

Neben- gebäude zur Kaserne

Kaser- nenhof

Gebäude der Kommandantur (im O.G. großer Saal)

Kaserne 1. u. 2. Kompanie (Ers.Abt.)

Ersatz- Komp. (Ers. Abt.)

Waffen- meisterei u. Instand- setzung (WiG) (Ers. Abt.)

Gärtnerei

Kranken- revier und

Offz. Kasino

Zahn- station

Gleis verlegt im Sommer 1943

Gebäude der Kommandan- tür

Kommandantur des Tr.Üb.Pl.

Gärtnerei Gebäude

ROB-Unter- kunft (Ers.Abt.)

Schwestern- heim

Stabs- gebäude (Ers.Abt.)

Unterkünfte Stammpersonal (Kommandantur u. Ers.Abt.)

Wach- gebäude

Sport- platz

Feld- Uffz. Schule

Tor

Schwimm- bad

Wohn- heim Stabshelferinnen

Nebengebäude (Geräte u. Fahrzeuge) für die Feld-Uffz. Schule

"Naumann"- Bahnhof

Ort Rembertow

Stadion

Bahnhof

Baracken - Lager für die Marsch-Kompanie (Frühjahr 1943 gebaut)

Bhf. Rembertow

been commanders of armored trains). Soon after the establishment, 1st Lt. Hermann Hoppe seems to have joined as engineer officer. The unit was subordinated to the commander of the Fast Troops (later the Armored Troops) of Recruiting District I in Insterburg (1943-44 Colonel Busse). Thus, at first the replacement framework for the armored trains was unified in competent hands. On October 1, 1942, a training battalion for armored trains was added at the same site. The commander was Captain Werner Franke; the two existing replacement companies were assigned to it as the 1st and 2nd training companies; the replacement battalion was to have a newly created cadre and a replacement and a recuperation company, but this measure never seems to have been fully carried out. The replacement company was set up at once under 1st Lt. Rudolf Oppenhorst. A cadre company can be documented only shortly before the reorganization of March 28, 1943; the recuperating men never formed more than a platoon within the replacement company. On March 10, 1943, a marching company was established in the Replacement Battalion; its commander was 1st Lt. (later Capt.) Rudolf Opitz, formerly commander of PZ 3.

On March 28, 1943, the staffs and the replacement and the training battalions were combined under the name "Armored Railroad Train Replacement Battalion." Major Naumann remained their commander. Captain Franke of the Training Battalion became his deputy as Ia and continued to remain responsible for questions of training (in October 1943 he was replaced by Captain Frank Drexler). Ib was 1st Lt. Hans Feuerlein, Adjutant (simultaneously IIa) was 1st Lt. Willi Leggewie, soon replaced in June 1943 by 1st Lt. Dr. Hans Klaus Hoecker. The battalion doctor was Dr. Jerg, the staff commissariat officer was Erwin Trzaska. The Replacement Company was taken over by 1st Lt. Grabke, who also had the duties of the Ic (after the attempt on Hitler's life on June 20, 1944, he also became the NS Command Officer of the Replacement Battalion). The 1st Training Company was now renamed the 1st (Inf.) Company (Chief: 1st Lt. Johannes Crasselt), and handled the training of the infantrymen, engineers, and radiomen. The second was now the 2nd (Heavy) Company (Chief: 1st Lt. Gustav Gelhaar) and was responsible for

the artillery training (cannons, A/A guns, later also tank destroyers) and those on the tanks. The composition of the armored train crews from the trained personnel took place in the March Company, still under the command of 1st Lt. Opitz. On September 1, 1943, a 2nd March Company was set up, at first led by Captain Albert Hollstein, but in November of that year he took over the command of PZ 30 (his successor is presently unknown).—For the training of the crews there was a training armored train on hand since the spring of 1943.

The entrance to the Rembertow camp, at which the Armored Railroad Train Replacement Battalion was located from April 1, 1942, to July 23, 1944. Photo: H. Stallknecht Photos/W. Sawodny collection

A look from the southeast at the northern part of the Rembertow camp. The line cutting diagonally through the picture is the Rembertow—Zielonka rail line; to the right of it is the training ground. The flat two story building in the center housed the two training companies of the Armored Train Replacement Battalion. The big building behind it belonged to the command of the training camp. Behind the trees at the left are the buildings of the sick bay. Photo: H. Jaeger/W. Sawodny collection

The courtyard of the training company's barracks building (east wing at the right edge of the photo; 2nd Heavy Company), looking east toward the armory (right behind the barracks) and other barracks for weapons and equipment. Opposite the barracks (left edge) are garages for vehicles. A swearing-in ceremony is just taking place in the courtyard; weapons used by the armored trains are on display. The railroad line over the yard (later approximately to follow the middle ruts) has not yet been built. Photo: W. Sinning/W. Sawodny collection

After the track was laid an armored train was driven onto it for such occasions (here Type BP 42, probably the practice train), as seen in this photo taken on October 13, 1943. It shows the west wing of the building in which the 1st (Infantry) Company was housed. Photo: K. Herbst/W. M. Koehler collection

While the training company's barracks building was probably built in the 1930s, many buildings at the Rembertow camp were older. Since a photo of the staff building of the Armored Train Replacement Company has not been found here is an example, the central part of the building in which the Field NCO School, which also included an armored train company, was located. Photo: W. Mauss/W. Sawodny collection

After the March Company was set up in the spring of 1943 barracks were built for it in the southern part of the camp, on the site of a former airfield. Photo: J. Kraemer/W. Sawodny collection

Besides the training and assigning of crews for the armored trains, the Replacement Battalion was to arrange for their equipping with all kinds of mobile material, from machine guns to bullets, from shear telescopes to screwdrivers. The vehicles (tanks, armored scout cars, trucks, and cars) were also assigned to the armored trains here. And all of this applied not only to new formations, for supplying to fill losses of materials on the front also operated through the Replacement Battalion. If damaged armored trains came back from the front minor repairs could be made at the OAW Pruszkow, where the Replacement Battalion had an extension site. For major repairs or rebuildings they were sent to appropriate workshops, mostly railroad repair works.

The enlargement of the Replacement Battalion resulted in constant expansion work at the Rembertow camp. The parking tracks for the armored trains (the so-called "Naumann" Depot) were expanded, equipped with ramps and finally equipped in part with wooden garages of the uniform field railroad type at their ends. Parallel to the connecting line to Zielonka, which formed the eastern boundary of the barracks area, one line was built into this area itself, with several parking lines at the end to serve the storehouse

of the Replacement Battalion there. In the southern part of the troop training area of the camp—branching off from the first—a second curved firing track was built. As the possibilities of housing were exhausted too, the barracks area was expanded to the southeast to the Warsaw—Siedlce line, where the March Company was situated. In the autumn of 1943 another barracks compound was built three kilometers to the east, in Wesola, at the southern edge of the training camp, for the newly established second March Company. There the crews were given their final training after their armored trains arrived, before the trains then went into action.—Along with the many types of training in Rembertow itself, trips were made to Palmnicken on the Baltic Sea for sharpshooting, and partisan fighting under realistic conditions could be practiced in the extensive wooded areas of White Ruthenia. The base for them was the Slobodka camp, 5 kilometers north of the Linovo depot on the Brest-Litovsk—Baranovici line, to which it had a rail connection.

But soon such possibilities were to take place much closer to Rembertow.

Before this is examined, though, another type of action in which members of the Armored Train Replacement Battalion were involved

A line protection train stands at Rembertow in the summer of 1942. Tank carriers and infantry cars with non-mobile 38(t) tanks from the former PZ 27 set on them; in back a car of the Austro-Hungarian type from the Polish PP "Pierwszy Marszalek," a flat car with a T 34 tank on it and a Soviet-type BP 35 gun car. Photo: G. Gayk/W. Sawodny collection

Armored Train PZ 42 (without locomotive) in the area of the Naumann Depot in Rembertow. Photo: Dr. H. K. Hoecker/W. Sawodny collection

The finished train shed with armored train cars in May 1944. Photo: R. Jendrossek/W. Sawodny collection

must be mentioned. After it became known among the Jews of the Warsaw Ghetto that their transports went to the liquidation camps, the remaining ones began to oppose such measures at the beginning of 1943. Therefore, the SS decided that the ghetto, still holding some 60,000 people, was to be liquidated by force beginning on April 19, 1943. The SS units chosen to do it, under Brigade Leader Jürgen Stroop, were given an engineer command from the Armored Train Replacement Battalion, which grew from a strength of two officers and 16 men to two officers and 42 men by the beginning of May (as of 6 May engineers and another Army unit, with a final strength of two officers and 37 men, were added). At first the engineers took part in putting down nests of resistance with explosives and flamethrowers. In the second phase, after the above-ground buildings had been systematically burned down and the Jewish fighters and civilians had been forced into the underground bunkers that had been prepared long before, their hour struck. Again and again, the wasteland of ghetto rubble was combed through by the SS to locate these bunkers, which succeeded bit by bit by following people going in or out,

by using listening devices and bloodhounds, and often enough by information from already captured Jews, who betrayed the hiding places out of fear or under torture. Of course attempts were made to open the bunkers and bring the people out, often by drilling holes through which lit fog bombs were thrown into the chambers, but no risk was taken. If such a risk was in sight, the engineers had to blow up the bunkers with their inhabitants inside, not just after emptying them. Stroop himself stressed again and again in his reports what high losses occurred, and in his final report he estimated the number of Jews who died there (of course, including those who died in the fires) at 5000 to 6000, a figure that is probably not too high when one considers that in many of the 631 blown up bunkers there were 200 to 300 people (others had already been abandoned before the Germans found them). He also praised the readiness to cooperate and the "joy in action" of the engineers in this operation, which ended on 16 May. Only a very few Jews escaped this inferno through the canalization and joined the Polish resistance movement, which had established itself in the hard-to-reach swampy woodlands along the Bug.

A Type BP 42 armored train turns from the firing track to the (electrified) Brest-Litovsk-Warsaw main line in the direction of Rembertow. Photo: K. H. Knapp/W. Sawodny collection

Below: A Type BP 42 armored train is seen while firing from the firing track at Rembertow. Photo: H. Bruntsch/W. Sawodny collection

This movement now became more and more active, and also carried out attacks on the Warsaw—Bialystok railroad line that ran by to the south, as well as the lines that branched off toward East Prussia in Tluszcz and Malkinia. Now securing runs on these lines that ran out from Rembertow, and action against partisans in the area were made by the Replacement Battalion. The partisan danger came nearer and nearer to Rembertow itself. On September 13, 1943, partisans had to be driven out of Zielonka, and on 8 October the situation in and around Warsaw became so precarious that the training activities were interrupted and the whole Replacement Battalion was placed under alarm status. In the fighting against partisans in Rembertow even a first lieutenant of the unit was lost. New and extensive fighting against partisans took place in the Praga—Rembertow—Zielonka triangle from January 2 to 18, 1944. The 2nd Company, which met a large partisan unit near Drewnica (south of Zielonka) on 5 January, had two dead and five wounded to report from the battle that ensued. Finally, the Replacement Battalion had to set up a place to stay overnight in Warsaw, so that the Rembertow men on short leave no longer had to travel the dangerous return route.

According to the ambitious expansion program for the armored trains in 1944, a second increase in the Replacement Battalion took place in the second quarter of the year. From April to June four additional training companies were set up. Of the company chiefs, 1st Lt. Helmut Röhm (also tank officer of the battalion), 1st Lt. Messer, and 1st Lt. Joachim Schönberg are known. In March 1944 the place of Captain Drexler as the major in the staff (also Ia and deputy commander) was taken by Heinz Dieter Becker, and the now-separated work of the Id—as well as ordnance officer—by 1st Lt. Horst Creutzburg. The Adjutant (and IIa) was now Captain Helmut Fischer. Around this time Captains Dieter Segel (motor vehicle expert) and Erwin Jähn (legal officer) were active in the staff. An officer list of July 12, 1944, includes, besides the two majors (Naumann and Becker), eleven captains and 28 first and 54 second lieutenants. Not

only were personnel reserves for new units trained as NCOs and men, but also veteran crews who came back to the Replacement Battalion more and more often on account of the strongly increasing losses of armored trains in 1944, to wait for a new train to be issued to them. The armored train crews were regarded as special troops that were to be returned to their units as quickly as possible, So in general—and until the war ended–they avoided the "hero claw," the reception staffs that gathered all available soldiers together in critical situations and sent them to the front as alarm units to fill holes there.

Meanwhile, the Replacement Battalion set up its own ROB (Reserve Officer Applicant) training, led at first by 1st Lt. Wilhelm Mauss and from the autumn of 1944 by Captain Hermann Hoppe. In September 1942 a training company for armored trains had been set up in the Field NCO School of the Fast Troops (later Armored Troops), which was housed in the same barracks area in Rembertow as the Armored Railroad Train Replacement Battalion. There the new subordinate commanders for these units were trained. The company leaders were Captain Paul Schüttke (Sept. 1942-May 1943), 1st Lt. Rolf Lorscheidt (May-December 1943), 1st Lt. Herbert Haschick (January-May 1944), and Captain Helmut Walter (June 1944-May 1945).

When the Soviet troops crossed the Bug south of Brest-Litovsk near Vlodava and Luboml on July 18, 1944, in the last phase of their summer offensive and, turning northward, overran the area between the Bug and Vistula, they also approached Rembertow dangerously. The Armored Train Replacement Battalion was at first to be thrown in for defensive fighting on the Vistula front south of Warsaw, and was alarmed for this early in the morning of July 23, 1944. After they had set out on the march the counter-order came two days later. The Replacement Battalion vacated Rembertow, Wesola, and Pruszkow and moved to Milowitz, 4 km northeast of Lissa on the Elbe (the transports passed safely through Warsaw, where the uprising of the Polish underground army broke loose a little later). The troop training camp there had been the base of the Czech armored trains before 1939. Since Milowitz was not big enough to house them, the barracks for the almost ready-to-march armored trains—as before in Wesola—was set up in Neuenburg on the Elbe (12 km east of Milowitz). The Armored Train Replacement Battalion was subordinated now to the commander of the Armored Troops (Colonel von den Decken) in Recruiting District IV.

At the beginning of September 1944 a new reorganization took place. The battalion (still led by Major Naumann and his staff) was now called the Armored Train Replacement and Training Battalion. The Replacement Company became the Staff Company, while the 1st (Infantry) and 2nd (Heavy) Company were now the 1st (light) and 2nd (heavy) Armored Train Training Companies. Along with them, the four training companies set up in Rembertow shortly before and the two march companies remained at first. In the process of reducing the armored train program, though, early in October 1944 two of the training companies and one march company were disbanded. As for the replacements in the command positions (First Lieutenants Crasselt, Gelhaar, and Messer, for example, received armored train commands) insufficient information is available.

The Commander of the Armored Train Replacement Battalion, Major Ernst Naumann. Photo: H. Becker/W. Sawodny collection

First Lieutenant Creutzburg took over the Staff Company (his successor as Ordnance Officer and Id was a Lt. Kürken), 1st Lt. Röhm took the 2nd Heavy Training Company, and 1st Lt. Johl the 4th Training Company. 1st Lt. Helmut Döhring was named as another company chief. Despite that, the Armored Train Replacement and Training Battalion still had a large surplus of personnel, including officers. Only in the last weeks of the war did Milowitz begin to empty, when everything that had wheels and could carry weapons was gathered to be used—sometimes in improvised form—as armored trains, and when the rigorous Commander of Army Group Center, Field Marshal Schoerner, ruthlessly combed out the backline services—many members of the Armored Train Replacement and Training Battalion had to go to the front, generally as tank destroyers. Major Naumann too, the commander of the Replacement Battalion since its establishment, left Milowitz with an armored train battle group at the beginning of May. His deputy, Major Becker, took his place but fell into the hands of Czech rebels on a scouting trip shortly before the surrender. After the surrender the members of the Battalion, like almost all other German troops in the area, tried to move southwestward and reach the U.S. lines, but were knowingly left for the Russians by the Americans.

The Armored Train Training Company of the Field NCO School of the Armored Troops in Rembertow was also moved with the school at the end of July 1944 to Wischau near Brno, and at the end of March 1945 to Wildflecken, where it was assigned to the 2nd Armored Division (Armored Grenadier Regiment 304) and in April 1945 carried on retreat fighting against American troops from the Rhoen into the Fichtelgebirge before it was compelled to surrender.

From August 1944 on the Armored Train Replacement Battalion was located in barracks at Milowitz. Photo: Dr. H. K. Hocker/W. Sawodny collection

Below: A map of the area around Milowitz. The Lissa-Milowitz line was used only for military purposes. Since the space at Milowitz was very limited, the place for the final equipping of the trains and the march company was located in Neuenburg. Reproduction: W. Sawodny collection

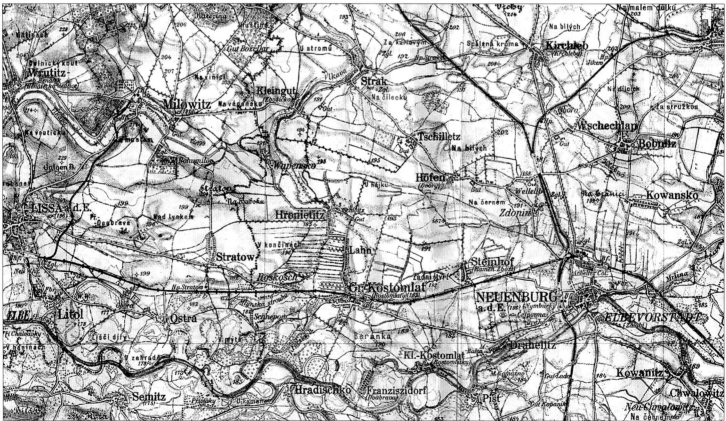

Construction History

1938-39: Rail Protection Trains

In 1937 the OKH had decided to depart from the earlier Reichswehr planning and not build any new armored trains, since the value of these weapons, which seemed obsolete in view of the development of tanks and aircraft—especially with the high amount of work and the considerable cost—was doubtful. Instead, it was considered sufficient to use some of the existing rail protection trains of the German

e seen in general as insufficient. Only
erg RBD stationed in Insterburg or
d the Munich protection train—were
r (in all cases, steel plates behind the
l met the set standards, and in 1937
General Command No. I (the two
Transportation of the Wehrmacht (the
eeded.

the skepticism about their usefulness,
ave armored trains, it was decided to
but—although less well equipped—
from General Command III (Berlin),
were to be put into service. All the
to set up armored trains—besides
Königsberg), VII (Munich), and VIII
ail protection trains in question, and
ns for their equipping and tell what

1938, and with partial consideration
r of all seven rail protection trains as
led for:

o. III. A.K., Berlin): rail
East from Frankfurt on the Oder.

o. IV. A.K., Dresden)—rail
Stettin, probably in place of
ich did not meet the requirements.

o. VII. A.K., Munich)—rail
Munich.

o. VIII. A.K., Breslau)—one
BD Breslau.

o. IX. A.K., Kassel)—rail
Nürnberg from Aschaffenburg;
ne of Gen.Kdo. No. IX, but the
aken for a less suitable one of

o. I. A.K., Königsberg)—rail
Königsberg from Insterburg.

o. I. A.K., Königsberg)—rail
Königsberg from Allenstein.

lso assigned the only remaining
1 (RBD Königsberg) as Armored

tion trains, equipped only for infantry,
control cars of six closed, armored
armament of artillery was wanted.
ere planned as weapons carriers, and
were to be placed at the outsides of both halves of the train—directly after the control cars, so as to have effect in the direction of travel as

well. The equipment and the formation of this added armament varied very much, though—as did the original cars themselves—among the individual trains. The Munich train already had two gun cars when it was taken over as an armored train (presumably built in 1937, when its use by the Wehrmacht was considered, but possibly earlier). They had a fully armored closed body, even with a limited-traverse turret, but were not fitted with guns, so that the Gen.Kdo. VII now had to come up with appropriate (7.7 cm F.K. 16) weapons.—Gen.Kdo. No. 1 equipped its armored trains (No. 6 and 7) with two O-cars each, with a gun on a turntable on a raised platform in the middle, but open (thus firing over the bench). The building of these cars seems to have begun only after the trains were taken over as armored trains, for the Insterburg train—although used in the Polish campaign—ran as a railroad repair train until October 3, 1939 (presumably without the gun cars); only as of the 26th of that month did it become PZ 6.—The other four armored trains were to have 3.7-cm Pak 35/36 and 7.5-cm I.G. 18 guns, and at first they were to be loaded onto stake cars as wheeled mounts. In PZ 4 (Gen.Kdo. No. VIII), special cars were then built with armored bodies, while the three trains added in 1938 (no. 1, 2, and 5) at first were given no guns at all; they remained in the condition of their rail protection days. The other armament of all the trains consisted primarily of old water-cooled heavy MG 08, likewise taken over from rail protection, their numbers varying between 6 and 16, and some light MG 08/15. There were also just four MG 34 per train installed on twin mounts for A/A use, after the originally planned equipping with 2-cm A/A guns was called off. There were also handguns for the combat crews.

While Armored Trains No. 3, 4, 6, and 7, intended for combat action and equipped with guns, carried permanent crews, for Armored Trains 1, 2, and 5, only the commanders were designated; their crews would be taken from the troops only in case of need. Accordingly, these three armored trains were not intended for combat action, but only for securing tasks behind the front.

It is of particular interest that a six-wheeled armored scout car (Sd.Kfz. 231) belonging to the police was assigned to PZ 3 as a reconnaissance vehicle as early as 1938. This scout car, armed with two MG (not the standard 2-cm gun) and carrying a five-man crew, could run both on the road and—since it was fitted with lowerable rail rollers—on the railroad. It was thus a forerunner of the later Panhard scout car, on which the road-to-rail change was made by changing wheels. This scout car was obviously a single example and was taken out of service in 1940-41 (possibly after being damaged in Holland).—Other armored trains (documented for No. 1 and 7)—in the spring of 1940 at the latest—had received MG-armed Skoda armored railcars captured from the Czechs and Polish as reconnaissance vehicles. Whether they were provided—as was urged by the K.St.N. in 1942—for all armored trains at the time is questionable.

Armored Trains No. 1 to 7, despite their same basic conception, each had an individual look, which could be changed by rebuilding and reequipping during the course of the war in those with a long life. Of the changes that could not be recognized externally, the notable ones were the replacement of the MG 08 by the Type 34 (1940-41) and the improvement and strengthening of the armor, especially on the trains that had been badly conceived in this respect, No. 1 and 2

(PZ 5 had been dropped already), which also took place before the Russian campaign began, but later changes of this type in all the trains are not ruled out.

On the very first day of the war, September 1, 1939, PZ 3 was badly damaged at Konitz. Provisional repairs at RAW Schneidemühl were followed by more basic work at the Schichau shipyard in Danzig. In particular, the gun cars were rebuilt. The armor, particularly the front parts, was strengthened. That of the gun turrets was also improved, although their turning mechanism was put out of order. Thus, the newly installed guns (7.5 cm F.K. 96 new type) only had a very limited field of fire to the front.

After its action in Holland on May 10, 1940, PZ 3 went to the car improvement works in Halberstadt, where the gun car was rebuilt again. It was now fitted with a ten-sided turning turret open at the top (a forerunner of the closed type used on the standard BP 42 armored train) on a firm armored base, in which an experimental gun made by Rheinmetall and planned for self-propelled mounts, a 7.5-cm L/41 cannon with a muzzle brake (forerunner of the Pak 40), was installed. A new observation stand and a platform for the 2-cm A/A gun were also added. To carry the increased axle pressure (presumably the armor of the entire car had been improved) the car was fitted with a third axle in the middle.

In the attack on Holland on May 10, 1940, Armored Trains No. 1 and 5 had been seriously damaged, the former by running onto a block and being derailed, the latter by artillery fire. PZ 1, its front half including the locomotive being unusable, was completed by the armored locomotive and still intact or reparable cars from PZ 5, which was dissolved, but also received an added G-car with brake cabin built into an armored car.

In the winter of 1940-41, all the armored trains were reequipped for the planned Russian campaign. Thus, Armored Trains 1 and 2 now received gun cars, in addition to heavier armor. While PZ 2 was equipped with the Czech cars of the out-of-service PZ 25 with their 7.5-cm Skoda cannons (there was, of course, only one gun turret per car; the second was removed and replaced with a platform holding a 2-cm A/A 38 gun), two flatcars fitted with low armor all around were added to PZ 1, along with a front-mounted 2-cm A/A and a 4.7-cm Böhler-Siderius M 35 infantry gun (Pak) in a turning mount with all-around armor. At the same time, the armament of PZ 4 was improved by replacing the 3.7-cm Pak with the same infantry gun.

Like Armored Trains 1-3, the other trains still in service were also fitted, in the course of this reequipping, with two 2-cm single A/A 38 guns. In PZ 6 these were first mounted on low-sided cars that ran ahead of the gun cars; later—as in Armored Trains No. 4 and 7 from the start—they were mounted on the covered freight cars, which had formerly been armed with twin A/A machine guns, after appropriate platforms had been built.

Later too—often after damage—ever-smaller revisions, often not documented in detail, were made. In the winter of 1941-42 PZ 3 was given a new command system made by Telefunken, and in the spring of 1942 PZ 1 received a quick-braking system. From that time on the 2-cm single A/A guns were gradually replaced on the still-active armored trains by quads, and were given rail-going Panhard scout cars as reconnaissance vehicles.

In July 1942 PZ 6 was damaged. In the course of large-scale repairs at the Pruszkow OAW much rebuilding and refitting was done. The command cars were equipped with new command posts

and a more effective radio system, and two G-cars were fitted with A/A mounts. The other two cars of the former rail protection train and the gun cars with the open platforms were scrapped. In place of them, two captured Russian railcars of the same type, which were introduced by the Germans as individual Railcars No. 17-23, were set up as new gun cars, each with two turrets with 7.62-cm F.K. 295/1(r) guns. The rear one of these two cars at first bore a big German-made frame antenna. This suggests that it may have retained its motor and was planned for individual use separately from the train. But such uses scarcely seem to have happened, or the motors may have become unusable, for this antenna was later (in late autumn 1943?) removed at the Marburg RAW.

After being derailed and bombed in December 1942, PZ 1 was thoroughly renovated at the Königsberg RAW in the first half of 1943. From the old train there remained by pictorial proof only the armored locomotive and two A/A cars, which were rebuilt as command cars. Two flak cars with 2-cm quads, two gun cars built on Russian four-axle chassis and each carrying two German-made armored turrets, and two armored carrier cars probably left over from PZ 26 with Praga 38(t) tanks loaded on them, plus the control cars, completed the new PZ 1. This rebuilding corresponded—though in a somewhat different order—to the K.St.N. 1169x for the standard armored train.

Most of the other still-available armored trains of the 1-7 series were also rebuilt later according to this uniform plan. To do this they were taken out of service, usually after damage, at the following times:

- Armored Train No. 2: June 5, 1944
- Armored Train No. 3: July 15, 1943
- Armored Train No. 4: mid-November 1943
- Armored Train No. 7: end of January 1944.

For No. 3, 4, and 7—and probably also for No. 2—the rebuilding was carried out at the Königshütte shops (which then belonged to the Röchling steel works). While the new PZ 3 was ready for action in July 1944, PZ 4 was ready only in January 1945, PZ 7 at the beginning of May 1945, and work on PZ 2 was halted in November 1944.

For PZ 1, tank-destroyer cars were built—probably on their own initiative—in the winter of 1943-44, with turrets of captured T-34 tanks mounted on flatcars. This measure was imitated at first by other armored trains on the eastern front (documented for PZ 26 and 61), and was later (summer 1944) introduced for all the armored trains (the further-developed standard BP 44 type and later rebuildings)—though with turrets from German Panzer IV tanks.

Taking over complete rail protection trains with their six internally armored freight cars called from the start for numerous infantry crewmen for the first armored trains of the German Wehrmacht (No. 1-7), though their effect from the trains themselves was naturally limited. This is why their main method of use was envisioned as using the train as a protected means of transport and an armed backup for the infantry, which generally had to leave the train for their combat tasks (to be able to do this as unseen by the enemy as possible the cars had floor hatches, which were built into boxes between the axles, and through which the men could get out as close to the ground as possible, so as to swarm out from them and go into action. There was also another task, taken over from the rail protection trains, of securing the repair of damaged rail connections. For this, part of the infantry crew was also trained in track laying (at first the main building troop included one NCO and 15 men), and the needed materials were carried on the control cars. On the other hand, little value was placed at first on the artillery, as shown by their being equipped with few small caliber and often obsolete guns. The concept that typified the German armored trains in World War I was also maintained in the considerable length of the trains, which had at least ten cars, including the gun and control cars (while the considerably more heavily armed armored trains of the enemy in World War II—Poland and the USSR—had at most half as many cars). If one adds the sometimes insufficient armor,

it is understandable that they had little success in offensive action in 1939-40. It is all the more surprising that these early armored trains—if not forced by damage to be rebuilt sooner, as were No. 1, 3, and 6—were, though modified often until 1943-44, essentially kept in their original composition. Their main task in the east as of 1941, of course, was the securing of back line rail connections from steadily increasing partisan activity, against which their equipment was sufficient, but even PZ 7, which was drawn more and more into the actual combat action in the southern sector of the eastern front, was able to survive until January 1944.

PZ 1 consisted in 1938-39, as in its rail-protection days, of five armored passenger cars and only one freight car (behind the locomotive). Photo: K. Fliegner/W. Sawodny collection

After being damaged in Holland on May 10, 1940, PZ 1 received the intact cars of PZ 5 for its front half. It was also equipped later with gun cars, on which a 2-cm A/A (left) and a 4.7-cm anti-tank gun (right) were installed, each with armor to protect the crew. Photo: S.I.R.P.A./E.C.P.A. Paris

In the rear half of PZ 1 were the original cars, plus another G-car with a brakeman's cabin rebuilt as an observation post (left of the tree) and the aforementioned gun car (far left). Photo: E. Grahl/W. Sawodny collection

The rear half of PZ 1, rebuilt in 1943 (the front half was identical except for the different command car). The tank carrier cars were taken from PZ 26, the two-turret gun cars were newly built on captured four-axle Russian cars, and the flak cars (right before and after the locomotive) were also new. Remaining from the earlier PZ 1 were only the command cars, though they were rebuilt. Photo: W. Sitzius/W. Sawodny collection

PZ 2 shortly after it was taken over from rail protection in Dresden. The lettering on the car shows that it comes from the Stettin RBD. Photo: H. Wenzel collection

The gun cars of PZ 2 were of Czech construction, and after it was disbanded in the summer of 1940 were taken over by PZ 25, with only the turning turret with the 7.5-cm cannon retained; the rear one had been replaced by a stand for the 2-cm A/A gun. Photo: G. Tomaszewski/W. Sawodny collection

In May 1944, after losing both gun cars, PZ 2 still looked like the earlier rail protection train. Soon afterward, though—as the last of the old trains—it was called in for rebuilding. Photo: W. Sitzius/W. Sawodny collection

The former Munich rail protection train as PZ 3, seen near Konitz on September 1, 1939. Photo: F. Englberger/W. Sawodny collection

Even before they were taken over by the Wehrmacht, gun cars were built for this train, with a swinging front section that held a 7.7-cm F.K. 16 gun. Photo: Military Archives, Freiburg

After being damaged near Konitz the armor was strengthened considerably, an open observation post was installed, and the turret was now fixed rigidly. Thus, the gun (now a 7.7-cm F.K.96 new type) had only a very meager traverse through the enlarged front port. Photo: W. Obermark/W. Sawodny collection

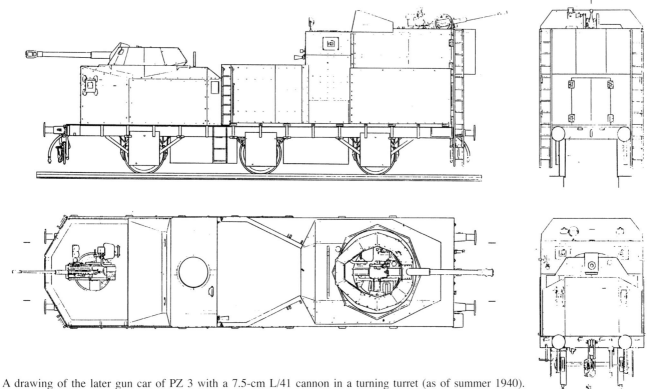

A drawing of the later gun car of PZ 3 with a 7.5-cm L/41 cannon in a turning turret (as of summer 1940). Drawing: P. Malmassari

In the summer of 1940 the gun cars of PZ 3 were rebuilt again. On the front part an open turret with a 7.5-cm L/41 cannon was mounted, the observation post was closed, and an A/A platform was built behind it. To reduce the axle load, a third axle was installed in the middle of the car. Photo: Imperial War Museum, London

Above: PZ 4 was formerly the rail protection train of the Breslau RBD. Photo: W. Obermark/W. Sawodny collection

The gun car of PZ 4 was built on a low-sided car. In the front one of the two octagonal turrets was a 3.7-cm anti-tank gun; in the rear one, mounted higher, a 7.5-cm infantry gun. In between was the ammunition bunker with its arched roof. Behind the raised gun turret was an armored position for a range finder. Photo: W. Obermark/W. Sawodny collection

Another picture of the gun car of PZ 4, now in Russia in 1943. In the front turret, in place of the 3.7-cm anti-tank gun, there is now a 4.7-cm infantry gun; on the G-car behind it a mount for the 2-cm A/A gun has been installed. Photo: G. Leinen/W. Sawodny collection

The former rail protection train from Würzburg (Nürnberg RBD) became PZ 5 of Wkr. IX (Kassel), and is seen in Poland in 1939. Photo: Truss/W. Sawodny collection

PZ 6 on June 21, 1941. At right are the three rail protection cars of the Königsberg train. The gun car (left)—a high-side O-car with an open-mounted gun (the shield can be seen over the edge of the car) in the middle—was added only after the Polish campaign. Photo: Library for History of the Times, Stuttgart

PZ 6 after being rebuilt in the autumn of 1942. The rail protection G-cars are modified, one with an A/A mount (covered gun) in the roof, the other with an observation post and frame antenna. At far right is a two-turret former Russian armored railcar (also with a frame antenna) modified as a gun car. Photo: E. Espey/W. Sawodny collection

This type of gun car is easy to see in the picture of the front half of PZ 6. The revised G-cars of the rail protection type behind it were modified in the same way as those in the back. Photo: H. Bruntsch/W. Sawodny colection

The front half of PZ 7 in the spring of 1940, with extended high antenna. The gun car (far left) is covered. Photo: W. Nöthen/W. Sawodny

PZ 7 is seen at Dinslaken in the same period of time. The picture shows, in the foreground, the rear half of the train. Photo: T. Schorlemmer/W. Sawodny collection

The same part of PZ 7 in Russia in the winter of 1942-43. In the gun car (left, exchange type Königsberg, note the armoring of the wall) there is now a 7.62-cm F.K.295/1(r) installed—but still open. Behind it (ahead of the following G-cars of the rail protection era) is an extra O-car rebuilt as an A/A car (A 10 type) with provisional partial roof and without axle protection. Photo: Federal Archives, Koblenz

Legend of the following schematic drawings
(applies equally to all following drawings of this type)

All black: documented clearly by photos
Diagonal: documented by pictures, but details unsure
Outlined: according to crew members, but no photos

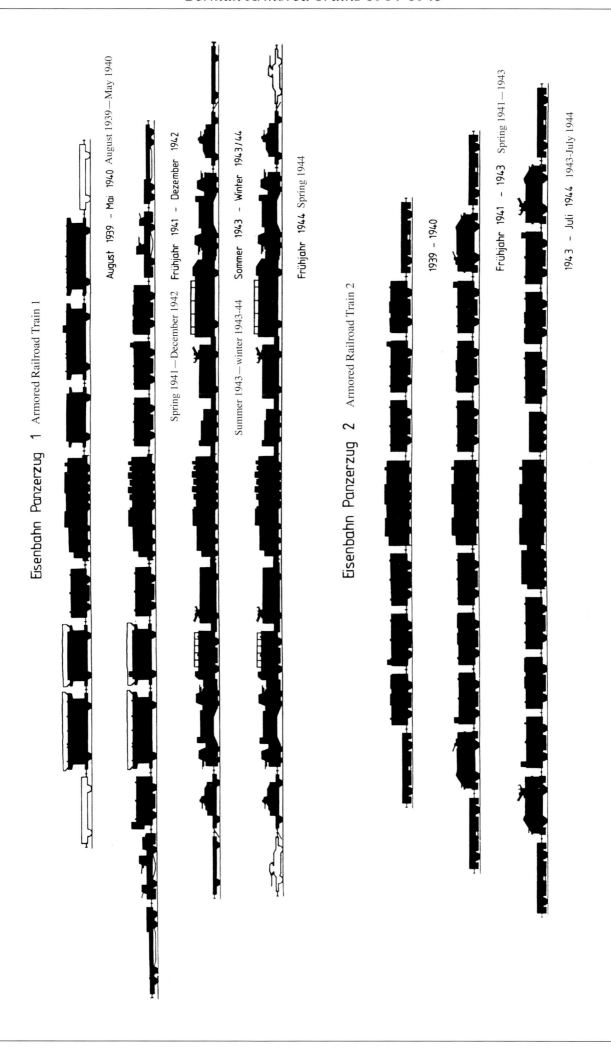

Eisenbahn Panzerzug 1   Armored Railroad Train 1

August 1939 – Mai 1940   August 1939—May 1940

Frühjahr 1941 – Dezember 1942   Spring 1941—December 1942

Sommer 1943 – Winter 1943/44   Summer 1943—winter 1943-44

Frühjahr 1944   Spring 1944

Eisenbahn Panzerzug 2   Armored Railroad Train 2

1939 – 1940

Frühjahr 1941 – 1943   Spring 1941—1943

1943 – Juli 1944   1943-July 1944

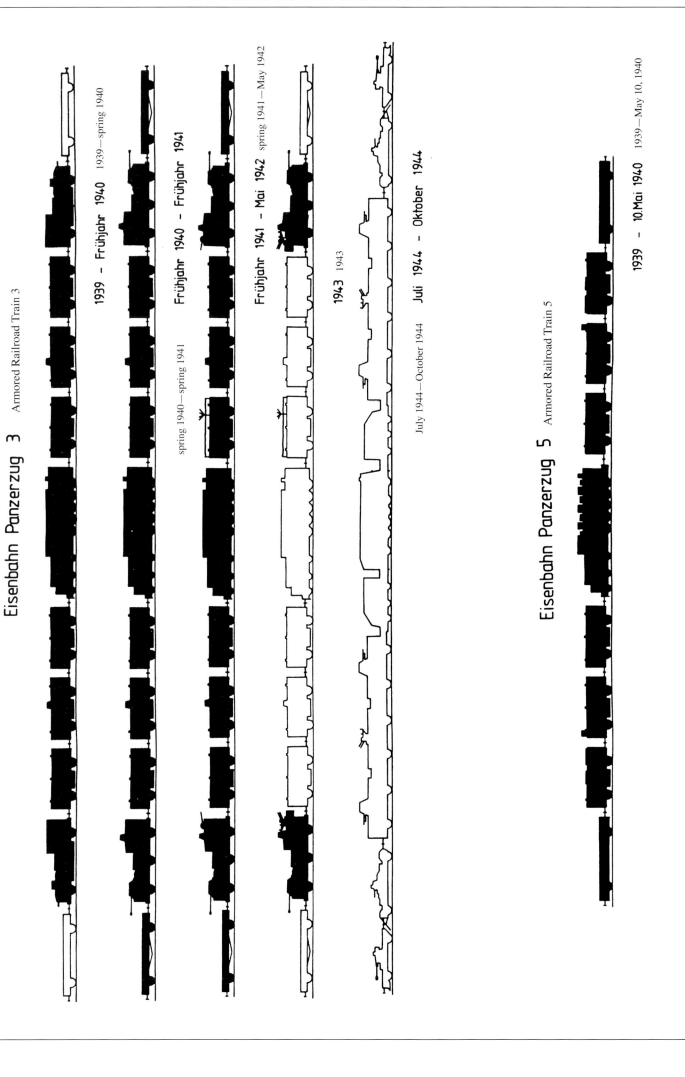

Eisenbahn Panzerzug 3 — Armored Railroad Train 3

1939 – Frühjahr 1940 — 1939—spring 1940

Frühjahr 1940 – Frühjahr 1941 — spring 1940—spring 1941

Frühjahr 1941 – Mai 1942 — spring 1941—May 1942

1943 — 1943

Juli 1944 – Oktober 1944 — July 1944—October 1944

Eisenbahn Panzerzug 5 — Armored Railroad Train 5

1939 – 10.Mai 1940 — 1939—May 10, 1940

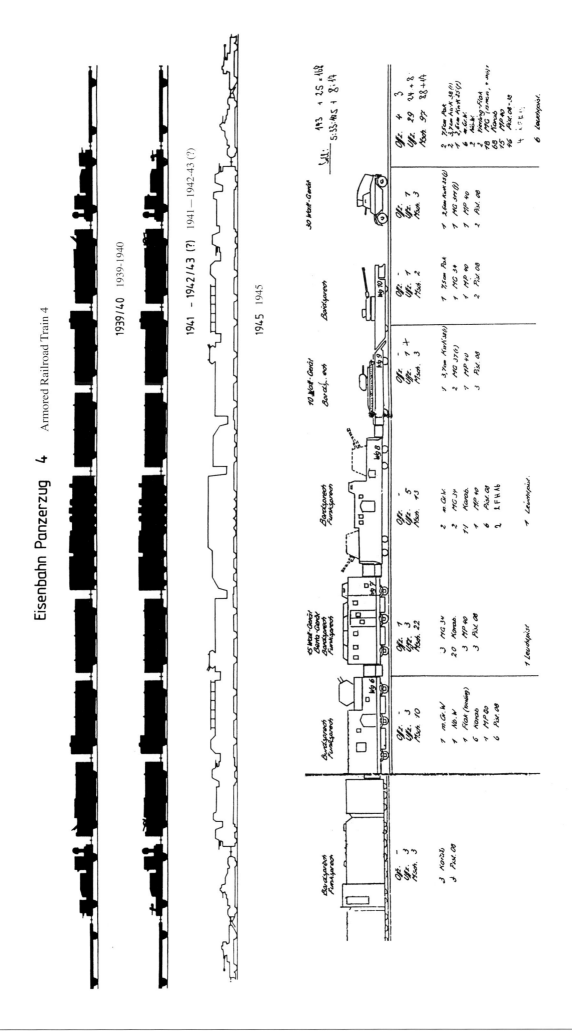

Eisenbahn Panzerzug 4   Armored Railroad Train 4

1939/40   1939-1940

1941 — 1942/43 (?)   1941—1942-43 (?)

1945   1945

The original scheme sketch of the rear half of the newly built PZ 4 (1945). The guns (four l.F.H. 16, right 18!) were added. Crew and armament of A/A and command cars are presumably different for the front half of the train. Three of the four officers (commander and artillery officer in the command car, doctor in the A/A car with medical compartment) were there. Drawings: W. Mausz/W. Sawodny collection

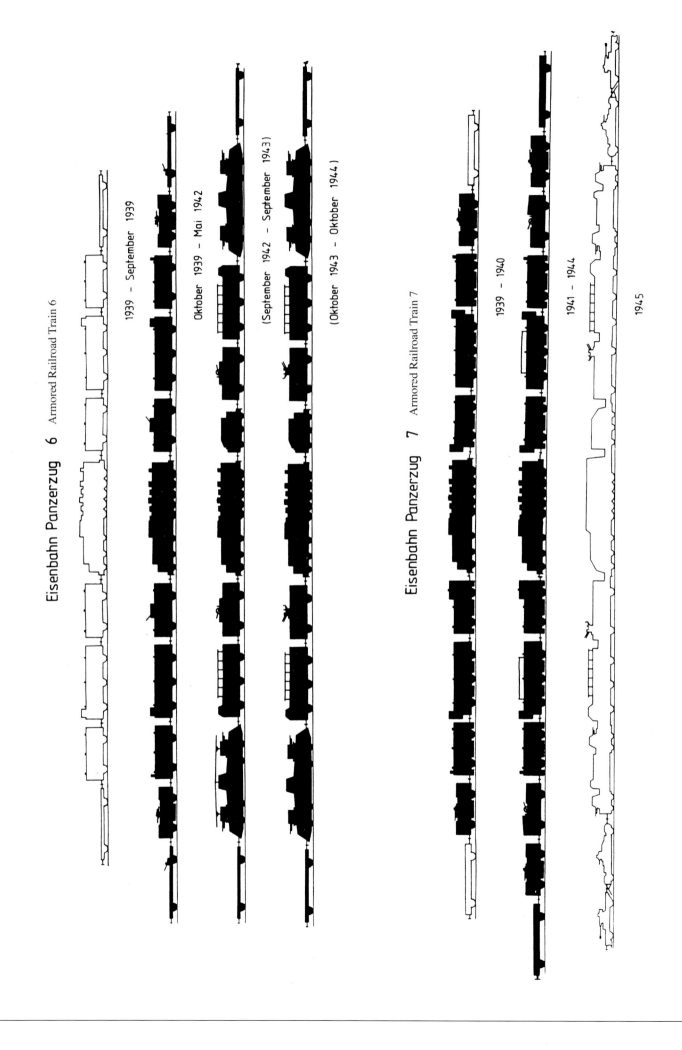

Eisenbahn Panzerzug 6 — Armored Railroad Train 6

1939 – September 1939

Oktober 1939 – Mai 1942

(September 1942 – September 1943)

(Oktober 1943 – Oktober 1944)

Eisenbahn Panzerzug 7 — Armored Railroad Train 7

1939 – 1940

1941 – 1944

1945

1940: Captured Czech and Polish Trains

In the occupation of what remained of Czechoslovakia in March 1939, all the available Czech armored train material fell into German hands at Milowitz, near Prague. There were five armored trains for combat purposes, plus a training armored train, including the following vehicles:

– Four armored locomotives of the 310.4 series, later designated, because their weight was increased by the armor, as 313.9 or 314.9 (ex MAV 377; three of former Austro-Hungarian origin, one similarly armored by the Czechs in 1919);

– possibly one armored locomotive of the 310.3 or 320.2 series (ex MAV 376);

– two former Austro-Hungarian gun cars of different construction, each with a 7.5-cm Skoda L/26 cannon;

– four Czech gun cars, each with two of these guns;

– five infantry cars of Austro-Hungarian origin, armed with machine guns;

– four Czech infantry cars armed with machine guns;

– one armored railcar of Skoda type, plus several contact cars.

During the Polish campaign in September-October 1939 armored train material was also captured. Of the ten Polish armored trains available when the war began, PP. 54 "Grozny" and one training armored train fell into German hands undamaged. PP. 52 "Pilsudczyk" was slightly damaged, and several more so (including PP. 11 "Danuta") or unusable (PP. 12 "Poznanczyk," PP. 13 "General Sosnowski," PP. 14 "Paderewski," and PP. 15 "Smierc"). Three armored trains, one of them with bomb damage (PP. 51 "Pierwzy Marszalek," the other two were PP. 53 "Smialy" and PP. 55 "Bartosz Glowacki") fell into Soviet hands in the occupation of eastern Poland. The still usable material was gathered in Krakow by the Germans.

By instructions of February 16, 1940, five armored trains were to be set up from the captured Czech and Polish material, and were intended for securing tasks in the occupied part of Poland (Oberost Zone). The two armored trains to be made up of Polish material, No. 21 and 22, were to be equipped by the Commander East according to the given possibilities (according to the available Polish material) and manned by him; they were set up on June 10 (No. 21) and July 10, 1940 (No. 22), by High Command XXXIV in Krakow; the crews were taken from Inf.Ers.Btl. No. 49 in Breslau (Recruiting District VIII), the technical personnel, as usual, from the Reichsbahn. For the three armored trains, No. 23, 24, and 25, the Czech material was repaired and rearmed at the workshops in Halberstadt. Then they were sent to Rehagen-Klausdorf, where the establishment of all three armored trains was done by Railroad Engineer Replacement Battalion No. 4 on March 1, 1940.

Oddly enough, these armored trains were by no means made up uniformly; No. 21 differed from No. 22 just as the three trains made of Czech material differed from each other. PZ 21 received not only the gun car of PP. 54 "Grozny," which carried both a 7.5-cm F.K. 02/26 (p) and a 10-cm 14/19 (p) howitzer (the car from "Grozny," which went to PZ 22, was armed with two cannons of the first-named type), but also a car, similarly armed with guns, from PP. 52 "Pilsudczyk." Along with the one-turret gun cars (7.5-cm F.K. 02/26), which probably came from the Polish training train, of which No. 21 and 22 each had one, there was the following artillery material:

– PZ No. 21: three 7.5-cm field guns and two 10-cm howitzers;

– PZ No. 22: only three 7.5-cm field guns.

In addition, PZ 21 also included the "assault" car of PP. 54 "Grozny" as a command car, the infantry car from PP. 11 "Danuta," and the Ti 3-13 (ex G 5.3 54 654) armored locomotive from PP. 52 "Pilsudczyk"; PZ 22 had the command car from "Pilsudczyk," another internally armored covered freight car (probably from one of the Oppeln rail protection trains) from this train. Two cars also went to PZ 23—see there), and the armored locomotive Ti 3-4 (ex G 5.3 54 651) from "Grozny."

The material from captured Polish armored trains, gathered in Krakow in the winter of 1939-40. Photo: G. Krause collection

The German armored trains made up of captured Polish material in the summer of 1940, No. 21 (left, rear part) and 22 (right, front part), in Krakow. Photo: A. Schwipp/W. Sawodny collection

The particularly insufficient armor (it was rolled steel kettle plate) was much strengthened at the end of 1941 during an overhaul at Schneider, Le Creusot (the trains had already been moved from the General Government to France in the spring of 1941), and the locomotive of PZ 22 was also fitted with armored aprons. At the same time, every train received two low-sided cars fitted with 2-cm A/A guns.—At the end of October 1942 PZ 21 was transferred to the eastern front. At this point the Polish Ti 3-13 armored locomotive was replaced by a Series 93 type (formerly of PZ 25). During repairs at the Kiev-Darniza EAW in February 1943, the single 2-cm A/A guns were replaced by quads, and one of these quads was mounted on the small gun car instead of the turret with the 7.5-cm cannon; the artillery of this train was thus reduced from the usual four guns. The train was also given a road-rail Panhard 204/38(f) scout car as a reconnaissance vehicle. In the period from October 1943 to June 1944, PZ 21 was again damaged by mines. Not all the cars are said to have been repaired; some were replaced by covered freight cars with concrete double walls. Apparently the train was also issued a flat car in 1944 with a captured Russian T 34 tank on it.—PZ 22 was also modernized in several ways. By the beginning of 1944 it received: a French 140 C series armored locomotive instead of the Polish Ti 3-4; a new radio set (which PZ 21 had also received); A/A quads in place of single guns; two carrier cars with Praga 38(t) tanks on them; and a Panhard scout car. When it was transferred to the eastern front in October 1944, it was also given two tank destroyer cars with Panzer IV turrets (7.5-cm KwK L/48).

The armored trains made up of captured Czech material had the following composition:

– Train No. 23: a former Austro-Hungarian gun car (from k.u.k. Armored Train No. II); a Czech gun car (one turret replaced by an A/A mount); two Czech infantry cars; two covered freight cars with inside armor (from one of the Oppeln rail protection trains); one of the old Austro-Hungarian armored locomotives (MAV 377; CSD 310.4 or 313.9) with tender; and besides the noted armament, 20 Czech 7/24 machine guns were on hand.

– Train No. 24: a former Austro-Hungarian gun car (standard type); a Czech gun car (three 7.5-cm cannons in all); four former Austro-Hungarian infantry cars; two armored locomotives (MAV 377.362—CSD 314.901 and MAV 377.483) with a tender; and 24 Czech 7.24 machine guns.

– Train No. 25: two Czech gun cars (in all, four 7.5-cm guns); two Czech infantry cars; one 313/4.9 armored locomotive (ex MAV 377) with tender; and 12 Czech 7/24 MGs.

The vehicles that came of earlier Austro-Hungarian origin had very effective two-layered armor of Martin cast steel; the Czech cars, on the other hand, had only a thin (8 mm) one-layer armor, though of high-grade nickel steel. Improvements may have been made when the trains were first set up under German command.—The earlier Czech guns (7.5-cm Skoda cannons) were retained as armament.

The small, old wet-steam CSD 313/4.9 (ex MAV 377) locomotives quickly proved to be too weak for the long German armored trains (their Czech forerunners had had at most three armored cars!). Therefore, and because there was no need in the summer of 1940 (the war was being waged only in the air and on the sea at that time), Armored Trains 23-25 (and Armored Railcar No. 15) were ordered out of service on August 14, 1940. The cars were kept at the Reichsbahn WAW in Königsberg (the gun cars of PZ 25, though, were rebuilt in the winter of 1940-41 and assigned to PZ 2), and the personnel trains and some of the crews were assigned to Trains 21 and 2, which were just receiving their final equipment.

On order of June 19, 1941, at the beginning of the Russian campaign Armored Trains 23 and 24 were made up anew. They were equipped where they stood, at the Königsberg WAW. As opposed to their former composition, the following changes were made: the weak Czech (ex-Austro-Hungarian) wet-steam MAV 377/CSD 313/4.9) locomotives were replaced by Series 93 German armored locomotives; all the Czech gun cars now had the rear turret removed and replaced by a platform for a new 2-cm A/A gun; for the second of these guns, a platform with armored sidewalls was built on the rood of the infantry car, which was placed in the other half of the train right after the earlier Austro-Hungarian gun car; and the Czech MG 7/24 were replaced by German MG 34, partly mounted behind new gun ports. Whether the armor was reinforced is not known. PZ 24 received two more infantry cars of the standard Czech type, which were probably not yet finished when the train was first set up. After equipping was finished at Königsberg, the two armored trains were sent to the Brandenburg-West WAW. There the final equipping and manning were done by Recruiting District III. The two trains were not sent to the eastern front, but to the Balkans.

On October 23, 1942, PZ 23 arrived at the Gleiwitz RAW after being badly damaged. There it was completely rebuilt according to K.A.N./K.St.N. 1169x; the same was done to PZ 24 at the Munich-Neuaubing RAW after a collision on February 14, 1943.

The third (PZ 25) of the armored trains made of former Czech material, taken out of service in the summer of 1940, could not be reactivated at the same time as the others, as its gun cars had meanwhile been used elsewhere (in PZ 2), so that only two infantry cars and the two control cars were on hand. Another old Austro-Hungarian MG car made of captured Czech material, which had not been included when PZ 23-25 were first set up, was still at the Halberstadt workshop. Only on November 21, 1941, was it decided to reactivate PZ 25 too, with its equipment based on experience with the broad-gauge armored trains developed for the Russian campaign (see next section). Two captured French Somua S 35 tanks were placed on flatcars, not only to replace the artillery with their 4.7-cm tank guns, but also to be operated away from the train, although their carrier cars in PZ 25 did not have the automatically lowering ramps of the broad-gauge armored trains, but a ramp of planks that had to be set up in case of such action. The Czech-Austro-Hungarian infantry car at the Halberstadt workshop was fitted with two platforms; on the rear one, somewhat higher, a 2-cm A/A gun was mounted, while the front one served primarily as an observation post. The train was to receive a second car of that type, as an armored train captured in

An armored train captured in Yugoslavia in April 1941 had former Austro-Hungarian cars. They were used in the reactivated PZ 25 in November. Photo: W. Fleischer collection

Yugoslavia in April 1941 was set up of the same type, and its gun car was similarly rebuilt. From this armored train two infantry cars (k.u.k. type) were also added to PZ 25. As a locomotive, the armored Series 93 type of PZ 24 (which had been replaced by a Series 57 type) was taken. Used at first in the back line areas of the central eastern front, it was later transferred to France in exchange for the better-equipped PZ 21. The aforementioned locomotive was replaced by a Series 57 type. Either at this point or soon after it arrived in France (in any case, before the summer of 1943), the Somua tanks were replaced by Praga 38(t) types, and 7.5-cm cannons (of the same Skoda type as on PZ 2, 23, and 24) were installed with gun shields on the front platforms of the A/A cars. Later (early 1944?) two additional 2-cm A/A quads—presumably mounted on a low-side car—were added. Before it was reassigned to the eastern front, PZ 25 was sent to the Leipzig-Engelsdorf RAW. The type and extent of the revision made there are not known. In any case, it received new gun cars (of the two-turret, four-axle type, with 10.5-cm F.H. 18/40 guns–which must have been completed already by that time, presumably for PZ 2, the work on which was halted at about the same time), and tank-destroyer cars with Panzer IV turrets (7.5-cm KwK L/48). The other cars—infantry and command cars, gun and A/A cars (cannons removed and single-barreled 2-cm A/A guns replaced by A/A quads)—may have been left essentially as they were in view of the short revision time of some eight weeks.

The captured Czech trains, No. 23-25, even after their original, very insufficient, weak MAV 377 series armored locomotives (built 1891-1900) were replaced, had thin armor and meager artillery (only two low-performance guns), and were suitable only for securing tasks in the hinterlands. This determined their areas of use (Denmark, the Balkans, France). No. 23 and 24 were thus rebuilt fairly soon into practically fully new trains that corresponded to K.St.N. 1169x, but PZ 25 had to make do with its old material until the late autumn of 1944, using cars that had in part been built in the k.u.k. monarchy in 1914!

The Polish armored trains with their good artillery equipment were quite ready for action after their armor had been improved and their unsatisfactory Ti 3 locomotives were replaced, especially the more strongly armed PZ 21, whose Polish 10-cm howitzer was later also used to arm the German standard-type BP 42. So they remained essentially unchanged until they were lost in action in 1944-45.

PZ 21 was transferred to France in April 1941, still without A/A cars. The gun car came from the Polish "Pilsudczyk" armored train, the command car from the "Grozny." Photo: T. Wiethoff/W. Sawodny collection

The front half of PZ 21. Before the armored Polish locomotive (Ti 3-13, ex-Prussian G 5.3) are the infantry car (assault car) of the Polish armored train "Danuta," the small (one-turret) gun car (probably from the Polish training train), and the two-turret gun car (from "Grozny"). On the low-side car, the Sd.Anh. 51 for the 2-cm A/A gun, which was already available at that time, is visible (set up at the head of this car). Photo: W. Mauss/W. Sawodny collection

For use in the Soviet Union, an A/A quad was installed on the small gun car with its turret removed. The second A/A quad remained on the four-axle low-side car, with an armored ammunition bunker on the rear part of the car. Photo: H. Bendl/W. Sawodny collection

PZ 22 is seen in France in 1942. Behind the gun car (which came from the Polish armored car "Grozny") is a former rail protection car (presumably from an Oppeln train). The locomotive (Ti 3-4) already has additional armor on the sides. Photo: Federal Archives, Koblenz

In the back part of PZ 22 were the command car from the Polish "Pilsudczyk" and the same small gun car (probably from the Polish training train) as in PZ 21. Photo: Federal Archives, Koblenz

Since 1942, the A/A gun was mounted on a two-axle low-side car of this train (note the armor of the car walls), which was coupled to the earlier four-axle contact car. Photo: Federal Archives, Koblenz

In the spring of 1944, PZ 22 had a French 140 C series armored locomotive in place of the Polish one. Note also the changed antenna position on the command car. Before the A/A car (now armed with a quad) is another contact car (the original four-axle car is behind it as an equipment car). Photo: Schueller/W. Sawodny collection

Even in action on the eastern front (here in Slovakia in November 1944) the wagons were the same. Before the locomotive (hard to spot here) are the two-turret gun car, the command car, and the A/A car. Coupled on in addition are a tank-carrier car (tank removed) and—at the right edge of the photo—a tank-destroyer car with a Panzer IV turret. Photo: B. Schaknies/W. Sawodny collection

PZ 23 saw its first service in Denmark in April 1940. The original camouflage paint of the Czech gun car and the infantry car behind it was also adopted for the Pg-car from the Oppeln rail protection train. On the gun car, the rear turret has been replaced by a mount for a twin A/A machine gun. Photo: W. Sawodny collection

Above: PZ 23 in Yugoslavia in the autumn of 1941. On the A/A platform of the Czech gun car there is now a single 2-cm gun. Behind the rail protection Pg-car is locomotive 93 220, which replaced the original too-weak MAV Series 377 armored locomotive when PZ 23 was put back into service in June 1941. Photo: Federal Archives, Koblenz

Left: In the rear half of PZ 23 were a three-axle G-car from the Oppeln rail protection train, a Czech-made infantry car with an A/A mount for a twin MG 34 installed on the roof, and the gun car of the Austro-Hungarian PZ II of World War I (later with the Czech PZ 1).

PZ 23 after total rebuilding in 1942-43. It now had a captured Russian four-axle car in each half with a new body and two gun turrets, a command car (a rebuilt rail protection car), an A/A car (a rebuilt Czech infantry car), and a Series 57 armored locomotive. At the ends were tank-carrier cars with 38(t) tanks and contact cars. Photo: H. Bruntsch/W. Sawodny collection

PZ 24 is seen after being set up in the spring of 1940, also in Czech camouflage paint. All the cars except one gun car came from Austro-Hungarian armored trains of World War I; here gun car 141.172 and behind it infantry car S 149.902 of the Austrian PZ VII or VI, as of November 1918 Hungarian PZ IV, as of 1919 Czech PZ 3, behind it (with observation turret and spotlight) infantry car 140.972 of the Austrian PZ 1, later Czech PZ 2; of the two locomotives in double traction with a tender between them, MAV 377.362 (Austro-Hungarian PZ IV, Czech PZ 2) points in the direction of the depicted train half. Photo: P. Bettner/W. Sawodny collection

The rear half of PZ 24 consisted of the MAV 377.482 locomotive (armored by the Czechs in 1919 for their PZ 6), infantry wagon 140.914 (formerly Austrian PZ II, then Czech PZ 1), and S 150.271 (Austrian PZ VII, later Czech PZ 2), as well as a Czech-built gun car. Photo: P. Bettner/W. Sawodny collection

In its second setup in June 1941, two former Czech infantry cars were added before and after the locomotive (now of Series 93). The rear turret of the gun car was replaced by an A/A mount with a single 2-cm gun. Photo: H. Röhle/W. Sawodny collection

In the front half of the train, the Czech infantry car had an A/A mount with a single 2-cm gun on the roof; on car S 149.902 there is also a mount for the twin MG. Since December 1941 PZ 24 used locomotive 57 2043, which was used with PZ 1 in 1939-40. Note also the antenna stretched over both infantry cars. Photo: Federal Archives, Koblenz

When it was rebuilt in 1943, PZ 24 received four-axle gun cars with two turrets, two each of the Austro-Hungarian cars served as command cars (note the new observation post), and the Czech infantry cars were rebuilt as A/A cars. The tank-carrier car was taken over by PZ 30. Photo: S. Maurischat/W. Sawodny collection

Right: Before PZ 24 was moved from France to the eastern front in November 1944 it was given tank-destroyer cars with Panzer IV-H turrets. Photo: E. Behling/W. Sawodny collection

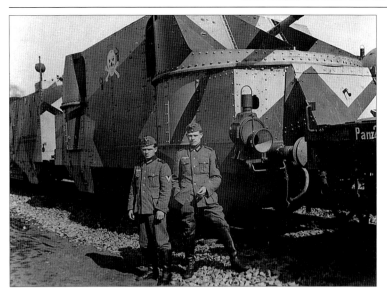

PZ 25, when first set up in March 1940, consisted, besides a Series MAV 377, of only a Czech infantry car and gun car (still with two turrets) in each half of the train. Photo: W. Fritzsche/W. M. Koehler collection

Second from top: In the second version of PZ 25 in December 1941 only the Czech infantry cars were still on hand, since the gun cars had been used on PZ 2. From the Czech material there was only the infantry car S 150.003 (from Austrian PZ I), which was modified by the installation of two high roof platforms (2-cm A/A gun on the rear one). Meanwhile, a Yugoslavian armored train (ex-Austrian PZ V) had been captured, and its cars (here infantry car 140.912) were added to the train. The armored locomotive is 93 298, which was formerly used for PZ 24. Photo: H. J. Schlichting/W. Sawodny collection

In the back half of PZ 25 there were, besides the Czech infantry car from the Yugoslav train (ex Austrian PZ V), the S 148.105 infantry car and a gun car, its number not known, which was fitted, as was S 150.003, with roof platforms (A/A stands). At this time the train did not yet have guns; the artillery was supplied by Somua S 35 tanks on the flatcars. Photo: E. Banser/W. Sawodny collection

During service in France (1943-44), the low platforms of both such cars carried 7.5-cm Skoda L/28 cannons (as on all gun cars of Czech origin) installed in open mounts. The Somua tanks had been replaced by 38(t) types, which were still carried on SSk Koeln-type cars without fixed unloading ramps. Photo: Federal Archives, Koblenz

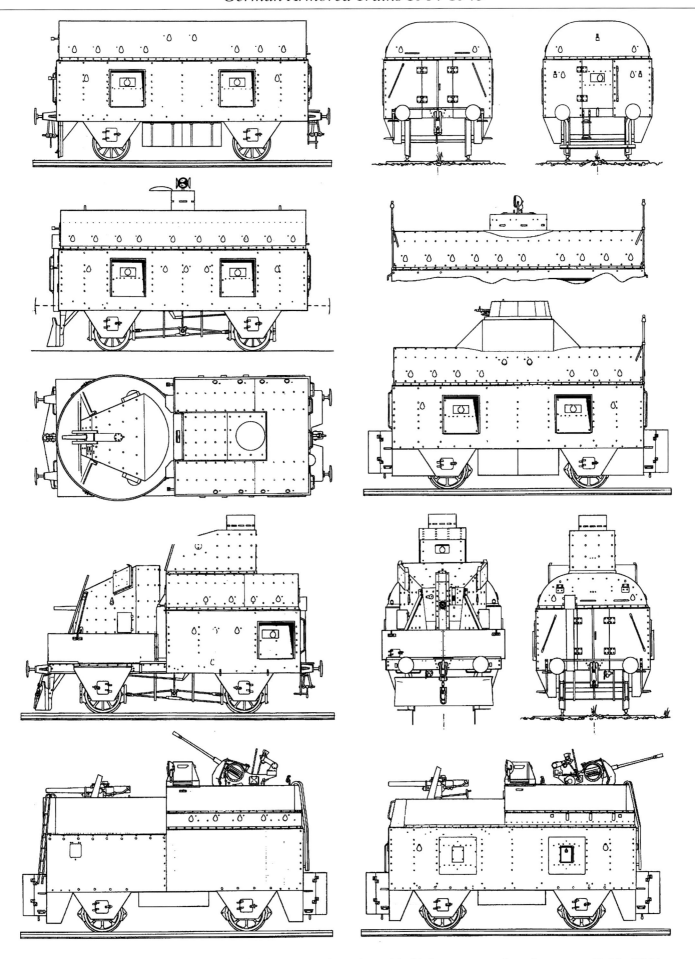

Austro-Hungarian armored train cars of World War I (*from top to bottom*): a. original infantry car types; b. roof structures added for PZ 24; c. gun cars (as in PZ 24); d. rebuilt gun/A/A cars of PZ 25, based on earlier gun cars (left) or an infantry car (right). Drawing: P. Malmassari

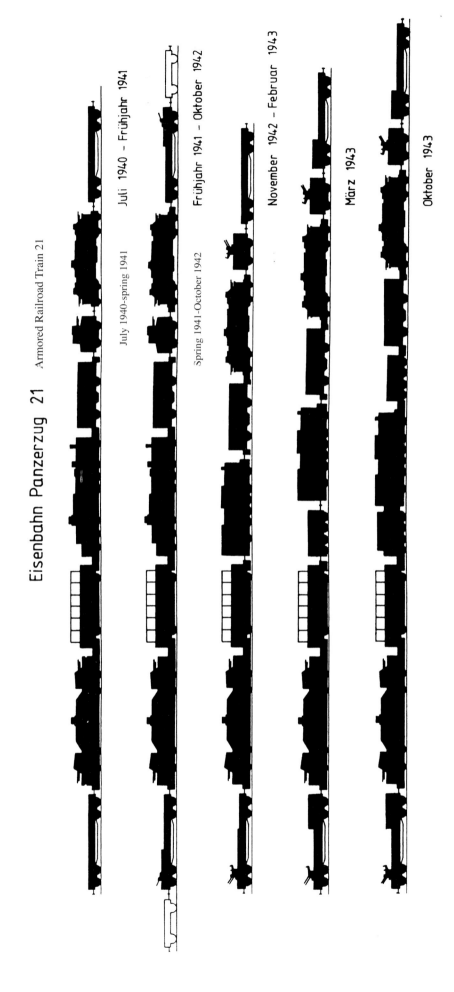

Eisenbahn Panzerzug 21   Armored Railroad Train 21

Juli 1940 – Frühjahr 1941

July 1940-spring 1941

Frühjahr 1941 – Oktober 1942

Spring 1941-October 1942

November 1942 – Februar 1943

März 1943

Oktober 1943

After being damaged in the summer of 1944, several temporary cars were used as substitutes, among others, ostensibly a flat car with a T 34 tank on it. The place of the damaged armored locomotive was taken by a "black one" of Series 52.

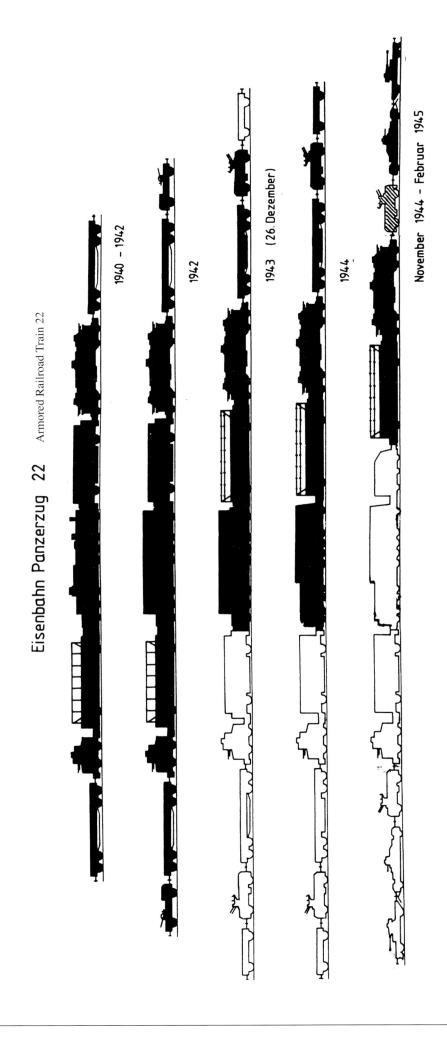

Eisenbahn Panzerzug 22   Armored Railroad Train 22

1940 – 1942

1942

1943   (26. Dezember)

1944

November 1944 – Februar 1945

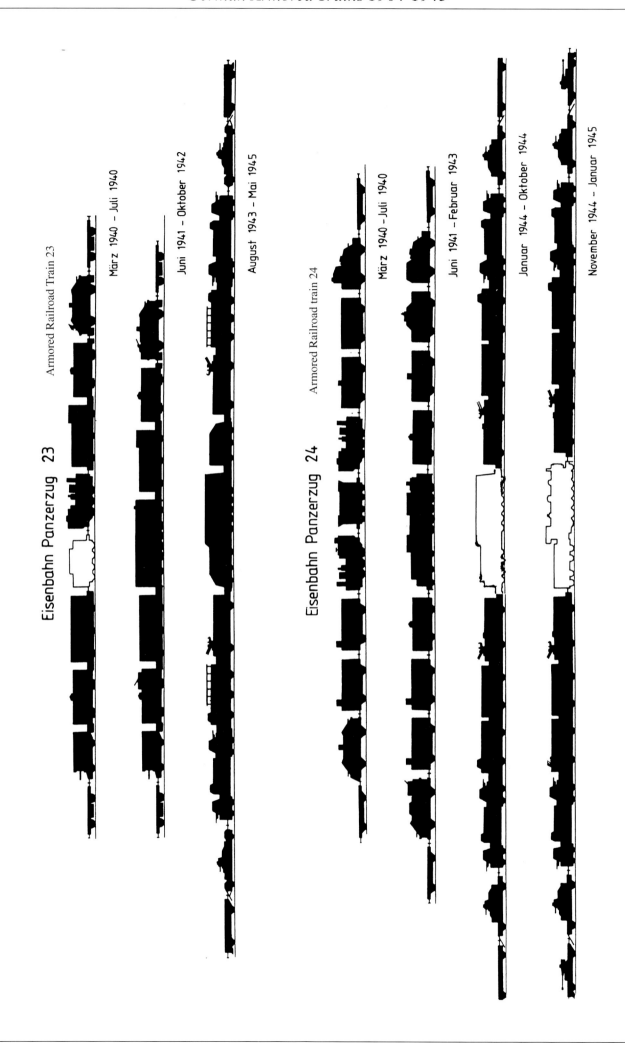

Eisenbahn Panzerzug 23

Armored Railroad Train 23

März 1940 – Juli 1940

Juni 1941 – Oktober 1942

August 1943 – Mai 1945

Eisenbahn Panzerzug 24

Armored Railroad train 24

März 1940 – Juli 1940

Juni 1941 – Februar 1943

Januar 1944 – Oktober 1944

November 1944 – Januar 1945

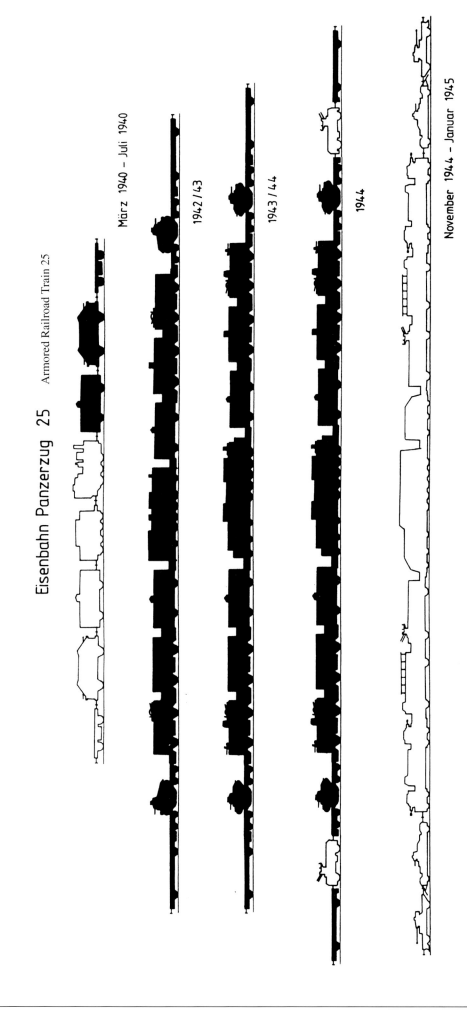

Eisenbahn Panzerzug 25   Armored Railroad Train 25

März 1940 – Juli 1940

1942 / 43

1943 / 44

1944

November 1944 – Januar 1945

In view of the short rebuilding time, the use of cars from the earlier PZ 25 can be assumed, at least for the A/A and command cars for the last rebuilding (as of November 1944).

1941-42: Broad-gauge Armored Trains and the Use of Captured Russian Material

When in the latter half of 1940 the planning for a campaign against the Soviet Union began, there were, after the disbanding of PZ 5 and the deactivation of PZ 23-25 and PT 15, only eight such units. Although at first there was optimism that the supply problem in the east could be overcome essentially by means of motorized groups on the highways—unbelievable in view of the means that were available, and as it later proved in practice, totally unjustified—it may have been the Chief of Transportation who, in view of the vastness of the area to be occupied—even in ignorance of the later threats to the back line connections by partisans—considered this number of armored trains insufficient.

The Inspection of the Railroad Engineers In 10 was therefore called on in November and December 1940 to develop concepts for new armored trains, whereby both a quickly realized instant solution and an interim emergency situation were to be offered. The requirements set up for this "Panzerzug 1941" were:

1. Armored railcars that could be used individually and also combined in a train.
2. Armored railcars as tank carriers.
3. Armored rail vehicles that could be used as combat cars both on rails and on roads, and could be put on and taken off the rails quickly, even under enemy fire.
4. Creation of a makeshift armored train before all these requirements were realized.

For the immediate solution, the placing of tanks on armored Ommr-cars was suggested. The next step (emergency solution) was to be placing the tanks on specially developed railroad cars pulled by an armored locomotive. In the next step, these trains were to be completed by shock-troop, kitchen, hospital, and other cars; in the last step, all cars were to have their own power, meeting the requirements listed as 1 and 2.

In longer terms (ready for introduction in the summer of 1943) there was another armored train (designated "SP 42") planned, for which these requirements were set:

1. Armored railroad chassis to hold tanks (Type IV) that could be unloaded onto a road within 10 minutes and loaded back on within 15 minutes (tank carrier cars).
2. Armored Diesel locomotives.
3. Armored cars for command, shock troops, and engineers with kitchens and quarters.
4. Armament with 7.5-cm tank guns (in Panzer IV turrets), 2-cm A/A quads, and machine guns.
5. Controlled uncoupling of every single car from the command post and from every car.
6. Switching to Russian (1524 mm) and Spanish (1668 mm) gauges.

The entire armored train should consist, besides the Diesel locomotive, of three tank carrier cars with Panzer IV tanks, a command car, an infantry car, and two control cars.

The contract to develop the Panzerzug 1941 and the SP 42 was given on December 13, 1940, to the Linke-Hofmann Works in Breslau for the cars (for the instant solution of the Panzerzug 1941 also to the Dessau Wagon Factory) and the Berlin Machine Building AG (ex-Schwartzkopff) in Berlin for the locomotives (later Krupp and Henschel were also to be included).

Although the development lines listed here could not be followed strictly and thus neither the Panzerzug 1941 nor the SP 42 went into production as originally planned (unless one wants to see the scouting trains not built until 1944, made up of cars with their own power, as late realizations of the Panzerzug 1941, which scarcely seems acceptable for other reasons), almost all the individual suggestions made in these plans were realized in some form, though often in a very different context. Thus, in what follows we shall often come back to them.

The central aspect of both designs is the carrying of tanks on suitable railroad cars. The model for them may be cars captured in the Polish campaign with unloadable Renault FT 17 or TK tanks. These cars were sometimes driven via a special drive directly from the tank motor (according to the requirement for a railcar as a tank carrier in the Panzerzug 1941). But while these tank carrier cars were just escort vehicles for usual armored trains, for the Poles they were raised to become the basic principle of the armored train itself, which did not carry any other built-in heavy weapons. Although fast loading and unloading is mentioned only for SP 42, it can also be assumed for the Panzerzug 1941, since the load of ready-to-roll tanks would make no sense otherwise. If one adds the requirement for armored vehicles quickly changed to be usable on both roads and rails, and the characterization of the infantry and engineer forces as shock troops (SP 42), it is shown that the train, seen only as a means of transport and base of action (command and communication central, kitchen and medical amenities, quarters), still was given the greatest possible value for the fighting troops in terms of independence from the rails, meaning also action outside the realm of the rail network.

With the solidification of the plans for operation "Barbarossa," the attack on the Soviet Union, the chief of Transportation came back on March 19, 1941, to the new establishment of armored trains, and in fact for the broad gauge (1524 mm) of the Russian track network, since the standard gauge armored trains could not be used on it (one assumed that one would capture enough broad gauge locomotives and cars to be able to keep traffic going without changing the gauge—an assumption that later proved to be false). At first five armored trains planned according to the makeshift instant solution for Panzerzug 1941 were turned to. Every armored train was to consist of one control car and three Om (or Ommr) cars, on which tanks were loaded and could be unloaded by a ramp onto the open road. The In 6 provided 15 captured French Somua S 35 tanks armed with a 4.7-cm cannon and a machine gun. Series 57 (ex-Prussian G 10) freight locomotives were to provide motive power; after their gauge was changed they were to be stationed in advance, as switch engines, at border depots chosen as starting points, and temporary cab armor was to be applied to them when they were taken over by the armored trains before the depot. The Operations Department of the Army General Staff, charged with setting up these trains along with the Planning Department of the chief of Transportation, insisted that the armored trains at once be assigned an infantry staff to take charge of mines, explosives, and fog laying equipment, so as to guarantee a manifold ability for action also off the rail lines. For this purpose, each of the five armored trains was also to include another contact car and two Om (Ommr) cars for the infantry, with their sides to be protected by armor plates from the fortress building contingent, but with their tops remaining open. In April 1941 it was decided to divide the cars among six instead of five armored trains.

The additional locomotive was a Wehrmacht Diesel of the WR 360 C series built by Henschel, adapted for broad gauge and intended to be delivered to the Soviet Union as part of the economic agreement, but it was held back on the German side of the border under the

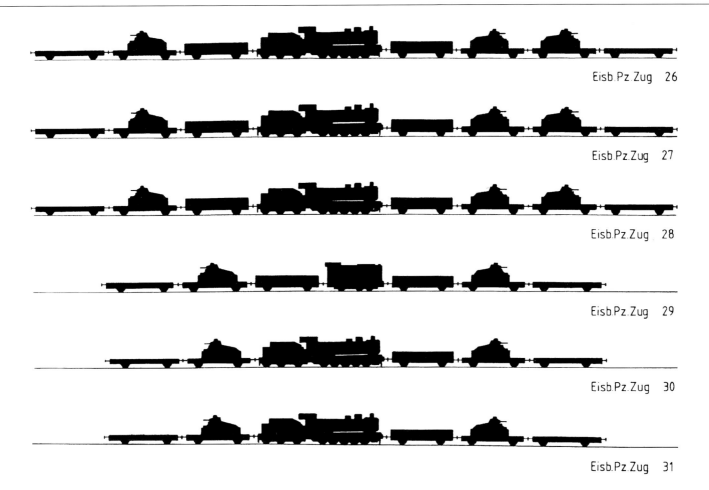

Eisb.Pz.Zug 26

Eisb.Pz.Zug 27

Eisb.Pz.Zug 28

Eisb.Pz.Zug 29

Eisb.Pz.Zug 30

Eisb.Pz.Zug 31

A scheme of the composition of the broad gauge armored trains set up for the Russian campaign (according to the immediate solution for "Panzerzug 1941" by In 10). The reduced numbers of cars for No. 29-31 resulted from the fact that the material to be divided evenly among the five trains originally (two infantry cars and three tank carriers each) now were used to equip six. Along with the five Series 57 steam locomotives, one WR 360 C Diesel served the sixth train (PZ 29). Drawing: U. Schwarze

pretext of further tests. On instructions of May 28, 1941, the setting up of the six armored trains (No. 26-31) by Recruiting District VIII (Breslau) was finally ordered. The training for the Somua S 35 of the personnel to be provided by Tank Replacement Battalion 15 in Sagan was carried out by Tank Brigade 100 in Paris; setting up the whole crews, which included the four-man crew of each tank, the command group of the commander, a radioman, a medic, and a fog laying man, the technical crew of two engine drivers and two firemen, plus two truck drivers for the baggage train (the troop units to which the armored trains were subordinated were to provide the infantry crews) took place in Teschen (Olsa region). (The infantry crews had to be provided by those troop units to which the armored trains were subordinated.)

According to the cars originally planned for five trains, Armored Trains No. 26-31 had somewhat varying compositions:

No. 26-28: 2 contact cars, 3 tank carriers, 2 infantry cars, one BR 57 steam locomotive.

No. 29: 2 contact cars, 2 tank carriers, 2 infantry cars, one WR 360 C Diesel locomotive.

No. 30-31: 2 contact cars, 2 tank carriers, one infantry car, one BR 57 steam locomotive.

The locomotive was always placed in the center; the cars were divided equally between the two halves of the train in the order: contact car—tank carrier—infantry car (from end of train to loco), and in case of an uneven number of cars, the front half included one more.

Transport of the 15 Somua S 35 tanks from Paris to Teschen (Olsa region) to equip the No. 26-31 armored trains. Photo: O. Schattmann/W. Sawodny collection

This ensemble deserved the name "armored train" only because of the loaded tanks (which obviously proved itself, for it became an integral part of all future German armored trains), but for the infantry on their open cars, the autumn rain must have been very unpleasant, to say nothing of the 1941-42 Russian winter. To improve or at least ameliorate the situation, the members of the armored trains were left to their own devices at first. They attached covers to the open infantry cars, at first tent canvas, later in fixed form. When possible they tried to obtain and include cars from captured Russian armored trains. PZ 28 was luckiest, for in the autumn of 1941, before the winter began, it secured a complete heavy Russian armored train, from which not only the two gun cars (each with a 10.7-cm F.K.M. 10/30), but also the fully armored locomotive (Series O) were taken over. Their own infantry cars, as well as the German locomotive, were turned over to the supply train but could be included if needed, but in general they kept only the three tank carrier cars with the Somua tanks and the two contact cars from the original equipment.—A captured closed infantry car was also added to PZ 31 in the winter of 1941-42. Another four-axle and two-turret gun car (one turret replaced by an A/A mount) may have been added only at the increase of the train's crew in the spring of 1942 (see below). Whether the car of the "Krasnoye Sormovo" type (guns removed and a 2-cm flak quad installed in one turret instead) was already in PZ 26 in the winter of 1941-42 or was added only when the crew improved the train in the spring of 1942 is not clear. The latter point in time may refer to the completion of this train with two makeshift armored freight cars. Whether PZ 29, shortly before its loss in January 1942, was reequipped with captured Russian cars could not be determined for sure. PZ 27 lost all its original cars at Suchinitshi around the beginning of 1942 and was equipped anew in January-February 1942 with two captured Russian two-turret gun cars and an armored and covered O-car. As for PZ 30, it added only a low-side car with a 2-cm A/A quad, although the train in this condition remained in service in the northern sector of the eastern front—under very rough climatic conditions—until November 1942.

For the armored trains of the 26-31 series that remained after the loss of PZ 29, the months of March to July 1942 brought essential changes. After the assumption that enough locomotives and cars would be captured to maintain action on the broad gauge railroads to the necessary extent had not come true, the conversion of the rails to standard gauge (1435 mm) was undertaken—beginning in the summer of 1941—in the occupied area. In the late spring of 1942 this measure had progressed so far that now the "Barbarossa" armored trains had to be converted to standard gauge to maintain their freedom of movement. The conversion of PZ 26 and 27 was done at Novosokolniki in April 1942, that of PZ 30 probably in Lyuban in July 1942, and that of PZ 28 and 31 in Kharkov about the same time. It is surprising that even the last two broad gauge trains stationed in the southern sector of the eastern front were converted, although the summer offensive moved in the directions of Stalingrad and the Caucasus and added another large area of broad gauge rail lines. This shows that it was no longer intended to use the armored trains right behind the front; on the other hand, though, doing the conversion so fast even in these areas meant that they could do their main job of securing the rail lines in the hinterlands better in standard gauge form.

In addition, the crews of all the armored trains—regardless of what cars they had on hand—were upgraded between March and

June 1942 to a strength of 6 or 7 officers, 27 to 35 NCOs, and 95 to 120 men. If the combat train did not have enough room to hold them all they were housed in the supply train. This shows that even at that time the full development of the named armored trains was considered. This point will be taken up later.

In the year and a half that followed the setting up of the "Barbarossa" trains (PZ 26-31) and the beginning of the Russian campaign until December 1942, along with the reactivated PZ 25 (in December 1941), just two new armored train units (one of which consisted of two combat trains) reached the troops along with the reactivated PZ 25, all made of captured material from the Soviet Union, though it had particular circumstances. When the Russians marched into Poland beginning on September 17, 1939, they captured three Polish armored trains: PP. 51 "Pierwszy Marszalek" near Poworsk, east of Kowel; and PP. 53 "Smialy" and PP. 55 "Bartosz Glowacki" in Lemberg. The first two—including their armament—were taken over by the Soviet NKVD, converted to broad gauge, and remained stationed in Lemberg. They fell into German hands at the end of June 1941. According to a directive of November 14, 1941, they were put into service by the German Wehrmacht as the two (broad gauge) combat trains of PZ 10. Thus, these captured Russian trains were really of Polish provenance, but only one of them was actually built in that country; the checkered career of the other deserves to be reported more thoroughly:

The armored train of the Soviet "Krasnoye Sormovo" type, built in Nizhni Novgorod early in 1919, was captured during the summer by the white Denikin Army, with which it saw service under the name "Dobrovolets." In the winter of 1919-20 it was recaptured by the Reds and bore the name "Im.Saumana i Dshaparidze." In the Russian-Polish war of 1920 it fell into Polish hands and remained active, first as "Strzelec kresowy" and later renamed PP. 51 "Pierwszy Marszalek" until 1939. As reported above, it fell back into Russian and, barely two years later, German hands, under whom it saw service—first as Combat Train II of PZ 10, and later as the independent PZ 11—until it was destroyed on January 13, 1945, almost at the end of the war.

Along with two contact cars, Combat Train I of PZ 10 included a Russian Type O armored locomotive and the two gun cars of the formerly Polish armored train "Smialy" (each with a light howitzer and a field gun); and Combat Train II had the old Polish Type Ti 3 armored locomotive (ex-Prussian G 5.3, probably Ti 3-2) and the two gun cars of the formerly Polish "Pierwszy Marszalek," each with two field guns. It appears that at first former Polish "assault cars" were used as additional ex-Polish combat cars (that of "Bartosz Glowacki"— later clearly provable—with Combat Train I, and in Combat Train II possibly that of "Smialy"; that of "Pierwszy Marszalek" turned up in the summer of 1941 in a German broad gauge line protection train), whereby neither radio equipment nor A/A guns (the "Smialy" (?) car has a roof mount—probably for a twin A/A-MG 34) could have represented the K.A.N. setup. Both combat trains of the broad gauge PZ 10 were converted to standard gauge in Kharkov, at the latest in the summer of 1942. They were assigned armored locomotives of the German Series 57 with additional tenders, and command and A/A cars rebuilt out of cars captured from heavy Russian armored trains, in which instead of a gun turret an A/A stand with a single 2-cm gun had been installed; Combat Train II had two of them, replacing the "Smialy" car; Combat Train I had one (the car from the former "Bartosz Glowacki" remained with the train), while the second 2-cm A/A gun was installed on an additional infantry car of a "Barbarossa" train (probably taken from PZ 31).

On January 3, 1942, a makeshift armored train, named at first after the city, was assembled by Recruiting District II in Stettin. On May 10, 1942, it was taken over as a regular armored train, at first called "A" and later PZ 51. For this train four-axle Russian freight cars were rebuilt at the Pruszkow OAW, and it is noteworthy that—as with the earlier rail protection trains and the armored trains that resulted from them (No. 1-7)—the wooden walls were kept and inside armor was applied. In all, PZ 51 included two gun cars that each had two turrets, at stepped heights, from Russian BT-7 tanks with 4.7-cm tank guns, modeled after Soviet wartime armored trains. Along with another four-axle car with a 2-cm quad, there was a command car rebuilt from a high-wall freight car and two contact cars. The armored locomotive—demonstrating the origin from a line protection train—belonged to the 38 (Prussian P8) series.

In all, two lines of development can be seen in this period. For one, the reequipping of the inadequate "Barbarossa" trains with captured Russian cars, seen in any case only as an emergency solution, followed the guidelines of the "Panzerzug 1941" concept, namely adding only closed cars for shock troops, kitchens, medical facilities, etc., while heavy weapons were provided only in the form of unloadable tanks (Armored Trains No. 26 and 31; PZ 25, returned to service in December 1941, can also be listed as this type). On the other hand, augmentation of the artillery armament according to the Russian model with four guns per car was undertaken (PZ 10, 27, and 51). In both cases, efforts were made to reduce the number of cars as compared to the earlier armored trains, even if it never equaled their opponents who fought with armored trains (Poland, Soviet Union). This last aspect was quickly given up again when the final development of the "Barbarossa" trains began; and of the two possibilities, the up-gunned version soon won out (in the first half of 1942 the development of the standard BP 42 armored train also prevailed, likewise with four guns, although two cars with unloadable tanks were also provided).

For the final reequipping PZ 27 was first in line; after serious damage at the end of May 1942, to which one of the gun cars in particular had fallen victim, it was moved to the Eberswalde RAW. The material from a line protection train which, after the opening of the pocket around Sukhinitshi had taken over a tank carrier car and an infantry car (which was now rebuilt as a second tank carrier) of the original equipment of PZ 27, and which went out of service at the same time, was used to rebuild it; thus, these cars returned to their original train. They were now loaded with Panzer 38(t) tanks. A similar captured gun car to the destroyed one (with round instead of square turrets) was also taken from the line protection train, as well as an early Austro-Hungarian infantry car from the Polish "Pierwszy Marszalek" armored train, which had fallen into Soviet hands in September 1939 and German hands in 1941, and which was fitted with an A/A platform (the second A/A car was a captured Russian one). For command cars, rebuilt G-cars (perhaps also from the line protection train) were used. The locomotive was now fitted with full armor. At the end of 1943 another four-axle freight car was added between the rear gun and tank carrier cars as a spotlight car.—PZ 27, badly damaged in March 1943, was rebuilt again (and ready for action at the end of April 1945), but information as to its composition in lacking.

PZ 28—probably when converted to narrow gauge in the spring of 1942—had to give up its scrounged-up gun cars because of their unusual caliber; they were replaced by two other captured cars originally with two turrets with 7.62-cm F.K. 295/2(r), one of which—as on the captured Czech trains of 1940—was removed and replaced by an A/A platform (one single 2-cm gun, one 2-cm quad). The earlier German Series 57 locomotive, with only its cab armored, came back, as did the old infantry cars, now with fixed roofs. In the summer of 1942 several minor improvements (modifying the observation posts on the gun cars, adding armored observation posts on the contact cars) were made to this train, but all in all it remained closest of all to the original version of the "Barbarossa" trains.

In November 1942 PZ 30 was sent to the Eberswalde RAW for revision. There it received two captured Russian two-axle gun cars (from the "Komsomol Chuwashy" armored train), each with one turret (7.62-cm F.K. 295/1(r) gun), which were somewhat modified (such as observation posts at the end of the car toward the train's end), and two four-axle cars from a former heavy armored train as infantry, A/A, and command cars. The tank carriers were the tub-shaped type of the standard BP 42, with Praga 38(t) tanks (the original tank carriers of this armored train—now also carrying Praga 38(t) tanks—came to PZ 24, which was rebuilt in the Munich-Neuaubing RAW at the same time). The still available original locomotive of Series 57 was now fully armored. In the summer of 1944 another revision took place, in which this locomotive, meanwhile lost, was replaced by a Russian armored type (see the locomotive chapter); the Russian gun turrets were replaced by ten-sided types (the guns were retained) like those of the BP 42 standard train, and the train also received tank-destroyer cars with Panzer IV turrets and 7.5-cm KwK L/48 guns.

When Armored Trains No. 26 and 31 (as PZ 1) were sent back for modernizing in November or December 1942 (the first to the Zwickau, the latter to the Gleiwitz RAW), a plan was applied that had been used already in the summer of 1942 in the rebuilding of PZ 6 (still without tank carriers) and 27 (which added a spotlight car later) that equaled the arming and manning of the K.St.N./K.A.N. 1169x of the BP 42 standard train, though it was planned for a different yet uniform arrangement. Its essential mark was the use of captured Russian four-axle cars as two-turret gun cars (uniformly fitted with 7.62-cm F.K. 295/1(r) guns). While they were taken over essentially unchanged for PZ 31—similar to the earlier revision of PZ 6 and 27—though with ten-sided German tank turrets, those of PZ 26 received a completely new armored body with an observation post in the center and two German-made turrets at different levels. From then on, only the second type of cars was used in revising armored trains. The A/A quad was mounted on its own cars, running before and behind the armored locomotive, with the kitchen and the medical room located in their other halves. These cars—the command cars stuck in between them—were rebuilt two- or three-axle freight cars. In all the following lineup was used, running from the locomotive out, in each half of the train:

A/A car—command car—gun car—tank carrier (for PZ 27, 28, and 31, and in the takeover of PZ 26 by PZ 1—still the type used before, but fitted with a fixed ramp and Panzer 38(t) tanks, otherwise the uniform BP 42 type with the same tanks)—contact car; later the last one was replaced by a tank-destroyer car.

This scheme for reconstruction based on the standard BP 42 type was used not only for PZ 26 and 31 of the "Barbarossa" series, but also—as already noted in the previous chapter—for all other older trains that were modernized since the end of 1942. Here is a complete list of them:

PZ #	Rebuilding began	Ready for Service	Workshop
1	12/14/1942	8/22/1943	RAW Königsberg
2	7/19/44	rebuilding stopped 11/2/1944	
4	12/23/1943	Jan. 1945	Koenigshuette RR Works
7	3/4/1944	5/1/1945	Koenigshuette RR Works, RAW Ingolstadt
23	10/23/1942	8/14/1943	RAW Gleiwitz
24	3/10/1943	1/26/1944	RAW Munich-Neuaubing
25	Sept. 1944	Nov. 1944	RAW Leipzig-Engelsdorf
26	3/8/1943	2/19/1944	RAW Zwickau
31	11/2/1942	10/14/1943	RAW Gleiwitz

Armored Trains No. 6 (rebuilt at the Pruszkow OAW, July-September 1942) and 27 (rebuilt at the Eberswalde PAW, June-September 1942), which varied only slightly from this scheme, were to match the K.St.N./K.A.N. 1169x fully in February 1944. Armored Trains No. 3 (rebuilt at the Königsberg Railroad Workshops, 9/11/1943 – 7/12/1944) and 30 (rebuilt at the Eberswalde RAW, Nov. 1942 – 2/8/1944) were also to be revised according to K.St.N./K.A.N. 1169x using rebuilt captured Russian cars, but with differently equipped cars in a different order (in particular, four two-axle one-turret gun cars instead of two two-turret, four-axle types). PZ 28's Somua tanks were intended to be replaced by T 34s in the early summer of 1943, but this did not take place (later it received the usual Praga 38(t) for the tank carrier cars). Its rebuilding (January-May 1944, started at the Nikolaiev EAW, finished at some unknown place after that was vacated on 3/9/1944) included mounting of 7.62-cm 298(r) antitank guns on the contact cars and replacement of the single 2-cm guns with another quad complied with K.St.N. 1169x, although equipped with varying guns. Since PZ 21 in December 1943 and PZ 11 in the summer of 1944 had been revised according to the K.St.N./K.A.N. 1169x (the latter only at that time by replacing the single 2-cm guns with A/A quads and adding carrier cars with 38(t) and tank-destroyer cars), the former variety of armored trains in armament and crews—though with the loss of other trains before that measure was planned—was almost completely eliminated. Only PZ 22 remained an exception, as its different artillery armament—only three guns—did not allow such a change, as it was likewise true of PZ 51 with its four small caliber (4.5-cm) guns in tank turrets, but which came closer to the K.St.N. 1169x in February 1944 with the provision of Praga 38(t) tanks on carrier cars.

Of the Soviet armored trains that fell into German hands in large numbers, especially in 1941 and 1942, though in very different conditions (from fully unharmed to totally destroyed), much was used to reequip the older German armored trains. Other material of the kind was also used in makeshift armored trains set up and operated by the troops (line protection trains); their composition, of course, was very heterogeneous, and also went through many changes.

It can be determined, though, that the captured armored trains—except temporarily in some line protection trains—were never reused in unchanged form. For one thing they did not conform, with

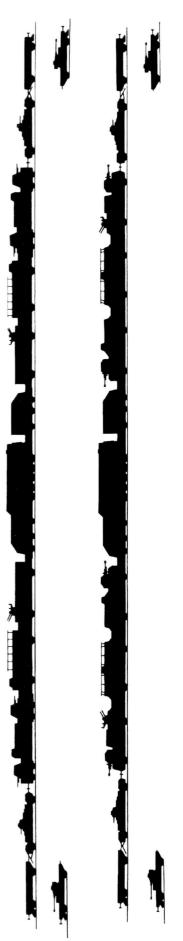

Composition scheme for most older armored trains (PZ 1-31) revised and reequipped according to K.St.N.1169x, compared with the standard BP 42 type or BP 44 (equipment with tank-destroyer cars). Drawing: U. Schwarze

their low numbers of cars (at that time they consisted of an armored locomotive, contact cars, and, at most, two two-turret—or four one-turret—gun cars) to the German concepts; for another, their later use, exclusively in standard gauge, required rebuilding in any case (for this reason, presumably, very few Russian locomotives were ever used). The primitive internal amenities also could not have satisfied German standards. For reequipping the very inadequately equipped "Barbarossa" armored trains, the captured Russian cars were, of course, very welcome, and even their broad gauge could be kept at first. When they were included in German trains, the number of gun turrets was sometimes reduced, or they were completely removed. From 1943 on only the chassis was used more and more often, with a new armored body built on it; the retained soviet guns were now housed in the ten-sided German-made armored turrets.

Like the Poles, the Russians preferred to use four-axle chassis in their armored trains, while two-axle types were commonly used by the Germans. This greater number of axles, even when two gun turrets were installed on a car, allowed heavier armor (up to 50 mm) than that of the German cars (30 mm, which was always a weak point of these designs) without letting the axle pressure become too great (20 tons was the upper limit). This improved equipping was naturally retained when they were used in German armored trains. On the other hand, the pivot mounting of the four-axle cars made derailed cars, which occurred more and more often as a result of partisan action as the war went on, considerably harder to get back onto the rails than two-axle German cars. This aspect was responsible for the fact that the Germans did not switch to four axles on German-built cars, but also limited the axles as much as possible on rebuilt cars.

PZ 26 at the start of the Russian campaign. The rear half of the train differed only in that it had only one (instead of two) tank carrier car with Somua S 35 tanks. Photo: P. Voneif/W. Sawodny collection

Later (early 1942?) a captured Russian "Krasnoye Sormovo" car was used with the front gun turret rebuilt as an observation post, the rear one as an A/A platform with 2-cm quad. The infantry cars show flat roofs. Photo: H. Jäger/W. Sawodny collection

In the rear half of the train two two-axle O-cars with steel walls were added, seen here behind the infantry car with its tent-canvas covering (in the foreground). Photo: H. Jäger/W. Sawodny collection

The rebuilding of PZ 26 in 1943 was done to the same plan as PZ 1 and 23; in each half of the train were now an A/A car (the rebuilt infantry car of the old PZ 26), a command car (rebuilt G-car), a four-axle, two-turret gun car (captured Russian car with new body), and a tank carrier car, now with Panzer 38(t) (of Type BP 42; the original tank carrier cars were transferred to PZ 1). Photo: H. Jäger/W. Sawodny collection

After PZ 27 had lost its original cars (like PZ 28, see next page, top) in the enclosure of Sukhinichi early in January 1942, it was equipped with two captured Russian two-turret cars (BP 35 type) at Roslavl. In the rear half of the train a two-axle O-car was added. The contact cars were also Russian-built; only the German 57 locomotive, with only its cab armored, remained when the train was still used on broad gauge. Photo: W. Hahn/W. Sawodny collection

At the end of May 1942 the front gun car of PZ 27 was destroyed. Rebuilding was undertaken at the Eberswalde RAW. The material of a deactivated rail protection train was used; several cars of the old PZ 27, recaptured at Suchinichi and taken along with this train, were again used as tank carriers, but now with 38(t) tanks. This train was also the source of the gun car with the round turrets and the former Polish "assault" car (from "Pierwszy Marszalek") that was rebuilt as an A/A car; it is seen here running between the command car (a rebuilt G-car) and the locomotive—still the old one, but now fully armored. Photo: R. J. Roddewig/W. Sawodny collection

Later (1943) a four-axle car with a spotlight mounted on it (recognizable by its dark color) was added to PZ 27. Photo: H. J. Roddewig/W. Sawodny collection

PZ 28 at the beginning of the eastern campaign. The frame antenna built on the tender is easy to see; the radio cabin was inside the tender. Here too, the open infantry car was already covered with tent canvas. Photo: Federal Archives, Koblenz

In the autumn of 1941, PZ 28 could already incorporate a complete captured Russian heavy armored train (two Type BP 35 cars with a 10.7-cm cannon in a turret). The German infantry cars were happily left with the quarters train and the Russian Type O locomotive was preferred to the 57 with only the cab armored. Only the tank carrier cars with Somua tanks (both edges of the photo) were left with the train. Photo: Federal Archives, Koblenz

In the summer of 1942 (upon its conversion to standard gauge) this captured material had to be given up. The Type 57 1653 locomotive, with only the cab armored, came back, as did the infantry cars. The Russian gun cars were replaced by others in which the front turret was removed, with an A/A platform installed in its place. Photo: B. Schultz/W. Sawodny collection

A little later the infantry cars at least received fixed gabled roofs. One was equipped as a command car (recognizable by the roof antenna). The picture also gives a good side view of the new gun car with the longer (L/40) 7.62-cm F.K. 295/2(r) in the turret and the A/A quad (the other had a single gun). Photo: E. Lehle/W. Sawodny collection

Only at a new rebuilding in the spring of 1944 did PZ 28 receive a second A/A quad. The locomotive was fully armored, and all the armor was improved. The Somua S 35 tanks were replaced by Panzer 38(t)s. In particular, the earlier contact cars were rebuilt. They received an armored body in which a 7.62-cm ZIS-3 or 298(r) Pak was mounted. In the back part is the ammunition bunker, on which the spotlight is installed. Photo: E. Lehle/W. Sawodny collection

Left: The first two digits on the turret of the Somua S 35 tank show that this is PZ 29 (shortly after the start of the Russian campaign). It is also easy to see that the crew of the infantry car was protected by the side armor only when they were lying down. Photo: Federal Archives, Koblenz

This picture of PZ 30 in action in the northern sector of the eastern front gives the same impression, but as a rear view, looking back on the locomotive 57 1504. Photo: Federal Archives, Cologne

The cars of PZ 30 had—though on the same Ommr Linz chassis—somewhat different bodies, and may have been the prototypes of the series. Here a Somua tank is being unloaded from the carrier car. Photo: Federal Archives, Koblenz

PZ 30—although in constant use in the northern sector of the eastern front—had no closed cars until the end of 1942. Only an A/A quad installed on a low-side car, possibly similar to this temporary solution coming from PZ 26, was installed. Photo: H. Jäger/W. Sawodny collection

Only when rebuilt in 1943 was PZ 30 completely equipped with new material—the closed cars were all captured from the Russians. In place of the tank carrier cars turned over to PZ 24 it received Type BP 42 cars with Panzer 38(t) tanks. The locomotive—still 57 1504—was now fully armored. Photo: Federal Archives, Koblenz

When it was reequipped in the first half of 1944 PZ 30 was given a captured Russian locomotive, new German-made gun turrets, and additional tank-destroyer cars. Photo: W. Conrad/W. Sawodny collection

In PZ 31 too, a four-axle Soviet armored train car was added in the winter of 1941-42 to protect the crew from the cold. Photo: H. von Heymann/W. Sawodny collection

In the spring of 1942 a Russian Type BP 35 armored car was also added, with one of its gun turrets replaced by an A/A platform. Photo: N. Bartel collection

In a total rebuilding in 1943, the later general plan was already followed—four-axle, two-turret gun cars, G-car rebuilt as a command car, A/A cars—but the gun car kept its boxy shape, although already fitted with German turrets. Thus, it represents a transitional stage from the former (PZ 6, 27, 28, 30) to the later (PZ 1, 23, 26) revisions. Photo: W. Sawodny collection

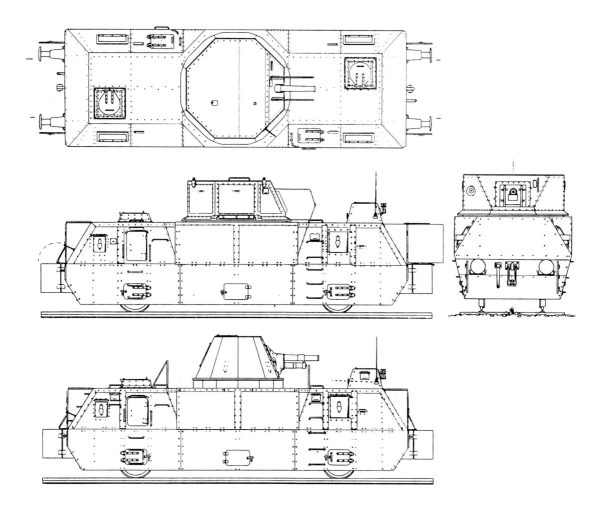

Soviet armored train cars used for reequipping. *Above:* One-turret, two-axle (top and front views, Russian type; side view: German modification with Soviet- or German-built turret) used on PZ 30 and 3. *Next page, above:* Soviet Type BP 35, also with round turrets as on PZ 27 and 31, as in one-turret heavy type in PZ 28 and—turret replaced by A/A platform—as command and A/A car in PZ 10, 11, and 30. *Below:* New German construction on Russian chassis, here from PZ 25; similar but with certain modifications in PZ 1, 4, 7, 23, 24, and 26. Drawings: P. Malmassari

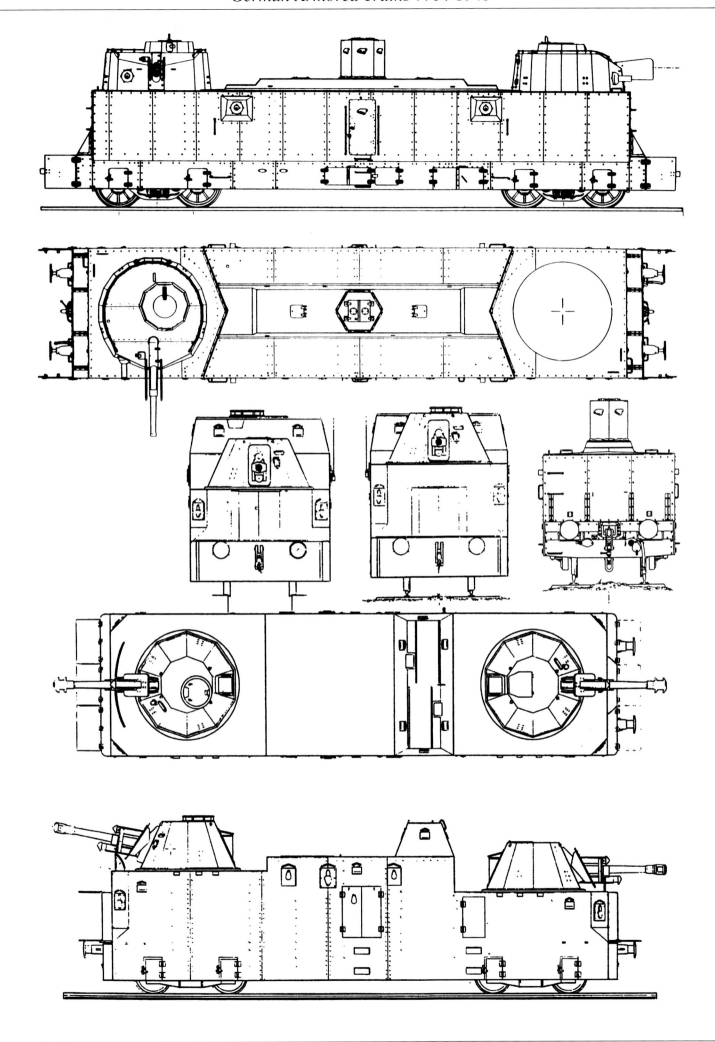

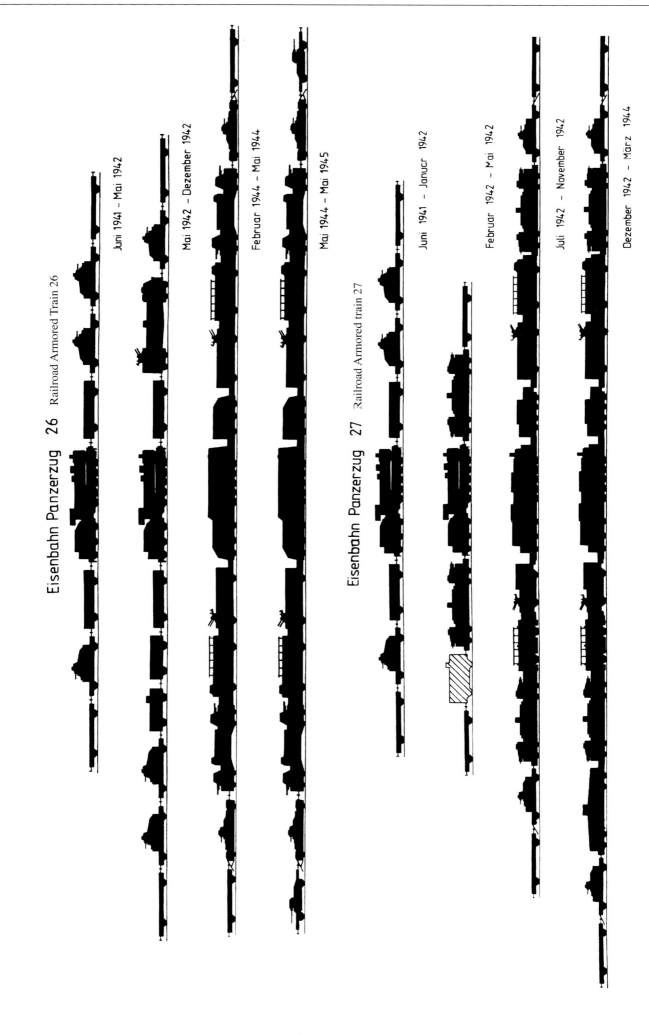

Eisenbahn Panzerzug 26 — Railroad Armored Train 26

Juni 1941 – Mai 1942

Mai 1942 – Dezember 1942

Februar 1944 – Mai 1944

Mai 1944 – Mai 1945

Eisenbahn Panzerzug 27 — Railroad Armored train 27

Juni 1941 – Januar 1942

Februar 1942 – Mai 1942

Juli 1942 – November 1942

Dezember 1942 – März 1944

PZ 27, badly damaged in March 1944, was built anew and ready for action at the end of April 1945. Nothing is known of the train's composition.

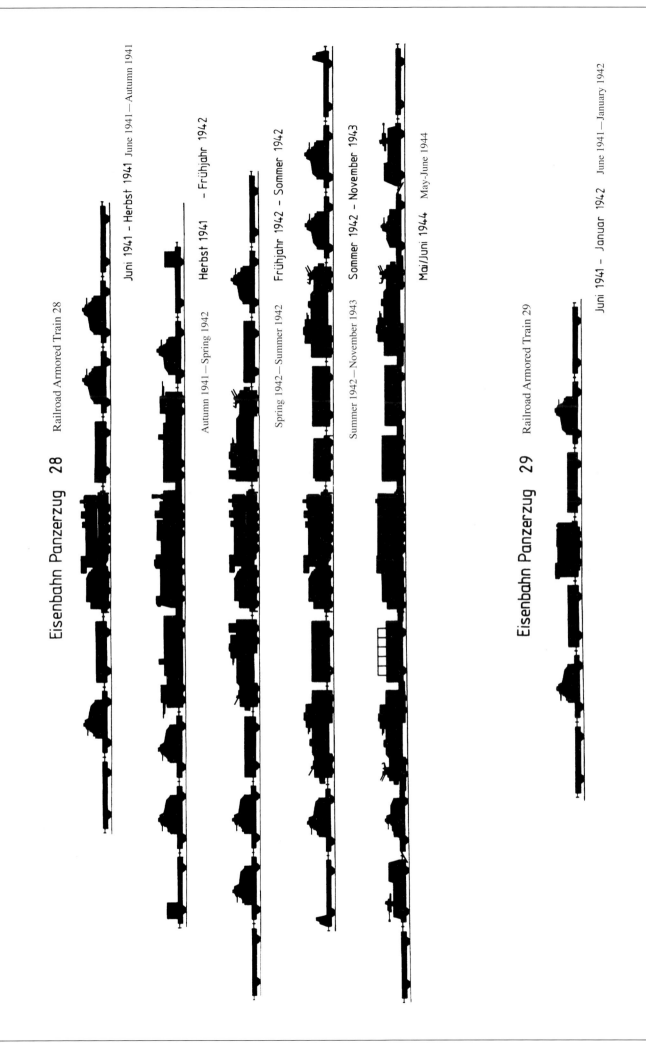

Eisenbahn Panzerzug 28   Railroad Armored Train 28

Juni 1941 – Herbst 1941   June 1941 — Autumn 1941

Herbst 1941 – Frühjahr 1942   Autumn 1941 — Spring 1942

Frühjahr 1942 – Sommer 1942   Spring 1942 — Summer 1942

Sommer 1942 – November 1943   Summer 1942 — November 1943

Mai/Juni 1944   May-June 1944

Eisenbahn Panzerzug 29   Railroad Armored Train 29

Juni 1941 – Januar 1942   June 1941 — January 1942

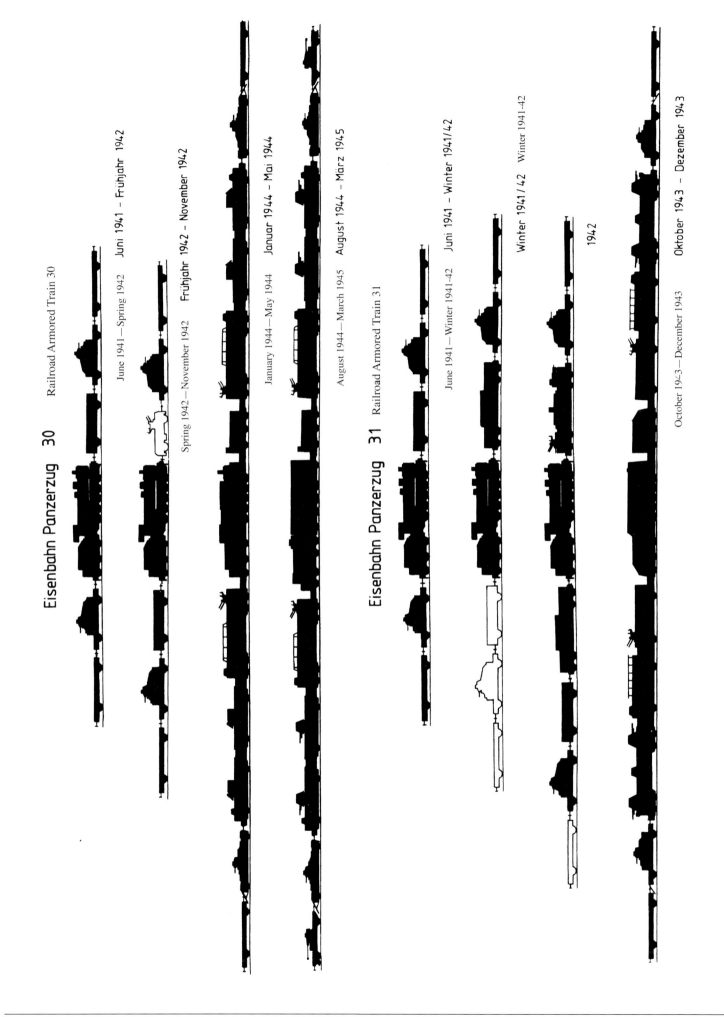

Eisenbahn Panzerzug 30   Railroad Armored Train 30

June 1941 — Spring 1942   Juni 1941 – Frühjahr 1942

Spring 1942 — November 1942   Frühjahr 1942 – November 1942

January 1944 — May 1944   Januar 1944 – Mai 1944

August 1944 — March 1945   August 1944 – März 1945

Eisenbahn Panzerzug 31   Railroad Armored Train 31

June 1941 — Winter 1941-42   Juni 1941 – Winter 1941/42

Winter 1941/42   Winter 1941-42

1942

October 1943 — December 1943   Oktober 1943 – Dezember 1943

Of the Polish armored trains that fell into Soviet hands in 1939, after being taken over by the Germans the "Smialy"—now with a Type O Russian armored locomotive—became Combat Train A of PZ 10 (left). Combat Train B (right) with the gun car of the "Pierwszy Marszalek" (Krasnoye Sormovo type) at first kept the Polish armored locomotive Ti 3(-2?) converted by the Russians to broad gauge. In the rear half of the train, another ex-Polish "assault car" ran next to the same gun car. Photos: W. Pflaumbaum/W. Sawodny collection

After conversion in the summer of 1942, Combat Train A received a Series 57 armored locomotive. A rebuilt heavy Soviet armored train car served as an A/A and command car (in front of the loco). Behind the loco is the "assault" car of the Polish "Bartosz Glowacki" armored train. In the rear half of the train, the A/A gun was mounted on an armored low-side car of the same type as the infantry car of the German broad gauge armored trains (far right in the photo). Photo: W. Pflaumbaum/W. Sawosny collection

Combat Train B also received a Series 57 armored locomotive during conversion in the summer of 1942. As in Combat Train A, heavy Russian armored train cars served as command and A/A cars, here in both halves of the train. This combination was also kept after it became the independent PZ 11 up to the summer of 1944.

Only during overhauling in Lemberg in the early summer of 1944 were the single A/A guns replaced by quads, and PZ 11 received additional tank-destroyer wagons with Panzer IV-H turret, visible in the picture. Photo: E. Wienss/W. Sawodny collection

PZ 51, built at Pruszkow in the summer of 1942, consisted of internally armored Russian freight cars. *Above and below:* Two GG-cars—lowered from the center back—carried two Soviet BT-7 turrets of different heights with 4.5-cm tank guns. In the rear half of the train was another GG-car converted to an A/A car (2-cm quad), and in the front an OOt-car made into a command car. The armored locomotive belonged to the German 38 series. In all, this armored train could not deny its origin as a line protection train. Photos: M. Streit and A. Hagemeier/W. Sawodny collection

In the spring of 1944, PZ 51 received tank carrier cars which were built like those of the earlier broad gauge armored cars (PZ 26-31), but with fixed side walls. Panzer 38(t) were used on them. Photo: W. Sitzius/W. Sawodny collection

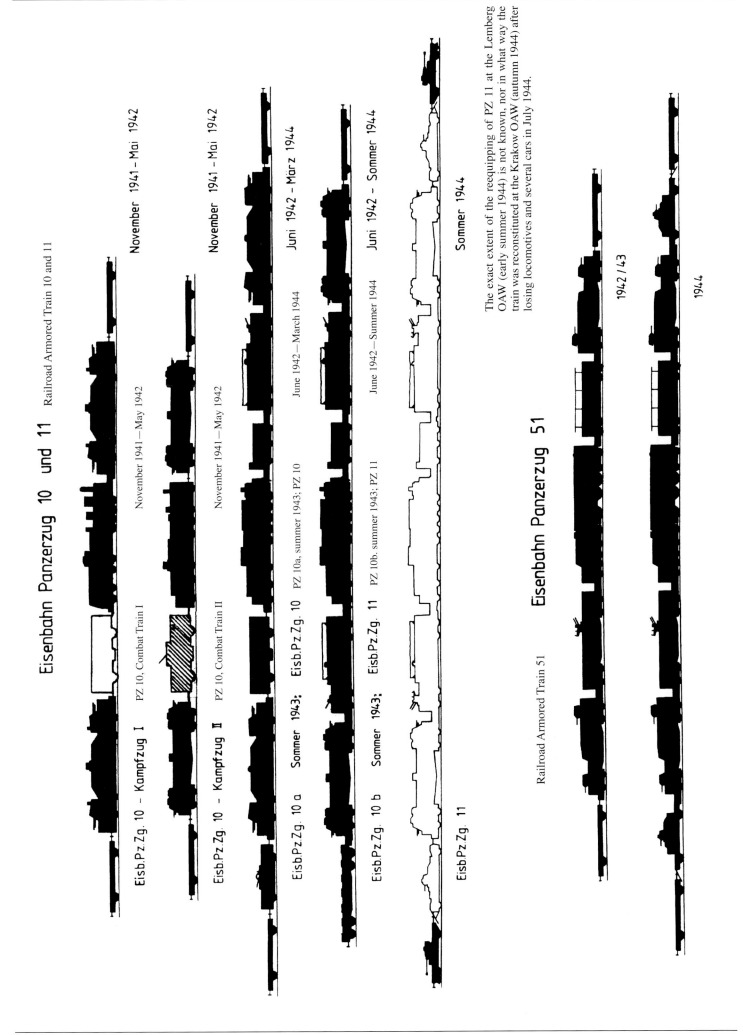

Eisenbahn Panzerzug 10 und 11   Railroad Armored Train 10 and 11

Eisb.Pz.Zg. 10 – Kampfzug I   PZ 10, Combat Train I   November 1941 – Mai 1942   November 1941 – May 1942

Eisb.Pz.Zg. 10 – Kampfzug II   PZ 10, Combat Train II   November 1941 – Mai 1942   November 1941 – May 1942

Eisb.Pz.Zg. 10 a   Sommer 1943;   PZ 10a, summer 1943; PZ 10   Juni 1942 – März 1944   June 1942 — March 1944

Eisb.Pz.Zg. 10 b   Sommer 1943;   PZ 10b. summer 1943; PZ 11   Juni 1942 – Sommer 1944   June 1942 — Summer 1944

Eisb.Pz.Zg. 11   Sommer 1944

The exact extent of the reequipping of PZ 11 at the Lemberg OAW (early summer 1944) is not known, nor in what way the train was reconstituted at the Krakow OAW (autumn 1944) after losing locomotives and several cars in July 1944.

Railroad Armored Train 51   Eisenbahn Panzerzug 51

1942 / 43

1944

1942-43: The Standard Type BP 42 and its Further Development to BP 44

Under the aegis of the competence of the Railroad Engineers (1938-1941) one was content to take over rail protection trains and captured Czech and Polish armored trains. Suggestions of In 10 from the end of 1940 were only realized in provisional form (the "Barbarossa" trains as an immediate solution to Panzerzug 1941) or not at all (Panzerzug SP 42). Thus, a collection of 18 armored trains was created which varied much in their numbers of cars and equipment, so that each one had its own individual character. This impression was strengthened later on with the inclusion of captured Russian material, whether for reequipping existing armored trains or creating new ones in 1942. In the meantime, the armored trains had been assigned to the Fast Troops in August 1941, and thus In 6 had become responsible for their further development so as to attain a uniform solution for the future, since in view of the extent of the area gained by then and the danger to the back line connections by partisans in Russia and the Balkans an increased use of armored trains was to be expected.

In the established requirements it was tried to unite all viewpoints as much as possible. A numerically strong infantry crew, armed with machine guns and mortars and able to operate outside the train, was agreed on. For their support, two unloadable Praga 38(t) tanks on their own carrier cars were included (taken over from the Panzerzug 1941 plan and the "Barbarossa" trains). An engineer troop was not only to make needed repairs to the tracks and the train (the materials were carried on the contact cars), but also to support infantry attacks on fortified places with flamethrowers and explosives. With Polish and Russian armored trains as models, the considerably strengthened artillery armament was developed using exclusively captured material. Every train was to receive two 7.62-cm Field Cannon 295/1(r) and two 10-cm Howitzer 14/19(p). Two 2-cm A/A quads were also provided, not only to fight off air attacks but also to intervene effectively in ground combat. To allow easy recovery in case of derailing, it was decided to build all the cars on two-axle Ommr Linz chassis (wheelbase 6.0 meters); only the tank carriers were a special design, with the same number of axles, but with the wheelbase lengthened to 7.0 meters. Because of the limitation of the axle pressure they could use only relatively thin armor, resistant to cored bullets and splinters (maximum thickness 30 mm), though they were also well aware of this weakness. It was stated in the requirements of In 6 "Makeshift armored train, SmK-secure." This word probably also brought about the choice of the abbreviation "BP 42" (= behelfsmässiger Panzerzug 1942) and shows that a different solution was envisioned in the future, which of course never happened; this type of train was built in this form, never improved in this feature, until the war ended.

The development contract for this BP 42 armored train was issued to the Linke-Hofmann firm in Breslau in January 1942, and one for the armor of the planned Series 57 (Prussian G 10) locomotives, with two tenders per locomotive, went to the Krupp firm in Essen. The design details were worked out by June 20, 1942, and a wooden model was built. According to this original plan the train included ten cars:

- 2 combat and infantry cars
- 2 command cars (one with built-in kitchen, one with medical room)
- 2 A/A and gun cars
- 2 tank carrier cars with Panzer 38(t) tanks
- 2 contact cars.

These cars were divided into two equal halves, in the order listed above, running out from the armored locomotive in the center (the second tender was coupled in front of it) to the ends. For reasons of weight, only one gun turret could be mounted per car. The car with the small-caliber 7.62-cm F.K. 295/1(r) could also carry a platform for the 2-cm A/A quad (A/A and gun car); the heavy 10-cm F.H. 14/19(p) was installed on the combat car. In series construction a change was made in the order, with the howitzer cars now taking the kitchen and medical cabins, while the infantry crews were housed in the command cars. The armor plates, with a maximum thickness of 30 mm, were supplied by a Ukrainian steel plant near Krivoy Rog. The weight of the two-axle cars was between 27.24 (tank carrier including tanks) and 37.29 tons (howitzer car), so that the heaviest cars had an axle pressure of 18.65 tons (the armored locomotive, for which exact data are not known, may have had a similar or slightly higher pressure). The speed of the BP 42 armored train was listed as 60 kph, its range 180 km, with water and coal supplies as limiting factors. The strengths of the crew and armament, as well as the other equipment, were regulated in K.St.N./K.A.N. 1169x of August 17, 1942, which was already replaced by a new edition on February 1, 1943.

The first six of these new armored trains were ordered by the OKH on July 17, 1942; they were numbered 61 to 66. Two per month (September, October, and November 1942) went into production at the Linke-Hofmann works in Breslau; they were to be finished at two-week intervals beginning on 10/15 and be sent to the Armored Train Replacement Battalion for final equipment and crews. Delays came up soon; though the first (No. 61) was ready for action on December 23, 1942, the last of the series (No. 66) was ready only on July 23, 1943 (the unknown delivery dates from the factory should be several weeks earlier, since the last period before action was used to train the crew on their armored train).—On April 27, 1943, the OKH ordered a second series of this type (Armored trains No. 67-72), which were to be ready for use in the field on the 30th of each month from July to December of that year. The delays in the start of construction were partly even greater (No. 67, 5/15; No. 68, 8/1; No. 69, 8/20; No. 70 and 71, 9/16; No. 72, 11/23/1943), so that the wait until they were ready for action was extended by two to three months.

In 1943 the eastern front, beginning in the southern sector, was moving back more extensively and quickly, and the armored trains—previously used mainly to secure the back line rail network from partisan attacks—were drawn more and more into the actual battles on the front. Here the insufficiency of the armored trains in terms of armor and weaponry became clear; the Type BP 42 armored trains were also no match for the growing numbers of Russian trains to oppose them. If no basic help was possible in the first case because of the two-axle design of the cars (improvement through the use of better steel might have been possible, but was not very likely in light of the lack of such material at that point in the course of the war), so attempts were made at least to improve the armament. The captured 7.62-cm F.K. 295/1(r) and 10-cm F.H. 14/19(p) guns were to be replaced uniformly by the German 10.5-cm Field Howitzer 18M (which could not be done in all cases, because of delivery difficulties), but above all, at the ends of the trains—in place of the contact cars (which were regarded as dispensable; the closer the war came to German soil, the less was the danger of partisan activity, and thus of mining the tracks; later, though, they were often brought back on the responsibility of the trains), based on front experience of the troops and makeshift constructions with captured T-34 turrets on tank destroyers, flat cars with the turret of a Panzer IV (usually Type H) with high-performance 7.5-cm KwK L/48 guns, effective even against Russian T-34 tanks, mounted on appropriately armored bases, were used. The other cars of the train were also improved, as shown by externally visible details, such as the MG ports now cut into the armor plate itself (formerly in screwed-on armor flaps) and the armored bodies now mounted symmetrically on the chassis (formerly moved to one side). But strengthening the armor was not possible for reasons of weight. A more effective organization of the crew was achieved.

On September 6, 1943, the OKH gave out orders for twelve (PZ 73-84) of this improved type, called BP 44, which were to be ready at monthly intervals through 1944 beginning in January. But the delivery of these trains began only in the late spring of 1944, and took until the end of the war, even with the last two trains dropped.

In both series—BP 42 and 44—not only were the combat trains built, but so was a train for the Armored Train Replacement Battalion for training purposes. At first this was PZ 60, but afterward PZ 75 (renamed Panzer-Lehr-Zug 5) was used for this task (later a replacement, PZ 75, was ordered). Of course, these training trains—the last one even overwhelmingly—also saw combat service.

PZ 32 formed a variation of the standard BP 42. The Military Commander of France received instructions to set up this armored train on February 4, 1944; on 11 February he was assigned four 10-cm 14/19 howitzers for it. The French 050 A series locomotive was armored by Schneider in Le Creusot, and the combat cars were built by Somua in Lyon-Venissieux. At first the plans for the BP 42 were followed except for small details, such as changed armor flaps for the MG ports. The armor consisted of chrome-nickel steel (Brinell hardness 80-100 kg) 20 mm thick (subframe 10 cm). An important development, though, besides the cars with a gun turret and a 2-cm A/A gun, which were taken over unchanged from BP 42, the two other gun cars were also fitted with A/A platforms on which a 3.7-cm Cannon 36 was mounted to meet the increased air raid danger in the west, especially after D-Day, was countered. Kitchen and medical compartments were located in the second tender. The two tank carrier cars were delivered by Linke-Hofmann in Breslau, but the Panzer 38(t) tanks that went with them seem not to have arrived on time, for later a Renault R 40 tank was used on the front car and a Gw.LrS self-propelled mount with a Russian 12.2-cm howitzer on the rear one, a unique solution for an armored train. The contact car ahead of the tank carrier car also did not have a Scharfenberg coupling, but was pushed ahead at a long distance by an iron rod, a sign of a temporary measure. To man this train, the crew of PZ 31, lost in Russia at the end of 1943, was transferred to France (which is why the train was also listed as "No. 31"; but one should, to avoid confusion, use the number 32 assigned by the OKH). It went into service in mid-July 1944.

Under the prerequisite of creating a train that was useful for all kinds of action, BP 42 or 44 (remember that all older armored trains were eventually reequipped according to the K.St.N. or K.A.N. 1169x , though in modified arrangements) was probably a tolerable compromise despite some weaknesses like the insufficient armor, but the practicality of this prerequisite itself can certainly be questioned.

For the tasks of securing the lines and partisan fighting, armor that was secure against S.m.K. bullets was quite sufficient, and heavy artillery was not necessary. But good mobility of the train itself (short overall length) and of the crew outside the train (equipped with tanks, armored scout cars, engineer equipment) were of value. The "Barbarossa" armored trains met these requirements sufficiently—after the infantry had been housed in closed cars in the first rebuilding phase, and A/A armament that could also be used effectively in ground combat had been added. Equipment that went beyond this just resulted in needless costs and the risk of more men and valuable material, especially in that it was never possible to prevent partisan attacks on the armored trains; on the contrary, they grew worse, what with war progressing through the strengthening of partisan bands, and their ever-better information services and growing experience in the use of special explosives. In a report on May 19, 1944, it was therefore recommended that makeshift track protection trains be used rather than armored trains.

For front duty, though (remember, this occurred only on the eastern front), not only was the armor insufficient, but so was the equipping with armor piercing weapons, although here the addition of the tank-destroyer car to the BP 44 brought a certain improvement. In addition, the mobility of the train in battle was also of decisive importance, so one may ask whether it would not have been practical to decrease the number of cars. This would have had to be done at the cost of the infantry and artillery. Although the effect of armored trains working together with infantry units in action was often desirable, it is questionable whether it was necessary to take them along in the train, or whether this could be achieved with temporarily assigned troops too. Still less insightful in hindsight, apparently, is the artillery (field cannons and howitzers), and one may keep in mind that they were at first very weak in the German armored cars in the early stages of the war, and only later—probably under the impression of the captured Polish and Russian armored trains—were strengthened considerably. Neither for line securing and partisan fighting (machine guns like the A/A quads were much more effective for this purpose) nor for front service (for which armor piercing weapons had more advantages by far) was equipping them with guns really necessary. It only allowed the armored train to be used as a mobile battery behind the front (which happened often); such an action, though, would have been just as possible with unarmored trains.—In August 1944 an armored train for front duty was suggested by 1st Lt. Rolf Lorscheidt, then Commander of PZ 11; besides a Type V 36 Diesel locomotive, a command car and two A/A cars fitted with 2-cm quads, which also contained a kitchen and medical compartment in the other half of the train (all three cars show four axles with a modest overall length of 7.7 meters, which suggests very heavy armor), it consisted of six tank-destroyer cars with Panzer IV turrets (7.5-cm KwK L/48). This surely would have been much better suited to combat purposes than the somewhat simultaneously delivered BP 44 armored train, even if

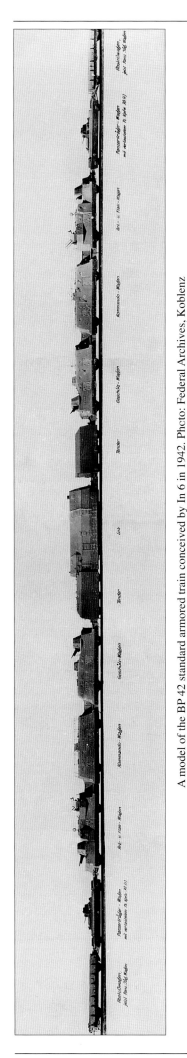

A model of the BP 42 standard armored train conceived by In 6 in 1942. Photo: Federal Archives, Koblenz

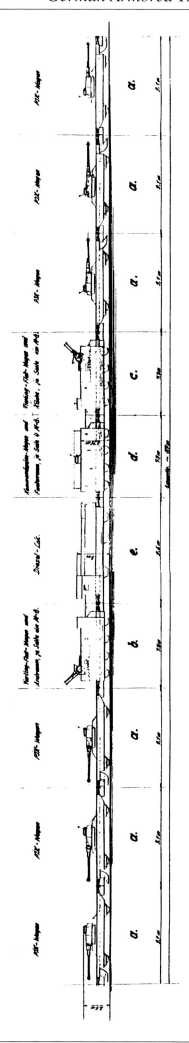

A drawing of an armored train for front duty by 1st Lt. Lorscheidt (August 1944). Drawing: R. Lorscheidt/W. Sawodny collection

the number of tank-destroyer cars had been reduced to four (which brought not only a saving of material, but would also have increased the mobility). In any case, such a train was never built.

The discussion shows that it probably would have been more practical two build two or three different kinds of trains instead of the uniform BP 42 or 44:

1. Line protection trains for securing rail lines and fighting partisans (lightly armored, equipped with machine guns and unloadable armored vehicles; infantry and engineers).
2. Armored trains for front action (heavily armored, armor piercing weapons, A/A equipment, also for ground action).
3. Perhaps light railroad artillery (unarmored).

Naturally their versatility, which allowed a quick change of type of action with one and the same train, would have been lost. But for the first-named use at least—whether at first for lack of armored trains, and later because of their described considerations—special line protection trains (in the Balkans, the light and heavy scout trains—see following chapter) were created along with armored trains.

It should not be ignored that the moral effect of strongly armed, outwardly imposing BP 42 or 44 armored trains, which supported their own forces' backbone (especially those without heavy weapons), at first scared the enemy—whether partisan bands or regular infantry units—until they had learned the weak points and attacked the armored trains with mines and delayed fuses or antitank guns, or even tanks—at least that was the situation at the end of 1943.

Despite that, the concept of the BP 42 armored train—too complex for one purpose, insufficient for the other, unlimited, usable only for that for which an armored train was not necessarily essential—had not, in the end, been a forward-looking design; its further development into BP 44 was a halfhearted measure that did not result in curing its faults. It remains to be affirmed that the Armored Inspection In 6 obviously had essentially more conservative concepts of armored trains than did In 10 of the railroad engineers previously for their suggestions for the Panzerzug 1941 or SP 42, which—taken to their planned conclusion—would have been a much more progressive solution, better suited to their primary task of securing rail lines.

An armored train of the standard BP 42 type. The lower photo—without the locomotive—shows the mirror-image look of the two halves with their howitzer cars. Photos: H. D. Becker and J. Dicke/W. Sawodny collection

The improved BP 44 type. While the cars show minor changes from those of BP 42, the armament (four 10.5-cm 18/40 light howitzers, added tank-destroyer cars with Panzer IV-H turrets (7.5-cm KwK L/48)) had been much strengthened. Photos: Federal Archives, Koblenz

[BP 42]

[BP 44]

[BP 44]

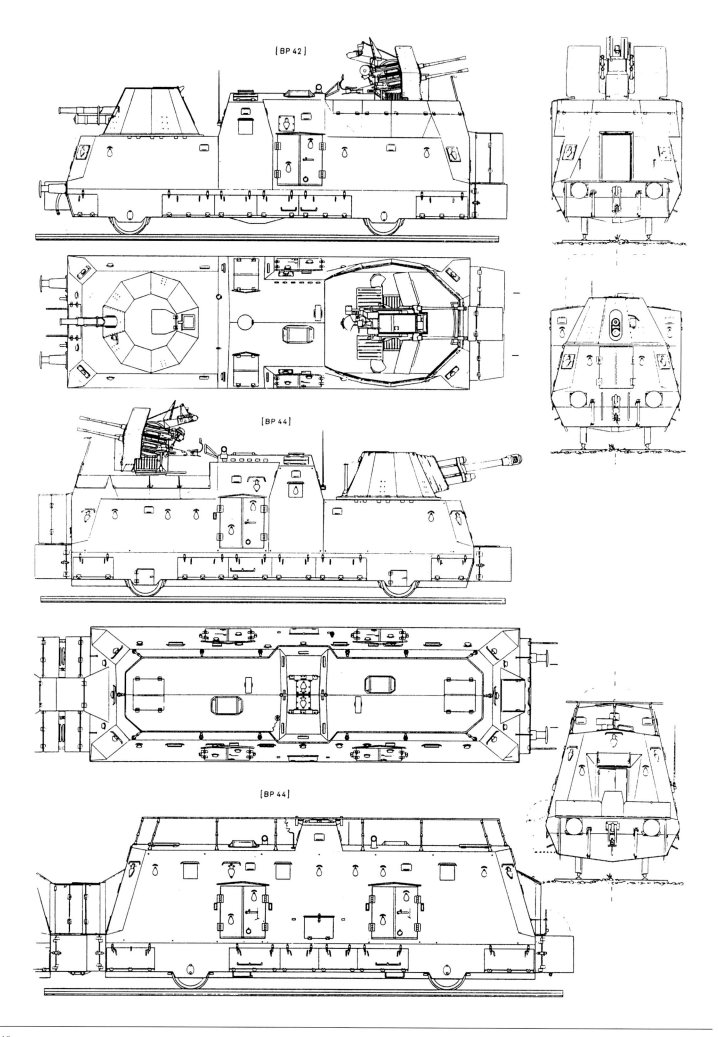

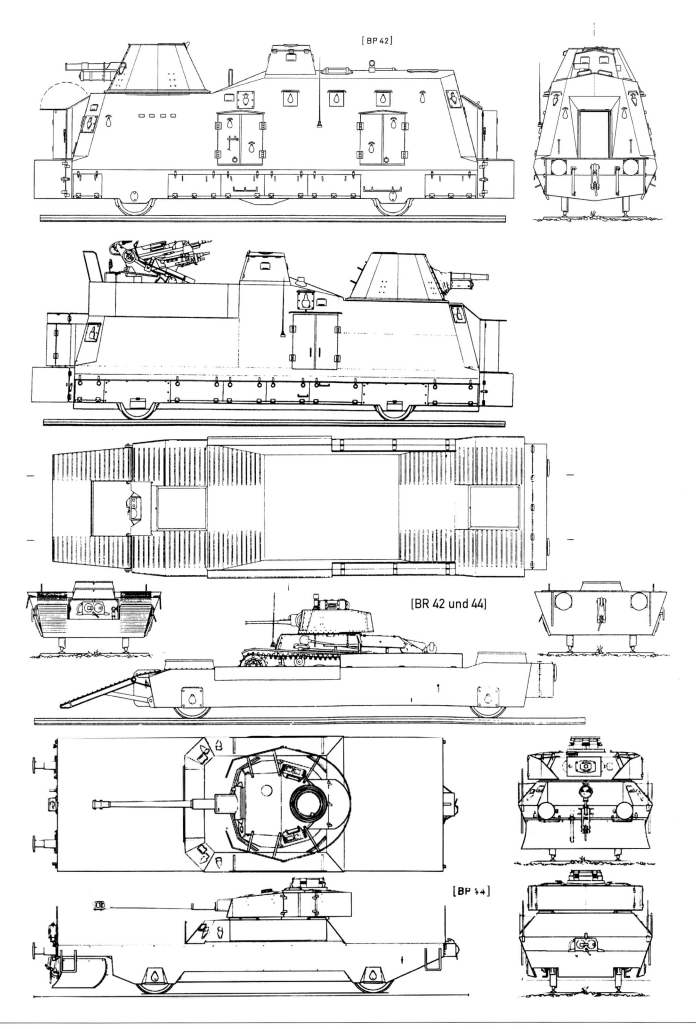

[BP 42]

[BR 42 und 44]

[BP 44]

A variant of BP 42 was PZ 32, built in France in 1944. Here the howitzer car in the other half of the train also gained a platform on which a 3.7-cm flak gun was mounted. The other cars were like those of BP 42. Photo: P. Sue/Malmassari collection

The tank carrier cars of PZ 32 were also supplied with unusual vehicles, like the self-propelled Lorraine-Schlepper LrS mount with a Russian 12.2-cm M 38 F.H. The photo was taken after the war, when the French displayed this captured armored train in their country. The cars were rearranged. In place of the second car with a 3.7-cm A/A gun, which belongs behind the locomotive, there was originally, of course, a car with a 2-cm A/A quad. Photo: "La Vie du Rail" Archives *Below:* This car is seen in the photo of the train's other half (likewise from after the war). Note the flaps of the MG ports, somewhat changed from BP 42. The train's artillery consisted throughout of 10 cm light F.H. 14.19 (p). On the tank carrier car (right) in this half of the train there was a captured French Renault R 40 tank. Photo: S.I.R.P.A./E.C.P.A., Paris

1943-44: The Light and Heavy Rail Scout Cars

In the spring of 1943, the danger of partisan attacks on supply lines in the Balkans and Greece increased greatly. The Commander Southeast thus called for additional armored trains. In June and July 1943 he received two BP 42 trains, but it was seen on a test run that they were too heavy for the light roadbeds and makeshift bridges in Greece. Therefore, an idea was taken up that had been initiated at the end of the twenties with the building of Czech Tatra type armored railcars, which could run either as motor-driven individual vehicles or be combined into columns or trains. Before the war, very flexible trains made up of such self-propelled vehicles were seen in Poland (which had obtained some of these Tatra railcars), as well as by the German General Staff, as superior to conventional armored trains with steam locomotives and cars, but in spite of this view no practical results were generated. In the final solution for the "Panzerzug 1941" suggested by In 10 at the end of 1940 trains based on this concept reappeared. One can assume that planning on this basis was followed further, for in August 1943 the Steyr firm was contracted with for the building of such motor-driven armored railcars, also called "armored rail scout cars," which could be coupled together to form trains.

Two types of them were developed, a light and a heavy armored rail scout car; later light and heavy armored trains were made up of them. The two-axle light armored rail scout car was built on chassis of the Steyr BM 40G passenger motor car. It had an overall length of 5.69 meters (body 5.50 m, wheelbase 2.20 m), and angled-walled armor had a thickness of 14.5 mm on the sides, 10 mm on the bottom, and 5 mm on top. The empty weight was 7.5 tons and the load limit was two tons, so that with a total weight of 9.5 tons an axle pressure of only 4.75 tons resulted. The air-cooled 3.5-liter 8-cylinder motor of Porsche design produced a sustained power of 70 HP (51.5 kW)

at 2500 rpm, worked via a four-speed gearbox with switched-in reversing gear, allowed equal forward and backward motion in all speeds, and drove both axles via roller chains. The top speed was 60 kph and the fuel consumption 35-40 liters per 100 km, so that with a tank capacity of 160 liters a range of some 400 km resulted. At each end of the car was a command post, and next to the driver's seat was another seat for the machine-gunner. Another seat for the fifth crewman was in the middle beside the off-center motor. In the body there were six cut-out MG ports with vision slits (two at each end, one on each side), and four machine guns were carried. On the roof were two symmetrically located observation turrets with folding-out covers, three vision slits each, and three brackets for machine guns for anti-aircraft defense, with a hanging seat below. The motor could be removed through the removable central part of the roof. The roof also carried the frame antenna for the 30-watt radio set. At each end there were two headlights with covers which could be operated from the driver's seat, plus a central coupling formed as a towing and pushing device. A five- or six-man crew was suggested. Ten of these light armored rail scout cars formed a light armored train (le.Sp.), two of them functioning as command cars (half-trains of five railcars were often used); the cars went into action separately, usually in pairs for mutual cover); of the other eight cars, two were manned by engineers, the other six by infantry, and the full crew including the supply train numbered two officers, 16 NCOs, and 53 men.—According to instructions from the OKH on August 25, 1943, four such light armored trains (No. 301-304) were built; they were finished and put into service during the first half of 1944. The total number of light armored railcars, which could also be used individually as command cars for armored train regimental staffs, may have added up to about 50 (including those for replacement).

The first prototype of the light armored rail scout car. Ball mantlets are provided for machine guns, and the headlights are mounted openly. The ventilator flaps in the door to the motor are open, and there are also two entry hatches on this side. Photo: Steyr-Daimler-Puch Archives

For the light armored scout car, the chassis of the BM 40G passenger motor car of the Steyr company was used. The off-center mounting of the air-cooled V-8 motor can be seen clearly. Photo: Steyr-Daimler-Puch Archives

Foot and Hand Controls of the rear driver's position

1. Clutch pedal
2. Foot brake pedal
3. Accelerator pedal
4. Hand brake lever
5. Reverse shift lever
6. Gearshift lever
7. Sand-strewing lever

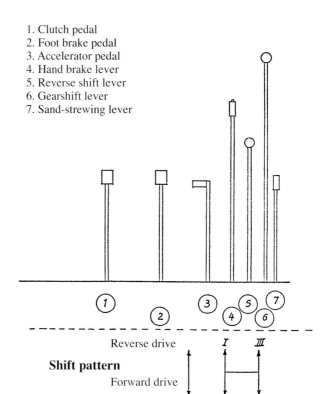

Left: Driver's position on the chassis of the BM 40G motor car. In the light scout car, the reverse and sand levers were added and the armature board was rectangular and upright. *Right:* Backward shift controls (schematic) of the light scout car. Levers 4-7 were mounted in the opposite order at the front driver's position, to the left of 1-3. Photo: Steyr-Daimler-Puch Archives

View of a late prototype of the light armored rail scout car, already with the frame antenna for the Fu 22 SE 30 radio. The headlights—just two in the lower body—are closed with square flaps. The automatic coupling that only these cars had is easy to see. The ventilator louvers for the motor are covered with rectangular armored flaps. Photo: Steyr-Daimler-Puch Archives

These rectangular covers of the ventilator louvers were also used in the first series model, but round armored flaps for the headlights are now present. Photo: J. Loop collection

Later (here in the last delivered railcar train No. 303) these three rectangular flaps were replaced by an arrangement of eight mushroom-like armored covers (as in the heavy railcar). Photo: P. G. Roemer/W. Sawodny collection.

A light railcar half-train consisted of five cars (the full train had ten). Photo: Federal Archives, Koblenz

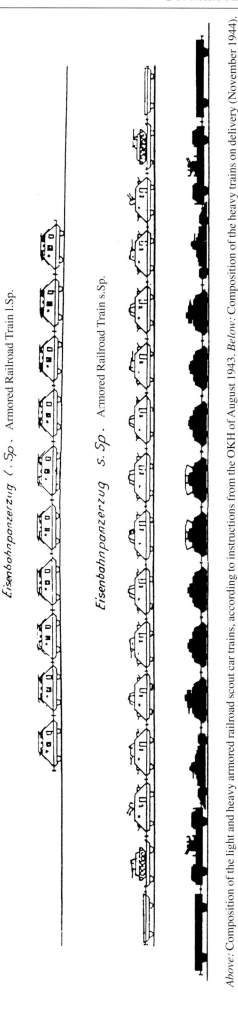

Above: Composition of the light and heavy armored railroad scout car trains, according to instructions from the OKH of August 1943. *Below*: Composition of the heavy trains on delivery (November 1944). Drawings: Federal Archives-Military Archives Freiburg and U. Schwarze

Eisenbahnpanzerzug l.Sp. – Armored Railroad Train l.Sp.

Eisenbahnpanzerzug s.Sp. – Armored Railroad Train s.Sp.

Drawings of the light armored railroad scout car. Drawings: P. Malmassari

Unlike the light scout car, information about its heavy counterpart is much more sparse and vague; from the course of events concerning these vehicles it can be assumed that difficulties became evident, leading to changes and considerable delays. On August 3, 1943, the OKH ordered the building of 100 heavy rail scout cars by the Steyr firm; an order for another hundred of these vehicles reached the firm on November 24, 1943. Of these, 16 armored trains (s.Sp.) of 12 scout cars each were to be made up. The instructions for establishing the first ten trains (No. 201-210) dated from September 24, 1943. That equally fast production to that of the light armored scout cars was expected can be seen that both of them were entered in Weapon Memo No. 14 of September 26, 1943, with which the higher commanders were instructed about new material that was either on hand or soon would be. On September 15, 1943, a war strength report (K.St.N. 1170x) for the heavy scout car train (s.Sp.) had already been made. From these documents, plus pictures of the prototype vehicle in the Steyr factory archives, the following can be learned:

It was intended that the same chassis and the same motor (though with fluid drive for the heavy type) be used for the light and heavy scout cars. On this chassis, an armored body with angled walls (20 mm thick) was set, its entire length measuring some 6.25 meters. The arrangement and structures of this armored body depended on the purpose of the vehicle, for unlike the light armored train, the heavy one consisted of differently equipped cars. The planned details were (with the structures on the middle of the armored body):

– Infantry car (octagonal observation turret)
– Engineer car (observation turret as on infantry car)
– Command car (observation turret as above, frame antenna)
– Artillery car (armored turret with 7.5-cm KwK L/24; the prototype had the Panzer IV F1 turret, the series production cars had that of the Panzer III N)
– A/A car (2-cm A/A Quad 38 or 3.7-cm A/A Twin 43)

Heavy armored rail scout cars with a 7.5-cm Geb.K. Skoda M 18 or a 12-cm mortar firing through an opening in the roof of the armored body instead of the turret were discussed, but in the end they were not built (the 12-cm mortar was carried only as a mobile weapon for the disembarked infantry troop).

All the cars were equipped with sprung front and rear buffers and normal hook couplings. They could be used either singly or as a coupled-together train, but in Weapon Memo No. 14 it says of their use "Action in principle as a complete armored train." This memo also states a gross weight of 18 tons for the individual car (it may have varied according to the equipment), which gives an axle weight of 9 tons. A top speed of 40 kph is stated, and a range of 700 km, but both values might have to be corrected downward to correspond to those of the light armored train (for these the Weapon Memo cites 70 kph and 1000 km, while actually only 60 kph and some 400 km were reached).

The K.St.N. 1170x of September 15, 1943 (just like the weapon memo), lists the following composition of the heavy armored train: Commander's car; platoon leader's car (infantry platoon); 2 infantry cars; one engineer car; platoon leader's car (artillery platoon); 4 artillery cars; and 2 A/A cars; there were also—as in the standard BP 42 series—2 tank carrier cars with 38(t) tanks on them and, as a reconnaissance vehicle, a road- and rail-capable Panhard 204/38(f) scout car. The combat crew is listed as 4 officers, 25 NCOs, and 89 men, plus 17 members of the supply train.

It can be suspected that the body of the heavy car on the chassis of the light scout car may have caused problems. With the greater car length, the short wheelbase of 2.20 meters caused big front and rear overhangs, which resulted, particularly from the necessity of mounting the motor to the left front of the car center because of the combat structures, outside the axle (as shown by the ventilator circles on the body), in an unfavorable division of the weight and probably poor running characteristics. The motor itself seems to have been too weak for the heavy scout car, and the top speed is correspondingly low. The U-shaped frame of two longitudinal and six transverse members (NP 14) of the light scout car also could not have been sufficient for

A prototype of the artillery car of the heavy armored scout train still had a Panzer IV F1 turret with a short 7.5-cm KwK L/24 gun. The corners of the body are angled. The motor ventilator (behind the soldier) is covered by a simple plate. Note the short wheelbase and the too-great front and rear overhangs. Photo: Steyr-Damler-Puch Archives

This prototype car was also shown to Hitler. Photo: W. J. Spielberger collection

the heavy box body, and certainly not for the pulling and pushing forces to be expected from a train made of twelve such cars coupled together, running on sloping tracks (note that the coupling hooks and buffers were not at frame height, but were attached considerably higher). Whether and to what extent changes were made on these points is not known; unfortunately, there are not enough pictures to confirm a possibly lengthened wheelbase. (Changes from the prototype and series model, like the aforementioned change of the turret on the artillery car and the elimination of angled corners on the armored body, are of a maintenance and production-technical nature and have nothing to do with the noted problems.) A strong indication of such problems and attempts to solve them is the extremely long time between awarding the contract and readiness of the first such vehicles for action. While six to eleven months passed between these dates for the light armored trains, the first two heavy trains were ready for use only in mid-November 1944, or almost 15 months after the Steyr firm received the contract to build them. Not only material shortages could have been responsible for this delay. On August 1, 1944, a new K.St.N. 1170x came into power with changes from the older one, reducing the four artillery cars with Panzer III turrets to two and replacing them with two launcher cars (8- or 12-cm mortars), as well as dropping the alternative of the 3.7-cm twins for the A/A cars. A further draft of a K.St.N. 1170x, undated but surely coming from 1944, retains the four artillery cars, but reduces the total number of cars from twelve to ten by dropping infantry and engineer cars. When the first heavy armored trains reached the troops in November 1944 they included only eight heavy armored cars: 2 command cars, 4 infantry and engineer cars, and 2 artillery cars. The 2-cm A/A quad was installed only on low-sided cars which ran at the ends of the armored trains. The planned armored scout cars with flak platforms thus had not been produced, although the OKH contract of November 24, 1943, expressly foresaw them as 20% of the total order. It is obvious that with such a delayed beginning of deliveries, even with the number of cars reduced by a third, only a fraction (6) of the originally ordered 16 heavy armored trains could be produced.

While the light scout trains, despite their armament of only machine guns, could prove their excellent suitability for track securing, even in low-visibility and partisan-infested areas, through their mobility and their extensive possibilities of providing cover in separated formations a just evaluation of the heavy armored scout trains can scarcely be made, for they came into action at a time when fuel supplies were so meager that their motor drive and its resulting increased radius of action, plus the possibility of action by individual cars or parts of a train—their real innovations—could scarcely be used any more. In order to start moving at all, an unarmored steam locomotive usually had to be scrounged up and be placed—as in earlier armored trains—in the middle of the coupled-together train. Therefore, the heavy scout trains—except in their lighter construction—do not differ from the old armored trains powered by steam locomotives.

A test run with a series production (no angled edges) heavy armored scout car. The structures atop the box body are still lacking. Photo: H/ Wülfing/W. Sawodny collection

The artillery car of the production version had the turret of a Panzer III N and the short 7.5-cm KwK. For the motor, which was located, depending on the direction, in the left front or right rear corner of the car body (and thus outside the axle!), three mushroom-like ventilator covers were attached at the front and seven on the side of the car. Photo: Federal Archives, Koblenz

The command car of the heavy armored scout train. The infantry car was built the same way and also had an octagonal turret with vision slits in the front, back, and sides, plus machine-gun ports in all four corners, but no frame antenna. Photo: Federal Archives, Koblenz

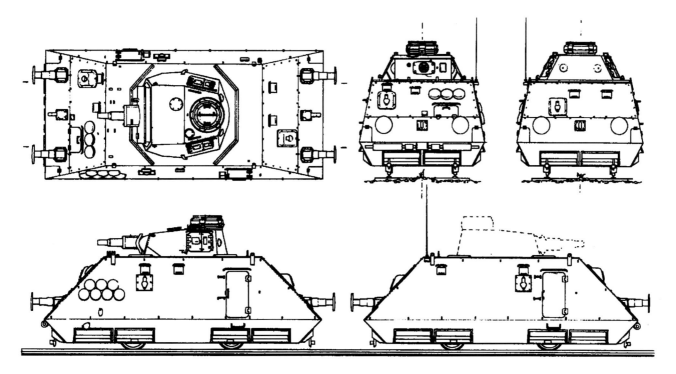

Drawings of the heavy armored scout car with Panzer III N turret and (next page) the infantry or command car. Drawings: P. Malmassari

Above: The heavy scout car trains that were delivered all had only eight cars: one artillery car, two infantry cars, and one command car in each half of the train. Photo: Federal Archives, Koblenz

Below: The A/A quad was not—as originally planned—mounted on any armored scout cars, but on a two-axle stake car (with an ammunition bunker on the rear half of the car), and the tank carrier car (slightly modified as compared to those of BP 42/44) was built somewhat differently with a fixed exit ramp—as shown here without a 38(t) tank. Photo: W. Obermark/W. Sawodny collection

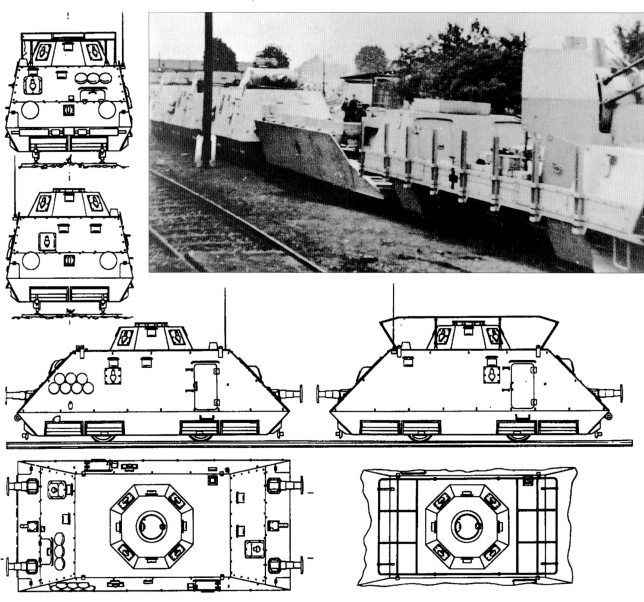

1944: Carrying out the Summer 1943 Building Program

Since the Russian campaign began, the significance of back line rail connections had become ever greater as a supply route for the fighting troops, but so had its risk of danger from stronger and better-organized partisan bands. Since guarding by place-bound security forces could not be done for lack of manpower, the armored trains, mobile and thus able to cover greater areas, gained more and more importance. A very similar situation also developed in the occupied Balkan areas. Since the winter of 1942-43 (the debacle at Stalingrad), the armored trains had also proved their value in front action, whether in fighting enemy breakthroughs, which were frequently carried out so that their advances also aimed at breaking the supply lines of the German troops, as reinforcement for retreating or moving units, or as support for counterattacks. These positive factors were very well known by the high command and manifested themselves in the reorganization of April 1943, in which the armored trains were not only taken into the armored troops, which had attained a special position through the particular position of their inspector-general toward the rest of the Army, with the Commander of the Armored Trains directly subordinate to the Commander of the Army or his general staff, who took on the function of a service-arm general, they themselves attained a special status within the armored troops.

This emerged in practice in the approval of a very ambitious expansion program in the summer of 1943, which will be summed up concisely here, although parts of it were already noted in preceding chapters. It envisioned the following details:

   12 new armored trains of the improved BP 44 type;

   4 new armored trains of light scout cars;

   16 new armored trains of heavy scout cars;

   5 new armored railcars fitted with guns;

plus the intensification of the total rebuilding of the older armored trains already in progress since November 1942, and the reequipping with tank-destroyer cars of them and the BP 42 armored trains put into service since December 1942. One characteristic of this expansion program is that the equipping with heavy weapons was no longer done with captured material, but with those from German production.

Of course, this exposed the armored trains much more strongly to the competition of other service arms, and by possible changes in priorities difficulties resulted. There were repeated delivery problems for the Light Howitzer 18/40, which made temporary solutions necessary. On the other hand, it seems that when 1945 began there was no shortage of armored turrets (for the tank-destroyer cars); on some armored trains built at that time even "Whirlwind" turrets were used for A/A quads. This was probably a result of the immobilization of the tanks, still produced in large numbers, by the systematic bombing of fuel production plants in the latter half of 1944. Transferring weapons systems to coal burning armored trains was seen as a possible way to make them somewhat mobile and use them against the enemy. This explains the documented growing preference for armored trains in the last months of the war (at the beginning of January 1945, the use of armored trains was designated "extremely urgent"), which suddenly seemed to go against the previous trend, although this did not have to be revised on the basis of what had happened meanwhile.

A comparable situation of competition for the weapons existed for the armored trains in the material sector (iron and steel) after the Ukrainian steel works at Krivoy Rog, which previously supplied these products for the German armored trains, was lost in February-March 1944. Here, too, the needed materials had to be obtained in competition with all others who needed them. It is thus no wonder that considerable delays occurred in the extensive building program. It is interesting here to compare the dates of readiness for use set in the contracts and in actual fact:

Armored Train No.	Readiness Contract	Date Actual	Difference in Months
301 (le.Sp.)	9/30/43	2/27/44	5
302	10/15/43	3/17/44	5
303	10/30/43	6/16/44	7.5
304	11/15/43	4/22/44	5
73 (BP 44)	1/1/44	7/7/44	6
74	2/1/44	7/20/44	6
75	3/1/44	7/20/44	5
76	4/1/44	11/18/44	7.5
77	5/1/44	1/19/45	8.5
78	6/1/44	2/6/45	8
79	7/1/44	2/6/45	7
80	8/1/44	3/-/45	7
81	9/1/44	4/-/45	7
82	10/1/44	5/-/45	7
83	11/1/44	–	–
84	12/1/44	–	–
201 (s.Sp.)	1/31/44	11/11/44	9.5
202	2/28/44	11/11/44	8.5
203	3/15/44	1/18/45	10
204	3/31/44	2/6/45	10
205	4/15/44	4/-/45	11.5
206	4/30/44	5/-/45	12
207	5/15/44	5/-/45	12
208	5/31/44	5/-/45	12
209	6/15/44	–	–
210	6/30/44	–	–

Thus, only the light scout trains were finished in a reasonable time (6 to 9 months) after they were contracted for; the originally planned building times of 6 to 12 weeks were surely set too short. Of the improved BP 44 type armored trains, only three (No. 73 to 75) went into action in June and July 1944 (10 to 11 months after the contract dates); the last two of them were not at all completely equipped as planned.

After that there was a four-month pause (until November 1944), in which only a few armored railcars captured from Russia joined the armored trains. In the much-enlarged gap between planned and actual finishing dates the shortage of material because of the loss of the former steel suppliers (for the heavy scout trains, also the mentioned production difficulties) can be seen, but other points of view may also have had an effect. Unlike the previous year, the armored trains operated more and more unluckily since the beginning of 1944; the loss rates rose sharply and culminated in the summer of 1944 when, beginning with the Russian offensive in the central sector of 22 June, in the next three months there and in other areas no fewer than eleven units were written off. Though attempts were made in the initial stage of this time period to make up the losses—in August the armored trains were listed in the second-highest stage of urgency, equal to the Tiger and Panther tanks—a more precise study of the combat reports probably awakened serious doubts on the front line usability of this weapon. In September the complete dropping of new construction was weighed. Although this skeptical view remained in the OKH, as shown by the lowering of the position of the commander of Armored Trains on December 7, 1944 (see previous chapter), the building program of 1943 finally seems to have been retained, as a decision of the General Army Office of October 2, 1944, shows, though, in view of the already occurring delays, a stretching of the program into 1945 was unavoidable. The following details were named:

8 BP 44 Armored Trains: Delivery in the last quarter of 1944; rest contingent. (Of the original twelve, three were already delivered; the fourth was nearly finished).

16 Armored Trains (s.Sp.): Delivery in the first quarter of 1945, already allocated: 11; still to be allocated: 5, 2 of them in the last quarter of 1944.

5 Armored Railcars: Delivery in the first quarter of 1945; rest contingent.

Suggested for reequipping of older trains:

46 Tank-destroyer cars: Delivery in the first quarter of 1945; still to be allocated: 8

6 Tank carrier cars: Production to begin in the first quarter of 1945; first contingent: 2

To replace destroyed vehicles (besides total destruction, the document lists 12 armored trains with vehicle losses up to 40%:

36 various cars: Delivery in the first quarter of 1945; still to be allocated: 18

There is also a contingent for the repair of armored trains and production of spare parts, as well as a remittance to the Deutsche Reichsbahn for eight locomotives for use in BP 44 armored trains. In all, the need for the last quarter of 1944 was calculated at:

3864 tons of unalloyed iron,
64 tons of alloyed iron,
2630 tons of coarse sheet metal, and
53 tons of fine sheet metal.

Naturally, this request also developed from illusory conceptions, as the comparison with the real figures, at least for new constructions by the end of the war on May 9, 1945, shows:

Armored Trains BP 44: 6 (No. 77-82, ready for action beginning at end of January 1945)

Armored Trains (s.Sp.): 8 (No. 201-208, ready for action beginning in mid-November 1944).

Of the five armored railcars, one was being finished by the Steyr firm at the end of the war; the others had remained in more or less advanced stages of construction at the Linke-Hofmann works in surrounded Breslau.

On the other hand, the armored trains No. 80-84, also being built there, were moved away earlier. Their further work was done by the "Bohemia" car factory in Boehmisch-Leipa. While no. 80 and 81 were finished, only some of the cars of PZ 82 were delivered. No. 83 and 84 were in such an early stage that work on them was halted in April 1945.

Of the eleven heavy armored scout trains already allocated in the last quarter of 1944, obviously only eight were in a state of being built by mid-January 1945, the beginning of two more was planned, but was halted by instructions on January 19, 1945.

Thus, the production of armored trains, even though under increasingly difficult conditions, continued to the war's end; in fact, in the last months there was even a growing interest in such units, reasons for which have been stated above. This need, above all in view of increasing losses, could not be met from the building program conceived in 1943, as the described losses and enemy occupation of production facilities hindered and halted its complete fulfillment.

1945: Line Protection Trains: Return to the Provisional State

To deal with this shortage, attempts were made to establish available line protection trains, after suitable reequipping when possible, as regular armored trains, a method that had been used in individual cases earlier, and that had already been characterized by raising the subordination conditions for these trains to higher and higher command levels.

To begin with let us follow the development of such units, although it must be noted that the information on them is much too spotty than that on the armored trains, so that one can scarcely attain a complete picture any more.

Along with the regular armored trains, which the OKH commanded as an army troop (and for which the staff officer of the armored trains—as shown—was responsible, subordinated to the General of the Fast Troops and later the commander of the Armored Troops in the Army General Staff), and were attached mostly to armies in case of need, makeshift (called auxiliary at first) armored trains were set up from—often captured—rolling stock, material, and weapons just at hand by individual units, at first naturally preferentially by railroad troops and securing units, but also by others, such as divisions and fortress troops. To avoid confusion with regular armored trains, the OKH issued an order on July 12, 1943, that these trains were only to be called "line protection trains," a regulation that will be retained below for the sake of clarity, although it was not always followed in the war, so that others, such as "makeshift armored train" or "auxiliary armored train" turn up again and again after that.

A further difficulty in limitation results from such trains also having been set up by the flak troops, which must be differentiated from the trains of the actual railroad flak, though they were referred to in eastern sources as "armored trains," without distinction as to whether they were armored or not. The latter—always gathered into batteries (although sometimes used as single cars for protection of certain objects!)—belonged to the category of railroad artillery, not covered here; their task was primarily anti-aircraft defense, although during the fast withdrawals of the last war years they often came near the front and could intervene in ground combat. But such units as were set up by the flak troops especially for such combat tasks are to be called "armored trains," although they usually lacked infantry components. Their armament generally consisted of mixed heavy (8.8-cm) and light (2-cm) A/A guns, both in low numbers (1 or 2 guns). More or less exact descriptions of a few such trains exist.

The first such flak armored train about which information is at hand was set up in January 1942 by the II. Battalion of Flak Regiment 4 for securing as well as freeing the only supply line from Wyasma through Sytshevka to Rshev for the 9th Army after the Russian winter offensive before Moscow circumvented the front bulge near Rshev and this line was constantly endangered. For it, two 8.8-cm and two 2-cm A/A guns were mounted on flat cars and provisionally (along with gun shields) protected by low walls of sandbags; an unarmored captured Russian locomotive pulled the train. The crew consisted of 40 men (commanded by 1st Lt. Langhammer) and had four machine guns in addition to the A/A guns. How long this train was in action is not known.

When the 707th Infantry Division took over the securing of the back land of the 2nd Panzer Army in the Bryansk region in May 1942 several line protection trains were extant. Between May and July 1942 trains called "Erika," "Marlen," "Lilli," "Luise," and No. 101 were mentioned. "Erika" was armed with an 8.8-cm and two 2-cm A/A guns as well as three light machine guns; "Marlen" had a 2-cm A/A gun. These two, at least, seem to have been armored flak trains (no information on the armament of the other three trains is at hand), but they were less heavily armed than the trains listed above in the Rshev area. None of these names reappears after July 1942.

In October 1943 an armored train was set up by the 9th Flak Division in Vladislavovka (north of Fedosia) in Crimea; it was commanded by Lt. Muhr. It consisted of two control cars loaded with planks, four open cars with breastworks of armored double walls—

the inner space filled with chalk rubble—on which two 8.8-cm and two 2-cm A/A guns were mounted, and one G-car, in which a radio station was installed. The locomotive and tender were unarmored. The train, which was used at the Perekop isthmus until then, moved back in the direction of Sevastopol when the soviets attacked in April 1944, and was surrounded and blown up in Sarabus on the way there.

Even in surrounded Breslau, workers at the FAMO works in the old RAW on Mathiasstrasse built an armored flak train between February 28 and March 20, 1945. The chassis of the cars were brought from the Linke-Hofmann works, already under fire (they had previously built armored trains; the unused material was obviously all transported elsewhere before the city was surrounded). The armament consisted of four 8.8-cm, one 3.7-cm, and four 2-cm A/A guns, plus two MG 42. The crew, commanded by 1st Lt. Paul Poersel, numbered 108 men, with 32 railroad men for the repair of possible rail damage. The train, which operated at first on the southwest and then the northeast of the encirclement front of Breslau, remained in action until the city surrendered on May 6, 1945.

The origins of line protection trains, though, were elsewhere. During the occupation of Denmark, a railcar (unknown type) taken over by the Wehrmacht was sent by ferry from Warnemünde to Gjedser instead of PZ 25 on April 9, 1940, and, manned by a shock troop, advanced to Vordingborg.—In the western campaign, too, several railroad engineer units were issued passenger railcars for shock-troop rail reconnaissance and capture. The railcars—probably of the VT 137 series—which were used by the Wehrmacht almost constantly throughout the war—were given camouflage paint and marked by the German cross, and were otherwise unchanged, thus not armored, but they were accompanied in front by low-side cars, which served not only as control cars, but also carried observation posts and machine gun mounts with a makeshift armor of railroad ties or double plank walls with sand between them. Some of them were secured by small railcars running ahead of them.—These cars were used only in the earliest days of the western campaign and were then returned to the Reichsbahn.

For the end of June 1941, thus shortly after the Russian campaign began, a report tells that railroad engineers set up an X- (work) car temporarily protected by railroad ties all around, a covered

This single photo of an improvised armored flak train comes from a German newsreel of 1944. Photo: Federal Archives, Koblenz

An unarmored VT 137 passenger railcar on the western front in May 1940. On the R-car in front is a machine-gun (MG 08) position "armored" with wooden planks.

Cars of the line protection train set up by the 221st Security Division in July 1941 and later passed to the 707th Infantry Division in Rembertow in the summer of 1942. In the foreground is a captured Type BP 35 Soviet gun car with round turrets, behind it the SS-car with a T 34 tank on it, then an ex-Austro-Hungarian armored train car (from the Polish armored train "Pierwszy Marszalek"). To the far left and hard to identify are the recaptured cars of PZ 27, probably also belonging to this line protection train. Photo: W. Rosner/W. Sawodny collection

freight car and a pusher locomotive. A similar ensemble, naturally consisting of captured broad gauge material, may have been used frequently for track surveillance and protection in the initial phase of the eastern campaign. The crew and armament soon grew. The 221st Security Division set up a broad gauge line protection train in the second half of July to secure the Pripyet line; it consisted of the following vehicles: a control car loaded with building material; a Polish "assault" car (presumably of PP. "Pierwszy Marszalek") armed with four machine guns and six rifles; a G-car with makeshift armor made of rails, ties, sand, and stones (8 machine guns, 6 rifles); a Polish Ok 1-90 (ex-Prussian P8) locomotive temporarily armored by the Lapy EAW; a G-car, also with makeshift armor, carrying a 10.5-cm F.H. 18 and two mortars; and a control car with railroad building material and tools. Later an XX-car that could carry a T 34 tank was added. The supply train of four passenger cars and a kitchen was soon expanded to five passenger cars and four G-cars (kitchen, weapons and ammunition, coal, spare parts). As time went by, the R-car with the howitzer was replaced by a captured Soviet armored car with two 7.62-cm F.K. 02/30 in turrets, and in January 1942 the train gained the cars of PZ 27, abandoned in the encirclement of Sukhinitshi and regained there when the pocket was opened, which were added to the train (one tank carrier and one infantry car, both carrying non-driveable Panzer 38(t) tanks).

An improvised broad gauge line protection train of the 3rd Company of Railroad Engineer Regiment 3 is seen in the southern sector of the eastern front, still with a "contraband" locomotive. The "armor" consists of concrete-filled double walls and sandbags. Photo: Federal Archives, Koblenz

Later a gun car was taken over from a captured Russian armored train; it had two turrets on different levels, of which only one was fitted with a 7.62-cm F.K. 295(r), and a Type O armored locomotive.

The train of the 221st Security Division, named "Leutnant Marx" after its commander, was turned over to the 707th Infantry Division on August 23, 1941, and is probably to be found among those listed for that unit in the early summer of 1942 (No. 101?). Soon after that it was assigned to the Replacement Battalion in Rembertow.

Documented in a picture is a train assigned to the 3rd Company of Railroad Engineer Regiment 3 of the Kleist Panzer Group, Army Group South, which was made up of several low-side cars with double walls, the space being filled with sand or concrete. The train is fitted with several machine guns—also for anti-aircraft defense—and a 3.7-cm anti-tank gun is set up in the first car. Later a captured Russian gun car with a 7.62-cm F.K. (a second gun of this type was obviously removed from the still-present turret) was added, and the locomotive, formerly temporarily armored, was replaced by a Russian Series O armored loco.

This shows the second step in the development of line protection trains. In the advance phase to the end of November 1941, a whole series of Russian armored trains fell into German hands; many were destroyed or damaged, others essentially unharmed. What was more obvious than to use them at once on the German side? A whole row of such German-manned Soviet armored trains of the most varied kind are verified in photos, and often their anti-aircraft defense, consisting only of A/A machine guns, was strengthened by 2 cm guns. All other data about their areas of action, names, etc. was usually lacking. The only exception is a train captured in November 1941 in the breakthrough to Crimea at Dshankoy. It was manned by Engineer Regiment 617 and fought at the end of December during the Russian landing north of Feodosia. Its later fate is not known, but it may have been disbanded soon afterward, as were all such trains that disappeared by the summer of 1942 at the latest. All Soviet armored train material had to be delivered to the OKH and was gathered and checked centrally. It was then—often rebuilt into very different form—assigned to the regular German armored trains. Only seldom did Russian armored train cars remain with line protection trains.

Such an example is found in the line protection train "Polko" (in some sources this unusual name is rendered "Polkow" or "Polkoff"). This had taken over the gun car, armed with two 7.62-cm tank guns in T-34 turrets of the Soviet armored train "Za Stalina" (for Stalin), captured in October 1941 between Wyasma and Gshatsk. Its armored locomotive, which will be mentioned in the appropriate chapter, had to be taken to the field workshop at Roslavl for repairs, and was at first replaced in "Polko" by another captured Russian Series O armored locomotive. This line protection train was completed with a two-axle low-side car, on which an octagonal concrete turret with

A Soviet armored train manned and used further by the Germans. The guns are French 7.5-cm Schneider M 97 cannons. The 2-cm A/A guns were installed in addition. Photo: Federal Archives, Koblenz

This Soviet armored train was captured in Crimea in November 1941 and used by the Wehrmacht. Photo: J. C. Gembe collection

a twin A/A MG 34 was mounted, and several flatcars as control cars on both ends, all captured from the Russians. At first it remained as a broad gauge train in the Wyasma area, but in any case—although documentation for 1942 and 1943 is lacking—with the Army Group Center, where it was converted to standard gauge. In February 1944 it turned up with the 9th Army in the Rogachev area; during the 1944 Russian summer offensive it went to the 2nd Army in the Pripyet district and withdrew to the Warsaw area. Between the A/A car (now with a higher armor wall added around the octagonal turret) and the gun car with the two T 34 turrets, four covered freight cars (armored inside?) were hitched; the locomotive in the middle, with a tender of Prussian type (presumably G 10/Series 57), was unarmored. In front

of the A/A car and behind the gun car were other cars, presumably carrying weapons; then the train ended with control cars at both ends. With this composition "Polko" was lost between the Vistula and the Oder in January 1945 during the Russian offensive.

The year 1942 brought the establishment of the most line protection trains. Along with the Russian offensives in the winter of 1941-42, which pushed the front back at various places, there came—especially to the Army Group Center—increasing partisan activity in the hinterlands, which threatened supply lines increasingly. On the other hand, in the first months of that year several German armored trains were so damaged that they had to spend long times being repaired or were completely destroyed; replacement by new trains did not take place that whole year.

Above: the Russian armored train "Za Stalina," captured east of Wyasma in October 1941. The anti-tank shots in the locomotive and cars, which put the train out of action, are easy to see. The armored locomotive, originally with G- and control cars, formed its own rail protection train. Later, after conversion to standard gauge, it was withdrawn and obviously served, with its armor, as a model for those German locomotives of Series 57 for the BP 42 armored trains. The car with two turrets from T 34 tanks was combined with a captured Series O armored locomotive and an X-car on which an octagonal weapon platform of cast concrete was mounted with twin A/A machine guns, to form a broad gauge line protection train that bore the name "Polko" (*left*). Photos: H. Finzel/H. Wenzel collection, and Federal Archives, Koblenz

The line protection train "Polko" west of Warsaw in late September 1944. The twin machine gun stand is surrounded with an armor wall. Four (inside-armored?) G-cars are still used. In front of the A/A car and after the gun car with the T 34 turrets are other cars which may have carried additional weapons. The loco, with armored cab, appears to be from Series 57. Photo: W. Conrad/W. Sawodny collection

The activity of no fewer than five line protection trains with the 707th Infantry Division in the Bryansk area in the early summer of 1942 was already noted.—In the 221st Security Division (based at Gomel) two line protection trains guarded the supply lines meeting at Unetcha in November-December 1942: "Zobten" (with Security Regiment 27) on the line coming from Kritchev in the northwest and "Rübezahl" (Security Regiment 45) the line from Gomel in the southwest. "Rübezahl" was later designated No. 45; whether "Zobten" was taken over as No. 350 when Security Regiment 27 was replaced by Grenadier Regiment 350 in the division or the latter was a new formation by this regiment is not known. Both line protection trains remained with the 21st Security Division until the summer of 1944. At the beginning of October 1944, when they were with the 390th Security Division in the Baltic area between Memel and Libau, the following composition, armament, and manpower were recorded:

Line Protection Train No. 45 (ex-Rübezahl): four combat cars with one Russian tank turret with a 4.5-cm gun; one 5-cm and one 8-cm mortar; five light MG 34 and five Russian machine guns; and four control cars; crew: one NCO and 15 men. Supply train with two personnel and three business cars.

Line Protection Train no. 350 (ex-Zobten?): five combat cars, with three Russian tank turrets with one 3.7 and two 4.5-cm guns; one Czech 7.5-cm cannon (Geb.K. M 15?); two Czech 2-cm A/A guns; one light Russian and two medium French mortars; eight light MG 34 and four Russian machine guns; and three control cars; crew: one NCO and 33 men. Supply train: four personnel, one business and one ammunition car. One of the combat cars and one armored locomotive joined No. 350 in Königsberg only in September 1944.

Since at least January 1943, the 201st Security Division in the Polozk—Newel area had the line protection train "Werner"; in the spring of 1944 it was still in the Polozk—Molodechno area. On November 1, 1943, the armament listed for this train was: two anti-tank guns, one heavy and one medium mortar, and three heavy and three light machine guns, all captured from the Russians. Later (in May 1944) it went to the 391st Security Division, the Security

Regiment 75, which also had the rail protection train "Heinrich," about which no details are known at that time.

For the 286th Security Division (Minsk—Borissow—Orscha—Smolensk line) no line protection trains are known. But in April 1943 it had several armored railcars. The indication that they were used exceptionally on the road allows the assumption that they were Panhard scout cars, usable on both roads and rails, such as were issued to armored trains as reconnaissance vehicles. Security Regiment 45 (221st Security Division) listed an armored railcar in December 1942 with a sergeant as commander, two drivers, and a machine gunner as its crew. Another—larger—vehicle of this type is shown in a picture; it has the turret of a BT-7 tank with a 4.5-cm tank gun as armament.

Another line protection train, named "Blücher," was assigned by the commander of the back line army zone of the 3rd Panzer Army (Korück 590) to secure the Jarzewo—Dorogobusch–Wjasma line in July 1942. It is said to have consisted, besides a cab-armored locomotive, of several covered and open freight cars, their double walls filled with cast concrete and fitted with shooting ports, plus a stake-side car at the end with a ready-to-roll Panzer 38(t) (on loan from the 20th Armored Division, later replaced by immobile damaged tanks), and naturally the obligatory control cars; the crew numbered 126 men. In October 1942 the number of cars was reduced. Now listed as armament were a 3.7-cm cannon, a 2-cm gun, two light and one medium mortars, and two heavy and 14 light machine guns; the crew had two officers (commander 1st Lt. Dümlein) and 71 men. One of the plank-covered tanks it carried is not clearly identifiable; the other is a German Panzer II. At the end of January 1943 the train was sent with the 3rd Panzer Army to the Witebsk—Polozk area, and was irreparably damaged in a collision with PZ 67 on the Polozk—Newel line in November 1943 (it fell down a railroad embankment). Afterward a new "Blücher" line protection train was built at the Dünaburg EAW. It was composed of four-axle (converted) Russian cars with armored bodies. The car order (symmetrical with slight variations in both halves) was, from the end to the loco: artillery car with three-level armored body, a T 34/76 tank turret on the front—lowest—part with a 7.62-cm gun, a Russian T 70 turret in the middle

A three-axle armored railcar of Russian origin with a BT-7 tank turret, used as a security vehicle. Photo: W. Sawodny collection

with a 4.5-cm gun, and a crew and ammunition cabin at the rear; an A/A and launcher car with an open-top front part (space for a mortar), on the rear A/A platform a single 2-cm (front car) or quad (rear car); a light gun car, on the lower front part the turret of a Russian T-26 tank with a 4.5-cm gun, with crew and ammunition space to the rear; the next infantry car in the front half was covered and fully armored, while the rear car was an internally armored, covered freight car, which contained the command post and radio station, perhaps also a kitchen and medical section. The locomotive in the middle had only its cab armored and came from the P 8 series (38 3504).

In the Army Group Center sector there were more line protection trains. Since the 1941-42 Russian winter offensive, the 83rd Infantry Division had been alone around Welikije Luki, on the boundary with Army Group North, but had no direct contact with other German units to either north or south. Its supplies came from Nowosokolniki in the west and Newel in the southwest. Both rail lines were constantly endangered and thus needed constant securing. In Nowosokolniki there was a line protection train, sometimes called "Novo" after its location, sometimes "Jansen" after its commander; it was probably set up and manned by the 6th company of Railroad Engineer Regiment 4, located there, or Field Transit Battalion 17. At first it ran on broad gauge lines, but it was converted to standard gauge in April 1942.

The line protection train "Blücher" (Loco 38 3504) at first consisted of inside-armored G-cars and cars with non-driveable tanks, for which protection was provided. Photo: P. Malmassari

After it had been irreparably damaged in November 1943, the line protection train "Blücher" was built anew at the Dünaburg EAW (*pictures below*). Now it had only Russian four-axle cars, armored outside except the command car (*left edge of upper photo*), and stepped lower bodies for tank turrets (first car: T 34/76 and T 70 turrets; car behind A/A car: T 26 turret). One of the A/A cars was armed with a single 2-cm gun and a quad, the other with a quad. Each had a mortar installed in the other half. The Series 38 locomotive had only the cab armored. Photos: W. Sitzius/W. Sawodny collection

One of the two gun cars of Line Protection Train No. 83 with the turret of a Soviet BT-7 tank. Photo: H. Giehl/A. Hellrung collection

Below: The Line Protection Train "Michael" was set up in the southern sector by the 6th Army in October 1943. The whole tanks (T 34 with cast turrets) were set on flatcars and surrounded by a shield of steel plates. The locomotive, of Series 38, is armored—unusual for line protection trains. Photo: Ullstein Picture Service

It was lost during the Russian attack at the end of 1942.—Both regular armored trains, No. 3 and 27, were used at first on the line from Newel. After they were damaged and withdrawn in May 1942, the 83rd Infantry Division set up a line protection train (commanded by 1st Lt. Lohmann) that was designated with the division's number 83. After Welikije Luki was lost it was transferred out of the 83rd Inf. Div. in the spring of 1943, though it kept the number, and for the rest of the year it was subordinated to the 3rd Panzer Army, which used it for security tasks in their back line area. Its armament as of November 1, 1943, corresponded to the more precise data from early 1944: along with three control cars, two four-axle gun cars, each bearing the turret of a Russian BT-7 tank with a 4.5-cm gun, and two G-cars, one set up as a radio station. Along with the two tank guns, the train had twelve Russian light machine guns; its crew, besides the commander, consisted of 4 NCOs and 32 men; the supply train had ten cars. In October 1944 it was taken out of service and delivered to the Armored Train Replacement and Training Battalion in Milowitz.

Just as Line Protection Train No. 83 bore the number of the division that established it, this was also the case for Line Protection Train No. 321, which was probably lost with the 321st Infantry Division in the Rogatschew area early in November 1943. The origins of the numberings of Line Protection Trains No. 223, 420, and 777 (the last assigned to Myslowitz at the eastern edge of the upper Silesian industrial area as of autumn 1944) could not be determined. On the other hand, a "Line Protection Train No. 102" mentioned in Budapest in December 1944 may have been a Hungarian armored train. On July 13, 1944, the Organization Department of the Army General Staff issued the order to avoid confusion with armored trains, and all line protection trains should have numbers from 600 up. In fact, such trains with numbers 601 (in the back line area of

the 2nd Army north of Warsaw in August 1944) and 607 (listed as a "heavy armored train" at the beginning of 1945, first in southern Poland and then in Upper Silesia)—both newly established—can be documented, and Line Protection Train No. 83 was renumbered 683. But this order could not be accomplished. Except for the noted new establishments, the line protection trains kept their old numbers and names; even 683 soon became 83 again.

In view of the fact that the partisans carried on their strongest attacks in the back lands of Army Group Center, it is not surprising that by far the most line protection trains were set up and operated in this area.—Very few data on line protection trains could be found for Army Group North. On January 19, 1944, the loco of such a train (its name unknown) fell into a mine crater between Dno and Wjasje; and on October 7, 1944, the 16th Army's Line Protection Train "Wespe" (Wasp) was mentioned.—At the end of March 1945 another line protection train was set up on the cut-off peninsula of Hela to defend the approaches. It consisted of a Series 50 (52?) locomotive and four cars, two of which were armed with 10.5-cm naval guns, one with an A/A (2-cm quad?) gun, and one with a mortar. During the withdrawal fighting early in February 1944 a unit set up for short-term scouting was active on the line south of Oredesch with a rail truck, a car with a 3.7-cm anti-tank gun, and an engineer shock troop (led by 1st Lt. Schrade). It can be presumed that such ad hoc and makeshift "armored trains," generally disbanded after their tasks were finished, were used on all fronts again and again.

For the southern region of the eastern front, the Line Protection Train "Michael," set up in mid-October 1943 by the 4th Company of Railroad Engineer Regiment 3, is known. It was with the 6th Army at first, which was then between the Dnjepr bend and Melitopol. When it withdrew to the lower Dnjepr, it was pushed onto the cut-

An unidentified line protection train with a Soviet T 26 tank mounted in an Rms-car. (The name "Moritz" applies to the tank, not to the train.) Photo: N. Bartel collection

off peninsula of Crimea, into the 17th Army's zone, at the end of the month. There the train took part successfully in the defensive combat at the Perekop narrows, which it helped to defend until April 1944. During the Russian attack in April the withdrawal toward Sebastopol succeeded, where the "Michael" train was blown up in a tunnel near the Mekensiewy Gory railroad station on May 8, 1944. The train consisted of the following cars: a closed car with cast T 34 turret; a car with an A/A platform (first a single 2-cm gun, later apparently 3.7-cm twins); a closed command car with machine guns (also twin A/A machine guns); an armored Series 38 (Prussian P 8) locomotive; a closed crew car with machine guns; a car with a platform for a 12-cm mortar (plus machine guns); a closed car with cast T 34 turret; and a control car. The two cars with the tank turrets had double steel walls with concrete filling, while all the others had steel plates with railroad ties behind them. Later, flatcars with a heavy machine gun stand (cast double sheet steel ring with cast concrete) were added between the gun cars and control cars. Otherwise, only the two line protection trains "Bär" and "Wolf" are known from the southern sector of the eastern front; they were stationed in Lublin in the spring of 1944.

The third and last step in the development of line protection cars on the eastern front—after sorting out the material from captured Russian armored trains—consisted of German-made armored bodies on converted Russian freight cars, using almost exclusively tank guns in the turrets of captured tanks as their armament, a method they took over from the wartime armored cars of the enemy. The exact makeup of the trains naturally varied very much depending on local conditions. The locomotives (apparently mostly P 8/Series 38) of these rail protection trains often had armor on only their cabs.

The development of the rail protection trains was also reflected in the regulations. The "Temporary Guidelines for Organization and Use of Railroad Armored Trains" of May 24, 1942, gives the following recommendation for their creation: In addition to the locomotive placed at the middle of the train, take two to four O-cars, at best coal cars with iron walls to a height of 1.80 meters. These are backed with a double layer at a distance, made of high-piled railroad ties held together by clamps. If available, a wall of sandbags can

be placed behind them as added protection. For use on endangered tracks, control cars loaded with sand, gravel, or soil (gravel or stake cars) can be placed at the ends of the train. Armament and crew depend on the circumstances (available captured weapons, tasks). The photos show that double walls filled in with concrete were also used as armor. Used as weapons, besides carbines and machine guns, were mortars and anti-tank and A/A guns up to 8.8-cm caliber. These recommendations represent the first phase of their construction. The OKW memo "Partisan Fighting" of May 6, 1944, adds under no. 143 that line protection trains should consist of G- and R-cars that have been made safe with available material, such as armor plates, concrete armor, connected with planks and ties, with sand filling (and if possible bottom armor against mines should also be provided), or by setting immobile tanks or scout cars on them. Possibilities of throwing hand grenades from the cars and exiting through the car bottom should be considered during construction. The Commander of Armored Trains in the OKH had prepared recommendations for their building and armament for command offices that intended to build line protection trains, even a frame K.St.N. or K.A.N. This corresponded to the third building phase, though on the eastern front, instead of mounting entire tanks or scout cars, usually their turrets (presumably available unharmed in greater quantities) were installed.

Whole tanks set on low-walled cars—as recommended in the memo noted above—were used for the line protection trains that were used in the Balkans (Yugoslavia and Greece) and Norway. Here only captured French tanks were used, preferentially the Renault FT 17/18 of World War I, but occasionally also the more modern Renault R 35, Hotchkiss H 35 and 39, and Somua S 35 types. For the "Igel" line protection train active south of Vinkovci in December 1944, data on ammunition consumption suggest that in addition to captured French tanks armed with a 3.7-cm gun they used 2-cm A/A guns, 8-cm and light Italian mortars, plus several British, Italian, and German machine guns.

In Norway, the first line protection train seems to have been set up at Oslo in 1942. It bore the name "Norwegen." In January 1944 54 men, commanded by Lt. Wildt, were named as its crew. In

the autumn of 1944 there were, besides this one, also the "Voss," "Grong," and "Narvik" line protection trains. They had obviously taken their names from the places where they were stationed. For January 1945 there are finally data as to their armament:
- "Norwegen": one 3.7-cm anti-tank gun, one 8.8-cm A/A gun, one 2-cm A/A and one 2-cm improvised A/A gun, two German 8-cm and two British 5-cm mortars, two heavy and 12 light machine guns, one Hotchkiss H 39/40 tank with 3.7-cm gun and machine gun.
- "Bergen" (ex-"Voss"): one Renault FT 17/18 with 3.7-cm gun, two 3.7-cm anti-tank guns, one 2-cm A/A quad, two German 8-cm and two British 5-cm mortars, two heavy and two light machine guns.
- "Grong": one tank with 2-cm gun (German Panzer II?), two 3.7-cm anti-tank guns, two 2.5-cm A/A guns, four British 5-cm mortars, two British anti-tank rifles, four French heavy machine guns, five light machine guns (four Norwegian, one German).
- "Narvik": one Renault FT 17/18 with 3.7-cm gun, two British 50cm mortars, two Norwegian heavy machine guns.

At this late point in time a fifth line protection train called "Mornardal" was mentioned, but its armament was not listed.

Surviving pictures of Norwegian line protection trains show in one case a train with six open cars provisionally armored with steel plates, covered with cord nets for camouflage material. Whether weapons were installed or building materials were carried on the stake cars at the ends of the train cannot be seen; on the car in front of the Norwegian loco and tender (probably like the one behind the loco) is a 3.7-cm anti-tank gun on a wheeled mount. For the other train, the exact composition cannot be fully determined from the photo. The front half consists of a stake car with rail material and two open freight cars with double wood-plank walls (space between filled in). On the front car a MG 34 for A/A and ground use is installed; a Renault FT 17/17 tank is loaded on the second car. Both trains are clearly not as well armed as the data above indicate; presumably this was an earlier stage of equipping.

After attacks by partisans on railroad lines took place in the Balkans in the summer of 1941 and these activities constantly increased, the few regular armored trains available there were supported by line protection trains, especially on the extensive narrow gauge lines not usable by the former. In the summer of 1941 such a train is mentioned for the narrow gauge lines west of Mladenovac. At the beginning of July 1943, in addition to three German and two Croatian armored trains (the latter on the narrow gauge Slav. Brod—Sarajevo lines) there were five line protection trains in the Croatian area. The Larissa line securing staff in Greece had four line

One of the line protection trains in Norway. Here the armor consists of half-height steel side plates. In the car before the unarmored Norwegian locomotive the barrel of a 3.7-cm Pak can be seen. Photo: Federal Archives, Koblenz

Another of the Norwegian line protection trains had only double wooden walls with filled-in spaces as armor. In the background a captured French Renault FT 17/18 tank is visible. Photo: Federal Archives, Koblenz

protection trains at the end of August 1943. A year later, in August 1944, an overall report on the entire Balkan area listed the following line protection trains: No. 101, 102, 104-109, 202, 203, 205-210 (209 listed twice), 214, and 222. The 100-series trains were narrow gauge, the 200-series standard gauge. The double numbering of 209 may he a writing error (for No. 204?). Gaps in the 101-109 (103!) and 201-210 series (201, maybe 204) could indicate losses. This may refer to trains in Croatia, where five were listed as present in July 1943, but only three a year later.

As for armament, two Renault FT 17/18 tanks are usually listed for narrow and standard gauge trains. Often only a 3.7-cm gun is listed, which suggests that in these cases the second tank is the type with machine guns. Equipping with tanks sometimes seems to have varied; for Line Protection Trains 202 and 208 in November 1943 an additional 4.7-cm gun (Somua S 35 tank?) is listed, while as of February 1944—as already in August-September 1943 only a 3.7-cm gun is named. Line Protection Train 209 was the only one to carry two Somua S 35 (with 4.7-cm guns) over the entire period; for No. 206, three 3.7-cm guns (two Renault FT 17/18 and one Hotchkiss H 39, as shown in the photo for such a train?) are listed for August 1944. Besides the tank guns, the line protection trains usually also had an 8-cm and a 5-cm mortar and 6 to 9 machine guns, of which up to three may have been heavy.

The armored infantry cars shown in the pictures could be captured Yugoslav types; the freight and passenger cars were surely equipped with radios—as the antennas indicate—but do not seem to be armored. The locomotives too (probably mostly Yugoslav—as

the HDZ-Series 20 in the photos) had armor only on the cab and the cylinder. Although not listed among the equipment, it appears that open cars with mounted 2-cm A/A guns were made up on their own account. There are indications that Croatian armored cars were used in line protection trains by the Germans too.

At the capitulation on May 9, 1945, another line protection train, "München," is listed for the occupied part of Yugoslavia, but it cannot be determined whether it was built new (in which case the name could suggest its place of origin), or might perhaps be the renamed Line Protection Train 206 (such a step seems plausible in view of the use of the 200 numbers by the heavy scout trains that were delivered to the Balkans as of November 1944).

In northern Italy, a line protection train stationed in Novara (Captain Both commanding) has been documented; in Istria two ("Adria" and "San Pietro"), and one in Friaul ("Pany"), plus two more in the German-controlled northern part of Slovenia, in Upper Carniola, and one "armored securing train" and a rail tank in Cilli. In Klagenfurt there was a "line securing train." No data survive as to their composition or equipment, so it cannot be decided whether the latter belonged to the line protection series. In France, after repair work had been disturbed regularly by attacks of the Maquis, the railroad executive of the Lyon EBD had equipped two repair shop trains ("Anna" and "Caesar") with armored and machine-gun-armed O-cars, thus converting them to line protection trains in autumn 1943.—A line protection train, its name unknown, consisting of O-cars with wooden double walls (probably with cast concrete) and added "armoring" of sandbags, was active from June to August

Tanks of the Renault FT 17/18 type were also used by the line protection trains in the Balkans. This is one of the 200 (standard gauge) series. The infantry car is probably from Yugoslavia and comes from an armored train built between the world wars. Behind it is a probably unarmored passenger car. Photo: Federal Archives, Koblenz

The variety of the materials used shows in this picture of a 200 series line protection train (No. 206?). After a row of four control cars come two cars with FT 17/18 tanks, then an ex-Yugoslav infantry car, a G-car as command car (antenna!), the cab-armored JDZ-series locomotive, and a passenger car. Photo: Federal Archives, Koblenz

The rear part of the same line protection train. Behind the passenger car are a Yugoslav-built infantry car, two tank carriers with Renault FT 17/18 or Hotchkiss H 39 tanks, a low-side car with unknown contents, a car with a mount for a 2-cm A/A gun, an O-car (with a mortar?), and another series of empty cars used to detonate mines. Note also the plank structure below the infantry car—protection against mines. Photo: Federal Archives, Koblenz

1944 on the Bordeaux—Perigueux—Brive line. Since it is known that the German troops withdrew from that area eastward through Bourges at the end of August 1944, it is not improbable that it could have been this same train that was the "auxiliary armored train" seen coming from Bourges at Saincaze on 2-3 September and at Moulins on 4 September, and the line protection train that was attacked and conquered by Special Air Service No. 3, a mixed British-French unit, in Montceau-les-Mines on 6 September.—In Dammerkirch, west of Belfort, a line protection train had to be given up on November 27, 1944, because bridges to both sides were blown up. The first car had an unloading ramp; a tank had probably been loaded on it. There followed several G-cars (with inside armor?) in the front part of the train (no data on the rear half exist). It was armed with an A/A twin (2.0- or 3.7-cm?). In surrounded La Rochelle there was an armored train in October-November 1944 armed as follows: one 8.8-cm C/35 rapid-fire gun, one 3.7-cm M 42 cannon, two 8-mm Hotchkiss machine guns, two fog systems, and a command communication system. A second train with unknown equipment followed later.

A the end of November 1944, an "armored train of the Hook of Holland Fortress" was set up in the Netherlands; it had a 30-man crew and was probably active until Army Group Netherlands surrendered on May 8, 1945.—On April 1, 1945, it was reported that the American troops advancing from Ahlen toward Beckum were fired on by an armored train on the Hamm—Gütersloh line; it was then silenced by U.S. tanks and abandoned by its crew. Whether,

even on the western front, such desperate means were taken to keep heavy weapons mobile on coal-fired trains in view of the massive fuel shortage, or it was a railroad A/A train from Ruhr area security could not be determined.

As the war moved on, a steady increase in the valuing of line protection trains can be seen. Though at first they were set up and used at most on the division level, the authority gradually moved upward to the armies, where the commanding general of the back line army zone (Korück) was usually responsible for them. Here they often took the place of lacking regular armored trains. The best example of this is the zone of the 9th Army in autumn 1944: in the area west of Warsaw, Armored Train Regiment No. 3 (Lt. Col. Dr. Günther) was to gather at first. When this was moved to East Prussia because of the Russian breakthrough in October-November, Korück 532 received, instead of it, the group of line protection trains No. 45 and 350, "Polko" and "Werner." Correspondingly, the interests of line protection trains, also after July 1944, were handled by the commander of the armored trains under the Chief of the Army General Staff—notwithstanding their subordination to the troops.

With the acute shortage of regular armored trains, available line protection trains were even turned into them. An early example is PZ 51. During the developmental and construction phases of the newly conceived BP 42 standard type, no new armored trains at all came to the front in 1942. Thus, in Recruiting District II, since January 1942, the line protection train "Stettin," just being established, was taken

Armored Train 51 (here entering the shooting line at Rembertow), with its freight cars, tank turrets, and—armored, to be sure—Series 38 locomotive, clearly shows its derivation from a line protection train. Photo: J. Kraemer/W. Sawodny collection

over as a regular armored train in May 1942, at first designated "A" and later No. 51. It was originally to receive the material from the line protection train of the 221st Security Division or 707th Infantry Division just delivered to Rembertow (see pp. 155f). Instead, four four-axle Russian freight cars (three GG and one high-wall OO) were armored inside at the Pruszkow OAW and turned into two gun cars, each with two BT-7 tank turrets (4.5-cm guns) on different levels, one A/A car with 2-cm quad, and a command car (a covered OO-car). There were also the obligatory control cars. The fully armored locomotive was of Series 38. Thus, PZ 51 looked like a line protection train and remained very short of the usual equipment of other regular armored trains, even after it had been reequipped in the spring of 1944 with two tank carrier cars and 38(t) tanks. With its light armament, it was even exceeded later by several line protection trains that had T 34 turrets with 7.62-cm guns. — Why the well-armed line protection train "Blücher" (see pp. 157f), built new in the winter of 1943-44, was called back early in June 1944 to the Replacement Battalion in Rembertow and, on orders from the OKH on July 19, 1944, was reorganized and renamed PZ 52, is not known. It is true that a mine exploded under it on May 28, 1944, but only one car was seriously (by no means irreparably) damaged. The losses of such Army Group Center units in the Soviet offensive may have been the reason for equipping it as an armored train. Of "Blücher,"

only the (now fully armored) Series 38 locomotive and the two cars with T 34 turrets were used, though replaced with German Panzer IV turrets and long 7.5-cm guns. The weapons were removed from the T 70 turrets, which served only as armored observation posts. On the rear half of the train A/A platforms were installed, one with a 2-cm quad, the other with a single gun of that type from the former line protection train. Since radio cabins were also installed in these four-axle cars they simultaneously served as tank destroyers, A/A and command cars. A four-axle Russian car with two turrets and with 7.62-cm 295/1 guns of the former PZ 27 (the car had just reached a back line workshop for repairs when the train was destroyed in March 1944) was added. Along with the usual control cars and two tank carriers of the standard type, with Panzer 38(t), there were also—just before and after the loco—two internally armored two-axle G-cars for the infantry, which also held the kitchen and medical sections. Obviously, these were preferred to the original four-axle cars of "Blücher" because they could be brought back to the tracks more easily in case of derailment. When the "Blücher" was rebuilt as PZ 52 is not known; it was ready for action in mid-October 1944.

In 1945 the shortage of armored trains became so great that large numbers of line protection trains—at first by command, then budgeted—were turned into regular units (subordinated as army troops to the Commander of Armored Trains under the Inspector-

PZ 52 was made of the line protection train "Blücher." Here is one of its combat cars; the T 34 turret has been replaced by one from a German Panzer IV H; the gun has been removed from the T 70 turret, which served only as an observation post; and on the back part of the car is a mount for an A/A quad. It also had a two-turret gun car from PZ 27, which was just being repaired when the armored train was destroyed in March 1944, and thus escaped its disaster. At the left is a two-axle G-car, at the right a tank carrier. Photo: K H. Klapdohr/W. Sawodny collection

This picture of the rear half of the train shows the second gun car (Panzer IV H turret) of PZ 52 and the tank carrier with Panzer 38(t) coupled to the rear end of the train. Photo: H. Mueller/W. Sawodny collection

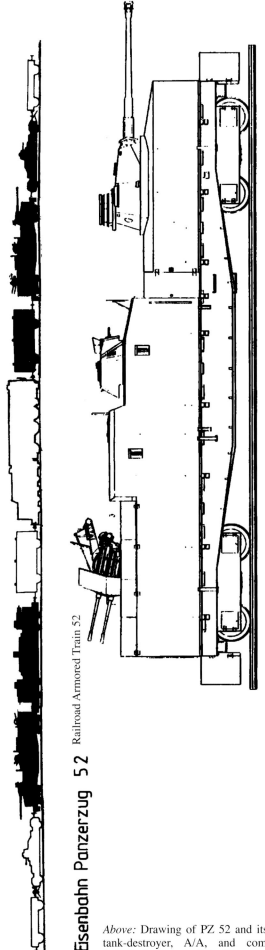

Eisenbahn Panzerzug 52 Railroad Armored Train 52

Above: Drawing of PZ 52 and its combined tank-destroyer, A/A, and command car (rebuilt from cars of the line protection train "Blücher." Train Drawing: U. Schwarze/W. Sawodny, Car Drawing: P. Malmassari

General of Armored Troops and his regimental staffs). This first applied to the line protection trains No. 83 and "Max," then with the Replacement Battalion in Milowitz. While the former, No. 83, was a veteran of the eastern front (nothing is known of this train's equipment except that it was powered by a fully armored WR 360 C 14 Diesel locomotive), the rail protection train "Max" was new, made up partly of material from the three armored trains that had been captured in autumn 1944 when the uprising in Slovakia was put down (the rebuilding is said to have been done at the Steyr works). The Slovakian armored trains each consisted of two double-walled (with concrete cast in between) coal cars with sheet iron covers, of which the lead car had a port in the front wall for an 8-cm Skoda M 17 field cannon (the rear wagon had only machine-gun ports). On two flat cars, undriveable Skoda 35(t) tanks were set and given sheet metal coverings. The exact composition of "Max" is not known, but it would appear that only the Slovakian cars with the tanks were used—and the rest were German-built. Early in February 1945 it reached the eastern front, but its armament and armor proved to be insufficient for use there, so it was transferred to the Balkans just a few days later. For its probably identical brother train "Moritz" the following composition was listed: at each end of the train a control car and a tank-destroyer car (Panzer IV turret), in between them armored G-cars with machine gun ports and A/A platforms (2-cm quads)—locomotive—two cars carrying Panzer 35(t) tanks captured in Slovakia. The train—it too was stylized into a regular armored train—saw service briefly in the Brno area in the last days of April.

When the Russians had reached the Oder early in February 1945, the Inspector-General of the Armored Troops and the Minister of Armament contributed the line protection train of that name to the defense of Berlin. Undriveable "Panther" tanks were even made available for it and loaded on flat cars. The train was built by the Krupp-Druckenmüller firm in Berlin-Tempelhof; it left the factory on February 12, 1945, and was later listed as a regular armored train. The Krupp-Druckenmüller firm also rebuilt two line protection trains that had been left in good condition when the 9th Army had hastily retreated from the Warsaw area. The repair of the line protection train "Werner" lasted from February 5 to March 2, 1945 (it went to the Balkans a short time later); that of Line Protection Train No. 350 from 6 February to the beginning of April 1945. The composition of the latter is known: it consisted of a Series 52 locomotive and, in each half of the train, an armored G-car as command car, an armored O-car with an A/A (2-cm quad) platform, a flat car with a Panzer IV tank (with hull but no running gear) and a control car. These two trains were also regarded as regular armored trains.

Several other line protection trains appear to have been assembled by the Armored Train Replacement Battalion in Milowitz shortly before the war ended, but no data have been found to date as to their numbers, names, composition, and equipment. A photo of the front car of a line protection train halted near Kralup on May 8, 1945, shows that light railroad A/A cars with their concrete A/A platforms were also used in this last offering. The train is said to have carried a 15-cm howitzer (presumably with a wheeled mount on an open car).

Line Protection Train No. 350 after its rebuilding in April 1945. The Series 52 locomotive had partial armor (cab, compressed air tank, provisional plank protection along the boiler). In front of it is the command car. Photo: E. Behling/W. Sawodny collection

This picture of the same train shows that the tank-destroyer car has a Panzer IV H tank without running gear set on a flat car. The A/A car is behind it. Photo: E. Behling/W. Sawodny collection

The Armored Railcars

When some of the German Reichsbahn's rail protection trains were taken over as armored trains by the Wehrmacht in 1938, only the RBD Königsberg's railcar (VT 811) of the five built in the early thirties was still available, left in Allenstein. This was also turned over to the Wehrmacht as Armored Railcar No. 15 and assigned to PZ 7 (ex-RBD Königsberg rail protection train), also stationed in Allenstein. The Diesel-powered vehicle (13.10 meters long, wheelbase 7.30 meters) with two 75-HP (55-kW) motors was armed at first only with four light machine guns. The crew consisted of one officer, 8 NCOs, and 16 men, of whom three NCOs were assigned to the technical crew by the Reichsbahn. This armored railcar, which was taken out of service from October 1940 to November 1941, was rebuilt either in that period or between October 1942 and March 1943, when it was in the workshop again. It was fitted with Diesel-electric drive, with two 150-HP (110-kW) motors (an electrical technician was assigned to the crew to service the electric parts); the armament was increased to six machine guns, and a round observation tower was built in the middle of the roof. So as not to let the increased weight exceed the allowed axle load, another axle (A 1 A) was installed in the middle of the vehicle. PT 15 remained the only one of its kind until the end of 1943 and saw service until the end of the war.

In December 1940 the Inspection of Railroad Engineers (In 10) commissioned a prototype of the SP 42 armored train. A Diesel locomotive of Series WR 550 D 14 (factory no. 21304) built by Orenstein & Koppel was armored for it in 1942 by the Berliner Maschinenbau AG in Wildau. The steel plate (50 mm thick) proved to be too heavy for the four axles. Thus, additional four-axle trucks were added to both ends of the vehicle, increasing its overall length to 2.20 meters. The armored platforms over it each carried a 2-cm A/A quad. This locomotive was finished at the end of 1942, but meanwhile the SP 42 armored train project had been dropped. On instructions from the OKH the locomotive was to be used as an armored railcar, but its final preparation ended only on January 27, 1944. The A/A quads on the platforms at either end were replaced with gun turrets with 7.62-cm F.K. 295/1(r) after a Russian model (see below); the sidewalls were covered with 50-mm armor plate, which raised the total thickness to 100 mm. The powerful MAN W 6 V 30/38 Diesel motor (107.9 kN pulling power) allowed the vehicle to reach 60 kph despite its total weight of 200 tons and the addition of two tank-destroyer cars (flat cars on each of which a turret of the Russian T 34/76 tank with a 7.62-cm tank gun was mounted). This armored railcar, which bore number 16 and saw service as of June 1944, was the best-equipped vehicle of the German armored train weapons with its thick armor, heavy armament, and speed.

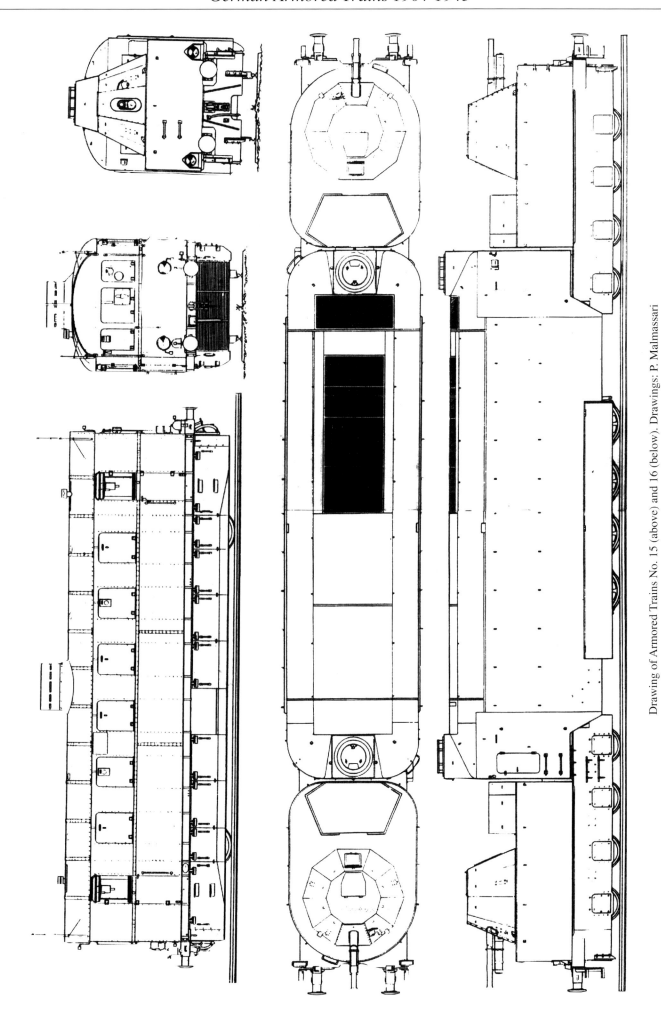

Drawing of Armored Trains No. 15 (above) and 16 (below). Drawings: P. Malmassari

The former rail protection railcar VT 811 as Armored Railcar No. 15 (it also bore the name "Seydlitz") of the German Wehrmacht after reequipping with stronger motors and an additional axle in the middle. Photo: Federal Archives, Koblenz

Armored Wehrmacht Diesel Locomotive WR 550 D as a towing machine for the planned SP 42 Armored Train. To decrease the high axle load caused by the heavy armor (100 mm on the sides), four-axle trucks with A/A platforms were built at both ends. Photo: J. Kraemer/W. Sawodny collection

As Armored Railcar No. 16 the A/A platforms were replaced by turrets with 7.62-cm 295/1(r) guns. Because of this equipment the vehicle was listed as a "gun" railcar. Photo: W. Herbst/W. Koehler collection

Before PT 16 went into service in June 1944 it had two tank-destroyer cars with T-34 turrets coupled on at both ends, of the type that were used by the Dünaburg EAW since the beginning of the year to reequip armored trains (No. 1, 26, 61) in the Polozk area. They were probably first meant for PZ 2, which was then withdrawn for total rebuilding. Photo: Federal Archives, Koblenz

It fell into the hands of the 1st Polish Army south of Neuruppin-Neustadt on the Dosse on May 1, 1945, and was used by the Poles against uprisings in the Ukrainian border area until 1946. Today it is exhibited in the Railroad museum in Warsaw as one of the very few remaining ex-German armored railroad vehicles.

Even before this Railcar No. 16 was finished, the German Wehrmacht put seven vehicles of the Russian Type MBW D-2 into service (two more went to PZ 6 as gun cars) as armored railcars. They came from NKVD armored trains captured in 1941 (although these also had a locomotive, the cars, built in 1932-35, had their own motors, as was considered in planning the German "Armored Train 41" in the final stage). These vehicles, weighing 34 tons in original form (with 20-mm armor), had an overall length of 10.30 meters, but a wheelbase of only 3.90 meters, which surely resulted in not very good running performance because of the long overhangs. They had self-bearing bodies and two gun turrets, each with a 7.72-cm M 02/30 (German 295/1(r)) field gun. When the Wehrmacht took them over modifications were made to the observation and gun turrets, and the four machine gun ports (now light MG 34), and both the motors and radio equipment were replaced. Instead of the earlier U.S. motors of the Hercules type, they now had under-floor Diesel motors of 180 HP (132 kW) with eight horizontally opposed cylinders (presumably 2 x 4 V 18 L produced by the Deutsche Werke in Kiel); the power was transmitted hydrodynamically and gave the vehicle a speed of 60 kph. The preparation of the first of these "armored gun railcars," No. 17, began on March 6, 1943; it was ready for action on 6 December of that year. In the period from July to November 1944 six more ex-Soviet vehicles of the same type were put into service (No. 18-23; No. 18-20 were ordered on November 20, 1943; No. 21-23 on January 27, 1944) from July to November 1944.

These Russian vehicles served as a model for new German production. Not only was PT 16—as already noted—fitted with similar armament, but on June 3, 1943, the OKH War Diary noted: "Request to Chief H. Ruest. u BdE, for the five Diesel railcars from the Siemens-Schuckert Works on hand, to have them equipped like Railcar No. 17 with two 7.62-cm F.K. 295/1(r)." On June 20, 1943, it was added: "For the five Railcar 17s under construction, each is assigned two heavy Pak 7.5 cm 40." The building of these four-axle railcars (estimated length with buffers 13.70 m, wheelbase within pivot mountings ca. 2 m, distance between their turning pins ca. 8.40 m), with their greater penetrating armament in the form of two Panzer IV-H turrets with their 7.5-cm L/48 tank guns, now called "Tank-destroyer Railcars No. 51-55," was so much delayed that the final instructions for their building were issued only in December 1944. In March 1945 three of them (No. 51-53) were budgeted and were to be finished shortly. But this happened to only one car before the war ended, and it fell into Allied hands at the Steyr works, ready for delivery. The others remained unfinished at the Linke-Hofmann works when Breslau was surrounded early in February 1945.

The Soviet armored railcars, which had a self-bearing armored body and two turrets with 7.62 M 02/30 (short) guns, fell—as did this one—to the Germans in large numbers. Photo: Federal Archives, Koblenz

Two of them were used as gun cars in PZ 6; seven others were taken over by the Wehrmacht as Armored Gun Railcars No. 17-23. The gun turrets were retained, but their lower parts were surrounded by an added armored shield, the observation towers built atop them, and the A/A machine guns were removed. A new radio set with a frame antenna and a new motor were installed. Machine gun ports and vision slits were fitted to the system used in BP 42. Photo: Federal Archives, Koblenz

These captured Russian vehicles served as a model for the German-built railcars, which had four axles and two Panzer IV H turrets with long 7.5-cm guns and thus were called "Tank-destroyer" railcars. Although five of them were contracted for in the summer of 1943, just one had been finished when the war ended. It is seen here at the Steyr works in Muenichholz. Photo: MVT Berlin

The others were being built at the Linke-Hofmann works in Breslau. Here one of these vehicles is shown at the works during their inspection by a Polish commission after the fall of Breslau in May 1945. Photo: J. Magnuski collection

Below: Drawing of Tank-destroyer Railcars No. 50-55. Drawing: P. Malmassari

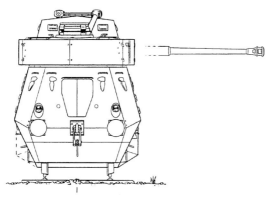

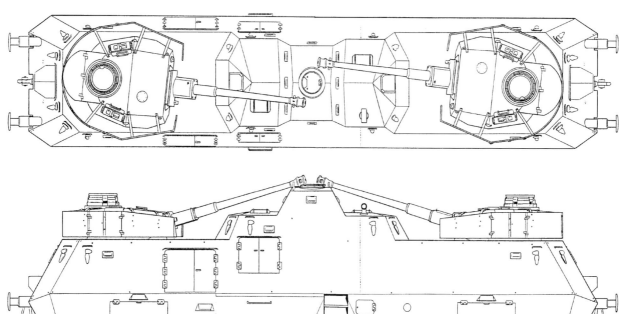

The "Littorinas" had two M 13/40 tank turrets with 4.7-cm guns. While the Italian vehicles also had two 8-cm mortars installed in the middle, all the vehicles used by the Germans were fitted with a 2-cm Breda M 38 A/A gun on a round stand. Photo: W, Herbst/W. Koehler collection

Below: Drawing of the "Littorina" railcar, side view. Drawing: P. Malmassari

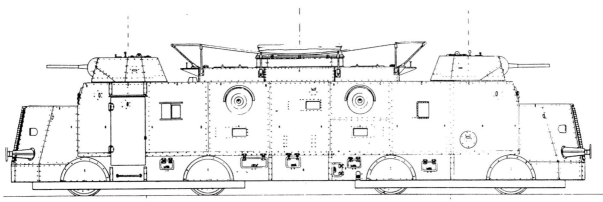

Both the captured Russian vehicles No. 17-23 and the German-built No. 51-53 had crews of one officer, 8NCOs, and 12 men. The same was true of Railcar no. 16, with the addition of 2 NCOs and 4 men as crews of the coupled-on tank-destroyer cars.

In 1944 the German Wehrmacht had also obtained a series of armored railcars from another side. In 1941 the Ansaldo-Fossati firm in Sestri Ponente had rebuilt several (data vary from 5 to 8) Type ALn 56 passenger railcars as armored cars for the Italian occupation troops in the Balkans. These cars had an overall length of some 13.40 meters and were driven by two 6-cylinder, 115 HP (84.5 kW) gas-oil motors (Fiat Type 356), which were mounted directly on two-axle trucks (distance of axles 2.88 meters) and allowed a speed of 50 kph. The armor was 15 mm thick; as armaments they had two turrets of the Italian M 13/40 tank, each with a 4.7-cm gun and a machine gun, and in the center a stand with a 2-cm Breda M 35 A/A gun or two 8-cm mortars. The vehicles with the A/A guns also had four 8-mm Breda machine guns in side ports; those with mortars had six of them. When the Italian troops were disarmed in September 1943 one such railcar came into German hands, and the Ansaldo-Fossati firm received a contract to build eight more vehicles of this type—exclusively with A/A guns–for the Wehrmacht in 1944. These railcars, called the "Littorina" type, were numbered 30 to 38. The crews of 7 NCOs and 23 men had two light MG 34 and one 8-cm mortar to use in addition to the already noted weapons.

Armored railcars were generally subordinated to armored trains. The "Littorinas" were intended to be used in pairs as escorts for light

The truck of the "Littorina" with the six-cylinder Fiat 356 gas-oil motor mounted on it. Photo: DB RAW Nürnberg

scout trains, but with one exception (PT 30 and 31 for PZ 303) they did not reach them, for war-related reasons, and were then assigned individually to other armored trains. Only PT 15 operated alone for a time to handle railroad securing tasks in Greece as of the summer of 1943, along with six Panhard scout cars, until the last light scout train (No. 301) was ready for action at the end of February 1944, and the "excess" Littorina PT 38, which was at first available to the Commander of the Armored Trains with the OB Southeast, remained independent after they received Command Train No. 1.

Trains of the Armored Train Regimental Staffs and Armored Train Replacement Battalion

For the planned establishment of three armored train regimental staffs in the spring of 1944, a fixed stationing in a building in Belgrade was intended for Regimental Staff I (Col. Becker), who took command of the armored trains in Army Group F in the Balkans in January 1944. The two staffs for the eastern front (No. 2, Lt. Col. von Türckheim, and No. 3, Lt. Col. Dr. Günther), though, were to be mobile. For this purpose, Armored Train No. 72 of the BP 42 standard series, just being set up in February 1944, was divided into two half-trains (72 A and B), each to serve as a command train for the regimental staffs. Although the final formation of these staffs was delayed until the autumn (Oct.-Nov.) of 1944, they went to work with these half-trains as command trains. While the armored cars formed the front part of the train, the rear part consisted of three G-cars (possibly earlier rail protection cars with inside armor), presumably serving as quarters for the crew, so as to make the staff more mobile and independent of a base station. The last car was fitted with a Panzer 38(t) turret. Command Train 72A had the original Series 57 armored locomotive, 72B had 93 220. Meanwhile, a new concept for mobile command centers of armored train regiments had developed. Unfortunately, no photo of Command Train No. 1, finished at the end of December 1944 and turned over to Colonel Becker's staff in the Balkans, has been found. But the surviving K.St.N. of the Armored Train Regimental Staff of November 5, 1944, can be used as a good contact point. Accordingly, next to the armored locomotive (surely Series 57) there must have been two tank-destroyer cars with Panzer IV turrets (7.5-cm L/48 guns), two A/A cars with 2-cm quads (the other half of one car probably held the medical station, the other the kitchen), and at least one but probably two command cars. The crew consisted of four officers (regimental commander, adjutant, train commander, and technical leader), 11 NCOs, and 17 men.

In 1945 such cars were too costly to be used in command trains, as they had no combat tasks, being stationed in the hinterlands of Germany at that time, where no attacks from partisans that called for countermeasures were expected. When a new battle group of armored train regiments was hastily set up to cover the Oder front at the beginning of February 1945 under Staff No. 2 (Lt. Col. von Türckheim), who had previously lost almost all his combat trains in the Russian January offensive, the former command train, the half-train No. 72A, had to be used as a combat train. The staff received a makeshift command train bearing the number II. Besides the control cars at both ends it consisted of three G-cars with inside armor and a low-side car, on which a 2-cm A/A quad was mounted. In the first G-car were the commander and technical leader of the train, and in the second the kitchen and medical station. The train was powered by a Polish Ti 3-13 (Prussian G 5.3, now 54 654) armored train locomotive, which had been captured by the Germans in 1939 and served with PZ 21 from the summer of 1940 to November 1942, but had then been mustered out because it was too weak. Behind the locomotive came the staff's command car with the radio station, then the A/A car. The crew (presumably not including the locomotive crew) consisted of 4 officers (regimental commander, adjutant, train commander, technical officer), 8 NCOs, and 7 men. Another command train (No. III), likewise makeshift and probably of similar composition, was set up for a short time in April 1945 and saw service with the new Regimental Staff No. 3 in the last days of the war in the Sudetenland and Protectorate of Czechoslovakia.

Command Train 72B in May 1944. Ahead of the 93 220 armored locomotive (the Series 57 loco pulled Command Train 72A) is a complete BP 42 half-train. Photo: W. Sitzius/W. Sawodny collection

The second half is more interesting, with three G-cars of rail-protection type (note also the boxes between the axles), which probably provided both living and fighting space. At least the last one has an armored rear wall with gun ports and a Panzer 38(t) turret on the roof. Behind it is a tank carrier car of the broad gauge type carrying a VW Kübelwagen. Photo: W. Sitzius/W Sawodny collection

Three command railcars for the armored train regimental staffs were also put into service in the early summer of 1944 (and a fourth probably for the commander of armored trains in the OKH). The crews are listed as a driver and a radioman (plus the members of the staff). These vehicles were very probably individual cars, as they were used in the light scout trains.

The armored train regimental staffs were also to include a workshop train in their area equipped with appropriate facilities, such as a machine shop, locksmithing, and carpentry shops, as well as electrical and gunsmithing works to be able to handle damage and defects that could not be repaired by the crews with their own means, to the extent that such work could be done with the equipment carried on the train without having to send the train to an EAW in the back lands (for major damage this remained unavoidable). Workshop Train No. 1, which was intended for Regiment Staff I in the Balkans, was finished in July 1944 and transferred to its area of action on 21 July. It included about 12 cars and a crew of about 35 men (Lt. Ermer commanding). Its main task was serving light scout trains No. 301-304, which had taken over the securing of the lines from Belgrade through Serbia to Greece and in that country itself since the spring of 1944. Thus, the workshop train was first stationed in Lapovo, south of Belgrade. But even before the Russians broke through into that area (on October 9, 1944) it was withdrawn at the right time. Three of the four light scout trains were also cut off, but the workshop train found a new task in serving the similar heavy scout trains No. 201-204, which were transferred in pairs to the Balkans in November 1944 and February 1945; thus it remained in action until the war ended.

Workshop Train No. 2, to be set up on order of the OKH as of August 8, 1944, was to be ready for use early in October 1944. But its final preparation was delayed until shortly before the war ended, when it was with the Replacement Battalion in Neuenburg and was taken by the Czechs there.

The commander of Armored Trains in the OKH used an express-train car (salon car?) and three railcars for his inspection trips early in 1944. One of the latter was replaced later by an armored command railcar (light armored rail scout car). As of early February 1944 (until his post was transferred to Potsdam in mid-July 1944) he had PZ 72, stationed in Allenbruch, at his disposal, of which both halves (A and B) were intended as command trains for the armored train regimental staffs, but their establishment did not take place at that time.

The Armored Train Replacement Battalion in Rembertow (in Milowitz as of August 1, 1944) had a BP 42 training train since the spring of 1943 at the latest. It bore no. 60, but was also known as "Rudolf," or "R" for short, by the first name of the marching company's commander, 1st Lt. Rudolf Opitz. On February 10, 1944, Training Train "R" had to go into combat service for lack of other trains for that purpose; it came back badly damaged at the end of March 1944. It does not appear again, so presumably was not reconstituted. PZ 75 of the improved BP 44 was to take its place, but its delivery, planned for March, was delayed until well into July 1944. And then, after the Soviets had already threatened the Warsaw area, it also had to be thrown into combat use. Its planned use was manifested in the name "Armored Instruction Train No. 5" given in August, but this did not change its further front service. Instead, PZ 72 B was sent back from East Prussia as a training train for the Replacement Battalion, which had meanwhile been transferred to Milowitz. It saw this service until mid-October 1944, when it was assigned to its

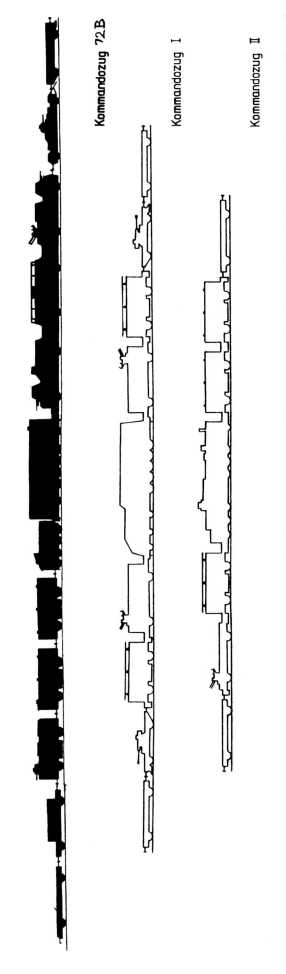

Schematic drawings of the command trains. Command Train No. 72A corresponded definitely in its front and probably in its rear half to Command Train 72B, but with the Series 57 armored locomotive of PZ 72. Drawings of Command Trains I and II (no photos available) are based on information from the K.St.N. or from former members. Drawings: U. Schwarze

The Type BP 42 armored training train, in use by the Replacement Battalion since the spring of 1943, was numbered 60 (car numbers 936 00x), but was usually known by the first name of the marching company chief, Captain Opitz, as "Rudolf" or simply "R." Photo: H. Wiese/W. Sawodny collection

intended use as command train for Armored Train Regiment Staff no. 3. On December 1, 1944, Armored Instruction Train No. 5 finally took its place as the training train of the Replacement Battalion, but only until January 28, 1945, when it had to go into combat service again. After it left, the Replacement Battalion had to get by without a training train.

Supply Trains

Since armored trains could stay in action for long periods but there was no place in the train for the crew to rest, the 1938 service instructions had recommended the provision of a living quarters train of passenger cars. It soon proved that the special nature of armored trains, their autonomy, intended only a temporary arrangement to troops for special tasks, so that amenities, like service areas, frequently changed, requiring an independent supply base. So in the first war years a supply train for every armored train was already formed. It included a living and a supplying part, and the combination of the two showed a certain variability.

The living quarters consisted of one or two officers' quarter cars and 6-10 crew quarter cars. The officers' cars included individual bedrooms and living rooms, while the crew cars had sleeping quarters with two- or three-layer bunks. At first the officers' cars were former express train cars and the crew cars former passenger cars; at the start of the war they were naturally German-built cars, but later most were taken from the occupied countries. As the war went on, the crew cars were more often closed freight cars, and the officers' cars were passenger cars or even freight cars. The living areas also included a writing room car, in which the paymaster, the master sergeant, and the bookkeeper had their places, and a kitchen car, in the other half of which were the medical facilities, and especially in the first half of the war there was a living room car (writing and socializing space originally in passenger cars, kitchen cars were freight cars). The cars had stove heating, so as to guarantee their independence from a heating locomotive.

The supply section consisted of at least one weapon and workshop car, a clothing car (tailor and shoemaker), an ammunition car, a provision car, a construction and equipment car (all closed freight cars), and two flat cars, on which motor vehicles belonging to the supply unit (usually production passenger cars of various makes, later usually VW Kübelwagen) and 1.5-ton (as of 1944 usually two-ton) trucks were carried. The supply sections of the light and heavy scout trains also included an extra workshop car for motor repairs. Naturally other transport cars could be added as needed, but it was required that taking them from general rail traffic be kept at a minimum—also through practical and space saving housing of men and materials.

Depending on its structure, the crew of the supply train (minus the combat train crew) included the paymaster (official at officer's rank), six NCOs (top sergeant, accounting and provision NCOs, a secretary and draftsman, armorer, equipment NCO, field cook), and seven men (two car and truck drivers, two armorer's aides, a cook, a tailor, and a shoemaker); in the light and heavy scout trains there was also a repair troop consisting of a wagon master at NCO rank and one or two mechanics (crew rank). In the process of thinning the supply trains, the positions of the accountant, one armorer's aide, and sometimes the cook at crew rank were eliminated.

The supply trains always stayed for a long time at the depot that served as the armored train's action base. Thus, they did not have their own locomotive, so one had to be assigned by the responsible service office in case of transfer trips. Because of this immobility they were threatened more and more as the enemy's air superiority increased during the war, with attacks on railroad stations—always a favorite and frequent target of air raids anyway. There were increasing losses of materials, and sometimes also of men. Thus, the supply trains went through ever greater changes by additions or new constructions, which the crews themselves often carried out right on the spot. In their mixtures of cars they formed a colorful, ever changing picture. The following pictures can offer only a very limited view of this.

Above: The cars of the supply trains formed a remarkably colorful picture, of which only a very small bit can be shown here. Here is a group of compartment and aisle passenger cars of the Prussian type as crew cars of PZ 23. Photo: H. Bruntsch/W. Sawodny collection

Six Saxon fourth-class passenger cars were used in PZ 1. Photo: E. Grahl/W. Sawodny collection

At first, express train cars were made available for officers, as here in PZ 3. In the foreground is AB 4ü bay.08. Photo: F. Englberger/W. Sawodny collection

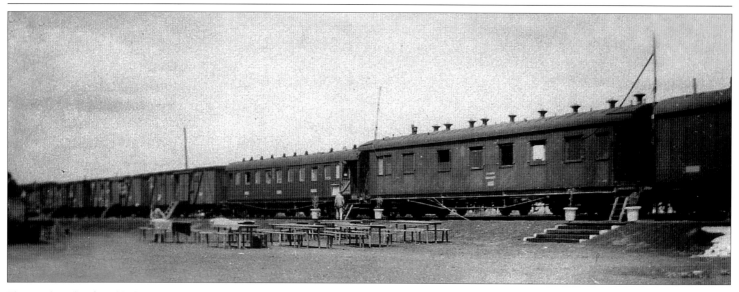

The supply train of PZ 28 shows, at far right, probably a baggage car (kitchen and canteen?), then a captured Russian car (writing and radio room, as shown by the antenna), an express car of Polish type (officers' car), and a series of Polish G-cars rebuilt as crew cars. Photo: B. Schultz/W. Sawodny collection

A French second-class compartment car of the "Est" type was used in PZ 19. Photo: J. Kraemer/W. Sawodny collection

If the quarters train—here that of PZ 51—was at one place for long, as was often the case in partisan fighting, the men settled down as best they could, adding steps and railings to the car doors, a log roadway along the train, and so on. Photo: G. Gayk/W. Sawodny collection

Later only rebuilt G-cars—even for officers in the end—were used for quarters, as here in PZ 63 on the eastern front. The smokestacks of the stoves extend through the roofs. The numbering identifies Wehrmacht property (with 900 numbers as "cars of private origin"). The first group of digits, 936, indicated armored trains in general, while 0 through 4 as the first digits of the second group were reserved for combat trains, and 5 and higher were used for quarters trains. Photo: H. Beckmann/W. Sawodny collection

In PZ 4, a four-axle B 9 yfi from France was taken to the eastern front. The heating, now needed, was done by coke stoves, whose smokestacks went out the windows. Photo: W. Sawodny collection

A Prussian 3rd class compartment car was used as a writing room in PZ (light scout train) No. 303. Beside it is a G-car rebuilt as a quarters car. Photo: P. G. Römer/W. Sawodny collection

Right and below: The interior of a well-furnished quarters car. Right: in front is the living room, in back the sleeping area with fixed three-layer bunks. The view of the setup (below) shows the crews' lockers. Note the stools hung on the ceiling. Photo: H. Bruntsch/W. Sawodny collection

The canteen car of PZ 3 with upholstered chairs and tables between them. In the background is the sales window with price list. At the upper left is a radio receiver. Photo: H. Bendl/W. Sawodny collection

Things are cramped in this crew car, with three-tier bunks set up on each side. Photo: Federal Archives, Koblenz

Below: The writing room of PZ 3 is located in a passenger car. The separated area in back was the commander's room. Photo: H. Bendl/W. Sawodny collection

An interior view of the commander's room of 1st Lt. Hans Bendl (PZ 3). Photo: H. Bendl/W. Sawodny collection

The canteen car of PZ 1—here decorated for Christmas—had only wooden benches; wall coverings and lamps gave it a more pleasant look. The picture of Hitler was a scarcely dispensable wall decoration in those days. Photo: W. Sitzius/W. Sawodny collection

The cook, on the other hand, worked in more prosaic surroundings, usually in a G-car. Photo: W. Sitzius/W. Sawodny collection

The workshop was also located in a G-car. This picture shows that of PZ 26, with the typical "cannon" stove and its smokestack to the outside. Photo: H. Jäger/W. Sawodny collection

The Production Facilities

The rail protection trains of the twenties and thirties—and thus also the first seven armored trains of the German Wehrmacht—were constructed and armored in workshops of the responsible district offices (for the armored trains: Königsberg, Osten-Frankfurt on the Oder, Breslau, Stettin-Dresden, Würzburg-Aschaffenburg, and Munich). The basis for them undoubtedly came from recommendations of the RVM. Thus, the halves of all the rail protection trains consisted, besides the control cars, of three covered, internally armored railroad cars, of which at least one had an observation post. Since the end of the twenties, the locomotives came almost exclusively from Series 57 and 93. The armoring of these locomotives was also done according to a uniform plan, probably recommended by the RVM. In detail, though, the preparation was left up to the workshop doing the job, so that despite these general specifications, each of the rail protection trains showed its individual character.

PZ 3, the only one damaged in the Polish campaign, was improved at the Schichau shipyards in Danzig after its initial repairs at the Schneidemühl RAW.

Of the five armored trains set up in the first half of 1940, those made of captured Polish material (No. 21 and 22) were obviously made up on site—presumably in Krakau—without great constructive changes. The captured Czech material was reworked at the Halberstadt construction workshop, which also assembled the armored trains No. 23-25 made of it.

At this Halberstadt workshop, the gun cars of PZ 3 were also rebuilt to hold the new 7.5-cm L/41 guns, delivered by Rheinmetall, in their turrets. On the other hand, the repair of PZ 1, damaged on May 10, 1941, is said to have been done at the Darmstadt RAW (or was it confused with the Halberstadt RAW?). PZ 7 was overhauled at the Leipzig-Engelsdorf RAW in the spring of 1941.

The new formation of Armored Trains No. 23 and 24 in June 1941, and that of PZ 25 later (November-December 1941), took place in the Königsberg car building works, where the materials of these armored trains were deposited when they were taken out of service in the autumn of 1940. The Halberstadt construction works provided additional captured cars for them.

The rebuilding of the armored trains captured in Lemberg at the start of the Russian campaign into the two combat trains of the German Armored Train No. 10 in November 1941 was done by the EAW there.—PZ 51, first planned as a line protection train, was made up of captured Russian material in the first half of 1942 at the Pruszkow OAW (west of Warsaw).

With the building of broad gauge Armored trains No. 26-31 for the Russian campaign a kind of series production began. The tank carrier cars seem to have been delivered by the Dessau Wagon Factory, the infantry cars by the Linke-Hofmann Works in Breslau. The latter firm was also, under contract from In 10, supposed to carry out the development of the "1941" and "SP 42" armored train projects, while the locomotives for them were to be armored by the Berliner Maschinenbau-AG (ex-Schwartzkopf) in Wildau (but there was only a single Diesel locomotive, the WR 550 D, which

saw service later as Armored Railcar No. 16). Also after the armored trains were turned over to the Fast Troops and the responsibility for them to In 6, the Linke-Hofmann Works in Breslau remained the developmental and construction firm for the armored trains of the BP 42 standard type (later BP 44, No. 61 ff.); the steam locomotives of Series 57 (Prussian G 10) were armored by Krupp in Essen. Production in Breslau ran until the end of January 1945; then, in view of the city being threatened by Soviet forces, the unfinished material there for Armored Trains No. 80-82 was taken to the area of the Protectorate of Bohemia and Moravia (when a makeshift armored train was made up there after Breslau was surrounded, nothing else of the kind was found at Linke-Hofmann, and it had to be built new). The further work on Armored Trains No. 80-82 was done at the "Bohemia" Wagon Factory in Böhmisch-Leipa. As an additional construction site—though mainly for line protection trains (rebuilt and new),—the Krupp-Druckenmüller firm in Berlin-Tempelhof was included as of the end of January 1945. A site for the final equipping of these trains built there and intended for the Oder front was set up in

Like interior photos of armored trains, photos of their construction are very rare. The light and space conditions were unfavorable for amateur photography. From the main production plant, the Linke-Hofmann Works in Breslau, there is just this picture of armored railcars of the 51-55 series as they were found after the city was taken in May 1945. Photo: J. Magnuski collection

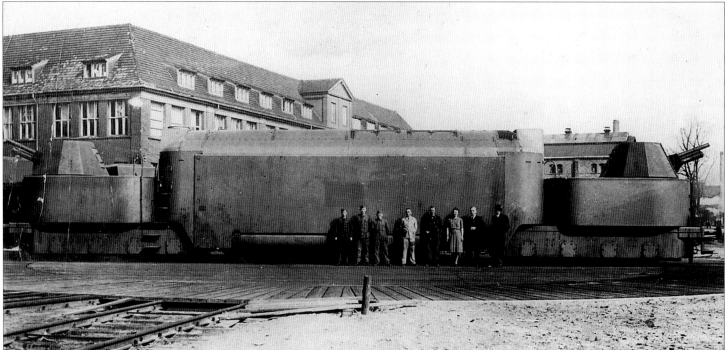

On the turntable at the Berliner Maschinenbau AG in Wildau, Armored Railcar No. 16 is seen in its full size with several factory employees. This was the firm's only contribution to the building of armored trains. Photo: S. Lauscher collection

Berlin-Hoppengarten, since transferring to the distant Replacement Battalion in Milowitz would have been too time consuming.

The development contract for the light and heavy scout trains was issued to the Steyr firm in the summer of 1943; the firm also provided the motors and chassis later. The armored bodies were built at the Nibelungenwerk in St. Valentin.

Of the armored railcars, No. 15 was a rail protection vehicle (VT 811) built by Wegmann in 1929, which was probably armored in Königsberg, since it served in that RBD.—PT 16 originated as a Diesel locomotive of the "SP 42" series—built by the Berliner Maschinenbau AG—as already noted. Railcars No. 30-38 were built by the Italian firm of Ansaldo-Fossati in Sestri Ponente. Railcars No. 17-23 were captured Russian vehicles, probably adapted at the Nürnberg RAW, which was responsible for repairing and overhauling all the armored railcars of the German Wehrmacht.

The German made railcars (No. 51-55) were built at the Linke-Hofmann works in Breslau. Whether the Siemens-Schuckert firm was involved in the interior work on these vehicles, as is first mentioned in the OKW war diary on June 3, 1943, is not known. The only completely built railcar of this series was at the Steyr works (Ball Bearing Factory, Münichholz) when the war ended. Obviously this firm was also involved in the final preparation of the railcars, possibly only after Breslau was surrounded and the original preparation site was lost.

The rebuilding of the early armored trains No. 2, 3, 4, and 7 was done in 1944-45 at the car factory in Königshütte, Upper Silesia,

which was run by the Röchling Works. While No. 3 and 4 were finished earlier and went into service, PZ 7 was taken away at the end of January 1945 as the Russians approached; it was finished at the Ingolstadt RAW. The rebuilding of PZ 2 was halted in November 1944.

The thorough rebuilding (which much resembled new building) of the old armored trains No. 1-31 was done in RAW facilities, especially Eberswalde (PZ 27: June-September 1942; PZ 30: November 1942-February 1944); Gleiwitz (PZ 23: October 1942-August 1943; PZ 31: November 1942-October 1943), and Königsberg (PZ 3: May-October 1942; PZ 1: December 1942-August 1943), but the Zwickau (PZ 26: March 1943-February 1944) and Neuaubing RAW (PZ 24: March 1943-January 1944) were also involved. From the realm of the General Government, only one site, the Pruszkow OAW, is known; the rebuilding of PZ 6 (July-September 1942) was done there. Where the rebuilding of the line protection train "Blücher" into PZ 52 was done could not be determined. For the involved railroad repair shops, these extensive rebuildings were surely an unusual task that tied up space, material, and personnel capacities and affected normal operations. That such problems became more serious as the war went on is shown by the steady lengthening of the building times: 4 to 6 months in 1942, but later almost always a year or even longer.

Smaller rebuildings or rearmings, as well as repairs, were also done in railroad workshops, usually the improvement works, but of course in those near the fronts—thus usually in captured enemy territory. In the east, the Königsberg RAW was also involved

Three pictures of the building of PZ 30 at the Eberswalde RAW in 1943; at left a command and A/A car (ex-Soviet four-axle car), below a two-axle gun car captured from Russia. Naturally, other DR vehicles were also given routine service. Here, too, women had to take part in war work (lower right). Photos: W. Conrad/W. Sawodny collection

The dismantling of captured Russian cars so the chassis could be fitted with new bodies was often done outdoors, as here on PZ 26 at the Zwickau RAW. Photo: H. Jäger/W. Sawodny collection

The gun cars for PZ 23 are being built in the Gleiwitz RAW. Photo: H. Radermacher/W. Sawodny collection

In the Neuaubing RAW, old Austrian infantry cars (two coupled together and fitted with an observation post) are being rebuilt for the new PZ 24. Photo: DB AW Neuaubing

(naturally, especially as of the summer of 1944, when the front neared East Prussia), but in the northern sector of the eastern front, the Dünaburg EAW also carried on such work. In the central sector such work was done in workshops at Roslawl and Baranovici, but the Minsk EAW may have been involved too. In the southern sector the Kiev-Darniza, Kharkov (where the tank factory were also involved), Poltava, Stalino, and Nikolayev EAW, and also Lemberg later, but this list—like the previous one—can hardly claim to be complete. For the armored trains stationed in the Balkans the Marburg RAW, then belonging to RBD Vienna, was responsible. In France, various modifications of the German armored trains stationed there were made in Parisian workshops; larger jobs were done at Schneider in Le Creusot. This factory, along with the Somua works in Lyon-Venissieux, also built the new PZ 32. The armored trains withdrawn from France in the autumn of 1944 were reequipped for service on the eastern front at the Offenburg and Schwetzingen RAW shops, while PZ 25 was rearmed at Leipzig-Engelsdorf. Servicing and repairing of the armored train locomotives were obviously done primarily at the Gleiwitz and Königsberg RAW shops.

Small scale repairs to armored trains which came back to the Replacement Battalion in Rembertow were made at the Pruszkow OAW, and at the Neuenburg EAW after the Replacement battalion was transferred to Milowitz at the end of July 1944.

When such work was carried out at railroad workshops—during the frequent rebuildings and new constructions, the crews of the armored trains were stationed at the site, and individual crewmen were called in to work on the basis of their ability to do the jobs, for which the technical leader of the train had essential influence. So it was assured that not only previously gained experience was included in construction, but the crews also experienced the creation of their train and thus became quickly and thoroughly familiar with its qualities and specialties. For factory rebuilding—such as at the Königshütte works—this was not the case; the crews remained at the Armored Train Replacement Battalion and the train was delivered to them when it was finished; then they could spend a long introductory phase becoming familiar with it.

A photo taken secretly by the Resistance shows PZ 32 being built (by Somua in Lyon-Venissieux). Photo: Service Historique de L'Armee Paris

The Armored Train Locomotives

The compiling of this chapter is difficult, because scarcely any documentation is available, and even the assembled photos give insufficient information. The locomotive numbers are almost always covered by the armor, and sometimes even the type of locomotive is scarcely recognizable.

In the early rail protection times the locomotives were very varied, but there are very few concrete data on them. In 1921 a Stuttgart rail protection train had a Württemberg T 5; until 1924 this office used 93 801 (still under its old number, Stuttgart 1447) as its rail protection loco, and later a Prussian T 14 of unknown number can be recognized in a picture. The Erfurt 93 285 was based in Grünberg (RBD East) at that time, and 93 191 can be identified as a loco of the Munich RBD. In the Hamburg-Altona RBD, 92 804 (Prussian T 13) served from 1924 to 1932, and a Series 75 (Baden VIb or c) armored locomotive, in use by the Karlsruhe BRD even after 1930, may also come from the early days. The inclusion of the rail protection trains in the Army's mobilization plans (1930) resulted in the rail protection trains usually getting fully armored Series 57 (Prussian G 10) or 93 (Prussian T 14) locomotives, while among the latter some earlier ones were probably retained. Type 57 locos are documented in the RBD of Berlin, Hamburg-Altona (57 2043), Munich (57 3293), and Regensburg, 93s in the RBD of Breslau and Stettin (93 058), and 93 060 was also an armored locomotive, but no definite use with a rail protection train (Magdeburg-Hannover?) can be documented to date. Whether a roughly equal division of the two loco types existed must remain unanswered; even the majority of 57s in the armored trains taken over from rail protection does not contradict it.

The 2-8-2 tender locomotives of Series 93, built in large numbers since 1914, showed good running characteristics in both directions as long as its speed was not too high, and satisfactory pulling performance, but also showed several weaknesses: weak driving gear, many hard-to-reach parts, an unsatisfactory water supply that limited its action radius, and above all a poor distribution of its axle loads (the front running wheel had the highest, 17.3 tons, the driving wheel had the lowest, 14.2 tons). The axle load, comparatively high overall (the two outside coupling axles and the rear running axle had values of 16.7 to 16.9 tons), allowed only thin armor (15 mm), and

the small radius of action made these locomotives appear ill suited for use with armored trains, but their noted weak points in normal use may have contributed to their frequent use in rail protection trains, for they sat in the roundhouse most of the time, and their armor and range seemed quite sufficient for securing use in their own area.

The situation was much more favorable for the robust and uncomplicated Series 57 freight locomotives that had 0-10-0 axle order and separate tenders. With a slightly lower top speed and good pulling power (1460 tons at 50 kph on the level), they had larger fuel and water supplies and thus a greater range. Above all, though, they had a low, evenly divided axle load of 15.4 tons at most, which allowed heavier armor (25-27 mm, as was also reported then for rail protection cars?).

Obviously, general guidelines had been issued by the RVM for the armoring of the locomotives of the rail protection trains, but they allowed enough play for individual formation of details, so that their appearance was largely similar, but each machine showed differences in details. The armor followed the external outlines fairly closely, and appropriate bulges were provided for additions to the frame (air and feed pumps, preheater) and the steam channels to the smoke chamber (in Series 57 they were on the left when facing forward—where the preheater and feed pump were located—but often the armor sheet extended along the entire boiler). The running gear was covered with vertical armor skirts, which—sometimes with a small offset—also ran over the cylinders. The boiler superstructures (sand boxes, steam domes) usually bore their own armored coverings, but were partly housed in a common armored box as well. For the parts of the locomotive that needed servicing there were doors in the armor to make them reachable—though certainly under difficult conditions. The armor of the cab was especially important. In Series 93 the coal box was fully integrated in it, forming a space enclosed all around that could be reached through an armored sliding door. In Series 57 the entrance was in a narrow area between the locomotive and tender, covered by a steel door—which ended at chest height. To the rear, the open space between the loco and the likewise armored tender was kept as narrow as possible by an armored flap on the back of the cab roof. The cab had a fairly large sliding side window, with a small window (in Series 93) with an armored flap to the front.

The partly armored 93 265—with protection for the cab, water tank, and cylinder, pumps, steam ducts, and air brakes—which was found at Halle when the war ended, might have been the locomotive of a line protection train. Photo: EK Archives

The rail protection locomotives retained their original armor throughout the war, as shown in this postwar photo of 93 058, which took over PZ 2 in the same form in July 1938 until it was taken out of service in June 1944, and then pulled PZ 78 in 1945. Photo: H. Wenzel collection

Two other 93s were armored in the spring of 1941 for the reconstituted armored trains No. 23 and 24, but in different ways. Here is 93 220 of PZ 23, which was replaced by a 57 when this train was rebuilt. Afterward, around the beginning of 1944, it pulled the remainder of PZ 68, later Command Train 72B (from which time the photo comes). Photo: W. Sitzius/W. Sawodny collection

Locomotive 93 298, armored in 1941 for PZ 24, is here with PZ 21 in February 1943. Photo: G. Leinen/W. Sawodny collection

Weighing data are known for 93 058 and 57 2043. 93 058 was weighed unarmored in 1926. With axle loads between 15.16 and 16.70 tons, the total weight was 96.30 tons. After being armored (1941) it had a total weight of 112.82 tons (with 16.52 tons of armor), with axle loads, except for the front running wheel (16.42 tons), between 18.77 and 19.71 tons. For 57 2043, one has to rely on the general data given for this type of locomotive in an unarmored state (totals of 76.6 tons for the locomotive, 45.8 tons for the tender, with all axle loads between 15.2 and 15.4 tons). After armoring (1938, tender 1941) the weights were: total weight of the loco 89.8 tons (armor 13.2 tons) and tender 53.3 (armor 7.5) tons, the axle loads, except the rear most loco axle (19.0 tons), including the tender were 17.2 to 18.1 tons, and clearly more favorable than those of the Series 93 locomotive.

When seven rail protection trains were taken over by the German Wehrmacht as armored trains in 1938, Series 57 — naturally — was given preference. They were either already with the trains (as was 57 3293 for Munich's PZ 3, and probably also the East Prussian armored trains, No. 6 and 7), or were taken from other rail protection trains (like 57 2043 from the Hamburg-Altona RBD, which presumably replaced 93 285 on PZ 1 in Frankfurt on the Oder). Armored Trains No. 4 (Breslau) and 5 (Aschaffenburg-Kassel) also used armored Series 57 locomotives; only PZ 2 (Dresden, the ex-Stettin rail protection train) kept its 93. — The locomotives remained with these armored trains for long periods, some during their entire existence, such as 93 058 with PZ 2 from 1938 until it went out of service in July 1944. At the beginning of 1945 it went to PZ 78, returned with it from southwestern Hungary to Styria, and stayed with the train when it was surrendered in Thalheim, near Judenburg. One exception is PZ 1; its loco was damaged by derailing on May 10, 1940, and replaced by the loco from disbanded PZ 5 (57 3301?). The repaired loco of PZ 1 (57 2043) was assigned to PZ 24 at the end of 1941; when that train was rebuilt in the spring of 1943 it went to PZ 25. Stopped with that train southwest of Kielce on January 13, 1945, it was used after the war as Tw 1-116 of the PKP.

Not included in the category of rail protection construction are two Series 93 locomotives which reached Armored Trains No. 23 and 24 in June 1941. They may have been armored just before being assigned to those trains in the spring of 1941, for an improved, smooth-walled version of armor was tested on them. For the PZ 24 loco (93 298), the vertical surface extended without any interruption from the coal box and cab over the whole power plant, including the cylinder onto the front of the smoke chamber on an even level over the water box. The upper part of the boiler was likewise armored in box form, but narrower. Only the upper part of the smokestack and the integral armoring of the steam dome and sandbox projected from the top. In PZ 23's locomotive (93 220), the smooth vertical sidewall extended up to the edge of the cab roof along the entire length of the vehicle. It joined a likewise full-length twice-angled roof-like closing, which also covered the steam dome and sandbox, and let the smokestack project only a few centimeters. Since the cab showed no lateral projection here, two small openings for sight were cut out of the armored wall ahead of the smoke chamber.

The course of Locomotive 93 298 can be traced easily at first, thanks to its characteristic shape. It remained with PZ 24 until December 1941, was then replaced by the aforementioned 57 of the earlier PZ 1 (57 2043), and joined the reconstituted PZ 25. In October 1942 it was exchanged there for the Polish loco of PZ 21. It can be documented with the latter train until July 8, 1944, when it was badly damaged by Russian tanks in an attack near Vilna. When the resulting repairs at the Königsberg RAW were finished in October 1944, PZ 21 had already been cut off in Courland, so that the loco could not return to it. It was later captured by the Soviets. The armored locomotive 93 220 remained with PZ 23 until, after being damaged, it reached the Gleiwitz RAW in October 1942, where it was to be fully rebuilt. In the winter of 1942-43 it helped PZ 68, and in April 1944 it went to Command Train No. 72 and took over Section B. It must have fallen into enemy hands in Gotenhafen (Gdynia) at the end of March 1945. It was definitely in Poland after the war.

The rebuilt PZ 3, finished in July 1944, is said to have had 93 1126 as its armored locomotive. It would have been the only case of the unfavorable T 14.1 type being used for this purpose, what with its even higher axle loads (3 axles over 18 tons!). PZ 3 was blown up in Weinoden, Latvia, on October 10, 1944; the locomotive, 93 1126, was in Soviet hands after 1945. Also noted as an armored loco in the east was 93 259. In October 1944 it was at the Königsberg RAW, and in 1945 with the PKP. After the war, the partly armored 93 265 was in Halle. It may — since thus equipped locomotives were often used there — have been assigned to a line protection train. — In all, only a few locomotives of Series 93 were used with armored trains, and even if there were more of which nothing is known, there could only have been one or two.

Armoring in rail protection style, as was used on Series 57 locos for Armored Trains No. 1-7, followed, in principle, the same plan, but showed minor variations which allow the locomotives to be identified and their histories to be traced.

57 2043 (above) was at first with PZ 1 (shown here); after its damage suffered on May 10, 1940, was repaired, it went to PZ 24 in December 1941, and to PZ 25 in 1943. Photo: K. Fliegner/W. Sawodny collection

The locomotive of PZ 3 (left) was 57 3293. Photo: H. Bendl/W. Sawodny collection

The number of PZ 4's armored locomotive is not known. Photo: P. Malmassari collection

The loco of PZ 5 (maybe 57 3301?) went to PZ 1 after PZ 5 was disbanded in the summer of 1940. Photo: EK Archives

Even in the armored locomotives of the two Königsberg trains there are small differences: while the coverings of the sandboxes on PZ 6 are flat (center), those of PZ 7 are sloped like roofs (below). Photos: P. Malmassari collection; Museum of Technology and Transit, Berlin

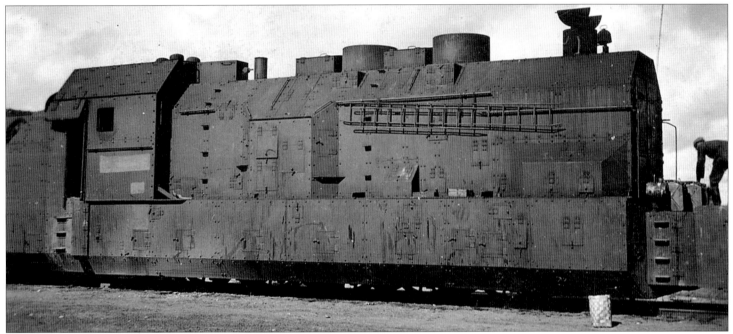

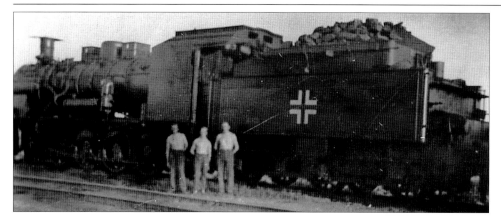

For the broad gauge armored trains set up in the spring of 1941 (PZ 26-31), the steam locomotives had only provisional armor on the cabs, as here on the 57 (number unknown) of PZ 31. Photo: H. v. Heymann/W. Sawodny collection

For the two combat trains of broad gauge No. 10, Series 57 locomotives were used when they were converted to standard gauge, probably at a workshop in Kharkov, in the summer of 1942. The free upper smoke chamber and the arched plate on the smoke exit channel are characteristic. Yet there is a difference: while the loco of PZ 10A (afterward PZ 10) had angular covering of the cab, that of 57 1064 of PZ 10B (later PZ 11) is round. Photos: Federal Archives, Koblenz and R. Lorscheidt/W. Sawodny collection

The same style—though with additional covering of the upper smoke chamber and a smooth upper edge of the side armor—is seen on 57 1653 (PZ 28), though it was only applied in Nikolayev early in 1944. Photo: E. Lehle/W. Sawodny collection

Similar armor, but running smoothly to the front, is seen on the two locomotives of PZ 27 (57 2300) and PZ 30 (57 1504) prepared by the Eberswalde RAW. Both have the upper half of the smoke chamber uncovered. Photos: H.J. Roddewig, W. Conrad/ both W. Sawodny collection

For Armored Trains No. 26-31, set up before the Russian campaign began, five Series 57 locomotives were converted to broad gauge in the spring of 1941 (57 2300 for PZ 27, 57 1653 for PZ 28, 57 1504 for PZ 30, and 57 2526 for PZ 31 (PZ 26 probably had 57 2658)). They were stationed—even before the armored trains were set up, which took place on the night of June 21-22, 1941—at their starting depots at the boundary (Eydtkau, Terespol, and Zuravica) as broad gauge shunting locomotives for transit traffic between the Soviet Union and the German Reich. The speedy night work of setting up the armored trains (the other materials—including the cars—arrived loaded on standard gauge freight cars only after darkness had fallen) allowed only provisional cab armoring with steel plates. Only when the armored trains were rebuilt, often much later (the time span reached from May 1942 to the beginning of 1944), were these locomotives, which had meanwhile been converted back to standard gauge, fully armored. Their armor shows various stages leading to the later construction of the locomotives for the standard BP 42 armored trains.

The locomotives that the two combat trains of Unit No. 10 (later Armored Trains No. 10 and 11—57 1064 is known for No. 11) received when they were converted to standard gauge in the early summer of 1942 (they used captured locomotives previously) also deserve mention here. Their armoring was probably done at the Kharkov workshops, and they represent a type of their own. Only the vertical skirts under the frame, which otherwise reached only slightly under the wheel axles and even had cutouts for the rear wheels, extended over the full length of the locomotive. A very slightly angled armor plate rose to just over the middle of the boiler, and did not cover the smoke chamber. The steam exit channels, though,

were protected by their own armored box, fitted in welded form. The upper part of the boiler protection was an equally long armor plate inclined at about 30 degrees, rising just barely above the height of the boiler, but in the area of the steam domes and sand boxes it was high enough to protect them. At the front end there was a transverse plate between the boiler and the smoke chamber; its height also enclosed the structures on the boiler. The upper part of the smoke chamber and smokestack thus remained outside the armor, which was also opened at the top in the boiler area. The armored cab, projecting slightly to the sides, had either an angled squared-off (PZ 10) or rounded roof shape (57 1064 of PZ 11).—57 1064 was damaged and remained in Lublin when PZ 11 retreated on July 24, 1944, and later turned up with the PKP as Tw 1-42.

The same pattern was followed in improved form much later (early 1944) for the locomotive of PZ 28 (57 1653), prepared at the Nikolaiev EAW. The upper part of the smoke chamber was now protected by an additional angled armor plate; the upper armor ran from the front of the loco to the cab at the same height, raised to cover the structures on the boiler (whether there was a covering cannot be seen). The armor plate in the lower boiler area was now mounted vertically.—The fact that 57 1653 was in a scrap yard in the Saarland after the war shows that it did not stay with PZ 28 until its loss (on June 29, 1944, east of Borissov).

A somewhat different variation is seen in the two locomotives of armored trains No. 27 (57 2300, May-November 1942) and 30 (57 1504, November 1942-February 1944) armored at the Eberswalde RAW. The drive cover was uninterrupted here and reached farther down. The vertical armor plate on the lower half of the boiler was extended to the smoke chamber, thus covering the steam exit channels. The—less inclined—armor on the upper part of the boiler

The locomotive of the rebuilt PZ 26, armored at the Zwickau RAW, already shows the fully smooth form of the standard BP 42 type. Only the cab, with its rounded roof, and the tender with its upper body, show variations.—The locos of Armored Trains No. 23 and 31—prepared at the Gleiwitz RAW—completely corresponded to the standard type. Photo: H. Jäger/W. Sawodny collection

and the superstructures, though, still left the smoke chamber and smokestack uncovered. The locomotive of PZ 30 (57 1504) was shot down by Russian tanks at Karpovo (north of Odessa) on April 6, 1944; PZ 27 was withdrawn after being badly damaged in March 1944; its locomotive (57 2300) may have gone to PZ 79, for it turned up in Hungary after the war, and No. 79 was the only train that had remained there.

The full armor on the locomotives of Armored Trains No. 26 (57 2658?, Zwickau RAW, November 1942-February 1944) and 31 (57 2526, Gleiwitz RAW, November 1942-October 1943) followed the smooth and all-enclosing form of the standard BP 42 type in terms of their running gear and boilers, including smoke chambers. Only the cab (of PZ 26) and tender still showed the older form of armoring.

All these locomotives received mostly armored auxiliary tenders of different types as time went by, including some from captured stocks.

For the standard BP 42 armored train conceived in 1942, only Series 57.10-35 (G 10) locomotives with tenders, including a second one running in front, were planned. The armoring was made at the Krupp works in Essen. The armor was all vertical in the running gear area, with doors at all axles and a separate armor plate with an opening panel over the cylinders. Above the frame—also running all the way to the cab—was a slightly inclined armor plate up to mid-boiler, and on it a second one at a greater angle of ca. 25 degrees, which enclosed the whole locomotive. In the cab area, the slightly inclined armor plate reached up to the middle of the more tilted one (in this area was a window closed by an armor plate), and the roof area was angled more flatly. The transition from the boiler armor and the cab was covered by two angled triangular armor plates so that no catches were formed; in the lower one a vision slit with a cover was inserted. The locomotive had a smooth armored roof, out of which only the smokestack projected, while everything else atop the boiler was covered but reachable through hatches. The front of the locomotive was covered by an angled armor plate into which a two-part smoke chamber door was fitted. Two ladders were attached to the sides: one just before the second axle and up to the roof, the other to the middle of the boiler at the fifth axle. The cab was closed off

at the rear by an armored cover that reached down to the upper edge of the tender. The narrow entrance to the cab could be closed by a horizontally divided two-part armored door. The tender had vertical side armor up to the level of the cab window; only then was it angled up to the roof edge. It was filled with coal from above and could be covered by armor plates. The back wall was flat below, more tilted above, with an armored door for the water tank. The front auxiliary tender was identical. In the all-enclosing, smooth and, when possible, angled form whose pattern can be seen in a Russian armored loco captured in 1941 (see below), an optimum may well have been found. As for thickness, the 30 mm that could not be exceeded for reasons of weight proved unsatisfactory.

The locomotive numbers of this type are all covered by the armor, so that no information can be gained from pictures. The following Series 57 locomotives were turned over to the German Wehrmacht by the Erfurt RBD (Gera workshop) on the stated dates:

57 1071 and 57 1585 on 2/21/43
57 1094 on 5/11/43
57 1280 and 57 2198 on 11/30/43
57 1913 on 12/24/43.

They were intended for the second series of BP 42 armored trains (No. 67-72). 57 1585 was with PZ 67 and, matching the location of its loss, found in Latvia after the war; 57 1913 pulled command Train 72A, which was lost in Kolberg, and was with the PKP as Tw 1-93 after the war. No postwar data remain for the other four locomotives. PZ 68 (57 1071) was lost in Königsberg early in April 1945, and PZ 69 (57 1094) was destroyed east of Tarnopol on March 21, 1944. Armored Trains No. 70 and 71, which had 57 1280 and 57 2198, were also lost, the first in Rasdelnaya early in April 1944, the other in Slanic, Romania, in August 1944.

The similarly armored 57 3070, from the Marburg RAW, was at Obdach, Carinthia, at the war's end. Presumably intended for another armored train previously, it was probably assigned to PZ 4, which reached Slovenia at the end of January 1945 and could withdraw to St. Andrä (Lavamünd-Wolfsberg line) as the war ended.

In addition, 57 1085. 1332, 2384, 3068, and 3301 are mentioned as armored train locomotives. 57 1085 was with the DB after the war, but it is not possible to assign it to a train. 57 1332 was subordinate

A Series 57 armored locomotive for a standard BP 42 armored train. In its smooth-sided form, even the cab is integrated without catching places. The photo also shows the slanted front end. Photo: A. Gardziella/W. Sawodny collection

The photo at right shows the second tender coupled in front of the locomotive, and of the same building type. The round door to the smoke chamber, set in the front armor, can also be seen. Photo: H. Beckmann/W/ Sawodny collection

to the General of Transport Southeast and remained with the Austrian Railways after the war. Thus, it belonged to one of the armored trains that were long active in the Balkans and remained on Austrian territory after the war, which suggests PZ 23 and 64. 57 2384 turned up in Poland as Tw 1-56 after the war, 57 3068 in the Soviet Union; so the former was captured on what was later Polish territory and the latter by the Red Army. 57 3301 is known to have been in the hinterlands of Army Group Center from August 1941 to July 1944 and was sent back from a gathering point to Reich territory on July 16, 1944. It may have belonged to PZ 1 (ex-PZ 5/Aschaffenburg rail protection train) but have been under repairs in Minsk when that train was lost (June 27, 1944).

Two other notations are hard to believe. 57 1067 is said to have been used as an armored loco east of Warsaw in July 1944 (with Armored Instruction Train No. 5, ex-PZ 75?). But in October 1944 this loco was in Ulm, and when the war ended it was in Aulendorf, damaged, which scarcely fits together. PZ 64 is said to have used 57 1696 or 1698 (it was being overhauled at the Gleiwitz RAW in January 1945). Both locomotives are documented as being with the General of Transport Southeast, but the first was lent to the CFR, the latter temporarily rented by the HDZ, neither being compatible with its use as an armored train locomotive (for PZ 64, see also above and below).

In all, nineteen Series 57 locomotives can be identified by numbers as armored train locomotives, though not all can be linked with definite armored trains. On the other hand, the total number of G 10s used as armored locomotives can be estimated as 30 to 32, 13 of which (nine of them known by number) can clearly be linked with armored trains up to No. 31 based on their characteristic structural details, even if their numbers are unknown.

It is certain that every armored train was assigned only one armored locomotive. When it was out of action for a long time and needed servicing because of breakdown or damage, an unarmored loco had to be borrowed from the Reichsbahn until the armored loco was ready to run again. Surely it would have been advisable if the supply train (which never had a loco of its own, but had to obtain one from the area for trips to new positions) had had a spare armored loco, but this would have meant that too much valuable equipment would have been out of action. The Reichsbahn was very reluctant to turn locomotives over to the armored trains. At first they—like the Reichsbahn's own rail protection trains that became armored trains—were only lent to the Wehrmacht. Requests to buy them were declined in 1942, and apparently only in September 1944 was it agreed on, for a number of armored train locomotives were listed on the 28th of that month as "sold to the Wehrmacht."

At first the temporary replacements wanted for damaged armored train locomotives were those of Series 57 (G 10), later also on the Series 52 (so-called "war locomotives") when they became available. It can be documented that PZ 21, from early July 1944 (after its own Series 93 armored loco had been shot down) until its loss at Moscheiken on October 30, 1944, used 52 6233, and PZ 24 had 52 5720 from October 1944 until it was blown up at Konskie on January 16, 1945, but these are just a couple of known examples out of several others.

Such locomotives were often provisionally armored. The full armor of the Series 52 locos for direct use in armored trains took place only in the last weeks of the war. It has been stated that, as early as the beginning of March 1943, 52 223 had its cab armored, as well as its smoke chamber, long boiler, and tender (which equals total armoring), but this locomotive, stationed at Bw Shlobin, cannot be

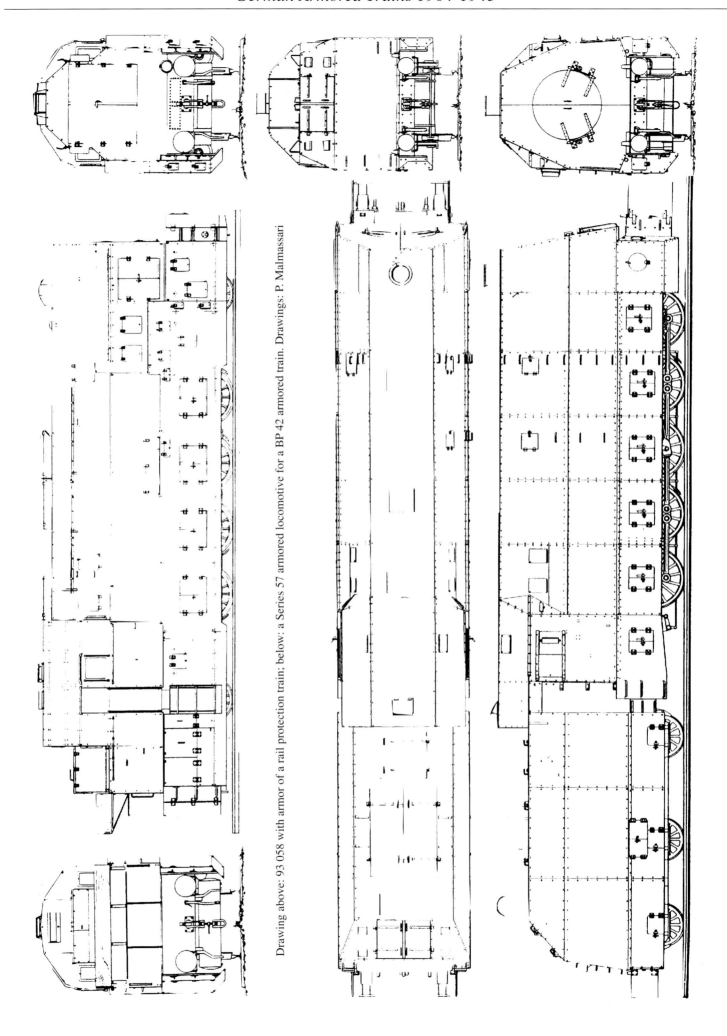

Drawing above: 93 058 with armor of a rail protection train; below: a Series 57 armored locomotive for a BP 42 armored train. Drawings: P. Malmassari

When an armored locomotive was out of action because of damage or overhauling, the armored trains were often assigned "black" (unarmored) locomotives temporarily. Here is one of Series 57 with PZ 2. Along the boiler a provisional "armor" of wooden planks was attached. The cab was simply protected with plates that were pushed behind the holding bars (covering the locomotive number). Photo: K. Böhringer/W. Sawodny collection

Above: For this purpose, more and more Series 52 war locomotives were called on; here is one with a 4 T 30 stiff frame tender with a standard BP 42 armored train. Photo: BFZ Stuttgart

Right: Loco 52 6233 with a 2'2' T 30 tub tender pulled PZ 21 as of July 1944 and was lost with the train at the end of October in cut-off Moscheiken. Photo: K. Böhringer/W. Sawodny collection

52 1489 became the locomotive of Armored Train 350, an upgraded line protection train, in 1945. The loco shows only cab armor, such as several in transport service were given to protect them from low-flying air attacks. Otherwise, the boiler was provisionally protected only by adding wooden planks, and the compressed air cylinder for the brakes by a steel plate in front of it.

proved to have served with any armored train. On the other hand, the armored trains from No. 80 on received fully armored locomotives of that type only in 1945. Locomotives 52 1965 (PZ 82?, with four-axle condenser tender) and 52 7021 (PZ 80) are documented; both were in Czechoslovakia at the war's end. While 52 7021 was taken to Russia, 52 1965, with series number 559.0, was still used for a time as an armored train loco by the Czech Army. Shortly before the war ended several line protection trains reequipped as regular armored trains were regularly assigned Series 52 locomotives; Train No. 350, as of March 4, 1945, was given 52 1489, with only its cab armored (the boiler was provisionally "protected" with a layer of wooden planks).

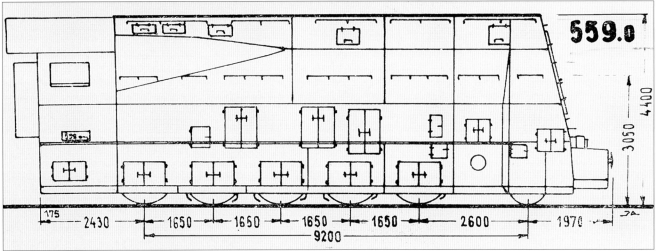

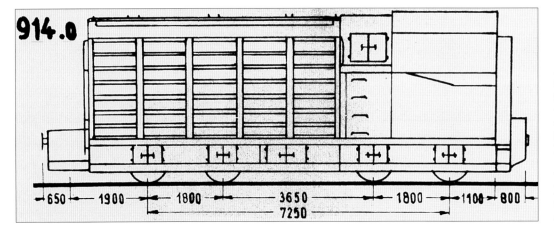

Just shortly before the war ended, Series 52 locomotives were armored for Armored Trains No. 80ff. 52 1695 with a four-axle condenser tender was used later (under series number 559.0) by the Czech Army as an armored train locomotive.

The photo and drawing show armored locomotive 559.0 and tender 914.0 (ex-series 52). Photo: J. Magnuski collection

Line protection trains often had Series 38 (Prussian P 8) locomotives—again with only the cab armored—like 38 3504 with line protection train "Blücher." Photo: W. Sitzius/W. Sawodny collection

Another Series 38 locomotive (38 2104?), this time fully armored, was used by PZ 51, which began as a line protection train. Photo: G. Gayk/W. Sawodny collection

At first the line protection trains naturally had a varied spectrum of locomotives—often captured ones from their stationing area. Later, at least with the line protection trains stationed in Russia, locomotives—often provisionally armored—of Series 38 (P 8) seem to have been preferred. One of them—though rebuilt with full armor—was with PZ 51, developed from the line protection train "Stettin" of "A" (38 2104? This armored loco, documented at Bw Vilna in the summer of 1943, could also have belonged to one of the numerous line protection trains in that area), and one with PZ 52 (ex-line protection train "Blücher," 38 3504). The line protection train "Michael" also had 38 1940, a fully armored loco. But the line protection train "Polko" seems to have had a Series 57 loco—with only the cab armored—in the summer of 1944, and a photo shows 55 042 with a line protection train in the central sector.

Thus, not only did the line protection trains and the captured armored trains retain their steam locomotives, but such were also used for newly built BP 42 or 44 trains to the war's end, although their use with armored trains showed considerable disadvantages. If the loco was parked cold it required a warming phase of several hours before being ready for action; if it was kept under steam it used up water and coal while standing, and had to be refilled even after a relatively short distance, even though the supplies were increased by using an auxiliary tender. Since similar arrangements were not always possible in combat areas, water and coal often had to be added under primitive conditions. Water often had to be taken from brooks or ponds. A pump was installed under the cab for this purpose (in some

captured locomotives hand pumps had to be used). And often enough coal had to be moved laboriously from the storage place to the tender by a bucket chain of crewmen. At intervals of one to three weeks (depending on distances) the locomotives even had to be brought to a railroad workshop for so-called "washing out," freeing the boiler from ashes, slime, and stone, a job that required two to three days. Again and again action had to be broken off for these reasons, and commanders to whom the armored trains were subordinated were very rarely informed of these necessary procedures.

Because of the much faster readiness for action, the greater range, easier supplying and servicing, but also the better starting procedure and the lack of telltale smoke (which was balanced by the equally noticeable motor noise), the use of Diesel locomotives to pull the armored trains would have been far preferable. In the new building plans of In 10 of December 1940, an armored Diesel loco was in fact foreseen for the "SP 42 Armored Train"; for "Armored Train 1941" no locomotive type was specified, but these were intended only as transitional solutions; in the final versions of these armored trains, an armored train was to consist of cars with individual motor drive, an idea that was realized only in 1944 in the light and heavy scout trains. In a memo from the Railroad Engineer Inspection in April 1941, a 1260 HP (925 kW) Diesel loco with a pulling power of 600 tons at 50 kph on the level was mentioned as being in the works for armored trains. This may have been a variant of the WR 1260 1-C-1.15 locomotive (weight in service 64 tons, pulling power 12 tons) intended for the "SP 42 Armored Train," which was fully

Supplying a steam locomotive with coal and water was a major problem when the train was in action. Here the coal can at least be loaded onto the tender mechanically. Photo: H. Beckmann/W. Sawodny collection

It could also happen that it had to be loaded laboriously by a human chain. Photo: R. Lorscheidt/W. Sawodny collection

The tender's water tank was filled via the rear flap (below). But often a depot crane was not available for loading water, and rivers or lakes had to be utilized. At left, the hose link for a water pump is being laid for this purpose. Photo: W. Nazarenus u.N.N./W. Sawodny collection

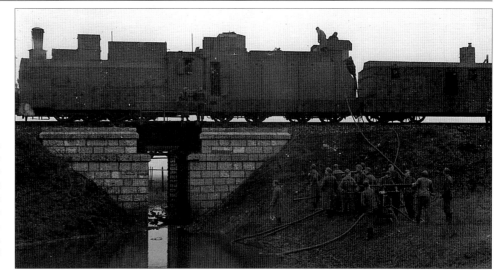

Sometimes only hand pumps were available, as with this captured Russian Type O locomotive that was also used gladly by the Germans in the broad gauge days—as here with PZ 28. Note the opened door on the locomotive and the observation turret on the command post in the front part of the tender (Soviet armored trains had no true command cars!), and the position for a twin A/A machine gun on the rear of the four-axle tender. Photo: Federal archives, Koblenz

From the engine driver's position in the locomotive at the center of the armored train there was only a very limited view of the track, or none at all. Thus, speaking connections between the observer in the front car and the train commander who gave the orders were vitally important, especially for the engine driver. Photo: Federal Archives, Koblenz

designed when the war ended but never went into production. Since this was not available, a WR 550 D 14 built by the Maschinenbau und Bahnbedarf AG (Orenstein & Koppel) for the prototype of the "SP 42 Armored Train" at the Berliner Maschinenbau AG (formerly Schwartzkopf) in Wildau in 1942 was fitted with 50-mm armor. Probably because of the weight, two four-axle pivot mountings were attached at the front and rear of this locomotive, with 2-cm A/A quads mounted on their superstructures. Since the "SP 42 Armored Train" project had meanwhile been halted, this one vehicle, after rebuilding, was put into service early in 1944 as Armored Railcar No. 16.

When the OKH recommended setting up six broad gauge armored trains for the Russian campaign in the spring of 1941, instead of the five requested by the chief of Transport, this sixth train was assigned, instead of the otherwise planned Type 57 (G 10) steam locomotives, a WR 360 C 14 Diesel locomotive (apparently from the lot made by Henschel), which had only cab armor. It actually pulled PZ 29 until the end of December 1941, but it is not known whether it was replaced then at Orel by a captured Russian O Series armored locomotive or was blown up with the train west of Kaluga on January 13, 1942.—A second, defective WR 360 C 14 (made by Deutz) was with the Armored Train Replacement Battalion as a target for armored train shooting tests. This loco was put back into service, even with upgraded engine performance, by a member of the Deutz firm in training with the Replacement Battalion. This WR

360 C 14 loco was then fully armored and sent to the eastern front in the autumn of 1943 (?) with the ex-Deutz man as its driver and a quarters and workshop car as an emergency loco for armored trains that had lost their locomotives in action. This Diesel loco's activities can be confirmed only at times: in March 1944 it brought back both the damaged practice train "R" and PZ 11 in the Tarnopol area; in the winter of 1944-45 it brought Command train No. 72A back from the Carpathians to Krakow. In February 1945 it was assigned to PZ 83 as its regular locomotive, reached the Oder front with it, and withdrew with it to Mecklenburg in April-May 1945, where it was turned over to the Americans near Holthusen-Hagenow on 2 May. To conclude the portrayal of the modest use of Diesel locomotives with armored trains it can be noted that the suggestion made by 1st Lt. Lorscheidt in the summer of 1944, but never carried out, to build a combat train which—consisting almost exclusively of tank-destroyer cars and with an armored WR 360 C 14 as its loco—would have suited the changed realities on the eastern front much better, surely a result of experience that the designer had gained as commander of PZ 11 with the replacement loco described above!

The locomotives of captured armored trains were also taken over and used by the Germans. With the Czech armored trains taken over in 1939 there came the C-n2t locos MAV 377.116, 362, 455, and 483, which were armored in 1914, in Imperial days (the last having been similarly armored by the Czechs in 1919) CSD 310.412, 440,

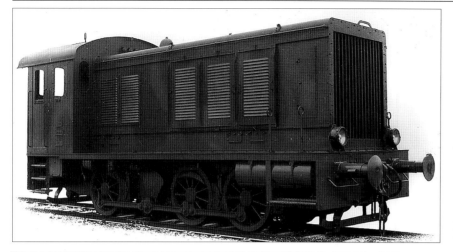

Two of the WR 360 C 14 Wehrmacht Diesel locomotives served with armored trains: partly armored in 1941 with PZ 29, fully armored in 1945 with PZ 83. Photo: Henschel factory/S. Lauscher collection

PZ 29 was the only conventional armored train that had a WR 360 C 14 Diesel locomotive. The radio set of this broad gauge locomotive was housed in its cab, and the frame antenna was mounted on the motor housing. Photo: Federal Archives, Koblenz

In the locomotive of the "SP 42" armored train—the later Armored Railcar No. 16—an armored hood (left and above) was simply erected over the larger WR 550 D (at right is the sidewall of the engine compartment, in the background the cab with its oval front window). Photo: M. Zimny/J. Magnuski collection

450, and 453, as armored locomotives 313.901 and 902 or 314.901 and 902, which were in fact first used with German armored trains No. 23, 24 (MAV 377.362 and 482 in tandem), and 25 in the spring of 1940. Their performance, fully insufficient for the long German armored trains (389 tons at 40 kph on the level), was surely one reason why these armored trains were taken out of service after a few months. On their reactivation in 1941 the trains received Series 93 armored locomotives. The Hungarian and Czech locos remained in Wehrmacht service as workshop vehicles; 313.902 and 314.901 were at the Glöwen explosives factory and were scrapped at Wegeleben in 1956, 313.901 was at the Austrian Ebensee at the war's end, and the fate of 314.902 is unknown.

From Polish armored trains to German there came the Ti 3-4 (German 54 4021 Type G 5.3, from the Polish "Grozny" armored train to German No. 22) and Ti 3-13 (German 54 4024, from "Pilsudszyk" to PZ 21) locomotives. These venerable 1'C freight-train locos of Prussian provenance had low axle weights (14.5 tons) and had much more pulling power—790 tons at 50 kph except on upgrades—than the MAV 377, but naturally far inferior to Series 93 and 57. All the same, Ti 3-4 pulled PZ 22 until the beginning of 1944; its further fate is unknown. Ti 3-13 switched in October 1942 from PZ 21 to PZ 25 and was replaced there in the spring of 1943 by a Series 57 locomotive. It was then assigned to the Armored Train Replacement Battalion, but took over the makeshift command train No. II in February 1945 and was still with it near Grevesmühlen, in northwestern Mecklenburg, on May 2, 1945. Another Polish armored locomotive of this type—presumably Ti 3-2—fell into Soviet hands in September 1939 with the armored train "Pierwszy Marszalek" and

For Armored Trains no. 23 to 25, made up of captured Czech material, the Hungarian Series 377 armored locomotives, dating from Imperial times and having type C axles, were originally used; PZ 24 even used one in tandem with an auxiliary tender in between. In front is 377.362, in back 377.483. Photo: W. Geipel/W. Sawodny collection

Armored Locomotive MAV 377.455 was used with Czech Armored Train no. 3 (or CSD 310.450 and locomotive 313.902); in 1940 it was with German PZ 23 or 25. Photo: Difrology Club collection, Prague

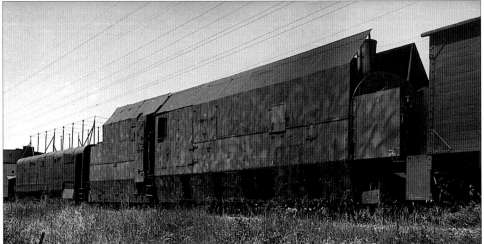

Armored locomotives of the Ti 3 type (ex-Prussian G 53) came with captured Polish trains to German armored trains. Ti 3-13 with PZ 21 (below) shows its original condition with an observation post for the commander (used by the engine driver in German service) on the tender. On Ti 3-4 (PZ 22, left), additional armor was added to the loco and tender later. Photo: Federal Archives, Koblenz, and F. Englberger/ W. Sawodny collection

was converted to broad gauge by them; in June 1941 the Germans captured it in Lemberg. It was included in Combat Train B of PZ 10, but was replaced by a Series 57 armored locomotive (57 1064) when the train was converted to standard gauge in the summer of 1942.

Almost all of the Russian armored trains had Series O locomotives (with their Od and Ov steering gear variations) with 0-8-0 axle order, which was well suited to these uses because of the low axle load (13.5 tons). In the early days of the eastern campaign in particular, a goodly number of them were captured and used by the Germans—especially as line protection trains—as long as the broad gauge rail network had not been converted. Such locomotives were used on regular armored trains at that time only for Combat Train A of PZ 10, PZ 28 (both only until the summer of 1942), and perhaps for a short time for PZ 29. With the conversion to standard gauge they were replaced by German Series 57 locomotives; their armor was probably removed and the locos then used for regular freight traffic.—In the spring of 1942 a different captured Russian armored locomotive was prepared at the Roslavl field workshop. It came from the "Za Stalina" armored train that fell into German hands between Vyasma and Gshatsk in October 1941. The locomotive, which was hidden under almost all-enclosing armor, has inspired many questions. The axle order seems to be 2-6-2 (Series S?), but behind the cylinders there could be another running axle (Series Lp?) or drive axle (Schtsch series with an added rear running axle?). According to newer data, it is said to be a 0-6-0 industrial loco with integrated coal box of Series 9P, with the relatively high axle load of 18 tons.

To bear the weight of the armor all the same, an additional running axle was installed in front and in back, the water tank and coal box were probably removed, and a separate tender coupled on instead. After being repaired at the Roslavl field workshop the locomotive formed a line protection train, at first with two G cars. It was then obviously converted to standard gauge and thoroughly examined, for the manner of its armoring apparently served as a model for those who received Series 57 locomotives for the standard BP 42, and later BP 44, armored trains. In the summer of 1944 this ex-Soviet armored loco was assigned to the rebuilt PZ 30 to replace its 57 1504 loco that was lost near Odessa. It was left behind after being hit in the steam dome by Russian tanks, rendering it immobile at the Allenstein depot, and was recaptured by the Russians there.

In the summer of 1943 two French locomotives of Series 140 C (140 C 117 came from the Niort depot, the other—whose number is unknown—from one of the Paris depots) were taken to Gleiwitz and armored there. In the spring of 1944 they went to armored trains that were being used (No. 22) or about to be used in France (PZ 24, which received 140 C 117, but was sent first to Italy and only reached its planned service area in July). These 2-8-0 locomotives had an original axle load of 16.5 tons and an in-service weight of 73.2 tons, and resembled the German Series 57 (G 10) type. Despite that PZ 24 was assigned, in place of 140 C 117, for reasons of performance, a makeshift and partly armored Series 52 loco in November 1944. 140 C 117 was sent to the Armored train Replacement Battalion in Milowitz; its later fate is unknown. Whether the other armored

Almost all the Russian armored trains used Series O locomotives with 0-8-0 axle order. Just as often they fell into German hands. But they were run (here with PZ 28) only as long as broad gauge was used. Photo: Federal Archives, Koblenz

This captured Russian locomotive, under whose armor a Type 9P shunting engine is probably hiding, had a front and rear running axle added to decrease the axle load, and its side water tanks and coal box removed and replaced by a towed tender. With its smooth armoring extending all the way up, it doubtless served as a model for the German Series 57 locomotives assigned to the standard BP 42 and 44 armored trains. In the front end, the two welded-up shot holes that put the loco out of action can be seen. Photo: Federal Archives, Koblenz

locomotive of the French 140 C series pulled PZ 22 until its end at Sprottau, in Lower Silesia, on February 11, 1945, is also not documented. — For PZ 32, built in France, a Series 050 A locomotive (an Austrian Series 80 Gölsdorf loco, delivered to France after 1918) with 0-10-0 axle order was armored. The locomotive number is listed as 31, but also as 33 or 35. It was unarmored after the war. For the 1945-47 display of the armored train that was captured at St. Berain on September 8, 1944, and its use in René Clément's film "Bataille du rail" though, 050 A 31 was fitted with authentic looking cardboard

"armor."–Still to be mentioned is that the Prussian G 8.1 5182 Cöln 1943/44 loco given to France as reparations in 1919 served with the Armored Train Replacement Battalion as an unarmored shunting engine under its French number 040 K 518.

The accuracy of the information that PZ 64, after its Series 57 armored locomotive was sent to be examined at the Gleiwitz RAW in January 1945, was given a Hungarian 4-8-0 Series 424 loco armored at the Nagykanisza heating house (and whether this loco was with the train until its surrender in Pernegg on May 9, 1945) still lacks confirmation.

For the armored trains used in France, two locomotives of the French 140 C series were armored in the winter of 1943-44. Photo: G. Guse/W. Sawodny collection

A locomotive of the French 140 C series. Photo: La Vie du Rail

The only Austrian-built Series 80 Gölsdorf 050 A 31 locomotive to be armored was prepared for PZ 32, which was assembled in France. Photo: La Vie du Rail

Soon after it fell into French hands in September 1944 this locomotive was unarmored. When the captured PZ 32 was used in the René Clément film "La bataille du rail" and put on display in France, a locomotive of the same type was "armored" with cardboard, obviously in the original form, as can be seen in comparison with the only authentic picture, though it shows only the cab and tender. Photo: La Vie du Rail

The Cars and Their Armor

(see pp. 97, 165 for drawings)

For the cars used in the German armored trains a three-way division can be made: first the taking over of cars from the Reichsbahn, naturally modified, but so that the original form is still easy to recognize; second, new constructions on car chassis, or completely new cars built for armored trains; third, captured cars, which can again be divided into original or adapted types of armored train cars that still show their origin, rebuilt freight cars, and new constructions on the chassis of armored trains, like freight cars.

Belonging to the first category are all the Reichsbahn's rail protection trains, as well as the seven that were taken over as armored trains in 1938; also some cars of Armored Trains No. 22 and 23, which were also taken from a rail protection train. All the cars bore numbers that were reserved for special vehicles of the Reichsbahn's administrative offices, including some of the 700 series (known are: Karlsruhe and Oppeln rail protection train.: 700 ..., Nürnberg rail protection train/PZ 5: 701..., Stettin rail protection train/PZ 2: 704..., Königsberg rail protection train/PZ 6, maybe also PZ 7?: 790..., Breslau rail protection trains, including PZ 4: 798...). In general, the cars of a rail protection or armored train were numbered consecutively by the last digit of the second group of numbers, while cars added later were given other numbers, such as the Königsberg rail protection train's 790 151 to 156, the gun cars added to it as PZ 6 (gun cars 790 210 (and 211?). The cars taken over by the Wehrmacht from the rail protection trains were—like the locomotives—at first only rented; only in September 1944 were they purchased.

The great majority of the cars in the rail protection trains, and thus also in the resulting armored trains, were two-axle, or at times also three-axle covered freight cars of various types, mostly old ones: Pg baggage cars (mostly three-axle), and even—as seen in the Frankfurt/Oder and Karlsruhe rail protection trains—various types of passenger cars. Of special interest in this respect was the rail protection train of Frankfurt on the Oder, the later PZ 1. It consisted of three two-axle uniform 3rd-4th class corridor cars of the 1928 type (exchange type, 13.92 meters long overall), two three-axle Prussian State Railroad 4th class corridor cars with end platforms and upper lights (overall length 12.20 to 12.80 meters), and one two-axle G-car as a command car. The armoring of the passenger cars was unusual in having externally attached steel plates; most of their windows were welded shut, the remaining ones in State Railroad cars were closeable by armored shutters, reduced in size in the uniform type to loopholes or observation hatches.—In the Karlsruhe rail protection train there was only one externally armored passenger car (type not identified because of the unfavorable perspective) with loopholes, plus a Baden P 3 (Group 133e) baggage car and four internally armored G-cars.

All the other known rail protection trains, including those taken over as Armored trains 2 to 7, usually consisted of six G-cars; the Regensburg and Stuttgart rail protection train as well as Armored Trains No. 2, 3, and 5 exclusively of such two-axle types, all of the older flat-roofed Prussian IIds or generalized A 2 type. The Breslau PZ 4, on the other hand, consisted only of three-axle types, including two baggage cars. An Oppeln rail protection train could have been similar; a G-car of it was with PZ 22, a baggage and a G-car (all

On this corridor car of the exchange type of 1928 used in PZ 1, external armor with new, small windows and ports for weapons was applied. Photo: E. Grahl/W. Sawodny collection

This car (there was only one left after the damage of May 10, 1940) was kept as a command car when PZ 1 was totally rebuilt in 1943. The entrance platforms were removed, the car was fitted with a new roof (with observation post and frame antenna). In the area of the command compartment and radio cabin the windows were completely closed; in the infantry section they were fitted with machine-gun ports. In place of the removed box between the axles a low side door was fitted. Photo: W. Sitzius/W. Sawodny collection

The windows of this Prussian 4th class corridor car with PZ 1 are partly closed, and partly equipped with armored shutters. Photo: E. Grahl/W. Sawodny collection

three-axle) with PZ 23. Another Breslau rail protection train had, besides two three-axle baggage cars (a somewhat different type from that of PZ 4), only two-axle G-cars. The cars of PZ 7 (Königsberg) were also mixed, with four two-axle G-cars, one three-axle baggage car (same type as PZ 4 and 23), and a three-axle G-car with a brake cabin. PZ 6 could also have had a three-axle G-car. It is notable that these three-axle (G- and baggage cars, but not corresponding to the Prussian IIc 13 type) turn up only in rail protection trains of the eastern border rail administrations.—Very unusual was a gathering of four Breslau rail protection cars shown in a photo from 1933. They have ex-Prussian iron O-cars of the IId1 or A6 type, two open on top (with armor shields and probably a weapon system in a wooden cover), two with roof structures of the World War I type. Could these have been leftovers from the disarmament of 1920-21?

These cars probably still had the usual two-walled armor common at that time. The rail protection cars, on the other hand, had only simple armor attached to the outside walls of passenger cars and behind the wooden walls of the much more frequently used freight (and baggage?) cars. The latter—important as camouflage in the rail protection days—proved impractical for combat duty because they were inflammable, but remained with these armored trains until they were thoroughly rebuilt, thus into 1944. More precise data

are available only for PZ 3's armor, which was all made of 26-mm chromium-nickel steel that offered protection against all types of infantry guns and splinters, but could be penetrated by low-caliber artillery guns, unless the shot struck at a very unfavorable angle (20 degrees at most). During the Polish campaign, the armor of this train's gun-turret, observation- and command-post walls was increased to 60 mm (double walls, hardened steel 30 mm thick outside, 30-mm soft steel inside with air in between). PZ 3, formerly a Munich rail protection train, ranked among the best armored of them, and Armored Trains No. 4, 6, and 7 may have had similar protection. The armoring of the other rail protection trains (and probably also of PZ No. 1, 2, and 5, which was strengthened later) was not sufficient to repel pointed bullets with cores. It is definite that not only the thickness of the armor plates, but even more the quality of the steel of which they were made, was decisive. Presumably there were also questions about the goodness of the armor carried by PZ 2 that led to the replacement of the originally planned Dresden rail protection train with the one from Stettin. Whether and how much the armor of these armored trains was improved during the first reequipping phase between the western and eastern campaigns in the winter of 1940-41 is not known.—The axle ends of the rail protection trains were covered by an arched or small boxlike plate, and in rebuildings or new constructions in 1940-41, such as the gun cars of Armored

This damaged car from PZ 3 shows the typical steel armor behind the wooden car wall in all former rail protection cars. As can be seen, this armor has remained unharmed despite the fully splintered outer wall. Under the door is the opened exit box. Note also the protector on the right axle (that of the left axle was probably shot away). Photo: W. Hahn/W. Sawodny collection.

Here a soldier is just leaving PZ 4 (which still has a freight train look) by the box between the axles. Here, too, the somewhat unusual axle protection can be noted. Photo: W. Obermark/W. Sawodny collection

Trains No. 1 and 3, plus an added G-car with a brake cabin in the first; larger armor skirts were hung in front of the wheels instead. The couplings between the individual cars were usually protected by side armor plates as well.

The cars had machine gun ports, rifle loopholes, and observation hatches of different sizes in the walls. For entry and exit they had floor hatches near the side doors which led to the boxes between the axles, through which the car could be left just over the ground, with the possibility of taking cover at once.—Weights could be found to date for two cars of PZ 22, but the stated 10.07 and 10.47 tons must refer to the empty weight of the unarmored cars (for reasons of camouflage?); with the armor and other equipment, one must surely assume that they reached the load bearing limits of 15 to 17 tons.

The formation of the observation posts with which one car in each half of the rail protection trains (and the armored trains that were made from them) was also varied. In most cases they were simply installed on the roof of a G-car (the rail protection trains of Regensburg and Stuttgart, Armored Trains No. 2, 3, 5, and 6). Sometimes brake

The interior of Car 1 of PZ 3. Photo: H. Bendl/W. Sawodny collection

The kitchen in Car 3 of PZ 3. Photo: H. Bendl/W. Sawodny collection cabins on G-cars were used (Karlsruhe rail protection train, Armored Trains No. 1 and 7), and the raised structures of baggage cars were also used for these purposes (Breslau and Karlsruhe rail protection trains, Armored Trains No. 4 and 7). If the trains did not run with these cars, used as command posts, on the ends of the train, then the cars in those positions were fitted with turning periscopes to observe the surroundings, particularly the rail lines, from inside (Armored Trains No. 5-7, later also No. 1). For observation purposes, shear telescopes could also be used in hatches made for them. The combat cars at the end of the train had spotlights.

The control (or protection) cars, on which railroad building equipment was always loaded, were two-axle low-side X- or S-cars of various types. Presumably they were at first not automatically uncoupling on the rail protection trains taken over as armored trains, but had to be uncoupled manually if necessary. Later the control cars were coupled to the trains by a Scharfenberg coupling that could be activated from inside the train, plus a pneumatic ejection system and a self-acting brake system that could be set in advance for a certain distance.

The very varied mounting of the artillery in the first armored trains is also interesting. For PZ 3 (Munich), armored gun cars had already been built in rail protection times (!), and the closed turret

The inside of a car on PZ 4. A machine gunner stands by the gun port in the car wall. The platform for the twin A/A machine gun, for which a hatch was built in the roof, rises at right. Photo: W. Obermark/W. Sawodny collection

On most former rail protection trains—as here on PZ 6—the armored observation posts were set on the roofs of the cars. Photo: W. Zimmer/W. Sawodny collection

Sometimes brake cabins—somewhat as on this newly prepared 1940-41 G-car of PZ 1 taken over after rebuilding in 1943—were expanded as armored observation posts. Photo: K. Böhringer/W. Sawodny collection

If Pg cars were used, as in the rail protection trains of the eastern railroad administrations, their raised sections were rebuilt as observation posts, as seen from the forward hatches. Here is a car from the former rail protection train of the Oppeln RBD with PZ 23. Photo: Federal Archives, Koblenz

for a 7.5-cm F.K. 16 (not installed in the rail protection era) could be turned 270 degrees by electric motors or hand controls. To the rear were a crew area, armored on all sides (with observation hatches), which also served as an ammunition bunker; between the crew area and the gun turret was an access passage protected with armor at the sides. When these cars were rebuilt in 1940 with a new gun in a turning turret on top they had a third, central axle installed for better distribution of the increased weight.—For Armored Trains no. 6 and 7, high-wall O-cars (PZ 6: ex-Prussian, Ludwigshafen type, overall length 9 m; PZ 7: Königsberg exchange type, length 9.10 m) were armored. The 7.5-cm gun on a socket mount was in the middle of the car (with a 360-degree traverse) and fired over the car wall. At the ends of the car closed, armored team cabins and ammunition bunkers were installed. The other armored trains were each to receive two 3.7-cm Pak 35/36 and 7.5-cm I.G. 18, which—in mixed pairs—were simply to be loaded unprotected with their wheeled mounts on stake side cars. While Armored Trains No. 1, 2, and 5 originally went completely without artillery weapons, PZ 4 had armored turrets for these guns (a lower one in front for the 3.7-cm anti-tank gun, a higher one in back—to allow firing over the front one—for the infantry gun) built on S-cars (presumably Augsburg type, overall length 14.10 m); in between was an ammunition bunker with an arched roof, and behind the infantry gun was another protected platform for the range finder. Similar S-cars were used when, in the winter of 1940-41, PZ 1 was equipped with guns. The cars were given knee-high all-around sheet-steel armor. The guns—a 2-cm A/A gun in front, a 4.7-

cm cannon behind—on socket mounts had only their gun shields in front; to the sides and rear there was additional shoulder-high armor (open above) attached; the rear (apparently longer) car also had an (also open-top) crew cabin, protected by armor plate.

When the rest of these armored trains were rearmed with 2-cm Flak 30 or 38 (as individual guns) in the spring of 1941, they could be mounted on platforms installed on the gun cars of PZ No. 2 (which had taken over the appropriate cars from PZ 25) and 3. For PZ 4, such possibilities were created by making cutouts in the roof and building platforms on two each of the G-cars, while for PZ 7 two additional O-cars (generalized Breslau or Essen types, overall length

In Armored trains No. 6 and 7 (here No. 6) the gun was mounted open in the middle of an O-car. At the ends of the car were covered cabins for crew and ammunition. Photo: Imperial War museum, London

On PZ 4 the gun car was fitted with two octagonal armored turrets at different heights (with a 3.7-cm anti-tank gun in front and a 7.5-cm I.G. 18 in back) on a two-axle S-car (Augsburg type?). Between the two gun turrets was an arched ammunition bunker; at the rear end was an armored range finder platform. Photo: W. Obermark/W. Sawodny collection

S-cars of the Augsburg type were also used in 1940-41 for the gun cars of PZ 1, with low steel walls and—open-top—turrets, their fronts formed by the gun shield—a 2-cm A/A gun in front, a 4.7-cm cannon in back. Photo: S.I.R.P.A./E.C.P.A., Paris

9.10 m), A/A guns were also mounted on added low-side O-cars for PZ 6 (later they were installed on the former G-cars of this train).

In the second category were the cars built for Armored Trains No. 26-31 for the Russian campaign. They were based on Linz-type Ommr-cars (overall length 10.10 m, wheelbase 6 m) with their walls removed. They were fitted with full length lower armor plates along the chassis offset slightly to the inside, with extensions down to the axle ends. The control cars, with hand-brake positions on the outsides, remained as flat cars. The infantry cars, weighing 21.8 tons, had steel walls 80 cm high all around, with sliding door gun ports (six in the sidewalls, three at the ends). They could cover the crews only when the men were lying down. For the Russian winter these open cars, at first coverable only with canvas, were naturally totally unsuitable, but fixed roofs were added to some of them later (flat ones as for PZ 26, inclined ones as for PZ 28, as can be seen in photos). The essential new designs, though, were the carrier cars for Somua S 35 tanks. They had armor walls some 5.75 m long and 1.10 m high, set in sockets in the car floor, covering the running gear of the loaded-on tanks. For the tanks, grooved plates and triangular rails were attached to the car floor to guarantee easy and safe movement and correct positioning on the cars. The also grooved two-part loading ramps (one part diagonally from the car to the ground, the other before it on the ground itself) were carried in transport on the front control car, which—now equipped with automatic Scharfenberg couplings and all other equipment—had to be uncoupled from the carrier car to load or unload the tanks. The ramp was attached by a clever device to the front of the tank, so that it lowered automatically when the tank moved forward on the car and was uncoupled when it was unloaded onto the ground; when the tank was loaded onto the car it could be lifted in the converse process. If two tank carrier cars were used, one after the other (Armored Trains No. 26-28), the tank from the second car had to be unloaded over the first one; for this, the two cars were linked by appropriate ramps. The cars with loading ramps weighed, without armor, 18.2 tons, those without, 14 tons; the loaded weight

For the broad gauge armored trains made up for the Russian campaign (No. 26-31), modified Ommr-cars of the Linz type were used as both infantry cars (far right) and tank carrier cars (with insertable and thus removable sidewalls) and control cars. The chassis armor, slightly curved to the inside, also covered the axles. Photo: Federal Archives, Koblenz

A variation was found on PZ 30; different vertical armor on the lower part of the car, screwed-on sidewalls on the tank carrier, and different ports for the infantry car. Presumably these were the prototypes for the series. Photo: Federal Archives, Koblenz.

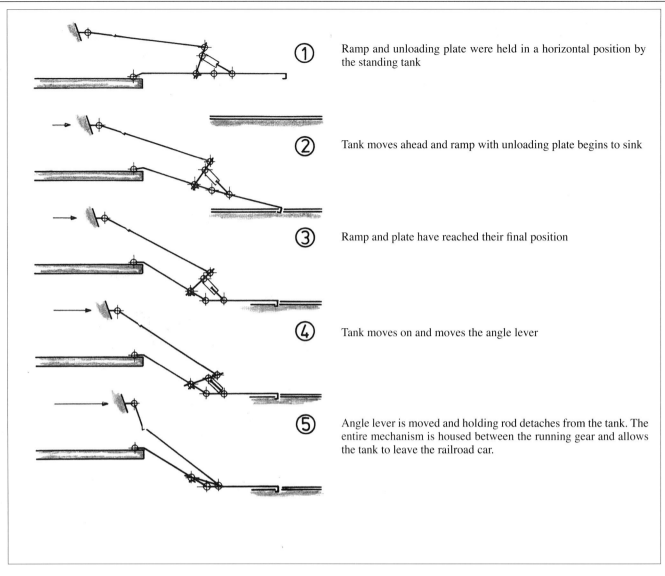

① Ramp and unloading plate were held in a horizontal position by the standing tank

② Tank moves ahead and ramp with unloading plate begins to sink

③ Ramp and plate have reached their final position

④ Tank moves on and moves the angle lever

⑤ Angle lever is moved and holding rod detaches from the tank. The entire mechanism is housed between the running gear and allows the tank to leave the railroad car.

The mechanism of the lowering unloading ramp used on Armored Trains No. 26-31. Drawing: U. Schwarze

This picture shows the holding and unloading mechanism of the unloading ramp attached to the Somua tank, as was used on Armored Trains No. 26-31. Photo: Federal Archives, Koblenz

of 21 tons was designed for the 20-ton tanks. The mechanism proved to be too likely to break down in use, and the loading ramps were not stable enough. A design that differed in minor details (different armor plates on the chassis, seven gun ports in the sidewalls of the infantry cars, fixed armor sidewalls on the tank carriers) was used for the cars of PZ 30; they may have been the prototype.

The closed cars of the standard BP 42 armored train had uniform two-axle chassis—probably also of the Ommr Linz type—with a wheelbase of 6.0 meters (the overall length, not listed, can be estimated at about 11.30 m). The armored body was not symmetrical, but offset some 50 cm from the axles, possibly because of the weapons' centers of gravity. Both the body walls and the chassis armor angled slightly to the inside from the baseplate of the car. The armor walls were listed as 15 to 30 mm thick, which may mean that the sidewalls were 30 mm and the roof 15 mm; they were simple walls of supposedly refined steel.

The command car had a smooth armored body 10 m long, angled at the ends, about 2.10 m high from the base, tapering inward about one meter (the outside width at the base was some 3.10 m). On the slightly angled roof in the middle of the car, an observation post extended over the full width of the body, about 1 meter long at the base and 75 cm high; running from the roof edge (and curving out at the observation post) an antenna was installed. The car's total height was about 4 meters, its weight 32.15 tons. (All measures of the car, as for all others, are estimates derived from the pictorial material). There were two of these command cars, one in each half of the train. One housed the commander and his staff, including the radiomen, the other the deputy commander (either the infantry or artillery officer). In addition, there were quarters for the infantry.

The howitzer car was of almost similar construction, but the observation stand did not extend the total width of the car, and in one half, the armored body was lowered by about 30 cm to create a

The command car of the standard BP 42 armored train. It is easy to see that the car body is offset somewhat to the right of the axles. Photo: H. Walter/W. Sawodny collection

The howitzer car of BP 42 had a 10-cm F.H. 14/19 (p) in a ten-sided turret. Note that the turret hangs over the car body sides. The open door offers a glimpse into the right section of the car (medical station or kitchen). Note the armor protecting the couplings and the crawl space between the cars made of hinged armor plates. Photo: Federal Archives, Koblenz

The cannon and A/A gun car of BP 42, with the 7.62-cm F.K. 295(r) in the same ten-sided armored turret at left and the A/A platform with 2-cm quad guns at right. In between is the slightly protruding observation post that gave the track observer by the turret a view to the front. Photo: Federal Archives, Koblenz

platform for the ten-sided turret, which was some 1.10 m high. Its base diameter of about 2.30 m (tapering to 1.30 m at the top) gave it a slight overhang at the side. In the other half of the car was the kitchen or the medical station. The total height was also about 4 m, the weight is stated at 37.29 tons.

The gun and A/A car had platforms about 3.60 m long for the weapons on both sides; the armored body below was about 1.20 m high. On the front platform was a ten-sided turning turret of the same dimensions as that of the howitzer car, now armed with a 7.62-cm F.K. 295(r) (Russian M 02/30); on the rear platform, which projected a bit to the sides, was the 2-cm Flak 38 quad, which was surrounded by a wall of armor plate some 80 cm high that could be folded in the upper part and which was on the same level as the middle section of the car (total height some 2.50 m, 2 m above the car bed, about 3.10 m above the rails). In the half with the A/A platform doors were cut in the tapering armored wall, while in the remaining part of the

armored body the walls were vertical, to give the observation stand more breadth and the track observer a chance to view the track ahead of the train beyond the turret. Since the A/A quad was higher than the roof of the middle section the total height of the car was some 4 m, and its total weight 35.75 tons.

While the cannon and A/A car had just one door on each side, the command and howitzer cars had two (symmetrically located on the first, while on the second the door to the medical or kitchen area was in the middle of that half of the car, while the door to the turret was offset to the middle between the turret and the observation stand). All cars (even the front cars!) had other doors in the front end, and they could be connected by folding steel plates to form a covered passage between the cars. The observation posts of all the cars had roof hatches, and spotlights could be mounted on the cannon and A/A cars and the command cars. On the roofs of the command and howitzer cars there were hatches near the ends (possibly also planned as ports for A/A machine guns and mortars). The gun turrets had a roof hatch and a rear emergency exit. The hatches in the armor of the chassis must have partially closed boxes for equipment and small objects, but some were exits for the path that led out of the car through floor hatches.

The car bodies had four other types of openings: machine gun ports in welded-on armor plate, enclosed by a two-part, upward- and downward-turning plate; loopholes, closed by a hatch cover attached on top and swinging to the side; windows in front of which a glass

A look through the open car door at the stove in the kitchen of the BP 42. Photo: H. Beckmann/W. Sawodny collection

A detailed picture of the cannon and A/A car of BP 42 shows the four small openings in the armor:
A. Window (closed by a forward-sliding armor panel, the glass could also slide to the side);
B. Vision slit with upward-folding armor plate;
C. Machine gun port with two-part cover sliding to the side;
D. Loophole with one-piece cover. Also visible is the upward-folding armor shield of the A/A position.
Photo: Federal Archives, Koblenz

pane or armor plate with a loophole of the above type could be slid; vision slits of armor glass with covers that swung upward.

The observation post of the command car had eight vision slits (three at each end, one on each side), that of the howitzer car had six (two at each end, one on each side). The command posts of the cannon and A/A cars, located on both sides of the central structure, each had one vision slit forward, sideward, and backward.—In the four angled corners of all car types there were machine-gun ports; only the howitzer car had vision slits above them on the end facing the locomotive. In the end walls of all cars was just one rifle loophole each to the right and left of the door (to the passageway), and also at the front of the cannon car at the end. The command car had machine gun ports above the end doors. In this car there were, in a row above the doors on the sidewalls: rifle loophole, window, machine gun port, vision slit, window, window, vision slit, window, and rifle loophole (on the right side moving forward; on the left side, instead of the third window, were two rifle loopholes: vision slits and machine gun ports were over the doors). In the two wings of the door there was also always a rifle loophole at offset heights (in the door without a machine gun port over it there was one set into the door in place of a deeper rifle loophole). In all, then, the command car had 12 machine gun ports (four in the corners, two to each side, one each to the front and back, plus two for A/A defense in the flaps of the observation post) and—including those in the window shields—23 rifle loopholes (two each to the front and back, ten on one side, nine on the other). In the sidewalls of the howitzer car there were in the higher part of the body, facing forward, to the right of the center: vision slit and machine gun port (over the door), three windows with rifle loopholes, and another rifle loophole. On the left side, the first window was replaced by a simple rifle loophole. Other rifle loopholes were located on both sides, at different heights, in the wings of the

two doors, plus another at the end of the car, under the gun turret. Thus, there were six machine gun ports in all (four in the corners, one on each side) and 22 rifle loopholes (two each in the ends and nine on each side). The cannon and A/A cars had a rifle loophole in the observation post on each side (under the vision slit), facing the front, and a window (with a rifle loophole) to the side. There were also in each side: under the A/A position, a vision slit flanked by two rifle loopholes; above the door a machine gun port and a vision slit; in each wing of the door a machine gun port (offset in height); and a vision slit in the armored body below the gun turret in the center of the car; plus a rifle loophole at the end of the car. Besides the six machine gun ports (four in the corners, one on each side) there were thus 18 rifle loopholes (four to the front, two to the rear, six on each side).

PZ 32 was built according to the BP 42 plans by Schneider in Le Creusot and Somua in Lyon-Venissieux in the spring and summer of 1944, but certain deviations resulted. The armor consisted only of 20-mm chrome-nickel steel (Brinell hardness 80 to 100 kg). The floor (and roof?) were 10 mm thick. The machine gun ports had differently shaped armor shields, larger in the lower part. The essential difference consisted of installing an A/A platform in the howitzer car (its overhanging side armor had the same level as the car wall, on which a 3.7-cm Flak 36 was mounted, while the actual A/A cars had 2-cm quads). Kitchen and medical areas thus had to be moved from the howitzer car to the added tender, which was thus robbed of its original purpose.

In the improved BP 44 model these car types remained the same as in BP 42 in principle, but now the armored car bodies were mounted symmetrically on the car floors, and the machine gun ports (with rain deflectors over them) were set directly into the armor wall. Strengthening the armor could not be done, for reasons of weight.

Only in PZ 32, built in France, did the howitzer car also have an A/A platform, with a 3.7-cm Flak 36 (the only actual use of this gun in the armored trains). The car body is mounted symmetrically over the axles. The machine gun ports are a type that varied from that of BP 42. Photo: La Vie du Rail

The armored bodies of the BP 44 cars were also mounted symmetrically over the axles. Otherwise they corresponded to those of BP 42, except for the modified machine gun ports now set directly in the armor. In the gun turrets there were only 10.5-cm light F.H. 18/40 howitzers. Photo: Federal Archives, Koblenz

In both train types the tank carrier cars carrying Praga 38(t) tanks were also identical. Unlike Armored Trains No. 26-31 built in 1941, these were now built as armored frames, some 9 meters long and 85 cm high, with the beds on which the tanks stood about at axle level. The wheelbase of the car had now been lengthened to some 7 m. Added side armored shields, some 30 cm high, with two folding panels, protected the entire running gear of the tank standing in the frame. From the tub, ridged surfaces angled upward from the floor level above the front and rear axles. In front was a fixed but flexible exit ramp some 1.80 meters long, which ended with no load some 20 cm over the rails (for heavy scout cars a variation with a fixed exit

ramp was made, which also had a lower front axle sill). Compared to the faulty mechanism of the broad gauge armored trains (No. 26-31) this was a much better solution; thus, when those trains were rebuilt, the retained tank carrier cars were also fitted with this simple but robust exit ramp. The tank carrier cars weighed 17.54 tons; along with the 9.7-ton tanks they had a total weight of 27.2 tons.

The presence of a fixed exit ramp on the tank carrier car, for which space had to be cut out on the car ahead, and its automatic uncoupling via a Scharfenberg coupling, required the making of special, correspondingly equipped control cars. Ommr cars of the Linz type were used, with low wooden walls and light armor for the

The tank carrier car conceived for BP 42, with a wheelbase extended to 7 m, was able to carry a 38(t) tank within an armor frame. With the added folding side shields the tank's running gear was completely protected. Photo: G. Krause collection

To use the exit ramp the tank had to climb over the raised panel over the front axle onto the ridged ramp. The jointed ramp ended some 20 cm above the rails. Photos: H. Beckmann/W. Sawodny collection; Federal Archives, Koblenz

Because of the exit ramp of the tank carrier car, the control cars of BP 42 also had to be of a special design (likewise Type Ommr Linz), which had a matching cutout at the rear. Here an added 2-cm A/A gun, provisionally protected by wooden planks, has been mounted on the control car. Photo: Federal Archives, Koblenz

running gear, which corresponded in appearance to the other BP 42 cars, but was fitted at the rear to the exit ramp of the following tank carrier car. These cars also were fitted with a shovel at the front.

In the BP 44, these control cars were replaced by tank-destroyer cars. These—with a length of about 9 m and a wheelbase of 5 m—also had strong, angled armor for the running gear, some 80 cm high, similar to that of the tank carrier cars, and a shovel at the front; they were angled off at the back to leave room for the ramp of a tank carrier car. On the flat car was an armored body 3.50 meters long at the base and 50 cm high, with angled walls—partly fitted with machine gun ports and vision slits to the front and sides—that bore the turret of a Panzer IV H tank with a 7.5-cm KwK L/48 gun. As usual with these tanks, there were often vertical armored aprons attached to the turret and lower structure. This lower structure naturally extended under the car level between the axles and could have had a total height of about 1.40 m. The car, which could be uncoupled and pushed away pneumatically, very probably had a battery powered electric motor giving it its own power for a short distance. The car, without added armor aprons, weighed 23.4 tons, and with them probably something over 24 tons.

Unlike the locomotives, which continued—until September 1944—to be on loan from the German Reichsbahn, the cars of the BP 42 and 44 armored trains were Wehrmacht property. They were marked with the letter "P" (as private vehicles), with Deipa (probably for "Deutsche Eisenbahn-Panzerzüge"), Berlin W 35, as the owner; their home base was the Wustermark depot. As private cars, they were numbered in the 900 series, and in fact, all vehicles belonging to armored trains had "936" as their first three digits. Of the next three digits, the first two were the number of the armored train, beginning with 01 + Armored Train No. 61, 02 = No. 62, 10 = No. 70, to 22 = No. 82. The last digit of this group showed the position of the car within the train; for example, 936 054 was the fourth car of Armored Train No. 65. The rebuilding of earlier armored trains or rail protection trains were now given 300 and 400 series numbers which, because of cars being destroyed or taken out of service, were sufficient; for example, 936 32 for PZ 22, 936 42 for PZ 52.—The cars of the supply trains for the armored trains were also given 936 numbers as of 1944, with 500 to 700 numbers as their second group of three. Previously the supply trains had kept their civilian numbers from their railway companies.

Owned by the Wehrmacht from the start and not numbered at all were captured armored train cars of Czech, Polish, Yugoslavian, or Russian origin. At the occupation of the remaining Czechoslovakia in March 1939, all six armored trains there fell into German hands. Of the Czech cars built in 1919, they included six infantry cars (CSD Ik 309,364, 314,850, 334,623, Ke 62,339, 302,591, 309,218) and four gun cars (Ik 307,901, 315,784, Ke 306,809, 335,267). But a goodly number still consisted of armored cars that Czechoslovakia had obtained from Austro-Hungarian stocks in 1918. These included five infantry cars (MAV cars numbered 140,914, 140,972, S 149,902, S 150,003, and S 150,271) and two gun cars (CSD 7-89499 and MAV 141,172). Other cars of the same type were taken by the Germans from Yugoslavia in April 1941 (infantry cars 140,912 and S 148,105, plus a gun car with an unknown number). The MAV cars of former Austro-Hungarian armored trains had an overall length of some 7.54 m (wheelbase some 3.60 m). The armored car box was 6.30 m long, 2.70 m wide, and 2.25 m high to the top of the high arched roof, with a height of 2.25 m for the vertical sidewalls (the light height inside was 1.90 m, the height over the rails 3.2 m without the roof structures, and with those of the infantry cars 3.66 m, of the artillery cars 4.55 m).

These cars still had the double-wall armor of the old days: outside a Martin cast steel armor 12 mm thick, behind it a 40-45-mm wooden wall, inside another steel plate 8 to 9 mm thick. Even with the later rebuilding of Armored Train No. 24 (1943-44) this armor was retained, but the observation turrets mounted on it were given simple, thicker steel walls. Otherwise these cars were largely unchanged in terms of types and numbers of rifle and machine gun ports and observation turrets. Only on the roof of one car of PZ 24 (former S 149,902) was a platform for a twin Type 34 A/A machine gun installed. In the mentioned rebuilding of this armored train, of course, major changes were made to the cars. In the second version of PZ 25 in December 1941 two of the former Austro-Hungarian cars were fitted with gun platforms surrounded by low walls. The infantry car S 150,003 gained a front one at the height of the roof edge and connected to the car body, while the rear one was mounted some 30 cm higher (so that the rifle loopholes remained above the roof edge), and projected—with angled edges—over the sides and rear. In the former artillery car (unknown number) the rear platform was formed in the same way. For the front one, the gun turret had been

The tank-destroyer car of BP 44 (that intended for PZ 74 did not reach its train before its premature action and quick loss), with the turret of a Panzer IV H, had a wheelbase shortened to 5 meters and probably a battery powered electric motor for short distances. The turret and lower structure had additional armored aprons. Photo: Federal Archives, Koblenz

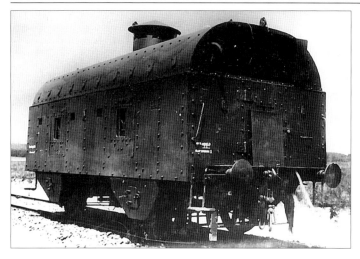

Upper left: The cars of the Czech armored trains were taken over unchanged for the German No. 23-25. Half of them were from former Austro-Hungarian armored trains of World War I. Here is MAV car 140,914 of Austrian PZ II with Czech Armored Train No. 1. Later it became part of German PZ 24. *Upper right:* The former Austro-Hungarian gun car, MAV 141,172 of PZ VII, was used in Czech Armored Train No. 3 and also joined German PZ 24 as of 1940. Photos: Difrology Club, Prague

Left: The German PZ 24 in the spring of 1940 with this gun car, behind it the former Austro-Hungarian MAV 140,972 and S 149,902 infantry cars. The train is still equipped with Schwarzlose 7/24 machine guns from Czech times. Photo: J. Kremer/W. Sawodny collection

Below: This picture of the rebuilding of the Austro-Hungarian cars of PZ 24 in 1943 shows that the original double-walled armor (12 mm outside, 40-45 mm space, inside 8-9 mm) of the car body and roof was retained, while the newly mounted observation post had a simple, thicker steel wall. Full length armor aprons were added before the running gear. Photo: DB AW Neuaubing

For the reestablishment of PZ 25 in December 1941, two such ex-Austro-Hungarian cars were modified more strongly by adding two platforms at different heights on the roof. On the back one a 2-cm A/A gun was mounted; on the lower front one a 7.5-cm Skoda cannon was placed later in an open mount. Photo: Federal Archives, Koblenz

The Czech gun cars kept their two turrets only partially in the first version of the German PZ No. 23-25. Photo: Difrology Club, Prague

Later, as here on PZ 2, which had taken over the gun cars of PZ 25, the rear turret was removed and replaced by an A/A platform for the 2-cm gun. Photo: K. Böhringer/W. Sawodny collection

replaced by a fixed, armored base—slightly drawn in at the front and sides—for the platform, which now also projected forward on these sides, again with angled corners. The platform was set at a somewhat lower level than on the infantry car, so that the height difference from the rear one was greater. To the front of the higher platform there was a closed, armored observation post, which rose above the low wall. On the rear platform of each car was a single 2-cm A/A gun, on the front one, a 7.5-cm Skoda cannon was later (as of Nov. 1942?) mounted behind a shield.

The Czech-type cars had roughly the same dimensions as the Austro-Hungarian ones, but because of their flat tent roofs with the same car height the straight sidewalls were higher (ca. 1.80-1.90 m). The armor consisted of simple plates of 8-mm nickel steel; the roof

armor was only 3.5 mm thick. Whether this very light armor was strengthened later is not known, but can be presumed because of the interior structure. In the originally two-turret gun cars with their unique turret design (the turning part cut about in half by a very raked front, and panels on both sides to protect the gun; the reason was to avoid an overhang of the gun barrel from the circumference of the turret), the rear turret was removed later and replaced by a platform for a 2-cm A/A gun. The infantry cars were used unchanged in PZ 23, but a platform for twin A/A machine guns was built on the roof of one car. The Czech cars added to PZ 24 in 1941 had larger ports cut into the sidewalls; here, too, one of the cars was fitted with a platform for a 2-cm A/A gun. In PZ 25 these cars had new machine-gun ports, those in the corners of the car being especially noticeable. A weight

The interior of a Czech infantry car while in use on a German armored train, once in combat setting and once at rest (such as in transfer trips), where sleeping provisions were made for the crew by stretching hammocks—though in the narrowest space. Photo: W. Sawodny collection

The Czech-built infantry cars sometimes were fitted with roof platforms for A/A guns, but remained unchanged otherwise, as here in PZ 23. Photo: Difrology Club, Prague

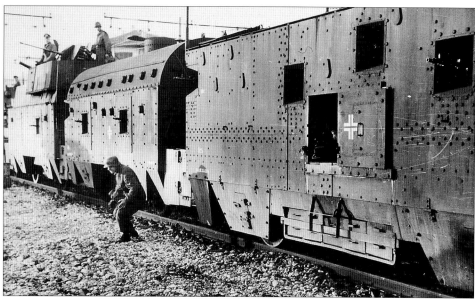

When PZ 25 was reestablished in December 1941, though, improved machine gun ports, especially more of them in the corners, were installed in the cars. This also applies to the ex-Austro-Hungarian cars (a left, MAV 140,912). Photo: Federal Archives, Koblenz

of 24.4 tons was listed for them.—PZ 25, when reestablished in December 1941, received two tank carrier cars with Somua S 35 tanks loaded on them. For them, though, simple four-axle SSk cars (joint Köln type design), wheelbase 6.15 meters, weight without tank 15.32 tons) without exit ramps; to unload the tank, a ramp had to be put together out of wooden planks that were carried.

The German armored trains made up of captured Polish material were connected with the Russian cars in two ways, beyond the general fact that the later Polish armored trains were modeled after the Russians, in the use of two two-turret, four-axle gun cars—the Polish armored trains had only an additional so-called "assault car" (infantry and radio car) in different two-axle lengths, some with flat roofs and antennas, others with barrel-shaped ones, both with antennas, which the Russian trains did not have. Three of the total of ten Polish armored trains even had direct Russian gun cars that had been captured in the Russo-Polish war of 1920, and one of them ("Grozny") had fallen into German hands unharmed in 1919. Also using material from the Polish-built armored trains "Pilsudczyk," "Danuta," and the practice train, Armored Trains No. 21 and 2 were made up in the summer of 1940. On the other hand, the Soviets had also captured three armored trains ("Pierwczy Marszalek," "Smialy," and "Bartosz Glowacki") during the occupation of eastern Poland in 1939, of which they used the first two themselves, converting them to broad gauge, and most of this material fell into German hands in Lemberg at the beginning of the Russian campaign. From it PZ 10 (with two combat trains, the second of which later being numbered PZ 11) was formed, which will be discussed better in the context of the Polish armored trains, although it also included captured Soviet cars.

In all, the following car types appeared in German Armored Trains No. 10, 11, 21, and 22:

- three four-axle Polish gun cars, about 17.20 meters long overall (armored body some 15.80 m long, 3.10 m wide; total height some 4 m), with two symmetrically arranged turrets (one 7.5-cm F.K. 02/26(p) and one 10-cm F.H. 16/19(p); two from PP "Smialy" in PZ 10, one from PP "Pilsudczyk" in PZ 21). Side armor: two 12.5-mm rolled steel plates with space of unknown width and filling; floor and roof of 5- to 8-cm simple armor;

- four four-axle gun cars of old Russian type; two each with one 7.5-cm F.K. 02/26(p), (only in the car from PP "Grozny" in PZ 21 was one replaced by a 10-cm F.H. 16/19(p)) in gun turrets on special substructures. Armor: two 10-mm boiler plates with 50- to 80-mm of space (filled with concrete), in PZ 11 two of the Russian "Krasnoye Sormovo" type from PP "Pierwszy Marszalek," overall length some 15.2 m, car body ca. 13.9 m, one each from PP "Grozny" in PZ 21 and 22, overall length 13.85 m;

- two small two-axle, one-turret gun cars with 7.5-cm F.K. 02.26(p), thinly armored, probably from the Polish practice train, one in PZ 21, the other in PZ 22.

- five assault cars of varying types, sizes, and probably armor;
- one from PP "Bartosz Glowacki" as an infantry car in PZ 10;
- one from PP "Grozny" as command car in PZ 21;
- one of PP "Danuta" (overall length ca. 10.7 m) as infantry car in PZ 21;
- one of PP "Pilsudczyk" as command car in PZ 22 (weighing 33.22 tons);

German PZ 21 took over this big four-axle, two-turret gun car from the Polish armored train "Pilsudczyk." At left is a 7.5-cm F.K. 02.26(p), at right a 10-cm F.H. 14/19(p). Photo: W. Geipel/W. Sawodny collection

– one of PP "Pierwszy Marszalek" or "Smialy" as A/A car in PZ 27 (type not clearly identifiable, the first named is documented as being sent to the Armored train Replacement Battalion in the summer of 1942; that of "Smialy" was probably in PZ 10 B at first). Armor and radios of these cars were insufficient, so that—sometimes more than one—reequipping was undertaken, in which the machine gun ports and observation turrets (sometimes replaced by observation cupolas of German Panzer III or IV) were also changed.

Along with the aforementioned, the following other cars were also in PZ No. 10, 11, 21 and 22:

– one ex-rail protection train (G-car, Oppeln train) in PZ 2;
– later (as of summer 1942), three four-axle cars from heavy Russian armored trains (gun turret replaced by platform for single 2-cm A/A gun), also used as command cars (one in PZ 10, two in PZ 11);
– six low-side cars with armored sidewalls, carrying single 2-cm A/A guns (two each in PZ 10, 21, and 22)—for one in PZ 22 a weight of 27.2 tons is listed; in the reequipping of PZ 21 with A/A quads one of these cars was dropped, since one quad replaced the gun turret with cannon of the small gun car).

This photo of a blown-up car of this type (presumably Polish PZ "Poznanczyk") also shows the double armor (two 12.5-cm drawn over curved double-T bearers). Photo: J. Wilhelm collection

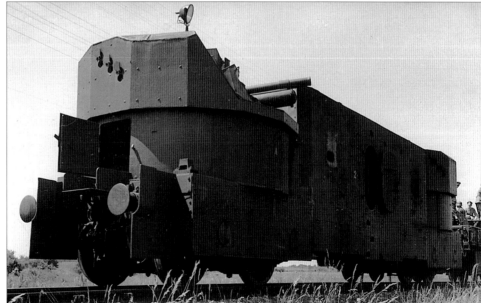

An ex-Polish gun car of Russian type (modified "Krasnoye Sormovo" type) from armored train "Grozny" armed with two 7.5-cm F.K. 02/26(p), in German PZ 22. Photo: Federal Archives, Koblenz

Such installations of 2-cm A/A guns (quads) on low-side cars were also done in the reequipping of PZ 25 in 1944 (in addition to the single ones mounted on the gun cars) and the heavy scout trains, instead of the originally planned but never finished structures on the scout cars themselves—the surviving photos show R-cars of the Stuttgart type with armored crew and ammunition bunkers in the rear part of the car, and a shovel at the front.

Aside from the reequipping of Armored Trains No. 11 and 22 with tank-destroyer cars in the summer and autumn of 1944, and the using of several G-cars provisionally armored with concrete to replace those of PZ 21 damaged in the summer of 1944, the cars of the four named armored trains were retained until their loss.

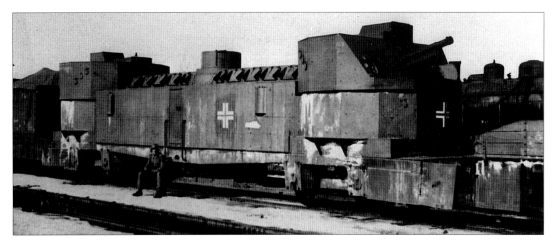

The Russian Revolution type "Krasnoye Sormovo" type, captured by the Germans in Lemberg after twice changing sides between Russia and Poland, turned up in PZ 11 (formerly a combat train B of PZ 10). Photo: W. Pflaumbaum/W. Sawodny collection

PZ 21 and 22 each received a small two-axle gun car that was probably in a Polish training train before. Photo: Federal Archives, Koblenz

The "assault" car of the Polish armored train "Bartosz Glowacki" was captured by the Russians in September 1939 and left in Lemberg. Falling into German hands there in July 1941, it was used as a command car in PZ 10. Photo: W. Pflaumbaum/W. Sawodny collection

The "assault" car of the Polish armored train "Pilsudczyk" served as a command car in PZ 22. Photo: Federal Archives, Koblenz

"Assault" car of the Polish armored train "Grozny" as command car in PZ 21. On the tender in front of it, the levers of the hand-operated water pump can be seen. Photo: G. Leinen/W. Sawodny collection

Below: Also running in PZ 21 (ahead of the Polish Ti 3-13 armored loco) were the "assault" car of the former armored train "Danuta" (without antenna) and the second gun car of "Grozny" with a 7.5-cm F.K. 02/26(p) (in the right turret) and a 10-cm F.H. 14/19(p). Photo: F. Englberger/W. Sawodny collection

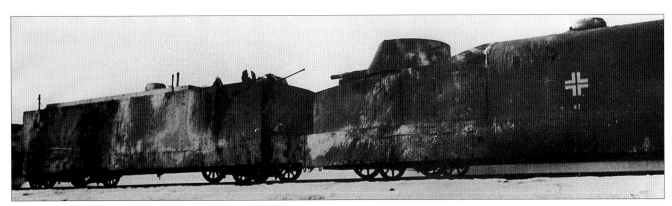

Above: In PZ 10 and 11 (ex-10B) Soviet cars from heavy BP 35 type armored trains were used as command and A/A cars, with an A/A platform (with single 2-cm gun) installed instead of the gun turret. At right is a gun car from the former Polish "Smialy" train in PZ 10. Photo: Prussian Cultural Photo Archives, Berlin

When older armored trains were equipped with A/A guns, and in the later heavy scout-car trains, they were installed on low-side cars. Here is one from PZ 22 with armored sidewalls and axle protection carrying a 2-cm quad. Photo: H. Schüller/W. Sawodny collection

Captured Russian cars, mainly unchanged, were used in the reequipping of older German armored trains, especially the broad gauge No. 26 to 31. In the spring of 1942 PZ 26 received a four-axle gun car of the same Russian Revolution type as PZ 11. Of course the guns had been removed; one turret was used as an observation post; in place of the other, a platform had been installed for a 2-cm A/A quad. Two more two-axle infantry cars cannot be identified definitely; they were probably improvised on the basis of O-cars, steel-covered and partly roofed. — PZ 27 received a similar car the same spring, plus two four-axle gun cars of the Soviet BP 35 type with two polygonal turrets holding 7.62-cm F.K. 02/30 guns atop a box-shaped armored structure with two angular turrets. This car was 13.70 m long overall and weighed 57.91 tons. — PZ 28 had already received two captured cars from a heavy Russian armored train in the autumn of 1941; they had four axles, box bodies with vertical walls, and a turret to one side with a 10.7-cm F.K. M 10/30. These were replaced in the summer of 1942 by two other captured cars, likewise four-axle types, originally with two gun turrets at different levels, with 7.62-cm F.K. 02/30. The lower turrets had been replaced by an A/A platform. — Whether PZ 29 had also been equipped with captured Russian cars shortly before it was lost in January 1942 is not definitely known. — In the winter of 1941-42, PZ 31 received a four-axle infantry car of Russian origin, and later also a two-turret car of the Soviet BP 35 type, with one

gun turret replaced by a flak platform. When the armored train was rebuilt in 1943 two four-axle gun cars of the same type as in PZ 27 were added, but the Russian turrets were replaced by those of the standard German type. — Two other cars of that type, possibly with single turrets (as in Armored Trains No. 10, 11, and 28, coming from Soviet heavy armored trains), were utilized as A/A and command cars when PZ 30 was rebuilt in 1943, with an A/A platform in place of the turret and an observation post added at the other end of the car. The gun cars of this armored train were four captured Russian two-axle, one-turret cars of the OB-3 type. These cars had an overall length of 3.10 m and a height of 3 m. The single-layer armor, angled except for the turret substructure, was 45 mm thick on the sides. They were reequipped with observation posts and improved communications; later (early in the summer of 1944) the Russian gun turrets were replaced by ten-sided German-made types. — The same type of two-axle gun cars — presumably also with German turrets — seem to have been added to PZ 3 after its rebuilding in 1943-44 (according to descriptions; pictures are not available). — A special case was PZ 6, which received two captured Russian armored railcars of the two-turret type as gun cars in 1942, which were also used later by the Germans as individual vehicles (German Armored Railcars No. 17 to 23). The motor seems to have been present in one of them at first, so that it could be used independently of the train, but later it was removed.

A captured Soviet car of the "Krasnoye Sormovo" type was assigned to PZ 26 early in 1942. The rear turret was replaced by a platform for a 2-cm A/A quad. Behind it is one of the original infantry cars with a canvas cover. Photo: H. Jäger/W. Sawodny collection

PZ 27 was equipped in February 1942 with two gun cars of the light Russian BP 35 type (two turrets with 7.62-cm F.K. 02/30 guns). Photo: H. J. Roddewig/W. Sawodny collection

One of them was destroyed by a mine explosion late in May 1942. PZ 27 was then given a car of the same type, but with round turrets, that had previously been used in a line protection train. Photo: H. J. Roddewig/W. Sawodny collection

For well over half a year, PZ 28 used two complete captured cars of the heavy Soviet BP 35 type, with a 10.7-cm F.K. M 10 gun in the turret. Photo: Federal Archives, Koblenz

In the summer of 1942 they were replaced by two gun cars of another Soviet type. It had originally had two turrets, but the Germans had installed an A/A platform (here with a quad, on the other car a single gun) in place of the front turret. In the turret was a long-barreled L/40 version of the 7.62-cm F.K. 02/30, 295/2(r) gun. Photo: B. Schultz/W. Sawodny collection

Above: PZ 31 also added a gun car of the two-turret Soviet BP 35 type after its rebuilding in 1943, but the turrets were replaced by ten-sided German types. Photo: W. Sawodny collection

Four cars of the two-axle, single-turret Soviet OB-3 type were added to PZ 30 when it was rebuilt. Observation posts had been added to the cars, which ran at the ends of the train. The guns were probably also the long-barreled L/40 type of the 7.62-cm F.K. 295/2(r). Photo: H. Plangemann/W. Sawodny collection

On its rebuilding in the spring of 1944, the Russian turrets were replaced by the German type, now with the short-barreled (L/30) version of the 7.62-cm F.K. 02/30, 295/1(r). Photo: H. Plangemann/W. Sawodny collection

PZ 30 had two captured four-axle cars, presumably former heavy Soviet cars from Type BP 35, as command and A/A cars, but more strongly modified than those of PZ 10. Photo: Federal Archives, Koblenz

PZ 6 was unusual in receiving two former Soviet railcars (the same type as the PT 17-23 used much later by the Germans) as gun cars in 1942. The antenna installed on one car indicates that it presumably retained its motor and could operate independently of the train. Photo: E. Espey/W. Sawodny collection

Later the four-axle Russian chassis had fully new bodies mounted on them. They consisted basically of an armored box with two German made turrets mounted on them at different heights. The (lower) front one had a 7.62-cm F.K. 295/1(r) gun, the (higher) rear one a 10-cm F.H. 14.19(p). In between was a raised command post. The cars, though the same in principle, showed minor differences in doors, gun ports, etc. in the individual armored trains. This is the gun car of the newly built PZ 1. Photo: W. Sitzius/W. Sawodny collection

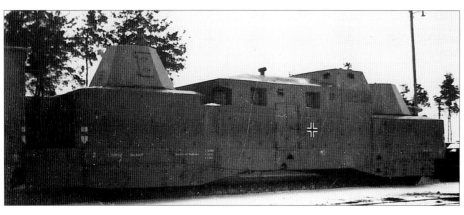

These differences can be seen clearly in the same type of car in PZ 26, shown in this picture. Photo: H. Jäger/W. Sawodny collection

In the rebuilding of older armored trains in 1943-44, only the four-axle chassis of the Soviet armored cars were usually used, with completely new bodies built on them. Despite differences in details this always showed the same general principle: a raised middle section with an observation platform built on it, and platforms for the two gun turrets (ten-sided standard German versions) at different heights (the front one lower than the rear one) at the ends of the car. The armoring all appears to be the double-layer type with concrete filling the space between them, probably stronger overall than on Armored Train 42 or 44. For these gun cars of PZ 26, 14.30 m long, 2.95 m wide, and 3.61 m high, a total weight of 60 tons is listed, but in PZ 23 the weight of these cars was 73.32 tons, which indicates a considerable difference in the details. This type of gun car was used in the rebuilt armored trains PZ 1, 4, 7, 23, 24, 25, and 26. Most of these gun cars—like the cars from Russian armored trains that were modified as command or A/A cars—had an approximate overall length of 14 m. But for the gun car at the Warsaw Railroad Museum (coming from PZ 24 or 25) the following data are stated: length (overall?) 13.0 m, width 3.20 m, height 3.90 m, weight 60 tons.

Since this rebuilding was combined with equating them to the equipment and manning of the standard BP 42 or 44 type (according to the K.St.N. and K.A.N. 1169 x), a constant scheme was also valid for the other cars, which was followed not only by the armored trains with the aforementioned gun cars, but also by others with less strongly modified captured two-turret cars: Armored Trains No. 6, 27, and 31. Along with the gun cars (and the obligatory control, tank carrier, and later tank-destroyer cars), it included a pair each of command and A/A cars. For them available cars were used (if for the former broad gauge armored trains No. 26-31, for which this was not completely possible, excess cars from former rail protection trains No. 1-7 were used, cannot be proved, but in view of the thrifty apportionment of cars by the Reichsbahn it is not improbable).

In particular the following correlations can be made, based on the photographs:

PZ 1: The remaining uniform corridor cars built in 1928 and the G-cars with brake cabins built new in 1940-41 had been rebuilt as command cars. Tank carrier cars were taken from PZ 26. The origin of the chassis for the A/A cars (G-cars of the previous train?) is not clear.

PZ 4: Only a schematic drawing for the rebuilding is available. But the command and A/A cars show a three-axle chassis, such as all the G- and baggage cars of the predecessor had.

PZ 6: Both the command and A/A cars were added to the new train by modifying earlier G-cars.

PZ 23: The three-axle cars of former rail protection trains were rebuilt as command cars; among the A/A cars are earlier Czech infantry cars (now weighing 30 tons).

PZ 24: Two cars each of Austro-Hungarian origin were united by short coupling for the two command cars; the Czech infantry cars were rebuilt as (30-ton) A/A cars. Received the tank carrier cars of PZ 30.

PZ 25: Here the very short time available for rearming did not allow any major modifications; at least the reuse of Czech infantry cars as command cars and the gun-flak cars as A/A cars is likely.

PZ 26: The earlier infantry cars of the broad gauge (Ommr Linz type) train were rebuilt as A/A cars (weighing 35 tons); the command cars were new (two G-cars of different types, one weighed 38 tons); Two of the three original tank carrier cars went to PZ 1, one probably to PZ 51 (replaced by those of the standard BP 42 type).

PZ 27: One of the A/A cars was of Polish origin, the other may have been a captured Russian car; the command cars were two newly rebuilt two-axle G-cars. The remaining infantry car of the original train was rebuilt as a second tank carrier car.

PZ 28: Both infantry cars (now with fixed roofs) and two of the three tank carrier cars remained with the train (the third may have gone to PZ 51).

PZ 30: The tank carrier cars went to PZ 24 and were replaced by those of the standard BP 42 type. The fate of the infantry cars is unknown.

PZ 31: Both A/A and command cars (G-cars) were new. The tank carrier cars remained with the train, the infantry car went to PZ 10 as an open A/A car.

As to the composition of PZ 3 and 7, nothing is known to date.

PZ 51, which developed from a line protection train, consisted exclusively of four-axle Russian freight cars with inside armor, three GG-cars (two as gun cars, each with two BT-7 tank turrets, the rear one on the roof, the front one on a low platform, one as an A/A car), and one high-wall OO-car (fitted with an armored roof) as a command car. At the beginning of 1944 it received two tank carrier cars of the broad gauge type (one each from PZ 26 and 28?).—In the second line protection train "Blücher," rebuilt as an armored train, only Russian four-axle cars were used at first, but except for one GG-car with inside armor, they all had special bodies made of steel. Only two of these cars (T-34 turrets replaced by those of German Panzer IV, and used not only as tank-destroyer cars but simultaneously rebuilt as command and A/A cars) went to PZ 52, which also received the remaining two-turret gun car from PZ 27 and two inside-armored G-cars and two tank carrier cars of the BP 42 standard type; thus its composition was very mixed.

Not much is known of the painting of the armored trains either, since only black-and-white photos have been found to date. The trains taken over from rail protection probably had their original colors at first, the brownish red of normal freight cars, but perhaps sometimes the gray-green of the managements' own trains (matching the color of the passenger cars as well), as the uniform gray tones of the passenger and freight cars in photos of PZ 1 lets one assume. PZ 3, on the other hand, seems to have been painted bluish gray already in 1938-39, as was later customary for the German armored trains. For the Polish campaign, some armored trains (proved for PZ 2 and 3) were painted in large spots of camouflage colors, while others (such as No. 1, 4, 5, and 7) still had their single-color paint in the western campaign.

The captured Czech trains (No. 23-25) retained their large-scale multicolored camouflage paint with straight borders when first set up (March 1940); the Polish ones (No. 21 and 22) were at first painted in small areas of two colors (probably also retained from former ownership). In PZ 22 an interesting transitional stage (from 1942?) is shown in pictures; only the (captured Polish) locomotive

The A/A cars resulting from this rebuilding were of very varied origins. For Armored Trains No. 23 and 24, Czech infantry cars were suitably rebuilt (here one from PZ 24). Photo: H. Röhle/W. Sawodny collection

For PZ 26, on the other hand, the A/A car was built on an Ommr-Linz chassis of a former infantry car. To the right is a command car whose origin is unclear. Photo: H. Jäger/W. Sawodny collection

had this paint, while the cars already showed the later uniform color (the G-car looks darker and probably still had the original "rail-protection color"). Before the Russian campaign began (in the spring of 1941), all armored trains—also the newly formed ones (No. 26-31)—were painted a uniform bluish-gray, as was also recommended in the current guidelines of May 1942. White camouflage color was whitewashed over it in the winter.

Captured Russian cars look brighter than the German cars of that time (1941-42); their paint was probably a brownish earth tone. This can be seen very well in PZ 28, where such cars were combined with the original tank carrier cars (note the particular camouflage painting on these cars, likewise taken over from Soviet times). Later (1943?) the situation changed for this armored train. The newly painted German cars now had a brighter color than the captured ones, which apparently retained their original color.

This change of color probably corresponds to the new sand-colored tone chosen when the standard BP 42 armored trains were introduced, after it had been found that the previous very dark gray did not offer enough camouflage, and which was also used on the

later BP 44 and light and heavy scout trains. In action, though, this color was frequently modified independently—from a wildly applied brush pattern in darker paint to a careful, possibly multicolored large- or small-spot pattern. Though such paintings were at first the exception (PZ 62 already had one before it went into action in February 1943), later (as of spring 1944) they became the rule. In the winter, the long-customary white camouflage was still used. But since the spring of 1944 the armored trains were usually camouflaged carefully with shrubbery applied to the outside walls (varying from bunches of grain to whole trees with wires stretched to attach them, so that the paint could scarcely be seen and thus did not play a major role).

The escort vehicles (tanks and armored scout cars) show the same spectrum of colors, and the same is true of the subordinated armored railcars up to No. 23. The Italian "Littorinas" (Armored Railcars No. 30-38), though, were given a special paint job of irregular large multicolored spots, set off from each other by light borders. They can thus be told clearly apart from the same type of vehicles used by the Italian Army, which also had multicolored painted spots, but with different shapes and no such borders.

The front half of PZ 51, at right a GG-car rebuilt as a gun car, with two turrets from Soviet BT-7 tanks on different levels, and behind it a roofed OO-car as a command car. Photo: A. Hagenmaier/W. Sawodny collection

Another GG-car (in the rear half of the train) had been rebuilt as an A/A and substitute command car. PZ 51 had the "freight train look" of the line protection trains, but with external armor plates added to the doors and machine gun ports. Photo: W. Sitzius/W. Sawodny collection

The Weapons

When the rail protection trains were taken over as Armored Trains 1-7 in the summer of 1938 they had no heavy armaments. Obviously, there was at first no uniform planning for arming them, so that the recruiting districts that set them up used what was available. In this way an extremely varied array of guns came to be used.

The two gun cars on hand for PZ 3 (Munich) were armed with 7.7-cm F.K. 16. After sustaining heavy damage near Konitz on September 1, 1939, these guns were temporarily replaced by the older F.K. 96 n.A. of the same caliber. In the early summer of 1940 its gun cars were thoroughly rebuilt, and as its final equipment it was fitted with experimental 7.5-cm L/41 guns in open-top turrets, forerunners of the long tank gun or Pak 40 intended for self-propelled guns, at Rheinmetall-Borsig. The armored trains equipped at Königsberg (PZ 6 and 7) surely had guns of similar calibers, but their exact type is unknown to date. The gun of PZ 6 shown on a socket mount in a photo could not be identified but may be an old naval gun. The first data on PZ 7, which name two 7.5-cm F.K. 02/26(p), come from the spring of 1942 and scarcely refer to the original equipment, which may well have corresponded to that of PZ 6 at first. For the other four armored trains, armament with two 3.7-cm Pak 35/36 and two light 7.5-cm

I.G. each was planned, but these were used only for PZ 4, while PZ 1, 2, and 5 remained without guns at first. — In the reequipping of the armored trains in the winter of 1940-41, this variety was not only retained but even increased. PZ 1 received two 4.7-cm Böhler-Sidius anti-tank guns captured in Holland, and the 3.7-cm Pak 35/36 in PZ 4 were changed to two of the same type, but later replaced by 4.7-cm Skoda A 5 (M 38) anti-tank guns. PZ 2 also received captured Czech guns, but of 7.5-cm (see below) caliber.

More uniform artillery weapons were provided for the armored trains (No. 23-25) made up of captured Czech material in the spring of 1940, although the view prevailed that two guns were quite sufficient for an armored train. The Czechs had armed all their armored trains with 7-5-cm Skoda D 28 guns, the bored-out 6.6-cm L/30 (1910) torpedo boat guns that had already been used in the Austro-Hungarian armored trains of World War I. Boring them out allowed the shells made for the 7.5-cm Skoda M 15 Geb.K. to be used (which was why these guns were often listed by that designation in German sources as well). There was no fire control system available for these guns; they had to be aimed directly. Of the six captured gun cars (two still from Austro-Hungarian times, four of twin-turret Czech design), each of the newly formed German armored trains received two with such guns; one of the two original turrets of the Czech cars was removed and replaced by an A/A platform. The gun cars of PZ 25 were turned over to PZ 2 in the winter of 1940-41; later PZ 25, rebuilt in December 1941, was equipped with the same type of guns in open mounts at the end of 1942, so that four armored trains then had identical equipment.

Besides their small numbers, the guns used up to then had low performance. In both aspects—as in armament in general—they remained behind the Reichswehr armored trains of 1918-1920 and apparently regarded this as sufficient even in 1939. The 7.5-cm caliber was seen as the upper limit; in fact, between the end of 1940 and mid-1942 a smaller caliber—even though in the form of quicker Pak and KwK guns—was even regarded as sufficient. This was shown not only by PZ 1, mentioned above, but especially by the broad gauge armored trains No. 26-31, set up in the spring of 1941, in which the dismountable two or three Somua tanks included the only guns (significantly, only explosive and small anti-tank shells

After PZ 3 had at first used 7.7-cm F.K. 16 or 96 n.A. guns, which had already been used in World War I and shortly afterward in German armored trains, it was fitted in 1940-41 with long-barreled (L/41) 7.5 cm experimental guns made by Rheinmetall, probably the forerunner of the later KwK L/48 or Pak 40 of the same caliber. It was already installed in a ten-sided turret, which was open at the top. Photo: W. Hahn/W. Sawodny collection

At a 90-degree position its long barrel extended considerably over the train's clearance. This was probably an early attempt to deal with the resulting problems. Still in all, enlarging the barrel lengths of the guns was considered only hesitantly. Photo: W. Hahn/W. Sawodny collection

Above left: The guns of PZ 6 (and probably also PZ 7), installed on socket mounts, could not be identified to date. They were presumably naval guns, with a fairly probable caliber of 7.5 cm. Photo: E. Espey/W. Sawodny collection *Above right:* The 3.7-cm Pak 35/36 was installed in the front turret of PZ 4. It can be seen here on a normal wheeled mount being used by a line protection train. Photo: Federal Archives, Koblenz

were selected as the only ammunition for them!) PZ 25, set up anew in December 1941, should also be included here, in which the Somua tank guns were also the only armament in its first year (until it was revised at the end of 1942), as should PZ 51, set up in June 1942, which had four 4.5-cm tank guns in turrets from captured Soviet BT-7 tanks.

On the other hand, the Polish armored trains which the Germans had fought against and captured some of in September 1939 had not only confronted them with a considerably higher firepower of four guns with 7.5- and 10-cm calibers per train (and these even with the meager number of three fighting cars per train), but also provided a uniform and effective equipment in this realm. When captured Polish material was used to make up German Armored Trains No. 21 and 22 in the spring and early summer of 1940, the 7.5-cm 02/26 (p) field cannons (reworkings of the proved 02 Russian gun designed by Putilov) used in them, and the 10-cm 16/19 (p) howitzer (built by Skoda and modified by the Poles especially for use in armored trains) were taken over, though the equipment of the two trains indicates uncertainty and willingness to experiment: while PZ 22 had three field cannons in two gun cars, PZ 23 had those plus two howitzers

Later the 3.7-cm anti-tank gun was replaced by a 4-7-cm cannon in PZ 4, installed at once in the gun cars of PZ 1 in 1940-41, where this picture shows them in an open-top turret, the front of which is the shield of the gun itself. The gun, a design of the Austrian firm of Böhler but modified for use in the Netherlands Army by Siderius, was used as both an infantry gun and an anti-tank gun. On the roof of the car behind it (taken over from PZ 5) are the spotlight at left and the periscope for line observation at right. Photo: E. Grahl/W. Sawodny collection

Above left: The 7.5-cm Skoda D 28 cannon taken from Czech stock and used in Armored Trains No. 2, 23-25 (here mounted open on PZ 25) was the old 6.6-cm L/30 naval gun of the Austro-Hungarian armored trains, bored out to 7.5 cm by the Czechs between the World Wars (reducing the caliber length to L/26) to be able to fire the ammunition of the Skoda M 15 mountain gun (thus it was also listed often in German sources as "Geb.K. M 15(oe or .t).") Photo: Federal Archives, Koblenz *Above right:* This picture, unfortunately taken without a flashbulb and thus strongly affected by light from outside, shows the mounting of this gun on a very low socket mount in PZ 23 (gun car of old Austro-Hungarian Armored Train II). Photo: H. G. Hartman/W. Sawodny collection

At the beginning of the Russian campaign tank guns were often used as armament, as in the broad gauge armored trains set up just for this campaign, which carried French Somua tanks (4.7-cm caliber, *left*), while PZ 51 had four Soviet BT-7 (4.5 cm, *above*) turrets. Photo: Federal Archives, Koblenz, and G. Gayk/W. Sawodny collection

In the Polish-made armored train cars—as here in PZ 10—the gun cradle of the Skoda 10-cm F.H. 14/19(p) was enclosed. Photo: W. Pflaumbaum/W. Sawodny collection

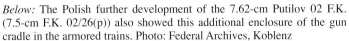

Below: The Polish further development of the 7.62-cm Putilov 02 F.K. (7.5-cm F.K. 02/26(p)) also showed this additional enclosure of the gun cradle in the armored trains. Photo: Federal Archives, Koblenz

When these 10-cm howitzers were used in the German BP 42 armored trains the enclosure was dropped, so that the barrel recuperator can be seen clearly. Photo: German Archives, Koblenz

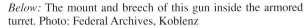

Below: The mount and breech of this gun inside the armored turret. Photo: Federal Archives, Koblenz

(in a total of three gun cars); in any case, the two-turret Polish cars were taken over without reducing their artillery. Only when, as 1941 turned to 1942, PZ 10—consisting of two combat trains and likewise made up of Polish material, which had fallen to the Soviets and then been captured by the Germans in Lemberg at the beginning of the Russian campaign—was put into service was the usual Polish and Russian number of four guns adopted; the first combat train of PZ 10 had two cannons and two howitzers, the second had four cannons of the Polish type cited above, each in two two-turret cars. PZ 7 was also—presumably in June or July 1941 at Cracow—reequipped with the 7.5-cm F.K. 012/26(p), although it had only two of these guns, and they were replaced on October 1, 1942, by Russian 7.62-cm F.K. 02/30 L/30 (s.u.) guns. When high-angle-fire guns were taken over for indirect fire the installation of a fire control system was necessary.

This increased total of four guns, corresponding to the Polish/Russian model, was then taken over for the BP 42 standard armored train developed in 1942, in which the frequent combination used by the Poles of two flat-trajectory and two high-angle guns (two cannons and two howitzers) was preferred. For this, the Czech/Polish F.H. 16/19 (p) continued to be installed; the Polish version of the improved Putilov cannon, though, was replaced by the Soviet (7.62-cm F.K./ 02/30 in L/30 short-barrel form, German type designation 295/1(r)), which had a greater aiming field, higher muzzle velocity of the shell, and greater range. This field gun was installed in many Russian armored trains, which often fell into German hands; thus Armored Railcars No. 17-23 (No. 16 was so armed later), which were of Russian origin, were armed with two of them.

Not only for the BP 42, but also for the rebuilding of older armored trains according to K.A.N. or K.St.N. 1169x, was the number of guns maintained until well into 1944, and the combination of two cannons and two howitzers was customary. The field cannons, being suitable for direct fire, were always in the turrets at the ends of the train, so that they could also be fired in the direction of movement. The howitzers, intended for indirect fire, were in the turrets nearer the middle of the train, no matter whether they were in rebuilt cars or BP 42 types, where the howitzer cars were right before and after the engine. Of the alternatives mentioned above, only PZ 32, built in France with many particular features, had four howitzers, and in only a few cases involving captured vehicles (PZ 6, 27, and 30) were there four cannons. Such captured cars also required a few other basic deviations from this ordained weaponry. PZ 28 had two armored cars, each with a turning turret, fitted with Russian 10.7.cm F.K. Schneider-Putilov 10 cannon from the late autumn of 1941 to the summer of 1942. Because of the caliber, unusual for German armored trains, these cars were replaced in the summer of 1942 by others of Russian origin, now using the long-barrel version of the 7.62-cm F.K. 02/30 (L/40); German number 295/2(r)). This gun was also used in the captured cars of PZ 27 (February-May 1942), and probably PZ 30 (February-May 1944), but were later replaced by the short-barrel type in both trains. This indicates the desire to keep the extension of the barrel in 90-degree position over the clearance of the cars as little as possible. To be sure, Polish and Russian armored cars had been encountered that—probably because of the wide space and the rarity of meeting limiting hindrances—were designed with more extent in this feature and had gained their own experience with the 7.5-cm L/41 guns, already installed in 1940, in PZ 3, but were reluctant to extend the barrel length beyond 2 m, a limit which

In the German BP 42 armored trains this gun was replaced by the more efficient Soviet development of the Putilov Cannon 02, the 7.62-cm F.K. 02/30 (German 295/1(r)), though the short-barrel L/30 variant was used. Photo: Federal Archives, Koblenz

In some of the German armored trains (No. 27, 28, and probably also 30) that used captured Russian cars, the long-barrel variant of this gun (L/40, German designation 295/2(r)) was also used. It is easy to recognize here on a captured Russian armored train car. Photo: B.f.Z.G., Stuttgart

Only temporarily was a 10.7-cm F.K.-M 10 (352(r)) used in a car from a heavy Russian armored train on PZ 28. Later the turret was removed and replaced by an A/A stand. In this condition they were used—also as command cars—in Armored Trains No. 10, 11, and in modified form also in No. 30. Photo: Federal Archives, Koblenz

Only with BP 44 had uniform arming with the more capable 10.5-cm F.H. 18/40 planned for all four guns. Photo: Federal Archives, Koblenz

Yet there were delivery difficulties for this gun, which resulted in makeshift solutions on the armored trains. On PZ 75 (later Armored Instruction Train No. 5) a report states that two Soviet 12.2-cm F.H.M 38 (396(r)) were installed, as seen here on a self-propelled mount which was loaded onto the tank carrier car of PZ 32. Photo: SIRPA/ECPA Paris

allowed the gun in a suitable mounting a full traverse within the train's clearance. For longer barrels in a perpendicular firing position, very exact observation of the track to be used, immediate reporting of any hindrances that appeared (railroad buildings, underpasses, nearby utility poles, etc.) to the gun crews, and prompt swinging of the barrel into the car's profile (the longer the barrel, the greater the swing), with equally quick swinging back into the direction of fire after passing through the danger area on combat trips was required. The choice of the train's position could also be limited by these conditions.

Although the German armored trains' artillery had been strengthened markedly in terms of the numbers of their guns, so as to equal the Polish and Russian numbers, they were actually well behind parity of high-powered modern equipment in their exclusive use of short-barrel (up to 2.40 m) guns of older types, with meager range and penetrating power. Only with the further development of the standard BP 42 to BP 44 types in 1944 were these guns replaced by the uniform German 10.5-cm F.H. 18/40 (barrel length 2.94 m). They not only had an increased range by three km, but their penetrating power was also sufficient to attack tanks with direct fire. But this task was now intended particularly for the added tank destroyers with their long-barrel 7.5-cm tank guns (barrel length 3.60 m). Thus, the change to exclusively howitzer armament as artillery seemed sufficient.

But from the beginning there were delivery problems again and again for the Field Howitzer 18/40. The first armored train of the new series, No. 73, finished in June 1944, actually seems to have had the new equipment. PZ 74 and 75, which had to rush into action when the Russians broke through to the Vistula at the end of June 1944, could not be armed according to plan. Still installed in the outer turrets of PZ 74 were the earlier 7.62-cm F.K. 295/1(r)—the guns in the inner turrets cannot be recognized from the photographs. For PZ 75 (later Armored Instruction Train No. 5), the armament was listed in February 1945 as two German howitzers (18/40) and two Russian ones of that type (12.2 cm?). In January 1945 a new delivery problem occurred. Thus, PZ 79 was sent into action without gun turrets (12-cm mortars were provisionally installed in the openings for the turrets); the guns were never delivered, as the train was soon lost.

The mass attacks of the outstanding Russian medium and heavy tanks, particularly the T-34, confronted the German armored trains, including the BP 42, with tasks they could scarcely carry out once they had passed more and more from the phase of fighting almost exclusively against partisans to front action as of early 1943, for they were hopelessly inferior to them in armor and armament. In the autumn of 1941 the Russians had already shown a pragmatic way that armored trains could be made equal to tanks in at least the second

aspect: they simply mounted turrets of tanks, with their penetrating guns, on railroad cars armored in the usual way. Remarkably this solution, as simple as it was effective, at first struck no chord in the regular German armored trains. On the other hand, turrets were soon used on line protection trains used by the troops, since appropriate captured material was being used there. Via this roundabout route they also reached the regular trains. Thus, the later PZ 51, originally conceived as a rail protection train (taken over in the summer of 1941), used two turrets from Russian BT 7 tanks. The 4.5-cm KwK L/46 guns in them, though, equaled only the 5-cm L/42 guns of Panzer III F-H in performance, and were thus also insufficient in the aforementioned sense. Then, too, it remained a single case. Thus arose the grotesque situation in which line protection trains equipped with T-34 turrets (such as "Polko," "Michael," or "Blücher") were far superior in firepower to several regular armored trains of the time.

The greatest weakness was always the lack of an armor-piercing weapon. Thus undriveable tanks were often carried. The 5-cm tank gun of the Panzer III—here on a line protection train, but also known to have been used on PZ 7, 28, and probably 27—were, alas, not penetrating enough for their specified use. Photo: S.I.R.P.A./E.C.P.A., Paris

The 7.5-cm L/48 tank gun of the Panzer IV H gave considerably better performance. Its turrets were used later on the tank-destroyer cars. Here such a tank is shown on the control car of PZ 62 in the spring of 1944, with added wooden plank protection on the sides. Photo: Ullstein-Bilderdienst

The armored train commanders helped their cause by taking it on themselves to "requisition" no longer operable tanks, setting them on flat cars and including them in trains. Panzer III, which is documented in photos from Armored Trains No. 7 (1943), 28 (winter 1941-42), and presumably 27, turned out, as noted above, to be scarcely effective. Panzer IV H, which was used by PZ 62 in the spring of 1944, was considerably better. It can be assumed that T-34 tanks were often used for this purpose as well, even though only one such use is documented, for PZ 21 in the late summer of 1944. After all, a T-34 loaded on a flat car was used by the Armored Train Replacement Battalion in Rembertow in the summer of 1942. Along with tanks, anti-tank guns were often carried on low-side cars—often with makeshift protection. In the spring of 1944 PZ 71 used the German 7.5-cm Pak 40, and the Russian 7.62-cm ZIS-3 was probably used on PZ 67 at the same time, with makeshift protection from tree trunks. The latter was also mounted permanently in the lead car of PZ 28—also early in 1944.

The breakthrough beyond these provisional uses was begun by a recommendation from the commander of PZ 1, 1st Lt. Helmut Walter, and was carried out when his train was modified by local technicians during an overhaul in the Dünaburg EAW at the end of 1943. They mounted the turret of a Soviet T-34 tank on a flat car set up for it. Under the car's floor was an armored box that held the traversing gear, crew, and ammunition. These cars were placed at the ends of the train. They proved themselves effective, and soon other armored train commanders from the region of PZ 1 also wanted to have them. Thus, early in 1944 the Dünaburg EAW also built a pair for PZ 61,

At times captured T-34 tanks were placed on railroad cars, as here on a line protection train. The width of the tank, though, allowed only flat cars without sidewalls. Photo: W. Rosner/W. Sawodny collection

Naturally anti-tank guns on wheeled mounts were also used provisionally. Here a Soviet 7.62-cm ZIS-3 division cannon is seen on the control car of an armored train (presumably PZ 67) in the spring of 1944. Note also the use of wooden planks and trunks for protection. Photo: W. Sitzius/W. Sawodny collection

At the same time, a German 7.5-cm anti-tank gun 40 was used on the control car of PZ 71. Photo: H. Griebl collection

and a few weeks later an improved type (the tank turret was no longer mounted directly on the car's floor, but on an armored structure with sloping walls, which offered more space inside) for PZ 26. In the spring of 1944 PZ 2 was also supposed to receive such cars, but it did not take place, since it was withdrawn for total rebuilding after losing both its gun cars. Meanwhile, the command office for armored trains in the OKH had taken notice, and the Dünaburg EAW delivered a pair of such cars to the Armored Train Replacement Battalion in Rembertow, where they were tested successfully (these cars were assigned to PZ 16 in June 1944). The Linke-Hofmann firm in Breslau was very soon instructed to build such "tank-destroyer cars" for the armored trains of the improved BP 44 type shortly before they were delivered, and from then on they were part of the standard equipment. The tank turret used was not that of the T-34, but of the German Panzer IV H with the long 7.5-cm L/48 tank gun. These cars, which replaced the control cars (later the latter were placed ahead of them

again), and could be uncoupled from the train automatically, were fitted with electric drive, which allowed them to move independently for short distances (such as back to the armored train). But there was no longer enough time to fit the first three new trains (No. 73-75) that were shortly to be delivered (in June-July 1944) with these cars. They were provided for No. 73 and 75 later. Only as of No. 76 (ready for action in November 1944) were they part of the original equipment, but as of late summer 1944 all the old armored trains that were sent in for overhauling or reequipping were fitted with these cars as well.

PZ 52 received the same Panzer IV H turrets on two normal armored train cars (taken from the line protection train "Blücher"— instead of the previously installed T-34 turrets). These turrets were also intended to be installed on Armored Railcars No. 51 f. But Armored Railcars No. 30-38 built in Italy were each given two 13/40 tank turrets with just one 4.7-cm L/32 tank gun.

The commander of PZ 1, Captain Helmut Walter, had an idea that brought definite progress, and which he undertook along with the engineers when his armored train was overhauled at the Dünaburg EAW in the late autumn of 1943. They mounted the turret of a captured T-34/76 tank on a flat car, which was added to the train in place of a control car. This design was so convincing that all armored trains that arrived at the Dünaburg EAW after that also wanted such "tank-destroyer cars." Here is one added to PZ 61 shortly afterward. Photo: W. Sitzius/W. Sawodny collection

The design of these cars was already improved at the Dünaburg EAW. As previously, a box for the crew had had to be added between the axles under the turret, which was mounted directly on the flat car, but now the whole tank, without its running gear, was mounted on such a car, which itself provided tapered side protection and side aprons over the wheel bearings, as seen here in a tank-destroyer car built for PZ 26 in the spring of 1944. Photo: H. Jäger/W/ Sawodny collection

The Commander of the Armored Trains in the Army High Command and In 6 were also quickly impressed by this idea, and within a few weeks they were prescribed as standard equipment for the improved BP 44, the first train of which was soon to be delivered, though with the turret of a Panzer IV H and a 7.5-cm L/48 tank gun on a specially designed undercarriage and car. Photo: Federal Archives, Koblenz

Naturally, the cannons of the Panhard Scout Car (2.5 cm) and the unloadable tanks (4.7-cm gun in the Somua S 35, 3.7-cm in the Praga 38 (t)) can also be ranked as guns of this type; the last of them could also fire from the train. But all of them were of small caliber, so that they could be used for direct fire on infantry, but no longer against tanks from 1942 on.—This was equally true for the turrets of the Panzer III N with their 7.5-cm L/24 cannons in the heavy scout trains; they were designed in the summer of 1943 but not delivered until the end of 1944. They formed the artillery of this train made up of motor-driven individual cars—tanks running on rails, so to speak. Four of them were planned originally, but—as in the "classic" armored trains—two of them were supposed to be replaced by high-angle weapons. At first the 7.5-cm Skoda M 15 Mountain Gun was discussed for this purpose. This plan was not carried out; instead, two cars were fitted with heavy mortars (12-cm Gr.W. 41, or alternatively the 8-cm Gr.W. 34). Their fixed installation was not done (except provisionally on PZ 79), and the heavy mortars were only used by the infantry outside the train.

The ammunition for the guns had been upgraded in 1941. It now numbered 250 shells for all cannons (whether field, anti-tank, or tank guns, including those installed in escort vehicles), for the howitzer 225, though the combinations of explosive and antitank shells varied greatly.

The Guns of the German Armored Trains (1939-1945)
A. Artillery

Caliber/type	3.7-cm Pak	4.7-cm I.G. Pak	4.7-cm Pak	7.5-cm Geb.K.	7.5-cm I.G.
German type	35/36	Kraftzug (holl.)	Kraftzug (t)	15 (t or ö)	18
Foreign type		Siderius	Skoda A 5	Skoda D 28	
Barrel caliber	L/45 (1.665)	L/39.4 (1.852)	L/43.4 (2.04)	L/26 (1.95)	L/11.8 (0.885)
Weight (kg)	450	373	570	799	400
Shell wt. (kg)	0.625[1] 0.354[2]	2.45[1] 1.47[2]	1.50[1] 1.65[2]	6.5	5.45[1] 3.05[3]
Velocity (m/s)	745 1030	320 660	660 775	345	220 345
Penetration	50mm/500m	44mm/500m	32mm/1500m		75-90mm/3550[3]
Max.range	7.2 km	7 km	5.8 km		3.55 km
Rate of fire	10-15/min				8-12/min
Ammunition	100[1] 150[2]		125[1] 125[2]	250	240 48[3]
Trains	PZ 4	PZ 1, 4	PZ 4	PZ 2, 23-25	PZ 4

Caliber/type	7.5-cm Vers.G	7.5-cm F.K.	7.62-cm F.K.	7.62-cm F.K.	7.62-cm Div.K.
German type	Rheinmetall	02/26 (p)	295/1 (r)	295/2 (r)	298 (r)
Foreign type	Putilov 02/26	02/30	02/30	ZIS-3	
Barrel caliber	L/41 (3.075)	L/30 (2.25)	L/30 (2.286) L/40 (3.048)		L/42 (3.20)
Weight (kg)	1040	1320	1350	1120	
Shell wt. (kg)	6.5	6.4	6.4	6.2[1] 3.05[2]	
Velocity (m/s)	580	593	635	680	680 965
Max. range	5.0 km	8.5 km	9.6 km	12.9 km	13.3 km
Rate of fire	30/min	10/min	6-10/min	6-10/min	15-25/min
Ammunition	125[1] 125[2]	125[1] 125[2]	250[1] PT: 200[1] 50[2]	226[1] 24[2]	
Trains	PZ 3	PZ 7,10,11,21,22	PZ 6,7, all BP 42, PT 16-23	PZ 27,28,30?	PZ 28, 67

Caliber/type	10.7-cm F.K.	10-cm F.H.	10.5-cm F.H.	12.2-cm F.H.
German type	352 (r)	14/19 (p)	18/40	396 (r)
Foreign type	M 10	Skoda 14/19		M 38
Barrel caliber	L/28.4 (3.04)	L/24 (2.40)	L/28 (2.94)	L/22.7 (2.77)
Weight (kg)	2180	1548	1800	2450
Shell wt. (kg)	16.4	16.0	14.8	21.76
Velocity (m/s)	579	395	540	515
Max. range	12.0 km	9.8 km	12.33 km	11.8 km
Rate of fire	6-8/min	6-8/min		
Ammunition		225	151[1] 18[4] 56[5]	
Trains	PZ 28	PZ 10, 21, 32, All BP 42	All BP 44	PZ 32, Training 5?

b. A/A Guns

Caliber/type	2-cm Flak	2-cm Flak	3.7-cm Flak
German type	38	36	
Foreign type		Breda	
Barrel caliber	L/112.6 (2.25)	L/65 (1.30)	L/98 (3.626)
Weight (kg)	420 (Q: 1540)	284	1550
Shell Wt. (kg)	0.132^1 0.148^2	0.135^1 0.150^2	0.623^1 0.658^2
Velocity (m/s)	900 830	830	820 770
Max. range	4.8	5.5	6.5
Rate of fire	220/min (Q: 800)	240/min	120/min
Ammunition	(see text)	720^1	80^2
Trains	all since 1941, Quad (Q) as of 1942	PT 30-38	PZ 32

c. Tank Guns

Caliber/type	2.5-cm KwK	3.7-cm KwK	3.7-cm KwK	4.5-cm KwK	4.7-cm KwK
German type	121 (f)	143 (f)	38 (t)	184/5 (r)	(it)
Foreign type	Hotchkiss	S.A. 38	Skoda A 7		
Barrel caliber	L/73 (1.825)	L/33 (1.111)	L/48 (1.776)	L/46 (2.07)	L/32 (1.504)
Weight (kg)			265		108
Shell wt. (kg)	0.32^2	0.70^2	1.42^1 1.47^2	1.43^2 0.855^4	2.45^2 1.5^4
Velocity (m/s)	920	705	705 740	760 970	630
Penetration	29mm/500m	23mm/500m	34.8/500 $30^{4)2}$	$60^2(82^4)/500$	48mm/400m^2
Max. range			7.4 km		7.0 km
Rate of fire					7-10/min
Ammunition	200^1 50^2 T	125^1	82^2	43^2T 200^1	50^2T
Trains	Panhard Scout	PZ 32	Panzer 38 (t)	PZ 51	PT 30-38
Caliber/type	4.7-cm KwK	7.5-cm KwK	7.5-cm Pak	7.5-cm KwK	7.62-cm KwK
German type	173 (f)	M 37	M 39	M 40	(r)
Foreign type	S.A. 35				
Barrel caliber	L/32.1 (1.509)	L/24 (1.80)	L/48 (3.60)	L/48 (3.60)	L/41.2 (3.139)
Weight (kg)		490			
Shell wt. (kg)	1.72^1	6.8^1 4.4^4	5.74^1 6.8^2 5.0^4	6.8^2 3.2^4	6.3^2 3.04^4
Velocity (m/s)	671	385 450	550 750 450	790 930	662 965
Penetration	50mm/500m	54mm/500m	130mm	151mm	69mm 92mm
Ammunition	250^1	125^1 125^4	40	125^1 $125^{2/4}$	
Trains	S 35 (f) tank	Heavy scout tr.	Jagd-PZ 38	PzJgWg (all PZ)	PZ 1,26, 61, PT 16

Notes:

Elevation and traverse figures were omitted, as they could be much influenced by installation in armored trains. The weight given for the entire gun is that in firing position in the field; it is merely an approximation for installation in armored trains. Barrel lengths are in meters. The stated velocity is the muzzle velocity in meters per second.

The penetration figures for anti-tank (Pak) and tank guns (KwK) indicates the mm of steel plate penetrated at a range given in meters (90-degree striking angle), unless otherwise noted.

Ammunition types: 1. Explosive shell; 2. Anti-tank shell; 3. Hard-core shell; 4. Hollow-charge shell; 5. Fog shell; T. Tracer.

Data for the F.K. 96 n.A. and 16 used on PZ 3 in 1938-1940 are found in the table on page 43.0

When the first armored trains were set up in the summer of 1938 arming them with 2-cm A/A guns was already planned. This was not done at first; they made do with twin A/A MG 34, of which each armored train received two pairs (which remained even after the trains were equipped with A/A guns later). Only in March 1941 were the existing armored trains (No. 1-4, 6, 7, 21, and 22) reequipped with two 2-cm A/A guns each. According to the K.A.N., Flak 30 or 38 could be used, but in practice the more modern model was always used (supplied with 1050 explosive, 60 anti-tank, and 240 anti-tank shells with tracers). This also applied to future new creations, with the exception of the broad gauge trains No. 26-31. The A/A guns—depending on the existing situations—were installed very differently. They could fire not only from the armored train, but each gun had a single-axle Trailer 51, which allowed transport away from the train. This possibility, though, seems to have been used very scarcely. As of May 1942, 2-cm Flak 38 quads were used on new armored trains (PZ 51, Standard Series BP 42/44) instead of single guns. Their ammunition supply was not quadrupled to match their guns, but was increased even more. It now included 6750 explosive shells (tracers) and 120 anti-tank shells and 1830 anti-tank shells (tracers); from 1944 on the proportions of explosive and anti-tank shells were changed as

follows: 2900 explosive shells, 2900 explosives with tracers, 2900 anti-tank shells with tracers. The quads were installed fixedly, with no possibility of use outside the train. The reequipping of older trains from single to quad guns took place very slowly, usually only when larger rebuilding was also undertaken. Thus, some armored trains used the single guns until well into 1944. Usually—especially in the standard versions like the BP 42—the 2-cm A/A quads had the usual shield. On the trains built new or rebuilt in the last months of the war, though, the A/A quad was usually mounted in the open-top "Whirlwind" turret. Whether a batch of them were built especially for the armored trains, or turrets made for A/A tanks were simply used in other ways because of the growing fuel shortage and the priority of tanks armed with cannons, is not known.—For the heavy scout trains (No. 201 f.), on which the A/A guns, contrary to the original plans, were not mounted on the armored railcars but always on low-side cars, the 3.7-cm twin gun 43 was considered as alternative armament to the 2-cm quad, but had been omitted long before production. The only armored train that had two single 3.7-cm A/A 36 guns (plus 2-cm quads) was No. 32, built and used in France in 1944.—A/A armament that differed from this in terms of type appeared only on the armored railcars No. 30-38 built in Italy, each of which had a 2-cm gun made by Breda.

On their establishment in 1938 arming the armored trains with 2-cm A/A guns was considered, but in the first two war years the twin A/A Machine Gun 34 was considered sufficient. This picture of PZ 22 shows the setup of these A/A positions: a round hole was cut in the roof and could be closed by sliding plates. In other cases (especially in captured Czech cars, whether of Austro-Hungarian or Czech origin) suitable platforms were built on the roofs. Photo: Federal Archives, Koblenz

Only before the Russian campaign began were the older armored trains rearmed with the 2-cm Flak 38. They were often installed on added low-side cars, sometimes protected by low armor on the sides. When possible, though, they were set up on their own positions in place of an individual A/A stand, as here on a captured car that served as command and A/A car in PZ 10. Photo: W. Pflaumbaum/W. Sawodny collection

The A/A guns, namely in the form of quads with their high volume of fire, proved to be highly effective. All through the war only two German armored trains were lost to air attacks: PZ 10—surrounded in Kovel and thus immobilized—fell to bombs, and light scout train No. 302 when a shot-down airplane fell on an ammunition train in Kosovo Polye, and the resulting explosion destroyed the railroad station and all the rolling stock that was there. On the other hand, the A/A guns of many armored trains were able to shoot down goodly numbers of enemy aircraft. In ground combat, too, the A/A quad proved to have a strong effect on the enemy's morale as well as a destructive practical effect.

In the autumn of 1944, rocket launchers mounted on railroad cars were also tested by the Armored Train Replacement Battalion. "Nebelwerfer" 41, from whose six mouths (two rows of three) of the launching rack either 28-cm explosive shells or 32-cm burning oil shells could be fired (range ca. 2 km), were mounted on SS cars. These cars were turned over to an armored train operating in the Bohemian area shortly before the war ended, but presumably were never fired.

The infantry of the armored trains used two of the 8-cm Gr.Wf. 34 mortars (supplied as of 1941 with 246 normal and 18 fog grenades per thrower). They were not attached firmly to the train (although flaps in several armored trains had been planned for such use), but were carried by the shock troop for use outside the train. Only in special cases were mortars used to fire from the train; thus they were

For the 2-cm single Flak 38 a two-wheel trailer (Sd.Ah.51) was carried, on which the gun could also be used in action away from the train. Photo: W. Hahn/W. Sawodny collection

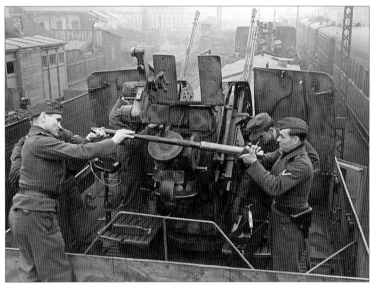

This possibility was eliminated when, in the latter half of 1942, the 2-cm Flak 38 quad was mounted on the standard BP 42 armored trains. Older armored trains were successively rearmed with them, as seen here in the A/A stand of the newly built PZ 23, where a barrel is being changed. The 2-cm quad with its more intense fire proved not only effective in anti-aircraft action but also in ground combat. Photo: S.I.R.P.A./E.C.P.A., Paris

In the last months of the war, the A/A quads were often mounted on armored trains in "Whirlwind" turrets, as here on the reequipped PZ 65 on the Oder front in the spring of 1945. These turrets were actually intended for A/A tanks, but the lack of fuel did not allow them to be used. Photo: F. Gruber/W. Sawodny collection

sometimes mounted temporarily on a flat or low-side car, standing on a bed of sand. In PZ 79, 12-cm mortars of type 42 were mounted in the same manner instead of gun turrets, to fire through holes provided in the roof of the car, but similar installation in cars of the heavy scout trains was not done. Until BP 42, the infantry also had three of the 7.9-mm Panzerbüchse 39 (each with 125 shells), which could not knock the more modern enemy tanks out of action since the French campaign; thus they were eliminated in the transition to BP 44 and the scout trains.—The engineer group of every armored train had one Flamethrower 41.

In the rail protection trains taken over as armored train in 1938, water-cooled heavy MG 08 were still on hand and continued to be used as heavy infantry weapons. Numbers exist for the following armored trains: No. 1: 6; No. 2: 10; No. 3: 16; and No. 5: 10; the other armored trains, being similar to No. 3, may have had numbers in the upper reaches. These machine guns were fixed in the trains and were kept until reequipping in 1940-41. As already noted, two of the twin MG 34 guns were also installed for anti-aircraft defense. In addition, the infantry crew of an armored train was also equipped with mobile heavy and light machine guns, the whole crew with rifles, pistols, and a small number of machine pistols. Only for PZ 3 does precise data exist: 6 heavy MG 08, 6 light MG 08/15, 6 machine pistols, 62 rifles, and 66 pistols.

The 8-cm Gr. Wf. 34 was ideally suited for action with infantry forces outside the train. Photo: W. Hahn/W. Sawodny collection

But the mortars were also used at times from the train, usually by rail protection trains. They were placed on a bed of sand. Protection was provided for the crews by armored sidewalls (that are missing here). Photo: B.f.Z.G. Stuttgart

The 12-cm Gr.Wf. 42, as tall as a man, was used by the heavy scout trains. They were originally to be installed in two cars, which was not done; they were used only outside the trains. But they were installed—out of necessity—in PZ 79; the openings of the armor provided for gun turrets instead of the temporarily unavailable 10.5-cm howitzer. Photo: W. Obermark/W. Sawodny collection

When the rail protection trains were taken over as armored trains their machine weapons were at first included. Here are three light MG 08/15 on a transport cart.
Right: The heavy MG 08 (here on a sled) was also used.
Photos: BPM Schwandorf

The ammunition supply for all ex-rail protection trains in 1938 was 180 rounds per rifle, 24 per pistol, 1536 per machine pistol, and 13,500 per machine gun (11,350 pointed, 1500 with core, and 650 with core and tracer). Data for heavy weapons are available only for PZ 3: 150 rounds per gun, 140 mortar grenades.—For the armored trains made up of captured Czech and Polish material in the spring and summer of 1940, the machine guns seem to have been retained at first (in the Czech cars, four Schwartzlose 7/24, in the Polish four Maxim 08 per "assault car" and two-axle gun car, 7 to 9 Maxim 08 per four-axle gun car). At the start of 1941, the older and water-cooled machine guns were replaced in all existing armored trains by MG 34, which from then on became standard infantry equipment for all new armored trains—aside from machine guns installed in captured armored vehicles. Only as of the summer of 1944 was this type gradually replaced by the MG 42.

Handguns and Machine Guns of the Armored Trains
(as of the beginning of 1942)

Pz	Rifles	Pistols	M.Pistols	Heavy MG	Light MG
2	101	66	14	4	22
3	92	79	13	8	26
4	108	69	12	4	18
6 (Aug. 1942)	77	76	13	2	20
7	103	70	13	4	26
10 (I & II)	102	113	8	-	38
21	111	75	13	4	16
22	103	71	13	4	16
23, 24	99	67	13	4	16
25 (Mar. 1944)	60	77	15	1	16
26-28	76	65	14	-	12
29-31	76	52	13	-	12
27 (May 1942)	93	69	13	-	18
51 (May 1942)	57	60	9	-	10

Light machine guns other than those built into vehicles (tanks and scout cars).

In both the Panhard scout car and the Somua S 35 tank there was always a French 7.5-mm machine gun, with 4500 rounds of normal

Later, inside and outside the armored trains—the air-cooled MG 34 was used, usually in the light version (seen here in the machine-gun port of PZ 1); a few of the heavy type were also on hand, but just one in the BP 42 trains.
Photo: S.I.R.P.A./E.C.P.A., Paris

and 4500 of tracer bullets for each. The supplies for the Czech MG 37 in the Praga 38(t) tanks were somewhat less: 4020 normal and just as many tracer bullets. In the Italian-made armored railcars No. 30-38 there were six 8-mm Breda M 38 machine guns installed (two in the tank turrets, two on each side of the vehicle). The ammunition supply for them is unknown.

Besides the machine guns, the armored train or railcar crews naturally had handguns: rifles (98K carbines), pistols (08), and machine pistols (39/40). For the older armored trains (No. 1-51)—depending on the varying numbers of crewmen—the numbers of machine guns varied just as did those of the handguns (see the table). The ammunition on hand, though, was identical per gun, but the 1942 standard was reduced from that of 1938: 75 rounds for the rifle, 16 for the pistol, 1024 for the machine pistol, and for the heavy and light machine guns 4750 rounds (4150 s.S., 450 S.m.K., 150 S.m.K. tracers). These numbers were retained when a standard for the BP 42 was set with the K.St.N./K.A.N. and gradually equaled by rebuilding almost all the older armored trains. The norm now included one heavy and 16 light machine guns, 59 rifles, 77 pistols, and 15 machine pistols.

A change was made with the modernization to BP 44, in that some of the carbines were replaced by the self-loading Model 43 (with targeting scope); for these, 120 instead of the otherwise customary 75 rounds were on hand; several rifle-grenade devices were also supplied (with 30 explosive, 20 large or 30 small anti-tank, 20 blind, and 20 fog shells per device). The ammunition supply for the machine guns was also changed. While only a change was made to 3950 pointed rounds, 450 with cores and 350 with tracers for the heavy machine guns, the supply for light machine guns was cut by more than one-third, to 2100 pointed rounds, 300 with cores, and 100 with tracers. These numbers also applied to the heavy and light scout trains. Their supply of infantry weapons consisted of:

Trains	Rifles (Carb. 43)	Rifle Gren.	Pistols	Mach. Pistols	Heavy MG	Light MG
PZ 22 (1944)	62 (3)	3	48	20	2	11
PZ BP 44	70 (5)	4	50	18	2	12
Heavy Scout	26 (25)	?	60	21	1	18
Light Scout	19	-	52	11	-	40

In addition, every armored train (from the beginning) carried 180 Type 24 stick grenades and 180 Type 39 egg grenades; the light scout train had only 60 stick grenades. The engineer group had a lot of explosives, not only to destroy rail lines and structures, but also to make their own weapons useless and destroy the entire train if it should get into a hopeless situation.

Naturally, there were very different numbers for the armored railcars with their smaller crews. PT 15, armed with only six light MG 34, had a crew of 26 men with 11 rifles, 12 pistols, and 3 machine pistols. While the ammunition for the machine guns, pistols, and machine pistols equaled the norm, only 20 rounds were on hand for each rifle, plus 60 stick and 60 egg grenades. The twin-turret railcars No. 16-23 had, besides the guns, four light MG 34 and had 21-man crews with 8 rifles, 10 pistols, and 3 machine pistols (same quantities of ammunition as PT 15: 60 stick and 30 egg grenades). The tank-destroyer railcars No. 51 ff. also corresponded to them. Whether the ammunition for those vehicles—like that of the armored trains—was reduced in 1944 is not known. The K.A.N. did not apply to the Italian railcars No. 30-38, thus their ammunition supplies cannot be cited. Along with the already mentioned Italian-built cannons and machine guns, the thirty man crew also had 8 rifles, 13 pistols, and 9 machine pistols (7 of them Model 43).

To conclude, it can be said that the armament with big guns was at first extremely varied. A certain simplification came with the captured Czech and Polish armored trains, but it was completed only with the standard BP 42 toward the end of 1942, since the equipment of the older armored trains was gradually—continuing until the war ended—made to equal it. Similarly to the escort vehicles, though, equipping with captured guns was maintained until well into 1944, and could not have made ammunition supply easy. To be sure, the ammunition of the same-caliber M 15 mountain gun could be fired from the 7.5-cm Skoda D 28 cannon (PZ 2, 23-25) throughout the war (which seems to explain the long use–to the end of 1944–of this antiquated gun). For the Polish 7.5-cm F.K. 02/26 French ammunition could also be used, and for the Russian 7.62-cm F.K. 02/30 the standard ammunition of that caliber, presumably captured in large quantities, was available. The caliber of the 10-cm F.H. 14/19, though, was unusual, and although this gun not only constituted the mass of the Czech artillery in 1939, and had been exported to several eastern and Baltic countries (Poland, Hungary, Romania, Yugoslavia) before 1939, production of suitable ammunition must have become more and more difficult as the war went on. Only with the BP 44 and the scout trains in 1944 was exclusively German armament (10.5-cm F.H. 18/40 and 7.5-cm KwK L/48) used. But even then, the Panhard scout cars and Praga tanks remained with the armored trains, which not only required the acquisition of suitable gun shells, but also that of special French or Czech machine-gun ammunition, along with German types for the armored trains themselves. In the "Littorina" type armored railcars (No. 30-38) only Italian weapons were on hand. To be sure, the K.St.N. for these vehicles bore the note: "Replacing the Italian weapons with German ones is foreseen when Italian ammunition is exhausted." But this step was not reached by the end of the war.

This picture of a line protection train shows almost all of the usual customary handguns used on these trains. The NCO at the right front holds a 39/40 machine pistol, behind the officer with the binoculars (the train leader) is a light MG 34 on a tripod (as also in the second car), and the other soldiers have 98k carbines. Photo: Federal Archives, Koblenz

Escort Vehicles

In the course of the war, the armored trains were assigned more and more independently mobile (on roads or rails) vehicles. This actually applies to the armored railcars as well, which with two exceptions (limited in time) were always subordinated to armored trains. Because of their significance, though, they were assigned a separate chapter.

Just shortly after it was set up, early in September 1938, to PZ 3 (Munich) was attached a six-wheel scout car (Sd.Kfz.231) with police registration number (former rail protection equipment?), which could be equipped to run on rails. This was probably a test vehicle, thus an individual piece. For travel on rails, lowerable rollers with rims were mounted before the front wheels and between the drive wheels. The power was transmitted to the rail by the friction of the road wheels, which were fitted to the railroad gauge of 1437 mm (the rear twin tires were eliminated). The drive was switched practically, on a road crossing of equal level to the tracks. The vehicle could be raised and turned by a jack mounted under it. The armor of the vehicle, which was 5.57 m long, 1.82 m wide, and 2.25 m high, was 14.5 mm thick in front, and 8 mm on the sides and rear; its top speed was 65 kph, its range was 260 km on the road, and 140 km off-road (and presumably on rails). The 2-cm cannon of Sd.Kfz.231 was replaced by a second machine gun (Dreiser type) in the turret; the crew numbered five men (one NCO as leader, two gunners, and two drivers). Damaged in Poland and the western campaign, it was taken out of service at some

unknown time, and whether it was ever again used in the Russian campaign could not be determined (if at all, then only in the very first phase).

Otherwise, only railcars with hand or pedal drive were available for trips on the rails (they were still on hand later), and certain numbers of bicycles were carried for trips on the roads.

The only T-18 railcar built by Tatra in 1926-27 that remained in Czechoslovakia had been captured, as had at least one of the six in Poland (perhaps more, as only one was definitely destroyed). These vehicles, 3.68 m long, 1.75 m wide, and 2.14 m high, with 5- to 8-mm armor and three-man crews (weight 3.7 tons, driven by an air-cooled 1.1-liter two-cylinder motor; speed 50 kph), were made available to the German armored trains as reconnaissance vehicles, and the machine guns originally in their turrets had obviously been removed. As of 1940, each armored train, according to K.A.N.,

The road- and rail-capable six-wheel scout car Sd.Kfz.231 assigned to PZ 3 in 1938 as a reconnaissance vehicle, shown at left with its rail wheels raised (and without weapons) and above with them lowered. Unlike the drawings (below), the vehicle when armed had no cannon, but only two machine guns in its turret.
Photos: F. Englberger and W. Hahn/W. Sawodny collection
Drawings: P. Malmassari

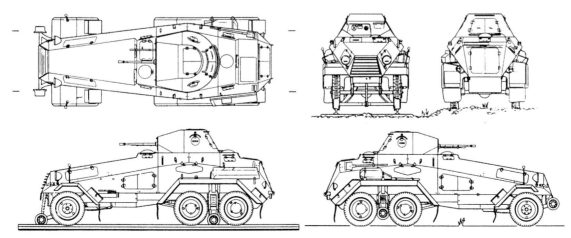

Of the captured Tatra T-18 armored railcars (only for rail use), at least two are documented as being used as reconnaissance vehicles by German armored trains until 1942: the ex-Czech one with PZ 1 (right, at the start of the Russian campaign) and one of the ex-Polish ones with PZ 7 (below, 1940).
Photos: K. H. Münch and T. Schorlemmer/W. Sawodny collection
Drawings: P. Malmassari

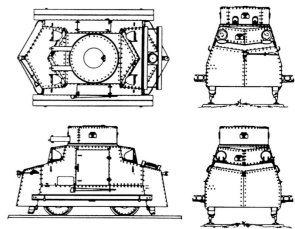

was to receive such a vehicle, but the number of captured railcars would not have allowed them all to be supplied. So the unarmored normal railcars driven by manpower were still used sometimes. Such armored railcars were also considered for the broad gauge armored trains (No. 10, 26-31). Corresponding Soviet vehicles were given to them, to the extent that they fell into German hands. Along with an armored railcar, the K.A.N. also lists a motorcycle adapted to run on rails for every armored train to the summer of 1942. Sidecar cycles would have been best suited for this use. The only pictorially documented vehicle of this type found to date, though, shows a simple 350-cc DKW cycle with its front wheel replaced by a pair

of railroad wheels. The board extension on the axle was presumably supported by another such wheel. The power was transmitted by the friction of the rubber-tired rear wheel on the rail.

During 1942, 40 of the 190 Panhard P 204 scout cars (German No. 38(f)) captured in France were equipped with special rail wheels by the Gothaer Waggonfabrik and the Bergische Stahlindustrie of Remscheid. The wheels could be changed in about 15 minutes, but taking the road wheels along during track travel was not possible. A 105-HP electric engine (77 kW) gave the four-wheel-drive scout car (length 5.14 m, width 2.01 m, height 2.36 m) a speed of 72.5 kph forward and 42 kph backward on the road and 50 kph on the rails.

After the Russian campaign began, captured vehicles of this type (left) were also used with the German armored trains, at right with PZ 10. Photos: Federal Archives, Koblenz, and W. Pflaumbaum/W. Sawodny collection

Along with armored railcars, the "rail motorcycle" was also used by armored trains until 1942. Remarkably, they were not only sidecar types, but—as in the only remaining photo of such a vehicle shows—a 350-cc DKW cycle, which had a wooden side frame added to carry objects. Photo: J. Netzer/W. Sawodny collection

The armor of the 8.3-ton scout car measured 20 mm on the front and sides, 7 mm on top and behind. In the turning turret were a 2.5-cm cannon 141 (f) and a 7.5-mm MG 311 (f); the crew numbered four men. As of the summer of 1942 all armored trains—including those newly put into service (except the light scout trains), as well as the existing ones, which gave up their former armored railcars and rail motorcycles—received two of these Panhard scout cars as reconnaissance vehicles. Although the number was reduced to one per train in 1943-44, the 40 scout cars originally equipped for this purpose, including the losses, could not have sufficed to provide all the trains, and others should have been reequipped too.

In the Russian-Polish War of 1920 several Polish armored trains had carried tanks on flat cars, which—unloaded by an external crane—could operate in the field. Around 1930 the Poles built special "tank carrier cars," which had hydraulic cranes or ramps for fast loading and unloading of the tanks and were even driven by the motor of the tank (TK types, Renault FT 17/18 or 7 TP). Every Polish armored train was assigned several of these cars, and in September 1939 the Germans captured a number of them.

Since 1942 the Panhard 38(f) scout car, captured from the French, which was fitted with additional rail wheels and thus could travel on both roads and tracks (time for change: 15 minutes), was used with the armored trains. Photos: G. Leinen & F. Brunner/W. Sawodny collection and Federal Archives, Koblenz

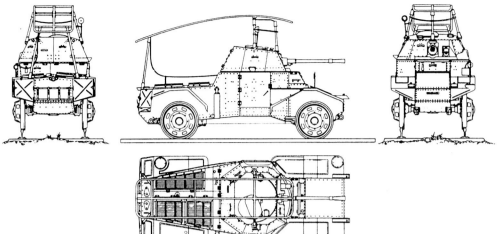

Drawing of the Panhard P 204 (38(f)) scout car. Drawing: P. Malmassari

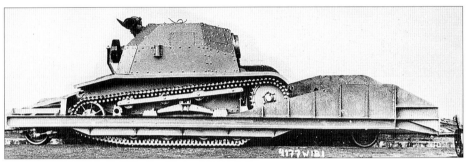

At the beginning of the 1930s, Poland built special cars for tanks (above the TK small tank, powered by the tracks of the tank running on the rails; below, the Renault FT 17 tank, driven by a jointed shaft between the tank motor and the car's rear axle), which—partly with a built-in hydraulic crane— allowed quick loading and unloading of the tank. The vehicles were also coupled together in TK-TK or TK-R-TK combinations. They were probably a model for the later though simpler German means of carrying tanks on railroad cars. Photos: J. Magnuski collection

In the "Panzerzug 1941" and "Panzerzug SP 42" of In 10 of December 1940, this idea of removable tanks carried on railroad cars—now, of course, integrated into the armored train itself—was taken up. The cars built for them were already described in the applicable chapter; they all allowed driving on or off via ramps in the forward direction of the train. This suggestion became reality in the spring of 1941 (with the immediate result of the "Panzerzug 1941") in the broad gauge armored trains set up for the Russian campaign (No. 26-31, instant realization of "Panzerzug 1941"), which received two or three thus-loaded tanks, but no other cannons. They used (as did PZ 25 at the end of 1941) captured French Somua S 35 (739 (f)) tanks. This 20-ton tank (5.30 m long, 2.12 m wide, 2.62 m high; ground pressure 0.85 kg/sq.cm.)—incidentally the first in which the turret and hull were made of cast steel—had armor 55 mm thick on the front and 45 mm on the sides of the turret, and 40 mm on the sides, 35 mm on the front and back, and 20 mm on the bottom of the hull, a 4.7-cm L/32 Tank Gun 173 (f) and a coaxial 7.5-cm MG 311 (f) in the turret. A V-8, 195 HP (143.5 kW) gasoline motor gave it a speed of 40 kph (power-to-weight 9.5 HP or 7 kW per ton) and a range of 260 km. The crew, originally of three men, was raised to four on the German armored trains (commander, loader, radioman, and driver). The Somua S 35 was not only the French Army's best

tank in 1940, but also quite equal to, and in some features (armor and range for example) superior to the German Panzer III, which still made up the mass of the German tank weapon at the start of the Russian campaign. This indicates that at first the use of these armored trains with their tanks in combat was probably considered. Against the new T-34 tank, which appeared with the Russian troops in growing numbers from late autumn 1941 on, the Somua—like the German Panzer III—was very inferior and could be used successfully only against infantry from then on. In partisan action, which was the main task of the armored trains in 1942, it could still be used with success.

The BP 42 standard armored train, which had artillery besides them, received two Praga TNHP-S (38(t)) as removable tanks; not only had great numbers of them been taken in the occupation of Czechoslovakia, but they were still being built until 1942. This 9.7-ton tank (4.90 m long, 2.06 m wide, 2.37 m high) had 25-mm armor on the turret and front and 17.5 mm on the sides. A six-cylinder, 125 HP (92 kW) motor gave it a top speed of 42 kph and a range of 230 km. In the turret it had a 3.7-cm Skoda Tank Gun A 7 L/40 and a coaxial 7.92-mm ZB vz/37 machine gun. A second machine gun of this type was originally installed in the front of the hull, and is also stated thus in the K.A.N. for armored trains.

For the broad gauge armored trains No. 26-31 set up in the spring of 1941, captured French Somua S 35 tanks were carried on specially built flat cars; here a tank is descending the ramp on such a car in PZ 28. Photo: E. Lehle/W. Sawodny collection

In PZ 25 this tank was carried on a normal SS car of the Köln type (here driven forward onto the control car in front). Photo: E. Banser/W. Sawodny collection

For the standard BP 42 armored train (and all later rebuildings), Czech Praga TNHP-S tanks, called 38(t) by the Germans, were carried on cars specially built for them (right). The picture above shows the tank in the hull of the carrier car. Although listed in the K.A.N., the machine gun has been removed from the front of the tank body in all pictures of these vehicles, and the hole is closed with a round steel disc. Photos: H. Hoffmann/W. Sawodny collection

The photos, though, show that this had been removed from all the 38(t) tanks assigned to armored trains and the port closed with a round armor plate. For fighting against tanks, the 38(t) was no longer suitable at the time of its first use on armored trains, what with its weak armor and armament. Its robust and reliable chassis, its high ground clearance (40 cm), and low ground pressure (0.57 kg/sq.cm.) made it a very off-road capable vehicle that remained usable even in the Russian mud season. Thus, it was predestined for partisan fighting away from the rails; it was also used by the advanced observers for the armored train artillery as a mobile support point.—Later Panhard scout cars and 38(t) tanks often successfully covered the breakthroughs of the crews to their own lines when armored trains were cut off and had to be given up.

A deviation from the usual equipment with two 38(t) tanks on the carrier car appeared in PZ 32, built in France and showing several other special features. On the front car was a French Renault R 40 tank; on the rear one, a very unusual self-propelled mount with a Russian 12.2-cm howitzer on a Gw. Lorraine tractor (f). Toward the end of the war it was planned to replace the 38(t) tank on the car with "assault guns." This actually concerned Type 38 "Hetzer" pursuit tanks, which could be loaded on the carrier cars despite their greater width. Of course, effective firing from the train was scarcely possible because of the fixed gun, but when unloaded they were a considerable advantage, especially in fighting against tanks. A report from PZ 64 on January 17, 1945, lists this equipment for it, but only a few armored trains could have been so equipped. In the last days of the war the crews and their "Hetzers" located with the Armored Train Replacement Battalion were sent to the front as anti-tank units.

In 1943 a rail running gear was developed for the Panzer III by the Saurer Works in Vienna. This four-wheel unit could be removed by lifting the tank hydraulically; one axle was driven by the tank

The vehicles on the carrier cars of PZ 32, which was built in France, deviated from the normal plan; this self-propelled mount with a Soviet 12.2-cm F.H.-M 38 on LrS(f) was especially unusual and obviously built only as a prototype. Photo: S.I.R.P.A./E.C.P.A., Paris

On the other carrier car of PZ 32 was a Renault R 40 tank. Photo: S.I.R.P.A./E.C.P.A., Paris

The Saurer Works had developed a removable rail running gear, which was tested on a Panzer III and—driven by the tank motor—allowed speeds up to 100 kph. As opposed to the plans only a few prototypes were built, and the intended use of this gear on other armored vehicles did not take place. Photo: Military Archives, Freiburg

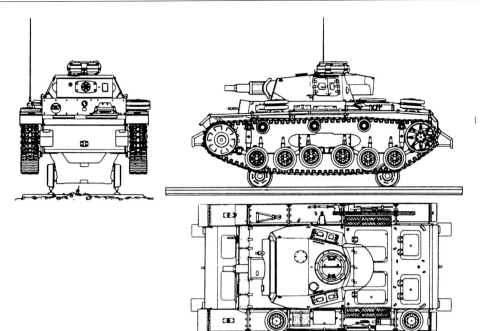

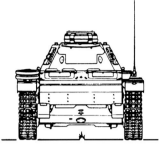

Drawings of the Schienen-Kampfwagen 1 (SK-1), a Panzer III tank with the Saurer rail-wheel system. Drawings: P. Malmassari

Every armored train was issued a sedan. These were usually passenger cars of various types. At left is PZ 28's car before the living quarters train. Later the VW Kübelwagen (above) was used, seen here being unloaded from a transport car. Photos: H. Jäger, E. Lehle/W. Sawodny collection

motor, and the vehicle could reach 100 kph on the rails. An iron model was introduced in October 1943, and in the spring of 1944 plans were made to supply every armored train with several such tanks. But there were never more than a few prototypes of this SK-1 (Schienen-Kampfwagen 1) made; one of these tanks seems to have been issued to Armored Train Regimental Staff No. 1 in Croatia at the end of 1944. Plans to equip other tanks than the Panzer III in this way never were carried out.

Along with these vehicles, the supply train of every armored train also had a light passenger car for the commander. At first these were various types of personal automobiles, then in September 1943 Tatra cars (probably Type 57) were prescribed for this use by the Organization Department of the OKH, and later, mainly the VW Kübelwagen (Kfz. 1, le.gl.PKW) was used. In addition, a light open truck was on hand for transport trips; at first the 1.5-ton Opel Blitz, as of 1944 the two-ton Citroen 23R, but variations from this norm frequently occurred in both cars and trucks. In September 1944 PZ 25 listed a Peugeot car and a Ford truck. A more extensive equipping with road vehicles was received by PZ 10 when it was first set up as two combat trains in December 1941. Not only two passenger cars (one light and one medium) and trucks were listed, but also a medium (350 cc) motorcycle and a heavy sidecar cycle. When the two trains were divided into PZ 10 and 11 in the summer of 1943 these escort vehicles were divided correspondingly; presumably the motorcycles were put aside.

Light trucks were also used; this 1.5-ton Opel Blitz was used by PZ 30. According to K.A.N. they were replaced by two-ton Citroen 23R trucks in 1944. Photo: J. Netzer/W. Sawodny collection

In conclusion, it can be determined that captured vehicles were used almost exclusively as escort vehicles for the armored trains—especially as combat vehicles. For 1939-41 the French Panhard scout cars and Somua tanks and the Czech 38(t) tank (with which several German armored divisions were equipped at the start of the Russian campaign) were considered excellent; at their introduction in the armored trains, though, they were—especially on the eastern

These vehicles were carried on R-cars on transfer trips. The photo shows PZ 26 with the automobile and truck on the front car coupled directly to the armored train, and the Panhard scout car with road wheels on the second car (the supply train followed behind). Photo: W. Hahn/W. Sawodny collection

Below: A four-wheel scout car, Sd.Kfz. 223, fitted with railroad wheels, bears a license plate (A-22 225) that offers riddles. Photo: K. H. Münch collection

Above: After Italy surrendered in September 1943 several armored rail vehicles of that country came into German hands (though the great majority went to Croatia). Here an OM Type 36 car is seen on the narrow gauge Sarajevo-Mostar line. Photo: Federal Archives, Koblenz

Left: During the North African campaign the Germans also ran this captured British Marmon-Herrington Mark 3 scout car on rails. Photo: Federal Archives, Koblenz

front—no longer suitable for front use, but still very useful for fighting partisans.

Finally, it should be noted that—independently of the armored trains—many other armored vehicles of the most varied kinds (armored railcars, scout cars, personnel carriers, etc.) were equipped to run on rails and used to secure rail lines. The surviving photos which have been found and reproduced here probably show just a small number of them.

These armored personnel carriers running on rails are presumably the Croatian "armored railcars" prepared in Slavonski Brod in the spring of 1943, probably built on Steyr 1500A chassis, which were also used as rail-capable trucks. Photo: G. Pehlke/W. Sawodny collection

Means of Communication and Observation

As was already known in World War I, and especially in the following years, the effective use of armored trains essentially depended on outside communication, and their striking power on the internal one. Thus great value was always placed on a variety of means of communication (so that even if one means was lost, communication could be maintained through others). The service instructions for 1938 and 1942 state:

– inside the train: telephone with loudspeaker, locomotive telegraph (only 1938), speaking tube (only 1942), acoustic signals (hooter/signal horn, bell, mouth whistle— the last only in 1938), light signals, messenger.

– outside the train: radio set, rail-line telephone, acoustic signals (locomotive's steam whistle, hooter/signal horn, fog signal), optical signals (flare pistol, signal flags, blinker— the last only 1938), messenger. Of these, signal horns, fog signals, and flags were typical and widely used means of railroad signaling.

Unfortunately, the data on the equipping of the German armored trains with means of communication are very spotty. The K.A.N. is not presented for all the armored trains; it is particularly lacking for the standard BP 42 type (but present for BP 44). For some units, such as the heavy scout trains or armored railcars, this equipment was governed by special regulations from In 7 (also not presented).

Within the train there were four means of command and information: 1. between the commander, technical leader, track observers at the ends of the train (later the subordinate reconnaissance and other armored vehicles were also included), the locomotive driver, and the deputy commander (usually the artillery officer); 2. from the artillery officer to the weapon positions; 3. from the commander to all the cars and their leaders; and 4. inside each car. At first all of them depended almost exclusively (other than mouth whistles and messengers) on wire or tube connections between and within the individual cars of the train.

An experience report on the action of PZ 3 in Poland in 1939 indicates that normal telephones were unsuitable for communication inside the train, since the noise of travel and battle made them very hard to understand; on the other hand, instructions given via microphone to loudspeakers were clear and easy to understand in all situations. The light-signal system proved to be very fragile, since connections and bulbs often fell out as a result of shaking. Horn signals were easy to give and to hear, but their possible variations and thus their usefulness were limited. The machine telegraph and speaking tube, taken from the early days of communication technology, were only used occasionally and soon disappeared. Acoustic signals were used by only a few armored trains as of 1942; they were on hand in the cars of Armored Trains No. 6 and 27. One problem was the communication cables between the cars (for all already noted means of communication); they had to be protected from disturbance or breakage.

An essential means of communication within the armored train was at first the telephone, later amplified to overcome the noise of travel and battle on a loudspeaker (right, upper edge). Photos: W. Obermark and G. Leinen/W. Sawodny collection

At first the most important connection within the train was the telephone network, which was linked, because of World War I experience, with loudspeakers in the cars. Depending on the type of train, there were 20 to 30 Feldfernsprecher, 33 telephones, and a similar number of headphones on hand. Also included in the telephone network was a switchboard with ten connections and two official links, which allowed transmission into the public telephone system.

In mid-1942—with the assigning of vehicles that could operate independently of the train (unloadable tanks, rail-capable armored scout cars)—radio communication joined the telephone. The sets used by the armored troops, the 1.2-watt type ultra-short-wave devices (10 channels between 24.1 and 25 MHz, range 1-3 km), were installed. For PZ 51 (which at first had no tanks) the five sets were distributed as follows: one on the locomotive, two in the command car, one in each Panhard scout car, meaning that the command path, reconnaissance-commander-driver, was first to be equipped. But in general, the total number of radio sets on hand was higher. For the heavy scout trains, which did not have direct connection between the cars, communication probably took place only by radio. The standard B 42 and 44 armored trains and all the older trains rebuilt according to K.St.N/K.A.N. 1169x—as the rod antennas on the individual cars prove—all had radio connections, with sets inside the cars coupled with loudspeakers. They were built in and listed in the K.A.N. records as "Far Reporting Device for Armored Train" (for BP 44—and probably also BP 42—with the suffix "BP"). For reasons of security they were still paralleled by a telephone network. Thus, only five field telephones were indicated (no more head sets), probably for future wire connection with disembarked troop units or connections with external networks.

For outside communication, though, the armored trains used radio almost exclusively. When the Munich rail protection train was taken over as PZ 3 it had a 20-watt radio set, probably the long-wave Tf 15 E, with 150-km range for telegraphy and 35 km for telephoning while standing (15 and 5 km when underway); it can be assumed that the other early armored trains had something similar. Nothing is known of the radio equipment of the captured Czech trains, and the Polish trains had similar equipment (transmission range unknown), with a roof antenna on each assault car; the commander, who was usually not in that car, but had his place in an observation turret on the tender (as in the Russian armored trains), was connected by a field telephone. He himself had a short-wave radio for communication with the escort vehicles (armored railcars and loaded tanks). There was a speaking tube connection with the other cars, and colored fans could be used for optical and horns and sirens for acoustic signals.—When this captured material was taken over for German armored trains, the earlier Polish ones (Armored Trains No. 21 and 22) at first used the materials on hand, but later replaced them with German devices, while the former Czech units were so equipped right away.

In 1940-41 PZ 3 was already equipped with a long- and medium-wave Fu 11 SE 100 radio (100 watts of transmitting power, with 0.2 to 1.1 MHz), for which the following ranges were stated: 450 km for telegraphy, otherwise 100 km with the transmitting mast (carried disassembled), with the roof antenna 60-75 km. There was also a canister radio (probably Torn.Fu. b) with a range of 8 to 12 km for telegraphy and 6 to 8 km otherwise, and 1 to 2 km for use inside the train (because of shielding by the steel walls). These figures come from a data sheet for the armored train and may state maximum values under optimal conditions. In the literature, average ranges of 200 km for telegraph and 70 km for telephone are given for the Fu 11 SE 100. One should keep in mind that the ranges were extremely dependent on the atmospheric and local conditions. The latter played

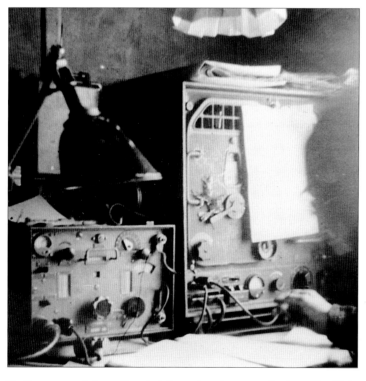

Radio was used from the start for external communication. The high-performance standard set was the Fu 11 SE 100 operating in the long- and medium-wave range. To the left is the all-wave Fu 1 E receiver, which could be used with it and with all radio sets used on armored trains (except the speaking radio in the ultra-short range). Photo: H. Jäger/W. Sawodny collection

According to K.A.N., only the Fu 11 SE 100 is always listed. The fact that other high-performance devices were also used is shown by this picture from PZ 23, stationed in the Balkans, in which a 150-watt short-wave naval transmitter of the Lorenz Lo 150 Fk 41 type is seen. The Fu 1 E receiver is on top of it again. Photo: Federal Archives, Koblenz

a particularly great role for the armored trains. There were great differences, such as whether the train was on an embankment or in a cut, whether, in view of the directional effects of many antennas (such as the frame antenna of the command car), the antenna was in line with its partner radio, and whether it was standing still (vital for long-range radio) or in motion, and these conditions changed constantly, quickly, and considerably. To be sure, a photo shows that in 1941 PZ 23 had a non-K.A.N. but powerful and long-range 150-watt Lorenz Lo 150 Fk 41naval transmitter (short wave 3-18 MHz) installed, but all available documents show that the Fu 11 SE 100 was standard equipment for the armored trains as of 1941 (whether there were deviations from the norm in other trains than PZ 23 cannot be determined for lack of word and photo documentation). Until the beginning of 1942 the kl.Fu.Trupp f (small radio squad) is mentioned, which had a 15-watt Transmitter/Receiver (3 to 7.5 MHz, range ca. 70 km for direct telegraphy, ca. 30 km for telephoning). Later the same device was listed as Fu 19 SE 15. Although it no longer appears in the 1944 K.A.N., other sources show that it was used at least to the end of that year—and probably to the end of the war, installed in the second command car. Despite its meager sending power, with the crank mast extended (8-9 meters) at night it allowed long-range radio communication by waves reflected from the Heaviside Layer by all armored trains on the eastern front with the staff officer, later the Commander of the Armored Trains at the General of the Fast Troops or the Ob.d.H. in Lötzen (partially in Vinnizia in 1942). When the office was withdrawn to Potsdam in the

In the broad gauge armored trains the radio shack was on the tender. Obviously, it was very cramped. Photo: Federal Archives, Koblenz

The radio shack in the command car of a standard BP 42 train did not offer much room either. On the back wall are the ultra-short-wave devices for radio contact within the train and with the armored vehicles; above is Radio Device a, below Fu 5 SE 10U. The main device (Fu 11 SE 100 or Fu 19 SE 15) was in front of the radiomen. Note also the window with the sliding armor panel behind the soldiers. Photo: Federal Archives, Koblenz

The slightly distorted perspective of this look into the radio shack of PZ 68 shows part of the Fu 19 SE 15 short-wave device at the left edge. Below in back is the Fu 5 SE 10U ultra-short-wave device over presumably the Fu 1 E receiver. Photo: O. Babor/W. Sawodny collection

The frame antenna on the command car limited the range of the radios. Thus, the armored trains carried an antenna mast (8-10 meters) which—when the train was stopped—allowed radio communication over longer distances. In PZ 22 the mast was mounted on the roof of the command car. Photo: Federal Archives, Koblenz

Below: On the standard BP 42 armored train the antenna mast could be mounted in a side bracket. Photo: H. Beckmann/W. Sawodny collection

summer of 1944, tests between the two command trains, 72 A and B (one in Berlin, the other at the farthest point on the eastern front), showed that communication was still possible. Thus, no reason was seen to equip the command trains with stronger radio sets.

For radio communication, a tall mast was originally attached to two cars of an armored train, at a suitable distance from each other, and an antenna stretched between them, which naturally had a strong directional effect, so that the position of the train was of great importance. Later telescopic crank masts (8 or 9 meters long) with star-shaped sprays at the end were used, and were attached to the command cars of BP 42 or 44 trains by brackets. To cross great distances, though, an antenna could still be stretched between the

crank masts on the command cars (depending on the differential characteristics). In transit, the roof antennas of the command cars (wires stretched between isolators on the older armored trains, tube frame antennas on the standard trains) were used. Naturally, they had a limited range.—The ultra-short-wave and voice communication was sent via two-meter rod antennas.

In 1944 the medium-wave Fu 22 SE 30 (Pzg) radio, a variation of the Fu 20 SE 39 (30 W, 1.12-3 MHz, range to 150 km for telegraphy, to 50 km for telephoning), was introduced. It was also used in the Panhard scout cars. The same Fu 22 SE 30 (Pzg) was used in the cars of the light scout trains (the equipment for the heavy ones probably corresponded to that of the BP 44 armored trains). Whether the armored railcars used this set or the Fu 11 SE 100 is not clear. Every armored train also had one or two all-wave (0.1-7.1 MHz) Fu 1 TE receivers, which were usable with all the named transmitters. One of them was probably used in the supply train, for which such a receiver was probably sufficient. But they usually had their own radios of the types already named, so that two-way communication was possible. The Fu 1 TE was also used to receive radio messages from disembarked troop units (shock troops, scouting troops, pursuit commands, advanced observers, etc.), for which each train had two canister receivers available, with ranges of 25 km for telegraphy and 12 km for telephoning. Later the ultra-short-wave knapsack devices Type d (100 channels from 33.8 to 38 MHz), with stated ranges of only 10 km for telegraphy and 4 km for telephoning, were also used. The unloadable tanks (Somua S 35 and Praga 38(t)) that were assigned to armored trains later had not only Funksprech a devices but also the 10-W ultra-short-wave Fu 5 SE 10U radios (frequency range 27.2-33.3 MHz, range 2-6 km depending on terrain) usually used in those vehicles. Naturally, a compatible set was used in the armored train.—To decode radio messages the "Enigma" decoding machine was introduced in 1944.

In a training report for PZ 22 on August 1, 1941, the following can be read: Contact with the train could be maintained at ranges up to 25 km with the Kleinfunkstelle a (5-W medium wave transmitter). Disturbances occurred, resulting from the shielding effect of the train's armor plates, the power lines of the electrified rail line, the effect of the train's roof antenna when directions were changed in transit (strong variations of the receiving strength), loosening of linking cables, and different wave settings of transmitters and

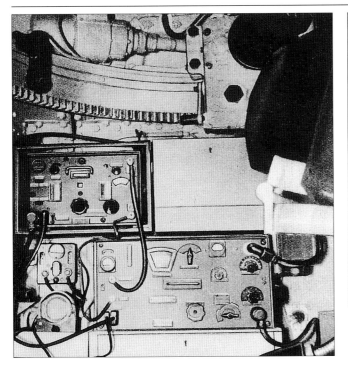

For communication between disembarked troops and the armored train, this short-wave Tornister Funkgerät b (knapsack device) was available. Photo: H. Schütz/W. Sawodny collection

This equipment inside a Panhard scout car shows the medium-wave Fu 22 SE 30 below, and the Fu 1 E receiver above it to the left. Photo: F. Trenkle collection

Right: The advanced observer position of an armored train (right) is connected by telephone wire to the train here. Photo: H. Beckmann/W. Sawodny collection

Below: The Commander of PZ 67, 1st Lt. Hermann Hoppe, with a Field Telephone 33. Photo: H. Hoppe/W. Sawodny collection

receivers (constant tuning was necessary), caused by vibrations during transit and combat, the noise of which also influenced clarity by sparklings and interrupting contacts in the train's internal signal system.

Many of these problems could be eliminated. Later the armored trains' means of communication were described as functional and very effective.

It was already noted that the armored trains' radio systems could be linked to the public network. The use of the railroad's own telephone lines (BASA) was more effective, as it allowed faster, broader, and less disturbed communication, though only with railroad operation offices.—Telephone communication was also available for disembarked troops, who usually carried a small device for this purpose; the light scout trains had two.

Along with the radio and telephone equipment, the armored trains also had other possibilities for outside communication. Naturally, the locomotive's steam whistle could be used anywhere to give acoustic signals. PZ 27 also had two sirens, as did PZ 10 and PT 15.

Every armored train had seven flare pistols and every armored railcar had three, with a collection of appropriate flare cartridges, and until 1943 the armored trains also carried ten sets of hand smoke signals. There were also two pairs of signal flags and a set of cloth signals on hand. Other optical signals could be given with spotlights and signal flashlights (in various colors).

To simplify giving orders a color code was introduced and posted in all armored train cars, which were numbered in order within the train: front (ahead of the locomotive) = yellow, back = green, right = red, left = black. "Move green" meant to go backward, while "disembark black" meant the troops were to leave the train to the left. There were similar simplifications for telegraphic, acoustic, or optical signals:

Attention:	—— —
Forward motion (white light):	... —- ... —- (vv)
Backward motion (green light):	. —- .. —- . (rr)
Stop (red light):	... ... (ss)

In great danger "s o s" was to be given. Other signals were to be agreed on for the occasion.

Like the means of communication, those for observation from the train were of great importance. For them, every armored train had at least two 14Z shear telescopes; in many trains periscopes were installed. There were also goodly numbers (18-28) of 6 x 30 binoculars; the commandant had a pair of 10 x 50 strength, and in the early armored trains so did the leader of the heavy machine-gun platoon. Later the numbers of stronger binoculars were increased. In 1944 the artillery and A/A leaders also received them. To lighten darkness, every armored train had two hand spotlights of 30-cm diameter, and in the light scout trains each of the ten cars had one. The heavy weapons had targeting scopes for direct aiming, and later panoramic scopes. Artillery, A/A guns, mortars, and—if there was one—the heavy machine-gun platoon had their own Type 14 or 34 range finders, later replaced in part by the newer 1 m R. 36 and 0.9 m R. devices.

Every armored train had several—at least two—swinging hand spotlights of 30-cm diameter. The spotter (with 6 x 30 binoculars) shows the equipment that was customarily used for communication with the inside of the train after the initial equipment—telephones with loudspeakers—was dropped, and remained until the end: headphones and strap with microphone. Photo: Federal Archives, Koblenz

Left: For observation purposes, every armored train was equipped with at least two 14Z shear scopes. Photo: federal archives, Koblenz

One of the range finders of an armored train in action, here with the 2-cm A/A gun. Photo: Federal Archives, Koblenz

The Crew

For the rail protection trains taken over by the Wehrmacht in 1938 there are only spotty—if any at all—references to the strength and structure of the crews available, with one exception: for PZ 3 (former Munich rail protection train) the proposal of the VII. Army Corps, which founded it, has survived, including not only a strength statement, but even a precise listing for all the train's cars. The strength is listed as follows:

	Officers	NCO	Men
Commander	1		
Deputy Commander (Artillery Leader)	1		
First Sergeant		1	
Machine-gun platoon leaders		2	
Messenger (repl.-telephone, 1 horn)			4
Command Group	2	3	4
Intelligence troop leader		1	
Radio & telephone troop			8
Knapsack radio troop		1	4
Intelligence Troop		2	12
Rifle group leader	1		
Troop leaders	2		
Riflemen (1 aux. stretcher bearer)			14
Rifle group (also trained as engineers)	3		14
Heavy MG half-platoon leaders	4		
Heavy machine gunners (2 stretcher bearers)			48
Messengers			4
Heavy machine gun platoon	4		52
Mortar group leader	1		
Gunners (1 stretcher bearer)			6
Mortar group	1		6
Gun leaders		2	
Cannoneers			8
Aux. artillery observer	1		
Calculators		2	
Artillery platoon	1		12
Gun leaders		2	
Cannoneers			8
A/A group	2		8
Medical officer	1		
Medics			2
Medical echelon	1		2
Cooks			2
Technical leader	1		
Track observers		4	
Locomotive drivers		2	
Firemen			4
Motor & light service (armorer's aide)			1
Technical crew (provided by Reichsbahn)	1	6	5
Group leader		1	
Construction workers			14
Construction troop		1	14

(provided by Reichsbahn, with infantry training, seen as second rifle troop)

The division among the cars was as follows: Total

1. Gun car — Gun crew (5 men)
A/A crew (1 NCO, 4 men) 10 men

2. Lead car — 2 track observers
1 telephonist
Heavy machine gun half-platoon
(1 NCO, 12 men)

2 messengers 18 men

3. Command car — 1 commander
1 machine-gun platoon leader
1 technical leader
1 telephonist
2 messengers
Half construction troop (1 NCO, 7 men)
Heavy machine-gun half-platoon
(1 NCO, 12 men) 27 men

4. Radio car — 1 intelligence platoon leader
2 radiomen
Knapsack radio troop (1 NCO, 4 men)
1 telephonist
Half construction troop (7 men)
1 mechanic
Relief locomotive crew (1 NCO, 2 men)
20 men

5. Locomotive — 1 locomotive driver
2 firemen 3 men

6. Medical/kitchen car — Medical echelon (1 officer, 2 men)
First sergeant
2 cooks
1 telephonist
Half rifle group (8 men)
2 messengers 17 men

7. Command car — 1 artillery leader (deputy commander)
1 machine-gun platoon leader
1 deputy artillery observer
2 calculators
1 telephonist
Half rifle group (1 NCO, 8 men)
Heavy machine-gun half-platoon
(1 NCO, 12 men)
2 messengers 30 men

8. Lead car — 2 track observers
1 telephonist
Mortar group (1 NCO, 6 men)
Heavy machine-gun half-platoon
(1 NCO, 12 men) 23 men

9, Gun car — Gun crew (5 men)
A/A crew (1 NCO, 4 men) 10 men

The heavy machine-gun half-platoons, the rifle group, the construction troop, the grenade-thrower troop, and the knapsack radio troop (along with their messengers)—thus the greater part of the crew (10 NCOs and 95 men)—could also be used outside the train. In all, the crew was to number 158 (4 officers, 23 NCOs, and 131 men), 27 of whom (1 officer, 7 NCOs, and 19 men) were to be provided by the Reichsbahn. A change was made, though, in that the equipping of the train with the planned 2-cm A/A guns was omitted at first, and their planned crews (2 NCOs, 8 men) were subtracted. This could be evened out in part by the added assignment of two twin A/A machine guns (probably each with a two-man crew) and the connection of the gun cars with the on-board telephone network (1 telephonist each). The track observers were surely soon moved from the lead cars into the gun cars, in which armored observations posts were built.

The same technical crews were assigned to all the other armored trains that were developed from rail protection trains, as were the construction troops (1 NCO and 15 men) provided by the Reichsbahn but also usable as a rifle group. In PZ 4—as in PZ 3—there were also four heavy machine-gun half-platoons, and one can assume that the entire crew would also have had about the same extent. Something

In the initial phase, the armored train crews were taken from the most varied troop units (infantry, artillery, engineers, intelligence troops, army A/A and medical units), and kept their service-arm colors on their shoulder flaps. Here is the crew of PZ 3 in March 1941. Photo: H. Bendl/W. Sawodny collection

similar can also be assumed for the armored trains (No. 6 and 7) equipped with guns (No. 6 apparently only after the Polish campaign). For Armored Trains No, 1, 2, and 5 (without gun crews), though, the upper limit of the crew (including the technical men) was stated as 130 men. In all armored trains the bulk of the manpower consisted of the infantry platoons, armed with the heavy Machine Gun 08 taken over from the rail protection trains and able to fight outside the train; they were amplified by rifle groups (with light machine guns), one of which was also the construction troop. Whether—as in PZ 3—a mortar group was on hand everywhere is possible but not probable. If one subtracts from the crew of PZ 3 the artillery personnel and the mortar group, one arrives at a strength of 127 men, which comes close to the stated limit for Armored Trains No. 1, 2, and 5. In PZ 3's experience report after the Polish campaign it is noted that the calculation leader on hand was merely one corporal, not trained for the job, was on hand. In view of the fact that the armored train was a fully independent unit subordinated to higher staffs, which had to carry out its salary payments and all calculations with financial offices, such as provision and medical offices, on its own responsibility, this was quite unattainable; apparently the supply situation in all was severely neglected in these early times—as can be seen from the portrayal above, no such personnel were included—it had all been severely neglected.

The only armored railcar then on hand (No. 15), set up by Recruiting District I, had as its crew a commander (Lt.), a sergeant (deputy commander), 4 NCOs, 8 light machine gunners, 6 riflemen, and 2 radiomen, plus a technical leader and two engine drivers, the last three all at NCO rank. In the K.St.N. of November 1941 only one more technician was listed; of the four NCOs of the combat crew, one was a railroad engineer, one a radioman, and one a medic; of the 14 men, now all listed as machine gunners (since these guns had been increased from four to six), one was also a field cook, one an armorer's aide, and two stretcher bearers. One of the radiomen was now listed as a messenger (by bicycle) and also a machine gunner.

The armored trains were supplied unmanned to the recruiting district to which they were assigned. Only when they were about to go into action were crews assigned to them from the responsible general command. At the beginning of World War II this was the case in the trains suitable for combat (PZ 3, 4, 6, and 7) up to eight weeks in advance (PZ 3: 7/5, PZ 4: 8/11, PZ 6: 7/10, PZ 7: 8/1/1939), in

order to have time to train the crews. The armored trains intended only for securing tasks, No. 1, 2, and 5, on the other hand, were manned only after the war began (on 9/7-8/1939). Except for PZ 5, the original cadres were to be taken from the replacement troop units (but presumably the first crews were supplied not by them, but by—unknown—active units):

PZ 1: Infantry Replacement Battalion 8 (Frankfurt/Oder)
PZ 2: Infantry Replacement Battalion 10 (Dresden)
PZ 3: Infantry Replacement Battalion 19 (Munich),
    Artillery Replacement Regiment 7
PZ 4: Infantry Replacement Battalion 49 (Breslau)
PZ 6: Infantry Replacement Battalion 43 (Insterburg),
    Artillery Replacement Battalion 37
PZ 7: Infantry Replacement Battalion 2 (Allenstein);
    Light Artillery Replacement Battalion 11 (Heilsberg)

The intelligence and medical troops were assigned from the corresponding replacement battalions of the responsible general command. On PZ 4, the guns (3.7-cm anti-tank and 7.5-cm infantry guns) were obviously manned by infantrymen.

The mortar platoon of PZ 4 with steel helmets. Photo: W. Obermark/W. Sawodny collection

In the already mentioned experience report of PZ 3 it is stated that the units providing the troops for the crew were instructed to assign only the best and boldest men to the armored train, but they did not always do that, but rather used the opportunity to get rid of inept and unpopular soldiers. The time of six and a half weeks allowed to train the crew (before the train moved out on 19 August) would have sufficed to accustom the men to the limited space and poor vision conditions as well as to cooperation, but this could have been done only on the standing train, as the technical crew reached the train only shortly before its departure. Thus, there was no chance for necessary practice runs, and especially for combat-like sharpshooting that could have demonstrated the effect of their weapons to the men. The lack of railroad engineers was also complained of. Neither the construction troop set up by the Reichsbahn nor the rifle group also trained in general engineering work could master their tasks sufficiently in action. It was recommended that crews, except for gun crews and intelligence troops, all be recruited from the railroad engineers. In fact, before the western campaign began in April 1940 the first troop units assigned to Armored Trains No. 1, 2, and 4 came from Railroad Engineer Replacement Battalion 1 (PZ 1 and 2) or Battalion 2 (PZ 4), instead of from infantry replacement units. But soon the railroad engineers formed only the engineer group, which in addition to their special railroad technical tasks of securing and restoring the usability of the lines also had to handle any other engineering tasks, and if need be the technical crew, while at the end of 1940 they returned to the infantry: PZ 1: Infantry Replacement Battalion 512 (Guben); PZ 2: Infantry Replacement Battalion 514; and PZ 4: Infantry Replacement Battalion 49 (now transferred to Strassburg).

In February 1940 Oberost was instructed to set up five armored trains, two of captured Polish (No. 21 and 22) and three of Czech material (No. 23-25). Recommended as a standard for the war strength of all these trains was: Command: one commander, one artillery officer, one medical NCO, two radiomen (NCO), one pay clerk (NCO), two messengers, and one cook; combat crew: one NCO and 6 men per gun, one leader, and two men per machine gun (all men by rank), one rifle and construction troop of one NCO and 12 men; technical crew: one technical leader (officer), two track observers, two locomotive drivers, one group leader (all NCOs), two firemen, one motor and light repairman (the technical crew, as from the beginning and until the war ended—to be provided by the Reichsbahn). For the captured Czech trains (No. 23-25), which were ready for action just a month later, for the available weapons (2 guns, 12 machine guns) there were 3 officers, 12 NCOs, and 66 men. Their combat crews were to be sent by Oberost for engineer training at Railroad Engineer Replacement Battalion 4 (Sperenberg, Recruiting District III), which functioned as the only replacement unit from then on. To be sure, these three armored trains were already disbanded in August 1940. A documented personnel transfer from Armored Trains No. 23 and 24 to PZ 21 and 22, according to this reason, indicates that the NCOs came from the Infantry School, the machine gunners from MG Replacement Company 8 (Zuellichau), the riflemen from Infantry Replacement Battalion 3 (Eberswalde), the artillerymen from the Artillery School or the Artillery Training Regiment in Jüterbog, and some engineers from Engineer Replacement Battalion 23 (Spandau); only the construction troop and technical personnel were actually provided by Railroad Engineer Replacement Battalion 4 (Sperenberg).—The captured Polish trains were set up at Cracow only in June and July 1940. In PZ 21 there were five guns on hand, in PZ 22 three, but the numbers of machine guns are unknown, so that the combat crews cannot be counted precisely. As replacement units, Infantry Replacement Battalion 49, the Light Artillery Replacement Battalion 18, Infantry Intelligence Replacement Company 221, and Medical Replacement Battalion 8 are listed.

When all the available armored trains (PZ 1-4, 6, 7, 21, 22) were finally rearmed with 2-cm A/A guns at the beginning of 1941, the crewmen all came from A/A Replacement Battalion (mot) 52 in Bremen. At that time, numerous other rearmaments (equipping PZ No. 1 and 2 with guns, replacing the captured machine guns and old German MG 08 or 08/15 by Model 34) were carried out. To what extent they influenced the strength and structure of the crews is not known.

In May 1941, the broad gauge armored trains No. 26-31 were set up for the Russian campaign. In them, corresponding to the instant solution of the "Panzerzug 1941" suggested by In 10, a new path was traveled not only in terms of equipment but also of crews. The constant manpower actually consisted only of the command group, the crews of the Somua tanks, the technical personnel, and a few supply train personnel. In detail, these were:

- Command group: one commander, one radioman, one medic, and one man for fog service (ranks of men except commander);
- Per Somua tank (three on PZ 26-28, two on PZ 29-31): one commander (NCO), driver, gunner, machine gunner (men);
- Technical crews: two locomotive drivers (NCO), two firemen;
- Supply train: Two truck drivers for supply trucks (men).

With the establishment of the broad gauge armored trains with the tanks they carried, the black uniforms of the armored troops mixed with the field gray Wehrmacht uniforms. Photo: H. Hoffmann/W. Sawodny collection

There were in all for PZ 26-28 one officer, 5 NCOs, and 16 men, and for PZ 29-31 one officer, 4 NCOs, and 13 men. The infantry crews had to be provided to the train by the unit to which the train was assigned for action.

At the beginning of the Russian campaign, the armored trains No. 23 and 24, which had been taken out of service, were reactivated. The war strengths named in the reactivation instructions was equivalent in combat crews and technical personnel to those of their initial establishment in February 1940, except that the command troop was expanded and restructured: one commander, one artillery officer, one staff sergeant (new), one medical NCO, one radio NCO, three radiomen (formerly two radio NCOs, two messengers), one telephonist (new), one cook, one pay clerk, and one truck driver (new). The Railroad Engineer Replacement Battalion 4 (Sperenberg) was now responsible only for the construction troop and the technical crew; otherwise there were replacement units: Infantry Replacement Battalion 68 (Brandenburg), Light Artillery Replacement Battalion 23 (Potsdam), A/A Replacement Company 104 (Döberitz, later A/A Replacement Battalion (mot) 66 in Wackernheim), Intelligence Replacement Battalion 3 (Potsdam), Medical Replacement Battalion 3 (Berlin-Reinickendorf), and later Fog Replacement Battalion 2 (Bremen). The availability of trucks as supply vehicles for Armored Trains No. 26-31, as for No. 23 and 24, indicates the expansion of the supply system.

Recruiting District III was also responsible for PZ 10, which was made up anew of captured Russian material in November

1941. The replacement units were the same ones as for the two previous trains, with the exception of the A/A guns, which were now supplied by A/A Replacement Battalion (mot) 47 in Würzburg. The specialty of this armored train, two combat trains combined under the same leadership, required a different personnel setup. Thus, the command group now included the commander (leader of the first combat train), deputy commander (leader of the second combat train), a first sergeant, a secretary and sketcher (NCO), four men for fog equipment, a medical officer (doctor), two medical NCOs, two stretcher bearers, the paymaster, a pay clerk (NCO), an armorer (NCO), two armorer's aides (men), one equipment and one provision NCO, one field cook NCO, and three field cooks, plus four truck drivers, two motorcyclists, one shoemaker, and one tailor. There was also the intelligence staff with three radio NCOs (one the leader), six radiomen, three telephonists, and one mechanic. The command and radio groups together thus had a strength of 3 officers, one official, 12 NCOs, and 29 men, in which the strong expansion of the supply train is noteworthy. The technical crew (for both trains) was formed of a technical leader, 4 track observers (NCOs), 4 (later 5) locomotive drivers (NCOs), 2 wagonmasters (motor and light mechanics, NCOs), and 5 firemen. The two combat trains were identically manned. Each included a machine-gun crew (lieutenant as leader, 4 NCOs as group leaders, 32 machine gunners; two of the group leaders and 10 of the gunners were railroad engineers; 6 of the machine gunners were also responsible for the 3 anti-tank rifles), a gun crew (artillery officer, one NCO as leader of the second gun car, 2 observation NCOs, 4 gun leaders (NCOs)), 24 cannoneers (two also range finders, one locksmith), and for the A/A guns one NCO as gun leader, one range finder, four gunners, and one ammunition loader. The combat crew of each train thus consisted of 2 officers, 13 NCOs, and 62 men.

The reestablishment of PZ 25 was done only in December 1941, now in Recruiting District 1. The replacement units named were Infantry Replacement Battalion 176 (Braunsberg), Motorized A/A Replacement Battalion 31 (Heiligenbeil), and Intelligence Replacement Battalion 1 (Königsberg). For the Somua S 35 tanks used at first instead of artillery, PanzerJäger Replacement Battalion 1 (Allenstein) was responsible. The technical crew, though, came from Railroad Engineer Replacement Battalion 1 (Fürstenwalde).

With the subordination of the armored trains to the Fast Troops in the summer of 1941, the variety of uniforms and service arm colors that previously prevailed because of the different origins of the individual crew members ended. The service arm color was now the uniform rose of the fast troops or armored troops, and a special marker was the Gothic "E" on the shoulder flaps.

On the shoulder flaps of this 1st Lieutenant (Friedel Wesche, Commander of PZ 63), the Gothic "E" of the railroad armored trains (combined with the rose service arm color) can be seen. Photo: Federal Archives, Koblenz

From 1943 on, the armored train crews wore the field-gray special clothing of the armored troops, with a short jacket and long trousers with laced boots. The crew of PZ 66 is seen wearing steel helmets. Photo: O. Babor/W. Sawodny collection

From 1943 on the special uniform of field cap, short jacket, long trousers, and laced boots was issued; technical personnel and gun crews wore black or light gray-green protective clothing.

On April 1, 1942, the Armored Train Replacement Battalion was set up in Rembertow and belonged to Recruiting District I. From then on it was the replacement unit for all armored trains and all involved troop branches. Only the medical personnel—also for all trains—was still provided by Medical Replacement Battalion 1 in Tapiau (Defense Zone I). On 1 October of that year a training battalion (which was later united with the replacement battalion) was added. In Rembertow, not only were soldiers assigned by other units for special service on the armored trains instructed, but so were recruits in growing numbers right after basic training. For a long time these two reservoirs more or less kept the manpower balanced. Simultaneously with the training battalion, an Armored Train Instructional Company, at which junior officers were trained, was set up at the Field NCO School for the Fast Troops (later Armored Troops) in Rembertow. Only for the officers did other sources have to be used at first. Then as of 1943 were ROB (Reserve Officer Applicant) courses given by the Armored Train Replacement Battalion, so that at least on the level of platoon leaders replacements could be drawn on internally, and only the company leaders (armored train commanders) had to be trained in facilities of the Armored Troops outside the Replacement Battalion. With the creation of the Armored Train Regimental Staff in 1944 and the paired use of armored trains, half of these company leader positions were upgraded to battalion leader positions, whose holders then led a pair of armored trains.—The members of the armored train service arm were classed as special troops who could not be used for any other purpose. Thus, if they had lost their train, they were to be marched immediately back to their train or to the Armored Train Replacement Battalion, and generally avoided, even toward the end of the war, the notorious "hero claw," those field police and other commands that gathered troops scattered in threatening front situations in the hinterlands, or others separated from their units, lumped them together into alarm companies, and sent them into battle.

For most of the armored trains that existed then (except No. 1 and 25, for which the same can surely be assumed), K.St.N. of February 1942 exists, giving information on the exact structure of the crews. It may even be that some of their features had not been instituted at that time, but even earlier—for Armored Trains No. 1-7 perhaps since their reequipping in the winter of 1940-41, but were not recorded until then. With the exception of the already noted special case of PZ 10 with its two combat trains, the composition from the individual service arms is very similar, and even in head counts only a few deviations occur on account of differences in the weapons they used.

The command group (including supply train) consisted of the commander, deputy commander, the first sergeant, a secretary and sketcher (NCO), a messenger (two on Armored Trains No. 1-7), two fog laying men, a medical officer, an armorer (NCO) with two assistants, an equipment NCO, a kitchen NCO with a field cook, a paymaster, an account clerk (NCO), two truck drivers, a shoemaker, and a tailor, making three officers, one official, 7 NCOs, and 10 men (11 in PZ 1-7). The intelligence troop always numbered 2 NCOs (troop leader and radio NCO) and 10 men (5 radiomen, 4 telephonists, and one mechanic). If two guns were carried, the artillery platoon included the platoon leader (Lt.), an aiming NCO, one gun leader (NCO), one aimer, and four cannoneers per gun, for a total besides the officer of 3 NCOs and 10 men; this was probably also true of PZ 25 when it was rearmed with two cannons at the end of 1942. In PZ 21 (5 guns) and PZ 23 (3 guns) there were, besides the gun crews numbering as above and the artillery platoon leader, also two aiming NCOs and one observer (NCO) on hand, so that the total strength of the artillery platoon was 1 officer, 8 NCOs, and 25 men or 1 officer, 6 NCOs, and 15 men. In PZ 4 there was no artillery platoon leader; each of the two anti-tank guns was operated by one NCO as gun leader, one range finder, one aiming gunner, and two gunners; each of the two infantry guns by one NCO as gun leader and 6 men. The anti-tank group probably numbered the same in PZ 1.

The infantry of the armored trains normally consisted of a rifle platoon armed with light machine guns, and also supplied with anti-tank weapons and mortars (one lieutenant as platoon leader, two messengers, four groups with an NCO as leader and 9 men, in all one officer, 4 NCOs, 38 men) and a heavy machine-gun platoon (one lieutenant as platoon leader, 2 messengers, 2 groups, each with an aiming NCO who was also the group leader, a range finder, two machine-gun leaders (NCOs), two aiming gunners and 8 men); in all one officer, 6 NCOs, and 24 men. On PZ 7 the heavy machine-gun platoon, which also had light machine guns, was increased by 6 men to 30. On PZ 3 both infantry platoons were equipped with heavy and light machine guns and thus had the same strengths: one officer, 6 NCOs, and 32 men (as the heavy machine-gun platoon, but 8 more men). All the armored trains also had a shock troop of one NCO and 11 men, mobile on bicycles and armed with light machine guns, an A/A half platoon (single 2-cm guns) with a half platoon leader, two gun leaders (all three NCOs), and 10 men, one engineer group armed with light machine gun and flamethrower (2 NCOs as group leaders, 9 men), plus the technical crew: technical leader (Lt.), 2 track observers, and 2 loco drivers (NCOs), one light and motor mechanic (NCO), and three firemen. For the entire crews of Armored Trains 1 to 24 there were thus 6 or 7 officers, one paymaster, 32 to 38 NCOs (11 to 13 of them sergeant positions), including besides the first sergeant in every case the armorer, the radio troop leader, and

In snow the disembarked troops put on appropriate camouflage clothing. Photo: W. Hahn/W. Sawodny collection

one of the loco drivers, who was simultaneously the deputy technical leader), and 124 to 140 men. From the men there were to be six auxiliary stretcher bearers chosen, and one officer and one NCO were responsible for gas protection, and a gas tracing troop of one leader and three men was likewise selected from the crew.

It is interesting that at the beginning of January 1942 there already appeared a K.St.N. for the broad gauge armored trains, oriented to the data above and also including a constant infantry crew (their temporary formation from the troop had not worked out). Thus, not only the command group, including the supply train and the technical crew, were envisioned as expanded, but a rifle platoon, a shock troop, an engineer group, and an A/A half platoon were also provided, as well as an intelligence troop, which was reduced by two telephones to one NCO and 8 men. There were also the crews of the Somua tanks (NCO as leader, loader, radioman, driver) with one NCO as technical mechanic for the tanks. Eliminated—in comparison with the other armored trains—were the heavy machine-gun platoon and the artillery platoon, so that the total strength was 5 officers, one paymaster, 27 (PZ 27-31) or 28 (PZ 26-28) NCOs, and 95 (PZ 29-31) or 98 (PZ 26-28) men. It is questionable, of course, whether these numbers were ever sustained. PZ 29 was lost in January 1942, PZ 27 and 28 already had gun cars at that time (for which a K.St.N. could be found only for PZ 27), and even PZ 26, which—with a captured Russian car and two makeshift armored infantry cars—still was quite ready to take this very expanded crew, shows one quad instead of the planned two single 2-cm A/A guns listed in the K.St.N. The surviving change reports of these armored trains let us conclude that expanding the crews took place only as of May (and extending to August) 1942.

At this time, PZ 51 was set up anew and Armored Trains No. 6 and 27 were rearmed; their K.St.N. survive, showing the transition to the crew structure of the standard BP 42 armored train, the first example of which was delivered in that same autumn of 1942. In the command groups of PZ 27 and 51 the fog service was dropped, and in PZ 6 so was the deputy commander. The fact that there was no radio NCO on PZ 51 is probably because of the limited space in that smaller train. Otherwise the intelligence troop, like the engineer group and the technical crew, were retained at their former extent.

Only PZ 27 had a full A/A half platoon; in PZ 6 the half platoon leader was dropped, while in PZ 51 a 2-cm quad replaced the two single guns with an NCO as gun leader, a range finder, a loading gunner, and four cannoneers. PZ 6 had two full infantry platoons, a light machine-gun platoon with a lieutenant as platoon leader, 5 NCOs, and 36 men, from which the three-man crew of the Panhard armored scout car already carried on this train was recruited, plus a heavy platoon which, besides the platoon leader (Lt.), a range finder, and two messengers, consisted of a heavy machine-gun group (3 NCOs, 10 men) and a mortar group (2 NCOs, 6 men)—the anti-tank rifles were also assigned to this platoon. Two infantry platoons of the same form were also listed for PZ 51, but the light machine-gun platoon is very limited, including besides the platoon leader (master sergeant) only two NCOs and 20 men, while the heavy platoon was increased to one officer, 6 NCOs, and 20 men by a specified group leader (NCO) and range finder for the mortar. In PZ 27 the infantry platoon had its full strength (1 officer, 4 NCOs, and 38 men), and there were also two light machine-gun groups adding up to 2 NCOs and 16 men (there were no heavy machine guns on that train). A special shock troop is no longer found anywhere; it was assembled from the infantry and engineer forces when needed. Although Armored Trains No. 6 and 27 were armed with the same guns (four 7.62-cm F.K. 295(r)), the strength of the artillery platoons varied: while PZ 27 had a platoon leader (Lt.), two aiming NCOs, and four gun leaders, plus another NCO as observer, plus four aiming cannoneers and 16 cannoneers, PZ 6 had an observer at lower rank (for special use), and the number of cannoneers was decreased to 12 (as later in BP 42). PZ 51, with its four tank turrets, naturally had a different crew: just two group leaders (NCO), plus four aiming and four loading gunners. PZ 27, like PZ 6, already had two Panhard scout cars, whose crews, like those of PZ 51, were taken from the infantry. There were also two Somua tanks (later replaced by 38(t)) loaded on carrier cars, with the usual four-man (one NCO) crews and an additional tank mechanic who was eliminated when the 38(t) tank arrived.—PZ 51 received its two unloadable 38(t) tanks only when rearmed early in 1944.—The total crew strengths (minus a tank group on PZ 51) were:

PZ 6:   6 officers, 1 official, 34 NCOs, 112 men
PZ 27: 6 officers, 1 official, 35 NCOs, 120 men
PZ 51: 5 officers, 1 official, 27 NCOs, 84 men

The officer corps of an armored train usually included six men. From left to right: the technical leader (special leader at officer rank), paymaster (official at officer rank), artillery officer, commander (Captain Heinz Becker of PZ 65), infantry officer, and doctor. Photo: W. Geipel/W. Sawodny collection

On February 1, 1943, the K.St.N. 1169x for the standard BP 42 armored trains (No. 61ff) appeared, to which, with very few exceptions (PZ 22 and 51, perhaps also PZ 25, 28, and 52), the older armored trains were also converted, a process that dragged out almost to the war's end.

The command group (including the supply train) in which a deputy commander (this job was done by the oldest platoon leader in service, preferably that of the artillery platoon) and the fog personnel were gone and only one messenger remained, had the same extent and composition as in PZ 6 (2 officers, 1 official, 7 NCOs, and 8 men). The intelligence troop, which was now subordinate to the command group, likewise equaled the earlier norm (2 NCOs, 10 men, two simultaneously radiomen for the Panhard scout cars). This applied equally to the technical crew (1 officer, 5 NCOs, and 3 men). All the infantry forces were combined in the first platoon. Besides the platoon leader it consisted of:

– Mortar group: 2 NCOs as thrower leaders (one also group leader), 8 mortar shooters (this group was also assigned the anti-tank rifles)
– Heavy machine-gun group: a troop leader (also aiming NCO), one machine-gun leader (NCO), one range finder (also for mortars), one aimer, 4 machine gunners, one messenger (2 NCOs, 7 men);
– Light machine-gun group: 3 NCOs (one group leader, 2 simultaneously leaders of the Panhard scout cars), 17 machine-gunners (4 also drivers of the Panhard scout cars on the road);
– Engineer group: 2 NCOs (one of them group leader), 9 armored train engineers (one also auxiliary fireman), one Panhard driver for use on rails.

The entire infantry platoon thus had a strength of 1 officer, 9 NCOs, and 41 men; a shock troop was to be formed out of these forces.

The second platoon (with a lieutenant as platoon leader) included:

– Artillery crew: two aiming NCOs, 1 observer (for special use), 4 gun leaders (NCOs), 4 aiming cannoneers, 12 cannoneers (6 NCOs, 17 men);
– A/A group: 2 NCOs as gun leaders, 12 men (two simultaneously range finders), quad gun crew as on PZ 51;
– Tank group: for each of the two 38(t) tanks two NCOs (driver and aiming gunner) and 2 men (driver and radioman); the total was thus 1 officer, 12 NCOs, and 33 men.

For the standard BP 42 armored train there was an entire crew of 5 officers, one official, 35 NCOs, and 95 men. Twelve of the NCO positions were sergeant ranks (including the first sergeant, the armorer, the radio troop leader, and one of the locomotive drivers): of the men, 8 were to be chosen as auxiliary stretcher bearers; one officer and one NCO handled the gas protection tasks, and a gas troop of one leader and 3 men was to be formed.—In the process of reorganizing the back line services (OKH command of December 5, 1943), in all armored trains, according to K.St.N. 1169x of December 5, 1943, the positions of the pay clerk (the work was to be taken over by the paymaster), one of the armorer's aides, and the field cook were eliminated.

From the first Wehrmacht armored trains (1938) to BP 42, the adapting to practical needs (such as in expanding the supply trains), the economic use of the positions (such as in reducing officers' positions or structuring the command group), and above all the shifting of weight from the infantry (which at first sometimes formed the entire combat group) to the heavy weapons (artillery, A/A guns, tanks) were very clearly meant to be carried out.

In the summer of 1944 the BP 42 armored train was upgraded to BP 44 (K.St.N. of 8/1/1944). Along with modernizing weapons, a reorganization of the crew (with almost the same number of men) was carried out. The supply train was taken out of the command group. The latter now consisted of the commander, the command troop with a troop leader (NCO) and three messengers, the medical officer and NCO, and the intelligence troop with a troop leader, a radio NCO, 8 radiomen (simultaneously telephonists), and a mechanic; in all 2 officers, 4 NCOs, and 12 men. The armored road vehicles (two 38(t) tanks and one Panhard scout car) were made into a tank and reconnaissance group, with two NCOs and two men for each 38(t) and one NCO and 3 men for the Panhard. The armored grenadier platoon included the leader of the action group (lieutenant, also platoon leader), the platoon troop (1 NCO, 2 messengers), two armored grenadier groups, each with a group leader (NCO), 4 machine gunners and 7 other gunners, an armored engineer group (1 NCO and 9 men) and a mortar group (2 NCOs as mortar leaders, one of them also group leader), and 8 gunners, totaling one officer, 6 NCOs, and 41 men (3 NCOs fewer than the infantry platoon of BP 42). A second lieutenant as leader of the heavy armored train weapons was also the leader of the armored train battery. This consisted of the battery troop (one battery NCO, an advanced observer (NCO), one messenger and likewise observer), and the gun echelon with four gun leaders (NCOs), 4 aiming cannoneers, and 12 cannoneers (with 1 officer, 6 NCOs, and 17 men, the same strength as in BP 42). Also subordinate to the leader of the heavy armored train weapons were the newly added heavy anti-tank half platoon (2 NCOs as gun leaders, 2 aiming cannoneers, 2 cannoneers) and the armored A/A half platoon (2 NCOs as gun leaders, 12 A/A gunners, two of them range finders, as in BP 42). The technical crew corresponded to the former status (1 officer, 5 NCOs, and 3 men), the now separately conducted supply train included the paymaster, the first sergeant, the NCO as secretary,

Since the locomotive personnel had no clear view to the front the track observer in the lead wagon was very important. Photo: W. Sawodny collection

Above left: The locomotive crew wore black overalls as their work clothes. Photo: W. Hartmann/W. Sawodny collection *Above right:* The gun crews too—whether artillery or A/A guns—wore overalls at work; here both black and light gray-green types can be seen. At right is presumably the Commander of PZ 51, Captain Paul Huhn. Photo: A. Hagemaier/W. Sawodny collection

the armorer with one assistant, the equipment NCO, the field cook NCO with one field cook, four drivers, one shoemaker, and one tailor (1 official, 5 NCOs, and 6 men). The now separate crew of the Panhard scout car and the new anti-tank half platoon not only made up for the three NCOs cut from the armored grenadier platoon, but also added seven men compared to BP 42 (BP 44: 5 officers, 1 official, 35 NCOs, and 102 men).

On the same date (August 1, 1944) the final K.St.N. 1170x for the heavy armored scout train (s.Sp.) appeared.

Command Group: one commander, one company troop leader (NCO, also railroad engineer), crew of the Panhard scout car (one NCO as leader, one aiming gunner and radioman, 2 drivers), one medical officer and one NCO, one switching and driving master (master sergeant), 2 track observers (NCO), radio troop, consisting of troop leader (master sergeant), radio NCO, 5 radiomen (one of them also mechanic), one driver for armored scout car (in all 2 officers, 8 NCOs, 9 men with one scout car).

Infantry platoon: One platoon leader (Lt.), one platoon troop leader (NCO), one messenger, mortar group with 2 NCOs as leaders (one also group leader) and 6 gunners; two machine-gun groups with 2 NCOs as group leaders, 8 machine gunners and 12 other gunners; engineer group with one leader (NCO) and 10 engineers; 4 drivers for armored rail scout cars (in all, 1 officer, 6 NCOs, 41 men with 4 scout cars).

Artillery platoon: one platoon leader (Lt.), 2 aiming NCOs (one also platoon troop leader, the other observer), one messenger; gun crew: 2 gun leaders (NCOs) and 6 cannoneers; mortar group: 2 thrower leaders (NCOs), 6 mortar gunners (for heavy mortars); A/A group: 2 A/A gun leaders (NCOs), 2 range finders, 10 A/A cannoneers; in all, 7 drivers for armored rail scout cars; tank group: 4 NCOs (2 commanders, 2 drivers) and 4 men (2 aiming gunners, 2 radiomen) for the two 38(t) tanks (in all, 1 officer, 12 NCOs, 38 men).

Supply train: one paymaster, one first sergeant, one secretary NCO, one armorer (NCO) with one helper, one equipment NCO, one field cook NCO, 2 drivers, one shoemaker, one tailor, repair troop with one NCO for vehicle service, and 2 motor locksmiths (in all, one official, 6 NCOs, 7 men).

The entire heavy scout train, according to the K.St.N., thus had a crew of four officers, one official, 32 NCOs, and 95 men. Of the

NCO positions 11 were for sergeants; among the men six auxiliary stretcher bearers and the usual gas protection personnel were to be chosen; in the supply train, two positions were to be filled by volunteer helpers. According to this K.St.N., the heavy scout train should have 12 cars, but in reality these trains never had more than eight. The quad flak guns were all mounted on S-cars; obviously missing were the two cars for the heavy mortars, which could not be deployed from the train out. The corresponding group was—for use outside the train—accommodated otherwise. From the previously named figures, the drivers for the corresponding scout cars were also dropped. On the other hand, the heavy scout trains immediately received an additional steam locomotive, since at the time of their first service (end of 1944) the fuel shortage allowed them to be motor driven only in exceptional cases. For the locomotive there was a technical crew of two loco drivers (NCOs) and three firemen; they came from the Reichsbahn, as did the scout car drivers, the switching and driving master, and the track observers.

In the light armored scout train (l.Sp.), on the other hand, all ten scout cars that formed it were equally crewed by an NCO as leader, four machine gunners, and the driver (who was also the radioman). In two of the cars, the NCO and machine gunners were also trained in engineering work (total 2 NCOs and 8 men). Only in the command car were there, besides the driver, the commander, one radio and one medical NCO, plus another radioman (also machine gunner); in the command car for the second half-train, besides an officer as platoon leader and the driver, a radio NCO, and three machine gunners. The scout-car drivers were provided by the Reichsbahn and had additional radio training; the machine gunners assigned as spare drivers belonged to the Wehrmacht but had been trained by the Reichsbahn as drivers. The combat crew of the light scout car train thus added up to 2 officers, 11 NCOs (three of them sergeants), and 46 men. Then came the supply train with a first sergeant, the bookkeeper (NCO), a secretary, the field cook NCO, the armorer (sergeant) with one helper, a motor locksmith (NCO) and a mechanic, two truck drivers, one shoemaker, and one tailor (in all, 5 NCOs and 7 men).

Of the armored railcars, the crew of No. 15, in service since 1938 and armed only with machine guns, was examined above. As of the end of 1943, the captured Soviet Railcars No. 17-23 were added, for which the K.St.N. of 1/1/1945 lists the following crew (which probably also applies to the similarly crewed PT 16): one artillery officer as commander, one medical NCO, the crews of the two guns numbering two gun leaders (NCOs), one aiming NCO, two aiming cannoneers and 6 cannoneers (one of them also the armorer's aide, one a radioman), a machine-gun crew of one gun leader (NCO) and 3 machine gunners (one of them also a messenger, one a field cook), two NCOs as railcar drivers (one of them also a motor locksmith), one radio NCO and one radioman; among the NCOs was one sergeant. The PanzerJäger Railcars (No. 51 ff., with two Panzer IV turrets) built shortly before the war ended had the same total crews (1 officer, 8 NCOs, and 12 men), but the gun crews included only two gun leaders, one aiming NCO, two aiming and two loading gunners (one an armorer's aide), but four (instead of three) machine gunners and two (instead of one) radiomen, plus two additional armored train engineers. Although the armored railcars of the Italian "Littorina" type (No. 30-38) had larger crews (7 NCOs and 23 men), they were only commanded by a first sergeant. Along with these commanders, the crew included one radio NCO, 7 radiomen (four also machine gunners), one intelligence mechanic, one mechanic, one NCO as gun leader, also another aimer and two loaders as the gun crew, one NCO, and two loaders as the A/A crew, one leader and three men for the mortar, one NCO as machine-gun group leader with seven machine gunners (two of them also railroad engineers), and two NCOs as railcar drivers (one also a motor locksmith).

When a task required it, the crew of an armored train could be augmented by further troops (infantry or engineers), but the cramped space inside the train limited the number to two or three groups. By hitching on more cars, which could require an additional locomotive, the transport capacity could—though without armor protection—be increased to the strength of a battalion.

A mottled camouflage suit is worn here by the Commander of PZ 11, 1st Lt. Rolf Lorscheidt. On the right side of the cap is a death's head, the unofficial emblem of this armored train. Photo: R. Lorscheidt/W. Sawodny collection

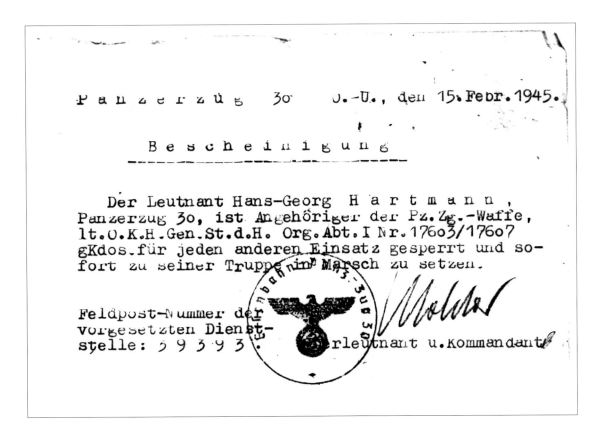

These certificates declared the members of armored train crews to be members of a special troop and protected them to the war's end from the so-called "hero claw" (Heldenklau). The staffs that gathered separated men in the hinterlands and sent them to the front as hastily formed alarm units. W. Sawodny collection

Combat History

Armored Trains Elsewhere in Europe—An Overview

Before the experiences of the German armored trains in World War II are recounted in detail, a brief outline of their development in other European countries will be given. Neither the western, northern, nor southern European lands had permanent armored trains at the end of World War I. In the Spanish Civil War, to be sure, the Republican side had put several such units (surely based on Russian examples) into service, but they remained fairly unsuccessful. When the Germans, in the western campaign, reached the Channel and Atlantic coasts and a crossing to Great Britain was feared, the British, at the end of June 1940, set up twelve armored trains (known by letters A to M), which were to protect the coast from the Channel to Scotland. A thirteenth "miniature" armored train was even placed on the 40-cm track of the Romney, Hythe, and Dymchurch Railway south of Folkestone. In the spring of 1941 the British crews, except the technical crews and, at first, the radiomen, were replaced by Polish troops. The trains remained in service until long after the time when an invasion threatened. The first was disbanded in April 1942, the majority between April and September 1943, and five only in November 1944.

In Eastern Europe, though, there was no country that did not have a more or less large number of armored trains since 1918. The leaders were the Soviet Union and Poland. In 1921—after the end of the Revolution—the former had more than 100 such units, while Poland had put a total of 85 of them into service between 1918 and 1921. In 1920-21 there were about 10 armored trains in Finland, ten in Estonia, at least six in Latvia, and three in Lithuania. Czechoslovakia had nine armored trains, three of which came from Austria-Hungary, just as in Hungary, where the total was twelve. Much less is known of the other Balkan states: Romania had four armored trains, two for broad and two for standard gauge (as of 1926), and Yugoslavia had at least one former Austro-Hungarian unit and four of their own construction; no data survive from Bulgaria.

The time of disarmament in the twenties, of course, brought a reduction in these figures. In the Soviet Union in mid-1931 there were still some 40 armored trains on hand. They were distributed among the army, navy, and NKVD, and organized in armored train divisions of three combat trains each, two light and one heavy, along with reconnaissance vehicles (armored railcars) and a supply train. The combat trains included—as already in the Revolution—besides the armored locomotive, which also held the command post, two armored cars, those of the light trains armed with two 7.62-cm cannons, those of the heavy trains usually with one larger-caliber

A light Soviet armored train of Type BP 35. Each car bore two turrets with short-barreled (L/30) 7.62-cm F.K. 02/30. Photo: A. Gutmann collection

The heavy version of the BP 35 carried only one turret with a 10.7-cm F.K. M10. Photo: N. Bartel collection

gun (10.7, 12.2, or 15.2-cm). In the thirties the armored train weapon was expanded, with the BP 35 armored train type following the same pattern. The four-axle cars were fitted with armored box bodies with a hexagonal observation turret in the center and either two turrets (of various designs), each with a 7.62-cm cannon (light train), or one turret with a heavy gun (heavy train). The number of Soviet armored trains was again around 90 as of June 1941 (still including many from the Revolution era), and there were also armored rail cars in large numbers. Of particular interest are twelve armored trains put into service by the NKVD in 1932-35, each of which included three armored cars (each having two gun turrets with 7.62-cm cannons) with individual motor drive, thus actually armored rail cars, but also had a steam locomotive to move the entire train.—In Poland, after the war with the Soviet Union (1920), most of the very differently composed armored trains were mustered out. Only two of these old trains were retained, along with three captured from the Russians, to which an infantry car (called an "assault car") was added. Following this pattern (two two-turret, four-axle gun cars, "assault car," armored loco and control car) they built one more armored train. This pattern was also retained in four trains built later (with Polish-developed streamlined gun cars), though two of the cannons (always the Polish 7.5-cm version of the Putilov 02 gun) were replaced by 10-cm howitzers, with which some of the older trains were also rearmed.

In the ensuing years, especially in the older trains, modernization was carried out. When the war began, Poland thus had ten armored trains and two training trains (made up of mustered-out older material).—In Finland only two armored trains were still on hand, and in the Baltic states, too, the numbers of armored trains had been much reduced, though they were increased in Latvia after 1928. In Czechoslovakia only five armored trains and one training train were in service in the thirties, in Hungary four. In these two countries, the concept of composition developed in the Austro-Hungarian monarchy was essentially maintained: besides the armored loco there were two infantry cars, in Hungary with guns installed; meanwhile, in Czechoslovakia with an added gun car with one or two cannons.

Al of the Czech armored trains fell into German hands undamaged in March 1939; the fate of the Polish trains, some of them destroyed, which fell to the Germans and Russians, will be described in the chapter on the Polish campaign. The armored trains of the Baltic states were seized by the Soviet forces after their occupation in 1940.—The two Finnish armored trains later took part in the 1939-40 winter war on the Karelian front, and in World War II, subordinated for a time to the German 163rd Infantry Division. Armed at first with 3.7-cm or 7.62-cm caliber guns, they were later rearmed with 4-cm Bofors A/A guns. While one was destroyed by its crew on June 23, 1944, the other remained in action until the armistice of September 4, 1944. Some of its cars can be seen today in the museum at Parola.

After the war began, large numbers of Type OB-3 armored trains with four two-axle, one-turret cars—here with long-barreled 7.62-cm F.K. (L/40) guns—were built in the Soviet Union. Photo: Imperial War Museum, London

In the war, the use of various tank turrets was preferred; the OB-3, like the BP-43, was fitted with T-34 turrets, and thus became the BP-43 type. The same armament was also installed on four-axle cars, as can be seen here. Photo: J. Magnuski collection

Above: The Polish "Grozny" armored train. The gun cars are of Russian origin ("Krasnoye Sormovo" type), but were much modified by the Poles. Captured by the Germans in September 1939, the cars were included in their armored trains No. 21 and 22. *Below:* The Poles equipped four armored trains with streamlined gun cars built in 1921. "Smialy" is shown here. From Russian possession (September 1939 to June 1941) it passed into German hands, and the gun cars were used in PZ 10. Photos: J. Magnuski collection

As soon as the Soviet Union was drawn into the war by the German attack on June 22, 1941, armored trains were built busily. Not only were the heavy losses in the first 15 months of the war quickly made up, but their numbers continued to increase. During the war the Soviet Union built some 200 new armored trains. Soon after it began a variation of the light armored train was introduced, which consisted, besides the locomotive, of four two-axle cars, each with one gun (7.62-cm cannon) turret (Type OB-3), the BP-35 being improved to NKPS-42. But the change was also made, especially in improvised types, to mounting Russian tank turrets on the cars in place of special gun turrets, which not only simplified production technology, but also equipped the armored trains with high-powered tank guns. From the BP-35 or NKPS-42 there came such an armored train, which consisted, besides the locomotive, of two four-axle cars with slightly angled armored walls 45 mm thick, and two T-34 turrets with 7.62-cm tank guns. The OB-3 became the BP-43 (four two-axle cars, each with one T-34 turret). From 1942 on the armored trains were equipped with an additional A/A car (usually with two 3.7-cm guns, sometimes also with a rocket launcher mounted on them). The locomotive, though, usually was still the Series O freight loco used since 1918-19. The "armored train division" consisting of three armored trains was also retained, though only light armored trains (with cannons up to 7.62 cm) were used later.

All of Germany's allies that saw action in the Balkans and on the eastern front, and were thus confronted with partisan activities, built armored trains, mostly improvised units in the manner of the German line protection trains. In the Balkans there were Croatia, Bulgaria, and Italy, and the latter's development of an armored rail car (Littorina blindata) is of special note. This type was taken over by the Germans

after Italy changed sides. On the eastern front, line protection trains of the Slovakian and Hungarian security units are known; Hungary in particular used only such new constructions in the hinterlands of Army Group Center and with the Wehrmacht Commander Ukraine, and not the already available four regular armored trains, which all remained in Hungary. Nothing has become known of the use of armored trains by Romanian units, but one may assume something similar for that country to what the other allied nations had.

Information about the composition of these trains is even scarcer, and can be gained only from the very few remaining photographs. At first the Italians used two-axle high-side O-cars with iron walls, which probably had added armor inside and were partly roofed; the weapon mounts (4.7-cm 47/32 antitank gun, 4.5-cm mine throwers, various machine gun types) were open at first. Later the cars were extensively roofed over, and similarly equipped G-cars were also used. — The Croatian armored trains for standard and narrow gauge consisted — as far as photos show — of special two-axle armored cars, which carried either two machine-gun turrets or one tank turret (French Type APX with 4.7-cm L/31.2 tank gun, but maybe others too). On the roof, besides the observation turret, was an open stand (for A/A machine guns?). Apparently each Croatian armored train included two machine-gun and two gun cars besides the control cars and locomotive. If necessary further freight cars were added. — The only available photo of a Hungarian line protection train on the eastern front shows in the front half of the train one (internally armored?) G-car with a weapon stand (machine gun?) on the roof, and in front of it a provisionally armored low-side car, on which a 4-cm Bofors A/A 28 gun is installed. It is known of a Slovakian line protection train that it carried a captured Russian T 26 tank loaded onto a railroad car.

A Croatian narrow gauge armored train, consisting of four armored cars, of which the inner two have two machine-gun turrets, and the outside ones a French tank turret with a 4.7-cm tank gun. The round roof structures were probably intended for A/A machine guns. The Yugoslavian Series 85 locomotive shows only cab armor. The added (unarmored?) G-car probably contained the kitchen and medical departments. Photo: Federal Archives, Koblenz

The same types of cars were also found in standard gauge Croatian armored trains. Here the two machine-gun cars are seen at the railroad station in Koprivnica. Photo: H. Griebl collection.

A Hungarian line protection train in the Ukraine. The R-car provisionally protected by wooden planks carries a 4-cm A/A gun, the G-car behind it has a machine-gun stand (?) on the roof. Photo: P. Malmassari collection

Orders and Instructions

When the rail protection trains were taken over as armored trains, the Army High Command promptly issued a "Temporary Service Instruction for Armored Railroad Trains" in June 1938. It was based on the already mentioned H.Dv. 300 of 1934, and thus completed it by including essential leadership, travel, and training decisions. The catalog of tasks, seen almost completely as defensive (securing of railroad transports, troop embarkation, destruction and repair work, supply and replacement, delivery and evacuation, covering withdrawals, mopping up insecure regions, use as a fast reserve), was now completed with more offensive possibilities of action:

- Investigation or possession of railroad stations or other railroad-technical structures by quick and surprising advances on short lines;
- Relief advances on the flanks of combat fronts;
- Support in continuing combat;
- Catch-up pursuit.

The description of the trains is oriented to the rail protection trains then on hand. Accordingly, an armored train should, in general terms, comprise:

An armored freight locomotive (top speed 65 kph, water supply 14 cubic meters, coal supply 4.5 tons) equipped with a pumping apparatus (to take on water, including from rivers and standing ponds), necessary tools and sufficient packing, thickening, and lubricating materials for long trips, in the middle of the train.

Six armored cars (three each before and after the locomotive) looking uniform and inconspicuous on the outside and equipped with steam heat, ventilation, and toilets inside. The installation of spotlights and shear scopes is considered purposeful. They are linked with the locomotive by a complete brake line; there is a braking apparatus in each car. The lead cars must have an uncoupling system for the control cars, activated from inside.

At each end of the train, as a control car, an open (Sml) car, on which building materials for improvement work and a removable derailing apparatus are carried.

It was made clear in general that armored trains should be short and easy to observe (a principle that was usually not followed by the German armored trains).

Armored railcars, which are especially suitable for reconnaissance work and to which all the instructions essentially apply, are generally used in connection with armored trains. They can be used either for reconnaissance tasks ahead of the train or as security vehicles behind it.

For the successful action of armored trains and for full utilization of their fighting power, strict leadership by the commander and friction-free cooperation of the crew, which was to be divided on the basis of combat roles—as in the Navy (!)—and who must know the equipment and performance of the train precisely, was considered necessary. For every car a car leader was to be designated, with a telephone operator assigned to him. The commander was the executive of the combat and technical crews; in his absence, the longest-serving member of the combat crew was to deputize for him, or in special cases the technical leader.

The latter—trained in operations and familiar with every detail of transit service and the applicable regulations—is absolutely the man in charge of the technical personnel, who is not only trained for running the armored train, but also, if needed, must be usable as the train leader, transit service leader, or switchman. He is the commander's advisor on all railroad-technical questions and responsible to him

for the technical leadership of the train. The commander's orders to the technical crew (for example, all instructions that concern the train's movements) pass as a rule via the technical leader, who must have them carried out in harmony with the railroad-technical requirements. The technical leader also has the trip report to make up and the leadership of the engineer troop to take on in their action.

The tasks of the technical crew and their leader are stated in detail in the "Service Instructions for the Technical Crew" of August 1, 1944, the only one that has survived from such a late time. Its rules may be added here. To be sure, the engineer troop, which had meanwhile been replaced by a railroad engineer group within the combat crew, no longer existed at this time.

From these instructions it is shown that the technical leader, regardless of his military rank, which could easily be lower, even below those of his subordinates, held an officer's rank as a special leader. The commander was to make sure that his regulations for railroad operations were followed by the crew, no matter what. The technical leader was not bound to any definite place inside the armored train. As long as his tasks allowed, he was either with the track observer or near the commander. In all railroad operational and technical matters he made contact, at the commander's bidding, with the responsible transport and railroad offices. Along with the development of his transit services and leadership of the technical crew, he was responsible for the train's railroad-technical readiness for action and for the training of the technical crew. The latter was to be organized so that further theoretical and practical training was guaranteed. To be able to repair damage caused by the enemy, thoroughgoing cooperation of every single member of the technical crew was to be striven for (for example, the fireman could also serve as the engine driver, or the track observer as car-master). The technical crew was also bound to participate regularly in military service activities (drill, weapon handling, marksmanship).

The technical leader was also responsible for the maintenance of the combat and supply trains. He was to be heard by the commander on all relevant questions, as well as those on the possible improvement of the loco and cars. He was to make sure that regularly scheduled tasks, such as washing out the boiler, brake testing, and checking of pistons, pushers, and bearings be carried out as nearly on time as possible; delays were allowed only for very urgent reasons. The technical leader was always to examine the making of repairs and avoid sabotage (by foreign or forced laborers). If tasks were assigned to the combat train that could not be carried out by the technical crew alone, soldiers from the combat crew were to be made available to him on request. The same applied to derailing-recovery work, which he was to lead. For this, a lifting tackle—the so-called "Deutschland" device—and a rail drag were available. On the other hand, repairs to the upper bodies or removal of mines from the roadbed belonged to the engineer group. The technical leader only checked the usability of the repaired track afterward.

The track observers were responsible for the conscientious observation of the tracks and railroad facilities. If a track observer spotted a danger on the tracks that threatened the armored train (obstacles, mines, vehicles) and required an immediate stop, he was obligated to apply the emergency brake immediately. If no corresponding instructions from the commander or technical leader were on hand, then the speed to be maintained by the driver was to be determined by the track observer. The track observer at the front of the train was simultaneously the train leader. He maintained communication with the operations officials in the railroad stations and reacted to written running orders.

The track observers, along with their main task, were also to be assigned to carrying out shunting tasks and the maintenance and care of the combat and supply train.

The locomotive crew was responsible to the technical leader for trouble-free, ready-to-run and neat condition of the locomotive. The oldest locomotive driver was his deputy and supported him in carrying out his tasks. The loco drivers were to make sure that all the repairs made in the AW or BW were carried out without problems. The locomotive crew could be called on for repair work to the locomotive and cars.—The motor and light mechanic, who was also the car-master, was responsible for the maintenance and care of all railroad vehicles except the armored locomotive. In addition, he was to assure all the electric power supply. To maintain the vehicles—especially when the person was an electric specialist—the track observers and—if necessary—the locomotive crew could be called on. Not among the tasks of the technical crew were the maintenance of the motor vehicles and the communication facilities; specialists from the combat crew were to handle those tasks.

For the armored train's readiness to march, the assurance of these matters was required:

1. Coal supply for at least 250 km of travel;
2. Water supply (including auxiliary tender) to be filled;
3. At least 8 atmospheres of boiler pressure;
4. Lubricating oil supply for 1000 km of travel;
5. Locomotive fully degreased;
6. Car axle bearings lubricated for at least 500 km of travel;
7. Air hoses in all the cars sealed;
8. Locomotive and car brakes trouble-free;
9. For the generator, fuel and water for at least 62 hours;
10. Checking the communication and radio equipment, means of observation and lights.

But now back to the current service instructions of 1938. In peacetime, movements of the armored train were to be undertaken with the responsible transport command in accordance with the Reichsbahn's order of priority as special train journeys. The regulations of the railroad personnel were to be followed strictly; neither the commander nor the technical leader could intervene in them, just as the commander had to follow the technical instructions of the technical leader. Non-regulation travel on their own was strictly forbidden. The same regulations applied in wartime to travel of the armored train in danger-free regions. In doing so, it was to be moved by an additional puller locomotive, whose personnel were familiar with the route, but at least one such escort was to be assigned.—For longer undertakings, the armored train could be assigned a living quarters train.

In wartime, all other affairs had to give way to the fulfilling of combat tasks. In urgent action trips, the movement of the armored train was to take place with priority over all other trains (according to instructions from the field transport department of April 6, 1943). In enemy-threatened regions (determined by the transport commands) the train was to be moved exclusively by the armored locomotive, which always had to be supplied sufficiently with water and coal. The crew was to take definite positions according to their combat roles, and all weapons and equipment (spotlights, telescopes, navigational aids, etc.) were to be kept ready for use. Entry and exit were done through the doors only in enemy-free regions, otherwise through floor hatches.

The responsibility for travel in enemy-endangered regions was borne by the commander alone. He could, in certain cases, also command the deliberate action of the train without regard for the otherwise customary regulations. The movements of the armored train were made, when possible, according to the plans of the responsible transport command, otherwise according to the commander's orders via the technical leader in accord with the station and track personnel, to the extent that they were present. All Reichsbahn offices were to accede to the requests made by the commander and carry out those measures that ruled out the endangering of both the armored train and any other rail transit on the traveled lines. The direction of shunting activity was generally to be handled by the station personnel; if they were not present, the technical leader or a delegate of his from the technical crew was to take over this task.

In action, the top speed of the armored train was to be 45 kph, to be sure only when the tracks were reported to be free. The lines before and behind the train, especially cuts and structures (the usability of bridges was, if necessary, to be tested by releasing the foremost car), were also to be observed, as were the nearby surroundings of the tracks and the air space. If the condition of the track was unknown, then—as long as the combat task did not require anything else—the speed was to be lowered enough so that the train could be brought to a stop at the right time if barriers or track damage appeared. It was expressly stipulated that the resulting loss of time was less important than the possibility of disrupting the carrying out of the task by incautious movement. If the train had to stop on an open track, then whenever possible, the regulations for unforeseen stopping were to be followed (naturally, the train was to carry the appropriate signals); acoustic signals, though, were to be used only when the combat situation allowed them. If the tracks were blocked or destroyed, then these hindrances were to be removed by the engineer troop on board or by disembarked members of the combat crew. This was to be done only when the establishment of mobility of the armored train required it, thus only in a makeshift manner, as the case might be.

If the train approached a suspicious vehicle on the track, the speed was to be reduced and a signal to stop was to be given (acoustic only when the enemy situation allowed). If the vehicle did not stop countermeasures were to be taken. If it occurred on the track on which the armored train itself was traveling, the derailment apparatus was to be ejected and, if necessary, the control car was to be uncoupled and applied. In railroad stations it could be switched onto another line.

When several armored trains worked together unified leadership was to be assured. The commanders and technical leaders of the trains constantly had to agree. In danger-free regions the trains moved at block intervals, one after another, in dangerous regions within sight of each other, but with a minimum interval of 300 meters at a speed reduced to 10 kph. On two-track lines—when other rail traffic was halted—travel could also be done in alternating formation.

Attempts to make the trains self-concealing by fog still applied. The resulting fog protection, which was effective only with favorable wind conditions—and even then limited by space and time factors—appeared insufficient. It could be applied only when the armored train was moving backward (since the train, when moving forward, would leave the fog cloud toward the enemy). The tracks leading into the fog area always gave the enemy tips as to the location of the train. Fogging in the enemy by firing suitable fog cartridges, on the other hand, seemed more favorable, yet the possibilities for this were usually lacking.

In the training of the crew, the precise knowledge of the train, its facilities—especially the means of communication within the train—and its possible performance, as well as the given conditions were the most important goals. Friction-free cooperation between the technical and combat crews was essential. Especially to be practiced were quick preparation of combat readiness, quick entering and leaving the train, conducting combat from both the standing and the moving train (school and combat shooting). Combat conduct outside the train, including cooperation with the members of the crew remaining in the train, the laying and removal of barriers, and the applying and removal of disturbances to railroad facilities, and cooperation with other service arms.

Some reminders of the troops to the armored train crews can be taken from the report of the 223rd Infantry Division concerning a drill with PZ 22 on August 1, 1941 (in which is should be remembered that PZ 22 had no combat experience at that time):

- The lack of an armored reconnaissance railcar is criticized; it was supposed to scout ahead of the armored train, report any hindrances at once and immediately begin to have them removed by an on-board engineer troop.
- The forward movement of the armored train at full speed is thereby made possible (in the drill, only 15 kph — accordingly, the combination of the armored train action is recommended above all for bicycle units.
- When advancing, no stops are to be made to pick up individual disembarked crew members. Time and the moment of surprise are lost thereby. They are to follow the armored train on foot, since it must be clear to them that its task is limited, so that they find it again in any case.
- When a hindrance is removed, the crew is to secure the work far-reachingly.
- In infantry action outside the cars, the crew has to proceed according to the instructions for an infantry company in a fire fight. Moving forward against the enemy in a row or a double row along the ditches beside the rails is impractical and results in losses.
- If the armored train encounters enemy resistance, all means of battle are to be used immediately and, if possible, at the same time and not one after another.
- The carrying of weapons when disembarking, including those of the engineer troop, is to be assured. It must be clear to the individual man that he is first of all an infantry fighter and not a technical personnel man.
- Giving commands must be done briefly, concisely, and clearly.

Toward the end of the advancing phase in Russia, on November 7, 1941, Halder, the Chief of the Army General Staff, sent out a memo on the offensive use of armored trains to all army groups and armies on the eastern front.

"Experiences of 1918 in the Ukraine (!) and the last weeks show that under certain prerequisites the use of armored trains can take on special significance.

In smaller undertakings the tasks of the armored trains can be:

a. Advancing surprisingly into enemy territory with destructive tasks, and returning after carrying the tasks out;

b. Rushing other forces out surprisingly to occupy important points and staying until reinforcements arrive.

Larger undertakings, especially in times when movements on roads and paths have become limited or impossible because of the weather situation, offer the possibility, by using slightly damaged railroad lines, of keeping the movements in progress, especially when only the appearance of small enemy groups is to be expected. Here the applied armored trains are to be strengthened by other forces, who are to be made mobile on trains, to form mixed railroad battle groups that are in a position to take over the spearhead of the attack for stronger forces following on the rails or, where terrain and road conditions allow, on both sides of the line."

In the appendix, an example of the structure of such a mixed railroad battle group is given:

In advance: Armored railcar with radio for reconnaissance (if available, or to be equipped temporarily).

1st Train: armored train (with snowplow, if possible), with leader and battle group and small construction command of railroad engineers.

2nd & 3rd Trains: Mixed crews from an infantry battalion, a tank company, a motorized battery with heavy howitzers (tanks loaded so that they can also have an effect from the train, one or two guns per train on platforms on reinforced car floors, to support the armored train under fire control from it by radio).

4th Train: Construction train with railroad engineers.

5th Train: One battalion with increased supply of heavy weapons and antitank guns.

6th Train: Supply train with ammunition, provisions, and fuel (depending on the situation, division among the individual trains is also practical).

7th Train: Same as 5th train.

In the notes thereon it is stated in detail that:

1. Reconnaissance by an armored railcar equipped with radio is desired, in order to avoid letting the trains get too close to each other if they encounter a barrier, with the chance of disadvantageous results (artillery fire, air attacks) (if no railcar is on hand, reconnaissance by an armored train moving ahead and amplified by aircraft);

2. If another armored train is available, it can be added purposefully at the end of the battle group with a construction command, in order to prevent damage behind the battle group;

3. The infantry on board must be protected against infantry fire by makeshift cover of logs and sandbags;

4. The troops on board should take along only very few vehicles (if possible, off-road-capable motorized Polish-type wagons or sleds), which are needed for movement in the vicinity of the destination to be reached;

5. The equipment of the entire battle group must be fully mobile in winter (showshoes or tires for infantry, light sleds for heavy weapons and equipment);

6. The contact of all the trains in the battle group by radio, also while underway, is necessary, and radio contact with assigned reconnaissance and supporting air forces must be assured (the radio sets of the loaded tanks can also be used; telephone contact within the trains);

7. The supply of the battle group with provisions depending on their task must be done so that they themselves and smaller battle groups left behind on the tracks remain alive and able to defend themselves for several weeks;

8. Additional forces must be kept in readiness, so that securing forces left behind can be relieved and the battle group can be brought back again;

9. Sufficient air defense of the trains, also while underway, must particularly be secured.

Prerequisites for carrying out such undertakings are:

1. The assignment must be limited;

2. Previous aerial scouting must show that no large destroyed objects block the tracks (smaller blockages are removed by accompanying construction crews, even with meager daily gain of area, large advances are thus possible in time);

3. Rail lines for action must be chosen that are of special significance for later supplying and connections, and the development of which is intended by the field transport chief'

4. To secure the most important objects until relieved by following troops. Sufficient forces must be taken along in the railroad battle group;

5. The attack spearhead must be closely linked with aerial reconnaissance and aerial fighting forces, so that any enemy resistance can be broken as quickly as possible, so that the enemy can find no time for extensive destruction.

For such offensive uses, of course, only the few (and badly equipped) broad gauge armored trains could be used, which are then to be replaced in railroad securing service in back land regions by normal armored trains or makeshift line protection trains (with wood and sandbag cover for tanks loaded onto O-cars).

The memo from the Chief of the General Staff, though, was illusory to the extent that there was scarcely any more time for such action by armored trains on the eastern front.

On May 24, 1942, the General of the Fast Troops issued the "Temporary Guidelines for the Structure and Action of Armored Railroad Trains" developed by his subordinate, the staff officer for armored trains, into which the experiences of the two- and three-quarter war years flowed. The possible types of action were seen as both offensive and defensive, with the emphasis on railroad-technical aspects, but also on general combat actions:

a. For scouting, securing and quick taking of railroad stations and structures, rail lines and other facilities, as well as for securing transports and loading and unloading in threatened regions,

b. For interruption and destruction of railroad facilities (structures, yards, etc.) or protection of rebuilding work in enemy territory,

c. For combat actions alone, within the framework of a railroad battle group, or in cooperation with other troops, especially on wings and flanks of battle fronts, above all in pursuit and withdrawal.

This essentially includes the tasks already formulated in H.Dv. 300 and "Temporary Service Instructions" of 1938, though in a different order, formulation and priority. In view of its date (after eleven months of the Russian campaign, including the reverses of the winter of 1941-42) the lack, or the subsuming in very weakened form, of possible actions previously stated *expressis verbis* is notable: cleaning up insecure regions (H.Dv. 300) and support during lengthy combat (for example, artillery support of infantry forces; Service Instructions, 1938), which in view of the already begun and constantly growing partisan action and the worsening front situation soon would rank among the most important tasks for armored trains.

The armored trains could cover long distances in a short time. Their possible use, though, was limited by their being bound to easily destroyed rail lines. This disadvantage can be balanced by cunning combat actions and by disembarking parts of the crews, especially loaded tanks, to fight outside the train. Required for their success are careful preparation for action, surprise appearance, and ruthless daredevil deeds, along with precise knowledge of the enemy's means of combat, the terrain, and the railroad network to be used. The success of their own and the difficult fighting against the Russian armored trains were cited as proof that with capable leadership, especially against already shaken enemies or those with few heavy weapons, significant gains could be made.

The information on the composition, armament, and manning of the armored trains in this document can be passed over, since they attempt to describe the very heterogeneous available material (former rail protection trains, captured Czech, Polish, and Russian trains, temporary broad gauge armored trains) imprecisely, and a very detailed discussion of these aspects has been made already in previous chapters.

The armored trains are army troops and subordinate in service to the Staff Officer of the Armored Railroad Trains under the General of the Fast Troops under the Commander-in-chief of the Army (later the Commander of the Armored Railroad Trains under the Commander-in-chief of the Army). Tactically they were subordinated to army groups, army high commands, or commanders of back land army groups and army territories; often a direct subordination to corps or divisions was required. For security of supplying, the subordination relationship needed to change as little as possible. They were not subordinated to railroad transport offices. Their railroad-technical maintenance, though, had to be cleared by the responsible command offices with the transport offices, which also had to undertake the railroad operational work.

Also included here is the assignment of a suitable shunting yard for the armored train, which must offer the possibility of taking on coal and water. At this railroad station the supply train, consisting of living quarters and business cars, and which every armored train took with it, in order to assure complete supplying (including postal service, canteen shops, etc.) of the train and its crew in view of the changing localities of action and situation conditions, was generally also to be kept. The commander was always to strive for this, and the responsible command offices were required to help to the greatest extent. Preparation and carrying out of all means of supplying were up to the paymaster, who had to be informed punctually of planned changes in location. The technical leader took care of the extremely important fuel supply (coal, water, gasoline, oil) in cooperation with the paymaster.

At the shunting yard, activity was to be covered from sight and attack by aircraft. For this it was necessary to take apart the combat and supply trains and park the cars in several pieces on various side tracks. Constant reconnaissance and securing had to protect the facilities from enemy surprise attacks. If the armored trains were endangered by enemy aircraft or artillery fire while at the railroad station, either position changes within the station yards had to be made or the train had to be taken out of the yard in agreement with the responsible railroad transport office.

When assigning a task to the armored train, it was to be kept in mind that it, through exclusive dependence on steam locomotives, had to be ready to roll in some 15 to 30 minutes when the loco was already under steam; if this was not the case, a time period of 6 to 8 hours had to be reckoned with. In that case, to be sure, a regular locomotive could save time and space by moving the armored train to the place of action while the armored locomotive was taken along, still in the heating phase. Further losses of time resulted from the fact that the armored train parked on side tracks—sometimes in several pieces—first had to be assembled and brought to the main line. It was to be assured that the armored locomotive's coal and water supply were always full, and if possible, a reserve had to be taken along in addition to the tender. It should also be considered that the locomotive waiting under steam used up coal and water even when it was not moving. A radius of action of 80 to 120 km was cited for the locomotive, depending on its type. Only in very special exceptions could the armored locomotive be used for other purposes (such as transport or shunting). Strengthening the armored train, whose composition could be changed only if cars were damaged, by coupling on additional cars (such as for added crew transport) must also be eliminated, so as to avoid overstraining the armored locomotive.

The travel instructions essentially corresponded to those in the 1938 service instructions, meaning that travel in the back lands could be done only according to the railroad activity regulations and with the permission of the Wehrmacht transport offices as to schedules, running speeds and stops; on lines in combat areas that were still occupied by railroad personnel, in agreement with them as well; in enemy action with combat tasks on the sole responsibility of the commander, who—as far as the situation allowed—could also order risky travel without following the operating instructions. But it was recommended that on combat trips a speed of 20-25 kph generally not be exceeded, so as to be able to stop in time if hindrances or track damage appeared.—A new addition was a warning for special caution toward native railroad personnel from occupied regions, which had already been called on in large numbers for assistance, since their knowledge of tasks, departure, running and stop times could lead to betrayal or even sabotage. Accordingly, giving such information via loudspeakers should be limited to the most essential because of the danger of being heard, and if possible, everything should be encoded.

The action of armored trains must be prepared carefully and kept secret. To be able to use the capability of the armored trains fully, the rail line chosen for the action must be investigated carefully by air reconnaissance, which must look especially for barriers and damage, and by as extensive ground reconnaissance as possible, on and near the line. Statements of prisoners and captured rail maps can also provide valuable experiences. It must also be determined whether the crew of the armored train must be augmented by additional forces in order to secure their own track route and carry out the combat task, and whether the armored train can be supported by other types of forces, so as to rule out surprises and break enemy opposition as quickly as possible. When orders are given, the commander of the armored train is to be informed steadily by the superior command office about the tactual situation, their own intentions, the railroad facilities to be covered—especially those in enemy territory—and the exact extent of the task. The communications with superior offices and all units involved in the task are to be assured. The preparations for the action are to be camouflaged carefully against enemy air reconnaissance and air attacks. The armored train generally carries its provisions with it (the supply train, with which constant communication is to be maintained, remains back at the base station). For longer undertakings, additional supplying on the traveled line is to be planned.

From the armored train too, careful reconnaissance along and on both sides of the line is to be done, both with the train's vehicles (armored railcars, rail motorcycles, etc.) and by disembarked scout troops. The first must advance quickly and boldly, with plenty of distance, but without losing contact with the armored train. The latter, generally at the strength of a squad, is to be given an exact schedule, especially as to where and when they will be picked up by the armored train. The enemy's position on the rail line and in the adjacent area is to be scouted, especially the positions of armor-piercing weapons, the condition of the line to be traveled, including the railroad structures and telephone lines, and line barriers, blocks or interruptions are to be spotted and, if possible, removed. The armored train itself can be used for reconnaissance, such as to determine whether the condition of railroad bridges, over- and underpasses allow their use, whether the railroad stations to be passed are occupied by the enemy, or whether antitank forces are present. Important results of reconnaissance must be reported to the responsible superior service offices at once and shared with the leaders of nearby units. The line behind the armored train is also to be secured by disembarked scout troops or accompanying rail vehicles, especially structures, over-

and underpasses. To secure the armored trains, tanks (possibly those carried on board) can be used along the tracks.

In combat, efforts must be made to rout the enemy by surprise by utilizing armor and speed, in order to avoid explosions and other track damage as much as possible. Clever utilization of the available rail network and constant movement of the train, in order to keep it away from enemy view and weapon effect as much as possible, are indispensable for successful combat. After pushing through enemy barriers, securing etc., the quick and extensive use of combat reconnaissance—especially on the flanks—is important. If armored trains are used to delay the advance of the enemy, their main task is the effort to stop them through constant surprise attacks and counterattacks by disembarked troops. Here the closest communication and cooperation with the troops fighting outside the train, which are to secure and support it, is necessary. It is also the armored train's task to draw the enemy's attention and fire to itself, to make it possible for the disembarked troops to approach the target of the attack.—The unloadable tanks carried on the armored train are, on the one hand, especially suited for attacking enemy installations (bunkers, machine-gun nests, etc.), which they must approach as closely as possible under the covering fire of the armored train so they can use their guns directly against the loopholes; on the other hand, for surprise attacks to capture railroad structures, particularly bridges. The tank must approach the bridge quickly and at the right time, so that any explosive charges that may be prepared to destroy the object can no longer be ignited.

If the approach of enemy armored trains is to be expected, then the rail line—when accessible—is to be broken or mined, but destruction of the line is allowed only on orders from the superior command office and in agreement with the responsible Wehrmacht transport offices. Using visible barriers or dummies, the enemy train is to be induced to stop, for which disembarked units of your own crew have been readied for a surprise attack, or at which fire from your heavy weapons can be aimed. If your own armored train must withdraw from the attack of an enemy armored train, this is best done by using smoke screens and blocking the tracks under cover of the fog (by dropping derailing devices such as drag shoes or derailed cars, such as your own control car). If it comes to combat, the locomotive of the enemy train should be fired on first, to make it incapable of movement.

For the cooperation of two armored trains, the rules given in the service instructions of 1938 were repeated. The formation of mixed railroad battle groups according to the already cited paper from Halder of November 7, 1941, was also described, which naturally had only a hypothetical character at the time when these guidelines appeared.

Finally, the use of armored trains to secure rail lines and rid them of enemy forces was mentioned. The section of line to be secured was to be patrolled with consideration of the transit situation by the armored trains, their reconnaissance vehicles (armored railcars, rail motorcycles), and perhaps other armed locomotives. Railroad stations and structures were to be occupied by members of the armored train crews or other assigned infantry troop units, in agreement with the responsible command and transport offices. The guarding of occupied rail facilities during the night by watchmen, sentries and patrols was especially important. Appropriate signals between them and the armed vehicles using the line (acoustic only when the situation allowed) were to be agreed on.

After completing a task, the armored train must be taken back to a railroad station with the facilities needed for restoring its fighting power (filling with water and coal, necessary maintenance of the locomotive and other vehicles, any repairs); as a rule, this is also the home station of the supply train. If this is not the case, then the transfer of the supply train to the new station is to be arranged.

Both the service instructions of 1938 and the guidelines of 1942 are designated "temporary." It is known that work was done on the final version of these instructions in 1943-44 at the office of the Commander of the Armored Railroad Trains in the Army High Command, but until now only the service instructions for the technical armored train crews, dated August 1, 1944, and already discussed elsewhere, could be located, and even former members could not remember the appearance of anything further on the subject. Only Training Advisory No. 18 of the Army High Command on February 10, 1944, "Experiences on the Action of Armored Trains," dealt with this subject, discussing in particular mistakes that had been made. Let us quote directly from it:

1. Armored trains were robbed of their most important means of reconnaissance and combat, their infantry impact and gun crews by transferring their armored combat vehicles, armored scout cars, armored reconnaissance railcars and infantry crews to other types of service, so that their effectiveness was limited and they were exposed to the danger of premature destruction. The armored train, with all the organic parts belonging to it, is a complete means of combat. Taking away individual weapons and parts of the crew makes it unusable for its real tasks and thus must not be done.

2. The armored train offers a large target, betrays itself easily by the smoke produced by its locomotive, has armor only secure from S.m.K. ammunition, and is easily immobilized by locomotive failure or track damage. The following actions, which have been ordered again and again, are therefore false:
   - Long reconnaissance trips on unsecured tracks,
   - Fighting enemy tanks,
   - Day-long advances one after the other on the same track.
   They will soon cause the destruction of the train.

3. Along with insufficient knowledge of the special qualities of the armored train, impractical subordination is often the cause of the above errors. Proved are:
   - Tactical subordination under command offices down to the division. Only this will result in the readiness for action considering the frequent changes of subordination. area, mobile combat and surprise attacks. Understanding the nature of the weapon can be a prerequisite.
   - Instruction for cooperation, exceptionally, with smaller groups for brief, clearly outlined tasks.
   - Instruction as to the supply and repair facilities of a corps or an army independent of the tactical subordination. Only this will result in the readiness for action, considering the frequent changes of subordination.

4. The following possible uses of the armored train, which correspond most with its special nature, were not always considered or utilized:
   - Cooperation with other forces, above all with troops that can mesh with its mobility. When the armor-piercing weapons of the enemy are knocked out by them, the great firepower of the armored train can take its full effect.
   - Support of withdrawal movements and counterattacks. Important here are:

- Timely direction via the usually heavily occupied railroad stations and rail lines near the front (cooperation with transport offices).
- Prevention of the negation of prerequisites for action by overly hasty destruction of railroad facilities, water sources, etc.
- Forward-looking training of battle groups of two armored trains, and possible reinforcement by railroad A/A guns. This results in:
- Considerable increase of firepower.
- The possibility of mutual support in combat and assistance in special cases (towing). In this way, immobile armored trains could be saved repeatedly from otherwise necessary self destruction. Hindrances, even on single tracks, did not occur.
- Use as mobile batteries and imitation of stronger artillery, especially on static fronts with appropriate rail lines. Fire control assured by artillery aircraft.

5. Various tasks have been assigned to armored trains without providing the necessary support to carry them out. Reinforcement of the armored train by infantry, engineers or railroad engineers has generally proved to be necessary for:
   - Independent combat tasks,
   - Special tasks such as repairing broken tracks, railroad service facilities, bridges, destruction of important rail facilities and structures, or laying mines in retreat movements.
   Additional carrying of two or three groups under armor protection, of forces up to a battalion without armor protection (on added cars) is possible.

6. As to the use of armored trains against partisans, the almost word-for-word inclusion appeared in the memo "Partisan Fighting" of the OKW of May 6, 1944, and will thus be dealt with later in this context.

Also worthy of note is a report of the Staff Officer for special use with the Commander of the Armored Trains (later Regimental Commander of the Armored Trains), Lieutenant Colonel Dr. Günther, of May 19, 1944, after an inspection trip in the zone of Army Group Center, in which similar points to those in the training instructions are made:

"The inspection . . . has shown that the fighting strength of the armored trains is not fully utilized. In all cases, the armored trains stood unused, parked at a railroad station, and their crews were deployed as infantry up to 25 km from the rail line, so that the heavy weapons (artillery and A/A guns) that constitute the strength of the armored trains could absolutely not come into action (author's note: Because of the quiet war situation no front action took place).

"Thus there is the danger that losses of long-trained, highly qualified and hard-to-replace personnel of the armored trains result from action for which personnel without special training are sufficient, and the possible success of which in no way equals the loss of the special personnel (Author's note: See Training Tip No. 18, No. 1).

"The armored trains were also used for securing rail lines. Armored trains are just as endangered by mines as other trains. For securing tracks, makeshift line protection trains suffice, the loss of which does not compare with that of an armored train. Through the use of armored trains in line protection and track securing, they suffer losses of the most valuable material and equipment (tanks, armored scout cars, etc.), whereby the readiness of the armored trains for action is put in question at the decisive moment.

"The advantage offered by armored trains over makeshift line protection trains was thus just in the moral effect that they had on their own and enemy troops. A disadvantage that must be considered, though, is that in this kind of action by the armored train, a part of its crew is always out in the country, so that the commander finds no time for training. The goodness and readiness of the crew must suffer from it. It is desirable that such armored trains as are not fully utilized in terms of their weapons are given the opportunity for training.

"Therefore it is suggested:

1. To use not armored trains but makeshift line protection trains to protect rail lines.

2. To use several armored trains in front action as armored train groups, together in overlapping use, under the leadership of an armored train commander who knows the type and strength of the weapons and can represent the wishes of the armored train to the superior command office (author's note: here, of course, the future regimental commander is speaking *pro domo*). The advantage of using several trains together is also that an armored train made immobile by shot damage to the locomotive can be towed out of the danger zone, and thus very valuable material can be saved. Then too, one armored train can still be used in front when another train must go, sometimes to a distant station, to fill up with coal and water. If possible, armored trains should be used at the front together with other weapons (such as infantry and tanks), so as to avoid cutting off a way back and secure flanks (author's note: for this whole section, see also Training Tip No. 18, No. 4).

3. Forming armored train groups for combined action also means that with their disembarked infantry platoons as lurking troops and armored trains as mobile support points, they can close off a large section of track between the trains."

There can now be no more talk of offensive combat tasks in view of the changed front situation; only the use of an armored train in local counterattacks can be seen. On the other hand, its use as a mobile railroad battery is formulated as a defensive task born from practice. The shortage of armored trains at that time—the lack of armor-piercing weapons and sufficient armor protection—was recognized. Therefore, great value was placed on their cooperation with other troop units, which could keep typical threats—especially by enemy tanks—away from the train. The always requested but only seldom practiced—often for lack of a suitable number—use of at least two armored trains was urgently called for. Its realization, as well as the elimination of the deficiency of giving orders, served the setting up of regimental staffs in the army groups, already considered since the start of 1944, and the now striven-for formation of armored train battle groups, means which, for lack of quantities, even now could, in part, only be carried out with great delays and, in general, much too late. A handwritten exercise for training purposes, from the end of 1944, stresses cooperation with other—preferably fast—troops, such as armored reconnaissance units, plus the particular suitability (on the basis of good radio equipment) for cooperation with the air force (if necessary, using control officers). Yet it is particularly stressed here that the armored train was not to be viewed as a mobile battery (!).—It can also be noted that the armored trains stationed in France—although not named in any document—were also considered for guarding the coast (much as in Norway, where this was handled by line protection trains). After the surrender of Italy in September 1943, they concentrated mainly on the western Mediterranean Sea, but in Italy itself they were soon frustrated by the intensive activity of the Allied air forces, which cut the armored trains' mobility by destroying rail lines. A serious application in this realm never took place, since at the time of the Allied landing in southern France all the armored trains had been sent inland to fight against partisans.

The Occupation of the Sudetenland and the Remaining Part of Czechoslovakia

The establishment of the German Wehrmacht's first seven armored trains by taking over the German Reichsbahn's rail protection trains took place in July 1938. For the march into Austria on March 12, 1938, these units were therefore not available.

Yet they could be included in the planning for a possible occupation by force of the German-speaking border areas of Czechoslovakia in September 1938. When this region fell to the German Reich without a fight in the Munich Accord early in October 1938, they were used in the occupation of the proper occupation zones:

Zone I (southern Bohemia, occupied on October 1 and 2): Army Group for special purposes (Linz): PZ 3 (Recruiting District VII, Munich)

Zone II: (Rumburg-Reichenberg region, occupied on October 2 and 3): Army Group 3 (Dresden: PZ 1 (Recruiting District III, Berlin)

Zone III (Eger-Karlsbad region, occupied on October 3-5): Army Group 4 (Schwandorf): PZ 2 (Recruiting District IV, Dresden).

Zone IV (northern Moravia, occupied on October 6 and 7): Army Group I (Oppeln): PZ 4 (Recruiting District VIII, Breslau)

The occupation took place without incidents; on October 14, 1938, all the armored trains were called back to their home bases.

The Czechs had also activated their armored trains during their mobilization in September 1938, one being transferred to Pilsen and three to Slovakia, while another, plus the training train, had remained at its peacetime base in Milowitz.

Without having taken part in any way in the course of events, these trains had been ordered back to Milowitz by the end of 1938. Along with these regular armored trains, twelve more makeshift ones had been set up in some Czech divisions during the mobilization, and

The gun barrel of PZ 3 rises threateningly toward St. Peter's Cathedral in Brno on the march into Czechoslovakia in March 1939. Photo: F. Englberger/W. Sawodny collection

some of them saw action against rebellious Sudeten German groups. That of the 3rd Division took part in the retaking of Warnsdorf and later of Rumburg, which had been occupied previously by Sudeten German free corps. The makeshift armored train of the 5th Division was used against free corps fighters near Hohenfurth on September 30; on 2 October, despite its cooperation, it did not succeed in driving the Germans out of Böhmisch-Krumau, but the Czech population was able to be evacuated.

When on March 15, 1939, the Czech President Haxha was forced to agree to the occupation of the rest of Czechoslovakia, German armored trains were again involved in the ensuing action. No. 3 had been transferred to the March Valley in Upper Austria and advanced from there to Brno via Lundenburg. PZ 4 first moved out of the upper Oder Valley through Prerau toward Olmuetz and then advanced farther in the direction of Prague. No information on the activities of the other armored trains is available, but it is easy to assume that at least one more (No. 1 or 2) may have proceeded along the Elbe valley from the north toward Prague.—In the turning of the Czech area into the Reich Protectorate of Bohemia and Moravia, all the Czech armored trains, along with great quantities of other weapons, fell into German Wehrmacht hands as captured goods; their material—including the four armored locomotives of Series 377 that remained from World War I—was combined into German Armored Trains No. 23-25 in 1940.

The Polish Campaign

In the preparation phase for the attack on Poland in July and early August 1939, the four armored railroad trains planned for combat tasks, No. 3, 4, 6, and 7, were already manned and the crews prepared for their actions. To be sure, PZ 6—as was shown later—seems not to have attained its full combat strength yet. So only Armored Trains No. 3, 4, and 7 saw action on the first war day.

PZ 7 from Allenstein took part in the failed surprise attack on the Vistula bridges in Dirschau. The group of Colonel Medem (Commander of Engineers in Recruiting District I) was sent to captured them unharmed. The 1st Company of Engineer Battalion (mot.) 41 was loaded into a regularly scheduled freight train, which was to run as usual from Elbing via Marienburg to Dirschau. It was followed by PZ 7, which carried an extra infantry shock troop and a platoon of the 2nd Company of Engineer Battalion 41. At the same time, another platoon of this company was hidden in a long-distance moving van and trailer to reach the road bridge. Exactly as the freight train and moving van arrived on the Vistula bridges, a Stuka group was to attack the railroad station at Dirschau and destroy the igniters for the explosive charges on the bridges. Thus the most exact timing was a prerequisite for the success of the undertaking. While the change to a Polish locomotive (with German personnel aboard) on the freight train took place smoothly in Marienburg, an unexpected delay occurred in Simonsdorf when a Polish railroad official handed over a transit permit. When the station in Liessau was reached at 4:42 A.M., the Stuka attack on Dirschau was already underway. Despite the signal, which was set on "stop," the train passed through the

The view from the front gun car of PZ 7 at the Vistula bridge near Dirschau, blown up at the right time by the Poles on September 1, 1939. Photo: J. Borgmann/W. Sawodny collection

When PZ 4 departed from the border station of Pawonkau on September 1, 1939, it met destruction that prevented its advance at this point. Photo: W. Obermark/W. Sawodny collection

Liessau station. When it approached the Vistula bridge, the bridge approach was found to be closed already by a steel and grid gate and secured by a track obstacle. It is very likely that not only the minor time delay in the arrival of the trains was to blame, but also that the Polish railroad official in Simonsdorf became suspicious—perhaps because of the armored train following the freight train—and alarmed the Liessau station and the bridge guard in time. So the freight train stopped about 100 meters before the bridge, and the crew had to get out and approach the bridge on foot. From there it immediately faced heavy fire. PZ 7, which had meanwhile come to a stop behind the freight train, was very limited in its weapons' effect by the train stopped in front of it. Only after switching the two trains could it give effective support. Although the bridges remained standing until after 6:00 (obviously, the igniters destroyed by the Stuka attack had to be repaired first), it was not possible to get to them. At 6:10 the Liessau side exploded, at 6:40 so did the rest of the bridges. Only in the afternoon were the engineers able to cross the river above and below the bridges. Dirschau could only be taken the next morning.— In connection with this undertaking, PZ 7 was transferred to the region north of Modlin until the fortress there surrendered at the end of September 1939. After that it took on line-securing tasks in the region northwest of Warsaw.

PZ 3 was supposed to capture the railroad station in Konitz in a surprise advance. The train, readied in Jastrow, was advanced to Linde in the night of September 1, 1939, and set out from there at 4:15 AM—the rail-running armored car (Sd.Kfz. 231) leading the way—in the direction of Konitz. Blessed by ground fog, it was able to cross three undamaged bridges beyond the border and arrive at

the railroad station in Konitz. Only when this was occupied by the rifle group from the armored train (5:10 AM) did the Polish defense begin, quickly increasing in vigor. Although the bridge just before the station had meanwhile been partly damaged by explosives, the armored train crossed the intact part from the station to gain a free field of fire. Meanwhile, though, the occupiers of the station had come under such pressure that the armored train had to approach again and evacuate them. Then it moved back onto the line ahead of the station again. From there and from the city, the Poles fired increasingly heavy weapons (infantry and antitank guns) at it. Despite vigorous enemy fire, damage and losses increased, and among others, the commander, 1st Lt. Euen, was killed by an antitank shell that hit the observation tower (Artillery Lt. Zettler took command). So as not to offer such a good target on the tracks, the train kept moving slowly but then came upon a bridge behind it that had meanwhile been blown up. The control car plunged off it, while the gun car running behind it was derailed. Uncoupling the car did not succeed, and thus the train was immobile and completely exposed to the Polish fire. When artillery also attacked, the crew left the train with their infantry weapons and, at first, took up positions beside it. Meanwhile it had become later than 10:00, and the spearhead of the infantry (III. Btl./Inf.Rgt. 90) had arrived. But they had to withdraw again under the heavy fire. When the Polish artillery fire blew up the front gun car and set fire to several other cars of the armored train, the train's crew moved off some 200 meters to the south. Only after the mass of the III. Btl./Inf. Rgt. 90 had arrived, and with artillery support, could the armored train be reoccupied and the station and city of Konitz taken. The rail-running armored scout car of PZ 3 had moved out past Konitz to

In battle at Konitz, PZ 3 drove onto a blown-up bridge on the first day of the war. The control car fell off and the gun car was derailed. Photo: F. Englberger/W. Sawodny collection

Thus immobilized on the track, PZ 3 was badly damaged by Polish fire. Photo: W. Hahn/W. Sawodny collection

the Brahe in the first approach, but the bridge there had been blown up at the right time. In an attempt to move the vehicle to the road at an overpass, the crew was killed and the scout car itself badly damaged.

Then PZ 3 was temporarily repaired at the Schneidemühl RAW and sent to the Schichau Works in Danzig for thoroughgoing repairs, in which the gun cars in particular were reinforced. In late September and early October 1939 it was assigned to the Kaupisch Corps for an attack on the Hela peninsula, but because of the track damage at Ceynowa it could not intervene directly. After the peninsula was taken, the armored train was stationed in Lublin.

PZ 4 was supposed to cross the border in the advance of the 3rd Light Division from Wildfurt and advance via Lublinitz and Herby toward Tschenstochau, inspecting and securing the rail line. But the tracks had already been destroyed so thoroughly by the Poles at the border station of Pawonkau that lengthy repair work was necessary. Therefore PZ 4 was transferred to Schneidemühl on 3 September and advanced slowly via Bromberg and Thorn to Kutno, but the pocket battle there had already been concluded (September 20, 1939). At the end of the month PZ 4 was in the Danzig-Gdingen region; as of October 7 it was stationed in Hohensalza, and carried out track security in this region until November 19, 1939.

The later PZ 6 was called "Railroad Repair Train Insterburg" during the Polish campaign, an indication that it was not fully equipped. Presumably it still lacked its gun cars, and the armor was also in an insufficient state. It was in Korschen at first, and was transferred to Lyck later. From there it supported the east flank of the Goldap Brigade forces already on the Narew and advancing as of September 10 as they took the border station of Grajevo and moved farther along the line to Bialystok (in Osoviec on 9/13, Knyszyn on 9/15). Then the train was transferred to Sudauen. Early in October it went to the Koenigsberg RAW for its final development, which lasted about a month.

The Armored Railroad Trains No. 1, 2, and 5, which carried no heavy weapons, were intended only for security tasks. Thus they were set up only in early September 1939.

From about mid-September 1939 on, PZ 1 secured the Schneidemühl—Bromberg—Laskowitz—Dirschau—Danzig line. As of November it was subordinated to the XXXVI. Army Corps in Radom. Securing trips took it through large parts of Poland. Its action area stretched from Kutno and Warsaw in the north to Kielce and Tschenstochau in the south.

PZ 2 arrived in Gleiwitz on September 14, 1939, and went on to Kattowitz to scout the line to Tschenstochau. As of 17 September it was stationed in Trzebinia.

One gun car was hit so badly that the ammunition in the turret blew up. Photo: W. Hahn/W. Sawodny collection

The Sd.Kfz. 231 used as a scout car by PZ 3 went out past Konitz, but was caught before the bridge over the Brahe and badly damaged, with its crew killed. Photo: F. Englberger/W. Sawodny collection

PZ 2 is shown at the end of September 1939 at the railroad station in Krenau (on the eastern edge of the Upper Silesian industrial area, known for its locomotive factory). Photo: G. Tomaszewski/W. Sawodny collection

From 25 to 30 September it carried out salvage work in Krenau. On 10 October it was transferred to Freistadt/Olsa to secure the line from Oderberg to Dzieditz. From 25 October on PZ 2 was in Minsk Mazowiecki, east of Warsaw, first to secure the rail lines between the Polish capital and the Bug.

Finally, PZ 5 started on September 15, 1939, in the hinterlands of Army Group South, from Tschenstochau via Cracow, Tarnow and Przemysl toward Lemberg. On 20 September PZ 5 was on the demarcation line in Zakopane to secure German-Soviet conferences; then it was transferred to the eastern part of the Upper Silesian industrial region. As of 22 September it was stationed in Sosnowitz. From 10 to 25 October PZ 5 was in Bielitz on the Saybusch-Dzieditz line.

Even before 1939 ended, all the armored trains except No. 2, which remained in Minsk Mazowiecki until the Russian campaign began, were transferred to western Germany. PZ 7, though, came back to Poland after the western campaign and was stationed in the Lublin-Cholm region until November 1940.

The ten armored trains of the Polish Army were organized in two armored train divisions (No. 1 in Legionowo, north of Warsaw, with Trains No. 11-15, No. 2 in Niepolomice, east of Cracow, with Trains No. 51-55). Each of these divisions had two trains built in Poland in 1921, two trains from the time of the Russian-Polish War (1920), and one small older armored train from the time when the country was founded. The 2nd Armored Train Division had another of these older trains as a training unit. All the trains had been modified in many ways during the twenties and thirties. The two Polish-built

ones of the 1st Division were subordinated to the "Posen" Army on September 1, 1939, while PZ 11 "Danuta" was in the northwest (Kolmar, across from Schneidemühl), No. 12 "Poznanczyk" was in the southwest (Rawitsch, on the Silesian border). No. 12, after border fighting near Rawitsch and Krotoschin, moved northward relatively quickly (to Wreschen) and then back to the east (via Kolo and Kutno), and on 7 September it was already near Blonie, west of Warsaw. There it was stopped by congested lines and cut off two days later. On the same day, though, it was badly damaged by German artillery near the town of Oltarzew (near the Ozarow station) and blown up by its crew. No. 11 came through withdrawal fighting near Schubin (Sept. 4) and Argenau (between Hohensalza and Thorn, on Sept. 7), on 9 September it arrived at Kutno. It stayed in the region from there to Sochaczew, where it was surrounded with the body of the "Posen" Army. When it was fired on and immobilized near the town of Raszno (on the Kutno-Lowicz line) on 16 September, it was made unusable and abandoned by the crew. No. 14 "Paderewski," at first held in reserve, was also advanced to Kutno on 9 September and operated from then on, along with No. 11; it met the same fate. Only a little east of its last stationing, in Jackowice, the crew blew it up on 16 September after it had been cut off on the way back from a vain breakthrough fight near Lowicz.—Another train of the 1st Armored Train Division, No. 13 "General Sosnkowski" belonged to the "Modlin" Army. At first it operated northwest of Warsaw in the Zichenau-Plonsk-Nasielsk region. On 7 September it was then transferred to the region northeast of Warsaw. On 9 September it fought near Wyszkow; one day later it was knocked off the rails and damaged by dive-bombers at the Lochow railroad station.

Hitler inspects the Polish armored train "General Sosnkowski," put out of action by a Stuka bomb at the station in Lochow on September 10, 1939.

The old No. 15 "Smierc," originating in Austro-Hungarian times, was kept in reserve at first and transferred to Modlin on 8 September when the fortress was threatened, surrounded with the rest of the troops, and surrendered with them on 28 September, but was obviously destroyed by the crew.

Of the trains of the 2nd Armored Train Division, the newer Polish-built No. 52 "Pilsudczyk" and No. 53 "Smialy" were with the "Lodz" Army north of New-Herby near Mokra on 1 September. There they and cavalry units inflicted heavy losses on the German 4th Armored Division. While No. 53 still had battles to fight with tanks of the 1st Armored Division as they advanced to Radomsk a little farther east, near Cykarzew, on the next day, No. 52 was already moved further north in the night of 1-2 September. On 5 September it fought in the Sieradz-Lask region. It was then transferred to the Warsaw area—east of it—where after using up its ammunition in Mrozy (between Minsk Mazowiecki and Siedlce), it was put out of commission by its crew. No. 53 also moved off to the north later. On 4 September it met the old No. 55 "Bartosz Glowacki" in Koluszki. Both were exposed to heavy bomb attacks there and were transferred to the Skierniewice—Zyrardow region, and later via Warsaw to Brest-Litovsk, where they were involved in combat on 14 September. Their way led next via Kowel to Lemberg (18 September), where they remained until the arrival of the Red Army, into whose hands they fell. The Armored Trains No. 51 "Pierwzy Marszalek" and No. 54 "Grozny," captured in 1920, were subordinated to the "Cracow" Army. No. 51 fought its first fights in the Sucha—Jordanow region, where it was damaged by artillery fire on 2 September. It was then transferred via Cracow, Tarnow, Debica, and Tarnobrzeg to Rozwadow, where it guarded the bridge over the San from 12 to 14 September. On 15 September it moved through Lublin and farther east to Kowel, and then reached the Sarny—Rovno region. On its return trip ahead of the advancing Red Army it got back to Poworsk (east of Kowel) and fell into their hands after being damaged by bombs (22 September). No. 54 was on the southern edge of the Upper Silesian industrial area on 1 September and was involved in heavy fighting in the Orzesche—Tichau—Kobier region, losing its commander in the battle. It had to endure further combat with German tanks near Wolbrom on 4 September. Then it moved off toward Tarnow. But since the bridge over the Dunajec was already destroyed it was abandoned by its crew in Biadolin. The training train of the 2nd Armored Train Division drew back in the direction of Przemysl, but before it could reach that city, it fell into German hands near Jaroslaw on 10 September.

From the material of Armored Trains No. 52 "Pilsudczyk" and No. 54 "Grozny" (plus the command car of No. 11 "Danuta" and presumably the gun car of the training train), the German Armored Trains No. 21 and 22 were set up at Cracow in the summer of 1940. They handled track securing tasks until their transfer to France in the spring of 1941.

The Soviets also used the Polish armored train material that had fallen into their hands, partly to set up two of their own armored trains, which—converted to broad gauge—were stationed in Lemberg. They were found there by the Germans when they occupied the city after the Russian campaign began (on June 30, 1941), and used by them by the end of the year as the combat trains of Armored Train No. 10 (Train 10A: gun cars of the ex-Polish No. 53 "Smialy," "assault cars" of No. 55 "Bartosz Glowacki"; Train No. 10B: Gun cars of the ex-Polish No. 51 "Pierwszy Marszalek," presumably "assault cars" of the "Smialy," plus the Polish Ti 3-2 armored locomotive, which surely came from one of these three trains).

After the Russian campaign began no armored trains of the German Wehrmacht were stationed for action in the territory of the General Government. But since April 1, 1942, until the evacuation on July 24, 1944, the Armored Train Replacement (and Training) Battalion was located in Rembertow, on the eastern edge of Warsaw. The armored trains constantly being set up there naturally made their test runs—particularly on the lines running eastward from Warsaw in the directions of Bialystok—Wolkowysk and Brest-Litovsk—Baranowici (on which a favorite practice site was located in Oranczyce), or branching off from Zabinka via Kobryn to the Pripjet region. Since the spring of 1943 at the latest (to February 1944) the Replacement Battalion also had a special training train, on which the crews could be trained on such runs before their own armored train arrived. After partisan groups made their presence known more and more in the Warsaw region and east of there, runs were made by the Replacement Battalion with the named trains, for both pure securing tasks and also direct action against these enemies.—When the fronts again approached the eastern border of the General Government during the German withdrawal after the successful Russian summer offensive of 1944, and had even moved far into it, the region again saw extensive armored train action by regular units. These events, though, are handled in the context of the eastern campaign.

The Polish armored train "Poznanczyk" was blown up by its crew after being damaged near Oltarzew on 9 September. Photo: J. Magnuski collection

The Occupation of Denmark and Norway

In March 1940 Armored Trains No. 23-25 were set up out of captured Czech material by Railroad Engineer Replacement Battalion No. 4 in Rehagen-Klausdorf. They were intended for the occupation of Denmark. Armored Trains No. 23 and 24 set out from their place of assembly to the gathering area at Bremen on April 5, 1940, were sent on the march on the evening of April 8, 1940, PZ 23 going with the advance battalion of Marching Group C to Flensburg (arriving between 3:45 and 4:15 AM on the morning of 9 April); PZ 24 went with the advance battalion of Marching group D to Niebüll-Süderlügum (arriving between 4:00 and 5:00 AM). At the beginning of the invasion, PZ 23 advanced to Fredericia on the east coast of Jutland, where it stopped and took over the securing of the bridge to Fyn. PZ 24 went up the west coast of Jutland, first via Tondern to Esbjerg. Later it was transferred to Holstebro, from which the bridge over the Lim-Fjord was secured. The two armored trains remained in Denmark until the end of May and beginning of June 1940; then they were called back to western Germany.

PZ 25 was supposed to take a ferry with the Buck Battalion of the 198th Infantry Division from Warnemünde to Gedser, and advance from there to Vordingborg to guard the bridge from Falster to Seeland. It might be mentioned that this use is the only one of a German armored train mentioned in Kurt von Tippelskirch's standard work on the history of World War II—except that it unfortunately did not happen. Late in the evening of 8 April, PZ 25 arrived at the Perleberg-Wittenberge gathering area on the quay to Warnemünde, but it was not shipped out. Instead, a normal passenger railcar was loaded onto the ferry "Mecklenburg." It was the first vehicle that—lying on the ground with a shock troop of the Buck battalion—rolled off the ferry in Gedser at 5:20 AM, followed by the rest of the troops on motorcycles and in motor vehicles. Presumably it was feared that the armored train on the slowly approaching ship would have aroused the Danes' suspicion, and thus its use was decided against.—This is what the records show. In the English language literature a picture was published (a copy fit to be reproduced could not be obtained) that appears to show an armored train being shipped out of Gedser. This is undoubtedly the complete Polish train "General Sosnkowski" that was put out of action by dive-bombers in Lochow on September 10, 1939. Even though it cannot be proved that this train was repaired and—although surely not with the first wave—could have

Left: PZ 23 at a railroad station on the east coast of Jutland in April 1940. Photo: P. Malmassari collection

Above: PZ 24, on the other hand, moved up the west coast of Jutland. Photo: P. Bettner/W. Sawodny collection.

Crewmen of PZ 24 in Esbjerg. Photo: W. Geipel/W. Sawodny collection

been sent to Denmark for line protection (for which, to be sure, no documentation is at hand!), there is one very suspicious circumstance: in the background of the picture, other armored train cars are shown being shipped out on the ferry, and of them, a third gun car of the "Sosnkowski" type is recognizable, but of these—since the train was unique—there were only two. So one might conclude that the picture was a photo montage that was made either by the Germans for propaganda purposes afterward to support the false report.

No armored trains were transferred to Norway, but on their advance along the rail lines the German troops already used makeshift armed trains. Later line protection trains were constantly being set up to serve on securing tasks. The train "Norwegen" is said to have been available already in the summer of 1942, but more precise data exist only from the last war years. In 1944 the line protection trains "Norwegen" (Oslo region), "Voss" (Bergen region), "Grong" (Namsos region), and "Narvik" (to secure the ore line from Sweden to there) existed. The trains (except "Norwegen") bore the names of the cities where they were stationed. Listed for January 1945 were: "Norwegen" (Armored Division "Norwegen"), "Bergen" (possibly the transferred "Voss," Field Command 188), "Grong" (XXXIII. Army Corps), and "Narvik" (199th Infantry Division), plus the probably newly established line protection train "Mornardal" with the LXX. Army Corps located along the Skaggerak coast between Kristiansand and Tönisberg. These trains, which were to protect the rail network from attacks by resistance fighters but also to fulfill tasks of coastal defense, all surely existed until the surrender and were then handed over.

Line protection trains in Norway:

Top: An armed railroad patrol during the occupation.
Above: Range finder and turret of a captured Renault FT-17/18 tank are aimed at a recognized target.
Upper left: On a tunnel-rich line in the mountains of central Norway.
Left: Heavily camouflaged on a securing run.
Photos: P. Malmassari and Federal Archives, Koblenz (3)

The Western Campaign and the Occupation
of the West European Countries

In the last weeks of 1939 the armored trains, with the exception of No. 2, were transferred to northwestern Germany. Their known stationing towns were Düsseldorf-Eller for PZ 1, Hamm for PZ 3, Hamm at first and then Osnabrück and Rheine for PZ 4, Mülheim/Ruhr, later Düsseldorf-Eller for PZ 5, Osnabrück, Oldenburg and Emden for PZ 6, and Lintorf or Dinslaken for PZ 7.

For the western campaign, these six armored trains were subordinated to Army Group B for the attack on the Netherlands. On May 3, 1940, the commanders, at a meeting in Dinslaken, were instructed as to their tasks for the attack day of 10 May. The armored trains were to make fast advances, take bridges over the Bulten Aa, Ijssel, and Maas, and push into the enemy positions, or break through them.

PZ 6, along with the 1st Cavalry Division, was to roll over the Dutch positions in Friesland and reach Harlingen by the evening of the first day, where it was hoped that they could capture the fortifications at the eastern end of the Zuider Zee dam in a surprise attack. In the train's advance from Weener, it already encountered a blown-up bridge over the Bulten Aa at the border town of Nieuwe Schans, which could be made passable for the armored train by engineers on hand there. But only a little farther, east of Winschoten, another railroad drawbridge was encountered that had been opened by the Hollanders. The Dutch troops posted on the opposite shore could at first drive back an attempt by the German troops, including the disembarked armored train crew, to cross the river. Thus, the surprise attack was ruined; the 1st Cavalry Division had to fight its way forward laboriously, and PZ 6 was called back to Wuppertal-Elberfeld.

The most demanding tasks were those of Armored Trains No. 3 and 4. The former was to advance from Borken via Winterswijk and Ruurlo to Zutphen, the latter from Bentheim via Hengelo-Almelo—Rijssen to Deventer, where the Ijssel bridges were to be taken unharmed if possible. This meant for both trains a trip of some 50 km through enemy territory before the actual action. The tracks had been scouted carefully in advance by officers of the armored trains riding in civilian clothing on regularly scheduled trains. The two trains crossed the Netherlands border at 5:35 AM.

For PZ 3, reported in advance as an express train, the undertaking progressed remarkably smoothly. At first it had a fully free run. Later it sufficed to aim its weapons (without firing a shot) at railroad buildings and facilities to persuade the Netherlands railroad men to allow it to run farther. Only in the last section did advance warnings by telephone cause the local personnel to leave their posts, but the line could be kept open by the railroad engineers of the armored train. Thus, the train approached Zutphen between 6:00 and 7:00 AM. But the warning of the approaching armored train had obviously also reached the bridge guards, for even before the armored train arrived in Zutphen the Ijssel bridges there were blown up. The armored train crew took possession of the railroad station there and advanced farther to the eastern shore of the Ijssel, where they came into combat with the Hollanders in bunkers on the opposite shore. The armored scout car (rail-capable Sd.Kfz. 231), which had advanced to the blown-up bridge, was immobilized there and shot down by enemy anti-tank guns. The armored train crew, scattered over about 1.5 km, fought with the Hollanders until units of the 227th Infantry Division and an SS battalion of the "Leibstandarte" arrived about 9:45 AM, but it still took until afternoon before, after knocking out the bunkers on the opposite shore, crossing the Ijssel was possible. PZ 3 was called back to Cologne-Brühl the next day.

The trip of PZ 4, which was followed by a troop transport train, did not run so smoothly. After it had crossed the border west of Bentheim at the attack time (5:35 AM), it ran into a jammed switch at the first railroad station in Holland, Oldenzaal, and one car was derailed. From there on, the engineers were sent ahead with cars and trucks to occupy the stations and thus assure open lines. Thus, the approach of a locomotive up the line that the armored train was using could be prevented. Thus PZ 4 reached Deventer only about 1:45 PM, after two battalions of the "Leibstandarte" had arrived there, but the Ijssel bridges were already blown up. The armored train crew took up a position along the Ijssel shore and fired at the Hollanders on the other bank (the other German troops had moved off to Zutphen), until they left their position on 13 May. Then the armored train crew crossed over in motorboats and advanced on bicycles to Apeldoorn. But just two days later they were gathered in Deventer again, and PZ 4 was sent back, first to Rheine, later to Wuppertal-Langerfeld.

PZ 4 (right) before Deventer. Behind it are the transport trains. Standing amid the crew, which has disembarked and awaits action, is Lt. Wieczorek, then the commander. Photo: W. Obermark/W. Sawodny collection

The blown-up Ijssel bridge near Westervoort, before which PZ 7 saw action and was damaged. Photo: T. Schorlemmer/W. Sawodny collection

PZ 7 had a considerably shorter route to its scene of action. Along with transport trains on which units of the 207th Infantry Division were loaded, it crossed the border from Elten after 5:35 AM and had reached Duiven around 6:20. The train got beyond Westervoort without trouble, where the troops were disembarked under fire cover from the armored train. They were supposed to cover the crossing of the Ijssel by the following SS Regiment "Der Führer," but its advance unit only arrived about 7:20 AM. On its arrival in Westervoort, the armored train had found the gates to the bridge closed, so that a surprise attack to take it was ruled out. The armored train was now supposed to support SS troops advancing on the bridge. A heavy fire fight developed with the casemates of the fortifications on the north side, in which PZ 7 was damaged. When the German troops approached the bridge it was blown up. The SS troops were able to cross the river only between 11 and 12 o'clock. Where PZ 7 was repaired is not known; it was then transferred to Poland.

South of the Rhine, the Maas bridges were the target of operations. To take the adjoining road and rail bridges near Venlo, which were only 5 km away from the German border station of Kaldenkirchen, 60 men of Engineer Battalion 156 (56th Infantry Division) were loaded onto a "Special Train W." By its description (freight cars with inside armor and machine guns, and a locomotive in the middle) it must have been one of the rail protection trains "borrowed" from the Reichsbahn and held ready in Krefeld. While the train stopped in Venlo to turn a switch the Hollanders blew up the bridges at 5:57 AM.

In two other cases, the bridges were supposed to be taken in surprise attacks before the attack time by shock troops of the "Brandenburger" dressed in Dutch mechanics' clothing (disguised as "Construction Training Battalion for special purposes 800"). In Roermond the troop dropped at the road bridge was recognized at the edge of town and driven away. The troop that was to march at 5:15 AM to the railroad bridge near Buggenum (north of Roermond) was also unmasked soon. To be sure, they overpowered the guards on the east bank and tried to storm the bridge, but it blew up more or less under their feet at about the official attack time (5:35 AM). PZ 5, which had a run of some 17 km ahead, had crossed the border and shortly after 6:00—after a blocked switch in Vlodrop had been opened and, after a quick ride through the Roermond railroad station—approached the bridge, the two eastern piles of which had remained intact. It was immediately taken under anti-tank fire from the casemates on the other side, whereby one of the first shells hit the brake line of the locomotive. Thus the train remained immobile on the approach ramp to the bridge and was—being only lightly armored—helplessly exposed to the fire, which set most of the cars afire, damaging some of them irreparably. The crew fled through the escape hatches, but five of them were dead and some 25 wounded. The transport train following in formation on the second line saw the disaster and pulled back under cover. From there the crew (II. Battalion., Infantry Regiment 59) spread out toward the Maas in order to fight down the Dutch positions on the west bank. Only between 9:00 and 12:00 were they able to cross a long stretch of the river and reach the Belgian border southwest of Roermond. The badly damaged PZ 5 was later disbanded; the reparable cars went to PZ 1.

On the other hand, the "Brandenburgers" were able to overpower the guards of the railroad bridge near Gennep and capture the bridge undamaged. At 5:28 AM PZ 1, waiting in Hassum and followed by a transport train carrying the III. Battalion of Infantry Regiment 481 (256th Infantry Division), started to move and crossed the Maas bridge at Gennep at 6:07. Both moved on quickly, broke through the Peel position of the surprised Hollanders near Mill, and advanced to just short of the railroad station in Zeeland, where the locomotive of PZ 1 also had taken a direct hit in the air ducting that stopped the train.

A car of PZ 5 prepared for the attack on May 10, 1940. Even at that time it still bore the Reichsbahn lettering "Repair Train." At far left is the train's commander, 1st Lt. Fritz Strauss. Photo: H. Popp/W. Sawodny collection

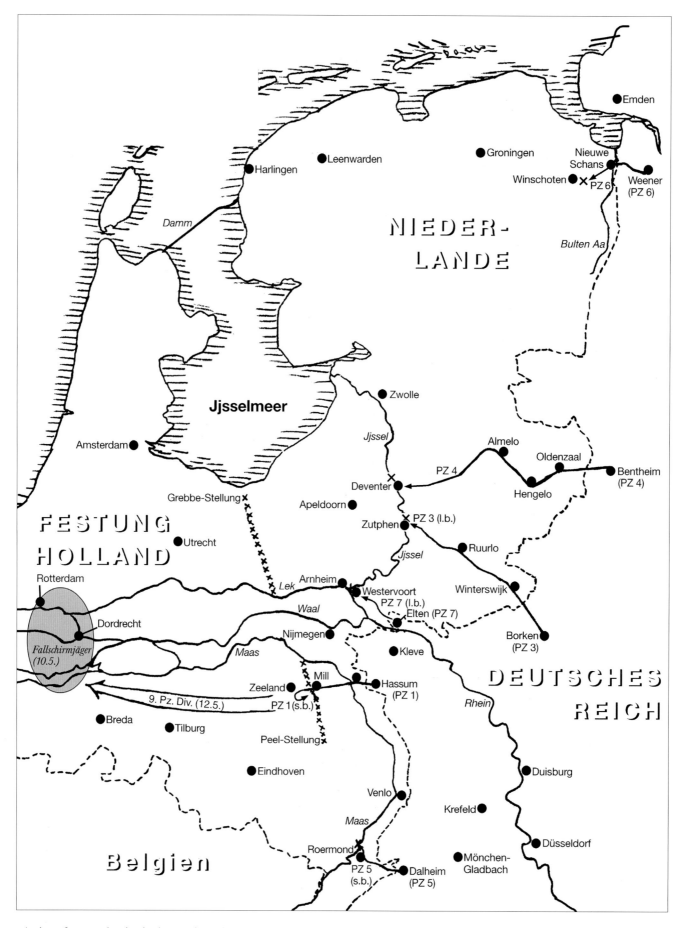

Action of armored trains in the attack on the Netherlands on May 10, 1940 (l.b. = slightly damaged, s.b. = badly damaged, X = bridge blown up).

The troops in the following transport train (which was later set afire by Dutch shock troops) left the train and attacked the surrounding enemies in fights with varying results. The locomotive of the armored train had meanwhile been repaired, and the train moved—now from the west, thus backward—back to the Peel position. There, to be sure, Dutch engineers had meanwhile closed the barrier and mined the tracks. The armored train drove at the barrier, which derailed half the train and the locomotive. The immobile train came under very heavy fire from the nearby Dutch bunkers, some of which had been put out of action by shock troops from the armored train crew. Although at attempt, at 3:50 PM, by the parts of Infantry Regiment 481 in front of the Peel position, to break through the position in order to approach the armored train and connect with the III. Battalion did not succeed, the Dutch counterattacks did not succeed in eliminating the German forces either, and toward evening the Hollanders drew back to the west. After German aircraft had bombarded the Peel position at 8:25 PM it was taken in a subsequent attack by troops of the 256th Infantry Division. Thus, PZ 1 could not only be rescued and the III. Battalion could rejoin the 481st Infantry Regiment, but the 9th Armored Division now had the possibility of making a fast advance to the west, and on the evening of 12 May it connected near Moerdijk with the troops of

For railroad inspection in the Netherlands, too, captured material was used. Here a Diesel switch engine and an O-car with a railroad engineer patrol are seen on May 17, 1940. Photo: Federal Archives, Koblenz

The front half of PZ 1 was derailed on May 10, 1940, by the barrier already closed by the Hollanders on its return trip after its breakthrough at the Peel position near Mill. In the foreground is a Dutch bunker captured by the armored train's crew; behind it one can see the rammed iron bars of the barrier (and another at some distance between the train and the crossing guard's house). Photo: H. Bendl/W. Sawodny collection

The place where PZ 1 was derailed is seen during cleaning-up work. The armored locomotive 57 2043 is already standing up again, but the cars have been tipped on their sides to clear the tracks. The explosion spot has been repaired already. Photo: S-MG The Hague

the 7th Airborne Division, who had landed there and were securing the mouth of the Vaal-Maas.

Despite this success, a negative balance has to be seen overall for the use of six armored trains against the Netherlands on May 10, 1940. Only one undertaking succeeded; all the others finally failed in their original intention, and this with a total of two badly and two slightly damaged armored trains with corresponding losses of manpower and material. PZ 1, badly damaged near Mill, was presumably sent for repairs at the Darmstadt RAW. For its restoration, the locomotive and the still usable cars of the disbanded PZ 5 (badly damaged north of Roermond) were used.

Unlike these actions within Army Group B, armored trains played only a non-essential role with Army Group A, which was to lead the main attack, and whose fast troops actually advanced through the Ardennes, crossed the Maas, broke through to the Channel coast and so cut off the main body of the French, Belgian, and British troops in Belgium. They carried out only scouting and securing tasks.

For this PZ 25, not used in Denmark, had been transferred from Warnemünde via Münster to Koblenz-Lützel earlier, PT 15,

which had been called in from its home base in Allenstein, and three Series 137 passenger railcars taken over from the Reichsbahn were made ready. Two of the railcars were assigned to the 1st company of Railroad Engineer Regiment 2, the other plus the armored railcar to the 4th Company of Railroad Engineer Regiment 3. On the morning of the attack day, May 10, 1940, the forces—led by the armored units—advanced over the border from Igel. Ahead of the railroad station in Wasserbillig they encountered a barrier, which was removed with explosives. At 6:55 AM they moved on to Luxembourg; PZ 25, whose locomotive came from an Austro-Hungarian armored train of World War I and was too weak, had to be given an extra loco to overcome the upgrades. After checking the bridges ahead of them for explosive charges (not present), the Luxembourg railroad station was reached at 10:45 AM. PZ 25 stayed in Luxembourg-Hollerich until June. On the same day (10 May) PZ 15 went on to the Luxembourg-Belgian border station of Klein-Bettingen. From there on major track destruction was spotted in Belgian territory and had to be repaired by the railroad engineers. The armored railcar secured the Klein-Bettingen—Pettingen—Differdingen line, brought materials from

PT 15 in the Ardennes in May 1940. This armored rail car too—like the unarmored ones—was given an R-car with a temporary gun stand (MG 08/15). Photo: Federal Archives, Koblenz

PZ 25 (background) in action in northern France in June 1940. Photo: N. Pignato collection

the last-named town, and transported engineer units to the site. On 17 May it covered the restored line via Arlon to Marbehan, on 18 May to Mellier, on 22 May to Libramont, and on 27 May—showing the progress in restoration—to Herbenmont. The other railcars, which were in the same area, were called back to Germany at the end of May.

Two such passenger railcars, painted field gray but unarmored, accompanied by O-cars with makeshift "armor" and machine guns, and manned by the 2nd Company of Railroad Engineer Regiment 4 and members of Infantry Regiment 45 (21st Infantry Division), advanced from the Prüm—Pronsfeld area toward the Belgian border at midnight on May 10. After capturing the railroad station at Lommersweiler, one turned southward but was stopped before a blown-up bridge near Oudler; the other advanced to before St. Vith, where a viaduct blew up before it. The crew was able to get out, overpower the bridge guards, and capture the town's railroad station. In that region both railcars provided security until 19 May; then they were called back.—Another such unit advanced from the Jünkerath—Stadtkyll region toward Malmedy on 10 May.

There is little information about the activities of armored trains in France in the second half of the western campaign, beginning on June 5, 1940. Around the first of the month, the two armored trains stationed in Denmark, No. 23 and 24, were summoned, but the armored locomotive of PZ 24, intended for securing tasks in the Liege region, broke down, so that it had to be taken to the Minden RAW for repairs. It was not used after that, but remained in Menden near Siegburg and was later located in Jülich. Nothing could be learned of the action and location of PZ 23, nor of the possible participation of PT 15 in this campaign. PZ 25, though, was transferred from Luxembourg to Charleville at the beginning of June 1940 and later moved up the Maas valley via Sedan and Verdun to St. Mihiel behind the front, which kept moving southward.

In the latter half of July, Armored Trains No. 23 and 25 and PT 15 were transferred back to Germany. Then they were disbanded along with PZ 24 and left in Koenigsberg.

On August 11, 1940, Armored Trains No. 3 and 4, then in Cologne-Brühl and Wuppertal-Langerfeld respectively, were transferred to occupied Holland for securing tasks. PZ 3 was stationed in Breda at first (until February 21, 1941), then in Eindhoven until it was transferred to the east on May 10, 1941. PZ 4 remained in Amsterdam for coast guarding until January 19, 1941, and was then transferred to Orleans, where it was stationed at Les Aubrais until May 10, 1941.

At the beginning of April 1941, Armored Trains No. 21 and 22, made up of captured Polish material, were brought to France from the General Government. PZ 21 was in Langres at first, and in Dijon-Porte Neuve from November 22, 1941, on. Its securing region was the entire eastern and northern French territory including Belgium, for which the train was often divided into two parts. For example, one half went from Paris (6/28/42) to Calais (7/2), Dunkerque (7/3), Bruges (7/4), Antwerp (7/5), Hasselt (7/6), Brussels (7/7), Liege (7/10), and back to Dijon on July 11. PZ 22 was stationed in Tours and made securing runs along the Atlantic and channel coasts in western France. On September 6, 1941, it was transferred from there to Niort. No special events were reported in that time period. It appears that at that time neither air raids nor activities of French resistance fighters resulted in noteworthy disturbances to rail transit.

At the end of October 1942 PZ 21, heavily equipped with artillery, was transferred to the eastern front. In its place, the much more lightly armed PZ 25 went to Dijon and was later kept in readiness at Nevers.

The snow-covered gun car (already with a 7.5-cm L/41 gun) is seen at a stop of PZ 3 in Breda in the winter of 1940-41. Photo: H. Bendl/W. Sawodny collection

PZ 4 (right) is seen in the Amersfoort yards while stationed in Holland in the autumn of 1940. Photo: W. Obermark/W. Sawodny collection

Above left: PZ 21 on its transfer run from Poland to France early in April 1941. Coupled on the front is the barracks train (with its own locomotive), and freight cars are hitched on behind the armored train. Photo: F. Englberger/W. Sawodny collection *Above right:* A rest stop on a securing run by PZ 21 in northern France, 1941-42. Photo: H. Wülfing/W. Sawodny collection

On November 11, 1942, both armored trains (No. 22 and 25) took part in the occupation of the part of France governed by Marshal Petain. On that day PZ 25 already reached Vichy, the seat of government. Both armored trains advanced to the Mediterranean coast, but PZ 22 was soon sent back to Saintes and later to Niort to carry out securing tasks in western France. PZ 25, on the other hand, stayed on the coast, which it was to guard from the Rhone delta to Nice (stationed in Barbentane, Miramas, and Nice). Its trips also took it into the French Alps, where it spent some time at Briancon.

When the fall of Mussolini at the end of July 1943 indicated a possible loss of Italy as an ally of the German Reich, the two armored trains in France were also alarmed for an advance into that country. PZ 25 was then in Miramas (Rhone delta), PZ 22, which had just finished a sharpshooting drill on the peninsula of Fouras, near La Rochelle, was transferred to Lyon. From the day of the Italian surrender (September 8, 1943), both took over the securing of the tracks from the Rhone delta to Genoa, and this remained in effect until March 1944. The trains were based at Imperia Oneglia, San Remo, Menton, Nicas-Cagnes (December 1943 to February 1944), Golfe Jouan near Cannes, and Les Arcs-Draguignan (securing the region from Toulon to Antibes, until July 1944); for PZ 25 the following

bases are listed: Alassio, Ventimiglia—Breil—Nice triangle (from November 1943 to March 1944).

In mid-March 1944 PZ 25 was transferred, at first via Marseille and Nimes to the western part of the French Mediterranean coast, where it secured the Montpellier—Beziers—Narbonne—Perpignan region. In May 1944 it went to Castres to protect the Narbonne—Carcassonne—Toulouse—Montauban region, but its action runs also took it to Bordeaux and Limoges. The last transfer was probably made in connection with considerably heightened Resistance activity in this region (on 19 July it carried out an anti-partisan action in Carcassonne, in which losses were recorded), but may have also been influenced by increased Allied air raids in the coastal area. This not only compelled the armored trains to be parked in tunnels during the day, but also narrowed their natural range through much destruction of tracks.

In June 1944 PZ 22 was also withdrawn from the coast. At first it went to Vienne, in the Rhone valley south of Lyon, later to Bourg-en-Bresse to secure transport on the Belfort—Besancon—Lyon line, as well as from Bourg via Chambery to Modane, a region especially threatened by partisans. On 14 June it was able to avoid a Resistance attack 10 km north of where it was stationed. In addition, PZ 24

PZ 22 on maneuvers in western France early in August 1941. Photo: Federal Archives, Koblenz

Above Right: PZ 22 at the railroad station in Nice in the winter of 1943-44. *Above Left:* PZ 22 at the station in Mentone in the autumn of 1943, after Italy surrendered. Photos: W. Grasst/W. Sawodny collection

PZ 25 was already used to protect the French Riviera coast since the end of 1942. After Italy surrendered its action area spread to Genoa—here on a securing run. Photo: Federal Archives, Koblenz

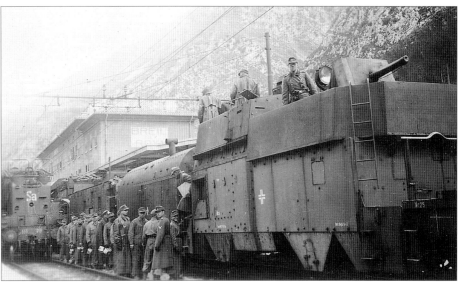

PZ 25 at the station in Breil in the winter of 1943-44. At left is an Italian 1'C1' Series 333 A.C. locomotive. Photo: E. Banser/W. Sawodny collection

was transferred from Italy to France at the end of July 1944. It was stationed in Bourges.

On February 4, 1944, the OKH advised the Military Commander France to set up an armored train of the BP 42 type. It was at first numbered 31 (the former armored train with that number had been lost in the east on December 28, 1943), but at the beginning of May it was renumbered 32. It was built by Schneider in Le Creusot and as of March 24, 1944, by Somua in Lyon-Venissieux. A bomb attack on this factory on 25 May did considerable damage and delayed the preparation of the train. PZ 32 was ready for action on July 10, 1944, and remained in the Lyon area. It was usually stationed in Villefranche-sur-Saone.

Besides the regular armored trains there were also line protection trains in France. On such (designated an "auxiliary armored train") operated as of June 1944 at the latest (but probably much earlier) in the Bordeaux—Limoges area. The train was able to fight off Resistance attacks at Mussidan on July 11, 1944, and Brive in August 1944.—The Railroad Authority at the Lyon Railroad Operations Office—presumably in the winter of 1943-44—re-equipped two auxiliary trains (for track rebuilding) with armed and armored cars as line protection trains, after they had repeatedly been attacked and brought into danger by French Resistance fighters. One of these trains (which were named "Anna" and "Caesar") was enclosed by rail destruction on both sides between Amberieu and Culoz (east of Lyon) in the spring of 1944 and besieged by the Resistance for three days before it could be freed—badly damaged—by the other train. There are no reports of other line protection trains in France, but that does not rule out the possibility that others could have existed.

The Western Allies had landed in Normandy on June 6, 1944, and in the last week of July the Americans were finally able to advance from the beachhead into the breadth of the region near Avranches, and soon to advance to the east quickly north of the Loire. On August 15, 1944, a second landing took place on the Mediterranean coast between Cannes and Toulon. The landed Allied forces immediately spread out along the coast to the east (Nice) and west (Toulon was surrounded on 20 August, Marseille two days later) and advanced northward, where they already reached Grenoble on 23 August, but they were not able to break the Germans' main retreat route, the Rhone valley, permanently.

At first PZ 25 was ordered back out of the Toulouse region into the Rhone delta. On 19 August it was already in the tunnels at Cassis, between Toulon and Marseille, but could scarcely move, on account of the total Allied aerial dominance. On 21 August it was attacked by low-flying fighter planes near Nimes and incurred losses. All that remained then was the retreat up the right bank of the Rhone, in which rail transports were accompanied and secured. On 24 August PZ 25 was in Le Pouzin, on 27 August in Tournon, and on 29 August finally in Lyon. The lines in the Rhone valley were broken again and again by bombs and Resistance fighters. Thus, the two repair trains of the Lyon railroad authorities had their hands full. On 24 August "Anna" protected rail repair work in Chasse, "Caesar" the rebuilding of the Isere bridge north of Valence. The next day "Caesar" was to escort a provision train to La Peage, but only reached Estressin, since the line to the south had been destroyed by bombs. On 27 August "Anna" was to pick up a gun transport in Givors, but came under such heavy fire from the Resistance at the edge of Lyon that it could not get through. On 28 August one of these line protection trains

escorted an empty train, but was forced to turn back by low flying planes south of Vienne.

On 30 August PZ 25—though without its additional A/A cars—was sent back to Macon and then moved on to Chalon-sur-Saone. On the next day its A/A cars protected the retreat of three locomotives from Lyon, which hauled two fuel trains in Belleville and Romaneche. The convoy, which a third train joined in Macon, moved from there to Chalon, Dijon, and Dole on 1 September, reached Besancon on 2 September, Belfort on 3 September, and German territory the next day. The rest of PZ 25 may well have arrived previously—presumably by the same route.—PZ 32 was also moved back from Villefranche via Macon to the Chalon—Chagny region in the last days of August, as were the line protection trains "Anna" and "Caesar," of which "Anna" had brought a fuel train back from Lyon-Brotteux to Macon (further data on the fates of these trains are lacking).

In the second half of August the Resistance was able to block the Chambery—Modane—Mont Cenis tunnel line completely, despite repeated action of PZ 22. At the beginning of September 1944 the Americans moved from Grenoble and approached Bourg-en-Bresse. Therefore PZ 22 was sent back via Macon to Dijon, where it was already located on 2 September. On 4 September it was documented as being in Auxonne on the way to Germany, presumably getting there via Gray and Vesoul to Belfort, since the line through Besancon was no longer usable.

The stationing of PZ 24 in Bourges was of special significance, for the retreat route of the remaining parts of the 1st Army, which had formerly been on the Biscay coast and was now in danger of being cut off between the spearheads of the Allies, which—one eastward north of the Loire, the other up the Rhone and Saone—both led to Dijon. It was not so much a matter of combat units as of many back line services, even civilian personnel, all of them naturally only mobile on foot and thus slow, as the march was constantly hindered by the Resistance. This gave special importance to rail transport running from the west and southwest to Bourges and Moulins. This route, like that going on from Bourges via Saincaze, Moulins, Paray-le-Monial, Montchanin, and Chagny, was cut several times a day by Resistance fighters and thus had to be repaired constantly. PZ 24 at first made chiefly securing runs between Bourges and Saincaze and Nevers; on 24 August it was ordered to Reuilly (on the Vierzon—Issoudun line), where a bridge had been blown up. On 29 August it began its retreat, which ran via Nevers (8/29-30) Moulins (8/30-31) and Paralle-Monial to Montchanin. There an explosion site was to be repaired before PZ 24 reached Dijon on 2 September as an escort for several transport trains. On the next day it was supposed to pick up other transport train at Paray-le-Monial but could only get to Montchanin, where the line had been broken by bombs. The return to Dijon on 4 September resulted, after track repairs in Chagny, in a low flying air attack in Beaune, in which two cars were lost. Meanwhile, French troops (which had landed with the Allies on the Mediterranean coast) advanced northward from west of Lyon between the Saone and Loire; the Americans approached the Doubs valley and Besancon, plus Langres to the north of Dijon. An attempt by PZ 24 to escape in the last-named direction on 5 September ended near Is-sur-Tille; the train had to return to Dijon. The next day the train went to Auxonne, where the line was blocked by a train collision. But a 300-meter detour line put the armored train on the track via Gray (9/7) and Vesoul to Lure (9/8), where the train again took on securing tasks and fought off several dive-bomber attacks. On

PZ 32 was abandoned by its crew at St. Berain (September 8, 1944). Photo: Viellard collection

September 10th it went on to Belfort, which could be reached only with difficulty, for a detour line again had to be built around a blown-up ammunition train, and the tracks between the tunnel and the station had to be cleared of the rubble of several collided trains. On 12 September PZ 24 finally reached the right bank of the Rhine safely.

PZ 32 had worse luck. It was also on the line from Dijon to Paray-le-Monial since 1 September and secured transports and track repair work. But unlike PZ 24, it did not return to Dijon at the right time. On 7 September it stayed in St. Berain (between Montchanin and Chagny) because the locomotive ran out of water. There it was caught up with and captured by French troops. Its supply train also had to be given up on 12 September. — A similar fate met the auxiliary armored (line protection) train that had operated in the Bordeaux—Limoges—Brive region in the summer of 1944 (see above). This was able to move to Bourges with the forces of the 1st Army, but they reached Bourges only on 3 September. The next day it was in Moulins, and on September 6, 1944, it too fell into the hands of French forces in Montceau-les-Mines. Still, these sacrifices helped to allow some 60% of the 1st Army to rejoin their own troops.

On November 14, 1944, the French 1st Army advanced out of the Doubs valley south of Belfort along the Swiss border, reached the Rhine on 19 November, and occupied Mülhausen. With the LXIII. Army Corps stopped on the front salient between that city and Belfort was a line protection train. On the French attack from the Altkirch region toward the west, this train was immobilized at the railroad station in Dammerkirch by blowing up the viaducts on both sides, and there—after running out of ammunition and probably being blown up by its own crew—it fell into enemy hands on 27 November.

The two armored trains set up in surrounded La Rochelle in the autumn of 1944 operated mainly in the Aigrefeuille region east of the city; on its surrender to the French on May 8, 1945, they were at the station in La Rochelle.

After British and Canadian troops arrived in Holland south of the mouths of the Rhine early in November 1944, a makeshift armored train, with a 30-man crew, was set up in the so-called "fortress" of Hoek van Holland. Other data on its equipment are lacking, as well as on its actions and its fate, but it can be assumed that it patrolled in the Hoek van Holland—Rotterdam—The Hague region, and it is not impossible that it did so until the time when the troops surrounded in the "Fortress Holland" surrendered on May 4, 1945.

Finally, it is reported that on March 31, 1945, a German armored train coming out of Neu-Beckum had fired on the American tanks advancing from Ahlen in the direction of Beckum and then was silenced and immobilized by fire from them. This too must have been an improvised unit (line protection train). — All of these reports show that even on the western front in the last months of the war, making heavy weapons mobile by rail was done again and again out of desperation, without, of course, being able to achieve any real success.

PZ 25 secures the Souillac—Brive line in southwestern France in the early summer of 1944. Photo: E. Banser/W. Sawodny collection

Armored Trains in the Balkans, Italy, Hungary, and Austria

The first two years in Serbia and Croatia—until the Summer of 1943

No German armored trains took part in the Balkan campaign in April 1941, but the Hungarians used theirs in the occupation of the area assigned to them between the Danube and Theiss.

To be sure, shortly after the occupation and division of Yugoslavia (into a separate Croatia allied with Germany and a Serbia occupied by Germany; the northern part of Slovenia had been added to the German Reich, the southern part to Italy, which had also appropriated Montenegro and Adriatic coastal areas; Hungary also received portions in the north and Bulgaria and Albania in the south), resistance groups became active, first the nationalist Chetniks, and after the Russian campaign began, also the Communists led by Tito, at first mainly southwest and south of Belgrade (the Tito partisans even ran an armored train for a short time on the narrow gauge line near Uzice, but had to give it up when they were driven out of that region). Through this district, though, there ran the important supply line for the German troops in Greece. Thus, in June 1941 the reactivated Armored Trains No. 23 and 24 were transferred to Serbia. PZ 23, after spending about four weeks in Belgrade or Topcider, was finally stationed in Mladenovac; PZ 24 in Nisch. Together they secured the line from Belgrade to Skopje, both the western line from Lapovo via Kraljevo, Raska, Kosovska Mitrovica, and Kosovo Polje, and the eastern one via Stalac, Nisch, and Vranje. PZ 23 was also assigned to guard the lines southeast of Belgrade in the direction of the Danube (to Smederovo and Kucevo) as well as the narrow gauge line west of Mladenovac (to Lajkovac with branches to Valjevo, Obrenovac,

and Cacak), for which a small "armored train" (O-cars with wooden sill reinforcement of the sidewalls, later probably included in the line protection trains) was set up.—PZ 24 also saw service on the line from Nisch to Sofia as far as the Bulgarian border, as well as to Zajecar and Negotin. Since the partisans seldom dared to attack the secured sections of the lines most of the runs were made without disturbance. PZ 23 reported eleven inspection runs in the period from October 15 to November 15, 1941, on two of which partisans were moved to flee, and twelve attacks by the shock troops outside the railroad area, in which partisan groups could often be positioned so that their attacks and explosions were considerably weakened. On 18 October a bridge was blown up between Aracicewo and Bagrdan immediately in front of the armored train; it was able to stop in time. On 28 November it was derailed on the Nisch—Skopje line, as the rail plates had been loosened. (It had previously secured the Nisch—Sofia line from 20 to 27 November in relief of PZ 24.) After repairs in Nisch it returned to its stationing in Mladenovac on 3 December. PZ 24 reported having covered 12,792 kilometers in action in the Balkans as of 15 November. Between 15 November and 14 December it made (besides two escorts of high officers to and from Belgrade) 15 securing runs from Nisch (mostly toward Skopje), twelve of which went without incidents. On 26 November a bridge had been blown up near Gramada, on 5 December the line south of Doljevac, on 14 December a partisan (infantry) action took place near Pesenjevci; in no case could partisans be captured. Previously, though, the two armored trains had taken part in mopping-up action in northwest Serbia, driving the partisans from there by the year's end. The disembarked crew of PZ 23 saw such action in the Jasenica valley between Rudnik and ToPola in late September and early October.

After the Balkan campaign in April 1941, Armored Trains No. 23 and 24—here PZ 23 on its transfer run—were stationed in Serbia two months later. Photo: H. Bruntsch/W. Sawodny collection

PZ 23 in action in the autumn of 1941. The infantry disembarks to attack partisans. Photo: Federal Archives, Koblenz

PZ 24—still with the Series 93 locomotive—in action in Serbia in the autumn of 1941. Photo: H. Röhle/W. Sawodny collection

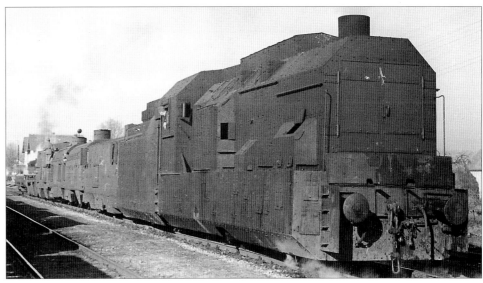

The rear half of PZ 24—here with Locomotive 57 2043—in 1942. Photo: Federal Archives, Koblenz

At first the partisans drew back to the west into the roadless regions of Montenegro and Herzegovina. Meanwhile, the Ustascha regime that ruled in Croatia had made so many enemies in the country by its bloody behavior, especially against the Serbs, that resistance spread throughout the land. Increasing attacks on the line between Agram and Belgrade now made them seem more strongly threatened than the lines in German-occupied Serbia, which had become more quiet. Therefore Armored Trains No. 23 and 24 were transferred into this region in the spring of 1942. At first PZ 23 spent a short time in Novska; it was finally stationed in Sisak. In addition to securing the main line from Agram toward Belgrade, it also made runs on the lines branching off from Sunja to Bihac or Banja Luka, though they usually ended at Kostajnica, as the Una bridge there was too weak for the armored train, and every crossing—even under appropriate cautionary measures—created a risk. At dawn on August 30, 1942, PZ 23 ran into a partisan ambush near Caprag, the first station east of Sisak. Setting off a detonation under the train threw the locomotive and all the cars except the gun-A/A car and the control car that went with it down a small embankment. A fireman who had jumped off the wrong side was crushed by the locomotive; and another member of the loco crew suffered severe injuries, from which he died later. Of the approximately 75 crew members carried on board, four more were badly and 62 slightly injured. Despite that, the crew of the

halted car was able to fight off the partisan attack on the wrecked train. After a crane train arrived two days later, the job of recovery began. The rest of the train remained in Sisak for some time before it was taken away to the Gleiwitz RAW, where an almost complete rebuilding of PZ 23 was undertaken.

PZ 24 was stationed in Slavonski Brod. Its region of action was likewise the line from Agram to Belgrade, and after PZ 23 went out of service also the lines from Sunja via Bosanski Novi and Prijedor to Banja Luka and from Sisak to Karlstadt, which were especially threatened by partisans, once the Tito bands had established themselves in western Bosnia in the autumn of 1942. In addition, PZ 24 also saw service in the Esseg—Dalj—Vinkovci region and on the Indija—Novi Sad line.

In place of the disabled PZ 23, PZ 6, newly equipped with captured Russian gun cars, came to the Balkans in October 1942. Its region of action was also the entire line from Agram to Belgrade, but for this armored train it also extended beyond to Nisch, for which it was stationed in Lapovo for a time. In mid-March PT 15 was assigned to this armored train.

As early as April 1942 three Croatian armored trains are also documented, one of them operating on the Agram—Belgrade line. At the beginning of 1943 the number of Croatian armored trains had risen to five. From that time on, armored railcars were also built in a factory in Slavonski Brod.

PZ 23 (right foreground) was called in the spring of 1942 to an explosion site near Rajic (east of Novska), where a transport train had been thrown off the embankment. Photo: H. Bruntsch/W. Sawodny collection

On August 30, 1942, PZ 23 itself fell victim to an explosion near Caprag (east of Sisak). The train was badly damaged. Photo: H. G. Hartmann/W. Sawodny collection

Cleanup work after the PZ 23 explosion. The armored locomotive 93 220 was righted with the help of the crane train and brought back to the main line on an auxiliary track. Photo: H. G. Hartmann/W. Sawodny collection

Below left: In October 1942, the rebuilt PZ 6 came to the Balkans to replace PZ 23. Photo: E. Espey/W. Sawodny collection

Facing page: Map of the railroad lines in the Balkan region.
Facsimile with kind permission of Musterschmidt Publishing, Göttingen, from Kreidler, E.: "Die Eisenbahnen im Machtbereich der Achsenmaechte waehrend des Zweiten Weltkriegs"

=== double-track line
---- single-track line
+++ narrow-gauge line
-.-.- German-Italian demarcation line
Status as of mid-1941

Through Rommel's advance toward Egypt the low-performance line to Greece appeared to gain greater significance, since the way from there to eastern North Africa was considerably shorter than from Sicily. Thus, an expansion program was decided on, which developed only in the summer of 1943—when the German troops had long since been driven out of Africa. On the other hand, this also encouraged the partisans to greater activity, by which the lines between Agram and Belgrade and those in Greece were hit particularly. Even after the main parts of the Tito bands were pushed southward out of northwestern Croatia and western Bosnia by Operation "White" in February and March 1943, there remained enough partisan groups in the region of the line from Agram to Belgrade to maintain a constant threat. The two German and the Croatian armored trains were not enough by far to be able to offer reasonable protection. Therefore additional makeshift armored trains—line protection trains—were equipped. On February 14, 1943 there were already four such line protection trains on hand in the Croatian region, and another had arrived by July 1943.—In the meantime, on February 13, 1943, PZ 24 was damaged in a collision during the anti-partisan Operation "Weiss" and had to go to the Maribor RAW for repairs. Meanwhile, it was decided to rebuild it completely in Munich, and it did not return to the Balkans.

How precarious the transport situation there was at that time is shown by many relevant entries in OKW war diaries, of which the following will be cited below, and from which the involvement of armored trains (unfortunately, no more exact details or even numbers of the trains are to be gained) can be seen:

12/14/42: South of Doboj (Brod—Sarajevo line), Croatian (narrow gauge) armored train derailed by sabotage.

12/17/1944: Between Bos. Novi and Bos. Krupa (line to Bihac) partisans attacked a Croatian armored train.

4/11/43: Near Nemila (in Bosna valley north of Zenica) a freight train was derailed and set afire by partisans; a Croatian narrow gauge armored train was used against them.

4/14/43: Through sabotage, two (Croatian) armored trains were derailed in the Bjelovar—Virovitica Slatina—Daruvar region.

April '43: The increasing partisan activity made securing the Saloniki-Athens line with line protection trains necessary.

5/16/43: An armored train was derailed by an explosion northwest of Novska.

5/20/43: A partisan attack near Mladenovac was beaten off by Serbian forces with the help of an armored train.

5/26/43: A (Croatian?) armored train ran onto a mine northeast of Daruvar; the locomotive and two cars were derailed. Fire fight with partisans.

5/28/43: A freight train was attacked west of Nova Gradiska; an armored train was used in a counterattack.

5/29/43: On the line from Sunja to Agram a line protection train ran onto a mine; two cars were derailed.

6/16/43: On the narrow gauge line from Lajkovac to Milanovac a sentry of the Serbian Volunteer Corps was attacked by a Chetnik group out of a train; it was pursued by an armored train.

6/19/43: An attack northwest of Nasice was broken up by an armored train.

6/29/43: Fighting around the railroad station at Lasva (south of Zenica) includes action by a (Croatian narrow gauge) armored train. Near Sunja an attack on a German munitions train was beaten back with the help of an armored train.

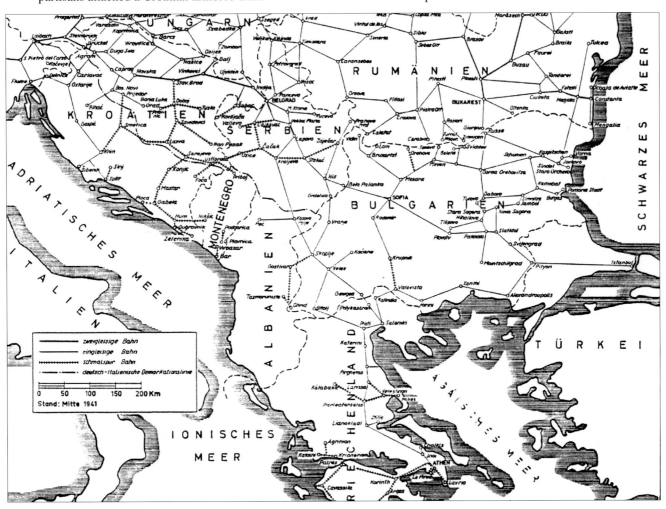

The Extension of Railroad Security to the Summer of 1944

The constantly growing influence on railroad traffic by partisan attacks caused the OKW to assign two armored trains of the new BP 42 series to the Commander Southeast. PZ 64 arrived in Croatia on June 22, 1943, and was stationed in Ruma (west of Belgrade). PZ 65, which was ready for action by mid-July 1943, was first supposed to go to Greece. Its run to Saloniki, though, showed that it was too heavy for the lines and bridges there. Thus it was ordered back to Croatia and was at the main depot in Agram as of mid-August. At the beginning of 1944 it was transferred to Popovaca on the northern line from Agram to Novska. In mid-August 1943 the newly built PZ 23 also appeared in Croatia again. It was first stationed at Sunja, as of 19 September in Novska (formerly the line protection train No. 206 was in that area; now it was transferred to the line from Sunja to Bosanski Novi).

The need to secure the Greek rail network as well, and the impossibility of doing so with a normal type of armored train, led to the hastening of plans to set up light and heavy scout cars for the Balkan area. The AOK order for the former was given in August, for the latter in September 1943. It was hoped that the four light trains would be ready for use as early as October and November, which was to turn out to be a false hope. As a temporary solution, PT 15 was assigned six road- and rail-going Panhard scout cars, and it was sent to Greece as an independent unit in August 1943. It remained there until the arrival of the first light scout train (No. 301) in February 1944. In addition, line protection trains had already been put into service in Greece in April 1943. The railroad security staff in Larissa, in addition to the aforementioned armored cars, had four such trains, numbered 202, 208, 209, and 214.

In August 1943 the transport system in the Balkans was reorganized. The Railroad Security Staff Croatia divided the Agram-Belgrade line into several security sectors, with an armored train in each of them:

Security Sector A: PZ 65, Agram
Security Sector B: PZ 6, Slavonski Brod
Security Sector C: PZ 64, Ruma
Security Sector D: Croatian Armored Trains No. 1 and 2, Line Protection Trains No. 104 and 105; Doboj (Slavonski Brod-Sarajevo narrow gauge line)
Security Sector E: PZ 23, Novska.

In the summer of 1943 the two new armored trains, No. 64 and 65, were transferred to the Balkans. PZ 64 is seen on the way to there, PZ 65 at its service post. Photos: W. Hartmann and H. D. Becker/W. Sawodny collection

On September 18, 1943, PZ 64 ran onto a mine. Several cars were thrown off the tracks, but were only slightly damaged. Photo: W. Hartmann/W. Sawodny collection

On August 4, 1943, it had also captured a Croatian armored train on the narrow gauge Bosanski Brod-Sarajevo line. Photo: Belgrade Railway Museum

In August 1943 the newly built PZ 23 appeared in the Balkans again. While the AA and command cars of the previous train had been rebuilt, the four-axle gun cars were fitted with two turrets; the armored locomotive, armor-bearing and control cars were those of the standard BP 42 type. Photo: J. Frings/W. Sawodny collection

In August 1943 PT 15 was sent to Greece with six rail-going Panhard scout cars. Before the railcar (left) is the commander, Oblt. H. Oppenhorst. Note that the crew (on the car) wear tropical hats. Above: Two of the Panhards assigned to PT 15. Photos: R. Reddin and L. Johnen/W. Sawodny collection

The Germans thus concentrated on this main line and the narrow gauge line to Sarajevo in Bosnia, while leaving the protection of the rest of the rail network to the Croatian allies.

On September 8, 1943, Germany's former ally, Italy, surrendered. The greatest part of the Italian troops could be disarmed by the prepared Germans, a few continued to fight on the German side, but some went over to the partisans, who thus gained considerable elbow room. The southern part of Slovenia was turned over militarily to the Commander, Adriatic Coastland, to whom the Italian provinces of Friaul, Görz, Trieste, and Istria were subordinate. In the Balkans, the entire west coast from Fiume down to Greece had to be occupied. As for railroad lines, the Italians had operated the coastal line from Fiume via Ogulin, Gospic, and Knin to Sibenik or Split, which had been shut down by permanent partisan activity between Gracac and Knin, the line from Ogulin via Karlstadt in the direction of Agram and that from Karlstadt to Laibach, plus the narrow gauge line from Dubrovnik to Mostar. Of them, the Germans undertook to keep only the Agram—Karlstadt—Ogulin line as Security Sector F (Line Protection Train No. 206—formerly transferred to the Sunja—Bosanki Novi region—was sent there on September 25, 1943) and the narrow gauge line that they tried to keep open from Sarajevo to Mostar and beyond. The Croatians took over line protection on the coastal line. In the first half of 1944, five Croatian armored trains operated in the district of the XV. Geb.K., which occupied Dalmatia between Sisak and Split.

One of the line protection trains used in the Balkans is on a securing run. It is pushing four control cars in case of mining on the line. Photo: Federal Archives, Koblenz

During a stop at a station, part of a line protection train's crew finds time for a card game on a car with an old captured Renault FT 17/18 tank. At right is a Mallett locomotive (axle type 0-6-0-0-6-0) of JDZ Series 31 (ex-MAV 651). Photo: Federal Archives, Koblenz

The leaders of a line protection train observe the terrain to the side. In the background are a locomotive of JDZ Series 20, a G-car rebuilt as a command car, and an infantry car built in Yugoslavia. Photo: Federal Archives, Koblenz

In their time, the Italians had used several makeshift armored trains, five armored railcars of the "Littorina" type and a number of rail-and-road armored troop carriers (OM Types 32, 35, and 36) and armored scout cars (AB 40, 41, and 43) to secure the rail lines, which were already severely threatened by partisans. When they surrendered, it is documented that one armored railroad coast battery and one armored train in Istria, plus numerous narrow gauge OM cars and one "Littorina" fell into German hands. Two of the railcars continued to be used by Italians on the German side; most of their other armored rail vehicles, unless they were destroyed, were taken over by Croats or partisans.

The first report of the General of Transportation in OB Southeast for the period between August 28 and September 10, 1943, reports on the situation:

"Considerable disturbance to railroad operations by frequent acts of sabotage on the Agram—Semlin main line. Operational development in Croatia thereby affected very strongly.... Operating situation in Serbia likewise tense at times resulting from bad moves in the direction of Croatia.... Leading and directing the railroad operations in New Bulgaria (the Macedonian part in southern Yugoslavia, which had been promised to Bulgaria in 1941; but the Bulgarians had already taken on line securing in Serbia south of Lapovo as an occupation troop) by the Bulgarian officials have been more and more faulty of late."

Here, too, the reports in which the participation of armored trains can be seen may be cited individually:

7/2/43: PZ 64 hit a mine near Nova Gradiska; partisan attack driven off.

8/18/43: In a night attack of the 1st Partisan Brigade on an airfield near Sarajevo, a line protection train was blown up.

9/18/43: PZ 64 hit a mine, slightly damaged.

9/21/43: Partisan activity by PZ 65 near Turopolje.

9/22/43: Partisan activity by PZ 65 near Mraclin.

10/14/43: Partisan activity by PZ 65 near Blinsky Kut.

10/29/43: Action of PZ 65 at an explosion site near Mraclin and against partisans near Lekenik; PZ 23 in action on the Brdani—Blinski Kut line.

10/30/43: PZ 23 secured repair work between Lipovljani and Banova Jaruga.

11/4/43: PZ 6 in action between Nova Gradiska and Petrova Selo.

11/11/43: PZ 6 was ordered from Slav. Brod to an explosion site near Okucani.

11/14/43: Croatian Armored Train No. 2 in action on the Doboj—Derventa narrow gauge line.

11/17/43: PZ 65 in action near Mraclin.

11/19/43: PZ 6 hit a mine east of Garcin; it exploded behind the locomotive; 2 cars badly, 4 cars slightly damaged; repaired until shortly before the end of the year. For this period Line Protection Train No. 206 was transferred into Security Sector B.

11/20/43: PZ 64 transferred from Vinkovci to Deletovci, evening action for line clearing near Kuzmin, where SF train was derailed by an explosion.

11/22/43: PZ 65 to an explosion site northwest of Zapresic.

11/25/43: PZ 64 cleared the Deletovci—Slakovci line after attack.

11/26/43: Line Protection Train No. 104 secured the Slav. Brod—Doboj line.

11/28/43: PZ 65 called to a blown-up passenger train 2 km north of Ivanicgrad.

11/30/43: Line Protection Train No. 104 secured explosion site between Rudanka and Johovac (north of Doboj).

12/2/43: PZ 23 secured repair work between Pescenica and Lekenik. Line Protection Train No. 104 south of Johovac for securing.

12/3/43: Line Protection Train No. 206 east of Garcin.

12/18/43: Narrow gauge armored train scouted Bradina—Brdani line (Sarajevo—Mostar line).

12/21/43: PZ 64 made securing run from Ruma to Kuzmin and back.

12/24/43: Narrow gauge armored train hit an explosion site between Ostrozac and Rama (Sarajevo—Mostar line).

1/14/44: Partisan action by PZ 6 near Sladinik.

1/26-3/1/44: PZ 6 repaired.

One can also refer to the diary of PZ 64, which offers a detailed view of the operations of an armored train in the Balkans.

These details show that reducing the endangering of transport traffic in Croatia was by no means successful—despite the action of the armored trains. Although resistance groups could be found and wiped out in occasional undertakings—usually away from the tracks and in conjunction with other units—which did not happen very often anyway, since they could usually get away from the attackers through

PZ 65 on the northern Agram-Novska line in the winter of 1943-44. Photo: H. D. Becker/W. Sawodny collection

their better knowledge of the localities, new ones quickly took their place. If an attack took place, the armored train—as long as it arrived on the scene promptly enough—could perhaps drive off the partisans and prevent the plundering of the attacked train, or at least protect the recovery and repair work against further attacks. Securing runs by armored trains usually got nowhere, for the local station personnel could, despite efforts for secrecy, report them at the right time to the partisans, who naturally avoided the part of the line being covered and moved their activities to other places. Such securing runs, which also served to clear already set explosive charges, meant delays in other traffic, which naturally had to be halted for the duration of the armored train's presence on the line. For example, in one week of December 1943 the Slav. Brod—Sarajevo line was closed for 37.5 hours because an armored train was guarding the Bosna bridge near Zenica. But on the other hand, the station and bridge guards, often very weak—and often the targets of partisan attacks—were very thankful for the appearance and presence of an armored train, for its effect in scaring off attacks was undeniable. This was also shown when armored trains escorted important transports, for as a rule they remained unharmed. This was surely the most effective use of the armored trains, and it permitted other traffic.

At the end of January 1944, the staff of the Commander of Armored Trains (Commander: Colonel Friedrich Becker) in Army Group F in Belgrade was set up to direct armored trains in the Balkans. After being bombed out, it moved to Indija in mid-April 1944.

In the Croatian area the stationings and securing sectors of the armored trains remained unchanged. With the occupation of Hungary on March 19, 1944, the four armored trains located in Croatia were transferred there briefly, with the two from farther east (No. 6 and 64) going to Kiskunhalas on the Belgrade—Budapest line, and the two from the Agram area (No. 23 and 65) to Fuenfkirchen. Their actions took place without combat, and after ten days the armored trains returned to their old bases. On April 23, 1944 PZ 6 was badly damaged by a mine explosion and had to go to the Maribor RAW for repairs.

The armored trains in Serbia and, above all, Greece were strengthened significantly in the first half of 1944, for at the end of February 1944 the first of the light scout trains (No. 301) finally arrived; it was first stationed in the Usje—Raska region on the western line from Belgrade to Skopje. PT 15 with its Panhard scout cars was thus sent back from northern Greece to the replacement battalion

Despite the armored and line protection trains, partisan activity in Croatia constantly increased. This strong mine explosion threw the G-cars of a transport train off on both sides of the line. Photo: J. Frings/W. Sawodny collection

Above left: The action of the armored trains against partisans took place not only on the lines, but also to the sides. Panhard scout cars of PZ 23 (the second is following in the background) are on a scouting trip through a Croatian village. Photo: H. Bruntsch/W. Sawodny collection *Above right:* An anti-partisan command from PZ 65 searches a farmyard in the winter of 1943/44. Photo: H. D. Becker/W. Sawodny collection

Light Scout Train No. 302, loaded on S-cars, passes through Fünfkirchen, Hungary, in March 1944 on its way to Greece. Photo: H. D. Becker/W. Sawodny collection

Below: To unload the armored rail scout cars (here, that of Light Scout Train 303) from the transport train, an angled ramp was built of rails. Photo: P. G. Römer/W. Sawodny collection

for refreshing. Some three weeks later it was replaced by the second light scout train, No. 302, with the rail securing staff in Larissa. In May, the light scout train No. 301 was moved up into the sector of the LXVIII. Army Corps in Attica. In the last week of April 1944, light scout train No. 304 with the overhauled PT 15 arrived in Croatia. At first it was stationed in Slavonski Brod (Securing Sector B) in place of the damaged PZ 6. At the beginning of July 1944 it was then subordinated to the Demotica Command in the Thrace region that was assigned to Bulgaria. Suflion became its stationing site (PT 15, now assigned to PZ 65 in Popovaca, remained in Croatia). The last of the light scout trains, No. 303, was delivered in mid-June 1944. Along with the armored (Littorina type) railcars No. 30 and 31, which were

subordinated to it, it arrived in the Bulgarian-occupied territory from Serbia. From the bases in Grdelica, Doljevac, Aleksinac, Zitkovac, Stevanac, and Bagrdan it secured the line from Belgrade via Nisch in the direction of Skopje to Vranje, but also saw service on the line from Nisch to Pirot in the direction of Sofia and from Lapovo to Kragujevac, and on the branch line to Krusevac. In mid-July 1944 the two "Littorina" armored railcars No. 32 and 33, intended for the light scout train No. 302, arrived in the Balkans. But they were held back in Croatia and assigned at first to PZ 64; from there they were often called on for inspection runs by the Commander of the Armored Trains in Army Group F in Indija.

The ten cars of the light scout trains operated as individual vehicles, but always in groups of two or three, so they could support each other. This was also true when transport trains were escorted, with one group in front and the other in back. On securing runs—including nights (later daytime action was no longer possible, because of low-flying aircraft danger)—individual scout cars stood by particular objects (bridges, railroad stations, frequent explosion sites, etc.) or ran back and forth on endangered lines; thus one scout train could easily watch over a sector 30 to 40 km long. Thus, these trains were very flexible and mobile; on emergency calls from sentries they quickly met at the site of the attack. Their modest armor generally sufficed completely to fight the small, lightly armed partisan groups that specialized in track destruction, so that they proved to be very effective. In the report of the General of Transportation in the OB Southeast for August 1944 it was stated: "The armored scout car train No. 303 has proved itself particularly in its actions. It has shown that the acts of railroad sabotage at the focal point of Stalac-Nisch (have)

Two cars of Light Scout Train 301 on a securing run in Attica (Greece). On the right foreground is a fortified dugout. Photo: Federal Archives, Koblenz

decreased strongly or were not carried out for days when the armored scout cars often made line protection trips." Of course, the action of the light scout trains suffered from the beginning from the ever-increasing shortage of fuel. In mid-July 1944 it was already suggested that at least two of the cars of the scout trains stationed in Greece be fitted with normal couplings with buffers (they originally had only an automatic middle coupling), to be able to be coupled to the trains to be secured during escort runs, so as to save fuel. Scout Train No. 303 could only be used within limits at the end of August 1944, since it lacked fuel. This situation got worse with the development of the war, and from November 1944 on Scout Train No. 303—just like the newly delivered heavy scout trains at that time—had to obtain a normal steam locomotive to be able to move at all. The advantages of its design were naturally lost to a great degree as a result.

Since the beginning of 1944, moreover, rail traffic in the Balkans had been influenced not only by partisan attacks that tended to increase, but also more and more by Allied air raids that came from their bases in southern Italy.

On August 15, 1944, the following armored and line protection trains were in the district of the Commander Southeast:
Commander of the Armored Trains at Commander of
Army Group F (Indija)
      Repair Shop Train No. 1 (Lapovo)
    XCI, Army Corps (Northern Greece):
      le. Sp. 302 (Katcrini)
      le. Sp. 304 (Command Demotica, Suflion)
      Line Protection Trains No. 202, 208, 222
    LXVIII. Army Corps (Attica):
      le. Sp. 301 (New Thebes)
      Line Protection Trains No. 209, 214
    New Bulgaria (Macedonia): several Bulgarian armored trains
Military Commander Southeast:
    I. Bulgarian Occupation Corps (Southern Serbia):
      le. Sp. 303, PT 30, 31 (Aleksinac Zitkovac)
      Line Protection Trains No. 203, 205, 207, 209, 210
    Line Protection Trains (narrow gauge) No. 101, 102, 106
    (Krusevac—Kraljevo—Cacak—Uzice line
Northwestern Sector (FK 816):
      Line Protection Trains (narrow gauge) No. 107, 108, 109
    (Mladenovac—Lajkovac—Valjevo line with branches to Cacak and Obernovac)
Railroad Security Staff Croatia: 6 armored railcars
    Security Sector A: PZ 65, PT 15 (Popovaca)
    Security Sector B: (PZ 6 then being repaired, RAW Maribor)
    Security Sector C: PZ 64, PT 32 and 33 (Ruma)
    Security Sector D: Croatian Armored Trains No. 1, 2 (Doboj)
                Line Protection Trains No. 104, 105
                (Slav.Brod—Sarajevo—Mostar line)
    Security Sector E: PZ 23 (Sisak)
    Security Sector F: Line Protection Train No. 206 (Karlstadt)

After it had already had several wounded to report in a fight with partisans near Voloder on 15 August, PZ 65 was badly damaged in a row explosion while leaving the Popovaca railroad station on 31 August with 6 dead and 12 injured. The still-usable cars (the rear half of the train) were set back on the rails at the site and repaired, the train was completed with provisionally armored cars and an unarmored locomotive until replacements were obtained, a sign that a lack of the train for long-term repairs could not be afforded. For its reinforcing, it received PT 32 (perhaps also No. 33?).

Increasing partisan activity, which even extended into Carinthia later, was also experienced in northern Slovenia, taken by the German Reich in May 1941, which had to be declared a "partisan fighting district" on June 21, 1943. The fighting was up to police units and home guards. In the part bordering on Croatia, the comparatively well-secured main line ran from Graz via Maribor and Cilli to Agram; the mountain line from Cilli to Unterdrauburg was considerably more threatened. Important transports were protected against direct attacks, often successfully, by adding armored cars armed with machine guns. In the summer of 1944 the railroad police in Cilli had an armored railcar (type unknown, armored personnel carrier like that on page 249, light road-rail armored scout car, or even Panzer III with rail running gear?) and an "armored securing train"; for Klagenfurt a "line securing train" with the code name "Diesel" was mentioned. These vehicles were obviously part of the railroad protection, but whether the trains were those of the prewar railroad protection and were presumably transferred to Carinthia for partisan fighting is not known.

Romania and Bulgaria Change Sides, and the Results

On August 24, 1944, the Romanians went from the German side to that of their opponents. This made it likely that the Russians, after marching through that country, would soon appear on the Danube and the Serbian border north of it, where a defensive front first had to be created.

Even worse was that Bulgaria also renounced its alliance with Germany on 27 August, and declared war on its former partner on 8 September. After the first date, the Bulgarian forces already withdrew from Serbia and Macedonia and left the field to the immediately advancing partisans. At the same time they disarmed German troops in their area. Scout Train No. 304, long since on the Turkish border, fell victim to them. It seems to have been blown up so as not to fall into Bulgarian hands. Of its crew, twelve were reported as missing in Lavara on 30 August; the rest could obviously fight their way to other German units that joined the armed withdrawal. This Bulgarian change of sides meant that an eastern front had to be built up not only in northern Serbia, but on down to the Aegean coast of northern Greece. Troops for it could come only from Greece. Not even Hitler, who held fast to every square meter of occupied ground, could reply to these arguments, and so—beginning on 5 September—the border areas of Greece and the Aegean islands were successively abandoned. On 3 October the order was then given to give up all Greece, southern Albania, and southern Macedonia; Attica was held longest (until 7 October), as air bases were located there, where the German troops landed when they were transported back by plane from the Aegean islands.

For the entire withdrawal of the German armed forces, naturally the only railroad line from Athens via Larissa, Veles, Skopje and Lapovo to Belgrade was of very decisive importance. Between Skopje and Lapovo a western line ran via Kosovo Polje and Kraljevo, an eastern one via Nisch. From September 1944 on these lines were the preferred targets of not only the partisans, but also the Allied air forces. Destroyed bridges in particular resulted in long-term delays. On these lines in the month named, only island traffic was possible. The Vitanovac—Kraljevo and Svecan—Kosovsko Mitrovica lines on the western branch and Jagodina—Cuprija, Mezgraja—Toponica and Nisch—Grdelica—Skopje on the eastern, plus Veles—Gevgelij, were out of service. In particular, the area between Nisch and Skopje was permanently occupied by partisans, so that the eastern link for the return of the German troops from the south remained unusable, as it was also occupied soon by Bulgarian and Russian troops in the northern area.

The Germans tried hard to maintain through traffic, at least on the western line. In the south, the strengthened actions of the security forces, including the light scout trains and line protection trains stationed there, were able to decrease the down time on the lines from more than 30% in September to under 7% in October, and between Veles and Gevgelij from 62% to 25%. By building up the Ibar bridge north of Kosovsko Mitrovica and the Morava bridge east of Kraljevo (as makeshift structures, over which trains could be moved only in pieces), the line between Athens and Belgrade was all usable again as of 3 October, even though it was broken temporarily more often by partisan attacks, especially in the Usje—Raska—Ibarska Slatina sector, and the considerable backlog that had built up south of Kos. Mitrovica could be cut down.

On the last day of September 1944, the Russian troops who had meanwhile marched in at the western border of Romania, broke into the Banat. PZ 6, stationed in Andrijevci again since its repairs were finished in September 1944, was transferred to Betschkerek on 30 September. On the next morning it encountered the Russian vanguard before Banatsko Aleksandrovo in its advance toward Lazarevo. It was immediately hit several times by antitank shells, which cost the lives of three men, including the commander and technical leader. In the further course of the fight, the gun turrets and the armored locomotive also took direct hits, so that the armored train was unable to fight and had to be towed away. What remained was taken back to Szöreg but had to be blown up there, since the Theiss bridge to Szeged was no longer standing.

All too soon thereafter, a surprising Russian advance took place from the Zajecar—Bor area to the northwest. On the evening of 8 October, its armored vanguard reached Markovac on the line from Belgrade to Lapovo, and on the next day the line from Velika Plana to Lapovo was in enemy hands. Thus, the most important link in the railroad connection between Belgrade and Athens was broken. Workshop Train No. 1 had been moved back to Ruma at the right time, at the beginning of the month; the Light Scout Train No. 303, though, was still right at the point of the break. Six scout cars and the quarters train in Lapovo had to draw back in the direction of Kragujevac—Kraljevo, where they were blown up, before the remaining crew members marched off toward Sarajevo (later some of them returned to the train via Slavonski Brod). The other four scout cars and the two "Littorina" railcars were in Markovac when the Russians appeared, they were able to move off to the north after a brief battle, but in Mladenovac they found the line barricaded by Tito's troops. On 11 October, though, in collaboration with assault tanks, the breakthrough could be accomplished. On 13 October they left Belgrade going westward; in the last days of October, what was left of Scout Train No. 303 was in the Ruma—Sid area, and on 31 October it was moved to its final site, Lipovljani (on the northern line near Novska), and brought back to a total of six light scout cars by two replacement vehicles.

The Retreat of Army Group E

By the Russian breakthrough at Lapovo, the unhindered withdrawal of the railroad transports from Greece, Macedonia and southern Serbia was broken again—and this time irreparably—a few days after the whole line had been made usable again. The northern terminus was soon Kraljevo, which was of particular importance because of the narrow-gauge line that branched off there to Sarajevo via Cacak, Uzice, and Visegrad. For to be able to connect with the German

units in Croatia, one now had to withdraw from the Ibar valley to the west in order to push along the Drina and Bosna in the direction of the Sava. This was done not only along the narrow gauge line from Kraljevo up the valley of the western Morava, for one part broke off already in Kosovsko Mitrovica to move via Novi Pazar through northeastern Montenegro to Visegrad. The troop units generally marched from Greece on the road, while the heavy weapons and, above all, supplies, were moved by train, for the cut-off army group could not depend on supplies from the direction of home, but in this respect had to depend exclusively on what could be brought along from the, thankfully, very richly stocked supplies in Greece, which they cleaned out completely. All of this now moved northward in an endless row of trains, and was—unless used up on the way—unloaded at the terminus of Kraljevo, where the no longer needed transport vehicles were destroyed. Thus not only did a gigantic stock of supplies build up there, but also one of the largest graveyards for railroad material. Despite numerous partisan attacks, plus bombing and low-flying fighter attacks, the line from Greece to Kraljevo could be kept open until the evacuation was finished, and all the Bulgarian attempts to break the withdrawal route near Skopje and Pristina, and those of the Russians in the Kraljevo—Cacak area, were in vain.

The end of this "army worm" crawling hundreds of kilometers broke out of Athens on October 13, 1944. On the 17th it was in Lianokladi, on the 19th in Larissa, on the 22nd in Katerini, on the 28th in Plati. On the 30th Saloniki was evacuated, and on 3 November the rear guards crossed the Greek border into Yugoslavian Macedonia. Further stations reached were Veles on 9 November, Skopje on the 11th, and Grlica on the 13th.

The light scout and line protection trains from Greece were also in this gigantic line. For lack of fuel, Light Scout Train No. 302 had been loaded onto a transport train, which brought it northward. On 12 November it was at the railroad station in Kosovo Polje along with the quarters train when an air raid took place. A shot-down plane unfortunately landed on three freight cars loaded with teller mines, and the explosion destroyed almost all the rolling stock at the station, including among others Light Scout Train No. 302 along with its quarters train. This event cost some 300 lives, plus 250 wounded, including many members of the armored train, whose commander was also killed.—Between Athens and Larissa Light Scout Train No. 301 had formed the rear guard. In the process, four scout cars were lost to defects or damage and had to be blown up for lack of opportunity to repair them. On 29 October what remained of the train was transferred to Skopje, from which part of it secured the line between Kacanik and Veles, while another operated on the line from Skopje to Kumanovo. On 7 November another scout car was lost in a collision with a locomotive at the Kacanik railroad station. The five remaining scout cars were transferred to Kosovo Mitrovica and Zvecan after Skopje was evacuated; they were to secure the barriers between Urusevac and Kraljevo during the withdrawal. After the abandonment of Mitrovica was planned for 20 November, Light Scout Train No. 301 was given orders on the evening of 18 November to transfer to Usce. Through carelessness, though, a bridge north of Zvecan was blown up. So the five scout cars still on hand, robbed of their mobility, had to be blown up in Zvecan on 20 November. The crew was added to the 4th Company of Fortress Infantry Battalion 1004, took part in the defense of Mitrovica, often served as a rear guard in the withdrawal to Sienica (which was reached on 26 November), and took part in securing the marching route in this area until 2 December. On 3 December the crew of the light scout train was sent on the march to Sarajevo, which it reached on 22 December. The supply train of Light Scout Train No. 301, carrying the crews of the five already destroyed scout cars, set out from Zvecan to Kraljevo on 17 November and reached it on the 18th. After the railroad cars had been turned over to the railroad guards for destruction, the march to the west on several motor vehicles was begun. When they reached Pozega (on the narrow gauge line between Cacak and Uzice), enemy forces had broken through to the north and threatened the line of march. In the defense, which lasted a week, the crews of the light scout train suffered losses (2 dead, 3 badly and 2 slightly wounded). Only on 29 November could they begin to march on to Sarajevo, which they reached on 9 December. From there the crew was sent on through Slav.Brod to Cilli. Nothing is known of the fate of the line protection trains. They surely carried out securing tasks along the withdrawal route and were then blown up—in Kraljevo at the latest.

The last troop units from the south arrived there on 30 November and marched off to the west. To be able to transport the supplies from Kraljevo as well, the use of the narrow gauge rail line running in the same direction was necessary. It led through a region controlled by Tito partisans and, for that reason, had been barred between Stambulcic (just a few kilometers east of Sarajevo) and Cacak early in October. After the combat units that had gone ahead on the road had opened the way and were able to hold it against later attempts by Tito's troops to retake it, the railroad engineers set out to make the line from Cacak to the west usable again, which succeeded as far as Visegrad. At the same time, troops had been sent out from Sarajevo to Visegrad, but this move had been so hasty that they were surrounded. Above all, they could not prevent the partisans from blowing up the large viaduct over the Drina at the mouth of the Lim (west of Visegrad). Thus travel from Sarajevo via Stambulcic became possible only in December, and the site of the explosion near Medjedja was not reached before 31 December. Though makeshift bridge building had begun earlier, it was not finished until January 1945. Meanwhile, the transports had been running from Karljevo for a long time. Presumably Line Protection Train No. 102, which was on that line, took part in securing them; it is possible that other line protection trains from the Lajkovac area or from Krusevac had reached Cacak or Kraljevo and were now present (news of them, unfortunately, is lacking). Because of the blown-up Drina bridge the trains had to be halted and unloaded on the east shore. When the withdrawal went on, the narrow gauge line in the east was given up. On 1 December Pozega was reached, on the 11th Uzice, on the 16th Kremna, on the 28th Mokra Gora, and on 31 December Dobrun. After the bridge was repaired all the goods and all the rolling stock—17 locomotives and 570 cars in all, including any present line-protection trains—could be moved to the west side and on to Sarajevo in the first half of January, although they could only be moved over the makeshift bridge one vehicle at a time. The bridge was finally dismantled, as the material was needed for other uses.

The narrow gauge line from Sarajevo to Slavonski Brod, which had previously served to supply the German troops in central Bosnia and Herzegovina, and now also the withdrawal of Army Group E (Sarajevo was the location of the staff since 16 November) and the units coming in from northern Albania and Montenegro, which had joined their marching columns in Visegrad at the end of December, was also of special importance. The line had long been disturbed by

bombings by partisans, who had strong centers in the Tuzla (between Bosna and Drina) and Jaice—Travnik areas. Their activities had increased much since mid-November and were constantly accompanied by low-flying air raids. In November the whole line was usable for only 201 hours; in December it was closed for 497 operating hours. In view of the limited numbers of rolling stock available, this was very unpleasant. 35 locomotives in November and 37 in the following month were so damaged that at first they were not usable. The vehicles that came from Visegrad in January 1945 were thus a welcome addition. Unfortunately, nothing has been learned of the activity of the armored (Croatian No. 1 and 2) and line protection trains (No. 104 and 105), plus presumably No. 102 and perhaps others, in January 1945) on this line at that time. News is also lacking of their whereabouts (the line was cleared only in April 1945, and the trains still present were surely blown up).

Events in the North of Serbia and Croatia

Northward of the breakthrough site in the Morava valley gained on October 8, 1944, the Russian units, supported by Tito's partisans, turned toward Belgrade and reached the southern edge of the city on 14 October. Until the 20th of that month Belgrade was completely in their hands. The staff of OB Southeast had only moved to Ruma on 13 October, while the General of Transport had moved from Belgrade to Esseg on the 6th, and the Commander of the Armored Trains in Army Group Γ had gone from Indija to Ruma in this period. Since half of the armored trains subordinated to him had either been lost or passed from his power when the lines were cut south of Belgrade in the events of early October, his office was dissolved on 14 October and the staff was transferred back to Germany, only to return to the Balkans with the delivery of the first heavy scout trains four weeks later.

Since a further Russian advance to the west was to be feared, the German command decided to give up the Danube—Theiss position north of Belgrade, which they still held, and to bring back the troops to a position running from the Danube bend near Vukovar, Sid, and the Drina from its confluence with the Save to Zvornik, which they held until April 12, 1945, except for the south wing, which had to be turned back to Brcko in December under pressure from Tito's troops, with minor deviations (on the main line, for instance, between Vinkovci and Sid). These movements began on 20 October. On 24 October PZ 64 still guarded the explosion sites in its previous base of Ruma and then left for Jankovci, east of Virovitica. From 26 October on it secured the staff of the OB Southeast. Field Marshal Weichs, who was temporarily in Slavonski Brod, then accompanied his command train to its final base at Agram on 29 October. On the journey partisans were encountered, but the armored train was able to fight them off. On 5 November PZ 64 was stationed in Andrijevci for the next two weeks.

In western Croatia, the last four months of 1944 were characterized by constantly increasing partisan activity and intensification of the air raids on focal point railroad stations and bridge building work, especially in the Agram—Novska area, but also on the main Graz—Maribor—Cilli—Steinbrück line. On September 1, 1944, the crew of PZ 64 suffered considerable losses in a low-flying air attack on the Ruma railroad station, but the combat train was only slightly damaged. On the same day traffic from Agram in the direction of Karlstadt, to Novska as well as via Sisak and Sunja and via Dugo

Selo and Banova Jaruga, was completely crippled by numerous explosions. The southern line was no longer completely usable, and the forces were content to maintain traffic from Novska to Sunja and on the connection from there to Bosanski and Novi and Bihac, but this line also had to be closed often for days, even weeks; most of the time only local traffic in parts of the region was possible, and similarly between Agram and Karlstadt. The northern line was also disturbed frequently, and often for long periods, but efforts were made here for instant repairs. As of the end of October, greatly increased low-flying air raids in this area, in addition to the cited actions, made themselves known very unpleasantly. PZ 65, which often saw action in the region west of Agram at that time, lost PT 32, which was subordinated to it and was badly damaged, in the explosion of a mine near Voloder. On the other hand, traffic between Novska and Slavonski Brod was only affected comparatively slightly, and on the line from Brod to Vinkovci, which had been greatly endangered by partisans previously, their activities decreased by much toward the end of the year, but bombing attacks of the railroad stations caused considerable damage. Especially noteworthy was the destruction of the Save bridge between Slavonski and Bosanski Brod on 8 September; it was restored only on 3 November. At the end of December a cableway over the Save was also built, so that the renewed bombing on January 18, 1945, had less serious results. Otherwise night rail traffic was completely halted, and in the morning hours the armored and line protection trains had to check the lines by letting their control cars roll forward, catching them and rolling them forward again, to set off time-fuse mines. The time required for this laborious activity was about forty minutes for ten kilometers of track.

Because of the remarkably serious disturbances to the line between Novska and Agram, attempts were made to circumvent the situation. At first a great part of the railroad traffic from the Slavonski Brod—Vinkovci region was sent over the Esseg—Fuenfkirchen route, but the Russian attack north of the Drava on 26 November ended that option. As of November efforts were made to reestablish the rail lines northeast of Agram in the direction of the Hungarian and German Reich borders. Through appropriate construction and security measures, the Dugo Selo—Krizevci—Koprivnica—Gyekenyes (Hungary) and Zapresic—Zabok—Varazdin—Csaktornya (Hungary, where instead of the Drava bridge blown up in 1941, a field railroad line over the road bridge connected the two last-named towns) lines were gradually put into service along with the branch from Zabok via Krapina to Grübel, and in January 1945 also the Varazdin—Koprivnica—Klostar—Virovitica—Slatina—Nasice—Esseg connection running behind the Drava front. The line protection train "Igel" went into service in December on the branch line running parallel behind the front from Vinkovci over the Sava to Brcko, which was especially severely threatened by partisans. It was heavily damaged in an air raid on 15 December and had to be towed out of action. It is unknown whether it was repaired and reused.

In mid-November 1944 the Armored Train Regimental Staff No. 1 (Col. Friedrich Becker) returned to the Balkans as Commander of the Armored Trains at OB Southwest, along with two newly built—the first—heavy scout trains (No. 201 and 202), plus two more "Littorina" armored railcars (No. 35 and 38; a third one—No. 34—was damaged during the transfer, and after being repaired in Vienna, arrived only in February). Since PZ 64 was stationed in Hungary around the same time this was the opportunity for a new arrangement of armored trains. Further deliveries and removals of armored trains took place in the next—and last—months of the war, and several stationing changes occurred, not all of which could be traced considering the time.

The Commander of the Armored Trains at OB Southeast set up first at Stockhammer near Cilli, then in Cilli itself. With the arrival of Command Train 1, the staff moved to Agram around the first of the year, and to Zapresic some two weeks later. At the beginning of February 1945, the staff and its command train took their apparently last station in Zlatar Bistrica on the line from Zapresic to Varazdin. PZ 65 remained stationed in Popovaca with PT 15 for longer—until January 18, 1945, when both were withdrawn and sent back to the Armored Train Replacement Battalion in Milowitz. The last scout train, No. 303, also remained in Lipovljani with both its railcars (No. 30 and 31). PZ 23 was transferred from Novska to Dugo Selo (branch of the newly repaired line to Koprivnica from the northern line). Around the first of the year it was in the Agram works to have its locomotive overhauled. After PZ 65 departed, it took up that's train's site in Popovaca. In mid-January 1945 PT 35, which had previously been repaired at the Maribor RAW, was assigned to it. Heavy Scout Train N0. 201 went at first to Slavonski Brod, until PZ 75, just arrived in the Balkans, arrived in January 1945. Then it secured the lines that ran behind the front toward Esseg and to Brcko from Vinkovci; finally it was transferred to the eastern part of the line from Esseg via Nasice to Virovitica south of the Drava. Heavy Scout Train No. 202 was at Cilli until Armored Train No. 4 arrived, and then in Agram. After the line from Zabok to Gruebel was repaired, it was transferred to Krapina to secure it; after the successful Russian offensive in southern Hungary it secured the Drava sector between Varazdin and Koprivnica until the end of May 1945. The independently operating PT 38 also remained in the Cilli area at first, and secured the Save bridges in Agram toward the end of the year. In February 1945 it took over the sector near Slavonski Brod from PZ 75 (see below).

Armored Railcar No. 38, which was directly assigned to the Commander of the Armored Trains in Army Group F for a time. Photo: W. Rösner/W. Sawodny collection

In mid-November 1944 the first two heavy scout trains arrived in the Balkans. Here is Heavy Scout Train No. 201, with the quarters train in the background. Photo: H. Schütz/W. Sawodny collection

Heavy Scout Train No. 202 was in the Krapina area in February 1945. The shortage of fuel caused it to be used with an additional steam locomotive. Photo: W/ Obermark/W. Sawodny collection

New armored trains also arrived in the Balkans in 1945. PZ 75, which came at the beginning of the year, has already been mentioned. It was stationed at Andrijevci. At the beginning of February, though, it was already sent back to Germany, but stayed at Maria Saal (north of Klagenfurt) at first during that month, probably because line bombings prevented its departure. — At the end of January 1945, Armored Train No. 4 arrived in Graz; it was originally intended for service in Hungary but was subordinated to the Commander of the Armored Trains in OB Southeast and stationed in Stockhammer. Its task was the securing of the line from Steinbrück via Cilli to Maribor, with the branches from Cilli to Unterdrauburg and from Pragerhof to Czaktornya. At the beginning of April 1945, the repaired PT 32 was assigned to it. — In February 1945 the heavy scout trains, No. 203 and 204, plus PT 34 were finally added. Scout Train No. 203 was stationed in Rain to secure the line from Agram to Laibach. For this, an armored railcar (No. 33?) was assigned to it. Scout Car No. 204, with PT 34, was on the line from Sunja via Bosanski Novi toward Bihac. Also transferred to the Balkans were the line protection train "Max" (along with PT 37?) at the beginning of February, and the line protection train "Werner" in March. In addition, by the war's end another line protection train, "München," was mentioned, but this may have been the renamed scout train No. 206 (the numbers of the 200 series had now been assigned to the heavy scout cars), which had been on the Agram—Karlstadt line in August 1944.

The main task of the armored trains was again line securing — with the results as before, thus in the end without penetrating success. The stationings show that partisan activity had now moved to western Croatia and Slovenia, the latter having been added to German territory, and in fact to beyond the Karawanken to Carinthia and southern Styria. In the reports from those last months, though, less of this activity, but rather defense against the omnipresent enemy air corps, was stressed more and more. Efforts were made to avoid it by carrying out securing runs at night and staying in covered places (such as tunnels) by day. The two 2-cm. A/A quads used on most armored trains, though, seem to have proved themselves splendidly in anti-aircraft defense, for losses and damage were reported only seldom (the worst event of this type seems to have been a gun and bomb attack on Heavy Scout Train No. 203 on March 20, 1945, which cost nine crewmen their lives, but large numbers of aircraft were shot down. In January 1945, though, the armored locomotive of PZ 75 was hit in an attack of American bombers on Slavonski Brod (the combat train, stationed in Andrijevci, remained unharmed).

The War's End in Croatia and Slavonia

The last phase of the fighting in the Balkans began at the end of March 1945, when the complete command was taken over by Army Group E (Generaloberst Loehr). At first the Tito partisans located in the Lika southwest of Agram attacked, and Bihac was abandoned before the month ended. Withdrawals also had to be made between Ogulin and Karlstadt, but the latter city remained in German hands. On 5-6 April Sarajevo was abandoned. Once again the very overloaded Bosna Valley line had to do its task. The troops and goods were brought over the Save successfully by 18 April; the narrow gauge armored trains still present were blown up. For on 12 April Tito's army had begun their offensive in Syrmia, attaining smashing success at once through landings across the Drave in back of the German front between Valpovo and Esseg and inducing a quick retreat. Heavy Scout Train No. 201 fell victim to it. Striking off from Nasice in the direction of Virovitica, it found itself cut off near Cacinci on 16 April by partisans who had destroyed the rail line. Thus the train had to be blown up; the crew joined Reconnaissance Battalion 55 and were able to withdraw with it to Carinthia, where they went into British captivity. PT 38 moved back from Slavonski Brod toward Agram. On 20 April Tito's troops approached Banova Jaruga through a gap in the front but were driven back again, so that the line from Novska to Agram remained open. Light Scout Train No. 303 moved there from Lipovljani on

26 April. On 30 April the front was roughly in a line from south of Karlstadt via Bosanski Novi, Novska and Daruvar to Virovitica. On 2 May the Heavy Scout Train No. 204 was able to relieve the withdrawal of the very hard-pressed troops from Bosanski Novi; then it dropped back in the direction of Sisak. On that day its further withdrawal was ordered, and PT 35 was cut off while securing by damage to the line west of Novska but was able to fight its way through. PZ 23, farther to the west, must have hit a mine and become damaged at that time. On 6 May the "Zvonimir" position was reached from Dugo Selo via Krizevci to west of Ludbreg. When the capitulation became known on 7 May, it was clear that by the time it went into effect (1:00 AM on 9 May) the former border of Austria, behind which the British waited and where they could be sure they had outrun Tito's troops, was no longer attainable for the greatest part of the German and allied Balkan troops. On 8 May all the armored trains received a radio message from the commander: "Armistice 9 May, 1:00; I wish you a happy return home." Cilli was named as the gathering place for the armored trains. The staff had already left Command Train No. 1 there the day before and gone by motor vehicles to Heilenstein, where they met the OB Southeast. The next day they were turned over to Tito's troops in Mies. Naturally the armored trains tried whenever possible to reach Austrian territory by rail. The most successful was PZ 4, whose commander had made radio contact from Cilli with the

Along with partisan activity, danger from the air increased more and more. This bomb damaged the front end of PZ 23 only slightly. Photo: G. Pehlke/W. Sawodny collection

While the locomotive was badly damaged in this attack on the Cilli railroad station in March 1945, PZ 4 (right rear) was unharmed. Photo: W. Mauss/W. Sawodny collection

---

Canadian Brigade of the 7th British Infantry Division, which voiced a keen interest in the unharmed turnover of the train. The armored train along with its subordinated PT 32 reached Maribor the next day, from which it took along a large number of German women in work service, and reached Unterdrauburg on 10 May. It was directed onward to St. Andrä on the line to Wolfsberg, where the Canadians took possession of the train. PZ 23 with PT 35 arrived in Maribor from Dugo Selo the day before (8 May) and the next day it took on passenger and freight cars loaded with fleeing civilians and left for Unterdrauburg. In the direction of Klagenfurt, though, it found the line choked with trains beyond Bleiburg. Thus the people left the armored train there and tried to go further on foot. During the night the crew encountered partisans and was scattered. Many found each other again as prisoners in Völkermarkt, where they were taken over by the British.

Heavy Scout Train No. 202 reached Cilli on 8 May but went on to Laibach. There PT 38, which had set out from Agram, joined it. Taking along Wlassow troops, it turned northward toward Assling, where the Karawanken tunnel was found to be blocked. The train and railcar were surrendered to the partisans, but the crew, along with the Wlassow troops, marched on through Kronau and the Wurzen Pass to Villach and was imprisoned by the British. Heavy Scout

Train No. 203 advanced from its last stationing in Eichtal to Cilli on 8 May and tried to reach Unterdrauburg on the main line. It was stopped in Schönstein-Warmbad and had to be surrendered to Tito's troops. While the officers remained in Yugoslavian imprisonment, the crew, led by Sergeant Truss, was able to reach the Austrian border on foot after coming through a firefight with partisans on 13 May. Light Scout Train No. 303 was supposed to pick up a hospital train in Laibach on 7 May, but did not find it. On the way back to Cilli, badly wounded men were picked up in Zagorje and a car with ethnic German families was hitched on. In Cilli the train, along with Armored Railcars No. 30 and 31, had to be handed over to Tito's troops. A large group of crew members led by the commander, 1st Lt. Römer, was joined by men from the line protection trains "Max" and "Werner," which had also surrendered in Cilli, found a good chance to leave the column of prisoners and were able to reach Austrian territory in Bleiburg and thus become British prisoners. The worst luck was that of Heavy Scout Train No. 204 with PT 34, which had fought its way from Sunja over the much-damaged and partisan-occupied Sisak—Agram line and from there via Steinbrück toward Cilli. The combat train was abandoned along the way, and the men tried to go farther in the quarters train. Shortly before Cilli they were stopped by a strong partisan group. After a shoot out they had to surrender and be marched into imprisonment.

Above left: In a fighter-bomber attack on the railroad station at Lipovljani on April 12, 1945, this car of Light Scout Car No. 303 was damaged. Hoto: K. Herbst/W. Köhler collection *Above right:* The last action discussion for the crew of PZ 4 before crossing the border to Carinthia near Unterdrauburg on May 10, 1945. Photo: W. Mauss/W. Sawodny collection

On the day of the capitulation, the crew of Light Scout Train No. 303 left the train and Railcars No. 30 and 31, which were turned over to Tito's troops, in Cilli. Photo: K. Herbst/W. Koehler collection

Armored Trains in Hungary and Styria

Except for the few days during the occupation in March 1944 (see above), German armored trains had not seen service in Hungary. When increasing Russian pressure made itself known on the Danube front north of the mouth of the Drava, the command area of the 2nd Armored Army to the line from the southwest end of Lake Balaton to the Danube north of Baja was extended to southern Hungary. The Soviet troops crossed the Danube to the west near Apatin and approached the Esseg—Fünfkirchen line, which had meanwhile become an important supply line for the central Croatian area. Thus PZ 64 was transferred on 12 November from Vinkovci via Esseg to the Danube front, where it fought the Russians near Batina in the ensuing days. On 19 November it was severely damaged. After being repaired at the Fünfkirchen works, the armored train reached the supply train in Beli Manastir, but just one day later it had to withdraw to Villany. On 27 November the armored train took part with its artillery and A/A guns in the fighting around Fünfkirchen, which lasted until the end of the month; then until 4 December there was withdrawal fighting around Szentlörensz and Szigetvar. From there the train moved on to Barcs the next day, but did not cross the Drava in the direction of Croatia, but was transferred northward again the next day to the Somogyszob region. East of there the Russian advance could be held and the front stabilized. PZ 64 was used for artillery support, mostly in Ötvöskonyi, with an advanced observer in Beleg. This activity lasted until February 15, 1945; then it was transferred to the line north of the Drava from Gyekenyes to Barcs, in the Vizvar region.

After Budapest was encircled and the Ardennes offensive failed, Hitler's attention turned almost compulsively to Hungary at the beginning of 1945. On February 6, 1945, the two new armored trains, No. 78 and 79, were sent on the march to Hungary (after PZ 4, intended for Hungary in January, had been transferred to Croatia—see above). Along with PZ 64, they were to protect the oil district of Nagykanisza—one of the last that the Reich controlled. PZ 78 was stationed at Balatonszentgyörgy at the southwest end of Lake Balaton; PZ 79 replaced PZ 64 near Vizvar, which was transferred to Nagikanisza. As of 8 March it, along with PZ 79, which had also been brought there, supported the German offensive from the Somogyszob region in the direction of Kaposvar.

The Russian counteroffensive began on 16 March. It spread quickly north of Lake Velencei to a break through into the depths of the region. To oppose it, Armored Trains No. 78 and 79 were also sent northward on 25 March. PZ 79 was supposed to reach Papa, but on the next day it encountered the advancing Russians east of Czelldoemoelk and fired on them. On March 27, after frequently firing on enemy columns, it was outflanked by the Russians west of Czelldömölk on the way back; the line was blocked by an approaching locomotive. After blowing up the weapons the crew left the train and tried to fight their way to their own lines, but they encountered a village occupied by Russians. In the ensuing fight the greater part of the crew was lost, and a small group was taken prisoner.

PZ 78 was ordered to go around Lake Balaton to its north shore (where the Hungarian armored trains No. 101 and 102 and their line protection train "Botond" were already present), to the line between Balatonszepezd and Dörgicse-Alkali. There it was involved in heavy artillery duels and had to withdraw to Tapolca on the evening of the next day. On 27 March the commander, 1st Lt. Crasselt, was killed in a bomb attack southwest of there. The armored train moved back via Keszthely and Balatonszentgyörgy to Nagykanisza, as did the Hungarian armored trains from this region. In the last days of March

PZ 64 saw action in Hungary south of Lake Balaton in the last months of the war. Photo: W. Hartmann/W. Sawodny collection

In February 1945 the two new armored trains, No. 78 and 79, were transferred to Hungary. Here the camouflaged PZ 78 is seen at the west end of Lake Balaton in March. Photo: H. Stallknecht/W. Sawodny collection

PZ 78 was used as a railroad battery near Zalaszentmihaly on the line to Szombathely. PZ 64 stayed east of Somogyszob in the meantime and made securing runs on the line from there to Gyekenyes.

Then, under the pressure of the Russians, who had already advanced far to the west north of them, the abandonment of the southwest corner of Hungary had to be decided on. PZ 64 covered the withdrawal from Somogyszob to Gyekenyes on 30 March, set out across the Drava the next day—the bridge was blown up behind it—and remained in Drnje on the southern shore on 1 April.—PZ 78 was able to move to Nagykanisza, which was already under artillery fire, at the last minute on 31 March. The next day it headed toward the Drava as far as Kotoriba, but had to use its artillery to support the front at Murakiraly-Perlak on 2-3 April, and then covered the withdrawal to Czaktornya. It stayed at that bridgehead until 9 April to protect the Drava bridge before leaving for Friedau as the rear guard after blowing up the railroad station at Czaktornya and the bridge. There it supported a counterattack, provided transport securing to Luttemberg on 11 April, was able to escape the Russians pushing into Radkersburg, and on 12 April reached its last action area in the Mureck—Gosdorf area.—PZ 64 had meanwhile moved via Koprivnica to Ludbreg (2-6 April) and was then transferred to Slovenia. On 8 April it hit a mine on the line from Varadzin to Zapresic and had to be repaired at the latter town (9-11 April). Its further course then took it via Steinbrück and Cilli on 13 April to Windisch-Feistritz. It was to be used on the line to Pettau, but it proved to be too weak for its weight. Thus it moved on 14 April via Maribor and Spielfeld to Mureck, where it joined PZ 78. The two armored trains spent the last three weeks of the war in that region, served as railroad batteries to support the front, but also received artillery fire and were hit by low-flying planes, though without notable damage. On May 4, 1945, PT 19, subordinated to PZ 64, arrived in Mureck (at the end of February PT 15 had been transferred to Styria, first to Graz; later it secured the line leading north from Unterdrauburg, and when the war ended it was in Wolfsberg).

PZ 78, on advance orders from the 2nd Armored Army, left its position near Gosdorf in the early hours of 7 May. When the capitulation of 7 May was learned of the train was already in Leoben, and the next day it went on to Thalheim, near Judenburg, in hopes of meeting the advancing British (who arrived the next day) in that direction. Presumably on hearing rumors that the Russians were at their backs, the crew abandoned the train and went off to the side into the mountains, marching overland by truck to reach the Enns, at which the Americans were. They succeeded on May 10, 1945. PT 19 had carried out supplying runs via Graz in the direction of Gleisdorf on 5 and 6 May. On the morning of 7 May it had drive trouble in Graz, but was repaired in one day. On its southward run on 8 May it met PZ 64, which had also left. Together they returned to Graz, where Austrians with red-white-red armbands wanted to stop the train. But they moved through the station with weapons in hand, cutting a switch. Beyond Graz there was one train after another, so that they moved ahead only slowly and reached Pernegg by evening. There the crew left PZ 64 at the capitulation hour (1:00 on 9 May) and moved ahead on the road. On the next day PT 19 went on to Leoben. There Austrian national groups also tried to stop the withdrawal of the German troops, but SS units ruthlessly made way by force of arms. For the following units this shooting led in part to panic reactions, as the men feared they were being rounded up by Soviet troops. Many went into the woods to the side and tried to reach either the Americans on the Enns or the British in the Knittelfeld area, which usually succeeded. A decimated crew that kept cool heads and stayed on board drove Railcar No. 19 to beyond Leoben, where it had to be left because of the choked line.

Armored Trains in Italy, Istria and Western Slovenia

After the surrender of Italy on September 8, 1943, the 71st Infantry Division, which had already taken over all railroad securing north of Görz and Trieste since the end of August, occupied all of Istria, and in the process captured an armored railroad coastal battery (15-cm guns) and an armored train, which they used in the ensuing mopping-up of partisans in that region. After that action ended in mid-November, the railroad battery could be returned to guarding the coast, while the armored train was turned over to Police Regiment 19 in Laibach and presumably took on line securing duties there.

PZ 78 was able to return to Styria by the war's end. In Thalheim the advancing British found it, abandoned by its crew. R.A.C. Tank Museum, Bovington

In December 1943, the OB Southwest had already requested armored trains for its zone in Italy, but had been refused, as no such units could be spared. He seems, though, to have kept on requesting them, for he was not only promised one of the new trains, but until its delivery in the summer of 1944 , the just-finished, rebuilt PZ 24, that was actually intended for France, was made available to him in February 1944. Its task was supposed to be securing the coast in the Toscana. On 6 February it reached its first stationing in La Rotta (on the line from Pisa to Florence) via La Spezia and Viareggio, on 12 February it was transferred to Torre del Lago, but just four days later it was called to the Udine—Görz region, into which partisan activity had extended from Slovenia. With its station in Cormons, it fought them on the line from Görz to Assling as far as the border near Piedicolle. On 25 February, though, it turned back to the Florence region. The coastal lines were now so bombed that PZ 24 went farther inland via Siena to Roccastrada. There were also tunnels there, in which one could seek shelter from the Allied aircraft, and in which the men stood around with nothing to do at first. Later came actions in Umbria, between Arezzo and Terni. In May, as the front south of Rome went into action, the armored train was finally transferred to Friaul. The securing runs now included the entire region from Görz— Udine—Casarsa to Tarvisio and Assling. The stations were Cormons, Spilimbergo, Resiutta and Fogaria. Along with much partisan action, bomb attacks were also experienced here again, hence tunnels had to serve as hiding places by day more and more often as time went by.

In July 1944 PZ 73, actually intended for Italy, arrived in the action area and replaced PZ 24, which now—as originally planned— could go to France. PZ 73 seems to have been stationed in Cormons and Görz from its arrival to the end of the war. On September 27, 1944, the supply train was attacked by fighter-bombers in Cormons, leaving five dead and seven wounded. From then on the train stayed in a tunnel near Görz. Another fighter-bomber attack took place at this site on January 14, 1945 (one dead, two wounded). For this train too, securing the rail lines in the Tagliamento and Isonzo valleys to the Reich border (Tarvisio and Piedicolle) was the task; in the first months in particular, though, runs were also made that extended from Verona in the west to Trieste in the east. Partisan attacks can be documented for 9 January (Vedrignano), 3 February (Lucinico),

20 February (Vilpucano), 2 March (Quisca), and 4 March (Colmo). Shortly before the capitulation in Italy on May 2, 1945, they wanted to move out, but got only as far as Udine, since the railroad station there was completely destroyed. The gun turrets were blown up, the other built-in weapons were made unusable. Then the crew drove in motor vehicles, including tanks and armored scout cars, via Piani and Tarvisio to Carinthia, where they arrived in Villach on 8 May and awaited the arrival of the British, to whom they surrendered. Tito's troops got the train back in action and used it for some years to patrol the border near Görz (Nova Gorica).

With the refusal to send armored trains to Italy in December 1943, the OB Southwest had probably been advised to set up line protection trains on his own to secure the rail lines against the increasing partisan activity. In Istria, Security Battalion 705, at least since the summer of 1944, had the line protection train "Peter" (or "San Pietro") on the line from Fiume to Rakek (in the direction of Laibach), and Security Battalion (M) 1209 had the line protection train "Adria" in the Trieste area. Both trains are documented shortly before the war ended. Also, in February 1945 another armored railcar is mentioned east of Trieste. Partisan activity was especially intense in the Julian Alps and their southern foothills. Along with the regular armored trains in service there (see above), another armored (line protection?) train, "Pany," can be documented in July 1944 on the Santa Lucia—Piedicolle line. In addition, the Italian "Mussolini" Battalion, involved in line protection from Görz since December 1943, had at least one (but probably two) railcars of the "Littorina" type. On the northwest Slovenian side, which joined the Germans in 1941, Home Guard Regiment 184, located in the upper Sava valley between Radmannsdorf and St. Veit, had two line protection trains.

It was probably one of these that, on August 11, 1944, aided the 1st A/A Training Battalion 699 in putting down a partisan attack at the Scheraunitz railroad station.

West of Milan, an "armored train" (line protection train, commanded by Captain Both), otherwise stationed in Novara—and also so named—took part in the operation against the partisan republic of Domodossola, but was derailed in Verbania in the early stages. — It can be assumed that besides this documented one, other such trains were used to protect important rail lines (such as the Brenner line).

The tanks of PZ 73 on a scouting run in Görz. Photo: Panzarasa/Stefano Digiusto collection

Armored Trains in Partisan Combat

With the taking of the Balkans and the beginning of the Russian campaign, armored trains were increasingly confronted with a task that was regarded as a borderline case for them from the start, the securing of the back line rail network, and in fact against a threat that had scarcely—if at all—been seen in their activities during high-level planning for the campaigns, that of partisans.

In the lands taken in 1939-40, there had already been occasional attacks on the occupying forces, but these actions remained at first so isolated that they could scarcely have been seen as a general problem, and they only rarely involved the transit routes and thus the rail lines. This changed essentially with the occupation of Yugoslavia and then of parts of the western Soviet Union. Both countries had a tradition of subversive action by irregular bands behind the front, and such activities were much encouraged by geographical circumstances—in the former, inaccessible, useless mountain regions, in the latter, the vast areas of impenetrable forest and swamp regions. There was also the extraordinary extent of the now-occupied regions, in an ever-greater imbalance with the number of securing forces available for its protection. In those lands a surface-covering occupation had to be dispensed with from the start, and securing had to limited to important places and the transit connections to and between them. Even for this, usually only over-aged and poorly equipped local defense units and, increasingly, those recruited from willing (and thus not very reliable) prisoners of war, were available. On the other side, the partisan movement in the occupied Soviet Russian regions, supported from the beginning by Communist party cadres as well as many strayed and disappeared Red Army officers and soldiers, immediately pursued operative goals. In Moscow, shortly after the war began, a central staff for the partisans was created, which organized their rigid command and gave them tasks in close agreement with the Red Army. They also took care of constant supplying of men and materials by slipping through weakly occupied front sectors, and by landing or dropping them from aircraft, and later—when the partisans had taken control of larger, connected areas, by direct air traffic. In Yugoslavia there were two partisan groups at the start, the Greater Serbian Chetniks and the nationally unconnected communistic bands of Tito, which sometimes fought against each other and thus did not go beyond tactical success at first. After the surrender of Italy (September 9, 1943), though, which the Chetniks had somewhat accepted and even promoted, and after the Western Allies (especially Great Britain) had dropped the Chetniks

in favor of Tito and had helped the latter with air-dropped supplies, the communistic units soon grew into a militarily organized army that was now quite capable of larger operations.

The unwise procedure of the German political leadership, which regarded the occupied regions as merely objects to be plundered, suppliers of cheap war, economic and agricultural products and of—forcibly recruited—work forces, and also persecuted as the contemptible targets of their racial madness, thus driving groups of the native populations, which had taken a friendly, even supportive position after the Russian campaign had begun, on account of their anti-Communist position, into the opposing camp, and the worsening of the general war situation, which likewise caused a thinning of the troops stationed there—along with the already mentioned securing troops, new or refreshed units of troops transferred there—encouraged the enemies of the occupying power—also in lands that had been peaceful until then—to increased and ever more vigorous action, which in time became an all-inclusive and scarcely quenchable fire, which sometimes took on the forms of a genuine revolt.

This cannot be the place to go into the partisan war in detail, its causes, history and effects, its conduct with mutual toughness, indeed grimness that took so many victims, including from the civilian population. A few aspects, though, that touch on the action of armored trains in these battles must be discussed, wherein the emphasis is placed on the Russian campaign. As everywhere, one of the main activities of the partisans—along with surprise attacks on individuals or small groups, and economic sabotage—here too was disrupting traffic, especially supplies for the front. After the poor condition of the Russian road network—especially in the mud periods in the autumn and spring—had become evident, supplies moved mainly on the railroad lines, which were thus increasingly exposed to the partisans' acts of sabotage. At the beginning of 1942 they were still limited mainly to roads and rail lines very close to the front, such as near Welikije Luki or between Dorogobusch and Wjasma, where armored trains were also used against them; later they increased particularly in the hinterlands of Army Group Center (the other two army groups were generally much less afflicted, and mostly in the territories bordering directly on Army Group Center; in the Army Group North area there was another herd of partisans in the region between Leningrad and Wolchow). The partisans improved their explosive techniques by using hard-to-find wooden mines which were ignited by either pressure or shaking, or had delayed or long-range fuses. After May 1942 this resulted in corresponding security measures by the Wehrmacht:

PZ 63 passes the ruins of a freight train destroyed by partisans in the northern sector of the eastern front.
Photo: H. Beckmann/W. Sawodny collection

- On both sides of the road, strips of 100 to 500 meters were freed of all sight hindrances; only guard personnel were allowed into this terrain.
- On especially endangered lines support points within sight of each other were set up and occupied; between these support points, ambushes for partisans were often set by patrols.
- At the railroad stations, watchtowers equipped with spotlights were set up; the buildings were secured with barbed wire, minefields and breastworks of tree trunks. The water towers were especially protected.
- The German station personnel were all armed; watchdogs were used. Each station was to work out defense plans.
- All important railroad bridges were guarded by sentries armed with heavy infantry weapons. They were also to patrol the surrounding areas regularly.
- Along the rail lines, mobile construction troops were stationed, equipped with all possible materials and reachable by telephone.
- The transport trains were accompanied by mobile guards; at least one car was fitted with a raised machine gun platform, which provided an opportunity to observe and rake the line.
- By day the transport trains were assembled into convoys that moved at slow speeds; on strongly endangered lines the train traffic was halted at night.

Several open cars loaded with sand or gravel were hitched to the front of every train to protect them from mines; the convoys often sent completely empty trains ahead. Later a special device was built that, mounted on an unmanned car at the head of the train, was to make mines explode.

Armored railroad vehicles, including armored trains, were included in these protective measures. The instructions for fighting partisan bands in the East, which the Wehrmacht command staff issued on November 11, 1942, say about this:

"Generous use is to be made of armored railcars, armored trains and makeshift armored trains. Their increase is to be striven for by all means. . . . Armored scout cars set on rails have proved themselves useful.

"Armored railcars, armored trains and makeshift armored trains and cars are to be used

a) to traverse the rail lines at irregular times for line protection,
b) for fast movement of combat-ready reserves and repair personnel to endangered places,
c) To protect supply trains by adding one of that kind of car to the train.

Fast use of all these special trains must be guaranteed at all times; sufficient alarm crews are to be kept ready.

The runs of the armored and special trains must be scheduled by the railroad service offices with consideration for rail traffic."

It appears from this that rail line and transport protection was regarded as the main task of the armored rail vehicles at that time. The armored trains often had an effect, simply by their presence, that restrained the partisans from attacking the lines they ran on or the transports they escorted (whereby one cannot avoid getting the impression that protecting trips by staffs or other high officers clearly enjoyed priority over trains with troops, weapons or supplies. To be sure, the armored trains were not at all enough for these purposes in the endangered regions, and so it is not surprising that the establishment of most line protection trains for which the cited combat instructions also include building instructions occurred in this period.

All of these measures resulted in a decrease in the number of partisan attacks on rail lines in the zone of Army Group Center in the last quarter of 1942, and that in December more attacks could be halted by guard personnel than were listed as successful. This favorable situation was sustained in the first two months of 1943; only from March on was a steep increase in attacks on railroad lines recorded, to continue and, in July, to exceed the number of 1000 attacks (meaning over 30 per day) for the first time. In them, the partisans turned increasingly to the serial blowing up of tracks, meaning that they placed whole series of explosive charges under the rails at short intervals and exploded them at the same time. The tracks were thus destroyed for long distances; repairs took correspondingly long (often up to 48 hours and more). In addition, deeply buried time-fuse mines with electric fuses capable of being set a long way ahead—from hours to several days--were used. On August 2, 1943,

To make it difficult for partisans to approach an armored train, safety strips were rid of sight hindrances on both sides. The line protection train "Polko" patrols. Photo: Federal Archives, Koblenz

the Soviets began a two-month "rail war" in which the partisan bands concentrated very specifically on destroying rail lines. There too, the focal point was in the sector of Army Group Center, the withdrawal of which after losing the battle of Kursk was supposed to be crippled, yet this action—although with considerably less intensity—also spread to the rest of the eastern front. It immediately elicited a German counter-reaction in the form of a call for intensifying railroad protection with all means. In the relevant Führer's Order No. 9 of August 5, 1943, it is stated under No. 4: "The armored railroad trains and line protection cars are to be gathered strongly on the most important and threatened lines (previously, Minsk—Gomel—Unetscha and Minsk—Orscha—Kritschew—Unetscha had been noted as such)." Although the destruction hindered German transport movements, in the end they could—of course with delays, of which the hours-long interruptions after the first and strongest strike were the most serious—be dealt with in the planned manner. In September the rail war was already drying down; in November the total number of attacks in the central sector fell back below 1000, remaining at about 800 until 1943 changed to 1944, and then climbing back to just over 1000 in April-May 1944. It is striking, though, that in this period the percentage of partisan actions stopped by German securing forces decreased, and particularly that the number of damaged locomotives remained equally high. This was partly attributable to the fact that now the partisans were shooting at them with antitank weapons to make their boilers explode. It also occurred now again and again that trains running alone, or the last one in a convoy, were attacked,

plundered and burned by large partisan groups after they had been derailed or stopped, signs that it was no longer enough to hinder their permanent presence near rail lines. In preparation for the Soviet summer offensive of 1944, the partisans carried out a further stroke in the rail war on the night of 19-20 June, and continued it the next two nights. And this time they succeeded in doing what had been prevented in the summer of 1943; they were able to cripple almost all the traffic in the backland area of Army Group Center and thus strongly hinder the bringing up of reserves in the first phase of the attack.

Compared to the events at Army Group Center, the railroad attacks by partisans in the other sectors of the eastern front remained comparatively meager. In Army Group North, the bordering region up to the level of Dno in particular was struck, but the partisans in the Wolchow region also remained active. A spread to the west, to the Narwa—Peipus-See—Ostrow line, took place only during the preparations for the offensive in January 1944; with the withdrawal to the former Baltic states the partisan activity died out extensively, since the anti-Soviet attitude of the people there offered no support. In the southern sector it was mainly the Bachmatsch—Woroschba region bordering the Brjansk partisan district that was endangered at first.

In general, partisan activities concentrated on the area that extended some 200 to 300 km back from the front and included the backline areas of the armies and army groups. The armored trains were also stationed there when they were not in front action.

Buildings along the rail lines were built up into fortified posts, as here in the wooded region northwest of Brjansk. Photo: H. Becker/W. Sawodny collection

In the spring of 1944, PZ 68 passes such a fortified building on the line through the Pripjet region. Photo: Federal Archives, Koblenz

Only in the central sector were there strong partisan bands from the beginning, also in the almost impassable Pripjet region that lay farther back, and they constantly threatened the Brest-Litowsk—Pinsk—Kalinkowitschi—Gomel rail line. This resulted in PZ 25 being transferred there as early as May 1942. On the other hand, the line from Brest-Litowsk via Baranowitschi to Minsk, also struck by attacks at times, remained at first a welcome destination for training runs by newly established armored trains from the Replacement Battalion in Rembertow. In the spring of 1943 strong partisan bands from the region south of Brjansk moved westward, settled south of the Pripjet region and disturbed the Kowel—Sarny—Korosten rail line. After an attack on the rail junction of Sarny in April 1943, Armored Trains No. 7 and 10 had to take over the securing of this line.

With the backward movement of the fronts, the partisans also moved farther and farther to the west. Thus after the withdrawal to the Dnjepr in September 1943, their activity increased in the Korosten—Schitomir—Berditschew region, and at the beginning of 1944 they increased sharply in the region between Lemberg and Kowel, and later spread out into the Polish territory between Lublin and Bialystok as well. When the western boundary of Russia was reached, the Soviet partisan movement came to an end; their units were absorbed into the Red Army. On the other hand, the Polish underground army, which had carried out attacks for a long time already—sometimes also on railroad facilities in the whole General Government—now emerged in Warsaw; and there were also uprisings in the region of the allied Slovakia; both uprisings had to be put down in long, exhausting fighting.

The role of the armored trains, which had changed through developments in 1943-44, is reflected in the corresponding excerpt from the OKW memorandum "Band Fighting" of May 6, 1944, which replaced the combat instructions of 1942 that were quoted above. It is stated therein:

"Armored trains are especially suited for partisan fighting. For large undertakings they are to be called in:

a) For advances into the enemy with independent combat assignments,

b) For artillery support,

c) For participation in operations with their disembarked parts (scout cars, tanks, infantry platoons, heavy mine throwers, engineer groups),

d) To prevent the retreat of bands over the rail lines. In no case may individual weapons or parts of the crew be taken away from the armored trains.

e) In special cases, when action by armored trains is not possible, as command centrals for the command staff of the operation by means of the numerous radio equipment.

Armored trains are particularly capable of carrying out independent small operations, especially as pursuit commands, as well as in combination with their own armored scout cars or tanks, depending on the terrain.

Securing runs promise success, taking in account the excellent information service of the bands only when they are kept as secret as possible, and thus are carried out

- preferably at night
- at irregular intervals
- and camouflaged by normal run numbers.

They are especially effective when the bands are constantly disturbed by patrols, scout troops, and lurking scout troops.

Timely intervention against surprise attacks on transports and moves on the rail lines presupposes:

- the highest level of constant alarm readiness,
- the fastest transmission of reports and commands, by radio when possible,
- prioritized movement of armored trains as "urgent assistance trains."

The presence of interlopers in the security strips on both sides of the rail lines was forbidden. Here a captured man is checked by the crew of PZ 63. Photo: Federal Archives, Koblenz

But also to the sides of the tracks, pursuit commands tried to apprehend partisans. Here a command from PZ 1 is moving along a brook in a swampy region of the central sector in the autumn of 1943. Photo: W. Sitzius/W. Sawodny collection.

The pursuit command of PZ 4 in the thick woods of the Brjansk region in 1943. Photo: G. Leinen/W. Sawodny collection

Possible special tasks for armored trains are:

a) Escort protection for important transport trains, courier trains, special trains of high officials.

b) Supplying embattled support-point crews on the rail line with weapons and ammunition, transporting wounded away.

c) Assistance in accidents after attacks on railroad trains including derailment and medical care.

d) Securing strongly threatened railroad stations, man-made structures and of work on and in the vicinity of the rail line.

e) Transport of infantry units up to platoon strength under tank protection, to battalion strength without it.

f) Distributing propaganda materials along the rail lines.

Calling in armored trains for these tasks is to be limited to especially justified special cases.

In each case, armored trains must be given clear combat tasks or other tasks. If two or more tasks must be given in exceptional cases, their order and urgency are to be commanded. Efforts must always be made to listen to the commander about the capability of his unit before assigning the task.

Unlike the armored trains, the armored (heavy and light scout) trains consist of 10 to 14 individual vehicles, each of which has its own power. Thus they can cover large diistances on the rail line (at 500-meter intervals between the separate cars, 5 to 6 km) and always gather quickly at endangered places by radio orders.

Line protection trains are armored in makeshift form; their crew is assembled through the chain of command . . . The action of the line protection trains in fighting partisans is done essentially like that of the armored trains under consideration for their usually much weaker fighting strength.

Armored railcars and rail-capable motor vehicles are to be used most extensively to secure rail lines.

(There follows a section on the use of line securing cars in transport trains.)

Completing this is the already mentioned report of the staff officer for special uses with the Commander of the Armored Trains, Lt.Col. Dr. Guenther, of May 19, 1944, after an inspection trip to the armored trains with Army Group Center, who notes that disembarked parts of the crew were used for infantry tasks far from the armored train, so that they can receive no support from the train's heavy weapons. It is to be feared that in actions for which normal securing troops were sufficient, unnecessary losses may occur among highly trained, specially qualified and only with difficulty to be replaced personnel. In their use for line securing, armored trains are exposed just as much to explosions of mines as the far less expensive makeshift line protection trains, which can fulfill such tasks just as well. Thus

The pursuit command of PZ 2 has located a supply dump of the partisans in the central sector; it will be destroyed. Photo: F. Brunner/W. Sawodny collection

Since lasting occupation of the vast space in Russia was not possible, villages in which partisans had been found were simply burned down, as here in the central sector by a command from PZ 66, whose 38(t) tank is just moving out. Photo: J. Kenter/W. Sawodny collection

unnecessary losses of valuable material and equipment (locomotives, cars, tanks, scout cars, etc.) occur, their loss being in no relationship to the higher moral effect that armored trains, as opposed to line protection trains, make on their own troops and the enemy. In partisan action as well, the formation of battle groups including several trains, since they—with disembarked infantry platoons as ambush troops, and disembarked armored vehicles as mobile support between the trains—can block large stretches of the rail line.

While in the Balkans, despite similar prejudices to those in the Russian theater, rail-line protection remained the main task of the armored trains (here, of course, the particularly suitable light and heavy scout trains were also used, the latter, to be sure, so late that they could no longer make use of their advantages), securing runs by armored trains played only a minor role on the eastern front from then on. Since native railroad personnel, among whom there were ever-increasing numbers of informants, had to be used at all railroad stations, such runs, which could not remain secret in view of the considerably preparation times, almost always became known to them at the right time. The explosion units could thus get away before the train arrived and—even worse—construct effective mine traps, which resulted in painful losses of men and material. The armored trains were too costly for this, even though their enhancement of morale for support-point crews and sentries along the rail lines was

still high. Attacks along the lines and the transports running on them could prevent the armored trains only in the fewest cases, since the partisans—informed of their coming—planned their actions so that they had already disappeared when the trains arrived, or they moved to other sections of the line, on which they could be active without being seen. On the other hand, the securing of rescue and repair jobs was practical, as the partisans tried more and more often to thwart their success by attacking those units.

Thus the armored trains were now called in more strongly for active partisan fighting. In the "small operations" mentioned in the memorandum, the armored train operated mainly on its own. The infantry platoon was disembarked and, along with the armored road vehicles, used as a pursuit command sideward of the tracks, when the terrain allowed it. This was supposed to drive out and destroy partisan groups that wanted to approach the lines or were sitting in their hideouts. The armored train, with which constant communication was maintained, could if needed (tough resistance) provide long-range support with its heavy weapons; in this respect, the pursuit command was also not supposed to go beyond their effective range (ca. 10 km). Naturally, previous information as to partisan locations and strengths were also very useful for such operations, whether gained from German reconnaissance or information from the native population, which came richly at first, but in time, because of the weakness of

After PZ 25 had been thrown off the rails by an explosive charge on the Pripjet line, two suspicious persons were captured and fastened to the derailed car with nooses around their necks. Photo: E. Banser/W. Sawodny collection

the German occupiers as well as the massive scare tactics of the ever-stronger partisans, became very sparse. As one can gather from the unanimous impression in diary notations of members of Armored Train No. 21 (involved again and again for long periods in partisan action at various places on the eastern front) from November 1942 to June 1944 and PZ 64 securing rail lines in Croatia from June 1943 to November 1944), they fought with very varying success. Some successful operations, in which they were able to apprehend and destroy partisan groups, are countered by a larger number of those that achieved nothing, because the enemies were able to get away at the right time. The particularly successful actions against partisans are reported in two brochures issued by the Commander of Armored Trains with the OKH, with the titles "Armored Trains," for Armored Trains No. 1, 2 (several times), 21, 27, 31, 64, and 66 (several times), and the commander of Armored Trains No. 26 (March 1942 to January 1943) and 1 (January 1943 to February 1944)—active exclusively in partisan fighting with them—he was later awarded the German Cross in gold for these actions.

In large operations (which took place in the Balkans so far from rail lines that armored trains could not take part in them), efforts were made to surround the partisans in their local areas and finally destroy them by systematically making the circle smaller. Here, of course, large numbers of troops were needed to make the encirclement as solid as possible (complete encirclement succeeded only in the rarest cases; with their much better knowledge of the region, the partisans almost always found an escape through which the hard core—though often with very heavy losses—could slip away). In order to save forces, it was practical to use a rail line (or main road) as one side of the circle, where by removing all sight obstacles for many meters to the side (to make it hard for partisans to approach), a wide coverless lane that could be watched with little effort was formed, which the partisans would have to cross if they were driven to it. Naturally, an armored train could not guard a long stretch alone; it had to be secured with support points within sight of each other, for their operation, disembarked parts of the armored train crew could be used. But the train could quickly be called in for fire support if partisans appeared and wanted to force a passage. The report from Lt.Col. Dr. Günther mentions that a battle group consisting of several armored trains could cover an ever larger section of tracks—and mainly with their own means. The most extensive action of this kind took place during

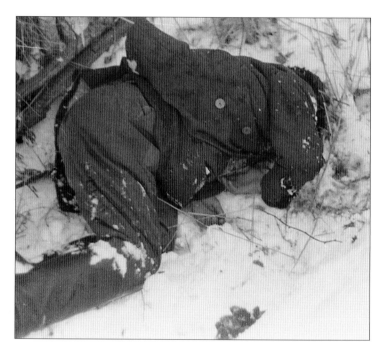

Above: A partisan fallen in battle with the pursuit command of PZ 71 in the Ukraine early in 1944. Photo: H. Griebl collection

Upper left: Although the orders from above existed from the start to execute all partisans outside the Hague Convention at once, they were often treated just like regular prisoners at first. Here captured partisans are taken away on PZ 63. Photo: H. Beckmann/W. Sawodny collection

Left: Later—since partisans also fought against their own people who cooperated with the occupying forces, as well as against the Germans, with extraordinary grimness—they were usually disposed of in short order. Here three suspected partisans ended on the gallows. Photo: W. Sawodny collection

Operation "Fruehlingsfest" against the partisan region around Lepel from April 16 to May 10, 1944, where the Molodetschno—Polozk rail line, against which the partisan were pushed, was barred with good effect by five armored trains and several line protection trains. The further tasks of the armored trains in such large operations were artillery support—naturally depending on the range of the weapons—and the participation of disembarked men including road vehicles with the encircling troops. In their framework, naturally the forces provided by the armored train could always be just a very small group, but they stood out because of their training and equipment and thus were highly valued. Of course this, as was variously criticized, included the danger that these parts of the crew would be drawn too far away from the armored train, and for too long, and thus affected its capacity for action. The armored train with its excellent communication facilities could also function as a command central for the action staff, especially when the events too place so far from the tracks that the armored train itself could not intervene. But the possibility of making independent advances against the enemy, discussed in the "Bändenbekampfung" memorandum, scarcely entered the picture. Aside from the fact that the partisans' locations were usually far from the—watched—transit routes, running on a line that led into a partisan area was only possible after intensive clearing measures and correspondingly great expenditures of time, as well as punishable silliness.

The success statistics of the Russian partisans in reference to the German armored trains are worth noting and discussing. As usual, the Soviet literature provides no inherently final statistics. For White Russia it is stated that from the beginning of the Russian campaign (June 22, 1941) to November 1, 1942, five armored trains were destroyed, from August 1, 1942, to July 18, 1943, five of them were derailed, and in the whole period up to the liberation of the area in July 1944, 32 armored trains had been blown up (notice the different terms for the types of success gained). In the Ukraine, partisans claimed to have derailed more than 60 armored trains during the entire eastern campaign, and the partisan leader Fedorow, active in the northern Ukraine, states in his report: "Eight armored trains with their crews flew into the air." Opposed to this, it is documented that not a single regular German armored train was lost to partisan activity, and of the line protection trains, for which an inclusive overview can no longer be gained, at most a very few (but none of those whose history can be traced over a long period). With the increasing progress of the war, it certainly happened more and more often that armored and line protection trains were blown up or derailed. But this happened only to a part of the train, and the derailed cars could certainly be rescued and rebuilt or replaced, so the train remained in action. Even taking this into account, and if one remembers that A/A trains of the armored trains were also counted by them, the Soviet reports seem to be much exaggerated.

All in all, it can be determined that the armored trains and other armored and armed railroad vehicles did their part in tireless, often frustrating action against enemies who are hard to catch, who damaged them again and again with explosives and caused losses by ambushes, that—although ever-increasing limitation of rail traffic was not to be avoided—the partisans' rail war against the railroad network could not achieve its final goal of cutting the front off fully from back line connections, except for a short phase in the central sector before the Russian summer offensive of 1944.

That partisans were not only "hunted," but that they also struck back strongly, is shown by this 38 (t) tank from PZ 66 that ran over a mine during such an action. Photo: J. Kenter/W. Sawodny collection

Three soldiers from PZ 63, who fell in a partisan attack near the Nowinka—Batezkaja line (northern sector) on August 19, 1943, are brought back to the train in tent canvas. Photo: E, Kwasny/W. Sawodny collection

The Russian Campaign

The 1941 Advance

Shortly after the end of the western campaign, the armored trains that served there were gradually transferred to East Prussia and the General Government (German-occupied Poland), where PZ 2 had already been in Minsk Mazowiecki since the Polish campaign. Armored Trains No. 1 and 6 went to East Prussia by September 1, 1940; while PZ 1 was stationed in Allenstein and later Heilsberg, PZ 6 was stationed in Tilsit. PZ 7—perhaps somewhat later, but in any case still in the autumn of 1940—came to Lublin; in the time period between the summer of 1940 and June 1941 it spent some time at the RAW in Leipzig-Engelsdorf, but it cannot be determined to date whether this was after the western campaign (to repair damage sustained there) or before the attack on Russia (for overhauling). In mid-May 1941, Armored Trains No. 3 and 4, which had carried out securing tasks in The Netherlands and France until then, finally were transferred to the East. PZ 3 was at first in Neumark, then in Thorn, PZ 4 went to Krakau.

In order to have armored trains available near the front at once, six such units were set up for the Russian broad gauge (1524 mm), according to the immediate solution for Project "Panzerzug 1941" suggested by In 10 in December 1940 (the available standard-gauge trains could be used only after the lines' conversion—involving delays, and farther in the backlands). Each of the three army groups involved in the attack was to receive two such trains; the two of Army Group North (No. 26 and 30, readiness site Königsberg) were to advance from Eydtkau in the direction of Kowno; those of Army Group Center (ready in Warsaw) were to set out for Baranowitschi; one (No. 29) from Platerow via Wolkowysk, the other (No. 28) from Terespol—Brest-Litowsk. For Army Group South (ready in Tarnow) one train (No. 27) was to advance from Cholm to Kowel, the other (No. 31) from Zurawica via Przemysl to Lemberg. But since the Cholm—Kowel line had been broken by the Russians, PZ 27 was supposed to cross the Bug from Terespol to Brest-Litowsk in the sector of Army Group Center and then go from there to Kowel (which, to be sure, was not actually done).

These broad gauge armored trains consisted merely of the new type of tank-carrier cars with captured French Somua S 35 tanks and open infantry cars. The training of the tank crews was done by Tank Brigade 100 in Paris; then they, along with their tanks, were taken to Teschen (Olsa district), where at the end of May 1941 the whole crews were assembled. The cars were placed at the readiness sites. On the other hand, the locomotives—unarmored and converted to broad gauge—had already been stationed at the border railroad stations as switch engines for some time before the invasion began. The

diesel locomotive intended for PZ 29 had even been promised to the Russians for use on their side, but had been held back on the excuse of insufficient testing. Officers of the armored trains—disguised as Reichsbahn train escorts for normal transport trains in the active freight exchange that went on until the last minute—examined conditions on the Soviet side. On June 21, 1941, the crews arrived at the action stations, the broad gauge cars only after night fell on the evening before the attack. An accompanying railroad engineer command with heavy lifting tackle assembled the armored trains during the night and protected at least the cabs of the armored train locomotives with armor plates they brought along. Thus on the early morning of June 22, 1941, they were ready in time for the attack at 3:15 AM.

In the region of the Baltic states, which only fell to the Soviet Union in 1940, as well as the northern Polish territory occupied by the Russians in 1939, the conversion work to broad gauge was not completely finished, or double-track stretches between the two border stations had one broad and one standard gauge track. Here several standard gauge German armored trains could also be used immediately when the war began.

PZ 3 is ready at the Prostken railroad station for the attack toward Grajewo on June 22, 1941. Photo: H. Griebl collection

PZ 1 at the railroad station in easily captured Augustowo on June 22, 1941. Photo: E. Grahl/W. Sawodny collection

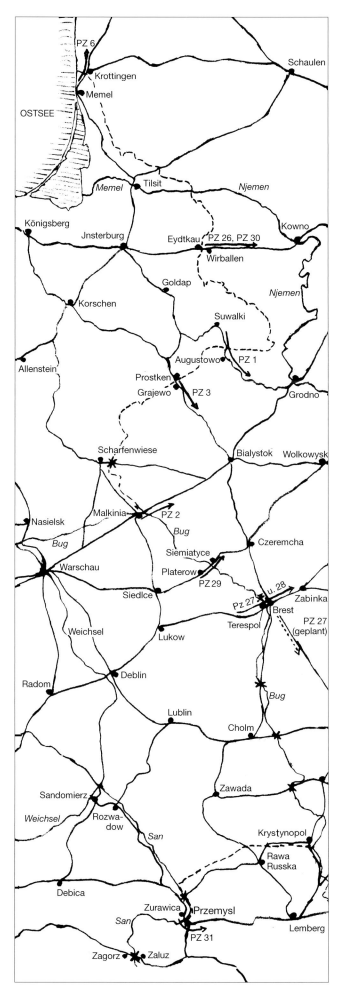

In the fighting near Grajewo on the first day, this Soviet flag was captured by the battle group of PZ 3. Photo: H. Bendl/W. Sawodny collection

PZ 6 advanced northward from Memel through the border town of Krottingen and took part in the fighting around Libau. PZ 1 was ready at Kruglanken and, proceeding from the Suwalki area, joined to the German Reich in 1939, took Augustowo, where the Russians, some still asleep, were surprised.; then it secured track repair work between Augustowo and Grodno and the rebuilding of the Memel bridge at the last-named town. PZ 3 pushed through the border position from Prostken and effectively supported the taking of Grajewo, which it then secured to the east. PZ 2 took part in the border battles on the Warsaw—Bialystok line, starting from Malkinia.

Of the broad gauge armored trains No. 26 and 30, ready in Eydtkau, the latter was delayed on the morning of the attack by a shell that hit its tender. The shell fortunately turned out to be a dud. Then it took part in fighting down the border fortifications. Thus in the zone of the 16th Army, only PZ 26 was able at first to advance toward Kowno, around which long battles took place. PZ 29 was able to cross the Bug railroad bridge unharmed in a surprise attack from Platerow on the morning of 22 June, and on the east bank, and after removing two camps of surprised Russians at the railroad station, to take Siemiatyce and fire on and rout an unsuspecting Soviet column going toward the Bug on a road that paralleled the rail line. Then the disembarked train crew was used to roll up the bunker line near Annusin, which was not done without some losses. On the other hand, Armored Trains No. 27 and 28, ready in Terespol, were obviously not used in the surprise-attack taking of the railroad bridge over the Bug in front of Brest-Litowsk by the 45th Infantry Division. Only on the night of 24-25 June was PZ 28 called to Brest-Litowsk to take part with its disembarked tanks (only one of which was ready to roll)

Action of the armored trains at the start of the Russian campaign. In the south the girder was formed extensively by the Bug and San rivers (otherwise shown by dotted lines). X = rail line broken.

in the hard fighting around the citadel, which lasted until June 29 (while PZ 27, planned for action in the direction of Cholm, probably waited in Terespol at first). PZ 31 as well, assigned to the 101st Light Division of the 17th Army, was not used in removing the railroad bridge to Russisch-Przemysl on the first day of the war. It remained in Zurawica until the Soviets had to vacate the region between Przemysl and the Carpathians because of the eastern advance over the San, and was then occupied with securing tasks in that region.—For the two standard-gauge armored trains with Army Group South (No. 4 and 7), there was at first no chance for action; they remained waiting in Cracow until the beginning of July 1941.

During the advance in the summer and autumn of 1941, the armored trains—also the broad gauge ones—were not active on the front. Their main tasks were scouting the rail lines in the conquered regions, securing repair and later regauging work, which soon became necessary, since contrary to what was originally expected from the Russians, only a little broad gauge rolling stock was left behind ready to use, fighting and capturing the enemy troops left behind in the back lands during the fast advance of their own combat troops, particularly in the course of the great pocket battles in the central sector, and to an ever-growing extent, securing transport against the already active partisans.

The armored trains' advance routes can no longer be reconstructed in all details. Precise locations are usually known only after the beginning of November 1941. These show that the units were all still serving in the army-group sectors to which they had been assigned at the beginning of the campaign. With the Army Group North, PZ 6—only later, after the line was regauged—made its way from Libau via Riga, Walk and Pleskau; it was already in Podsewy, on the line to Batezkaja, on September 3, 1941, and shortly thereafter had reached its final action area for the rest of the year, the line between Batezkaja and Dno, which it secured along with the lines that ran toward the front from Batezkaja to Nowgorod and Dno to Staraja Russa. PZ 26 also moved from Kowno through Wilna, Dünaburg, Rositten, Idritza, and Nowosokolniki, already reaching its final stationing, the line between Nowosokolniki and Dno, at the beginning of September. PZ 30 took the same route at first, but then continued from Rositten via Pleskau in the direction of Luga, where it was spent the time before the offense resumed in August. After the advance around Leningrad in October came to a stop, PZ 30 was transferred to the region of the 18th Army between Leningrad and Wolchow, where it was stationed at Ljuban and patrolled the line from there to Tosno and farther north to Mga.

PZ 30 advances on the double-track Pleskau—Luga line in Juny 1941. Photo: Federal Archives, Koblenz

After regauging, PZ 6 follows the front in the northern sector on the line from Pleskau to Dno to take over its securing tasks north of that city. Photo: Federal Archives, Koblenz

South of Dno the broad gauge was retained at first. Here PZ 26 had its action region in the autumn of 1941. Photo: P. Voneif/W. Sawodny collection

The route of PZ 27 can no longer be determined precisely. But it did not go, as intended, from Brest to Kowel, but rather remained in the sector of Army Group Center. Presumably it advanced through the Pripjet region (Pinsk—Kalinkowitschi) and via Gomel and Brjansk to Orel, where it was stationed at Seminarskaja on the line from there to Jelez as of mid-November 1941. In December it was transferred to Ponyri to secure the line to Kursk. After the fighting in Brest-Litowsk, PZ 28 advanced via Baranowitschi and Minsk to Orscha, but was then ordered via Witebsk into the Newel—Welikije Luki area in the late summer. PZ 29, reaching Baranowitschi via Czeremcha and Wolkowysk, followed it into the Witebsk region. In September, after the rail lines coming in from the west were regauged, they were replaced there by standard-gauge Armored Trains No. 1 and 2,

and both armored trains advanced into the Brjansk region after the resumption of the offensive at the end of September, via Smolensk and Roslawl (PZ 28) and Orscha, Kritschew, and Unetscha (PZ 29). PZ 28 was able to bring in many prisoners in the breakthrough of the pocket formed there, and in the process of its further advance, reached Orel in October. Here it gained the vehicles of a captured Soviet armored train, and from 10/31 to 11/3, along with two strengthened battalions of Infantry Regiment 521 (296th Infantry Division), parts of the 4th Railroad Engineer Company (motorized Railroad Engineer Regiment 8) and a railroad operations company, plus intelligence troops, carried out an operation to take possession of the Orel—Kursk line (between Orel, in German hands since 3 October, and Kursk, taken on 2 November, there were as yet no regular troops), on which two detailed reports are available.

In the period from 10/29 to 11/1 the Soviets had moved back to the east and made the double-track rail line between Jeropkino and Glasunowka unusable by destroying the railroad stations, blowing up signals and switches and removing the western rail line for 30 km. The armored train (whose Russian guns were still unusable; the three Somua tanks it carried also could not be unloaded because of defects) moved ahead with an infantry platoon and the railroad engineers. The armored train stopped before breaks in the line, the infantry swarmed out for securing, and the engineers took up the job of eliminating the damage (the average time for it is listed as two hours). The transport train (one locomotive with 37 G-cars, four of them for ammunition, two for provisions and one as a radio shack, three X-cars, each with two field kitchens, and two X-cars on which six light infantry guns and three antitank guns were mounted) moved up according to visual conditions. If the distance to the next railroad station was not too far, units were sent ahead on foot or on bicycles to mop up the villages on the rail line and perhaps catch the enemies at their destructive work. Reconnaissance in the area of the battle group, once up to 30 km to the east, was also carried out. Twice—at Smiewka and Kurakino—there were firefights, in which the armored train took part, with mounted militia and partisan groups which tried to disturb the Germans' work. They suffered losses, but some of them were able to escape to the east, since pursuit was not possible. In addition, 359 prisoners, mainly scattered men who had lost contact with their units, were brought in. At the railroad stations that were reached, support-point crews of one or two platoons were left behind; they also had the tracks between them to patrol. On 3 November the blown-up Snowa bridge near Solotuchino (40 km from Kursk) had been reached; its rebuilding would begin immediately, and the same was true of the Tuskorj bridge near Worobewka 12 km further, the work being done by an advance command. Except for 5 November, the enemy made no more attempts to disturb rail traffic on this line.

The broad gauge PZ 29 moves ahead in alarm readiness in the central sector of the eastern front.
Photo: Federal Archives, Koblenz

In the same sector PZ 28 also steams eastward.
Photo: Federal Archives, Koblenz

In Orel in October 1941 a captured Soviet armored train was added to PZ 28. It is seen thus here while mopping up the Orel—Kursk rail line. Photo: Federal Archives, Koblenz

It is stressed positively that the battle group was to be made up according to the length of the line and the number of railroad stations to be occupied, the necessary repairs were top be begun promptly by the railroad pioneers directly assigned to the armored train (for whose transport internally armored G-cars were to be planned on), and all communication links were to function trouble-free. It was reminded that the weapons of the armored train were not fully usable and no sufficient crew was available, so that it could only move a maximum of 15 km in daylight and with good vision (taking a second armored locomotive along was recommended); for the transport train, the loco was to be old, not overhauled and not leak-free, which resulted in high water use, which could not be made up from bodies of water for lack of pumps (requested were two trouble-free locomotives carrying water and coal supplies plus pumps), further, that through insufficient advance planning, when encountering a triangle turn, and by reverse shunting of the locomotive, the staff car had been placed at the end of the train, and the ammunition, provision and gun-transport cars right behind the locomotive of the transport train. Also requested for such operations were a cavalry platoon, a bicycle squadron, two or three jeeps, and vehicles for antitank guns (unloadable on open tracks), so as to make scout troops more mobile and allow better and further pursuit of a sighted enemy, a mine-seeking troop, an intelligence reconnaissance platoon with a security officer and interpreter, an A/A

machine gun platoon for aerial securing, pontoon bags for crossing rivers when bridges were destroyed, one or two railcars to maintain communication along the lines, and the guns carried on the transport train should be able to fire from it. — Afterward PZ 28 stayed on with stations in Orel itself, Solotuchino and Ponyri for securing on this line.

In mid-November PZ 29 was still securing the Brjansk—Orel line from Karatschew; later it advanced from Orel as far as Gorbatschewo in the direction of Tula with the 2nd Armored Army (stationed at Stalinojkonj), then eastward from there to before Teploje in the last offensive effort.

With a certain delay in time (because of the necessary regauging, in the case of two-track lines was usually done first to only one track, so as to move forward faster), the standard-gauge armored trains moved farther and farther eastward into the occupied territory. PZ 1 first moved from Grodno to Bialystok in July and then in the same month—following the regauging—advanced via Wolkowysk and Baranowitschi in the direction of Minsk; in August it was on the line from there to Orscha, in September in the Smolensk—Jarzewo—Dorogobusch region, where infantry action against partisans took place. A short action on the Smolensk—Witebsk line early in October finally brought it to its longtime stationing in Krasnoje, from which it had the line from Orscha to Smolensk for the rest of the year.

After the later regauging, the standard-gauge armored trains followed; here is PZ 1 behind the central sector of the eastern front. At right the Tatra railcar is returning from a scouting run. Photos: E. Grahl/W. Sawodny

After the border fighting near Malkinia, PZ 2 had been transferred to Brest-Litowsk to await regauging. Then it was transferred from there via Baranowitschi, Minsk, Borissow, and Orscha (between Bobr and Slawnoje at the beginning of September) to Witebsk, then finally, as of October 1941, to guard the Polozk-Witebsk line from Sirotino. PZ 3 was also moved to Brest-Litowsk at first, from where the crew carried out mopping-up actions on foot in the Pripjet district east of there. At the beginning of August it was transferred to Ossipowitschi, where the Minsk—Bobruisk line, and later the line via Schlobin to Gomel, were to be secured. At the end of October 1941, though, PZ 3 was called back to Koenigsberg to have a new radio system installed.

With Army Group South, PZ 31 crossed Galicia south of Lemberg and Tarnopol; around 6 July it took possession of a captured Russian armored train between Czortkow and Husiatyn, presumably receiving from it the infantry cars that are documented for it. Later it followed the main line from Lemberg to Odessa. During the pocket battle near Uman (at the beginning of August) it secured the construction on the Wapnjarka—Ladyschin line. Only after the Bug bridge was rebuilt could it advance in the direction of the Dnjepr. In mid-October it was in Krjukow opposite Krementschug, as of mid-November, after the Dnjepr bridge was rebuilt, it secured the line from there to Poltawa.

The standard-gauge armored trains, No. 4 and 7, first went into action at the beginning of July 1941, after the regauging of the Ukrainian rail network. PZ 4 crossed the Bug near Cholm and went to Kowel. From there it secured the line to Brest-Litowsk. Since it had to go back to Krakau for repairs, a makeshift train, equipped with machine guns and given the ingenious name "Fortschritt" (Progress), was given this task temporarily. The further course of PZ 4 led via Rowno, Schepetowka, and Schitomir to Fastow. PZ 7 also advanced along this line, with side trips to Sarny and stops in the Schitomir—Berditschew—Kasatin region. In mid-October both armored trains were located on the Fastow—Bobrinskaja—Pjatichatki—

Dnjepropetrowsk connecting line behind the Dnjepr, which they patrolled—after the first partisan attacks had been reported—along with their armored railcars. While PZ 4 stayed on that line, stationed in Bobrinskaja, but had to be sent back for repairs on 16 November, first to the Kowel EAW, later to Lemberg, PZ 7 crossed to the east shore early in November, after the Dnjepr bridge at Dnjepropetrowsk has been made usable and, stationed in Nischnednjeprowsk-Usel, secured from there to Sinelnikowo and further to Tschaplino or Saporoschje.

Soon after the border was crossed, it was found that the number of broad gauge armored trains put into service was not sufficient for scouting and securing the captured railroad network. Thus captured Russian armored trains were put into service for such purposes by the Germans. Although several pictures prove their existence, documentation of them is almost completely lacking. But soon the captured material had to be turned over to the collecting sites of the OKH. In addition, even at this time makeshift armored trains (line protection trains) were put into service, such as one broad gauge train used by the 221st Securing Division to secure the Kobryn—Pinsk—Luniniec line (stationed in Pinsk) at the end of July 1941 and named "Leutnant Marx" after its commander. A month later it was turned over to the 707th Infantry Division. How long it remained there—under other names and perhaps regauged later—is not known. At the end of January it must have been between Brjansk and Suchinitschi, since it included the cars of PZ 27 that were abandoned there at the encirclement and then recaptured. In the summer of 1942 it was left with the Replacement Battalion in Rembertow.

As opposed to the German armored trains that were not involved in combat directly on the front other than in the border fighting, the numerous—and constantly strengthened by new construction—Soviet armored trains saw much combat service during the withdrawal phase of their army. There is scarcely any German eastern front division that had nothing to do with Russian armored trains at some

The A/A crew of PZ 3, which was stationed in Ossipowitschi as of August 1941. Photo: H. Bendl/W. Sawodny collection

When PZ 4 reached the Bug east of Cholm in July 1941, the bridge over the river was already usable again. Photo: W. Obermark/W. Sawodny collection

When PZ 4 had to go back to Cracow for repairs in the autumn of 1941, an "auxiliary armored train" of freight cars, which was given the ingenious name "Fortschritt" (Progress) and manned for securing the Brest-Litowsk—Kowel line. Photo: W. Obermark/W/ Sawodny collection

In the southern sector, a line protection train armed with a 3.7-cm antitank gun guards regauging work in the summer of 1941. Photo: Federal Archives, Koblenz

Below: Thus did the battlefield look through the gun port of an armored train. Photo: Federal Archives, Koblenz

time. Although surely far from being complete, just their mention, found in war diaries of the OKW and in Wehrmacht reports (added to by a few further discoveries in documents of such events), gives an impression of the numbers of Soviet armored trains and the frequency and intenseness of their use:

6/23/41: A Soviet armored train (Type BP-35) is captured at Grodno.

6/25/41: In the interruption of the railroad connections leading to the Duena, the Luftwaffe also destroys two Soviet armored trains.

6/27/41: NKWD-PZ BP 76 lost near Smolewitschi (east of Minsk).

6/28/41: In trying to break out of the pocket at Bialystok, an armored train is destroyed by units of the 29th Infantry Division near Zelwa.

7/2/41: An armored train (NKWD BP 73 near Swislotsch?) is destroyed by the Luftwaffe.

7/6/41: An armored train is captured by the 17th Army near Kopyczince (south of Tarnopol) and turned over to the German PZ 31. In the advance of the 11th Armored Division on Berditschew, an armored train is destroyed at the railroad station in Michailenki.

7/8/41: In the advance of the III. Armored Corps on Schitomir, one armored train each is destroyed in Babiczowka and Dubowec (Nowograd—Wolinsk—Schitomir line) (one of BP-35 type).

7/9/41: Also after reaching Schitomir, Russian counterattack including the use of armored trains.

7/15/41: NKWD-PZ BP 53 lost near Polozk.

7/17/41: In the taking of Gdow, among other things, an armored train is captured.

7/24/41: An armored train is captured at the railroad station of Sucholesy (southeast of Fastow).

7/31/41: Near Demenka on the Ptitsch the 45th Infantry Division destroys an armored train.

8/7/41: During the pocket battle near Smolensk, continuing since 7/11, six Soviet armored trains were destroyed by the German Luftwaffe.

8/8/41: Among other things, an armored train is captured near Roslawl.

8/15/41: At the Dnjepr bridge east of Kanew, a derailed and overturned armored train is captured

(presumably NKWD BP 56).

8/19/41: In combat in the Kiev—Korosten region an armored train is captured. In an advance from Nikolajew to Cherson, remains of a Russian armored train are captured near Kubalkino.

8/20/41: In the battle in the Gomel region, two armored trains were captured.

9/1/41: In the battles around Reval, two armored trains were captured.

9/6/41: Two Russian armored trains are the backbone of the defense of the Desna bridge near Makoschin, important for the withdrawal; they are destroyed by Stukas.

9/10/41: In the attack out of the bridgehead of Krementschug a derailed armored train is captured near the Potoki railroad station.

9/12/41: The attempt of the Reconnaissance Battalion of the SS "Leibstandarte Adolf Hitler" Division to capture the entrance to the Crimea at Perekop in a surprise attack breaks down under fire from a Russian armored train.

9/15/41: A Russian armored train intervenes late in the fighting around Priluki; it is driven off by artillery fire the next day and later captured near Pirjatin.

9/22/41: In an attempt to break out of the pocket east of Kiev, four armored trains and three transport trains are destroyed near Perejaslawskaja.

9/23/41: Russian counterattacks under influence of armored trains on the bridgehead of the 295th Infantry Division (17th Army) near Krasnograd.

10/1/41: The 16th Armored Division (Pz.Gr. 1) is attacked by Russian units, supported by an armored train, northeast of Sinelnikowo.

10/10/41: A heavy two-day counterattack with the support of two armored trains on the bridgehead of the III. Armored Corps (Pz.Gr. 1) over the Mius prevents a further advance.

10/12/41: In counterattacks the Soviets successfully use two armored trains near Gawrischi (south of Bogoduchow). In the defense against these attacks, an armored train is later destroyed.

10/14/41: A Russian armored train is captured in Kolesniki (east of Gschatsk).

10/16/41: In the taking of Odessa, two destroyed armored trains are discovered in the northern fsector.

10/24/41: For four days the Russians have used several armored trains in defending the Kolmyzkaja—Tschaltyr sector

near Rostov stubbornly against the attack of the III. Armored Corps and hindered its further advance.

10/30/41: An armored train is captured in a surprise attack between Lakes Ilmen and Ladoga.

11/2/41: In the breakthrough of the 11th Army through the Juschun position (approach to Crimea), two Russian armored trains are destroyed; in the following advance two more are captured near Kurman-Kemeltschi and north of Alma.

11/8/41: The 16th Army captures NKWD-PZ BP 51 in the taking of Tichwin.

11/13/41: NKWD-PZ BP 82 is lost near Myslino (Wolchow region).

11/14/41: The III. Armored Corps is fired on by a Russian armored train while preparing for an attack on Rostov.

11/19/41: In front of the IV. Army Corps, belonging to the 17th Army, three Russian armored trains are spotted firing on Golubowka.

11/25/41: An armored train used against the bridgehead of Jachroma is destroyed by German fire.

A captured Soviet armored train of the Civil War type. Behind it a second, of Type OB-3, is recognizable. Presumably photographed in the attempted breakthrough from the pocket near Kiev on September 22, 1941. Photo: H. Griebl collection

In crossing the Beresina at the beginning of July 1941 this heavy Soviet armored train was destroyed near Borissow. Photo: J. Wilhelm collection

A destroyed Soviet armored train of BP 35 type in the central sector of the eastern front. Photo: Federal Archives, Koblenz.

This—certainly not complete—list counts 44 destroyed or captured Soviet armored trains for the first five months of the Russian campaign. On the other hand, it shows that they could also gain success again and again—especially in surprising appearances against unarmored units. So it is no wonder that the Soviets tries to balance these losses as quickly as possible by building new ones, for which the simple construction—tank turrets were simply mounted on armored car boxes—and the low numbers of cars offered the best prerequisites. Thus a decrease in the number of Russian armored trains would only have been temporary.

For a conference on November 7, 1941, with the chiefs of staff of the army groups and armies on the eastern front about the goals of the renewed offensive, the Operations Department of the OKH had prepared a memorandum. This foresaw that after reaching a resting position when the bad weather period began, they would be far to the east of Moscow(!), and carry out further combat actions with the help of armored trains and "pursuit commands". On the other hand, Army Group Center expected to be able to convince the OKH that their forces were only sufficient for an attack-like attainment of a semicircular enclosure of Moscow from the Volga-Moscow Canal in the north to Kolomna in the south; in their "Guidelines for Waging War in Winter and Particulars of the Winter War in Russia" of November 10, 1941, which considered building up a deeply structured position system to be possible only at the focal points of the front, otherwise settled on a mobile defense, depending on individual support points, from the Soviets, primarily with attacks made with tanks and armored trains along the roads and rail lines.

If the planning of the OKH for an offensive action was illusionary from the start in view of the small number and insufficient equipping of the German broad gauge armored trains—and only those could have been employed on the front—even on the assumption of a

rearming with captured Russian material and the additional use of such captured armored trains (Armored Train No. 10, made up of two such combat trains, was supposed to reach the combat zone by the first of the year), then the Soviets soon were also to teach Army Group Center, whose attack proceeded very well at first, that they were capable of much more than locally limited defensive actions along the traffic routes.

Several captured Soviet armored trains were also kept in use on the German side at first, until they had to be turned over to the OKH reserve. Photo: Federal Archives, Koblenz

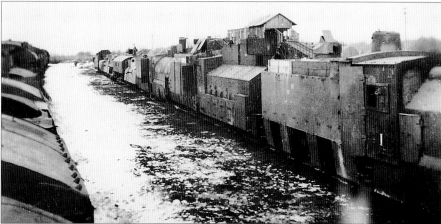

A railroad station in the back land area of the central sector, where captured Soviet armored train material was collected at the end of the year. Photo: F. Englberger/W. Sawodny collection

Another collecting site—this one mainly for captured NKWD armored railcars—in the Kharkov area in the winter of 1941-42. Photo: W. Pflaumbaum/W. Sawodny collection

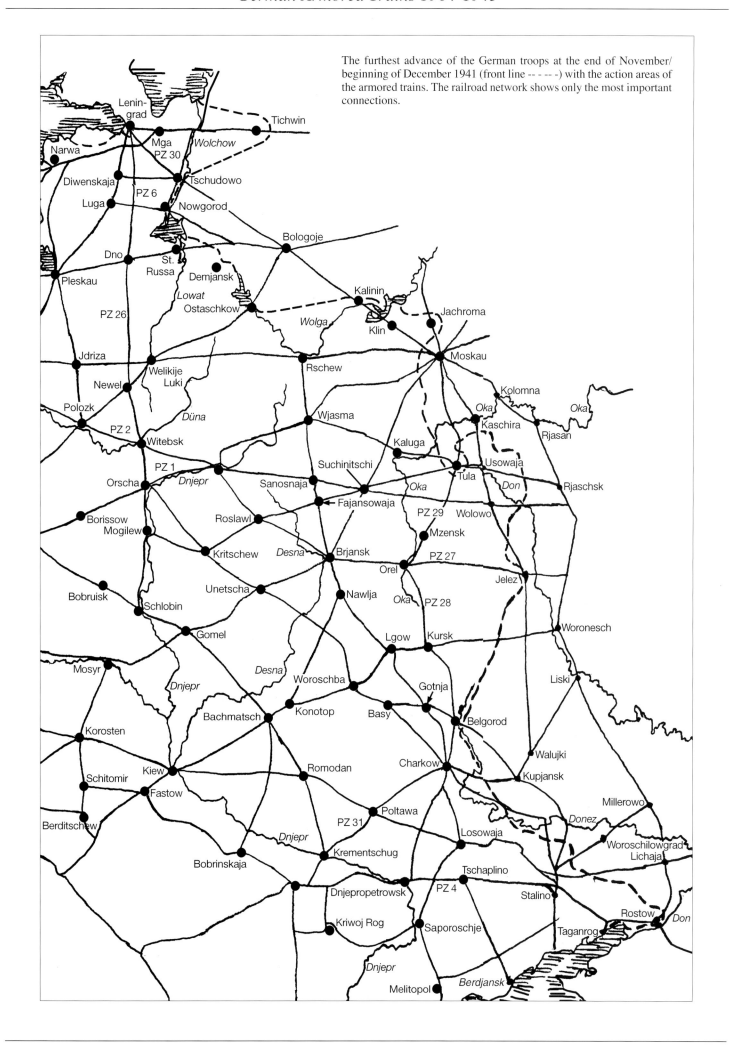

The furthest advance of the German troops at the end of November/ beginning of December 1941 (front line -- - -- -) with the action areas of the armored trains. The railroad network shows only the most important connections.

From the 1941-42 Russian Winter Offensive to the Encirclement of Stalingrad

As early as November 1941, the German 1st Armored Army, which had pushed ahead to the mouth of the Don, was first hit by a counterattack on its overextended flank and then thrown back to the Mius, having to give up Rostov. The ensuing battles on this front saw not only the activities of additional Russian armored trains (during December, no fewer than three were reported in constant action northeast of Debalzewo, one of which could be destroyed by artillery fire on 28 December), but the German PZ 4 was also transferred on 24 December from the Dnjepr via Stalino to Amwrosiewka (on the line to Taganrog), in order to take over securing directly behind the front, along with the SS "Wiking" Division, with a week long action directly into the front line being made by disembarked troops.

On December 6, 1941, a great Soviet counteroffensive began in the sector of Army Group Center. By this the armored trains were at first drawn particularly into the territory of the 2nd Armored Army for assistance. PZ 29 already suffered losses on December 7 from a bomb attack on the quarters train in Teploje, while the combat train was able to fight off an attack by Siberian infantry east of there. The readiness of the armored trains, even in the extreme winter cold, saw them in constant action, in view of the failure of weapons and road vehicles in those weather conditions, with supply trains and troop transports to the fore, wounded men transported to the rear, but also combat action against the advancing Russians. Only when they threatened to cut off the rail lines was it called back to Orel in mid-December. In view of the further enemy advances, especially

in the territories of the 4th Army and 2nd Armored Army, did PZ 29 reach the line from Brjansk to Suchinitschi on 21 December. On the way to there it lost its front control and tank-carrier cars, which fell off at a blown-up bridge. A little later it went to Kaluga to support the German units that were retreating in flight; there it was involved in vigorous defensive fighting from 29 December on, which took it to the rail triangle west of the city (Muratowka—Tichonowa-Pustyn—Gorenskaja). After an advance to the south had failed near Worotinsk on January 1, 1942, and a withdrawal toward Wjasma was made impossible by a destroyed bridge, PZ 29, in the withdrawal of the XLIII. Army Corps behind the Ugra and Schanja, was blown up, along with the other rolling stock that remained in that region, in Gorenskaja (the locomotive, no longer operable, in Muratowka) by a command of the 7th Company of Railroad Engineer Regiment 1 under Lt. Bölke. At first there were plans to reestablish this armored train with captured Russian material, but the plan was given up on February 25, 1942 in favor of PZ 27, and PZ 29 was removed from the list of armored trains.—PZ 27 was transferred out of the Orel region to Brjansk on December 30, 1941, and on the evening of the next day it made a reconnaissance run to Suchinitschi. It was prevented from returning immediately by blown-up places. In a renewed attempt on the morning of January 2, 1942, it lost all its cars south of Suchinitschi (some of them were regained in the relief of Suchinitschi in the latter half of January). The crew rode the remaining locomotive and one quarters car to Sanosnaja (since the line to the south was broken once and for all) and were transferred back to Roslawl on 7 January, where PZ 27 was equipped anew with captured cars at the field workshop.

The mine-thrower group of PZ 4 in infantry action on the Mius front in the winter of 1941-42. Photo: W. Obermark/W. Sawodny collection

PZ 1 on the Smolensk—Wjasma line in February 1942. Photo: E. Grahl/W. Sawodny collection

The Russian breakthrough in the territory of the 3rd Armored Army and the 9th Army did not involve the armored trains at first. The halted corner post of the 9th Army near Rschew, to be sure, gathered around the rail line from Wjasma to there, essential for supplying but always endangered, which was defended at first only by a makeshift armored train hastily assembled and armed with A/A guns (two 2-cm and two 8.8-cm, plus machine guns) by the II. Battalion of A/A Regiment 4. But soon the approach line from Smolensk to Wjasma was exposed to the constant danger of being blocked by the enemy forces who had broken through to the north and south (strengthened by partisan bands and paratroopers). PZ 1—after being repaired in January—was just brought forward onto the Smolensk—Wjasma line on February 1, 1942, and—often divided into two parts for a more extensive effect—formed the backbone of the alarm units deployed on both sides of the rail line. A special task was the protection of the Dnjepr bridge near Isdjeschkowo, which the Russians repeatedly tried to take or at least destroy by surprise attacks, which did not succeed. After it had already been used since 26 January to secure rail lines in the Rudna region between Witebsk and Smolensk, PZ 2 was also transferred on February 25, 1941, to the line from Smolensk to Wjasma and was particularly active in the Dorogobusch region. The enemy forces had already been cut off from their backline connections in February, but they were still able to stay near the railroad and thus still threaten the line. Thus the two armored trains remained in the Smolensk—Wjasma region. A partisan action near Kulewo—Dorogobusch on March 21, 1942, with heavy losses, is worthy of note for PZ 2, but on 5 April it was transferred from its last stationing in Jarzewo into the partisan area around Brjansk. PZ 1, which was overhauled in Warsaw again in April, later secured the

lines toward the front, running southward (Sanosnaja), southeast (Kaluga) and east (Gschatsk), from Wjasma. On 20 May it was then subordinated to the XLVI. Armored Corps and operated between Wjasma and Rschew. On June 11, 1942, though, it was transferred to the backline area of Army Group Center and saw service with the 286th Securing Division again between Orscha and Smolensk, as well as the line from Orscha to Mogilew.

PZ 30 came near the front with Army Group North when Soviet troops broke through the Wolchow front, pushed forward to the Jeglino rail intersection and turned onto the Ljuban—Tosno line. The armored train guarded the line, but the crew also had to disembark and strengthen the front at times. Only as the Russian troops were cut off in mid-March and then wiped out was the danger eliminated.

South of Lake Ilmen the Russians advanced over the ice of the lake and behind the German front on January 7, 1942, threatening their corner post, the city of Staraja Russa. The commander of the backline area of the 16th Army took command until the arrival of the 18th Motorized Infantry Division, and also had PZ 6, subordinated to it, advance from Dno to Staraja Russa. On 11 January it fought Soviet troops east of Polist and Ljadniki, but fired mistakenly on German troops—hard to distinguish because of the snow shirts they wore—in Sabolotschje. On the very same day it went back to Wolot to take on water, and the next day it reported locomotive damage. On 17 January at the latest it was back in Staraja Russa to reinforce the artillery of the units there and secure the rail line leading to it; in mid-February it was in Tuleblja. After the situation had stabilized, it was called back to Dno. Afterward it secured both the line from Pleskau via Dno toward Staraja Russa and the northern part, already converted to standard gauge, of the line from Dno toward Nowosokolniki, while the broad gauge PZ 26, at first stationed in Sustschewo and Loknja, then backing off more and more before regauging, and guarding its southern part. The conversion of the line to standard gauge had reached Nowosokolniki, where PZ 26 was also converted to it (see below), at the beginning of April; then it returned to its original action region on 23 April. The railroads in this region were of special significance, as since the end of January and beginning of February the two pockets of Demjansk and Cholm were to the east of it, but three months later they could be relieved, though they still remained focal points in the front. An added task for the armored trains was assisting the passage of transports with heavy artillery, which was being transferred from the Leningrad front to Crimea.

Since the end of February 1942, PZ 2 operated in the Dorogobusch region. Here its gun car is seen in the railroad station there after its axle bearings had been damaged. Photo: K. Böhringer/W. Sawodny collection

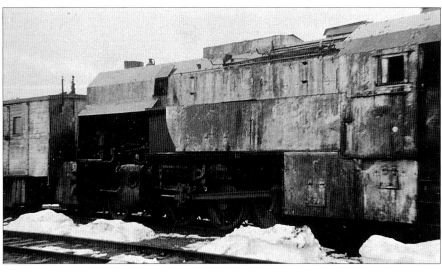

Locomotive 93 058 of PZ 2 had part of its armor torn off in a mine explosion. Photo: K. Böhringer/W. Sawodny collection

On 23 April 23 PZ 6 lost two dead in a partisan attack near Dudino (in the vicinity of Tschichatschewo); in mid-May it was transferred (probably because of damage) back to the Pruszkow OAW near Warsaw. To take its place—only in August, to be sure—the line protection train "Stettin" or "A," now upgraded to PZ 51, came to Dno to secure the lines that went out from there, especially in the direction of Nowosokolniki and Pleskau. PZ 26—except for being equipped with additional cars in the Duenaburg EAW in May—remained long in this region, suffering losses in partisan action near Sudoma (south of Dedowitschi) on June 21, 1942.

Russian breakthroughs in December 1941 and January 1942 had overextended the front so much that it was often occupied only at support points. One such place was Welikije Luki, where the 83rd Infantry Division occupied the dividing line between the Army Groups North and Center without having contact with other combat German troops to the left and right. This allowed Russian units, in cooperation with partisan bands, to trickle in and endanger the division's supply lines. They included the broad gauge line that came into the city from Nowosokolniki, as well as the line from the southwest, coming from Newel. This double-track line—as often in the transitional phase—had had only one track converted to standard gauge, while the other had kept the broad gauge. To support the weak securing forces who had these lines to guard, a broad gauge line protection train had already been made up at Nowosokolniki; it is sometimes called "Nowo" (after its stationing) in German files, but also sometimes "Jensen" (after its commander). After PZ 2 had

already been used from Sirotino on the line between Newel and Welikije Luki for a short time in February 1942, the broad gauge PZ 27, newly equipped with captured Russian cars in Roslawl, arrived there on the 22nd of that month. Its daytime duties were checking the line by shuttle runs at irregular intervals, preventing explosions and cleaning out villages suspected of partisan presence along this line. At night it was to strengthen the crew of the support point at Tschernosjem; the steady supplying of the combat troops in Welikiji Luki with food and ammunition, which it was also to secure, was done from there. Its appearance led to a temporary lull in partisan activity in this region. In the first days of March, the standard-gauge PZ 3, equipped with a new radio system in Koenigsberg, arrived; its first task was to be transporting a newly formed partisan pursuit battalion of the 83rd Infantry Division from Welikije Luki to the action region southwest of the city. Still on its run to Welikije Luki for loading, it was able to take part in the successful repulse of an attack on the support point of Tschernosjem that morning, and it remained there for securing until 9 March, then being transferred to Welikije Luki. PZ 27, which was ordered to the line from Witebsk to Rudnja for partisan action from 8 to 10 March, was stationed in Opuchliki, the site of the division's command post, after its return.

Meanwhile, the partisans began to concentrate on fighting off the armored trains. When they again attacked the Tschernosjem support point on 16 March, they blew up rail lines leading to there so that no armored trains could intervene (but the attack was driven off by the support-point crew).

PZ 27 is ready to depart from the Tschernosjem support point on March 8, 1942. Photo: W. Hahn/W. Sawodny collection

PZ 3 was also on the Newel—Welikije Luki line since the beginning of March 1942. Photo: W. Hahn/W. Sawodny collection

On 24 March the track was blown up 20 meters in front of PZ 27; the locomotive suffered a broken axle. On the way back from a successful partisan action near the support point of Münsingen (between Tschernosjem and Welikije Luki), PZ 3 hit a mine on 1 April, reporting considerable damage and five wounded. In the pursuit of the partisan group that had carried out the attack, seven Russian fighters were killed.—In Welikije Luki, Russian artillery fired on the armored trains as soon as they appeared in the railroad station there; thus on 23 March they were assigned stopping places outside the station. On 10 April PZ 3 was finally restationed from there to Opuchliki. Despite this, the 83rd Infantry Division continued to consider the presence of the armored trains extremely important. At the beginning of April, when the intention to withdraw PZ 3 was voiced, it insisted on its presence and named not only participation in A/A protection from Welikije Luki, but also called this armored train "the most effective protection to date of the Welikije Luki—Newel rail line" and the "only support for the few week support points, the daily occurring work on the tracks, etc." The division was also convinced "that the frequent explosions in the last days are attributable to the lack of PZ 27 (which will be discussed just below). If PZ 3 is also taken away now, then as the division sees it, the methodical track destruction will take on an unbearable extent; it must be reckoned on that the line might be fully lost to supplying and traffic. The removal of PZ 3 from the named line will also presumably be the signal for the enemy to knock out, in particular, the hated support point."

The intention—then not carried out—of transferring PZ 3 away came at a particularly unfortunate point in time, for since 27 March the remaining broad gauge track between Newel and Welikije Luki was also converted to standard gauge. Thus on that day the broad gauge PZ 27 had to be taken to Nowosokolniki. From there it was able, along with the line protection train "Nowo/Jansen," to relieve the Partisan Pursuit Battalion 83, meanwhile operating out of Nowosokolniki and northeast of Schubino, which had encountered strong enemy forces and thus come into urgent need of help. At the beginning of April the line leading north from Nowosokolniki to Dno was also regauged. This brought the broad gauge PZ 26, standing on that line and subordinated to Army Group North, temporarily to Nowosokolniki for the use of the 83rd Infantry Division, but now only the line from Nowosokolniki to Welikije Luki remained usable by the broad gauge trains. On 21 April PZ 27 was derailed there; shortly after that it too was regauged. Thus on April 11 the conversion of the broad gauge armored trains had also begun at Nowosokolniki. "Nowo/Jansen" was already finished on 15 April; PZ 26 on 23 April, but then it moved back to Army Group North on the line to Dno. The conversion of PZ 27 had just begun at that time; when it was finished, it was to be transferred back to the line from Newel to Welikije Luki.

This was all the more necessary, as PZ 3 had hit a remote-control mine 1 km north of the Münsingen support point on 22 April. The explosion of ammunition fully destroyed one gun car, and the two

On April 22, 1942, the gun car of PZ 3 was destroyed by a remote-control mine, and the following cars slid down the slope. Photo: W. Hahn/W. Sawodny collection

These cars were recovered only a month later—after a crane train had arrived. Photo: W. Hahn/W. Sawodny collection

following cars of the train fell down a slope (although they were in a heavily partisan-endangered region, they were recovered only on 24 May, as no suitable crane was available before). The incident cost seven dead and nine wounded; the rest of PZ 3 was ready for only limited action afterward and should have been sent out for repairs, but waited for the recovery of its cars that lay near Münsingen. It canceled its daily runs and limited itself to combing through the area around its station of Opuchliki and putting securing troops on the line at night. On 28 April rumors were heard of Soviet operations planned for the beginning of May. Armored Trains No. 3 and 27 (meanwhile returned to Opuchliki) were put in alarm readiness. An attack on the Schwedriko support point (between Opuchliki and Tschernosjem) on 1 May was driven off by PZ 27, and two days later a Russian 7.62-cm battery that fired on the support point was silenced. PZ 3 had less luck, as it hit another mine as it entered Münsingen on 2 May, but only slight damage was done.

As of 13 May a large-scale operation with the code name "Schnepfenstrich" tried to accomplish the cleaning-out of the region between the Tschernosjem—Opuchliki rail line and the Lowat. Disembarked members of the crews of Armored Trains No. 3 and 27, under the command of the commander of PZ 3, 1st Lt. Opitz, were to cross the Lowat near Staraja Reka on the morning of 15 May, along with half a company of Engineer Battalion 218 and police troops from Schwedriko, then turn southwestward the heavily enemy-occupied Klewniki and open the way there for other units attacking from the west. PZ 27 provided artillery support from Schwedriko and took over the radio command of the group. The operation was a complete success, so that the disembarked armored train crews could return to Schwedriko the same evening. On the other hand, PZ 3, which was to secure the rail line between Opuchliki and Tschernosjem during Operation "Schnepfenstrich" was immobilized on the same day, again by a remote-control mine under the locomotive. On 16 May it was towed back to Opuchliki, where it remained until being taken to Koenigsberg for repairs on 28 May (after the recovery of its two cars left near Münsingen). PZ 27 carried out a strong shock-troop operation, supported by the armored train's artillery, on 27 May, moving from Schwedriko in the direction of Sokolowo and Lissi Hory; on 30 May, though, it too met its fate near Münsingen. It struck a mine 1.5 km north of there; the front gun car was blown into the air. Among the four dead (besides five wounded) was its commander, Lt. Behrens.

With the departure of what remained of this armored train to Dünaburg on June 17, 1942, the use of regular armored trains in the Welikije Luki area ended. To protect the rail line between that city and Newel, the 83rd Infantry Division now set up its own line protection train, which bore the division's number (No. 83) as its identification (first mentioned on July 6, 1942; commander 1st Lt. Lohmann). It was also stationed in Opuchliki. Little is known of its activities. On 5-6 August it carried out a troop transport from Opuchliki to Welikije Luki, on 11-12 September it secured a large horse-drawn column moving southeast along the tracks between the same cities.

On November 25, 1942, the Russians took the offensive in the Welikije Luki region, leading in a short time to the encirclement of the city.

On May 15, 1942, PZ 3 again hit a mine, which blew the armor off the locomotive and caused the loco itself to derail. Photo: W. Hahn/W. Sawodny collection

The detonation of a mine under PZ 27 on May 30, 1942, included the train's commander, Lt. Behrens, among its victims. Photo: T. Schorlemmer/W. Sawodny collection

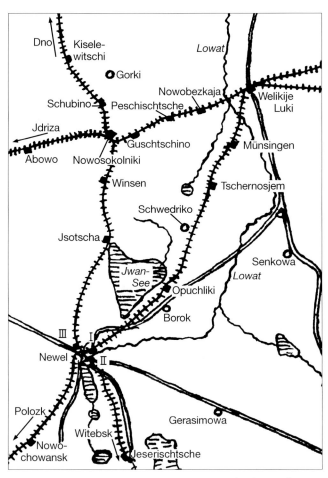

The Welikije Luki—Nowosokolniki—Newel action region.

On the 27th the line protection train "Nowo/Jansen", still located in Nowosokolniki, was to advance to Welebezkoje (ahead of Welikije Luki), but only got as far as Peschischtsche. On 3 December it took over the flank protection in a counterattack near Borowinka and Podoly. The locomotive was hit, immobilizing the train. After the other cars had also been hit by antitank shells, the train was abandoned and—after an attempt by a locomotive from Nowosokolniki to tow it back had failed—it was completely destroyed by German assault guns, so as not to let it fall into enemy hands. Nothing is known of activities of the line protection train No. 83 from this time, but it was able to withdraw during the Russian advance heading for Newel and came under the command of the 3rd Armored Army, which now used it—separated from the 83rd Infantry Division—for rail-line securing in its backline army sector. After this entire depiction of the events in the Welikije Luki region, though, let us return to the beginning of 1942 and the events in the southern sector of the eastern front.

On January 15, 1942, the 2nd Army was put under the command of Army Group South, and with it PZ 28, which was in the Kursk region and presumably took part afterward in the counterattacks to mop up the Russian breakthrough near Obojan on the line leading toward Bjelgorod in the Schumakowo—Solnzewo region.—Eastward of Kursk in the Tim sector, a Russian armored train made itself unpleasantly noticeable in from 25 January on, coming out from Golowinka and firing on the German positions again and again. An attempt to put it out of action west of Tscheremissinowo on 30 January with an explosive charge failed, but on 4 February, on its renewed action near Golowinka, gunfire was able to set the locomotive afire. Just a few days later (on 10 February), the Russians had replaced it with another armored train.—Further actions by Russian armored trains in this period are mentioned throughout January west of Bulazelowka (on the Kharkov-Kupjansk line) and on 26 January on the south wing of the 1st Armored Army (Taganrog—Rostow).

PZ 28 in the Kursk area early in 1942. A Russian XX-car with a Panzer III set on it was added to the original cars. The train was pulled by a captured Series O locomotive. Photo: E. Lehle/W. Sawodny collection

Combat Train B of the broad gauge Armored Train No. 10, newly established in January 1942, is seen during a partisan operation in the Lgow region at the end of February 1942. The infantry car in the right foreground (on which a 2-cm A/A gun is mounted) was borrowed from PZ 28 for this action. Photo: Peters/A. Gutmann collection

At the beginning of 1942 PZ 10, consisting of two broad gauge combat trains (A and B), came into action anew. It had been equipped at the Lemberg OAW and taken to Kiev-Darniza, where the crew, set up in Recruiting district III (Berlin), took over the train. Combat Train B was already ready for action on February 5 and went first to the backline district of the 2nd Army west of Kursk, in the Lgow—Woroschba region, where strong partisan activity was making itself known. On 10 March both armored trains (No. 10B and 28) were transferred from the Kursk area to Kharkov in the district of the 6th Army, where the other combat train (A) of PZ 10 had arrived from Darnia two days before.

The concentration of armored trains in the Kharkov region was doubtless influenced by the danger to that city, which, after the Russian offensive that began near Isjum on 15 January, was threatened by the thereby gained expansive breakthrough area which reached beyond the Kharkov—Losowaja rail line. PZ 31 had advanced from Poltawa via Krasnograd to Losowaja when the Russians threatened the city as of 24 January. In the defensive combat that took place there and the ensuing withdrawal fighting in the direction of Kharkov, it was damaged and then repaired in Kharkov. PZ 28 strengthened the northern corner post of the breakthrough area near Balakleja, held by the 44th Infantry Division, as of mid-March, interrupted only by a stay in Poltawa-Sortirowka for overhauling at the end of April. PZ

4 was called back from there after the Mius front was stabilized, in order to secure the Dnjepropetrowsk—Tschaplino—Stalino region, just a bit south of the region recaptured by the Soviets, and the only supply line of the German troops in the Donez basin, as of March (stationed in Uljanowka). Both combat trains of PZ 10 remained in Kharkov at first, but were transferred to the Belgorod region on April 23, 1942. There it was exposed to repeated air attacks, which grew stronger particularly before the renewed Russian offensive began on both side of Kharkov on May 12, 1942. On 16 May disembarked men from the armored train were used to fight off the Soviets, who were pushing forward over the Donez near Woltschansk, and suffered losses near Schurawiewka; on 18 May a combat car of PZ 10B was badly damaged by a bomb attack. The German troops were able not only to drive off this attack north of Kharkov, but also to encircle and destroy the strong Russian forces located south of the city west of the Donez. The following German advance to the Oskol at the end of May saw PZ 31 on the Kharkov—Tschugujew—Kupjansk line, while PZ 28 remained in Balakleja and PZ 10 in Belgorod.

In the offensive that began on June 28, 1942, which was to bring German troops to Stalingrad on the one hand and to the Caucasus on the other, the armored trains in the southern sector of the eastern front did not take part at all. The Russian armored trains were all the more active.

Later PZ 10 (here again Combat Train B) was transferred to Kharkov, where this photo was taken at one of the railroad stations; several captured locomotives are seen at right. Photo: J. Dicke/W. Sawodny collection

PZ 28 is seen at a station in this region. At right is a Russian Series Schtsch freight locomotive. Photo: Federal Archives, Koblenz

Here again, the relevant entries in the OKW diary and the notations in Wehrmacht reports offer an impression:

7/19/42: An armored train was destroyed near Schachty.

8/5/42: Two armored trains were destroyed by the Luftwaffe in the foothills of the Caucasus.

8/10/42: An armored train is destroyed by bombs south of Stalingrad (a similar report on 8/12 may be just a repeat).

8/30/42: The attack of an armored train is driven off by German tanks near Tscherwlennaja south of the Terek.

9/1/42: An armored train is destroyed by German infantry south of Stalingrad.

9/8/42: An armored train is captured in Woroponowo, also in Noworossisk (an identical report from 9/9 may be a repeat).

9/12/42: An attack with armored train support north of Grosnij is foiled by blown-up tracks.

11/1/42: West of the Terek two armored trains are destroyed in collaboration between Army and Luftwaffe.

11/3/42: East of Alagir (Caucasus) an armored train was destroyed by the Luftwaffe (identical report on 11/7).

12/23/42: North of the Terek German armored troops fire on an armored train, setting it afire.

On the other front sectors too, the Russian armored trains kept busy, as the following, scarcely complete reports show:

5/2/42: On this and the following day, several attacks by an armored train northeast of Mzensk (2nd Armored Army).

5/22/42: An armored train is captured while mopping up the Kertsch peninsula (Crimea).

7/28/42: At the Wolchow bridgehead at Solzy an armored train fires on the positions on both sides of the track.

7/31/42: Near Urzik (western suburb of Leningrad) and approaching armored train is compelled by gunfire to withdraw.

8/17/42: An attack on the Wolchow bridgehead at Solzy by an armored train is driven off.

9/14/42: An attack with armored train support on the Finnish southeast front (Karelian isthmus) is driven off, part of the armored train is destroyed.

9/15/42: North of Rschew an armored train is destroyed by bombs.

9/17/42: On the rail line south of Nowosil (east of Orel) repeated attacks by two enemy armored trains are repulsed on this and the next three days.

It is moreover noteworthy that after January 1, 1943, only a single German report has surfaced that mentions a Russian armored train: On August 2, 1943, the Luftwaffe reported one hit by bombs southwest of Orel. This indicates that the Soviets used armored trains almost exclusively defensively—and naturally for securing tasks—a concept that the Germans had meanwhile developed as well, as can also be seen by the fact that in the southern sector their armored trains remained in their stations during the 1942 summer offensive.

There in May and June the crews of Armored Trains No. 28 and 31 were considerably increased (after PZ 28 in early March had taken on part of the crew of PZ 29); in July and August all broad gauge trains in the Kharkov district (No. 10, 28 and 31) were converted to standard gauge, and were rearmed in several stages, except for PZ 31 (which was transferred back to the homeland in November for a total rebuilding). Meanwhile, only a few securing runs from Kharkov took place. This shows that partisan activity in the southern sector of the eastern front was slight at that time and resulted in no major disturbances of rail traffic. Thus PZ 4 was also transferred from its former action region northeast of the Dnjepr

On the advance between the Don and Volga this Soviet armored train (BP-35 type) was captured. Photo: J. Wilhelm collection

On this armored train captured in Schachty on July 19, 1942, the Russians had replaced the original gun turret with that of a KW 2 tank with a 15.2-cm howitzer. In place of the command turret too, a tank turret (presumably of the A series, with a 4.5-cm gun) was installed. Photo: W. Sawodny collection

In the foothills of the Caucasus this armored train was destroyed by the direct hit of a dive-bomber attack. Photo: Federal Archives, Koblenz

Also on the steppes north of the Caucasus, a bridge was destroyed along with the armored train that was crossing it. Photo: Federal Archives, Koblenz

The control car of PZ 10 B was derailed by a rail gap created by partisans in the Woroschba region (autumn 1942). Photo: W. Sawodny collection

bend near Dnjepropetrowsk into the strongly partisan-endangered Orel—Brjansk region (Army Group Center) on July 1, 1942. Only PZ 7 remained in constant action in the southern sector of the eastern front; after its overhauling it was stationed first, as of the end of January, in the Krementschug--Poltawa Romodan triangle, then at the beginning of July on the Kiev—Kursk line, on which—especially in the Bachmatsch—Woroschba region and on both sides of the Desna north of there—in which the constantly increasing partisan activity in the backline area of Army Group Center, adjoining on the north, spread out more and more. The following months saw it in constant securing and partisan-fighting action in this region along with the Hungarian occupation troops stationed there. Still the numbers and actions of the partisans constantly increased, so that on October 25, 1942 PZ 10 was also transferred to Belopolje (to secure the Woroschba—Lgow line); as of 2 November 1942 it was stationed in Makoschino on the Bachmatsch—Gomel line, while in its place PZ 28, called in from Kharkov, supported PZ 7 on the Bachmatsch—Lgow line.

PZ 28 is seen in Kharkov in the summer of 1942 after its conversion to standard gauge and rearmament. Now it is pulled once again by its original Series 57 locomotive with only its cab armored. Photo: B. Schultz/W. Sawodny collection

In the summer of 1942 PZ 25 secured the Pripjet line from Luminiec. Photo: E. Banser/W. Sawodny collection

On May 22, 1942, the reactivated PZ 25 and the subordinated PT 15 were stationed in Luminiec to secure the rail line through the Pripjet region between Brest-Litovsk and Kalinkowitschi, which was impossible to reconnoiter, rich in woods and swamps, and thus an ideal hiding place for partisans. Despite this, attacks on the line scarcely diminished. Thus in July units of the Slovakian Securing Division, which also had a makeshift armored (line protection) train, were also transferred there. In the first half of August attempts were made to encircle the partisans south of the rail line and push them toward it, as it was barred by PZ 25 and the Slovakian armored train, but the results were insufficient. The Army Group Center, in whose sector the partisans were most active, had—after Armored Trains No. 10 and 28 moved with the 2nd Army to Army Group South and into the Kharkov region, and Armored Trains No. 3 and 27 were badly damaged south of Welikije Luki at the end of May—only Armored Trains No. 1 and 2, the first of which being stationed in the Smolensk region in April, the latter having to be transferred to Schukowka on April 5, 1942, to secure the strongly partisan-endangered line from Roslawl to Brjansk. In the Brjansk region their activity had increased so much that as of July 1 PZ 4 was also called in from Army Group South, but it was damaged by a bomb attack at the Brjansk railroad station on 11 July, so it was only fully ready for action on 29 August and could replace PZ 2 in Schukowka. The latter now went to Brjansk to secure the many lines that went out from there to the north, east and south. In the second half of September both armored trains were obviously involved in a partisan action in the Sineserki—Rewny region south of Brjansk, in which they incurred losses. On November 16, 1942, PZ 4 defended Kletnja against attacking partisans, who were then pursued by disembarked infantrymen. On 24-25 November the region southeast of Schukowka was combed

through in Operation "Zeisig," but no partisans were found. Yet a strong partisan group attacked the railroad bridge near Polstinka on the evening of the 25th; PZ 4 was called in and was able to drive them away with heavy losses. On 30 December this armored train hit a mine and the locomotive was damaged.

In view of the fully insufficient number of armored trains for thorough track securing and the strongly increasing activities of partisans in the central sector of the eastern front, it is no wonder that the railroad engineer and securing troops who were responsible for the use and protection of the lines tried to help themselves and set up a series of makeshift armored trains (also called "line protection trains" in the later terminology) on their own. For the 707th Infantry Division in the region of the lines running from Brjansk to Roslawl and Unetscha, no fewer than five different such line protection trains (No. 101, "Erika," "Lilli," "Luise," and "Marlen") were mentioned from May to July 1942. In the second half of May the "Luise" and "Marlen" trains supported Operation "Luisenthal" in the Schukowka region with their artillery; "Marlen" was derailed there after a mine exploded. Train No. 101 was on the Pilschino—Krasny-Rog track section southwest of Brjansk on 31 May, and "Erika" and "Marlen" were involved in a partisan operation in the Borodino—Krasnoje region at the beginning of June 1942.

The 221st Securing Division, adjoining on the southwest (staff in Gomel) maintained two line protection trains in the autumn of 1942: "Zobten" (commanded by 1st Lt. Rogoll) with Securing Regiment 27 in Unetscha, and "Rübezahl" (commanded by 1st Sgt. K. Eckert) in Dobrusch, which since September 1942 guarded the lines in the division's zone by day and night (there were also attack commands that were transported by rail-capable trucks). For the two line protection trains of the 221st Securing Division, activity reports

In July 1942 PZ 4 was transferred from the southern sector into the Brjansk region, but suffered damage from a near-miss bomb at the Brjansk railroad station on July 11. Photo: W. Obermark/W. Sawodny collection

PZ 2 was also transferred to the Brjansk region as of April 1942. Here the officers (Commander, Captain Peters, third from left) and NCOs pose before and on the train's gun car. Photo: K. Böhringer/W. Sawodny collection

for the last five weeks of 1942 have survived, allowing an interesting insight into the actions of these trains and thus shall be reproduced here:

Line Protection Train "Zobten":

11/3: Manned by men of the engineer platoon of Securing Regiment 27.

11/15-16: Trips to transfer the II. Battalion, Grenadier Regiment 930 in the Surasch—Kommunary—Klimowitschi region.

11/17-18: Inspection trip by Finnish Major Alanko from Unetscha to Klimowitschi and back. On 11/18 partisans made an attack on the support point, Schurbin. When the train, stationed in Belinkowitschi, arrived, the attackers were already gone.

11/19: Theater group is taken from Kommunary to Klimowitschi; in Kommunary inspection of the III. Battalion, French Infantry Regiment 638 by officers of Securing Regiment 27.

11/20: Overhauling of the locomotive and repair of the train in Unetscha.

11/21: Trip with regimental adjutant to Kommunary (II./930).

11/22: Trip with ordnance officer to Surasch (Securing Battalion 743).

11/23-25: Transport of III./French Regiment 638 from Kommunary to Surasch.

11/26-27: Securing of repair work at an explosion site near Schurbin. Night inspection trip with Regimental Commander 27 (Colonel Hegedüs).

11/28: Regimental Commander 27 brought to II..930 in Kommunary. Transfer of III./French 638 to Surasch.

11/29: Train is called to Belinkowitschi after attack on railroad station. Further transfer transport of III./French 638 to Surasch.

11/30: Regimental Commander 36 taken from Unetscha to Kommunary.

12/1: Securing runs between Kommunary and Surasch.

12/2: Regimental Commander 27 taken from Kommunary to Unetscha. Visit to Pestschaniki support point on the way.

12/3: Securing runs between Unetscha and Kommunary. With officer group with Regimental Commander 27, visit to support points between Unetscha and Rassucha.

12/4: With same officer group, visit to support points between Rassucha and Potschep.

12/5: Regimental Commander 36 taken from Unetscha to Kommunary.

12/6: Visit to support points between Schurbin and Kritschew with Battalion Commander II./930.

12/7: Securing runs between Kommunary and Surasch.

12/8: Battalion Commander II./930 taken from Kommunary to Unetscha.

12/9: With Regimental Commanders 27 and 930, support points between Unetscha and Kommunary inspected.

12/10: With the same officers, support points between Unetscha and Schudilowo visited.

12/11: Support-point inspection between Unetscha and Surasch. Picked up Battalion Commander III./930 there.

12/12: Service trip of Regimental Commander 27 to division staff in Gomel.

12/13: Return trip with Regimental Commander 27 from Gomel to Unetscha.

12/14: One car with building material brought to Support Point 29.

12/15: Escorting a horse transport to Dobrik, tracks blown up there.

12/15-16: Partisan action between Irschatz and Schurbin.

12/17: Return trip from Schurbin to Unetscha.

12/18-20: Train overhauled in Unetscha operations workshop.

12/20-21: Partisan action near Korobinitschi.

12/22: Train in Unetscha operations workshop.

12/23-24: Support-point inspection with Regimental Commander 27 between Unetscha and Kritschew.

12/25: Train in Unetscha.

12/25-26: Partisan action near Kommunary.

12/26: Service trip with officers to Osmolowitschi.

12/27: Return trip to Unetscha.

Line Protection Train "Rübezahl"

11/22: Body of a fallen man brought from Slynka to Gomel.

11/23: Officer from division in Gomel brought to regiment in Dobrusch. 10 cars for transport of 8th Company, Securing Regiment 45 taken along. Checking trip to Nowosybkow.

11/24-25: Trip to Kommunary and transport of the 8./45 back from there to Dobrusch. In Slynka Regimental Commander 45 (Colonel Wiemann) picked up and brought to Gomel. 11/26: Return trip to Dobrusch. Beginning of overhauling and building up of the train.

11/27: Trip to Nowobelizkaja, locomotive change there and planks for building up the train fetched.

11/28-29: Building up the train. Evening trip with Regimental Adjutant to Slynka and back.

11/30: Building up the train. Trip to field workshop in Gomel. Evening brought officers to Belinkowitschi.

12/1: Return trip Belinkowitschi to Gomel.

12/2: Receipt of winter equipment. Trip back to Dobrusch. Evening checking run to Unetscha, took along two cars of coal.

12/3: Return checking trip from Unetscha to Dobrusch, with (practice) sharpshooting of the train.

12/4: Regimental Commander 45 picked up in Gomel and brought to Nowosybkow.

12/5: Weapon cleaning and re-munitioning. Trip to Gomel.

12/6: Return trip from Gomel to Dobrusch with 8 cars for troop transport.

12/7: Trip with the 8 cars to Nowosybkow. Loaded paratroop company there and brought to Gomel.

12/8: Brought orchestra group from Gomel to Nowosybkow.

12/9: From Gomel to Nowosybkow with officer.

12/10: With him, support-point checking between Nowosybkow and Unetscha. Then brought him back to Gomel.

12/11-13: Trip with officer from Gomel to Kommunary and Klimowitschi and back.

12/14: Checking the support points between Gomel and Slynka. Back to Dobrusch.

12/15: Regimental Commander 45 picked up in Nowosybkow. Checking trip to Potschep and back.

12/16: Train stays in Gomel.

12/17-19: Inspection trip with Commander 221st Securing Division (Lt. General Lendle) to Unetscha, Rassucha, Starodub, and Pogar. Back to Gomel.

12/20: From Gomel to Dobrusch. Supplied the train.

12/21: Checking trip with Regimental Commander to Pestschaniki and back.

12/22: Coaled in Gomel. Trip with Division and Regimental Commanders to Sakopytje and back.

12/23: Repairs to the locomotive. Transport of supplies for the regiment from Gomel to Nowosybkow.

12/24: Bathing and delousing the men in Gomel. Checking the train. Back to Dobrusch at midday.

12/25: Trip to Gomel for crew's visit to movies.

12/26: Personnel change. Coaling. Back to Dobrusch.

From this overview it can be seen that checking trips took place very often, but direct partisan actions in named times and places—perhaps for that very reason—were not needed very often and apparently were limited to the single-track line from Unetscha to Kritschew.

In the Smolensk—Wjasma region the withdrawal of PZ 2 had left a gap. The commander of the backline area of the 3rd Armored Army (Korück 590) thus also instituted at the beginning of August 1942 the establishment of their own line protection train, "Blücher" (Commander 1st Lt. Dümlein), which in the time that followed (until the 3rd Armored Army was transferred completely to the Witebsk—Polozk—Newel region at the end of January 1943) secured the rail line between Smolensk and Wjasma. Also PZ 1, which had at first been stationed between Orscha and Smolensk again after being overhauled in Warsaw, often had to be used on that line.—After the Soviets in their August offensive had come dangerously close to the main artery for the Rschew bridgehead, the rail line from Wjasma to there via and north of Sytschewka, PZ 1 was moved forward to there on 17 August, and took part in the successful defense against the attackers, and then in securing the line and transport in that region.

In the summer of 1942 the danger to the rail lines by partisans had also increased so much in the Polozk region that the Germans were compelled to transfer PZ 25—at first with the subordinated PT 15, which was withdrawn, though, on 26 September—from the Pripjet region to the 201st Securing Division for the guarding of the rail lines leading out of Polozk toward Dünaburg, Newel, and Witebsk. The 201st Securing Division, since the withdrawal of PZ 2 from their territory (in February 1942), had likewise set up their own line protection train called "Werner."

In the last months of 1942 the situation in the territory of Army Group Center relaxed somewhat, since further armored trains could be introduced. Thus on October 10, 1942, PZ 3, rebuilt after being badly damaged south of Welikije Luki (May 1942), replaced PZ 25 in Polozk; the latter train was transferred in turn to France. In its place PZ 21 came from there, first stationed in Krupki and securing the Borissow—Orscha line, which it covered every night.

Since 25 November the Russians had made another attempt to cut off or compress the salient in the front near Rschew. Hard fighting thus developed in the Belij region. PZ 21 was therefore transferred to the side line from Durowo to Wladimirskoje, and successfully took part there at the beginning of December in the defensive fighting near Nikitinka (it also stayed on that line afterward for securing and

In the summer of 1942 PZ 25, seen here unloading a Somua tank, was restationed from the Pripjet line to the Polozk region. Photo: E. Banser/W. Sawodny collection

As of the end of November 1942, PZ 21—coming from France—saw service on the Durowo—Wladimirskoje side line. Photo: A. Schwipp/W. Sawodny collection

After PZ 1 was derailed in heavy defensive fighting south of Rschew, it was hit by a bomb in Wjasma after being recovered. Then it was sent back for a total rebuilding. Photo: E. Grahl/W. Sawodny collection

After PZ 1 was lost, PZ 27 came to the line from Wjasma to Rschew. Here it is seen without a locomotive in Novoduginskaja early in December 1942. Shortly afterward it too was damaged. Photo: H. J. Roddewig/W. Sawodny collection

partisan fighting until its transfer on February 1, 1943).—PZ 27, after the damage sustained south of Welikije Luki at the end of May 1942 had been repaired, also came into this region—on the line leading northward from Wjasma. During their offensive, the Soviets were again able to reach the rail line north of Sytschewka. PZ 1 was used there and succeeded in scattering the enemy forces who had broken through and fighting to clear the line again on 28 November. On the next day, though, it was badly derailed on a blown-up railroad passage near Nikischkino. Eight cars and the locomotive jumped off the rails. The ensuing recovery and repair work, in which two auxiliary trains were also involved, had to be carried out under constant enemy threats, but they succeeded through the effect of the heavy weapons from the train and the train's disembarked infantrymen, which cleaned out the town of Nikischkino and were able to keep the enemy away from the scene of the crash for some time despite enemy counterattacks and thus finish the work. The damaged PZ 1 was sent back to Sytschewka at first, later to Wjasma. At the railroad station there, though, it took a direct hit from a bomb on 10 December. After that it was taken to Königsberg for a complete rebuilding. PZ 27 took its place, but was damaged by enemy artillery fire near Nikischkino on 14 December, so that it had to be towed back to Smolensk. With defensive fighting it was possible to hold the Rschew salient before it was voluntarily abandoned in March 1943 to gain forces for the collapsed front in the southern sector.

Thus the presence of the armored trains with Army Group Center could be strengthened to a modest degree by the end of 1942. At the end of December 1942, the first train of the newly built BP 42 standard series, PZ 61, finally was delivered there, namely to the 201st Securing Division in Polozk, in order to work together with PZ 3 and the line protection train "Werner," especially in covering the approaches to the Newel region, endangered by the Russian breakthrough around Welikije Luki.

The stationings and tasks of the armored trains with Army Group North remained unchanged in the latter half of 1942. PZ 26 secured the Nowosokolniki—Dno line. This was crossed by enemy forces very often as they slipped through the front on the Lowat and the adjoining swamps, which was occupied only at support points, and recruited younger men in the German hinterlands to replace their own forces, bringing them back by the same routes. Since they were clever enough not to cross the rail line in sight of the armored train, its commander, receiving appropriate reports, developed a successful technique of moving in disembarked infantry troops, supported by unloaded tanks. In this way several such enemy groups could be spotted, wiped out or captured. Particularly from mid-May (departure of PZ 6) until into August, PZ 26 was also used from Dno in the direction of Staraja Russa. After that the newly arrived PZ 51 essentially took over this important line, over which—on the 60-cm field line branching from it near Tuleblja—the supplies were to be brought for the pocket of Demjansk, through a small pathway, but it

In December 1942 the first armored train of the BP 42 standard series, PZ 61, finally reached the front in the central sector, in the Polozk region. Photo: W. Sawodny collection

In the northern sector, PZ 26 collided with a freight train near Schubino on August 21, 1942. Photo: H. Jaeger/W. Sawodny collection

was also supported there at times by PZ 26. PZ 51, stationed at Dno, also secured the approach line from Pleskau, as well as to Batezkaja to the north and sometimes also—along with PZ 26—to the south (Nowosokolniki). With the traffic on this line as heavy as ever and the armored trains likewise having to guarantee its protection, PZ 26 collided on August 21, 1942, with a transport train which had come to a stop before getting a signal to move from the Schubino railroad station. Several persons on the transport train lost their lives or were injured. In the 1942-43 winter combat the two armored trains were again able to provide valuable defensive help on the Lowat front south of Lake Ilmen.—The backline region of the 18th Army, from Luga and Gatschina in the west to the Wolchow—was still covered from its stationing in Ljuban by PZ 30. In October 1942 it was transferred from there to Nowinka, and two months later—in December—it was decided that the armored train, being quite insufficiently equipped for the Russian winter, should be sent home to Germany for rebuilding. In was followed for the same purpose in January 1943 by PZ 26, which was in a somewhat better state after its reequipping in May 1942, so that for several months after that PZ 51 remained the only one in the zone of Army Group North.

PZ 51 was the only armored train remaining in Army Group North area at the beginning of 1943. Photo: M. Streit/W. Sawodny collection

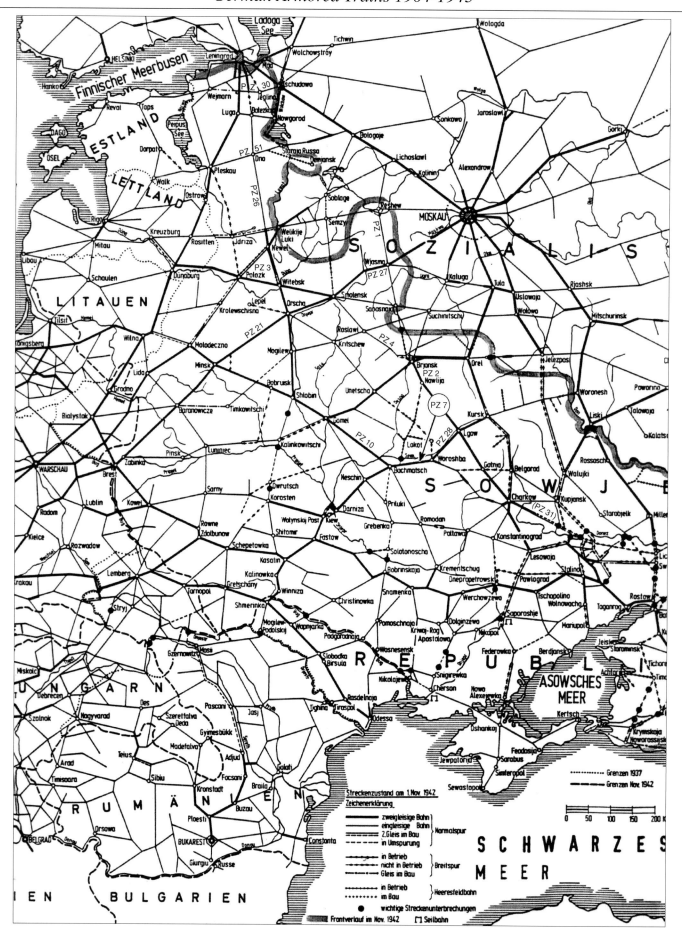

Stationings of the armored trains at the beginning of November 1942. South and east of Kharkov there were no armored trains stationed. (Map excerpt with the kind permission of Musterschmidt Verlag, Göttingen, from E. Kreidler, "Die Eisenbahnen im Machtbereich der Achsenmaechte während des Zweiten Weltkriegs")

From the Enclosure of Stalingrad to the Kursk Combat

Although the main events of this period took place in the southern part of the eastern front, the events in the northern and central sectors will be examined first for the sake of continuing from the previous chapter.

PZ 51, remaining alone in the territory of Army Group North in January 1943, continued from its station in Dno or from Roschtscha to the west to secure the rail network going out in all four directions against the constantly increasing partisan attacks, which more and more often could not be prevented, while subsequent pursuit usually remained fruitless. Pursuit commands which—usually based on reports from village officials—were sent out from the train to fight the partisan groups found to the sides of the tracks, were somewhat more successful. From February 10 to 18, 1943, the armored train with its disembarked units took part in the large-scale partisan operation "Wintermärchen" in the Porchow—Pascherwizy region, where on the first day of action near Marschowina one dead and one severely wounded man were to be reported. On 23 February the train hit a mine near Aschewo (on the Dno-Nowosokolniki line); on 13 March it was bombed in Dno. In June 1943 at the latest it was stationed in Tschichatschewo to protect the important cross link to Nowosokolniki for the coming months.—At the beginning of May 1943 the 18th Army received the new PZ 63 to replace PZ 30, which had been withdrawn four and a half months before. It was stationed at Kusnezowo, west of Diwenskaja. Since the partisan activity in the army's sector was then very meager, the armored train looked into the possibility of combat action on the lines running to Leningrad. This, though, had had to be limited to defense against enemy breakthroughs (which did not succeed), since active support of their own troops was not possible because the enemy could view the tracks and its hasty interruption did not allow a closer approach to the front. At the beginning of June, stronger partisan activity made itself known in the Nowinka—Batezkaja—Jeglino—Nowgorod region, making the constant action of PZ 63 on these lines, especially in the Jeglino—Ogorelje and Nowinka lines, necessary for the next two months. On 23 July it was transferred to the Mga region to provide artillery support for the German troops struggling in difficult but successful defense in the third battle of Ladoga. But after the end of the battle, it returned to its original station and its old action area five days later. There its activity was concentrated in partisan defense along the line from Nowinka to Batezkaja until October. On August 19, 1943, an infantry group from the armored train was caught in a partisan trap during pursuit southwest of Tschaschtscha and had to withdraw, suffering losses. Another advance with stronger forces on the next day found the partisan position abandoned, but the same enemy group (recognizable by the plunder it took with it) could be caught later.

In the sector of Army Group Center, the presence of armored trains was concentrated above all in two particularly partisan-threatened districts: the Polozk—Witebsk—Newel triangle and the area around

This photo of PZ 51 from 1943 shows that at times a gun car was made up of captured Soviet material. Photo: H. Griebl collection

In May 1943 the newly built PZ 63 was transferred to the northern sector. Here it is examined shortly after arriving in Diwenskaja by the Commander of Army Group North, Colonel General Lindemann. Photo: H. Beckmann/W. Sawodny collection

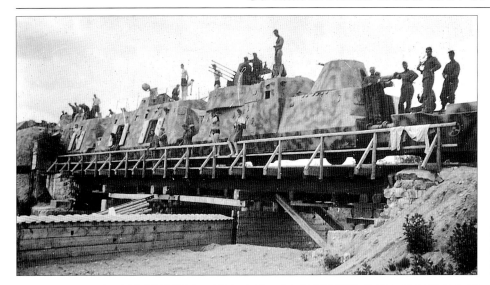

In the summer of 1943, PZ 63 was used to secure rail lines behind the Wolchow front, such as the line from Jeglino toward Nowgorod (here in Radofinnikowo). Photo: H. Beckmann/W. Sawodny collection

During the Lagoda battle at the end of July 1943, PZ 63--with men on the tank carrier and control cars—brings reinforcements to the front. Behind the control car is a rail-capable truck. Photo: H. Beckmann/W. Sawodny collection

Brjansk. Another focal point of armored train action, the Wjasma—Rschew front projection, was evacuated in March 1943. Even before that the armored trains stationed there had been withdrawn. The line protection train "Blücher" already left for Polozk with the Korueck 590, PZ 21 was transferred on 2 February to the Woronesch—Kursk region to take part in the heavy defensive fighting with the 2nd Army there, PZ 27 was subordinated to the 286th Securing Division to guard the Minsk—Orscha line from Krupki, and somewhat later (as of 30 April) Mogilew (Orscha—Schlobin line) became its station. It took part there in the partisan operation "Maikäfer" as a mobile radio center. On June 17, 1943, it was assigned to the 203rd Securing Division in Schlobin; on the trip there it hit a mine near Buda,, which caused two cars to derail, but did

not damage the train otherwise. After that it remained with the same securing division in the Schlobin region and was used there for line securing and partisan fighting.

PZ 61 (since Christmas 1942) was with the 201st Securing Division in the region south of Newel as 1943 began, along with the line protection train "Werner," on the line from Polozk to Newel, while PZ 3 and Line Protection Train No. 83 were under the von der Chevallerie Corps Group on the line from Witebsk to Newel, close to the front. Their purpose was at first the securing of supplies for the relief troops at Welikije Luki, and—after that city was lost—to stop a further Soviet penetration to the west and southwest, as well as to guard the lines coming in from Dünaburg, Molodetschno, amd Idritza.

In the early summer of 1943, PZ 27 secured the Schlobin region. On 15 July it hit a mine on the line to Kalinkowitschi. Photo: H. J. Roddewig/W. Sawodny collection

PZ 61 guards the improvement of a rail line broken by partisans in the Polozk region. Photo: Federal Archives, Koblenz

A number of large-scale operations were carried out against the partisans who were very active in this area, and armored trains took part in them. One of them, under the code name "Schneehase", ran from January 24 to February 12, 1943, directly on the Polozk—Newel line. Part of the crew of PZ 61, disembarked west of Kljastizi, took part, and one of the Praga tanks broke down in ice and had to be blown up, since recovery was not possible. The line protection train "Werner" was able to stop a partisan attempt to break out across the rail line near Polota toward the end of these actions (on 7 February). Right after that (15 February-11 March), the operation "Kugelblitz" took place in the Witebsk area; in it, PZ 61 was used for support on the line toward Polozk and PZ 3 on the line to Newel; in addition, the line protection train "Blücher" was also used. PZ 61 and the line protection trains "Blücher" and "Werner" also took part in the mopping-up operation "Donnerkeil" afterward (March 21-April 2, 1943) in the Dretun—Newel—Gorodok region. "Blücher" was on the Polozk—Newel line in the Dretun—Nowochowansk region, along with "Werner." In the final phase (on 30 March) the station towns of Polota (No. 61), Gorjany ("Werner"), and Obol ("Blücher"—the latter two on the Polozk—Witebsk line) were assigned.

While these three trains remained in the same area until the summer of 1943, and Line Protection Train No. 83 stayed with the II. Luftwaffe Field Corps for support southeast of Newel, PZ 3 was

PZ 4 (at right in the photo) at the Schukowka railroad station in the spring of 1943. Photo: G. Leinen/W. Sawodny collection

The Panhard scout car of PZ 4 at the stopping place of Rschanitza on the Schukowka—Brjansk line. Photo: H. D. Becker/W. Sawodny collection

PZ 21 on the transfer run out of the Smolensk area to Kursk in February 1943. Photo: H. D. Becker/W. Sawodny collection

transferred to Sebesch to protect the line from Rositten via Idritza to Nowosokolniki, on which heightened partisan activity had also appeared meanwhile. With the all too regularly conducted checking runs of the train, the partisans were in a position to derail it again and again with mines detonated at the right moment—for the first time already on 31 March near Maximkowo. Cars thus damaged had to be taken back to the Dünaburg EAW for repairs. Finally the train was so decimated that it was decided on July 13, 1943, to take it back to Germany for a complete rebuilding.

In the Brjansk region the armored trains remained unchanged in the first half of 1943. On 18 January PZ 2 was transferred from Brjansk to Komaritschi on the line to Lgow; on 17 February it returned to Brjansk, where it was used especially on the line there from Unetscha. PZ 4 stayed in Schukowka on the rail line to Roslawl, from which the line to Kletnja branched off, while a connecting line was being built from Rschaniza, southeast of it, to Djatkowo. On March 1, 1943, losses were incurred from partisans near Wyschkowitschi (west of Schukowka), and on 14 March by a bomb attack on Schukowka. On 13 June a disembarked group from the armored train took part in a partisan operation northeast of Schukowka, on June 17 PZ 4 was transferred to the region north of Staraja Lawschina to secure the work on the line being built from Rschanitza to Djatkowo, but toward the end of the month it had already returned to Schukowka.

When the 2nd Army had to push through toward Kursk and retreat after being encircled near Woronesch at the end of January 1943, PZ 21 was transferred from the area north of Dorogobusch into its zone. In the trip via Smolensk—Roslawl—Brjansk the train was attacked by bombs in the last-named city, with two quarters cars burned but the combat train unharmed. It went on to Kursk and, from 4 February on, covered the withdrawal movements there, at first to the east, then to the west of the city. Between Ryschkowo and Djakonowo in particular, successful withdrawals could be achieved through the effective cooperation of PZ 21 during and after the evacuation

of Kursk from 8 February. In fact, the armored train suffered hits from antitank shells to the locomotive and one car in a Soviet attack, supported by tanks, on Okolodok on 11 February. Then it was taken back to Konotop and repaired afterward at the Kiev-Darniza EAW. After being finished on 14 March, the train first moved to the Kiev—Korosten line at Teterew in the western Ukraine. From there it made extensive securing runs on the Kiev—Korosten—Kasatin triangle, but on 23 March also from Kiev in the direction of Kharkov (Grebenka—Romodan). On 14 April, though, PZ 21 was transferred via Kiev and Konotop to the southwest corner of the Kursk salient, to Sumy, to secure the Woroschba—Kharkov line. When the train came under artillery fire in Sumy, it went to Syrowatka on 24 May; on 30 May the train was attacked by low-flying planes in Grebenikowka, and two crewmen were badly wounded. In June it was finally stationed in Basy. From there it made securing runs on the line to Woroschba until the end of July 1943, as well as to Tetkino and Konotop.

On November 19, 1942, large Soviet units had broken through the front at the Romanian armies both northwest and south of Stalingrad, and just three days later they joined hands near Kalatsch and had enclosed the German 6th Army. To close the hold torn open in the front, all available units capable of fighting had to be gathered together. On 20 November the 6th Army asked Army Group B for armored trains (which were all in the Bachmatsch—Woroschba area) to protect the only rail line in this region, from Belaja Kalitwa via Parschin to Tschir. To secure to Tschir railroad station, a makeshift armored train with undriveable T 34 tanks loaded onto them was to be assembled, a measure that was no longer carried out, probably in view of the rush of events. Army Group B immediately sent Armored Trains No. 7 and 10 on the march; they were subordinated to the Stahel Group on 23 November, which held a bridgehead on the rail line east of the Tschir with alarm units and anti-aircraft troops of the Luftwaffe (This line had now gained particularly in importance as the big airfields for aerial supplying for Stalingrad, Tazinskaja, and Morossowskaja were on it). At this very bridgehead— characterized by the place names

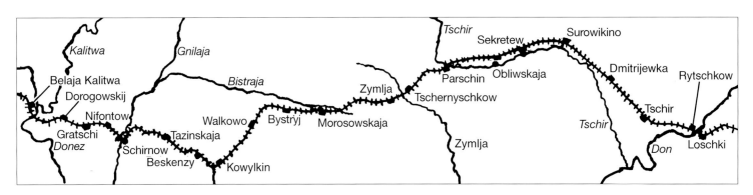

The railroad line between the Donez and Don (toward Stalingrad), on which PZ No. 7, 10, and 28 were used in the winter of 1942-43.

After the enclosure of Stalingrad, PZ 7 operated at first at the Tschir bridgehead, then near Rostov, and finally in the Donez Basin, and was constantly in combat until March 1943. Photo: Federal Archives, Koblenz

of Sekretew, Obliwskaja and Kowylenski—the two armored trains, No. 7 and 10, were used in direct action, the disembarked infantry units in the front lines, the armored trains themselves as artillery support behind them, along with the Luftwaffe and alarm units. In hard fighting, very costly for both sides, they were able to hold this bridgehead for a month, while the armored trains shot down several tanks and low-level planes. Only in the last weeks of December did they finally have to withdraw over the Tschir. Meanwhile, though, the Soviet troops had broken through the 8th Italian Army's front on the Don on 16 December and streamed southwards to the west of the upper Tschir; on 22 December they were already approaching and threatening the Donez bend and the aforementioned rail line east of it. On 23 December PZ 28 was hastily transferred from the area

northwest of Kharkov to Belaja Kalitwa, where the line crossed the Donez. The next day the Russians pushed through to Tazinskaja, took this important supply center with its large storehouses, destroyed the airfield from which flights to Stalingrad had taken off, and thus broke the rail line. Neither PZ 28, coming in from Belaja Kalitwa, nor one combat train of PZ 10 sent in from the Tschir front could stop this. Only on 28 December could the fully destroyed Tazinskaja be won back and, in connection with it, the rail line from Belaja Kalitwa to Tschernyschkow be cleaned up and put back in action with the help of the armored trains. The first days of 1943 saw Armored Trains No. 7 and 10 in hard defensive fighting around Tschernyschkow west of the Tschir, where PZ 10 was already hit by an antitank shell on January 1. As of 4 January the armored trains covered the slow withdrawal along the rail line, whereby as of 7 January a stable front,

PZ 10—here Combat Train A—supported PZ 7 in its actions between the Don and Donez and later in the Donez Basin. Photo: Federal Archives, Koblenz

Combat Train B of PZ 10 passes a capsized and burned-out freight car in its actions early in 1943. Photo: Federal Archives Koblenz

PZ 28 was also transferred to the Donez—Tazinskaja line on December 23, 1942, and took part in the fighting there; later it was in action near Rostov and in the Donez Basin. Photo: B. Schultz/W. Sawodny collection

Some of the gun car crew of PZ 10A stand before their car in the snow of the Russian winter. Photo: W. Pflaumbaum/W. Sawodny collection

at which the armored trains were also present, could again be held forward of Tazinskaja. On 16 January the final withdrawal to the Donez took place. PZ 28 was among the last that fought their way out of Tazinskaja that day. In this withdrawal fighting the armored trains were able to bring back several transport trains of valuable materials from already enemy-occupied territory. In crossing the Donez near Belaja Kalitwa on 18 January, a disembarked infantry group from PZ 28 did not arrive in time for the departure and was first thought to be lost, but were able to fight their way to it by other routes.

While PZ 10 remained on the Donez front with the Fretter-Pico Army Section and secured the area around the Lichaja rail intersection, Armored Trains No. 7 and 28 were transferred to Rostov, where the Russian advance along the lower Don threatened to cut off the withdrawal route of the 1st Armored Army from the Caucasus. Since this could at first be held by the 4th Armored Army at the right time, their duties consisted at first of securing transport on the marching route from Rostov toward Taganrog and guarding the line that ran behind the front from Rostov to Nowotscherkassk (PZ 28 also secured transport back from Tichorezk to Rostov). A critical situation developed when after the last parts of the 1st Armored Army passed through and the blowing up of the Don bridges, the Russians crossed the Don downstream of Rostov at the beginning of February and threatened to cut off the German forces still in the city. Armored trains No. 7 and 28 went into combat action, and it was PZ 7 in particular that, in fights near Martinowo (2/9), Chapry, and Sapadnji (2/10), was able to keep the northern line from Rostov open until these units withdrew, although it was damaged itself. On 11 February it was transferred to Stalino; two days later PZ 28 followed it there.

South of the central Donez the situation had meanwhile become very threatening after the Russian forces had broken through the 2nd Hungarian Army south of Woronesch and the 8th Italian Army south of Kalitwa in mid-January 1943, and now streamed westward, not only toward Kharkov through the wide open front almost unhindered, but also turned toward the Donez and crossed it, not only on 2 February near Woroschilowgrad, but in the following days to the south and southwest on its entire breadth between Isjum and Lissitschansk. PZ 10, remaining in the Donez Basin, was moved westward from Lichaja in view of this situation. Combat Train A was already in battle near Sol, north of Artemowsk, on 4 February, and was transferred the next day from Debalzewo to the Konstantinowka region, where it was involved in heated battles lasting for days west of that city (near Krasnotorka) on the east flank of the breakthrough area, where on 12 February it took a direct hit from an antitank shell that put it out of action; it had to be towed back to Konstantinowka for repairs. But on 11 February advancing Russian cavalry forces from Voroshilovgrad had already reached the region east of Debalzewo and broken the rail lines from there to Manuilowka and Schterowka; further to the west Soviet tank units had already broken through from Slawjansk to Postyschewo and had blocked the main supply line of Army GroupDon (renamed South the next day) from Dnjepropetrowsk to the Donez Basin. On 13 Febnruary PZ 10A was able to open the line east of Debalzewo again briefly, but then was ordered to Grodowka, on the eastern edge of the breakthrough area near Postyschewo. There PZ 7, transferred from Rostov to Stalino, arrived on the same day; as no time remained for its repairs. PZ 28, also coming from there, was at first sent to take the place of the damaged No. 10B on the line west of Konstantinowka, but went to Debalzewo two days later to help destroy the enemy troops who had meanwhile been encircled there. Near Postyschewo too, the SS "Viking" Division had succeeded in enclosing the enemy and finally cleaning out the city by 23 February; the rest were then destroyed in a pocket battle north of the rail line near Grischino. While PZ 10A stayed in and near Postyschewo at first, PZ 7 was ordered via Stalino, Pologi, and Tschaplino to Sinelnikowo, the railroad junction east of Dnepropetrowsk, on the evening of 16 February. A Russian armored formation, which had advanced from Isjum via Losowaja, approached it from the direction of Pawlogrod. The armored train, along with the few other alarm units, was actually able to hold Sinelnikowo against the attacking Russians on 19-20 February, and secure the transport of the 15th Infantry Division, brought in as reinforcements, on 20 February. The Russians in fact slipped past Sinelnikowo farther to the south, but could be caught and destroyed before Saporoschje—cut off from their connections to the rear. For the successful battles at the Tschir bend, near Rostow, Postyschewo, and now Sinelnikowo, the Commander of PZ 7, 1st Lt. Helmut Vögler, received the German Cross in gold.

On 20 February PZ 28 was likewise sent on the march from Debalzewo (at that town it was relieved by PZ 10A—previously at Postyschewo—which secured the line from there toward the front—in the direction of Petrowenki), likewise via Stalino and Pologi to Tschaplino. It was supposed to secure the approach of the 4th Armored Army—especially by guarding the Woltscha bridge near Wassilkowka—as was PZ 7 farther westward in the Sinelnikowo region. This army, along with the SS Armored Corps, which was coming toward it—after the Kempf Army Secttion had to give up Kharkov on 16 February—had been assembled southwest of the city near Krasnograd, and were to destroy, once and for all, the Soviet troops flowing in from the Donez in the direction of Dnjepropetrowsk. The new PZ 62 arrived in Krasnograd on 18 February, at just the right time for the planned attack of the SS Armored Corps. Two days later, along with the advance units of the SS Division "Das Reich," it was able to push forward successfully to Satschepilowka (on the afternoon of the next day a battle group of this division already reached Sinelnikowo), but on the same day PZ 62 had to be transferred to the Poltawa—Kowjagi line, since the Russians were advancing farther to the west in that region. On 21 February it was able to rub out a strong enemy group in an hours-long fight near Wodjanoje, still fought in this area until the 23rd, and then had to go back for more ammunition, destroying the switches behind it. Defensive fighting in the Kotschubejewka region followed until March.

After destroying the Soviet forces between the Donez and Dnjepr, the 4th Armored Army attacked from the Krasnograd region northward in the direction of Kharkov. The success of this operation resulted in the Russian troops north of Poltawa also being forced to retreat. Thus PZ 62 could now advance via Kowjagi to Ljubotin along with the Kempf Army Section. By 15 March the SS Armored Corps had recaptured Kharkov; three days later the Armored Grenadier Division "Grossdeutschland" also retook Belgorod. Thus the winter war in the southern sector came to an end.

In the territory of the 1st Armored Army in the Donez Basin, PZ 10A (No. 10B was being repaired since 13 February) had been transferred from Debalzewo back to Postyschewo to secure the line in the direction of Tschaplino. At the beginning of March it also had to be repaired, and was replaced by the meanwhile restored No. 10B, which was stationed in Meschewaja. The armored trains No. 7 and No. 28 stayed in the Dnjepropetrowsk—Nowomoskowsk—Sinelnikowo--Pawlograd region until 23 March, then PZ 7 was stationed with the 1st Armored Army in Losowaja. PZ 10B was transferred to Artemowsk on 27 March to secure the lines from there toward the Donez; its place in Meschewaja was taken at the beginning of April by the overhauled PZ 10A. On 30 April PZ 7 was called back to Korosten for track securing in the area of the Wehrmacht Commander Ukraine. In its place PZ 10A was now stationed in Panjutino, while PZ 10B remained in Artemowsk. On June 1, 1943, the two combat trains of the now-reunited PZ 10 were transferred to the Sarny region of the western Ukraine, where partisan activity had increased very sharply. Armored Trains No. 7 and 10 carried out track securing from then on in the territory of the Wehrmacht Commander Ukraine south of the Pripjet from Kiev to Kowel. Combat trains of PZ 10 ran into mines between Maniewicze and Sarny on 19 June and in Biala (north of Sarny) on 8 July, but were only slightly damaged.

The new PZ 62 arrived in mid-February, at just the right time to be able to intervene in the fighting south and west of Kharkov. Later it was stationed in Merefa (southwest of this large city). The picture shows it there. Photo: H. Hoffmann/W. Sawodny collection

PZ 62 on one of its securing runs south of Kharkov in the early summer of 1943. Photo: H. Hoffmann/W. Sawodny collection

In April 1943 PZ 7 was transferred to the Korosten region of the western Ukraine for track securing. In front of the gun car is an additional low-side car with a tank (presumably Type III Q) set on it. Photo: P. Nett/W. Sawodny collection

Left: PZ 28 on the Sea of Azov coast while stationed in Berdjansk. Photo: B. Schultz/W. Sawodny collection

PZ 10 — here Combat Train A — also reached the Sarny region in the western Ukraine in June 1943. Photo: W. Pflaumbaum/W. Sawodny collection

At the end of March PZ 28 was supposed to be transferred out of the Dnjepropetrowsk area to the Kempf Army Section in the region around Kharkov. This apparently was not done, for it is still listed as subordinated to OFK 397 (Dnjepropetrowsk) in July 1943. According to statements from crew members, though, it stayed for some time in Berdjansk on the Sea of Azov in between. As of July 11, 1943, it was then in Losowaja. — PZ 62 was stationed in Merefa in March 1943, after the conquest of Kharkov. It covered the lines in the direction of the Dnjepr, but escorting transports took it as far as Odessa.

From the Kursk Battle to the Stalemate in the Spring of 1944

On July 5, 1943, the German Wehrmacht began its last great offensive on the eastern front, the attempt to cut off the Kursk salient by a pincer movement from the north and south. After just a few days the northern attack group of the 9th Army was halted by the well-prepared Russians. On 12 July, when the Soviets in turn attacked and broke through the 2nd Armored Army, which covered the rear of the 9th Army in the German front bulge near Orel, and the Allied landing in Sicily on 10 July made a transfer of German forces to there necessary, Hitler decided on 16 July to give up his offensive — in the southern area as well.

This was all the more necessary as the Russians achieved significant breakthroughs both on the central Donez east of Slawjansk and on the Mius front. To mop these up, troops from the southern Kursk attack group had to be called in. Armored trains were involved in these counterattacks — as opposed to the Kursk battle itself. Thus PZ 28, stationed in Losowaja, had moved forward to secure the Barwenkowo — Slawjansk line for the incoming troop reinforcements; on 27 July it was subordinated to the combat commander from Slawjansk on the west flank of the breakthrough area, which could not be wiped out any more. — With the III. Armored Corps, PZ 62 went from Kharkov to the Mius front on 24 July. There it was able, in the counterattack that began on 30 July, to restore the situation.

On 3 August, though, the Soviets accomplished a much more serious breakthrough on the dividing line between the now-weakened 4th Armored Army and the Kempf Army Section on both sides of Belgorod. On the north flank, PZ 21 (subordinated to Army Group Center) was already near Solotnizkij on that day in both artillery and infantry action against Russian units, which were already feeling their way ahead in this region too, but the expected attack on the Basy

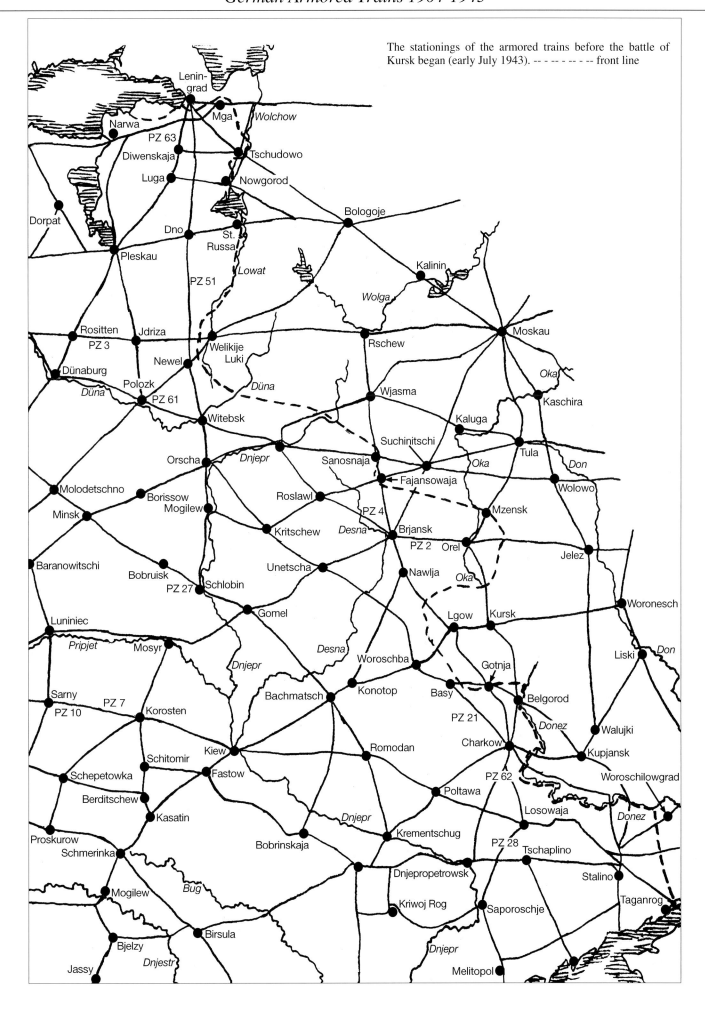

The stationings of the armored trains before the battle of Kursk began (early July 1943). -- -- -- -- -- front line

railroad station was not made. On the next three days it was exposed to steady air attacks, which actually did no damage. On 8 August the Russian advance along the Worskla in full strength had reached the region north of Achtyrka. Heavy artillery fire covered the region in which PZ 21 was located. Still on the same day it was involved in heavy defensive fighting before Boromlja, but could was able to pick up the guards of the Worskla bridge near Smorodino. When it tried to go back to Boromlja with them on the morning of 9 August, it already found itself cut off, but in a costly fight it accomplished the breakthrough. On the next two days it moved back to Sumy as the rear guard, destroying the railroad line, attacked several times by low-level planes. On 11 August it was moved back to Chutor-Michailowsky and there subordinated to the Korück 580 (2nd Army) for securing tasks.

The Kempf Army Section was pushed back by the Russian advance in the region north and west of Kharkov and saw itself exposed to the danger of being surrounded. The III. Armored Corps was hastily brought back from the Mius front, and PZ 62 along with it, which went into battle against advancing enemy forces in Solotschew (on the Kharkov—Gotnja line) on 6 August, but was mistakenly attacked by its own fighters and suffered losses. On 8 August it was in action south of there, near Dolschik, where it not only lost two guns but the locomotive was also damaged. Then it departed; the locomotive went to the Poltawa EAW for repairs. On that day PZ 28 was also transferred from Slawjansk to the area west of Kharkov. It took an effective part in the withdrawal fighting east of Bogoduchow and was between Maximowka and Repki on 9 August. On 12 August it supported the counterattack of the SS "Das Reich" Division from Maximowka in the direction of Bogoduchow. It remained on the Ljubotin—Maximowka line until 16 August, on which day it went from Mertschik toward Dnjepropetrovsk for repairs. Meanwhile PZ 11 (Combat Train B, now finally separated

In the second battle around Kharkov too, in August 1943, Armored Trains No. 11, 28, and 62—here PZ 11—saw action. Later they operated behind the Dnjepr line. Photo: T. Schorlemmer/W. Sawodny collection

Below: The combat area west of Kharkov (August 1943). Front line: -- - -- - -- August 3, 1943; -- . -- . – August 23, 1943.

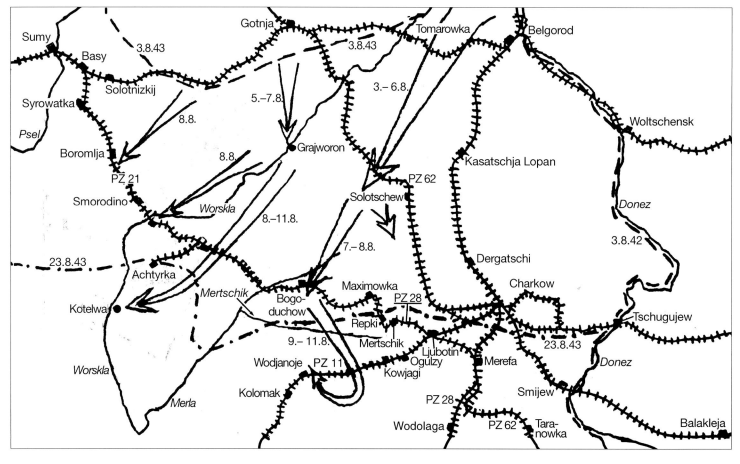

and independent from PZ 10) arrived in the Kharkov area from the western Ukraine on 11 August, just at the right time to take part on the same day in the fighting against the Soviet tanks that had broken through southward to the west of Kowjagi. In Kowjagi it took a direct hit from a Russian T 34, but could still maintain its position there and secure the approach from Ljubotin. After shattering the penetrated enemy forces west of Kowjagi, it inspected track-rebuilding work as far as Kolomak on 16 August. On 18 August PZ 11, located in Ogulzy, was transferred to replace the withdrawn PZ 28 on the line toward Bogoduchow, where the enemy attacked again. It strengthened the defenses with its artillery and was able to shoot down two Russian fighter planes in Repki on the 18th. It brought down another airplane near Maximowka on 22 August, but went to Poltawa for repairs on the same day after two guns had been knocked out. Thus the front west of Kharkov could be somewhat stabilized through the effective cooperation of the armored trains. To be sure, the enemy had also attacked eastward and southeastward of Kharkov; the city had to be evacuated on 22 August. Armored Trains No. 28 and 62, now ready for action again, were transferred to the line from Merefa to Krasnograd (south of Kharkov) on 21 August (No. 28 to Wodolaga, No. 62 to secure around Taranowka), but PZ 62 had to go back to Poltawa on 24 August for repair work that lasted until 19 September. Since PZ 11 was also there for the same reason until September, only PZ 28 remained in action south of Merefa.

In view of the withdrawal of the 6th Army and the south wing of the 1st Armored Army, approved on 8 September, the repaired PZ 11 and PZ 28 were transferred to Dnjepropetrowsk on 11 September. From there they reconnoitered in the direction of Tschaplino and were to protect the Woltscha bridge near Wassilikowka. On 14 September PZ 28 advanced near Pismennaja without encountering enemies, but had to vacate and repair the line, mined and destroyed by partisans, again; on the same day the armored railcar subordinated to it was able to reach the bridge near Wassilikowka. The next day PZ 28 itself got there after shooting down a lone T 34 on the way. But it had to go back to Sinelnikowo for coaling and was thus replaced by PZ 11. The latter even advanced to Tschaplino and was able to help the 9th Armored Division fight off an enemy attack there and then cover the destruction of the rail facilities and the withdrawal to Wassilikowka.

On 17 September the general retreat of the German troops to the Dnjepr and the Saporoschje—Melitopol line was organized. Armored Trains No. 11 and 28 were drawn back to Dnjepropetrowsk. PZ 11 was stationed in Suchatschewka, PZ 28 at first in Diewka (both a bit west of Dnjepropetrowsk), but PZ 28 was already transferred on 23 September to Choritza, opposite the bridgehead of Saporoschje, to help protect it, but above all the dam there. On that day PZ 11 reached Werchowzewo to secure the Pjatichatki—Dnjepropetrowsk line. — The repaired PZ 62 left Poltawa in its evacuation on 22 September and withdrew via Krementschug to the west shore of the Dnjepr; it transferred to Kamenka (26 September) and on 28 September to Bogdanowka (between Snamenka and Dolinskaja).

Above: 1st Lt. Frank Drexler—here in front of the armored locomotive—commanded PZ 62 until August 1943, when he was replaced by Capt. von Wedel. Photo: K. H. Knapp/W. Sawodny collection
Upper right: PZ 28. An armored booth for the track observer was already installed on the control car in the summer of 1942. Photo: B. Schultz/W. Sawodny collection
Right: Captain von Wedel (fourth from right) with the radiomen of PZ 62, which was at the Cherson bridgehead in the winter of 1943-44. Photo: K. H. Knapp/W. Sawodny collection

At the end of September the Russians had already succeeded in pushing two bridgeheads over the Dnjepr that could not be eliminated, one north of Kanew and the other between Krementschug and Dnjepropetrowsk. While it was possible to compress them tightly in the first one, the enemy proved to be active at the second one at the beginning of October and tried to advance to the nearby rail connection in the Woskobojna—Auly region (between Dnjepropetrowsk and Werchowzewo). On 3 October PZ 11, present there, was able to achieve complete defensive success with its disembarked infantry and supporting heavy weapons from the train; in the following days it remained lurking there and smashed known enemy readiness sites with its artillery. Enemy attempts to cripple the train with track blasts and destroy it by low-level planes or gunfire gained no results. On 15 October, though, the Soviets were able to cross the Dnjepr with strong forces east of Krementschug and break southward through the line between the 8th Army and 1st Armored Army. Within a few days they had reached the transverse line behind the Dnjepr in the area between Koristowka and Werchowzewo. While PZ 62 helped to cover the left flank of the breakthrough area near Protopowka and Alexandrija in the territory of the 8th Army on 19 October, PZ 11 (which was actually supposed to have been transferred to Schepetowka in the western Ukraine) was pulled out of its station near Auly via Werchowzewo and Erastowka in the direction of Pjatichatki, since Russian tanks had broken through east of that city. Early the next morning it approached this position between Kassinowka and Pjatichatki and was able to observe enemy troops north and south of the line and take them under fire. Suddenly the Panhard scout car, running some 500 meters ahead, took a direct hit and went up in flames. The train stopped and sent out infantry troops to reconnoiter and recover the Panhard crew, and they were able to roll up the Russian infantry, reinforced by partisans, along the line. But the train was suddenly covered by tank fire. The locomotive took one direct hit, the front gun car two. With its last steam it made the trip back to the nearest railroad station with three dead and thirteen wounded to report. The train was drawn back to the Dolginzewo—Apostolowo region. Since there was no longer any possibility of making repairs there, it was finally taken to Nikolajew on 30 October.

On 15 October the Saporoschje bridgehead had been abandoned under heavy enemy pressure; PZ 28, on the western shore there, was called two days later from the south via Apostolowo and Dolginzewo to Pjatichatki, which had been taken during the morning of 19 October by the enemy, who now pushed farther forward. PZ 28, with the 23rd Armored Division, delayed the withdrawal via Sawro and Radowaja to Wesselje Terny from the early afternoon of that day to 22 October. Then it was subordinated to the combat commander at

Kriwoj Rog and took part in the defense against the Soviets, who had advanced to the northwest edge of the city, and even to the inner city at times. On 30 October it was transferred to secure the line from there to Dolinskaja that was threatened by the Russians, who had broken through farther to the south from west of Kriwoj Rog. The German counterattack, on the move since 28 October, in which PZ 28 was not directly involved, stabilized the front on the Ingulez and also pushed the enemy back several kilometers north of Kriwoj Rog. On 2 November PZ 28 was again subordinated to the 23rd Armored Division there. Stationed in Rokowataja, just behind the front line, it helped to defend against the constant enemy attempts to attack in this area and was damaged on 14 November, but remained in action. On 5 December the Soviets broke out of their bridgehead on the upper Ingulez and had already broken the Dolinskaja--Snamenka rail line; afterward they pushed southward along this line to Kuzowka; between 16 and 18 December they even approached Dolinskaja. PZ 28 had already been transferred to the LII. Army Corps on the endangered line when this fighting broke out, and took an active part in its defense, as also in securing the railroad station of Dolinskaja-Schewtschenkowo, vital for unloading reinforcements. Later, from Kuzowka, its artillery supported the counterattack of the 17th Armored Division, which led on 20 December to the cutting off of the Russian breakthrough area and the emptying of the pocket. In these combat actions PZ 28 seems to have been damaged, for after being in Dolinskaja as the year ended, it was sent to the Nikolajew EAW for repairs at the beginning of 1944.

On November 18, 1943, PZ 62 had been replaced by the repaired PZ 11 in the Snamenka—Bobrinskaja area. PZ 62 was transferred to the XLIV. Army Corps in the 6th Army to support and secure the supplying of the Cherson bridgehead. During 1942 armored trains had been stationed in the 6th Army region only for short times (PZ 28 in the spring and early summer, PZ 62 for a few days at the end of July and beginning of August). Thus it was decided to set up the army's own line protection train, which was equipped by the 4th Company of Railroad Engineer Regiment 3 and put into service at Melitopol on 19 October, just at the right time to intervene in the withdrawal fighting in that area. On 23 October Melitopol had to be given up, and in the next days the train covered the withdrawal toward Crimea. Just one rail line led there, and so it crossed through the Siwasch isthmus into the territory of the 17th Army on 31 October. That army—meanwhile cut off on Crimea—gave it the name "Michael" and sent it on to the Perekop isthmus. There the provisional A/A armored train of the 9th A/A Division (under the command of Lt. Muhr, who later received the Knight's Cross) had already been present since 30 October, and had been able to shoot down 24 Russian tanks by 1 November. On

The line protection train "Michael", set up by the 6th Army in October 1943, had captured T 34/85 tanks set on flat cars and surrounded by sheet steel. Later it was cut off in Crimea. Photo: J. Magnuski collection

that day, along with the line protection train "Michael," which had been put into service as soon as it arrived, it fought off a Russian attack near Armjansk. The trains were able to repeat this success one day later and support a German counterattack on the citadel and brickyard of Armjansk the next day. They took part in further, ever-changing combats on the Tatar Wall until the year's end; then that sector of the front became quiet for the time being.

PZ 11 had reached the 8th Army in Snamenka on November 17, 1943 to replace PZ 62, but was sent on to the Bobrinskaja region one day later, where strong partisan activity had appeared. Wits its repulse, the armored train was busy to the north of Smela, particularly after an enemy attack on 29 November had broken the line between Smela and Tscherkassy, which—though only for a few days—could be restored, and also east of there near Kosary or southward near Serdjukowka. Meanwhile, though, enemy troops pushed westward from the Krementschug—Koristowka region, taking Snamenka on 8 December and being before Funduklejewka on the 13th and near Kamenka the next day. PZ 11 took part in the defensive fighting along the rail line; on December 14 it supported an attack by the 3rd Armored Division near Kamenka, which pushed the front line eastward to before Sosnowka. On December 21 PZ 11, then in Schpola, could finally—as already planned in October—be moved to Rowno in the western Ukraine. In place of it the 8th Army received the new PZ 70, but it was stationed in Pomoschnaja to secure the lines from there via Kirowograd toward Snamenka and via Nowji Mirgorod to Bobrinskaja.

North of Kiew, too, the Russians had already conquered the Dnjepr river barrier by the end of September 1943 with a large bridgehead on the border of Army Group Center in the Pripjet mouth area and a smaller one just a little north of the Ukrainian capital. In the territory of the Wehrmacht Commander Ukraine, Armored Trains No. 7 and 10 had been active in line-securing and partisan action since May-June 1943; PZ 10 (whose second combat train, to be sure, had been separated after explosion damage on June 16 and its repair as the independent PZ 11, transferred to the Kharkov region on 16 June was repaired at the beginning of August), was used in the Sarny—Kowel region and PZ 7 in the Owrutsch—Korosten and especially on the line from the latter to Kiev. In mid-October 1943, PZ 31, newly rebuilt completely at the Gleiwitz RAW, joined them and essentially guarded the Schmerinka—Kasatin—Berditschew line, but also undertook a securing run from Schmerinka toward Odessa as well as several successful partisan actions in the Schitomir region.

On November 3, 1943, strong Russian forces broke out of their bridgehead and through the German lines north of Kiev. Just three days later Kiev, circumvented to the west, fell, and one day later the Soviet troops occupied the railroad junction of Fastow, 60 km to the southwest; on 13 November they had reached Schitomir. PZ 31 was immediately sent to the line from Kasatin to Fastow, and was able to set fire to a fuel train in an advance 9 km behind the enemy line and contribute through its combat actions to holding the front near Popelnja. PZ 7 supported the withdrawal fighting on the line from Kiev to Korosten and had heavy and costly fighting to endure, especially near Spartak on 10 and 11 November. But on 11 November the XLVIII. Armored Corps, gathered in the Berditschew—Kasatin region, began its counterattack to the north. PZ 31 accompanied the advance on the right flank of this spearhead in the Popelnja—Koschanka--Fastow region and was able to roll up a part of the Russian front line with a surprise breakthrough. On 16 November the new PZ 69 arrived in Berditschew. It followed the troops of the XLVIII. Armored Corps in the direction of Schitomir and secured the rebuilding work on the blown-up railroad bridges. Just one day after Schitomir was regained on 20 November it also arrived there. In the following weeks PZ 69 first supported the Cavalry Regiment South in the Gorbascha—Tschernichow region with its artillery; after driving the Russians out of the area of the rail line, it secured the line toward Korosten, working from Schitomir. PZ 7 was busy all the time in the fighting around the last-named city, suffering damage and losses particularly between 24 and 26 November.

Again the Russian advances were held back in the zone of Army Group South, both west of Kiev and between Tscherkassy and Kriwoj Rog, and—although losing ground—a somewhat cohesive front was held. The armored trains used there—No. 7, 10, 11, 28, and 62 ever since 1943 began, while only in the last three months had the totally rebuilt No. 31 and the new No. 69 and 70 had arrived as reinforcements—had been able to come through the manifold defensive fighting with occasional damage, but without serious losses. Both were soon to take a turn for the worse.

On December 24, 1943, the 1st Ukrainian Front began to attack the German 4th Armored Army east of Schitomir and had achieved a deep breakthrough in a short time. PZ 69, used until then between Schitomir and Korosten, was transferred along with the XLVIII. Armored Corps to the Berditschew region for defense. PZ 31, formerly located near Popelnaja, unknowingly moved into one of the Kasatin railroad stations already occupied by the enemy during the defensive fighting on 28 December. Surrounded by superior forces and robbed of a chance to move backward, the commander ordered to crew to disembark. Although the train itself was allowed to fall into Russian hands unharmed, the crew could fight their way to the German lines and, in infantry action that cost losses, take part

The rebuilt PZ 31 arrived in the Schmerinka—Kasatin—Berditschew region in mid-October 1943. Soon it was involved in defensive fighting and fell into Russian hands in Kasatin on 28 December. Photo: H. von Heymann/W. Sawodny collection

At the end of December 1943, the new PZ 70 came to Army Group South and was stationed in Pomoschnaja. Photo: Becker/W. M. Kohler collection

in the defense of Kasatin until it was finally abandoned on January 3, 1944. The Russian breakthrough quickly spread westward from Korosten, which will be mentioned later, and from Kasatin to the southwest, where the Soviets, going around the strongly defended Winniza, could even block the important Lemberg—Odessa supply line briefly. To the southeast, thus in back of the German troops still in the Kanew—Tscherkassy region on the Dnjepr, they put pressure on the Taraschtscha—Schaschkow line. For the counterattack which was able to ease the strain northwest and north of Uman from mid-January 1944 on, PZ 62, removed from the 6th Army after its task at the Cherson bridgehead on December 20, 1943, was transferred to Christinowka on the 11th of that month.

On 5 January the Russians also began to attack on both sides of Kirowograd, and three of their divisions had surrounded the city two days later. Nothing concrete has become known of PZ 70's further action on the line from Pomoschnaja via Ukrainka to before Kirowograd. It may have supported the counterattack of Securing Regiment 331 west of Kirowograd near Schestakowka on 9 January, which made possible the escape of the surrounded units on the next night, and it was probably also involved in the defense near Nowo Mirgorod as of January 25, 1944, when the Russian 5th Guard Armored Army advanced on Schpola north of there, in order to close the pocket around the German units of the XLII. and XI. Army Corps in the Korsun area three days later by joining with the 6th Soviet Armored Army that came eastward from the area near Swenigorodka. PZ 62, operating before Talnoje, also saw itself cut off by tanks of the last-named Russian army, but was able to slip away at night and break through to its own lines—taking along an immobilized hospital train. The armored trains could take part in only a limited way in the efforts to open the pocket in February 1944, which took place away from the rail lines, by securing the Christinowka--Talnoje approach line (PZ 62 with the II. Armored Corps) and north of Pomoschnaja (PZ 70, subordinated to the 8th Army). They remained in these regions until the beginning of March.

On 5 March the Soviets began their next stroke. From the area west of Swenigorodka they moved southward, crossed the rail line west of Talnoje on 7 March, wherein PZ 62 was involved in the vain defense near Potasch, and on the next day they were already approaching Uman, which was lost on 10 March. On 6 March the Russians had already broken out of the Kriwoj Rog region (which they had already taken at the end of February), had reached Nowyi Bug on 8 March, and turned toward the west. Thus for the 8th Army,

far to the north of it, a withdrawal on the Bug line had to be ordered to avoid encirclement; it began on 11 March, but on the same day the first Soviet advance units already reached the river east of Gaiworon, which they crossed to the south bank two days later. PZ 62 crossed the Bug near Ladyschin and was transferred via Wapnjarka into the zone of the 1st Armored Army to the Schmerinka—Proskurow line, already threatened by the Soviets, just in the nick of time, for the railroad junction of Wapnjarka was already taken by the Soviet forces on 16 March and thus the link with Odessa was cut once and for all. They moved farther westward to the Dnjestr, which they crossed near Jampol on 18 March. Thus the gap in the front between the 1st Armored Army and the 8th Army was torn open irrevocably for 100 km. The 8th Army was forced to extend their north wing farther and farther to the west, and thus PZ 70, which had crossed the Bug near Perwomaisk along with an endless stream of retreating German troops, was sent to secure the line from Slobodka to the northwest. On 19 March it already had an encounter with Russian tanks near Popeljuchi, on the next day it had partisan groups, who had become active again, to fight with south of there, and who joined with advancing regular troops to take Kodyma, the station of the armored train, and compel it to withdraw to the southeast. It seems to have stayed in Slobodka for the next few days. On 26 March it tried to bring back, from east of the Balta railroad station, a hospital train cut off by a Russian advance near Scherebkowo, but after antitank shells hit the locomotive near the Perelety railroad station it had to turn back; a day later it was damaged again by hitting a mine near Birsula. With the front moving back toward the south, it found itself in Satischje on 31 March and then moved back to Rasdelnaja in the zone of the 6th Army.

At this army, which was still on the lower Dnjepr despite the abandonment of the Nikopol and Cherson bridgeheads at the beginning of March 1944, the fully reconstructed PZ 30 had arrived in Nikolajew on 21 February—since PZ 28, at the Nikolajew EAW for repairs, was not yet finished—instead of PZ 62, which had been withdrawn on January 10, 1944—to take over the securing of the line from there to Cherson. Even after the evacuation of Cherson at the end of February, it still stood as an advance post at the spearhead railroad station of Kopani until, after the breakthrough southwest of Kriwoj Rog to Nowyi Bug as of 8 March, a spearhead along the Ingul turned to the south and rolled up the front of the 6th Army, which had also been penetrated from the east. PZ 30 was transferred to the line to the north on that day and stationed in Wodopoj and already made

In February 1944 the newly built PZ 30 had been sent to Nikolajew. On 11 March it collided with an ammunition train near Lozkino, with the control car being pushed up onto the tank-carrier car. Photo: H. Plangemann/W. Sawodny collection

contact with the enemy near Lozkino on 11 March. In a collision with an ammunition train, the front control car was pushed onto to the tank-carrier car. On the next day they successfully supported the infantry in a breakthrough to Jawkino, but the armored train took two hits in the command car, in which the commander was wounded. After returning to Wodopoj it turned out that the workshops (and the still-unfinished PZ 28 with them) had been evacuated to Odessa already. While the locomotive of PZ 30, likewise damaged, went there for repairs, the combat train again had to escort a transport train to Lozkino on 15 March and then go on to Marjunka. Only on the 16th did it move back over the Bug to the connecting line from Nikolajew to Odessa near Trichaty, and was then in Kortschinskoje, from which artillery actions to the Bug front took place. The cars damaged on 11-12 March were sent to Odessa for repairs. From 20 to 26 March the combat train was in Dombrova Verde for aircraft protection (the quarters train was in Kolosowka). On 27 March the line to Odessa was successfully regained; the train stayed there for three days and received its now-repaired cars (armored locomotive and car) again. On 29 March it was supposed to go on via Rasdelnaja and Tiraspol, but because of the hopelessly jammed line (evacuation trains from the north (Birsula) and south (Odessa) met in Rasdelnaja) the train remained in Eremejewka until 2 April. On 3 April it could finally get to Tiraspol, but turned around when the news arrived that the Russians had broken into the railroad junction town of Rasdelnaja.

They could be driven back again; PZ 30 returned to Eremejewka with a freight train hitched on. In the night of 3-4 April PZ 70 had to enter Rasdelnaja from the north. On that morning the Soviets again launched an assault on Rasdelnaja, and the departure of the trains from the congested station was prevented from 7:00 to 10:30 AM by an accident before the next station, Macis, in the direction of Tiraspol. Even after this line was reopened, only a single hospital train could escape, for shortly after 11:00 the Russians fired a rocket launcher salvo right into the north end of the railroad station. A train just about to leave had to move back, whereby two cars were derailed and not only blocked the exit completely but also took the field of fire on the attacking Soviets away from PZ 70 and twelve A/A cars near it. After the southern exit—in the direction of Odessa—had meanwhile been blocked by Russian tanks and cavalry troops, a panic flight from the railroad station began; PZ 70—as well as the A/A cars—had to be blown up, but the crew was able to get through to the west. PZ 30 received an order on 4 April to hold the railroad station at Karpowo until the XLIV. Army Corps still to the east had passed through. On the morning of 6 April the armored train encountered Russian tanks while on a scouting trip near Eremejewka; around noon they had also reached Karpowo, and in the fight that developed there, the locomotive of the armored train (57 1504) was shot to pieces, the rest of the train was damaged, but the disembarked infantry along with eastern riders, and supported by the separately set-up combat cars of

PZ 30 in Tiraspol early in April 1944. Photo: H. Schaarschmidt/W. Sawodny collection

On April 13, 1943, PZ 30 was the last train to cross the Dnjestr-Liman on the ferry southwest of Odessa.

Left: On April 6, 1944, the locomotive of PZ 30, 57 1504, was hit by four tank shells (the photo shows one, to the left of the engine-driver) and put out of action. Photo: H. Plangemann/W. Sawodny collection

the armored train, were able to hold the site until, in the night of 7-8 April, units of the XLIV. Army Corps got through. In the return trip on the morning of April 8, the disembarked infantry, supported by the armored train's heavy weapons, had to fight off another enemy attack. Early the next morning they left Odessa, after blowing up the quarters train, in the direction of the Dnjestr-Liman, so as to cross it on the railroad ferry to Akkerman. In the huge jam that had formed there, they could only move forward slowly — constant air attacks caused losses — until on the afternoon of 13 April they could finally become the last train to leave the eastern shore of the Dnjestr. The newly repaired PZ 28 had chosen the same route out of Odessa a few days before. Both trains reached the Armored Train Replacement Battalion in Rembertow at the end of April or beginning of May 1944 by way of Romania and Hungary.

On 8 April the Russians also began to attack Crimea. At the Perekop narrows the line protection train "Michael" and the provisional A/A armored train of the 9th A/A Division supported the defense between Armjansk and Budanowka, against which the enemy could gain ground only slowly. The A/A armored train was hit by a bomb and had to be withdrawn for a day. Farther to the east, though, the enemy was able to break through over the Siwasch and was already approaching the rail line to Dschankoj east of Magasinka on 10 April. "Michael" and the A/A armored train went into action here as well, but then had to withdraw quickly when they were threatened with being cut off by the loss of Dschankoj on 11 April. The Soviet advance along the rail line to Sarabus could at least be delayed slightly. While the line protection train "Michael" withdrew farther to Simferopol, the A/A armored train supported the defense of Sarabus, was surrounded there and had to be abandoned when its crew broke out on 14 April. On that day "Michael" took part in fighting around Bachtschissaraj, and on the next day it occupied the high position on the south edge of the Belbek Valley. Its last station was the tunnel before the railroad station at Mekensiewy Gory. From here it moved farther ahead on the high ridge to fire on the Belbek

Valley, particularly, of course, after the Russians had begun the final attack on Sewastopol on 5 May. While the north front at the Belbek Valley was held, the enemy achieved a breakthrough at the Sapun Heights in the south on May 7, which compelled a withdrawal. On 8-9 May the quarters train of the line protection train "Michael" and a lot of other rolling stock was pushed into a ravine over a ramp, the combat train was placed in a tunnel near Mekensiewy Gory and blown up along with it. The crew moved back via Sebastopol to the Chersones peninsula, where on 11 May a group of some 20 men, along with the commander were picked up by a naval lighter and taken across to Romania.

On the north wing of Army Group South, the XLVII. Armored Corps had been transferred to the southeast into the Berditschew region after the successful Soviet attack east of Schitomir on December 24, 1943. The Russians utilized the weakness of the 4th Armored Army's left wing — the XIII. Army Corps was around Schitomir the LIX. around Korosten, neither was especially strong; to the north of them, until the 2nd Army of Army Group Center connected with them at the Pripjet Marshes, there was just a thin veil of securing forces — to make a massive assault in that direction too. It quickly spread westward along the Korosten — Sarny — Kowel line; Korosten fell on 29 December, Olewsk on 3 January, and Sarny was already in enemy hands on 10 January. PZ 7, located in the Korosten area, was involved in the defensive fighting from the start; after being damaged by a mine explosion while on a securing run between Olewsk and Belokorowitschi on December 17, 1943, it was again drawn into the affray in the fighting around Sarny. Then it was sent home for a thorough rebuilding. With that the history of one of the first armored trains, a former rail protection train that, basically still consisting of the same cars, that had been in the war since the failed surprise attack on the bridge near Dirschau on September 1, 1939, and in the past year — beginning with the defense at the Tschir bend, through the action near Rostow, in the Donez Basin, the successful defense of Sinelnikowo and, since November, the changing battles around

In the winter of 1943-44, PZ 10 was in the Sarny region, as of the beginning of February 1944 in Kowel. Photo: W. Pflaumbaum/W. Sawodny collection

Korosten—was found again and again at focal points in the war's events--ended for the time.—PZ 10, stationed in Sarny since June 1943, had secured not only the Cholm—Kowel—Sarny—Korosten line but also the Rowno—Sarny—Luniniec connecting line against the much-increased partisan activities, seems not to have been involved in the combat events, but to have been taken back previously. From February 5, 1944, on it was subordinated to the von dem Bach Battle Group in Kowel, to which the enemy had already approached as far as Styr and Stochod. The Soviets had thus not only advanced more than 300 km to the west, but had also expanded their breakthrough area to the north, where they had advanced west of Mosyr to the Pripjet (which—as will be shown later—led Army Group Center to transfer armored trains to the Brest—Pinsk—Luniniec—Ptitsch rail line) and to the south. The latter soon led them to the Kowel—Rowno—Schepetowka—Berditschew line, which they had already broken east of Schepetowka on January 8, 1944. PZ 69 had moved back there from Berditschew. It secured the line, extensively emptied of troops, from Schepetowka to Rowno, from the latter of which Armored Trains 11 (stationed in Rowno since the end of December 1943, subordinated to the combat commander in Zdolbunow) and 71 (newly arrived on Jamuary 12, 1944) came toward it. While PZ 69 was transferred from Schepetowka to Proskurow to secure the line from there to Tarnopol at the beginning of February, PZ 11 and 71 got into the battle with the approach of the Russians to Rowno at the end of January. At first they had to move back from Iwaczkowo, on

31 January also from Zdolbunow. While PZ 11 went to Dubno, PZ 71 covered the blowing up of the Rowno—Zdolbunow line on February 1 and was between Ulbarow and Zdolbunow a day later, where on 3 February it took part in fighting off a Russian attack east of Glinsk. On 4-5 February the two armored trains again brought a supply train to Zdolbunow, but on the 5th the city was finally evacuated. On the 6th PZ 71 blew up the bridge north of Lipa; then the armored trains covered the withdrawal to Dubno with artillery support and defense against enemy attacks. After the front had stabilized before that city, both trains remained in the Dubno—Brody—Krasne region for securing. Since artisan activity had meanwhile—as always—spread out behind the German front and grown considerably stronger, especially in the area northwest of Lemberg, the training armored train of the Replacement Battalion, as Armored Train "R" (after the first name of the commander, Captain Rolf Henning) was subordinated to the OFK 395 (Lemberg) on 10 February for service on the Lemberg—Sapiezanka and Lemberg—Krasne lines; in its place, PZ 71 was transferred to the area northeast of Tarnopol (Maksymowka—Zbaraz) to fight partisans.

As of February 27, 1944, the Russians began to push to the south and southwest from the Jampol area on the upper Horyn; their attack quickly took the form of a breakthrough. Soon they approached Tarnopol and the rail line east of it (to Proskurow) from the northeast. PZ 71, then stationed in Zbaraz, made a scouting trip to Mosurowce, and on the next day the train's disembarked infantry

PZ 11 operated in the Zdolbunow region in January 1944. Photo: R. Lorscheidt/W. Sawodny collection

In mid-January 1944 PZ 11 was joined by the new PZ 71 in the Zdolbunow region. Photo: H. Griebl collection

In one of their joint actions, the Panhard scout car of PZ 71 got between the armored trains and was thrown off the rails along with the control car. Photo: G. Beschorner/W. Sawodny collection

encountered strong enemy forces east of that town and had to retreat; on the same evening, enemies who had already broken through to Zbaraz were fought. In the morning twilight of 6 March, PZ 71, lurking at the railroad station in Zbaraz, came into combat with Russian tanks. After changing locomotives in Kurniki, it advanced toward Zbaraz again, along with assault guns, but was halted at the edge of the woods west of the city by enemy tanks, which shot down the locomotive. The mobile part of the train was towed back firing, the part left behind was secured by infantry and could be recovered during the following night. PZ 71 escorted a transport to Jezierna on 7 March and then went on to Krasne, where it was repaired hastily. In its place, PZ "R" was moved forward from the Lemberg area. On 7 March it also attacked Zbaraz, but also had to withdraw to Tarnopol after a costly fight with Russian tanks. On 3 March PZ 11 had already been transferred from Tarnopol to Podwoloczyska in the direction of Proskurow; a day later PZ 69 also arrived there from Proskurow, being able to use the line still unhindered. A scouting advance of PZ 69 on 5 March led to Wojtizi, but the enemy had already approached to within a few kilometers of the line. In the night Wolotschisk and Frydrychowka were secured. A new advance of both armored trains on the next morning showed that the enemy east of Wolotschisk had already crossed the line with strong tank forces. After a short fight, the armored trains moved back to secure the bridge over the Zbrucz west of Podwoloczyska. Toward evening there came the news that the Russians were already on the line west of Podwoloczyska. The two armored trains set out at once, moving side by side on the two-track line and received heavy fire from Rosochowaciec and Bogdanowka.

Returning it from all their guns, they were able to break through to Maksymowka. On 7 March the armored trains attacked Bogdanowka but could not capture it and withdrew to Maksymowka. When PZ 69 wanted to go to Tarnopol for supplies, it turned out that the Soviets had already blocked the line between Stryjowka and Kujdance with infantry and antitank guns. Firing from all its guns, it was able to push through, but took several hits. It immediately radioed PZ 11, which set out immediately and—warned in advance—was able to take the antitank-gun barrage under destructive fire. So it too was able to break through. While PZ 11 remained to secure the line north of Romanowka, but withdrew to Berezowica before the attacking Russians on 8 March, PZ 69 was transferred northward from Tarnopol on that day, since the enemy had already arrived on the Sereth and threatened to break the line to Krasne and Lemberg. Along with PZ 71, which had just arrived with a transport of reinforcements from Krasne, they drove the enemies out of Biala, held them down near Czystylow and secured the road and river bridges. PZ 69 had to go back to take on water and, since the railroad station and yards in Tarnopol were destroyed, went to Berezowica, where it met PZ 11. On the night of 8-9 March the Soviets surprisingly burst into Tarnopol itself. The commander of PZ "R" (which was at the northern edge of town), Captain Henning, wanted to scout the situation in the morning twilight, but was captured with the three men who accompanied him. The train itself was able to go northward out of the city; a planned relief attack from that direction, in which PZ 71 was also to take part, did not happen. PZ 69 too, which tried to reach the railroad station in Tarnopol from the south, could not get through. Yet it was possible

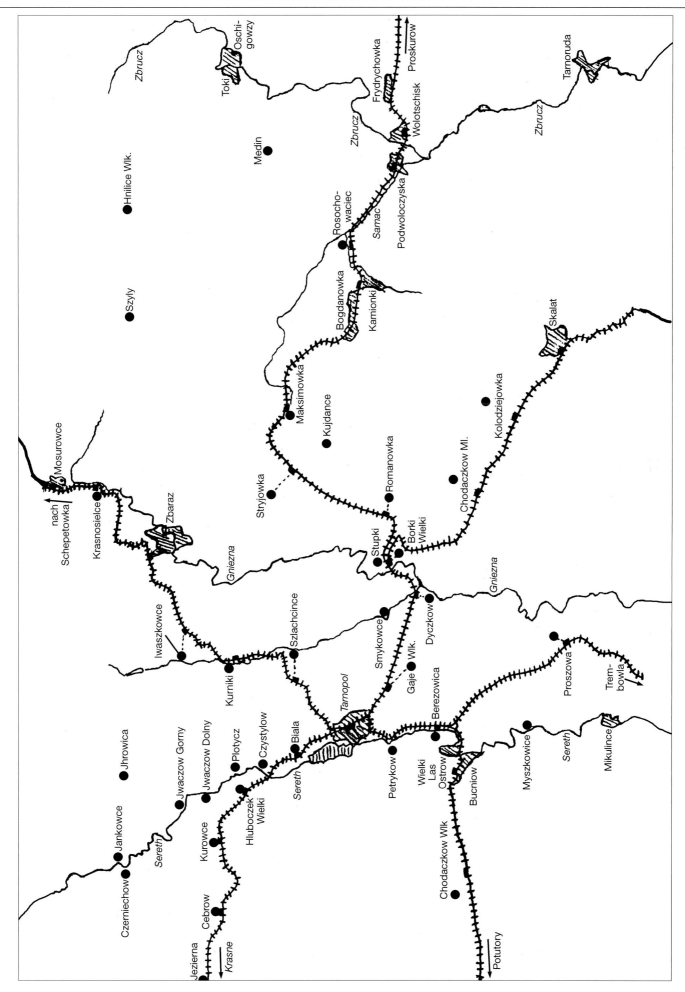

The Tarnopol battle area (March 1944).

An armored train in night action in the Ukraine early in 1944. Photo: Federal Archives, Koblenz

PZ 11 took part in the heavy fighting in the Tarnopol region in March 1944. Photo: H. J. Roddewig/W. Sawodny collection

to throw the enemy out of the city on that day. On the trip back to Berezowica, PZ 69 was fired on by Soviet units that approached the runway and railroad line from the east; later they crossed them and, turning southward, pushed forward to Wielki Las just north of Ostrow and Bucniow. PZ 69 then got acquainted with the situation in that region but had to return to Potutory for overhauling.

On the morning of 10 March the Soviets pushed into Biala (north of Tarnopol) again. The armored trains No. 71 and "R," that were at the bend in the track near Hluboczek Wielki, naturally attacked but could not drive the enemy away. So the line from Tarnopol to Krasne now remained blocked for the duration and was in German hands only from the north to the Sereth bridge. The two armored trains remained at their appointed station in Jezierna and went at the enemy forces on the east shore of the Sereth from Biala to Ihrowica with frequent artillery fire. On 13 March, with the help of the armored trains, a Russian breakthrough near Kurowce could be disposed of. Then one of the armored trains always took up securing positions in that town. On 17 March PZ 71 was called away, though, to secure the transport of relief troops from Cholm for the surrounded Kowel. For the next few days PZ "R" did its service alone. After the Russian breakthrough farther to the north, it set out for Jezierna on 22 March. Since its armored locomotive had become damaged and needed major repairs, this train was also withdrawn and returned to the Armored Train Replacement Battalion in Rembertow.

South of Tarnopol efforts were made on 11 March to clean out the Russian breakthrough near Patrykow. PZ 11, firing all its weapons, moved northward from Berezowica but stopped before an explosion site. The further attack from there was supported by flank fire and

was able to cause the Russians, fleeing back from Petrykow, major losses. The Soviets located at Wielki Las attacked southward again for relief and threatened the line, especially the bridges near Ostrow. A driveshaft on the locomotive of PZ 69, called in from Potutory, broke, so it had to go in for repairs again. Thus PZ 11 had to clean out the situation north of Ostrow, which succeeded. On the evening of 13 March it reported that in the constant combat of the past three days it had used 1300 rounds of artillery, 2600 A/A shells and 4000 machine gun bullets. On 14 March the explosion damage north of Berezowica was repaired. PZ 11 went to Tarnopol and was to go eastward immediately to take part in an attack by the 359th Infantry Division. But the train soon stopped before mines and explosion sites that had to be disposed of first. This also happened to PZ 69, which likewise arrived in Tarnopol on the evening of 14 March. Since the line repair work was being done slowly, both armored trains at first could only support the 359th Infantry Division's attack with artillery. When PZ 11 came back to Berezowica to take on water on 16 March, it found the railroad station deserted and had to be towed to Denysow. On 17 March it could finally advance into the captured Borki Wielki. PZ 69, on the other hand, was readied at the northern edge of Tarnopol for an intended attack toward Zbaraz, which then did not take place. Instead of that, on 18 March it relieved PZ 11 in Borki Wielki, which was transferred via Potutory, Lemberg, Krasne, and Brody to Rudnja, and was there posted in a cut by the railroad bridge. On the morning of 21 March the Russians attacked. At first PZ 69 had to withstand eight air attacks of up to 30 low-level fighters each with cover, which it was able to do without being damaged. Then it successfully took the enemy forces, who had already pushed

While the other armored trains in service there were withdrawn at the right time, PZ 69 remained immobile east of Tarnopol on 22 March and was blown up by the crew. Photo: W. Sawodny collection

into Stupki and Borki Wielki, under fire, and brought them to a stop. It covered the later withdrawal with fire from all its weapons, and thus moved back to the bridge north of Dyczkow. Meanwhile the enemy advanced southwestward from Smykovce toward the rail line with infantry covered by tanks. The armored train opposed them. In the vigorous firefight the rear A/A car was set afire. The armored train tried to depart in the direction of Tarnopol, but was stopped by an explosion under the locomotive (a dud bomb?) at the level of the village of Gaje Wielki. The loco and several cars were derailed. The train stood there fully exposed to enemy fire and was shot to pieces. The disembarked crew, though, could at first protect the train from being taken by the Russians. It was even possible in the night of 21-22 March to recover the front control, tank-carrier and A/A cars, though they were damaged. When the Germans withdrew further on the evening of 22 March, the burned-out and shot-up remainder of the train was blown up and the crew taken back to the quarters train, which departed for Rembertow. When Tarnopol, declared a "firm place" (an absurd new idea of Hitler's—the troops in such places were supposed to hold out to the last man, even when enclosed and surrounded—by which he hoped to stabilize the German eastern front, which was compelled to retreat again and again because of their inferior forces) was surrounded on 24 March, not one of the four armored trains subordinated to the combat commander 16 days before was still present.

Two of them had been transferred to other "firm places". PZ 11 was before Brody, where the locomotive had been shot up already during the defensive fighting on 19 March, so that it had to be towed away. Of course even then it could not be released for the urgently needed workshop visit that the commander had already requested on 25 February. Because of the heightened partisan activity in the area northeast of Lemberg, it had to continue to do securing tasks in place of the departed training PZ "R," meanwhile badly damaged in the fighting around Tarnopol, until at the end of April it was finally relieved by the newly summoned PZ 63 in Sapiezanka and could be sent to the Lemberg OAW for repairs.

PZ 10 had already been assigned to the other town declared a "firm place," Kowel, which was defended only by weak police units, at the beginning of February 1944. At first it secured to the east (action at Bielin on 25 February and Poworsk on 4 March). During the March offensive the Soviets also moved toward this city. The action of PZ 10 near Maczejow (west of Kowel) on 16 March could not prevent the meeting of their pincer arms and the surrounding of Kowel. The train itself remained inside the narrow pocket and gave the weak occupiers its best artillery support, but soon ran short of

ammunition. Its movements drew enemy fire to it, and on 21 March two cars of the train were fully destroyed by a direct bomb hit; the others (there was only one intact gun on hand) remained in action but were gradually put out of action by enemy fire. Then the armored train's crew took part in infantry action to defend Kowel. From 26 March to 5 April, on which the relief forces broke the ring around Kowel, they had four more dead, five badly and 21 slightly wounded to report. Although several cars of the armored train were still on hand after the liberation, it was not restored again. The relief forces for Kowel, brought in from Cholm, were very hindered in their movements by strong partisan forces east of the Bug, so the rail line was blown up again and again. Thus PZ 71 was called in from the Tarnopol region to secure the line and the transports running on it. It took on this task on 21 March, but was damaged by low-level planes in Luboml on 27 March and by bombs in Paryduby on 31 March, and after the liberation of Kowel it had to the railroad works in Lublin for repairs.—The Russian advance in the Kowel region aroused fears

PZ 10 was enclosed in Kowel in mid-March 1944 and supported the defenders with its artillery fire until it was put out of action by bombs and shells. Photo: Federal Archives, Koblenz

of a further advance, also northwestward toward Brest-Litovsk. The Army Group Center, to which the Kowel combat zone had been added anyway at the end of March, thus gathered the greater part of their armored trains in the Brest—Pinsk region, which will be dealt with later.

The greatest military disaster seemed to be taking form east of Tarnopol at the end of March 1944. Between the Russian forces that had crossed the Dnjestr on 18-19 March in the gap between the 8th Army and the 1st Armored Army between Jampol and Mogilew-Podolsk and then pushed forward to the west, almost unhindered, between the Dnjestr and Pruth, and those who had broken through southward east of Tarnopol from 21 March on, had already reached the Dnjestr north of Horodenka on 24 March and, after crossing it on 29 March, had been between Czernowitz and Kolomea on the Pruth, the entire 1st Armored Army was threatened with encirclement. PZ 62, being in their territory, was sent from Proskurow via Jarmolinzy

to the Husiatyn—Czortkow region to oppose the second pincer arm, but was pushed to the west, in the direction of Stanislau, by the superior Russian forces. Opposite the enemy troops who were also following in that direction, it was able to retake the railroad junction at Chryplin. Following this, it secured the transport of relief troops coming in on the line from Lemberg and took part in counterattacks southeast of Stanislau, which finally resulted in the 1st Armored Army regaining contact with the German forces to the west and thus being able to avoid defeat. On 17 April PZ 62 had to survive another costly battle near Czerniejow; after repairs it stayed—subordinated to the 1st Hungarian Army—on the line from Stanislau to the Tatar Pass threatened by the enemy forces west of Kolomea.

With the relief of Kowel and the integration of the pushed-back 1st Armored Army, the southern sector of the German eastern front became quiet for several weeks in April. For the armored trains, the balance for the first quarter of 1944 (counted from December 25, 1943, to include the loss of PZ 31) was certainly depressing. Of the eight armored trains on hand at the beginning date (No. 7, 10, 11, 28, 31, 62, 69, and 70) and the subsequent additions (No. 71, 30, R, and 63), Armored Trains No. 31, 69, and 70 were total losses, No. 7, 10, 11, 28, 30, 71, and R were so damaged that at least weeks-long if not months-long repairs were necessary (PZ 10 and the Training Armored Train "R" were obviously not repaired at all). Thus in mid-April there remained only two armored trains, No. 62 (southeast of Lemberg on the Chodorow—Stanislau—Tatar Pass line) and 63 (northeast of Lemberg, stationed in Sapiezanka; at the beginning of May it was occupied near Kamionka—Strumilowa with blocking the rail line in fighting against the Naumov partisan group, known by their long march—always in the hinterlands of the German front withdrawing toward the west—from Sumy via Poltawa, Kiev, and Schitomir to the area west of Brody). The establishment of a regimental staff in Army Group South to direct the armored trains (since the end of March, Northern Ukraine) that was planned for the spring of 1944 was thus illusory and had to be postponed for months.

In the territory of Army Group Center, the armored trains remained in their previous sectors, not involved in the Kursk battle at the beginning of July 1943: PZ 61 (along with the line protection trains "Blücher". "Werner" and No. 83) with the 3rd Armored Army in the Polozk—Witebsk—Newel triangle, PZ 27 with the 203rd Securing

PZ 62 in action southeast of Stanislau early in April 1944.
Photo: A. Popp/W. Sawodny collection

In a hard fight, PZ 62 was able to regain the railroad station at Chryplin. Photo: A. Popp/W. Sawodny collection

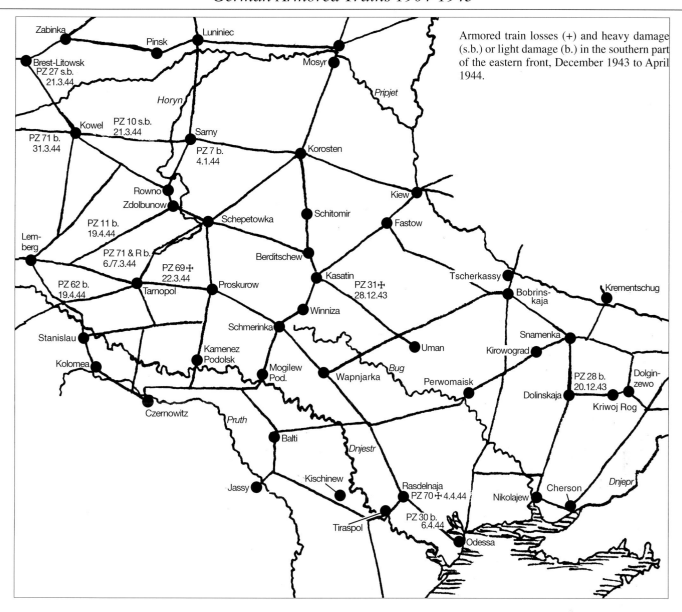

Zabinka
Pinsk
Brest-Litowsk
PZ 27 s.b.
21.3.44
Luniniec
Mosyr
Horyn
Pripjet
Kowel
PZ 10 s.b.
21.3.44
Sarny
PZ 71 b.
31.3.44
PZ 7 b.
4.1.44
Korosten
Rowno
Zdolbunow
Kiew
Schepetowka
Schitomir
Fastow
PZ 11 b.
19.4.44
Lem-berg
Berditschew
PZ 71 & R b.
6./7.3.44
PZ 69 ✚
22.3.44
Kasatin
Tscherkassy
Krementschug
PZ 62 b.
19.4.44
Tarnopol
Proskurow
PZ 31 ✚
28.12.43
Bobrins-kaja
Winniza
Schmerinka
Snamenka
Stanislau
Kamenez Podolsk
Uman
Kirowograd
Kolomea
Mogilew Pod.
Wapnjarka
Bug
Perwomaisk
PZ 28 b.
20.12.43
Dolgin-zewo
Czernowitz
Pruth
Dolinskaja
Kriwoj Rog
Balti
Dnjestr
Jassy
Kischinew
Rasdelnaja
PZ 70 ✚ 4.4.44
Cherson
Dnjepr
Nikolajew
PZ 30 b.
6.4.44
Tiraspol
Odessa

Armored train losses (+) and heavy damage (s.b.) or light damage (b.) in the southern part of the eastern front, December 1943 to April 1944.

Division in Schlobin, Armored Trains No. 2 and 4 in the Brjansk region (the latter stationed in Schukowka), PZ 21 on the southwest corner of the Kursk salient, and close to the dividing line with Army Group South; PZ 3, stationed in Sebesch has already been sent to the homeland on 13 July because of serious damage from mines in partisan action. The Russian attack on the 2nd Armored Army in the northern part of the Orel salient, which quickly brought operations in the direction of Kursk to a standstill for the 9th Army, which was threatened from the rear, at first saw only PZ 2 in front action. From 15 to 20 July it fought hard defensive battles on the western edge of the breakthrough area between Schisdra and Bolchow, at first near Elensk (15th-16th), then near Tereben (17th-18th), finally on 20 July near Malyi Orjewo (between Tereben and Resseta), where it was able to stop an enemy attack that had already led to panic flight. The Russian spearhead then turned to the south and threatened the Brjansk—Orel rail line. Therefore not only PZ 2 was sent there (on the western part of the line), but so was PZ 61 from the zone of the 3rd Armored Army; it took up its station in Orel itself. With its help the rail line could be kept open at first, but at the end of the month the evacuation of the Orel bend had to start. PZ 61 covered the destruction of the railroad facilities in Orel itself at first, which was occupied by the Russians on 5 August, then along the line to Brjansk, where Narischkino was given up on 10 August, Karatschew on the

15th, and the new defensive position before Brjansk, the "Hagen" line, was set up on 18 August. Thus PZ 61 was given back to the 3rd Armored Army in the Witebsk region on 19 August. PZ 2, which had previously been released, had already been transferred to Unetscha for securing tasks on 15 August.

This had become necessary because since 22 July the partisans had increased their activities very sharply in the region from Sewsk to Roslawl, using not only new mines but also new tactics, with rows of explosions, thus disturbing German transport movements very seriously; many lines were knocked out for days. PZ 21, after returning from the Sumy region, which has already been noted in the context of the breakthrough near Belgorod in the area of Army Group South (see above), was transferred to Chutor-Michailowsky on 12 August. Along with many securing runs, at first especially in the direction of Nawlja, it was exposed to frequent air attacks, which did no damage other than setting one control car afire. In the second half of August 1943 Army Group Center was able to have two armored trains sent to it: the new PZ 66 was stationed on the Minsk—Orscha line on 17 August, at first in Tolotschin, then some four weeks later in Krupki; the totally rebuilt PZ 1 on 23 August in the Gomel region, where it was subordinated to the Hungarian 23rd Light Division. Both were in permanent partisan action, not only on the rail lines, but also with disembarked troops in pursuit of the enemies to the sides of the tracks.

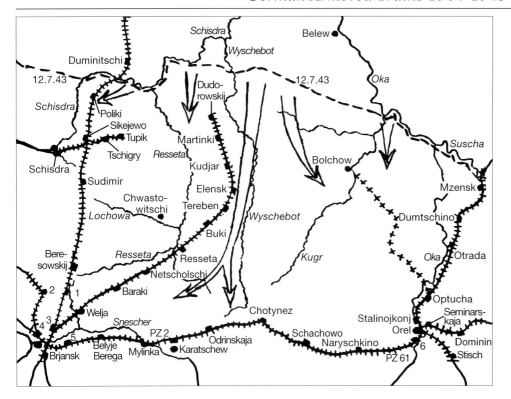

Soviet breakthrough at the 2nd Armored Army's front (July 1943), with the Brjansk—Dudorowskij branch line, not shown on many maps, on which PZ 2 operated.

- - - - - - Front line on July 12, 1943
++++++ Field rail line
1. Bagatowo
2. Fokino
3. Polpinskaja
4. Orlowsky
5. Sneschetskaja
6. Seminarskaja

PZ 21 near Wassilewitschi at the end of September 1943. Photo: H. Wenge/W. Sawodny collection

At the end of August 1943 the totally rebuilt PZ 1 came to the Gomel region. Photo: W. Sitzius/W. Sawodny collection

There it was assigned to the Hungarian 23rd Light Division, whose commander, Major General Mayjar (left), stands on the observation post of the command car of PZ 1 with the commander of the train, 1st Lt. Walter (right). Photo: H. Walter/W. Sawodny collection

Meanwhile the Soviets had extended their offensive from Army Group South border to Dorogobusch. PZ 21 moved back from Chutor-Michailowsky to the Desna overpass (and later bridgehead) of Witemlja. There it first took over the anti-aircraft securing of the bridge, then it guarded the approach from Unetscha, and in the withdrawal finally the blowing up of this line. On 10 September it set out for Newsorowo, on the 11th it made a securing run via Unetscha to Slynka and was transferred the next day to the Gomel—Bachmatsch line in the Snowskaja—Mena region. Via Gomel (Sept. 18) and Nowobelizkaja (Sept. 21) it reached Wassilewitschi, which was to remain its station for some time, on 25 September.

At the beginning of September PZ 4 was still in Schukowka. On 10 September a Russian breakthrough took place near Oslufjewo. The armored train advanced to there and first pulled a transport train with heavy bombs out of range of the Soviet weapons. Then it was able to drive the enemy back in a surprise attack from a covered waiting position and to advance 2 km beyond the town. In the ensuing hard firefight it was damaged but was able to make a quick withdrawal and escape the attempt to immobilize it by destroying the line behind it. After being hit in the locomotive's smoke chamber by antitank weapons, the train moved first into an ambush position on the Wetma

bridge and then away to Schukowka, which was also under enemy fire already. The quarters train, which was still there, was taken away to Unetscha. After exchanging fire with Russian tanks, PZ 4 slowly moved back to Brjansk on the morning of 11 September. On that evening it crossed the bridge between Brjansk I and II stations just before it was blown up (the explosive charges were already exploding in the later station as well; only one line was usable), and went on to Poluschje (Brjansk could still be held until 17 September). Later PZ 4 went to Unetscha, while PZ 2, which was there, was transferred back to Bobruisk on 23 September.

East of Smolensk, the Russians had taken Jelnja on 29 August. That was the reason that PZ 61, then with the 3rd Armored Army, was transferred to the line from Smolensk to there one day later (the line protection trains "Blücher," "Werner," and No. 83 remained to secure the Polozk—Witebsk—Newel triangle). The Soviet attack could be stopped at first, but was taken up again with increased power on 14 September. PZ 61 took part in the defense; on 18 September it was in battle between Dobromino and Pridneprowskaja. The enemies could be stopped again, but only for three days; then they renewed their attack and were soon before Smolensk, which had to be evacuated on 24 September, while the armored train covered the destruction of the rail facilities. Afterward it drew back in the direction of Witebsk before the Russians, who were advancing farther, but remained on the line from there in the direction of Rudnja.

As October began, the German front stabilized for several weeks ahead of the Witebsk—Orscha—Mogilew—Gomel line despite further Russian attacks. This and the arrival of armored trains No. 2, 4, and 21 in the region west of Gomel, as part of the withdrawal, allowed a rearrangement of their assignments, which was especially necessary because of the continuing partisan "rail war" against the supply lines of the front troops. Thus PZ 1, formerly stationed in Gomel, was transferred to the Bobruisk—Ossipowitschi region, but replaced there in mid-October by Armored Trains No. 2 (in Bobruisk until 27 October, then in Ossipowitschi) and No. 4 (securing the Ossipowitschi—Minsk line). They carried out a series of operations—sometimes working together—against the partisans operating there, in which PZ 4 was damaged in the Talka region on 8-9 November and then was sent home for a total rebuilding. PZ 1, after a short stay in the Pripjet district (Pinsk), was stationed on the Molodetschno—Polozk line, where the partisan activity had grown much stronger, especially between Polozk and Krolewschisna after the Russian breakthrough in the Newel region (see below). PZ 1—after visiting a workshop at Dünaburg in November—was very successful in its combat; especially noteworthy is the operation "Hochszeitsreise," carried out at the beginning of December. PZ 27, formerly located in Schlobin, was already transferred back to Baranowitschi at the beginning of

On October 7, 1943, PZ 21 ran onto a mine between Retschiza and Wassilewitschi, seriously damaging the cars in the front half of the train. The armored ammunition bunker and crew compartment for the A/A gun on the low-side car are easy to see. Photo: A. Schwipp/W. Sawodny collection

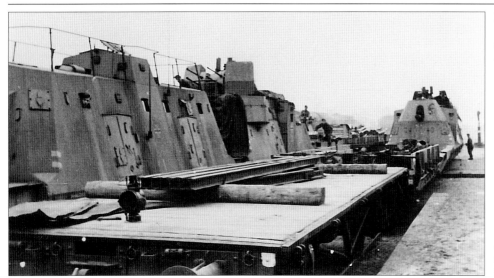

In October 1943 PZ 66 (with Army Group Center since August) and the newly delivered PZ 67 met on the Minsk—Orscha line. Photo: W. Hahn/W. Sawodny collection

Below: PZ 66 in Prijamino (Minsk—Orscha line) at the end of 1943. Photo: J. Kenter/W. Sawodny collection

October to secure the line from there toward Minsk as well as to Luniniec.—PZ 21 was in Wassiliewitschi at first to guard the rail line between Kalinkowitschi and Gomel. On 7 October it hit a mine on the way back from Retschiza, and three cars were badly damaged. On 10 October it was transferred to Kalinkowitschi, and from then on it essentially ran on the line from Luniniec to Wassiliewitschi.

As for the armored trains No. 61 and 66 as well as the line protection trains "Blücher, "Werner," and No. 83, everything remained as before at first, but the three line protection trains were now under the 201st Securing Division and used to guard the Dünaburg—Polozk—ahead of Witebsk line after the Newel district had been assigned to Army Group North. Early in October the newly finished PZ 67 was sent in. At first it was kept in the Molodetschno—Minsk area. Thus armored trains were now on all Army Group Center's important approach lines.

- Dünaburg—Polozk—before Witebsk line with branches to Newel: line protection trains "Blücher", "Werner" and No. 83, PZ 61.
- (Wilna)—Molodetschno—Minsk—Ossipowitschi—Schlobin—Gomel line with branches: Armored Trains No. 67, 4, and 2.
- Molodetschno—Polozk line: PZ 1.
- (Brest)—Baranowitschi—Minsk—Orscha line: Armored Trains No. 27 and 66.

PZ 68, which reached the 2nd Army new in mid-November 1943, was badly damaged already in a fight with the advancing Soviets on the 18th. The locomotive was shot up and unable to run, two combat cars burned out; here the destroyed command car is shown. Photo: O. Holbein/W. Sawodny collection

- (Brest)—Luniniec—Kalinkowitschi—Gomel line: PZ 21.

But this pause in the war's events at the front lasted only briefly. After the Russian offensive over the Dnjepr north of Kiev at the beginning of November 1943 proceeded well over a large area, it was extended into the territory of the German 2nd Army from the 1st White Russian front by an attack to the northwest from 10 November on. On 15 November the Kalinkowitschi—Gomel rail line was already broken, the Russian tank spearhead approached the Schlobin—Kalinkowitschi line south of the Beresina crossing near Schazilki. On the same day PZ 2 was transferred there from Ossipowitschi for bridge securing. In place of PZ 4, sent to the homeland for rebuilding shortly before, the new PZ 68 was immediately sent into battle ahead of Kalinkowitschi. On 18 November it had its baptism of fire near Wassilewitschi. Its locomotive was destroyed by several hits and two cars were set afire. But the engine driver was able to bring a civil (so-called "black") loco from the nearest railroad station to the rear and haul the rest of the train back (the badly damaged cars could also be recovered later in the course of a counterthrust). But there was no time for repairs. Later equipped with a replacement armored locomotive, the remainder of PZ 68 joined PZ 2 at the Beresina bridge near Schazilki. On 23 November the Russians had already crossed the rail line south of Schazilki and surrounded a grenadier battalion in the Scherd—Ostankowitschi region. In a joint operation, the two armored trains were able to break through to it the next day, pick it up and bring it back through the Soviet lines. The next day the Russians took the town and railroad station of Schazilki. PZ 2 supported the counterattack in a successful recapture, but was damaged and immobilized by shots to the locomotive, but could be brought back by PZ 68.

But the damaged cars could be recovered later; here they are being taken away. Photo: O. Holbein/W. Sawodny collection

The rest of PZ 68 remained in service with the spare armored locomotive 93 220 (with auxiliary tender). Photo: Federal Archives, Koblenz

Along with PZ 2 (right), PZ 68 (left) at first protected the Beresina crossing near Schazilki. Photo: G. Tomascewski/W. Sawodny collection

Below: On November 24, 1943, they were able to liberate a surrounded grenadier battalion south of there. Photo: O. Holbein/W. Sawodny collection

Later PZ 2 (and probably PZ 68) saw service in the withdrawal fighting between the Beresina and Schlobin, but the Russians halted their attack around the end of the month. Thus PZ 2 was moved back to Starye Dorogi on December 20, 1943, to secure the Ossipowitschi—Sluzk line, PZ 68 was sent to join PZ 21, which had played no role in the previous defensive battles, on the Luniniec—Kalinkowitschi Pripjet line (later brought back to Ptitsch) to fight the very active partisans there.

The 3rd Armored Army, in the northernmost zone of Army Group Center, between Smolensk and Newel, had at first been spared from attacks in the summer of 1943. Only in the process of moving its neighbor to the south, the 4th Army, from Smolensk to Witebsk at the end of September 1943 did it—at first undisturbed by the enemy—have to move back to the west. The Newel district had been assigned to Army Group North on 14 September. Just at this new boundary line south of Newel did the Soviets go on the offensive on 6 October, and they were not only able to take the city on the same day, but also to tear a gap between the two army groups, which led to the backward bending of their wings—that of Army Group Center pointing northward and extending westward. The Soviets constantly tried to extend this breakthrough to the west and south, so that along with the rail line from Witebsk toward Newel, the one running there from Polozk would also come into their action area soon. To what extent the three line protection trains ("Blücher", "Werner" and No. 83)—subordinated to the 201st Securing Division—were involved in the defensive fighting is not known. Of the regular armored trains, No. 67, which had already been advanced from the Molodetschno—Minsk region to the Orscha area, was taken via Witebsk to the line running toward Newel until north of Gorodok to support a barricade with its artillery. After just a few days, though, it was transferred to the line north of Polozk, along which the Russians also tried to advance. On 2 November it was in battle near Turitschino and was hit by an antitank shell, which cost it five dead and ten wounded. In the subsequent defensive fighting it was repeatedly able not only to liberate already enclosed troop units in counterattacks (sometimes in cooperation with the line protection train "Blücher"), but to use its heavy weapons to allow the German troops to hold a narrow lane, about 25 km long, along the rail line and parallel road between Polota and Dretun, in the midst of enemy-occupied land, for several weeks (until mid-January 1944). In this period (November-December) the line protection train "Blücher" ran into the stopped PZ 67 one night. While PZ 67 remained largely undamaged, "Blücher" fell down a railroad embankment and was so badly damaged that it then had to be built completely new at the Dünaburg EAW. The base of PZ 67 at that time was Polozk. When on January 10, 1944, the

aforementioned front lane to north of Polota was evacuated and the area around Polozk was likewise assigned to Army Group North, the armored train was also assigned to it, but remained in service on the Polozk—Polota line.

PZ 61, still with the 4th Army west of Witebsk at the beginning of November, was to be transferred to Mogilew to fight partisans on 3 November, but the critical situation in the area north of Witebsk made it necessary to turn it over to the 3rd Armored Army instead. It first replaced the withdrawn PZ 67 on the Witebsk—Newel line north of Gorodok (see above).

When the Russians crossed the rail line from Witebsk to Polozk in the Lowscha—Obol area at the end of November, it took part in

As of the end of October 1943, PZ 67 saw service in the area north of Polozk. A bore explosion badly damaged a gun turret. Photo: W. Hahn/W. Sawodny collection

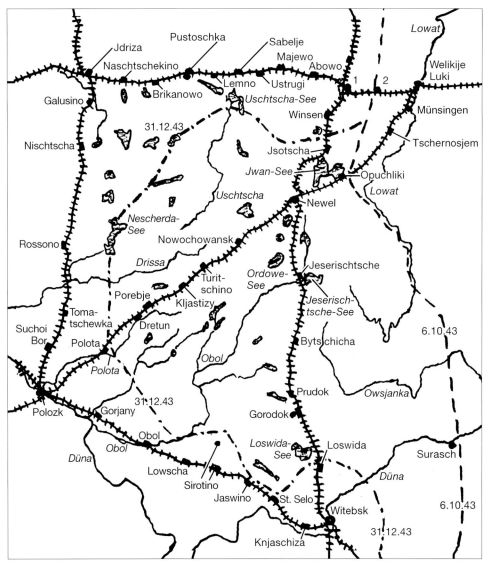

The Newel—Witebsk—Polozk battle area.
Front line:
-- -- -- -- -- --: October 6, 1943
-- . -- . -- . --: December 31, 1943
1. Nowosokolniki
2. Peschischtsche

In the winter of 1943-44, PZ 61 had heavy defensive combat to bear again and again. As of the beginning of 1944, the armored trains were so camouflaged with trees and shrubs in combat so that details of the trains can scarcely be recognized. Photo: W. Sawodny collection

On December 7, 1943, the first of the captured Russian gun railcars, PT 17, was assigned to it. In the middle is its commander, 1st Lt. Warda. Photo: Federal Archives, Koblenz

its liberation—along with PZ 67, which had also been sent there for a short time from the region north of Polozk. PZ 61—reinforced by the assigned PT 17 on 7 December—also remained afterward on this constantly endangered line, which ran so near the front that the normal rail traffic had to be halted on 1 November. Again and again it had to fight off enemy attacks that reached to the rail line or even across it. Only on January 17, 1944, did the Russians give up their attacks on the 3rd Armored Army.

Although the Russian breakthrough near Newel early in October 1943 was also aimed at the right flank of the 16th Army of Army Group North and the left of the 3rd Armored Army, the action of PZ 51, stationed north of Nowosokolniki, was undisturbed by it. From then on it went from its station, Tschichatschewo, to its line-securing and partisan-fighting tasks between Dno and Suschtschewo. Sometimes it was also in action on the line from Pleskau via Dno in the direction of Staraja Russa, as on 13 November near Porchow and on 27 November near Morino, where it was able to drive off a partisan attack on the railroad station. On 23 December its disembarked infantry were able to fight off an attack on Ljubony, but the armored train itself ran onto a mine, though without being seriously damaged.—With the 18th Army, PZ 63 remained on the Batezkaja—Nowinka rail line until 6 October, then it was transferred to Pleskau to secure the lines from there to Luga, Dno, and Ostrow. Around the first of the year it

was also used from Pleskau in the direction of Petseri and Dorpat (Estonia).

In mid-January 1944 the Russian offensive against Army Group North began in the Leningrad region, but also near Nowgorod. In the latter district, PZ 63 was immediately advanced from Pleskau via Luga and Batezkaja and took part in the defensive fighting with the XXXVIII. Army Corps. On 18-19 January it successfully helped in the defense of the Naschtschi railroad station, but suffered considerable losses. On 20 January—already passed by the enemy—it had to fight its way back to its own lines. Then it was used in the Batezkaja region. When the Russians broke the rail line to Dno south of that town at the end of the month, it fought near Peredolskaja on 29 January and took an antitank hit in the artillery car. PZ 51 was brought to the breakthrough site from the south and subordinated to the combat commander of Utorgosch already on 18 January. On 29 January it suffered losses in the defense of that town. North of Batezkaja too, the Soviets advanced over the rail line early in February. For reconnaissance purposes a hastily improvised "armored train"—consisting of a rail-running truck and a car armed with a 3.7-cm antitank gun—was assembled. Meanwhile the Russian troops were already approaching Luga from the north. PZ 63 was transferred there and later covered the withdrawal in the direction of Pleskau. In that city it was slightly damaged by a bomb on 18 February. Of course the front had stabilized at the beginning of March, but at the

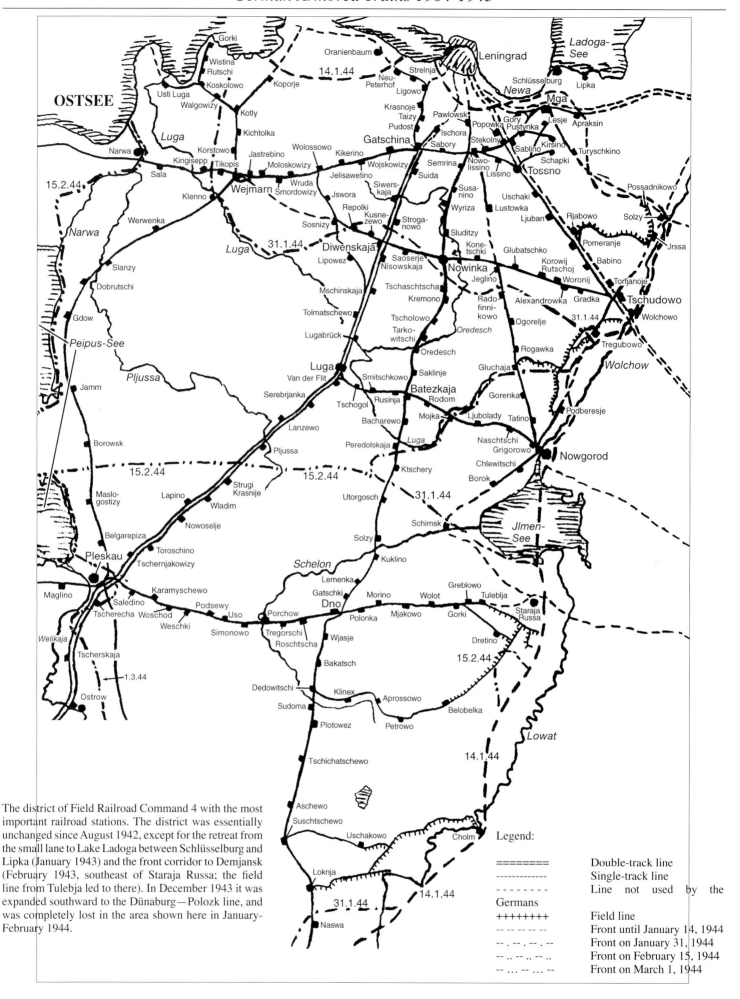

The district of Field Railroad Command 4 with the most important railroad stations. The district was essentially unchanged since August 1942, except for the retreat from the small lane to Lake Ladoga between Schlüsselburg and Lipka (January 1943) and the front corridor to Demjansk (February 1943, southeast of Staraja Russa; the field line from Tulebja led to there). In December 1943 it was expanded southward to the Dünaburg—Polozk line, and was completely lost in the area shown here in January-February 1944.

Legend:

========	Double-track line
-------------	Single-track line
- - - - - - -	Line not used by the Germans
++++++++	Field line
-- -- -- -- --	Front until January 14, 1944
-- . -- . -- . --	Front on January 31, 1944
-- .. -- .. -- ..	Front on February 15, 1944
-- ... -- ... --	Front on March 1, 1944

In the autumn of 1943 and the beginning of the following winter, PZ 51 was still to be found on the lines around Dno. Photo: M. Streit/W. Sawodny collection

Below: Here PZ 51 is coming into a large railroad station--presumably Dno—in the winter of 1943-44. Photo: M. Streit/W. Sawodny photo

called in from Polozk for a few days, but on 9 March it was already relieved by PZ 26, which had been assigned to Army Group North on February 20, 1944, after being fully rebuilt, and had first been used as an army group reserve in and around Rositten, so that No. 67 could return to its regular action area north of Polozk. PZ 26 could also be transferred to the quarters train in Sebesch on 16 March, after the front had stabilized east of Idritza. In April it replaced PZ 51 on the Idritza—Polozk line, and PZ 51 was now stationed in Rosenow and secured the Sebesch—Rosenow line, but also took over the securing from there to Dünaburg, and even occasionally from Dünaburg toward Polozk.

In Army Group Center, too, the pause in the Witebsk region did not last long. On February 3, 1944, the Russians attacked again northwest and southeast of the city. Since the combat at the second site developed unfavorably and the line south of Witebsk in the direction of Orscha was soon broken, PZ 61 was transferred there on 8 February to strengthen the defenses. After shutting off the Soviet attacks, it was taken to the Dünaburg EAW for overhauling on 22 February, where it was also rearmed with tank-destroyer cars (home-built with T 34 turrets). PZ 2 was also supposed to receive such vehicles, but that did not happen. After it had lost both gun cars in battles at the end of March, it was decided to rebuild it completely. In view of the tense situation, though, it had to hold out until the beginning of June before its transfer to the homeland wasp possible.

On February 21, 1944, the Russians advanced near Rogatschew, took the city and formed a bridgehead over the Dnjepr. PZ 66, which had been used since November 1943 not only to secure the Borissow—Orscha line but also repeatedly for partisan fighting between Orscha and Mogilew (among others, on February 13, 1944, in operation "Eisvogel" southwest of Mogilew), was brought in from the north to the breakthrough site near Lagodowa south of Stary Bychow. On the same day it was able to liberate an already surrounded regiment, and took part until 10 March, with great success, in the ever-changing

end of that month the Russians tried to move farther west between Pleskau and Ostrow. In the process, PZ 63 was damaged by artillery fire 10 km south of Pleskau on 31 March and was withdrawn for repairs. Afterward it did not return to Army Group North, but went to the southern sector of the eastern front (see there).—PZ 51 moved from Utorgosch to Dno at the beginning of February and later back to Pleskau, where it supplied rear-guard actions; as of 27 February it was transferred for securing to the Idritza—Polozk line, which was exposed to heightened partisan activity as usual, in view of the approach of the front.

The way back from Pustoschka to east of Idritza was at first covered, in the beginning of March 1944, by PZ 67, which was

During the Russian offensive in January 1944, PZ 63 had hard defensive fighting to bear on the line from Batezkaja toward Nowgorod. Photo: H. Beckmann/W. Sawodny collection

Toward the end of February 1944, Army Group North was assigned the rebuilt PZ 26, which was used at first for defense in the area east of Idritza. Photo: H. Jäger/W. Sawodny collection

On the transfer trip from the Molodetschno—Polozk line to the Soviet bridgehead near Rogatschew in February 1944, PZ 1 ran into a transport train. Photo: W. Sitzius/W. Sawodny collection

Below: PZ 2 on a securing run on the Krolewschisna—Glebokie line. Photo: G. Tomaschewski/W. Sawodny collection

defensive fighting in that area, serving as support for the hard-pressed infantry, covering the withdrawal and the accompanying track destruction, fighting off frequent air attacks and Russian attempts to cut it off. On 10 March it was transferred back to Mogilew. To the breakthrough site via Schlobin from the south there was summoned the line protection train "Polko" subordinated to the 9th Army—not the nearby PZ 2 from Ossipowitschi, as it, with its equipment that went back to 1940-41, was no longer capable of handling combat tasks under the conditions now prevailing on the eastern front, and the already modernized PZ 1, supplied in November 1943 with tank-destroyer cars (with T 34 turrets), which ran into a transport train on its way and was damaged, but still went into action (its securing tasks in the Krolewschisna—Glebokie region were now taken over by PZ 2). It was decisively involved in the defensive fighting with the 296th Infantry Division, so that the Russians could no longer expand their bridgehead from Rogatschew farther to the south; here the tank-destroyer cars proved themselves so well that they were made standard equipment for the Type BP 44 armored trains that were already being built.

The link between the 2nd Army and 4th Armored Army had never been properly restored after the Soviet attack of November 1943. The renewed Russian offensive around the change from 1943 to 1944 not only gained ground quickly to the west southward of the Pripjet, but had already expanded on 8 January to the exposed position of the 2nd Army in the Kalinkowitschi—Mosyr region. PZ 21, stationed in Schitkowitschi, suffered losses from bombing in Kopzewitschi on 13 January, in Ptitsch on 14 January, where it obviously covered

the successful withdrawal to just east of that city. Meanwhile the Russians had advanced far to the west south of the Pripjet; on 12 January they had already reached Sarny. The southern flank of the 2nd Army had thus spread to almost 200 km; the rail line leading north of the Pripjet from Brest to the east, its main supply line, was not only endangered permanently by the strong partisan bands hiding in the trackless swamp and wooded areas, but also by regular cavalry units slipping in. PZ 27, covering the western Pripjet line from Zabinka to Luniniec since the first of the year, was transferred to the line from Luniniec to the south in order to work against the Russians who were groping their way northward from Sarny.

In fact, it was able to fight off an attack on the bridge over the Horyn near the town of that name on 18 January. PZ 68 secured the line between Luniniec and Schitkowitschi, while PZ 21 was in action defending against Soviet units in the Ptitsch—Korschewka region until well into March. On 20 January PZ 27 was replaced by PZ 68 at Horyn; then it had to secure the partisan-threatened Baranowitschi— Luniniec line. On the Zabinka—Pinsk rail line after the departure of PZ 27 at the beginning of the year there was only the Hungarian line protection train "Botond," PZ 68 was transferred to Pinsk for track securing on 3 March, after the Russians had meanwhile advanced west of the Horyn to the upper course of the Pripjet.

This advance cut the rail line from Kowel to Brest-Litowsk on 15 March; a day later Kowel was surrounded. These events caused Army Group Center to fear that the Russians could move on to the big supply support point and traffic junction of Brest-Litowsk. Thus covering troops were hastily sent in, including—since they could be sent on the march especially quickly—all the usable armored trains subordinated to the army group. Thus on 17 March PZ 27, meanwhile

returned to the line east of Brest-Litowsk, was subordinated to the Combat Commander of Brest for action in the direction of Kowel. On the Pripjet line, PZ 68 was sent to Kobryn, PZ 21 to Drohitschin on 19 March; two days later the latter went to Zabinka. PZ 2 came directly from Krolewschisna to Brest. PZ 1 was transferred from the area south of Rogatschew onto the line to Beresa Kartuska, PZ 66 from south of Mogilew to Iwazewitschi; but PZ 1 was already subordinated to the OFK 399 (Brest) on 18 March.

PZ 27 undertook a reconnaissance run in the direction of Kowel on 19 March. It first ran onto a mine between Chotyslaw and Zablocie, but it continued its scouting. On the return trip on the night of 20-21 March it found itself cut off by Russian troops in Zablocie. PZ 2, which wanted to come to its aid, ran onto a mine north of Maloryto and had to turn back. When PZ 27, after fighting off constant enemy attacks, tried to break out to the south around 2:00 PM on the 21st, its locomotive was hit by antitank fire and immobilized, and also seriously damaged otherwise. The weapons of the armored train were then blown up and the train was abandoned by the crew, which fought

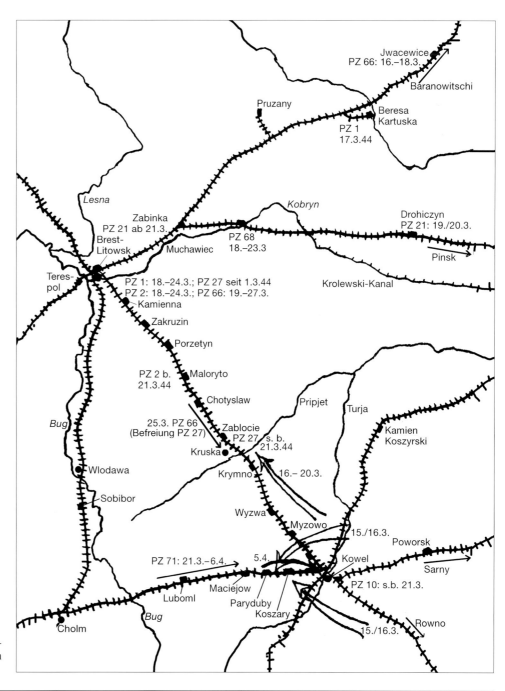

Concentration of armored trains in the Brest-Litowsk area after the enclosure of Kowel (March 1944).

The command car of PZ 68 was derailed by a mine explosion north of Luniniec early in May 1944. Photo: O. Holbein/W. Sawodny collection

In May 1944 PZ 28 arrived anew in the Pripjet region. Photo: E. Lehle/W. Sawodny collection

its way back to its own lines. Since their own troops were hanging on in Kowel, the Russians could not take the armored train away either. On 23 March the 5th Jäger Division began their counterattack, in which PZ 66, already transferred to Brest on 19 March and advanced to Chotyslaw on 22 March in place of the damaged PZ 2, took part along with the escaped remainder of PZ 27's crew. They were in fact able to drive the enemy back and recapture and bring back PZ 27, which was defended by the Russians and thus badly damaged again, presumably a unique experience in the armored train history of World War II.

This—as well as the mutual assistance of Armored Trains No. 2 and 68 near Schazilki in November 1943—were probably decisive in the introduction of the long-promoted pairwise use of two armored trains whenever possible.

On 24 March the dangers were over for Brest-Litowsk and the first countermeasures against the enclosing ring from Kowel were introduced. The remaining armored trains—with a certain rearrangement—could be returned to their securing areas. PZ 1 went to Ossipiwitschi to secure the Minsk—Bobruisk line, PZ 2 to its earlier action area of Krolewschisna—Glebokie, PZ 68 to Parochonsk near Pinsk. Armored Trains No. 21 and 66, though, remained in the area east of Brest. PZ 66, stationed in Beresa-Kartuska, secured the line to Baranowitschi, PZ 21—along with the Hungarian line protection train "Botond"—that to Pinsk.

The next three months were characterized by a multitude of operations against partisans, since their activities were constantly

increasing and were no longer to be kept under control. At the beginning of May, PZ 68 ran onto a mine north of Luniniec and was taken to Baranowitschi for repairs. In which it also received replacements for the cars that were burned out near Wassiliewitschi in November 1943. In its place, PZ 71 (which had been assigned to Army Group Center because of the temporary southward shift of the army-group border), having been repaired at the railroad works in Lublin, went to the Pripjet line. It too was damaged by a mine explosion near Mikazewitschi on 11 May. After being repaired, though, it was transferred to Romania and replaced in the Pripjet region by the meanwhile finished PZ 28 (evacuated from Nikolajew during rebuilding in March 1944).

After being repaired (including re-equipping with T 34 tank destroyer cars) at the Dünaburg EAW, PZ 61—along with the line protection train "Blücher," likewise newly rebuilt—was subordinated to the 221st Securing Division (which also had its own line protection trains, No. 45 and 350) in the Wilna region early in April 1944. On 10 April it carried out a successful partisan action near Kirnowo (on the line toward Lida).

Besides such individual actions by armored trains against partisans, there were also a number of combat measures of a larger extent—with the participation of numerically stronger securing units and several armored trains. One such was "Frühlingsfest" (April 16 to May 10, 1944), the attempt to encircle and destroy the strong partisan bands in the Lepel region. They were supposed to be pushed from the east toward the Polozk—Molodetschno line

The armored trains in the partisan operation "Frühlingsfest" in April and May 1944. PZ 2 (above), PZ 61 (center), and the line protection train "Blücher" (below) secured on the Ziabki—Krolewschisna—Parafjanow line. Photos: W. Sitzius/W. Sawodny collection

At the Farinowo railroad station south of Polozk at the beginning of May 1944, Armored Trains No. 26 and 67 were inspected by Lt.Col. von Türckheim. In front is his command train, No. 72 B, at the left edge is PZ 26. PZ 67 is out of sight behind the quarters train at right. Photo: W. Sitzius/W. Sawodny collection

To catch them there, Army Group North stationed Armored Trains No. 27 and 67 near Farinowo—Orechowo—Wetrino (already set up there in the previous limited operation "Regenschauer"), the 3rd Armored Army the armored trains assigned to it, No. 2 and 61, plus the line protection train "Blücher" in the Ziabki—Krolewschisna—Parafjanow sector. To what extent the line protection train No. 83, and the 391st Securing Division's "Heinrich" and "Werner" (the latter sent over by the 201st Securing Division) in Glebokie were involved is unknown. For Armored Trains No. 26 and 67, whose disembarked crewmen took part in combing through the areas bordering on the rail lines, there were losses from mine explosions; among others, the commander of PZ 26 was fatally wounded on 16 April. On the other hand, the armored trains in the Krolewschisna area were actually able to attack and destroy a large partisan group that was trying to cross the tracks near Kuhaje to avoid being surrounded.

During operation "Frühlingsfest," one of the designated regimental commanders for the armored trains, Lt.Col. von Türckheim, with his command train No. 72B, not only inspected all the involved armored trains in the Molodetschno—Polozk area (No. 2, 26, 61, 67, line protection train "Blücher"), but also PZ 51, which was with Army Group North not far away. The other of the planned regimental commanders, Lt.Col. Dr. Günther, made such an inspection trip with the command train No. 72A from 12 to 19 May to Armored Trains No. 21 (Iwazewitschi), 66 (Beresa Kartuska), 68 (Baranowitschi), and 1 (Ossipowitschi). His report has survived and was already discussed at length elsewhere.

After the conclusion of operation "Frühlingsfest," PZ 26 of Army Group North's armored trains went to the Dünaburg EAW for overhauling (where it was—like Armored Trains No. 1 and 61 before it—re-equipped with tank-destroyer cars (T 34 turrets); then it was transferred back to the Polozk—Idritza line; likewise PZ 67 returned to the line from Polozk in the direction of Newel. In Army Group Center the reassignment of armored trains to their units (for example, PZ 61 to the 221st Securing Division at Landwarow) was only of short duration. The line protection train "Blücher" remained with the 391st Securing Division in Woropajewo and must have been damaged again in May, for it was withdrawn on 1 June in order to be rebuilt into Armored Train No. 52, in which only a very small part of the previous rolling stock reappeared.

To smash the partisan groups that had slipped out to the south in "Frühlingsfest," operation "Kormoran" was begun on May 22, 1944. For it, Armored Trains No. 2 and 61 formed a western securing line between Molodetschno and Parafjanow, while line protection train No. 45 was already transferred to the line from Minsk to Schodino at the beginning. It was followed to there by PZ 61 on 25 May, and finally Armored Trains No. 21, 28, and 61 were united at the end of the month as a battle group, which set up a blockade line between Smolewitschi and Krupki under the command of Lt.Col. Dr. Günther (Command Train No. 72A). The securing between Molodetschno and Parafjanow was strengthened by two line protection trains ("Werner" of the 391st Securing Division and No. 83 of the 3rd Armored Army?). On 5 June the entire armored-train battle group transferred to the Molodetschno—Polozk line; PZ 2, stationed there, was—as the last of the 1938 armored trains—sent to the homeland for rebuilding. After the armored-train battle group could not stop a partisan group from escaping to the west between Kniahinin and Kriwitschi on 8

A look at the railroad station exit at Farinowo, at left the front end of PZ 26, in the background a radar device mounted on a railroad car. Photo: W. Sitzius/W. Sawodny collection

Below: At this time PZ 67 was pulled by a civil "black" locomotive (Series 57). Here too, a large radar device can be seen in the background. Photo: W. Sitzius/W. Sawodny collection

June, it was transferred one day later to Marina Gorka on the Minsk—Bobruisk line. In the region east of Minsk the partisans could be considerably decimated by 20 June. The armored-train battle group temporarily disbanded on 16 June; Lt.Col. Dr. Günther went back to East Prussia with his command train No. 72A, Armored Trains No. 21 and 28 went back to the Molodetschno—Polozk line. But on 19 June they again received the order to gather in Minsk, now under the command of the longest-term armored train commander, Major Linke of PZ 61. PZ 21 was supposed to guard the line from there to Molodetschno, PZ 28 that to Marina Gorka and PZ 61 that to Borissow. Along with the armored trains already mentioned, the

following ones were also in the sector of Army Group Center at that time: PZ 1 (Ossipowitschi—Bobruisk—Schlobin line), PZ 66 (securing the Brest—Baranowitschi line, with station in Beresa-Kartuska) and PZ 68 (being repaired in Baranowitschi).

In all, the status had been maintained in the previous year. Of the armored trains present in the army group at the beginning of July 1943 (No. 2, 3, 4, 21, 27, 61). To be sure, the obsolete No. 2, 3, and 4 had of course been sent back to the homeland for rebuilding; in place of them, the rebuilt or reequipped Armored Trains No. 1 and 28 plus the new BP 42 type No. 66, 67, and 68 (of which No. 67 was later turned over to Army Group North) were introduced. The only loss

PZ 72—later divided into command trains 72A and 72B—arrives intact at the OKH in East Prussia in January 1944. At right is an armored A/A train. Photo: Federal Archives, Koblenz

The command train 72B is camouflaged during its inspection run to the armored trains in the Polozk district (early May 1944). Photo: W. Sitzius/W. Sawodny collection

Lt.Col. Dr. Günther (fifth from left), with Command Train 72A (recognizable behind the group of people at left), inspects PZ 66 in Beresa Kartuska in May 1944. Photo: H. Brueckner/W. Sawodny collection

to be reported was PZ 27, though most of the trains—some several times—were more or less badly damaged in combat action or by explosions on securing runs. The spectrum ran from derailments or damage that could be repaired with on-board means to lengthy stays at workshops for either individual cars or whole trains.

For Army Group North too, the year's score did not look bad. Of the two armored trains on hand at the beginning of July 1943, No. 51 and 63, of course No. 63 had been taken away after being damaged in April 1944, but in January and February the army group had already received Armored Trains No. 26 and 67. On June 20, 1944, these trains had the following stations: No. 26 in Sawaruika (west of Idritza), No. 51 in Rosenow (east of Rositten), and No. 67 in Polozk.

Here too, this was to change soon, and so thoroughly that the planned installations of the armored train regimental staffs in the Army Groups North and Center, that had been indicated in the activities of the commanders planned for them, had to be postponed for several months for lack of material.

From the Russian Summer Offensive to the End of 1944

Exactly on the third anniversary of the German Wehrmacht's attack on the Soviet Union, the great Russian offensive in the sector of Army Group Center, which was to lead to its virtual destruction, began on June 22, 1944. On the night of 19-20 June, the partisan units operating behind the German front had crippled practically the entire rail network east of the Baranowitschi—Wilna—Dünaburg for many hours with far more than 10,000 track explosions. The armored trains could do nothing to stop them, and were themselves similarly limited in their mobility. After the Russians had attacked the 4th and 9th Armies from Orscha to south of Bobruisk on the day after their attack on both sides of Witebsk on 22 June, the armored-train battle group gathered in Minsk (PZ 21, 28, and 61) was sent on the march toward Bobruisk. On the same evening, though, Armored Trains No. 21 and 28 ran onto mines near Kola and had to return to Minsk for repairs. So at first only PZ 61, with the subordinated PT 17, could follow PZ 1, which had advanced from Ossipowitschi via Bobruisk toward Schlobin. Both trains went into battle on 25 June. PZ 61 was in combat with the T 34 tanks of the 1st Guard Armored Corps at the southern breakthrough site near Tschernje Brody toward evening. It was able to shoot down several tanks, but the train was also damaged; among other things, it was rammed by a T 34. Although cut off, it was able to break through to Bobruisk, but it could not hold up the flood of Soviet tanks streaming toward the west on that or the next day any more than PZ 1 could. In the early hours of 27 June the Soviets were already in back of the Germans near Jasen and Mirandino on the line from Bobruisk toward Ossipowitschi and Minsk. At first PZ 1 and later also PZ 61 tried to fight the line free again. The Russians could be thrown out of Mirandino briefly, but the line was fully jammed and impassable for kilometers by abandoned and destroyed evacuation trains. The armored trains (including PT 17) thus had to turn back to Bobruisk and were blown up there on the afternoon of 27 June. The crews were used in ground combat. When they tried to break out of Bobruisk, most of there members ended in Russian imprisonment.

In the spring of 1944, armored trains were damaged more and more frequently. Here are such cars as arrived at the Replacement Battalion in Rembertow. Photo: K. Herbst/G. Krause collection, and L. Johnen/W. Sawodny collection

PZ 21 (with "black" locomotive 57 3181), which was sent on the march from Minsk in the direction of Bobruisk after the Soviet offensive began, hit a mine on 23 June and—just like PZ 28—had to return to Minsk for repairs. Photo: K. Böhringer/W. Sawodny collection

Below: The A/A stand of PZ 26 after six enemy airplanes were shot down near Barawucha on 3 July. Photo: H. Jäger/W. Sawodny collection

The armored trains that remained in Minsk for repairs (No. 21 and 28) were to be assigned to the von Gottberg group, which was not able to stop the further advance of the strong Soviet tank forces, that broke through between Witebsk and Orscha, on the Beresina on both sides of Borissow, but was at least able to slow them down. But only a part of PZ 28 could be repaired for this task in makeshift form. During the following battles it was outflanked and surrounded by Russian troops between Krupki and Prijamino and had to be blown up. When the crew tried to reach their own lines on foot, many were captured.—PZ 21, only ready for action later, was sent to Lida on 29 June to secure the headquarters of Army Group Center, of which Field Marshal Model had taken command the day before.

The south wing of Army Group North, hanging on before Polozk, and having all the armored trains with it, was also touched by the Russian offensive. PZ 67, stationed in Polozk itself, already took part in the defensive fighting in the Obol region on 23 June,

and withdrew toward Polozk two days later. Meanwhile the Soviet forces that had broken through the front of the 3rd Armored Army had already advanced to south of the city. Thus PZ 67 was transferred to the rail line from there toward Krolewschisna and Molodetschno. On 29 June it was attacked by the Russian tank spearhead near Wetrino. The front half of the train took a number of hits and burst into flame. Fortunately the locomotive was only slightly damaged and was able to take the rest of the train out of the danger zone after uncoupling the burning cars. The remaining part of the train was pulled back to Kreuzburg, where the quarters train was, and was originally to be sent back to the homeland for rebuilding, but the later unfavorable development of the situation forbade that; it was only repaired in makeshift form at the Riga EAW. While PZ 51 remained on the Idritza—Rositten line, PZ 26 was transferred from Sawaruika to Polozk on 29 June and covered the evacuation of Barawucha (west of Polozk, which was abandoned on 2 July) from 1 July on. On 3 July it was able to bring down six attacking Russian planes. From 4 to 7 July it secured the withdrawal and the track-destruction work from there to Bigosowo.

Meanwhile the Soviets continued to move forward ceaselessly west of Bobruisk. On 2 July they had already surprised and taken Stolpce and thus broken the rail line from Baranowitschi to Minsk (though the cars of PZ 28 that were left in Minsk for repairs could be taken away via Molodetschno). Farther to the south a defensive line was supposed to be formed along the Baranowitschi—Luniniec line. For this PZ 68, its repairs in Baranowitschi just having been finished, was subordinated to the weak securing forces in Gansewitschi; one day later the line protection train "Polko," that was on the Pripjet line with the 203rd Securing Division, followed it there. But on this 4th of July the Soviets were already able to cross the rail line near Talminowitschi (between Gansewitschi and Baranowitschi) and could not longer be driven away from there. Thus the planned defensive line could not be held. The armored train and line protection train covered the removal from Gansewitschi to Luniniec of the forces, who had meanwhile been brought in, as of 6 July, and the destruction of the rail lines in this region that was also to be given up. On 9 July they moved back over the Jaselda bridge to Pinsk. The Russian breakthrough south of Baranowitschi, and later also north of the city, made it impossible to hold it, though it had been declared a "firm place." On 7 July PZ 66 was alarmed in Beresa Kartuska and advanced to Byten, but got into an air attack there, where it was able to shoot down two Russian planes. Since Baranowitschi was abandoned on July 8, PZ 66 was

The command car of PZ 68, damaged by a mine, is repaired in Baranowitschi. Photo: O. Holbein/W. Sawodny collection

transferred back to Beresa Kartuska on that day. After that PZ 66 and 68 and the line protection train "Polko" (which had been transferred from the Pinsk area to the Brest—Beresa-Kartuska line with the 203rd Securing Division) secured the withdrawal to Brest-Litowsk. The front line ran along the rail line on which PZ 68 stood, as follows: 12 July Pinsk, 15 July Drohitschin, 18 July Horodec—Kobryn, 21 July Zabinka; on the line toward Baranowitschi: 11 July Iwazewitschi, 12 July Beresa Kartuska, 15 July Oranczyce, 18 July Las, and 21 July Zabinka, but at least PZ 66 still operated out of Brest since 15 July.

PZ 21, stationed in Lida, was at first used in the direction of Baranowitschi, and later in the direction of Wilna when the Russians turned up there. Finally on 6 July it was transferred to Wilna itself via Mosty and Grodno, because of the threat to that city, but taken back to Landwarow on 7 July, at the right time to escape the encirclement of the following day (within the encircling ring there remained only the line protection train "Heinrich" of the 75th Securing Regiment, which was used east of the city and blown up before the breakout on 12-13 July). PZ 21 made another attempt on 8 July to push through to the railroad station at Wilna, but its locomotive and tender were shot up. It was possible, though, to pull it back; it was taken via Kowno to Wirballen to be refreshed there.

In mid-July 1944 the Russians extended their offensive to the entire eastern front. As of the 13th they advanced against the 16th Army in the Dünaburg—Rositten region. On 17 July PZ 26 got into the attack of the "Stalin" Tank Brigade near Bigosowo. It was able to shoot down six tanks, but it took a hit in the command post, and when it had to move back, the disembarked infantry could no longer be picked up and were captured. PZ 51 was in battle near Ludsen on the following days and later moved back to Rositten. What was even worse was that the Russian units streamed westward unimpeded through the uncloseable hole between Army Groups North and Center, the so-called "Baltic Hole" between Dünaburg and Wilna in the Ponewisch area, and reached Schaulen on 26 July. South of there, in the territory of the 3rd Armored Army, as of 22 July, PZ 21, joined by the newly built and assigned PZ 3, took part in the defensive fighting around Kowno; the preferred firing position for artillery support of the front was near Palemonas (east of Kowno); both were drawn back before the city was abandoned (30-31 July) when the Russian breakthrough appeared in the Schaulen area. North of there, with the 16th Army, Armored Train No. 26 was in battle near Ponemunek (west of Dünaburg) on 22 July; its damage made a stay at the Riga EAW necessary.

The Russian breakthrough at Schaulen and their ensuing penetration to the north, in which they reached the Baltic Sea near Tukkum on 1 August and thus cut off the entire Army Group North, made the alarm bells ring for all the armored trains of that army group. What remained of PZ 67, repaired at the Riga EAW, was already alarmed and transferred to Mitau on 25 July, to take part in a counterattack from Joniskis in the direction of Schaulen the next day, but it had to be cancelled. PZ 67 received an order to move off to Elley, but got into a race with Russian tanks that were pushing forward toward Mitau on the road that ran parallel to the rail line there. In the running fight, three tanks could be shot down. On a limited-sight curve just before the Mitau railroad station entry, the armored train, rushing at top speed, ran into a bomb crater. It was blown up, the crew took part as infantry in the defense of Mitau on 30-31 July, it was used in the same way near Modohn (east of Riga, between Stockmannshof and Schwanenburg) on 7-12 August, suffering considerable losses.—PZ 51 had also been transferred via Jakobstadt to Salite east of Mitau, where the Soviets had crossed the Aa toward the north, on 31 July. In the first days of August it was involved in cleaning out this breakthrough, and gave artillery support to the regaining of Mitau on 5 August, just as did PZ 26, which had meanwhile been repaired in Riga and had steamed from there toward Mitau on 2 August.—On the west flank of the breakthrough area too, with the 3rd Armored Army, Armored Trains No. 3 and 21, which had been called back from the Kowno area to Tilsit, were alarmed. PZ 3, whose quarters train remained in Tilsit, was sent via Krottingen and Telsche on 1 August, where it then stood as an advance guard. PZ 21 was supposed to reconnoiter from Tauroggen in the direction of Widukle, but was then stopped by a blown-up bridge and thus remained in the Tauroggen region.

Meanwhile, a Russian breakthrough was made in the area of Army Group North west of Pleskau. The two remaining armored trains (No. 26 and 51) were already given marching orders from the Mitau area onto the line from Walk toward Pleskau on 6 August. On 11 August PZ 26 gave artillery support to the weakening front near Lepassare and then drew back to Husari. An action conference of the two armored-train commanders took place there the next day, during which numerous crew members and the leader of PZ 51 were badly injured in an attack by low-level planes. On 13 August both armored trains got into a Russian tank attack near Soemerpalu.

PZ 21, whose locomotive was shot up in battle near Wilna on July 8 (thus seen here with "black" 52 6233) and had also added other makeshift-armored cars since the explosion on 23 June, is seen in action east of Kowno at the end of July. Photo: E. Böhringer/W. Sawodny collection

Bomb hits at a switch derailed PZ 51. The attempt of PZ 26 to tow it out of the danger zone failed, as a coupling broke. While PZ 26 moved out, PZ 51 stayed there and was surrounded. After nightfall the train was blown up; the crew fought their way to their own lines in a two-day march with the unloaded tanks and Panhard scout car — though also with losses. The returning PZ 26 already had to shoot its way through the Antsla railroad station, which was occupied by Russian tanks, and then was in Anne to support the stabilized front with artillery until 20 August; then the train was sent back to its quarters train in Kiefernhalt for about three weeks; the crew was brought up to full strength with former members of the lost armored trains, No. 51 and 67.

In the first half of August the 3rd Armored Army had assembled two armored corps on the Kelme—Telsche—Moscheiken—Frauenburg line to regain the connection with Army Group North. On 10 August Armored Trains No. 3 and 21 were sent marching to the XXXIX.

Armored Corps, with which they — PZ 3 von Schrunden toward the east, PZ 21 from Moscheiken to Autz — were to support the attack planned for 16 August. But PZ 3 was derailed on the transfer trip just a few kilometers beyond Krottingen and had to return for repairs. Thus only PZ 21 could take part in the attack on Autz with the 12th Armored Division as of 18 August. Autz was actually taken on 24 August (PZ 21 remained in that area afterwards). The hinterlands were secured by the line protection trains subordinated to the 390th Securing Division: No. 45 (Krottingen—Plunge line), No. 83 (Krottingen—Skuodas line), and No. 350 (Libau—Schrunden line). The breakthrough to Army Group North succeeded on 20 August only in a narrow strip of coast land between Tukkum and Kemmern, where the heavy cruiser "Prinz Eugen" could give artillery support. This corridor could be extended to the south only as far as the Doblen—Mitau line. Since the rail junction of Mitau was meanwhile back in Russian hands, the problem resulted that the only line leading

There the newly built PZ 3 joined it. Photo: J. Lutter/W. Sawodny collection

PZ 26 — its tank-destroyer car fitted with a T 34 turret — is seen in September 1944 near Apschuppen on the Tukkum—Mitau line. Photo: H. Jäger/W. Sawodny collection

PZ 63—seen here in western Ukraine a few weeks before—was shot down by Soviet tanks west of Krasne on 17 July. Photo: H. Beckmann/W. Sawodny collection

westward out of Army Group North's territory ended at the port of Windau but had no connection to the rail network leading toward the Reich from Libau. Thus a makeshift line was built hastily between Schlampen (Tukkum—Mitau line) and Elisenhof (northern link from Libau to Mitau), as well as the Riga—Mitau and Mitau—Kreuzburg lines were connected by a newly laid track east of Mitau. This allowed the troops of the 18th Army to retreat from Estonia and northern Latvia to the Baltic in the second half of September.—PZ 26 had already been moved up to Apschuppen on the Tukkum—Mitau line to give artillery support to the front and cover the construction work on the Schlampen--Elisenhof connecting line. On 18 September it was transferred via Riga and the eastern makeshift line (where it was derailed) to the Mitau line in the direction of Kreuzburg to support the hard-fighting front against the Russians, who tried to push into the Riga bridgehead from the south. Only on 4 October was it withdrawn to Dubbeln (between Riga and Tukkum).

Only one day later than with Army Group North—on July 14, 1944—the Russians also cut loose between Tarnopol and Kowel against Army Group North-Ukraine. PZ 63 (since June 5, 1944, on the Stanislau—Buczacz line, while PZ 62, which had been there earlier, had been sent farther to either the west or the south with the 1st Hungarian Army), was immediately transferred to the Lemberg—Tarnopol line. It was supposed to bring back a stuck hospital train from the Zloczow area, which was no longer possible. But on the next day it was able with a surprising forward move to almost completely rub out an enemy infantry battalion that had advanced to Skwarzawa. But fate caught up with it on 17 July. In the early morning hours it found itself surrounded by T 34 tanks of the 56th Army Brigade of the

Soviet VII. Armored Corps at the railroad station of Kutkorz (west of Krasne), and was shot down after a short exchange of fire. The crew, which had already sustained losses, was able to disembark, but only part of them could fight back to the German lines in the following night; many went into Russian imprisonment. This loss prevented PT 16, assigned to PZ 11—and replaced there by PT 18, which had just arrived at that time--from going to join PZ 63 as planned.

So both railcars stayed with PZ 11 when it moved northward from its station in Zolkiew to fight the Russians, who had already crossed the Bug. In Rawa Russka the vehicles found themselves enclosed but, after a Stuka attack, could break through to the north. Further costly defensive battles followed in Zamosc (east of Zawada); then they were given the task of blocking the rail line between Lublin and Cholm after the Soviets had crossed the Bug near the last-named city on 22 July. Once again PZ 11 was damaged—including the armored locomotive and an A/A car—but was able—pulled by an "unofficial" locomotive—to cross the San to Rozwadow along with the armored railcars at the right time before Lublin was taken on 24 July. The A/A car was destroyed at the Lublin railroad station; the armored locomotive presumably remained in that city, Russian sources report that on 23 July several T 34 tanks and SU-85 assault guns of the 49th Guard Army Brigade ambushed and destroyed an "armored train" pulled by a Diesel locomotive on the line leading from Deblin—Pulawy to Lublin. This was presumably PT 16 with its tank-destroyer cars but, which was not lost in this action (it could also have been a line protection train documented in Lublin in May 1944, called "Bär" or "Wolf," though according to contemporary knowledge of this type of trains it is unlikely that one should have a Diesel locomotive). For

Thus PT 16 (with two tank-destroyer cars with T 34 turrets coupled to it), which had been sent new to Lemberg at the beginning of June 1944, no longer reached it. The railcar remained with PZ 11. Photo: W. Umlauft/H. J. Wenzel collection

When the news came that the Russians had broken through, PZ 11 set out on a march to the north (toward Rawa Ruska) on July 17, 1944. Photo: R. Lorswcheidt/W. Sawodny collection

Below: PT 16 is seen during the combat in southern Poland in the summer of 1944. The Commander, 1st Lt. Patzner, is holding the rod. Photo: R. Lorscheidt/W. Sawodny collection

PZ 11 there followed further defensive battles on 27-28 July on the San line southeast of Rozwadow, in which the command car was destroyed, and on 3-5 August near Mielec. Again Russian sources report that an armored train was rammed and derailed there by a tank of the 47th independent Armored Regiment, and thus fell into Soviet hands. But PZ 11 and the two railcars, No. 16 and 18, remained in German hands. Here too, it may have been one of the Lublin line protection trains, which may have been used along with the armored train. After stabilizing the front east of Tarnow, PZ 11 was sent back to Cracow for repairs.

At this time no information is available on PZ 62, which was subordinated to the 1st Hungarian Army north of the Carpathians. Only at the end of August 1944 does it appear on the Preschau—Kaschau line in eastern Slovakia. Whether the armored train reached this region while coming back on the line north of the Carpathians (the south wing of the army group located there was attacked comparatively late and was still holding the Przemysl—Sambor—Stryi line at the end of July) or had turned onto the southern line from one of the Carpathian passes (Beskid, Uszok, Lupkow) already is not known.

The Russian advance over the Bug west of Kowel also brought the 2nd Army of Army Group Center, then in the Brest-Litowsk area, into great difficulties. On July 16-17, 1944, Soviet forces had already broken through the German front north of Brest, had occupied the Brest—Czeremcha rail line near Lyszczyce and advanced to the Bug. Another Russian spearhead pushed out of the Hajnowka district through Kleszczele to the Bug in the Drohiczyn—Siemiatycze area on 19 July and formed a bridgehead there. While the front could be reclosed behind the penetrating Russians in the first area, this succeeded near Kleszczele in the second for only a few hours; the two groups of Russian forces could also make contact with each other in the Nurzec area (on the Platerow—Czeremcha line). Despite this the 2nd Army tried to shatter these enemy units, which had a particularly threatening effect because of their bridgeheads across the Bug. Of the armored trains in or near Brest-Litowsk around this time, PZ 68 and the line protection train "Polko" may have been involved in the successful cleaning-out of the Brest-Litowsk—Wysokie Litewski--Czeremcha line on 21-22 July. PZ 66, on the other hand, was transferred to Platerow on 21 July to support the newly arrived 541st People's Grenadier Division in compressing the Russian Bug bridgehead at Drohiczyn and the attack from their own one located across the river near Fronolow. On the morning of 22 July it undertook an advance into the main enemy battle line after firing on it, and was still in battle there on the next two days, accompanying the advance of that division from Fronolow and being exposed to several air attacks in the process.

During these actions, the Soviets had crossed the Bug near the neighboring 4th Armored Army near Wlodawa (south of Brest), pushed through the German defenses and streamed not only to the west in the direction of the Vistula, which they reached on the Deblin—Pulawy region on 25 July, but had also turned toward the north and approached the important Warsaw—Siedlce—Brest-Litowsk supply line. PZ 68 and the line protection train "Polko" were sent on the march on 24 July to protect this line at its most important southern point, Lukow. They reached the city at the right time, to be sure, before the Russians, but even they could not strengthen the hastily assembled alarm units and retreating stragglers of the German troops enough to hold their own. They had to back off to Siedlce. There the first units of the SS "Totenkopf" Armored Division had arrived. An exploratory advance of PZ 68 managed to go two kilometers north of Lukow at 6:00 PM before it was fired on, but only a few hours later the first Soviet tanks already appeared a few kilometers south of Siedlce. The Russians also reached the line west of there, but could be thrown back, so that on the morning of 25 July reinforcements could be brought to Siedlce by rail. But in the afternoon of that day

PZ 74 (BP 44 type, but still with 7.62 cm guns, was in Rembertow for its final equipping, but when the Soviets approached, it had to go into action hastily southeast of Warsaw, but was destroyed by Russian tanks on 29 July. Photo: Dr. H. K. Höcker/W. Sawodny collection

the enemy already came back onto the line, which was not freed again. PZ 68, which stayed in Iganie until 28 July for those purposes, was involved in defense and counterattacks from Siedlce. On that day it had to go back to Siedlce for overhauling and was replaced by the line protection train "Polko." On the morning of 26 July the Soviets had also advanced northward east of Siedlce and cut the connection between there and Mordy. Since the latter town was only weakly occupied, PZ 66 was hastily called in from the Bug. Of course a unit of "Panther" tanks could break through to Mordy that evening (and back on the 28th), but a permanent connection between Siedlce and Mordy could no longer be established, so that PZ 66 remained cut off. In the next four days it was constantly in defensive combat around and east of Mordy, until it had used up its ammunition on 30 July. On the afternoon of that day it was blown up. The crew got back to Sokolow Podlaski in road vehicles.—When the Soviets, having pushed past Siedlce, also temporarily broke the connection between it and Sokolow on 28 July, PZ 68 and the line protection train "Polko" were withdrawn to Malkinia on the Warsaw—Bialystok line after fighting their way free, in order to protect them from a possibly threatening surrounding.

The strong Soviet forces advancing farther to the west southward of Lukow were just 60 kilometers southeast of Rembertow, where the Armored Train Replacement Battalion was located, on the morning of 23 July. It was alarmed early that morning, and its units set out on the march to the front. But halfway out, the command "turn" came, for it had meanwhile been decided to evacuate the Replacement Battalion intact to Milowitz near Lissa (east of Prague), which went on until July 26. On the morning of 25 July a reconnaissance advance with Panhard scout cars was undertaken from Rembertow to the east; it showed that the line to Siedlce was still free of enemies. The new armored trains still being equipped at Rembertow, No. 74 and 75, had to go into action at once—though they were not yet complete. PZ 74 was assigned to the 73rd Infantry Division, which was to set up a defensive position near Garwolin, southeast of Warsaw, on both sides of the line to Deblin. The armored train made exploratory runs toward Deblin, where it was able to fight against heavy artillery going into positions, but on the way back it was almost captured by Russian tanks. As of 27 July it covered the withdrawal of the 73rd Infantry Division in the Otwock area. On 29 July, Armored Train No. 74 was apprehended and shot down by Russian T 34 tanks that had broken through the German front and entered a patch of woods near the rail line at Pogorzel—a few kilometers ahead of Otwock; many crew members lost their lives; some were taken prisoner.

At first PZ 75 reconnoitered from Rembertow in the direction of Minsk Masowiecki, until that city was abandoned on 30 July;

then it was transferred back to Praga, the eastern suburb of Warsaw. When the Soviet III. Armored Corps, which had broken through, approached the Warsaw—Bialystok rail line on 29 July, PZ 68 and the line protection train "Polko" attacked from Malkinia, though without being able to stop the enemy from crossing the line and spreading out northward of it. While the line protection train "Polko" was then stationed on the likewise endangered line from Praga to Modlin, PZ 68, with the Felzmann battle group, covered the Bug crossing near Wyszkow, which the Soviets were threatening from Radzymin. When the Soviet III. Armored Corps, on the first days of August, had been cut off between Okuniew (on the eastern edge of the troop training camp at Rembertow) and Stanislawow, and was wiped out in the area north and south of Wolomin, PZ 68 secured the Wyszkow—Tluszcz line, took part in the defense of the latter town when the Russians renewed their attack on 15 August, and then drew back to Wyszkow, where it again defended the Bug crossing in the last ten days of August. After that was given up, it served with the Cavalry Corps at the Scharfenwiese—Nowawies Narew crossing.

After the Russians had come so close to Warsaw, the Polish underground movement believed the time to rise up had come. After the first indications on 30 and 31 July, which did not go unnoticed by PZ 75 in Praga, the revolt broke out in full strength on 1 August. The Polish underground fighters were able at first to occupy parts of the city and enclose or take out a series of German facilities, though many others were able to defend themselves. PZ 75 took part in the successful defense of the railroad bridge over the Vistula (the road bridges also remained in German hands). On 3 August the line protection train "Polko," steaming in from Modlin, prevented the taking of Legionowo (north of Warsaw) by the "Grosz" insurgent group. Massive German countermeasures began on 4 August. PZ 75 was assigned to the troops of SS Gruppenführer Reinefarth, attacking from the west, and was subordinated to the Schmidt Battle Group (Securing Regiment 608); it was on the western part of the ring line in the Wola area and supported the attack of the German troops there with artillery and machine-gun fire; and on 6 August, from the southern curve of the ring line, the Dirlewanger Brigade's attack on the tobacco factory in the Ochota district of the city. On 8 August it cooperated with the advance of the Schmidt Battle Group on the cemetery region on the northwest curve of the ring. On 9 August the line protection train "Polko" was also transferred from Legionowo to the northern ring line in Warsaw, but switched briefly to the other bank of the Vistula into the suburb of Praga on August 16 to fire on Soviet positions, and at the end of the month it was withdrawn from Warsaw to take on securing tasks in the area west of the city as far as Lawitsch—Koluszki. PZ 75, on the other hand--renamed Armored Instruction Train No. 5—remained in Warsaw until the end

The railroad lines and city districts of Warsaw.

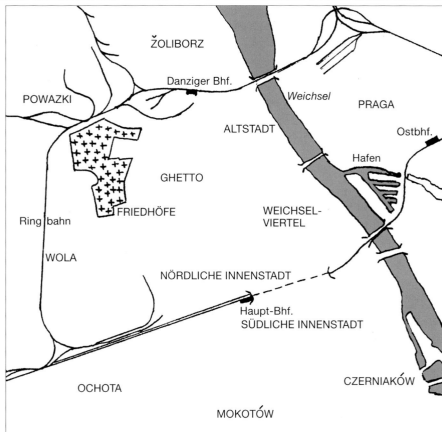

Below: Operation "Sternschnuppe" against the Polish insurgent group "Kampinos" (September 28-29, 1944).

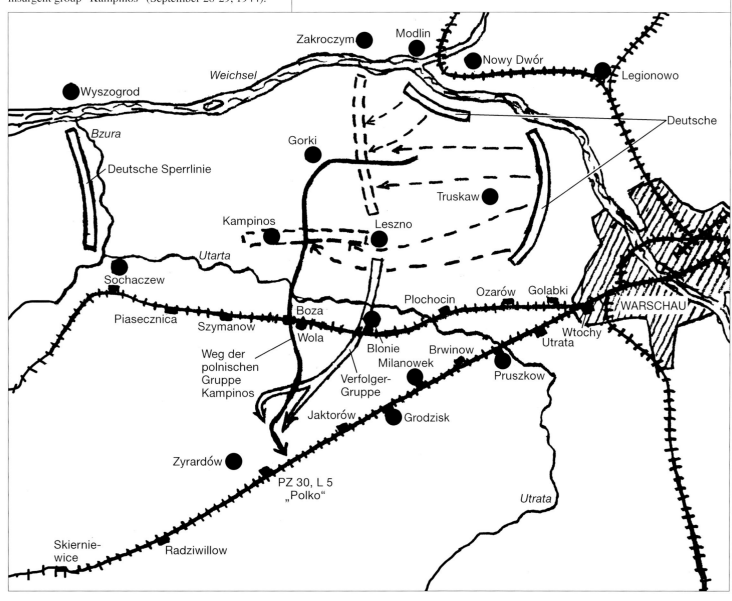

Left: At the end of August 1944, the 9th Army had been assigned the overhauled PZ 30, newly equipped with tank-destroyer cars (Panzer IV turrets). Photo: W. Conrad/W. Sawodny collection

Right: On September 29, 1944, the strong Polish resistance group "Puszcza Kampinoska" ran into a securing line composed of PZ 30, Instruction PZ 5 and line protection train "Polko" during a disengagement movement and was rubbed out. Horse-drawn wagons of the insurgents are being collected. Photo: J. Kraemer/W. Sawodny collection.

Below: Captured Polish insurgents are being taken away. Photo: W. Conrad/W. Sawodny

of September. From 13 August on, the armored trains used artillery fire on the old town again and again from the northern part of the ring line and the Danzig Station to give help and support to the Schmidt Battle Group, especially after the main attack on that part of the city, which lasted until the end of the month, had begun on 19 August. Much more significant than these cannonades, though, was that the trains, by moving around the ring line, prevented the insurgent units in the suburbs—at first in Wola to the west, later particularly in Zoliborz—from being able to unite with those fighting in the old town. Thus on 8 and 9 August the Poles made repeated attempts to either blow up the armored trains directly or at least immobilize them by destroying the tracks, but all these remained fruitless. Especially in the nights of 20-21 and 21-22 August, the trains brushed off the

desperate attempts of the Polish relief group "Puszcza Kampinoska" to get from Zoliborz into the old town, with the heaviest losses for those near the Danziger Station.—On 19 September the Instruction PZ 5 ran into heavy Soviet artillery fire there, with which the vain attempts on the 1st Polish Army to cross the Vistula in the district of the northern railway bridge, after the loss of the suburb of Praga to the Red Army on 14 September, were supposed to be covered. Training PZ 5 can still be documented on the Warsaw ring on 21 September, still giving artillery support to the German troops.

With the beginning of the operation "Sternschnuppe" on 27 September, through which the Polish insurgent group "Puszcza Kampinoska" was to be wiped out in the wooded area of the same name south of the Vistula near Modlin, Instruction PZ 5 was transferred westward from Warsaw and, along with the line protection train "Polko" and PZ 30 (this had been assigned to the 9th Army on 28 August and had, stationed in Opoczno and Petrikau, carried out securing tasks on the Koluszki—Starzysko Kamienna and Petrikau—Koluszki—Skierniewice lines, likewise threatened by partisan attacks) formed a barricade line between Zyrardow and Jaktorow. In fact, the Polish insurgent group ran onto this on 29 September and was almost completely rubbed out.

Next all three trains took on securing tasks in the area west of Warsaw to the Petrikau—Lawitsch line.—As of 21 October, though, PZ 30 and the Instruction PZ 5 were used in front of the Russian Narew bridgehead in the Nasielsk—Modlin region. Around this time, Regimental Staff No. 3 for the armored trains was finally to be installed in Blonie west of Warsaw (Lt.Col. Dr. Günther with Command Train No. 72B), but the events in East Prussia, which will be noted later, made an immediate move to there necessary.

PZ 30 (with the subordinated PT 19 in the background) returns to its station of Petrikau after action in Zyrardow. Photo: J. Kraemer/W. Sawodny collection

PT 19, assigned to PZ 30 at the end of October 1944, is seen in Modlin. Photo: J. Kraemer/W. Sawodny collection

Before the role of the armored trains in another rebellion operation is to be portrayed, one should think of PZ 71, which was active in Romania since mid-May 1944. From Galatz it secured the supply lines of the 6th and 8th Armies After the striking success of the Russian offensive that began on 20 August and the resulting side-changing of Romania on 24 August, the armored train moved back from Galatz via Braila and Buzau to Ploesti, coming through several fights with small Romanian units. The train was to go on over the Predeal Pass to Kronstadt but was ordered back to Ploesti to free some hospital trains surrounded there. Next it was given the task of bringing out the Luftwaffe mission that had gone from Ploesti to Slanic. This became its fate, for it was cut off on that branch line. So PZ 71 had to be blown up in Slanic on 31 August when the Russians attacked the town; some of the crew became prisoners; the others tried to fight their way through the mountains toward Neumarkt, but many of them had to share the lot of their comrades who were captured in Slanic.

The German military mission returning from Romania, along with the Soviet forces approaching the Carpathian ridge in the area of the Dukla Pass, gave the partisans who were active in Slovakia the impetus to rebel, and regular units of the Slovakian army soon joined them. The German military mission was arrested in St. Martin on 27 August and their members were shot the next day. The few German troops in Slovakia itself and the vicinity were alarmed on the evening of 28 August, including PZ 62, which was probably involved in opening the important east-west Kysak—Deutschendorf—

Rosenberg—Sillein line in the first two weeks of September (though its western section from Rosenberg to Sillein could be opened to traffic only on 11 October), and had this plus the cross line running from Neu-Sandec via Kysak to the Preschau—Kaschau region of Hungary to secure. In western as in eastern Slovakia the insurgent elements could be disarmed quickly, but the available German troops there were not sufficient to occupy the entire region. So the insurgents in the mountainous region of the Lower Tatra, the Great and Small Fatra, the Neutra Mountains and the Slovakian Erzgebirge were able to consolidate with those centered in Neusohl and hold out for eight weeks. Since they had only a few tanks, they built three armored trains in Altsohl, which consisted, besides the armored locomotive and three provisionally armored freight cars—the one at the front (behind the control car) carried a gun (8-cm Skoda M 17 cannon) firing through the front end, while the others just had machine guns with side ports—of two flat cars with undriveable Skoda 35(t) tanks set on them and surrounded by armor plate. The first of these armored trains, "General Stefanik," was finished about 18 September and was used immediately near Priwitz, where it was able to move forward, surprise the German Schill Battle Group heading eastward and drive it back ten kilometers. After that the armored train, moving back to Hronska Dubrava, was spotted there by the German Luftwaffe and so damaged in repeated attacks that it had to go to Altsohl for repairs. Later it was used on the line from Altsohl in the direction toward Lizenz in the Krivan region, a district that remained quiet until the final German attack in the second half of October. At the

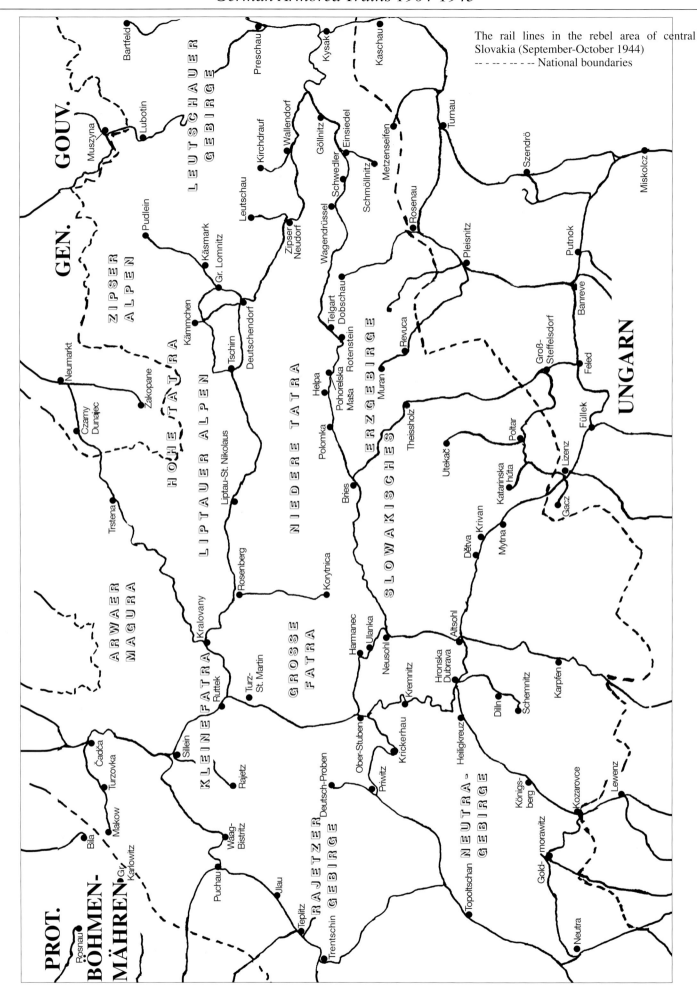

The rail lines in the rebel area of central Slovakia (September-October 1944)
-- -- -- -- -- -- National boundaries

At the end of August 1944 the Slovakians rebelled against the Germans. The insurgents built three armored trains at Altsohl. Here the "General Stefanik" train is seen in action. Photo: J. Meister collection

The rebel armored train "Hurban" was camouflaged with branches in the German manner. Photo: J. Meister collection

end of September the next armored train "Hurban" was finished at the Altsohl workshops—with the same composition but an improved version. It had its baptism of fire in the storming of the German "Tatra" Division in Ober-Stuben and Ceremosna on 4 October. There it was badly damaged. After being repaired it remained in action on the Neusohl—Harmanec line, where the front remained stable for the last weeks. The third—also similarly built—armored train "Masaryk" was finished on 13 October and transferred to the east end of the territory held by the Slovaks, near Telgart. There they still had the hope that the Soviet troops, who had attacked the German Carpathian front almost ceaselessly for four weeks would be able to break through successfully and connect with the rebelling Slovakian Army. It was in vain. Instead, the German units, who had meanwhile surrounded the entire rebel district, made a final attack on 18 October. PZ 62, to which PT 20 had been assigned at the end of September, secured the Deutschendorf—Tschirn region. The main German advance unexpectedly was made in the eastern part of the Slovakian Erzgebirge from the southeast, out of the Gross-Steffelsdorf –Pleisnitz area. On 21 October the attacking 18th SS "Horst Wessel" Armored Grenadier Division had reached the Telgart and drove its defenders back. The already damaged armored train "Masaryk" moved out to Rotenstein and then to Pohorelska Masa. There it was supposed to support the Slovakian counterattack, but the locomotive was hit by several artillery shells and was barely able to pull the train back to Helpa. In the next days this train was near Bries, where it tried to hold a last defensive position in the Gran valley. When the Germans captured Bries on 25 October, it was taken to Neusohl. The left column of the SS "Horst Wessel" Division had set out from Lizenz only on 22 October, reaching Mytna the same day and Podkrivan the next. The armored train "General Stefanik" may have taken part in the defensive fighting in the Krivan—Detva region, which lasted until 25 October. By 26 October it got back to Neusohl, where all three Slovakian armored trains met shortly before the collapse of the rebellion. On that evening they took part in the evacuation measures by moving wounded men and materials from Neusohl to Ulanka. While the remaining Slovak fighters moved into the mountains to the northeast, the armored trains were placed in the tunnel beyond Harmanec and fell into German hands there. They were taken to the Replacement Battalion in Milowitz, where some of their material was used later in the line protection trains "Max" and "Moritz."

At the beginning of November 1944 PZ 22, which was withdrawn from France, and to which PT 22 had been assigned, arrived in Slovakia. It relieved PZ 62 in its northern region, securing from Sillein to Preschau and from Altsohl to Kaschau. PZ 62 seems to have been transferred to the northern part of Hungary, where the Russians had reached the line from east of Nyireghaza to the Theiss south of Miskolc at the end of October. In their renewed offensive in December 1944, the right wing of the 1st Armored Army in eastern Slovakia, with which PZ 22 was also present in Kaschau then, was able to hold its ground, while the 8th Army—and PZ 62 with it—was pushed toward the Hungarian-Slovakian border. On 21 December this armored train was exposed to a bomb attack in Füllek; on the next day it suffered considerable losses in a fight south of Gross-Steffelsdorf. Before the year ended, PZ 62 was ordered to Poland (PT 20, assigned to it, had already broken an axle and had to be taken to the Nürnberg RAW, as repairing it in Ruttek was impossible), while PZ 22 alone remained in Slovakia.

Meanwhile the other armored trains that were formerly stationed in France had arrived in southern Poland. PZ 24 arrived in Cracow on 23 October and was transferred to its station in Makow (on the rail line to Chabowka). From there it secured the lines toward Neumarkt—Zakopane and Neu-Sandec. In November it was replaced in Chabowka by PZ 25, also returning from France; and now secured the line from Cracow to Sucha and was stationed in Kalwaria. Through these additions it was finally possible to set up the long-planned Regimental Staff No. 2 for Armored Trains (Commander Lt.Col. von Türckheim) with Army Group A (to which Army Group North Ukraine had been renamed in September). Its command train, No. 72A, was stationed in Cracow. At the end of 1944 a new distribution of the armored trains was undertaken, representing a division into "battalions" of two trains each. The Armored Trains No. 24 and 62 were stationed in Jelen (Koluszki—Skarzysko Kamienna line, thus in the hinterlands of the Russian Vistula bridgehead near Pulawy); PZ 25 was paired with PZ 11, which had been near Kielce—near the Baranow bridgehead—with railcars No. 16 and 18 since being repaired in Cracow. Only PZ 22 and its railcar—also subordinated to the Cracow staff—remained alone in Slovakia.

In the sector of Army Group North, to which the 3rd Armored Army had been subordinated since mid-September, the Russians attacked again on 5 October, the same day as the evacuation of the Riga bridgehead, to gain forces for the support of the other fronts. They assaulted the 3rd Armored Army between Schaulen and Raseinen, broke through it, and five days later they had reached the Baltic near Polangen, enclosed the city of Memel, and were on the lower Memel near Tilsit. Army Group North was thus cut off again—and this time permanently. On the north flank of the breakthrough area they tried to build up a defensive front with what remained of the left wing of the 3rd Armored Army and the troops of the 18th Army who were brought in from Riga, under the command of the latter. It ran more or less along the (Schaulen)—Papile—Moscheiken—Weinoden—Prekuln rail line. The Russians sent forces against this line again and again and tried to advance as far as possible to the north. PZ 3, serving since mid-September with the 201st Securing Division between Akmene and Papile, was at a vital point there, the southeast corner post of the breakthrough area, from the beginning. On 5 October the disembarked crew had to come through a costly fight near Gumbaikiai (southwest of Papile) against the Soviets, who had crossed the Windau and were advancing toward the rail line. On the same day there came the news that the enemy was also advancing northward to the east of Vieksiniai. PZ 3 went back there and came under fire already near Viliosiai (9 km east of Vieksiniai). Early on 7 October the Russians approached the line in the Weinoden area. PZ 3 was transferred there at once but could not prevent the enemy from crossing the line between Luse and Venta. On the next two days they tried in vain to reopen the line to Moscheiken. When the Soviet tanks also crossed the rail line west of Elkuzeme (toward Prekuln) on 10 October, thus holding PZ 3 in Weinoden, and the conquest of the city

itself was just about to take place as well, the train was blown up.—PZ 21, which was near Autz, was transferred to Moscheiken at the beginning of the Russian advance. From 8 October on it tried from there—as did PZ 3 from the west—to reopen the line to Weinoden, but the blowing up of the bridge over the Windau near Venta soon brought an end to these efforts. Thus it too was cut off. At first it still had a little moving space, reaching from Venta via Moscheiken to Vieksniai, but on 17 October the Russians advanced from the west to the edge of Moscheiken. Thus the railroad station also fell into their effective area. PZ 21—divided into individual cars—was posted on the station grounds; the crew disembarked and took infantry positions. The city could be held until 30 October, when as part of the second battle of Courland the withdrawal to the north became unavoidable. The crew of PZ 21 left with the rest, but only part of the train was blown up.

PZ 26—as long as the evacuation transports ran from Riga toward Tukkum—remained on this line in Dubbeln. Only on October 12 did it travel over the makeshift line south of Tukkum to Sexanten on the line toward Libau. At first it was intended for action in Prekuln, but was then stopped and transferred to Elisenhof to protect the still-open makeshift line toward Tukkum, when the Russians attacked this area as of 16 October. From 20 to 26 October Armored Train No. 26 was in Arasieli and gave the front artillery support; in the second battle of Courland starting on 27 October the front was pushed back to Bixten in that area. In the front position there, PZ 26—after the planned transfer of the armored train back to the Reich had been ruined again—saw 1944 become 1945.

In the southern district of the breakthrough region there were only line protection trains at first. The three of the 3rd Armored Army (No. 45, 83 and 350) moved to East Prussia, but No. 83 was transferred to the Armored Train Replacement Battalion in Milowitz, since no further need of it was seen. On 7 October the line protection train "Wespe" of the 16th Army was ordered from Courland to Krottingen. Whether it could still save itself at the Memel bridgehead or fell into Russian hands on the way is unknown; after that date it no longer appears. On 10 October, when the Russians had reached the lower Memel, PZ 52, rebuilt from the line protection train "Blücher" and just finished, was transferred to Tilsit along with PT 21, which was assigned to it.

On 19 October the Russians began their offensive against East Prussia from the Schirwindt—Suwalki area. The advance extended over the Gumbinnen—Goldap line until 22 October and was aimed at Königsberg. On that day PZ 52 was stationed on the Insterburg—Gumbinnen line, while PZ 68, called in from the 2nd Army, was

The newly assigned PZ 52 in Tilsit in October 1944. Photo: H. Müller/W. Sawodny collection

The combat car of PZ 52 was hit by a shell in a fight near Goldap on November 3, 1944. Photo: H. Müller/W. Sawodny collection

PZ 30 in East Prussia, where it belonged to the Armored Train Regiment Battle Group of Dr. Günther since November 15, 1944. Photo: G. Schaefer/W. Sawodny collection

placed on the Insterburg—Angerapp line. After they had succeeded in cutting off the Russian spearhead south of Gumbinnen, they also wanted to regain Goldap, which had fallen into Russian hands on 22 October. To do this, PZ 52 took a position on the Angerburg—Goldap line, while PZ 68 was to advance from Angerapp toward Goldap; a first advance on 26-27 October failed. In the last days of October the Regimental Commander of the Armored Trains with Army Group Center, Lt.Col. Dr. Günther, arrived in Angerburg with his command train No. 72B, which was originally supposed to have its command post in Blonie west of Warsaw, to take command of the armored trains in that district. The renewed attack began on 3 November.

While other army units closed their pincer arms behind the city from the north and south, Armored Trains No. 52, 68, and 72B (in this order on the line), accompanied by Assault Gun Brigade No. 259, advanced from Angerapp toward Goldap. The disembarked crews with their combat vehicles (tanks and armored scout cars), supported by the trains' heavy weapons, broke through the Russian position system on both sides of the rail line and advanced to a blown-up bridge one kilometer before the Goldap railroad station. Thus they contributed decisively to the retaking of the city, concluded on 5 November. The operation cost the armored train crews one dead and 19 wounded; one of the 38(t) tanks ran onto a mine and was lost. The

On December 1, 1944, Instruction PZ 5 was replaced in this Armored Train Battle Group by the new PZ 76 (seen here in November during a drill with the Replacement Battalion in Milowitz). Photo: H. D. Becker/W. Sawodny collection

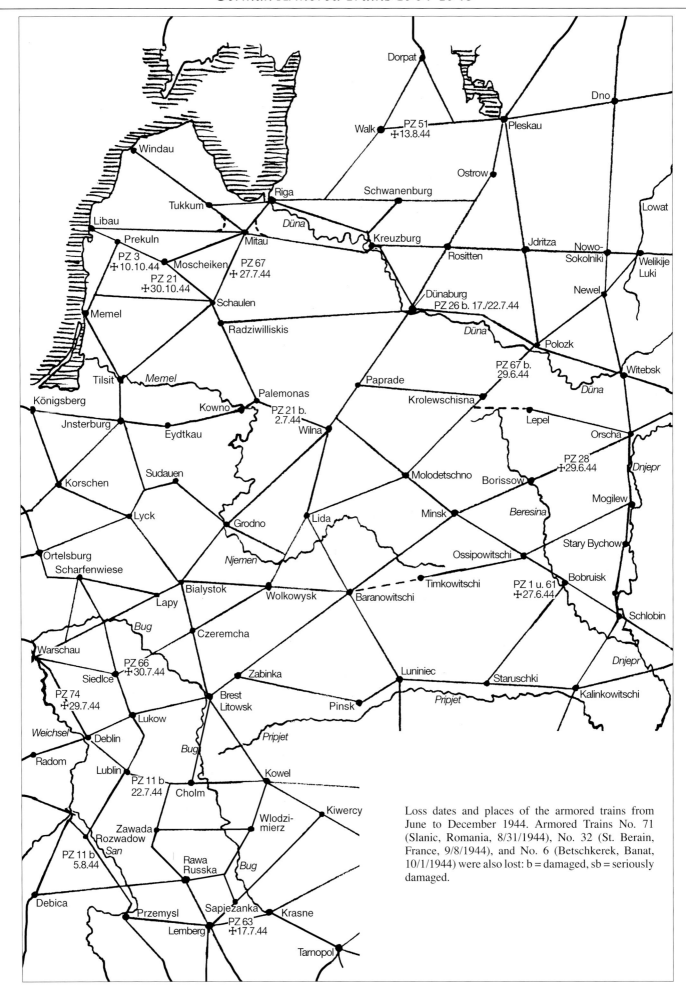

Loss dates and places of the armored trains from June to December 1944. Armored Trains No. 71 (Slanic, Romania, 8/31/1944), No. 32 (St. Berain, France, 9/8/1944), and No. 6 (Betschkerek, Banat, 10/1/1944) were also lost: b = damaged, sb = seriously damaged.

statistics for ammunition used in the period from 26 October to 4 November are available and are cited here:

10-cm howitzer shells:	209
7.62-cm cannon shells:	685
7.5-cm antitank shells:	143
8-cm mortar shells:	382
2-cm anti-aircraft bullets	9,300
Rounds of machine-gun ammunition	13,900

After the attack, the armored trains turned out to need overhauling. While this could be done on the spot with on-board means for Armored Trains No. 68 and 72B, PZ 52 had to be taken to the Königsberg RAW (until 17 November). Meanwhile it had been decided to assemble the entire Armored Train Battle Group of Army Group Center in East Prussia. Therefore PZ 30 (with PT 19) and Instruction PZ 5 were also transferred from the Narew bridgehead near Nasielsk to the Treuburg region (in their place the 9th Army. In the area west of Warsaw, received the line protection trains No. 45 and 350 from the 3rd Armored Army, as well as the line protection train "Werner," which joined the already present line protection train "Polko." With the Command Train No. 72B in Kruglanken, there was to be one armored train pair ("Battalion") in service on the Treuburg—Goldap line (Armored Trains No. 52 and 68, stationed in Stosnau/Kalkhof and Reimannswalde) and one on the Treuburg—Raczki line (PZ 30 and Instruction PZ 5, stationed in Reuss). Often, though, only one armored train was in the action area, since the other needed refreshing in the hinterlands.

On 1 December the Instruction PZ 5 was replaced by the new PZ 76 (with subordinated PT 23). On 12 December a new distribution of the armored trains was undertaken. The Command Train No. 72B was now in Allenbruch, PZ 52 in Jorken, and PZ 68 on the line from Kruglanken (where both supply trains were stationed) to Treuburg, Armored Trains No. 30 and 76 were used in Urbansdorf (near Goldap) with the supply trains in Passdorf and Grossgarten or later Rosengarten. Around the first of the year, Armored Trains No. 30 and 76 were with their supply trains. PZ 68 went to the Königsberg RAW for overhauling; PT 21, assigned to PZ 52, had gear trouble and was taken to the Nürnberg RAW for repairs. It might also be noted that on 30 November a Russian armored train fired on the German positions east of Osowiec (Lyck—Prostken—Bialystok line).

Of the 13 armored trains on hand at the eastern front in June 1944 (No. 1, 11, 21, 26, 28, 51, 61-63, 66-68, 71), only four (No. 11, 26, 62, 68) still existed whole at the year's end. With the addition of the newly built No. 74-76 and the rebuilt No. 3, 30, and 52 (of which, to be sure, No. 3 and 74—the latter after just a few days—were lost in the time period in question), but especially through the transfer of Armored Trains No. 22, 24, and 25 from France, then despite eleven losses (PZ 75 left for other reasons during this period), a total of ten armored trains could be attained. In November this finally allowed the long-planned establishment of the Armored Train Regimental Staffs with Army Groups Center and A, though on a reduced basis (each staff was originally supposed to have three "battalions" of two armored trains, thus a total of six combat trains; Staff No. 2/Army Group A had five, Staff No. 3/Army Group Center four combat trains, not counting the command trains No. 72A and B.

1945—The End of the War in the East

The Russian offensive, which was to carry the war far into the eastern part of the Reich, began on January 12, 1945. The stationings of the armored trains corresponded to those from the end of 1944. On the named date the Soviet troops broke out of the Baranow bridgehead and immediately tore a wide gap in the German front, through which they could stream westward unhindered. The spearhead was pointed directly at the Kielce—Tunel rail line, on which the group of Armored Trains No. 11 and 25 with railcars No. 16 and 18 stood near Checiny. On 13 January the report arrived that Russian tanks had been sighted on the line near Sobkow. PT 18 was sent ahead to reconnoiter but soon came back with shell damage and losses without being able to offer a conclusive report. Then PT 16 was sent out. Struck by low-level planes, it moved fast. Soon it saw a whole armada of tanks rolling onto the tracks, which were blocked already by two tanks that had come on from the left and right. Thanks to its high speed and strong armor, it was able to break through to the south, cross the Nida bridge and beat back the advancing Russian infantry with its fire. On the other track the scheduled passenger train from Tunel was steaming up unexpectedly; it could be stopped. Meanwhile PZ 25 had followed PT 16 from Checiny, and in two kilometers it met the mass of Russian tanks, which shot it into immobility. Although the train took a series of hits—among others, in the command car, costing all the officers—it was able, thanks to its intact guns, to fight off the Russians, which then surrounded it. At its call for help, PZ 11 also went into action to tow it away, but it suffered the same fate. Now PT 16 was supposed to tow the trains out. But German engineers had meanwhile blown up the Nida bridge, so that the trip back was impossible. The armored trains were made useless after night fell and abandoned by the crews, who fought their way to the German lines. PT 16—the only one to escape the disaster (after the damaged PT 18 could no longer be driven out of Kielce and thus fell into Russian hands there) at first covered the railroad crossing near Jedrzejow and later set out in the direction of the Upper Silesian industrial region. There it took part in stopping the Soviets, who were advancing from the east, near Szczakowa on 20 January, and was damaged in the process. The repairs made in the Gleiwitz RAW had to be interrupted when on 23 January the Russians approached that city from the north; thus the railcar was transferred to the Wittenberge RAW. –The Command Train No. 72A left Cracow, which was lost on 19 January, at the right time. Whether it took part in the fighting in the industrial region is not known, but at last it moved to the left bank of the Oder before the region was encircled on 27 January.—In the Upper Silesian industrial region the line protection train No. 607 (also called a "heavy armored train") and the armored train "Myslowitz," which had been built there ad hoc, saw action; their fates are unknown.

On 14 January the Russians also attacked from the Pulawy bridgehead. The armored trains near Tomaszow, No. 24 and 62, were alarmed that morning and, after an intermediate stop in Kamienna on account of trouble, reached Radom shortly after midnight. They were sent farther on the line toward Deblin and took up firing positions in Jedlnia on the morning of 15 January to prevent a breakthrough of the enemy on the road running parallel to the track some four kilometers to the south. But before they made contact with the enemy, they were ordered back about midday to the line from Radom to Kamienna, where the approach of Soviet tanks was reported. Yet everything remained quiet there too until afternoon; around 4:00 PM the trains returned to Kamienna to take on water and coal. The railroad station was so overfilled with removal trains that refueling the locomotives

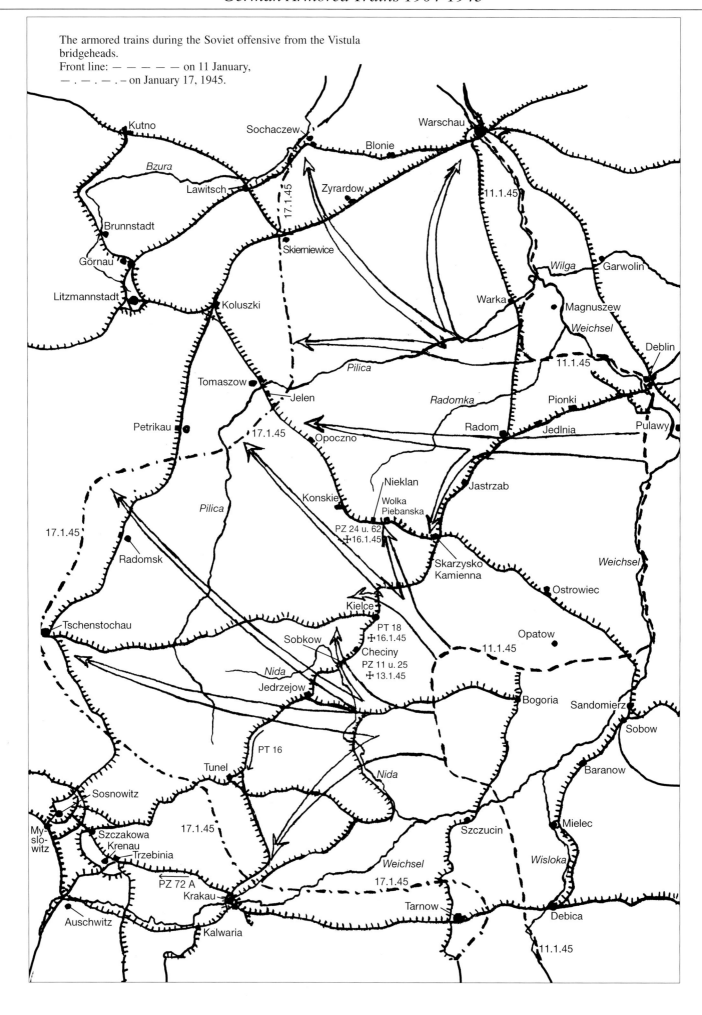

The armored trains during the Soviet offensive from the Vistula
bridgeheads.
Front line: — — — — — on 11 January,
— . — . — . – on January 17, 1945.

took until evening. Meanwhile the armored trains received the order to set out for Opoczno. Their trip was interrupted early on the morning of 16 January in Wolka Piebanska, as two ammunition trains had collided and gotten thoroughly wedged into each other there. The rest of the day would have been needed to clear the track. It was learned that the Soviets had meanwhile crossed the line northwards to the west of Wolka with strong armored forces and placed T 34 tanks along the tracks at the next railroad station—Nieklan—to catch trains that might come through. Since the single-track line back to Kamienna was meanwhile filled with abandoned removal trains, the commander of the battle group, Captain Popp, decided to blow up the two armored trains, which had not fired a single shot through the entire action, about 7:45 AM. The crews took their infantry weapons, radio and optical devices, and the road vehicles and set out, despite several air attacks, for their own lines and their supply trains west of Litzmannstadt.

Around 25 January, PZ 22 (with PT 22, which was taken away for other use at the beginning of February) was transferred from Slovakia to Silesia. It went to Liegnitz and fired from the line toward Lüben on the Russians marching in at the Oder bridgehead in Steinau. When the Soviets advanced from this bridgehead on February 8, it went to Sagan on 10 February, after the fall of Liegnitz, and was east of the railroad station of Sprottau on 11 February to cover the departure of an overfilled refugee train. It was shot down by fire from approaching Russian tanks at the edge of the woods on the other side. Thus all the trains of the Armored Train Regiment Battle Group with Army Group A (Center as of 25 January) except the command train No. 72A were destroyed.

On both sides of Warsaw the Russians cut loose on 14 January; on 15 January they broke through the German front and forced the Germans to abandon the city on 16 January. Through a front gap west of the city the Soviet tank units poured to the northwest and west. On 23 January they had reached Posen and Bromberg, on the night of 31 January 1-February they were even on the Oder near Küstrin and formed bridgeheads on the west shore of the river both north and south of that city as well as south of Frankfurt on the Oder. What happened to the four line protection trains stationed west of Warsaw in those days is not known. Two of them (No. 350 and "Werner" were able to cross the Oder; what became of the other two (No. 45

and "Polko") is not known for sure. Of course, Russian sources report two destroyed trains; one was shot down by tanks of the 2nd Soviet Armored Army on the Stettin—Küstrin line during the capture of Königsberg/Neumark on 4 February, and the other one—enclosed in Schneidemühl—was caught during an escape attempt on the line toward Schoenfeld on 12 February by JSU 122 pursuit tanks of the 47th Russian Army and fell, demolished, down the rail embankment. It is probable that these were the line protection trains No. 45 and "Polko."

Unprotected Pomerania (a gigantic hole gaped between the right wing of the 2nd Army west of Bromberg and the 9th Army that had moved back to the Oder) and the appearance of the Russians on the Oder east of Berlin—and thus only about 80 kilometers from the Reich capital—naturally inspired the greatest concern at the Führer's headquarters. Hitler created the new Army Group "Weichsel" (Vistula), whose leadership, out of mistrust of the Army generals, he entrusted to the military dilettante Himmler, the Reichsführer of the SS. The 2nd and 9th Armies were subordinated to him, and under the newly created command of the 11th Armored Army he tried to push additional forces into the hole. The armored trains were among them. On 29 January the Instruction PZ 5, used as a training train by the Replacement Battalion in Milowitz, was reactivated for combat action and reconnoitered from Arnswalde in the direction of Woldenberg; on the 30th it was able to take refugees fleeing ahead of the approaching Russian tanks to safety. On the 31st it was able to fire on a Russian infantry battalion near Reiherort, but on the same day it ran onto a mine near Augustwalde but could be made mobile again quickly. On the first days of February it took part in the defensive fighting around Arnswalde, so that on 4 February it was able to cover the withdrawal from Stargard and the blowing up of the tracks behind it. On 2 February the new PZ 77 also arrived. It came just at the right time to take part in the evacuation on the line from Pyritz toward Stargard. On 8 February it tried in vain to use its artillery and disembarked infantry to stop Russian tanks near Warnitz-Damnitz; the next day it had a costly fight with Soviet tanks near Gross-Schönfeld. On 16 February a counteroffensive was begun from Stargard, but it came to a stop in the western district near Warnitz-Damnitz, but at first broke through to Dölitz in the direction of Arnswalde. The two armored trains, which could not advance because of the destroyed tracks, took

At the beginning of February 1945, the just-finished PZ 77 was transferred to Pomerania for the newly created Army Group "Weichsel" (Vistula). Photo: H. Schüller/W. Sawodny collection

PZ 77 took part in the defensive fighting south of Stargard in February. On February 27, 1945, it was destroyed between Drawehn and Bublitz. Photo: H. Schüller/W. Sawodny collection

part on 17-18 February in the defensive fighting near Strebelow and Collin, where the Russians tried to cut off the German spearhead. The German offensive soon had to be stopped.—From reports on the action of the 1st Polish Army it can be seen that from 5 to 21 February a German "armored train" had also been active in the Märkisch-Friedland—Falkenburg—Tempelburg district. This was surely not one of the regular ones, but possibly—though not probably—a line protection train or even an anti-aircraft train (eastern sources do not differentiate among them all—anything that fired from railroad rails was an "armored train"!).

On the Oder front too attempts were made to get a group of armored trains together, but there was not very much available there at first. On 2 February only the line protection trains "Max" (newly assembled out of captured Slovakian material) and No. 83 (left with the Replacement Battalion) and the armored railcars No. 22 (taken from PZ 22 in Upper Silesia) and No. 37 ("Littorina" type) could be sent. The Reich Ministry for Armament and War Production (Albert Speer) and the Inspector-General of the Armored Troops decided hastily in Berlin to another line protection train, which should bear the name of the Reich capital, built (it was ready for action by 15 February). In command of all the armored trains assigned to Army Group "Weichsel" (thus on the Oder front and in Pomerania) was to be the Armored Train Regimental Staff No. 2 (Lt.Col. von Türckheim)—who had been out of work with the loss of all his trains in Poland and

Upper Silesia—was to take over as commander of this army group. On 3 February he received the makeshift Command Train No. II, so that his previous command train, No. 72A, could be added to the battle group (though it was transferred to Pomerania at the beginning of March). On 6 February PZ 65, overhauled by the Replacement Battalion, could be sent to the Oder front to replace the line protection train "Max," which was unsuitable for service on the eastern front, but which (along with PT 37?) was soon transferred to the Balkans. Further reinforcements were PT 16 around 20 February and PT 21 at the beginning of March. The commander and his command train were at first stationed with Army High Command 9 in Fürstenwalde; when General Henrici took over the army group, he was ordered to Army Group Command in Prenzlau and set up his command post in Beenz southwest of there. The fighting vehicles were at first on the Muencheberg—Werbig—Küstrin (Line Protection Train No. 83) and Fürstenwalde—Rosengarten—Frankfurt an der Oder (Line Protection Train "Max," later replaced by PZ 65, PZ 72A and PT 37). A record dated 19 February shows the trains essentially on the line connecting Rosengarten and Werbig: Line Protection Train No. 83 on the Werbig—Gorgast line, Line Protection Train "Berlin" at the Seelow railroad station, PZ 72A at the Schönfliess station and PZ 65 at the Boossen station. The assignments of the armored railcars are not known. The combat report of the Armored Train Battle Group for the month of February includes the fighting of enemy positions

The repaired PZ 65 was sent to the Oder front in February 1945. Note the "Wirbelwind" A/A turret and the tank-destroyer car. Photo: F. Gruber/W. Sawodny collection

The camouflaged PZ 65 is west of Frankfurt an der Oder on the main line to Berlin. Photo: F. Gruber/W. Sawodny collection

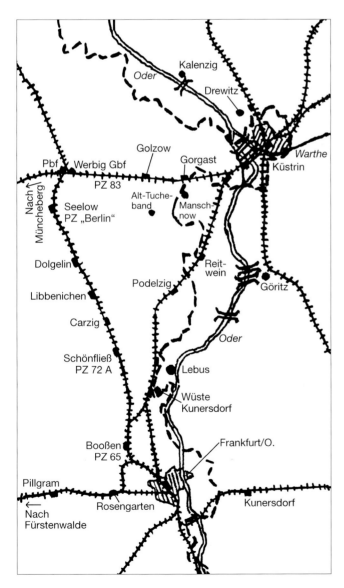

The Oder front between Küstrin and Frankfurt in February 1945. (The front line — — — — — showed only very few changes that whole month.)

east of Gorgast by PZ 83, in which one antitank gun was destroyed, on 5-6 February. On 7 and 12 February this armored train supported an attack in this area (on Manschnow on the 12th) with artillery fire. From 15 to 20 February Armored Trains No. 65 and 72A fired on enemy positions in the Lebus—Wüste Kunersdorf region as well as the approach routes to the bridgehead. On 16 February they supported an attack on Elisenberg and smashed an enemy counterattack the next day. On 28 February these armored trains, along with the Frankfurt fortress artillery, fired on enemy movements and trench work on the southern edge of the enemy bridgehead. The line protection train "Berlin," stationed in Seelow, fired its A/A guns on Soviet aircraft on 17, 20, and 22 February, of which only that of 20 February crashed on the German side of the front near Alt-Tucheband. Shot totals cited for that month (minus PZ 72A, which was withdrawn as February turned to March): 556 10- and 10.5-cm howitzer shells, 360 shells from 7.62-cm cannons, 51 from 7.5-cm tank guns, and a total of 1695 rounds of 2-cm anti-aircraft ammunition.

PZ 72A was also transferred to Pomerania at the beginning of March. PZ 83 seems to have been called in from the Werbig—Gorgast line top the Frankfurt an der Oder area in place of it, but exact data for the six weeks after 1 March are lacking. Thus it is not known either if the armored trains were in action in the area west of Küstrin when the Soviets surrounded that city and vain attempts were made to reopen the way to it. In general, the lack of ammunition, which grew more and more tangible, led to the fact that artillery actions were no longer carried out, but enemy air attacks had to be fought off more and more often. Before the Russian offensive began in mid-April 1945, the line protection train "Berlin" was in Seelow again, while Armored Trains No. 65 and 83 were on the southern part of the Werbig—Rosengarten line.

Just as it had done from the Vistula bridgeheads south of Warsaw against Army Group A, the Red Army had also set out to storm East Prussia on 13-14 January. The thrusts were directed frontally at first from the Schlossberg—Goldap area toward Königberg and from the Narew bridgehead northward from Warsaw toward the lower Vistula. Thus the region around the Masurian Lakes, in which the armored trains of Army Group North were located, was quiet at first. The 17th of January still saw them in the previous positions: Armored Trains No. 52 and 76 (with PT 23) in Urbansdorf ahead of Goldap, No. 30 (with PT 19) and 72B in Reuß east of Treuburg (PZ 68 was being overhauled at the Königsberg RAW). Only on January 19 were Armored Trains No. 30 and 72B alarmed and transferred to the 2nd Army in the Soldau breakthrough area. On the way to Deutsch-Eylau the armored locomotive of PZ 30 was left in Allenstein; it was pulled farther by an unarmored spare locomotive. On the morning of 20 January the group undertook a reconnaissance run in the direction of Soltau. Near Hartowitz they came upon a group of enemy tanks with infantry on them; in the fire fight that developed, PT 19 took a direct hit but could be towed away. They returned to Grodden, where enemy tanks soon turned up; later the trains went to Deutsch-Eylau. PZ 68 had arrived there meanwhile, having escorted and important transport westward from Königsberg (two not yet finished cars and the train's locomotive had remained in Königsberg, though). The next two days saw the three armored trains in action before Deutsch-Eylau, but it was already circled on both sides by the Russians on 21 January. On the night of 22-23 January as many women and children as possible were taken into the trains, which broke through to Charlottenwerder; there was only a brief exchange of shots with the enemy, but a blown-up track at one place had to be repaired with securing by the disembarked infantry. On 23 and 24 January the armored train group was still on the line between Riesenburg and Marienburg; on 25 January—previously attacked strongly in Marienburg—it crossed the Nogat.

Armored Trains No. 52 and 76, which remained in the Masurian Lakes area on 19 January, were subordinated to the 3rd Armored Army on 21 January and ordered into action on the Friedland—Wehlau line. Apparently, PZ 52 did not trust the situation. It sent one more radio message, in which it asked about the location of the Armored Army High Command 3, but set off quickly to the west itself. Taking along a hospital train in Schlobitten, it was able to reach Marienburg before the enemy broke the link near Elbing and join the Eylau armored train group. Thus only PZ 76 went with PT 23 to Königsberg; it was sent into action near Labiau on the northern line to Tilsit, where it was in combat on 25 January. Dropping back to the edge of Königsberg on 28 January, it was then transferred to the meanwhile threatened line from Königsberg to Pillau, but could not prevent it from being broken near Metgethen on 30 January. PZ 76 stayed outside the enclosing ring in the Fischhausen area. In the German attack on 19 February, which restored the connection between the Samland and Königsberg, PZ 76 saw service near Forken. The rest of PZ 68, which had remained in Königsberg, was stationed at the north station during the first encirclement of Königsberg and supported the defenders' north front. After the pocket was broken open it went to Fischhausen and was coupled to PT 23 there. Along with PZ 76 it secured the line between Königsberg and Pillau in the following weeks, but was also used on the fronts around Königsberg again and again. When the Soviets began the final storming of Königsberg, it gave artillery support in the suburb of Rosenau at first. Then it fought—while the ring closed again in the west—in the area of the rail triangle north of the main railroad station and experienced the end at the north station, near which the crew fought until the surrender. PZ 76, on the other hand, found itself outside the enclosing ring again this time. It made several vain attempts to break it. When the Soviets attacked the Samland, it was immobilized by shots in Seerappen on 14 April, made useless by the crew, and abandoned. Later the abandoned train was totally destroyed by low-level Russian planes.

There were still four of the five armored trains (No. 30, 52, part of No. 68, and the command train No. 72B) of the Regimental Battle Group of Lt.Col. Dr. Günther that had been able to cross the Vistula near Dirschau and thus avoid encirclement in East Prussia. Next they protected the Vistula line from Dirschau to Laskowitz west of the Graudenz bridgehead, with the focal point at the latter town.

When the Russians pushed northward through the Tuchel Heath, the armored train battle group was transferred to the Konitz area on 13 February and used for defense on the line from there to Czersk. It should be remembered that Konitz was the place where PZ 3 had crossed the Polish border when the war began on September 1, 1939, and became involved in heavy fighting. Now they were at the same place again, but now in the backward movement. Konitz itself was lost of 15 February. On 19 February the armored trains returned to the Dirschau area, where they were exposed to strong air attacks; on 23 February they went to the Preussisch-Stargard area, where the Russians tried to break through northward in the direction of Danzig. In firing positions near Hoch-Stueblau and Dreidorf they took part in the successful defensive fighting. On 27 February they received the OKH's order to march out; the entire armored train group was to be transferred to the Bautzen area in Lusatia. But the 2nd Army refused to give in and kept the armored trains there one more day, until the night of 1 March; that was to become their ruin.

On 24 February strong Soviet forces had entered Pomerania to break through toward the Baltic Sea, and quickly gained territory from the Preussisch-Friedland—Schlochau line to the northwest. The armored trains in Stargard (No. 77 and Instruction Train No. 5) were sent on the march to the west flank of the breakthrough area on 25 February. The next day PZ 77 was able to ward off the attack of Russian tanks on the Bublitz railroad station in an all-day fight; then it returned to Drawehn. In an attempt to go back toward Bublitz the next day it came into a trap probably set just for it. Twenty T 34 tanks and six antitank guns had driven to the tracks and took it under concentrated fire. Soon it was made immobile and destroyed more and more. The commander and infantry officer were killed, the rest of the crew disembarked and were able to get away from the train despite losses.—The Instruction PZ 5 went to Neustettin and escorted a gun transport from there to Belgard on the night of 26-27 February. Then it stayed—subordinated to the von Tettau Corps Group—in that area, took part in defensive fighting around Köslin on 3 March, and after the city fell on 4 March it returned to Belgard. Meanwhile the Russians had advanced from the south to the Treptow—Belgard line and reached the Baltic Sea on both sides of the thus encircled Kolberg. The von Tettau Corps Group thus found itself cut off in the Belgard—Köslin area and decided to break out. The Instruction PZ 5 was therefore blown up in Belgard on the night of March 4-5 before the crew started out with the others. In an adventurous march right through the Russian-occupied district, they were able to reach the Baltic Sea near Horst (northwest of Treptow) on 8 March, move along the shore, and on 11 March reach the Dievenow bridgehead, where there were still German troops.

When the loss of PZ 77 became known, it was decided to send PZ 72A from the Oder front to Pomerania in its place. Arriving in Köslin on 2 March, it was able to set out for Kolberg on the morning of 4 March, shortly before the city was surrounded. On 5 March PZ 72A—along with the 3rd Company of Railroad Building Battalion 408—was to set out from the Siederland railroad station to beyond Neugeldern to be able to give flank support to the advance along the Treptower Chaussee planned for the next morning. Since the destroyed tracks had to be repaired first, the action could take place only after night had fallen. After 6 kilometers it came upon Russian tanks dug in on both sides of the line, secured by strong infantry forces. Despite repeated advances, they could not get through, and the armored train was hit several times in this operation. It then returned to the Siederland railroad station and was to fire on Russian tanks near

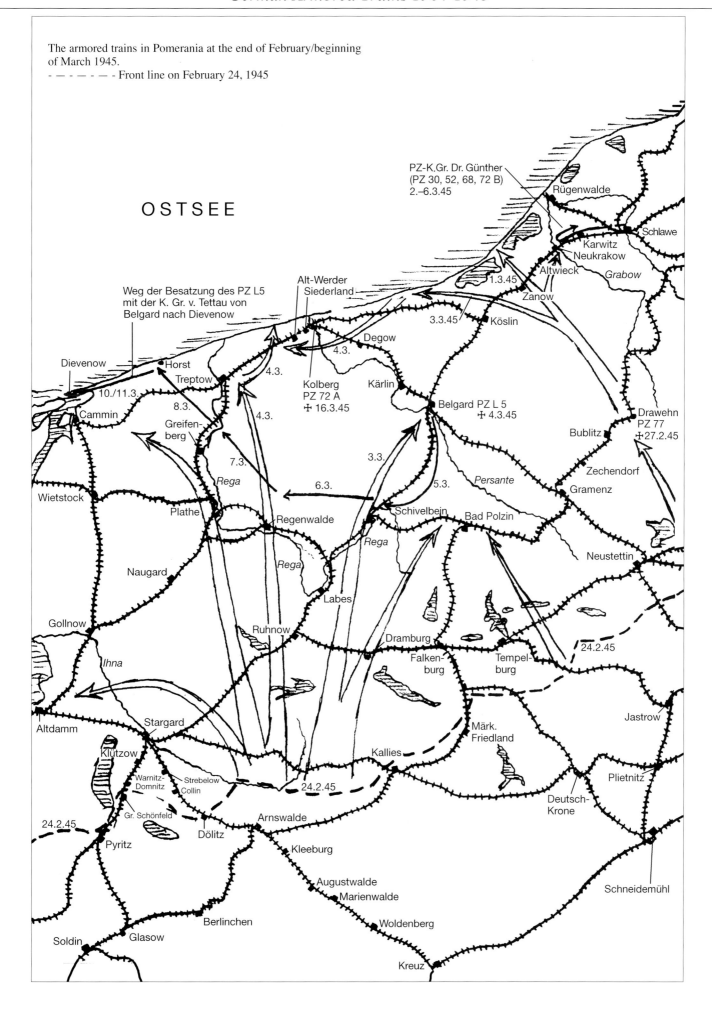

The armored trains in Pomerania at the end of February/beginning of March 1945.
- — - — - — - Front line on February 24, 1945

OSTSEE

PZ-K.Gr. Dr. Günther
(PZ 30, 52, 68, 72 B)
2.–6.3.45

Rügenwalde

Schlawe

Karwitz
Neukrakow

Altwieck

1.3.45

Zanow

Grabow

Alt-Werder
Siederland

Degow

3.3.45

Köslin

Weg der Besatzung des PZ L5
mit der K. Gr. v. Tettau von
Belgard nach Dievenow

Dievenow

Horst
Treptow

4.3.

4.3.

Kolberg
PZ 72 A
✝ 16.3.45

Kärlin

Belgard PZ L 5
✝ 4.3.45

Drawehn
PZ 77
✝ 27.2.45

10./11.3.

Cammin

8.3.

Greifen-
berg

4.3.

3.3.

Bublitz

Zechendorf

Gramenz

7.3.

Rega

Persante

Wietstock

Plathe

Regenwalde

6.3.

Schivelbein

5.3.

Bad Polzin

Neustettin

Rega

Rega

Naugard

Labes

Gollnow

Ruhnow

Dramburg

Falken-
burg

Tempel-
burg

24.2.45

Ihna

Jastrow

Altdamm

Stargard

Kallies

Märk.
Friedland

Plietnitz

Klützow

Deutsch-
Krone

Warnitz-
Domnitz

Strebelow
Collin

Gr. Schönfeld

Dölitz

Arnswalde

24.2.45

24.2.45

Pyritz

Kleeburg

Augustwalde

Marienwalde

Schneidemühl

Berlinchen

Woldenberg

Soldin

Glasow

Kreuz

Altwerder from there. This was unsuccessful, but the armored train drew the fire of the Russian artillery to itself. Thus on 7 March, when the enemy had come within 300 meters of the Siederland railroad station, it went back to the main station. German sources mention only that the train had been blown up there several days later, but Polish sources indicate that it had very vigorous activity before that on the eastern front of the enclosing ring. From 9 to 11 March—located in the eastern part of the freight station—its fire halted the attack of the 3rd Polish Infantry Division on St. George's Cemetery. From 13 March on it defended itself in the area of the locomotive roundhouse. Even the support of heavy "Stalin" tanks could not advance the Polish infantry's action against it. Only on 16 March could it be damaged so severely by massed fire of Field Artillery Regiment 6 that the crew had to give it up; they were transported out of Kolberg by ship.

When Lt.Col. Dr. Günther's Armored Train Battle Group set out westward from Preussisch-Stargard on the night of 1 March, a day late, the Russian tank spearhead had already reached the Baltic Sea between Köslin and Schlawe (the supply trains, sent out earlier, made it through!). So the Armored Train Battle Group, when they reached Schlawe on the afternoon of 2 March, saw that they were cut off from their further way back. While Armored Trains No. 52 and 68 immediately went on in the direction of the breakthrough site, No. 30 and 72B at first went toward Stolpmünde, and followed the other two trains only late in the evening. On 3 March Armored Trains No. 52 and 68 were in Neukrakow, while No. 30 and 72B were in Schlawin. The Russians blew up the railroad bridge over the Grabow. The attempts to rebuild the bridge in the next three days failed; they were given up because the Soviets, who were now on the Baltic in a broad front extending to far west of Kolberg, made a breakthrough illusory. Since the Russians had meanwhile pushed eastward as well to the north of Schlawe, the armored trains were transferred to defend the line from Schlawe to Stolpmünde; on the morning of the 7th they were already near Strellin heading from there to Stolp. That evening they reached the Russian advance units on the town's western edge, and the armored trains then went off toward Lauenburg. On 8-9 March they were in firing positions there near Neuendorf on the branch line to Leba; then the Russians were there too. Their further trip back led via Neustadt and Rheda to Gotenhafen, which they reached on 11 March. The armored trains were used as of 12 March to support the front forward of Gross-Katz. The action was taken in alternating pairs, two armored trains being in combat while the other two took on water, coal and ammunition in Gotenhafen. The heaviest fire hit the armored trains' position almost ceaselessly; they tried—as well as they could—to return it. On 19 March the Russians attacked. Gross-Katz had to be given up. Armored Trains No. 30 and 52 were in action then and were able to shoot down several Russian tanks and antitank guns on 20 March, but a bridge was blown up behind them, so that they were in a trap. The cars of the armored trains were set up separately while the locomotives were pushed over the blown-up bridge. On the next morning these armored trains were assaulted by Russian infantry; some of the crewmen were able to fight their way to Gotenhafen and via Zoppot to Neufahrwasser and be shipped home.—Armored Trains No. 68 and 72B were also in action behind the explosion site on that day. Lt.Col. Dr. Günther was fatally wounded, apparently by a splinter from a shell fired by the heavy cruiser "Prinz Eugen" in support that fell too short. These trains continued to take part in the defensive fighting ahead of Gotenhafen until the city was finally taken by the Soviets on 28 March; then the armored trains went back

to the Oxhöfter Kämp and were finally blown up there. The crews were ferried across to Hela.—On the Hela peninsula in April 1945 there was also a makeshift armored train built and equipped with naval guns, meant to strengthen the defense of the railroad area. It was also manned by former crewmen of Armored Trains No. 68 and 72B and remained active until the surrender on 9 May.

This requires us to remember another makeshift armored train that was set up in the last days of the war. Breslau, the home of the Linke-Hofmann Works and thus the production site of the standard armored trains since 1942, was already near the front at the end of January 1945. The material for Armored Trains No. 80 to 82, still under construction, was thus evacuated (while the also unfinished Railcars No. 52-55 were left there, only No. 51 got out). Breslau itself was encircled by Russian troops on 13 February. The fortress commander was Engineer General von Ahlfen, who had commanded armored trains in 1918-20 and had always expressed an interest in such units. So even in the surrounded Breslau on 28 February he ordered the building of such a train at the FAMO Works. Several still-available car chassis were brought from the nearby Linke-Hofmann car factory, and appropriate bodies were built for them. The armament consisted of four 8.8-cm, one 3.7-cm and four 2-cm A/A guns plus two MG 42. The assembly was done at the old RAW on Matthiasstrasse. On 20 March the train was ready and went into action with a 106-man crew. It was named Armored Train "Pörsel" after its commander. The train was first used in the southwest part of the city in the Mochbern district, in the direction of Schmiedefeld. Attacking with guns firing in a surprise advance, it was able to bring relief to the defenders again and again, especially those at the Gandau airport. By the end of the month it had shot down seven tanks and three airplanes. In the preparatory fire for the Russian attack on 1 April, though, its locomotive was hit, which made its withdrawal necessary. Since the armored train's previous action area had been lost in the Russian attack, it was transferred to the northern sector after being repaired. From then on it moved along the branch line parallel to the front from Breslau-Burgweide to Rosenthal and gave fire support to the Sauer Regiment located there. One of its cars with an 8.8-cm A/A gun was set up, well camouflaged, at the Burgweide railroad station and barred the line coming in from Oels. The Armored Train "Pörsel" apparently remained in action there until Breslau surrendered on 6 May.

Eastern sources mention two other German "armored trains." On 23 March Polish units in Kopitz, on the east bank of the mouth of the Oder, were fired on from Ziegenort on the opposite shore by one such—it was very probably an anti-aircraft train that was there to protect the Hydrogenation Works in Pölitz. At the end of March a T 34 of the 56th Armored Brigade claimed to have destroyed an armored train at the Lauban railroad station. Here too it may have been an (unknown) line protection or anti-aircraft train.—An actual addition occurred in March, though, in the transfer of PZ 75 from the Balkans to protect the OKH headquarters in Zossen and the office of the Inspector-General of the Armored Troops in Wuensdorf. From then on it was on the line from Zossen via Baruth to Golssen.

On 16 April the Russians began the final attack on the Oder and Neisse, which in a short time, in conjunction with the Allied movements from the west, was to result in the occupation of all of northern and central Germany and the surrender of the German Wehrmacht. In the vigorous fighting around the rail triangle near Werbig, the line protection train "Berlin" intervened from Seelow; it is said to have shot down no fewer than 56 Soviet tanks. Later, damaged in the fight and by low-level planes, it moved back into

Just one day after the Soviet offense began on the Oder front, on April 17, 1945, the line protection train No. 350, rebuilt at Krupp-Druckenmüller in Berlin, was ready for action as a makeshift armored train. Its command car is seen here. Photo: E. Behling/W. Sawodny collection

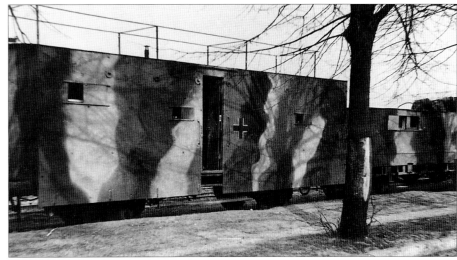

Below: Subordinated to the Steiner Group, from which Hitler hoped in vain for the relief of the Reich capital, it operated in northern Brandenburg. Here the commander, 1st Lt. Packheiser, stands before the tank destroyer car. Photo: E. Behling/W. Sawodny collection

a railroad cut south of Seelow and had to be abandoned there after the Russians had also reached the rail line near Dolgelin. The rest of the battle group (PZ 65, Line Protection Train No. 83, and Railcars No. 16, 21, and 22, perhaps also 37) were apparently all in the area around Frankfurt an der Oder. There they took part in the defensive fighting in the Boossen—Rosengarten region, which could be held at first. On 19 April, at the right time before the Soviet forces that had broken through near Seelow turned to the southwest and crossed the Frankfurt—Berlin line west of Fürstenwalde, the battle group drew back toward Berlin and was in Erkner on 20-21 April. Their further path led through the Reich capital and via Spandau to Nauen, then they turned to Mecklenburg. Armored Trains No. 65 and 83 (and presumably also the armored railcars) were at Lake Mueritz in Waren on 24 April.

At the same time as the White Russian Front on the Oder east of Berlin, the 1st Ukrainian Front on the Neisse between Forst and Muskau began to move on 16 April and immediately achieved a breakthrough in the direction of Cottbus and Spremberg. On the morning of 20 April the spearhead of the 3rd Guard Armored Army was already near Lübben and moved farther that day through Baruth to shortly before Zossen, the seat of the OKH. Before that city, though, it was held up, possibly with the cooperation of PZ 75, which also moved out of its station in Baruth to Zossen. This made possible on the same evening the—very rushed, to be sure—evacuation of the headquarters. The next day the Soviets stayed in the Zossen area and, along with the forces of the 1st White Russian Front which had advanced from Müncheberg via Fürstenwalde, closed the ring around the 9th Army near Königswusterhausen. On 22 April they moved on toward Berlin and reached the Teltow Canal. PZ 75, drawing back to Berlin, provided a withdrawal fight near Gross-Beeren and then set out at the right time, before the line was broken near Nauen on 23 April, out of Berlin via Spandau.

On 17 April, thus one day after the Russian offensive began, the rebuilt line protection train No. 350 was finished in Berlin. It went to the north flank of the breakthrough site, to the south wing of the 3rd Armored Army at Bad Freienwalde. On the 19th it had to retreat toward Eberswalde already. Assigned to the troops of Obergruppenführer Steiner there, by whom one—then abandoned for lack of forces—attack in the direction of Berlin was expected, it made advances in the direction of Melchow and Niederfinow, but went back to Templin on 22 April. Along with the Steiner Battle Group, it was transferred on 23 April to the Neu-Ruppin—Oranienburg region. There PT 16 met line protection train No. 350; both units were stationed in Beetz-Sommerfeld on the Neu-Ruppin—Kremmen line. PT 22 was also assigned to the Steiner Battle Group on 23 April and was on the line from Löwenberg toward Oranienburg, which was taken by the enemy on 24 April. Whether other vehicles of the armored train group gathered in Waren were also transferred there is not known. Again great hopes were placed in Berlin on relief attempts by the Steiner Group, but after initial success east of Oranienburg on 24 April and near Kremmen on 27 April, they were quickly driven back by the Soviets. Line Protection Train No. 350 and PT 16 were taken back to Radensleben on 27 April; from that day on, PT 22 secured the line from Neustadt/Dosse via Rhinow in the direction of Rathenow, which had been reached by the Russian advance units on that day. According to Polish sources, on 30 April an armored train coming from Neustadt/Dosse supplied flank cover for a—repulsed—German counterattack from Friesack toward Braedikow and then, after being damaged, steamed back to Neustadt; this was most probably PZ 75, which may have stayed in this region after leaving Berlin. On the afternoon of 30 April—as the Russians, who had broken through into the zone of the 3rd Armored Army from Fürstenberg and Zehdenik approached—Line Protection Train No. 350 and PT 16 set out for Neu-Ruppin, and on the next day for Neustadt/Dosse. While Line Protection Train No. 350—like PZ 75 and PT 22—went on from there to Wittenberge, PT 16 must have either (perhaps with some damage) stayed in Neustadt or even gone on southward in the direction of Rhinow (to replace PT 22?), for it was captured by the 1st Polish Army, which occupied that area. Information is lacking for the other units of the Armored Train Group (PZ 65 and 83, plus PT 21 and perhaps 37) that was in Waren on 24 April, but an armored train seems to have been in the Karow—Parchim region around 30 April. On 2 May the veil was lifted. All the still-available vehicles of the Armored Train Group, Armored Trains No. 65 and 75, Line Protection Trains No. 83 and 350, and Armored Railcars No. 21, 22, and perhaps 37, had gathered on the Ludwigslust—Parchim line. On the afternoon of that day they moved on together via Ludwigslust in the direction of Schwerin. In Holthusen they met units of the 8th U.S. Infantry Division, which had crossed the Elbe near Bleckede and moved forward via Hagenow to Schwerin. They surrendered to them. The trains and railcars were instructed to go to Hagenow-Land, where they were finally turned over to the Americans and the crews were sent to the collecting camp for prisoners.

Command Train No. II of the Commander of the Armored Trains in Army Group Weichsel took a different course. Only when the Russians broke out of the bridgehead on the Oder, formed near Gartz on 20 April, to the west on 24-25 April and approached Prenzlau from the northeast on 27 April, having already advanced far beyond it to the north, did Army Group Staff and Commander leave their quarters in Birkenhain and Beenz. The route of the command train led via Templin, Fürstenberg, and Neustrelitz to Waren, in the vicinity of which Army Group Staff settled for a short time on 28 April. With the removal of Heinrici as Commander of Army Group on 29 April, the Commander of the Armored Trains seems to have sought his own route with his command train. He traveled westward via Karow, Goldberg, Sternberg, Bad Kleinen, and Grevesmühlen, and apparently tried to reach the Schleswig-Holstein area. On 2 May, though, the train was blocked by several trains near Boerzow on the line toward Luebeck. The Americans had already advanced to the Baltic Sea in the east. Lt.Col. von Türckheim disbanded his staff and train crew. In small groups they tried to get through either southward or westward. Most of them went into American or British captivity sooner or later. A few were actually able to go home without trouble.

Since the beginning of October 1944, Army Group North was cut off in Courland and had to be supplied by sea. The request, submitted over and over, to take the troops there back to the Reich, where they were needed urgently, came to nothing because of Hitler's stubbornness. So they stayed there—far to the east of the main front—until the surrender on 8 May. PZ 26 was with them. In a series of attacks, the enemy tried to smash the Courland pocket. The offensive that was carried out since 22 December on both sides of the Doblen—Frauenburg rail line, in which the armored train normally stayed in its firing position ahead of Bixten, saw the train go to be overhauled in Libau. Thus it could take part only in the final phase from 29 December on. The position before Bixten could be maintained. On 1 March the Soviets again attacked in this region. This time, after tough defensive fighting, in which PZ 26 was

involved, the Germans were drawn back to Blieden. On 18 March the Russians renewed their offensive. The front was pushed ever farther to the west. On 22 March PZ 26 was in direct front action near Brotzen. It was considerable damaged in the process. The burning artillery and command cars had to be uncoupled. While the infantry crew remained in trench action in this sector until the end of April, the armored train was taken to the Libau RAW. The repairs lasted until shortly before the capitulation date, so that it never went back into action.

The only large area that the German Wehrmacht could hold until the capitulation, besides the Austrian-West Yugoslavian region, was Bohemia and Moravia. In the middle of it, the base of the Armored Train Replacement Battalion had been located at Milowitz, near Lissa on the Elbe, since August 1944. At the end of January, to be sure, the most essential production facilities for the armored trains, the Linke-Hofmann Works in Breslau (producing the standard BP 44 armored trains) and Königshütte Wagon Works (rebuilding older trains) had had to be evacuated, but the work—even though with inevitable delays—could be done at other places (the BP 44 armored trains were built at the car factory in Boehmisch-Leipa). In addition, the Steyr factory in St. Valentin still delivered heavy scout trains. Since the crews of armored trains lost in the winter of 1944-45 were sent back as special troops to the Armored Train Replacement Battalion, there was no shortage of personnel, and in the last days of the war a whole series of new armored trains could be put into action, but necessarily had to stay in the Bohemian-Moravian region. Yet the rebellion of the Czech railroad men grew ever stronger as the war's end approached. At first railroad stations and tracks were so filled with the great quantities of locomotive and car material evacuated from areas farther east, often no longer fully usable, that the transport routes were crippled. On 2 May this resistance in eastern Bohemia grew into an open revolt. Now tracks were also blown up, transports stopped by force of arms and their personnel taken prisoner. In the next few days this uprising spread, and culminated on the morning of 5 May in the bloody events in and around Prague. Armored trains in and of themselves would have been a good means of at least keeping the transport routes open, and a convoy system seems to have been organized in some areas, in which armored trains ahead were supposed to open the way for a row of following transports. It soon became evident, though, that even with these units, in view of the evident end and the uncertain fate, confidence had disappeared and the will to fight had been crippled. The events there, to be sure, could not be made clear in every detail any more (for instance, no trace of Armored Train No. 99—named in a field post list for April 1945—could be found to date). German documentary material from this period is not available, Czech material from the immediate postwar phase gives only very insufficient data, and the memories of the former members of armored trains of those days, when they can be located, scarcely apply to the trains and their equipment or the places where they saw action, but only to the question of how one could somehow save his skin in view of the imminent collapse and its results.

Armored Trains (BP 44) No. 80-82 are documentable; No. 81 and 82 had personnel assigned to them by order of the OKH of April 5, 1945, but PZ 82 was never finished. The rebuilt armored trains No. 7 and 27 still saw service, as did the line protection train "Moritz." The reequipping of the heavy scout trains No. 205 and 206 was also finished at the Replacement Battalion. At the end of April the makeshift Command Train No. III was put into service. It was originally intended for the Armored Train Regimental Staff No. 3, which had meanwhile gone down to defeat near Gotenhafen. There are indications that such a regimental staff, under the leadership of the former commander of the Armored Train Replacement Battalion, Major Naumann, was in service and active in the last days of the war; it is said to have departed from Milowitz at the beginning of May, along with another armored train (Type BP 44?, No. 81?), obviously to Reichenberg, where two armored trains are said to have been in the very last days of the war. After the war the Czechs found a single light rail-capable armored scout car (Steyr type) there, such as was used as a command railcar by the armored train regimental staffs. Beyond that, found stationed in Friedland at the end of May 1945 with the Czech armored train "Sokol"—as proved by photos—was a gun-A/A car of the German BP 44 type, which it could have taken over in Reichenberg. Czech sources report on an "armored train" abandoned by its crew in the Upper Georgenthal (Ober-Leutensdorf—Komotau line); this could have reached this area in flight from Reichenberg to the west (perhaps Command Train III?). But it must be remembered that the Czechs also called anti-aircraft railroad trains "armored trains" and put captured ones into service under that name.

The just-finished PZ 80 was driven out of Breslau at the end of January. Then came the final equipping and running-in at the Replacement Battalion before it went into action at the end of March in the Mährisch-Ostrau region. In April it was withdrawn to Olmütz. There PZ 80 was relieved by PZ 7 on 2 May. It began the trip back via Böhmisch-Trübau toward Kolin. The Czechs had already rebelled in eastern Bohemia. On the way, it was able to liberate an engineer battalion who had been disarmed by Czech insurgents near Chotzen; in Pardubitz they had to struggle to go farther. Since the direct route to the west was impossible because of the rebellion in Prague, the armored train went via Deutsch-Brod, Iglau, Pilgram, and Tabor, leaving behind the armored locomotive (because it was too heavy for the Moldau bridge) to Pisek, where there were American troops, to whom they tried to surrender on 10 May. But the train, along with the crew—like all German units in that area—was turned over to the Russians.

PZ 7, finished at the Ingolstadt RAW, was ready for action at the beginning of May and replaced PZ 80 in the Olmütz area on the second of that month; the supply train was left in Müglitz. Its actions on the next day took it from Schwarzbach to Stefanau in the direction of Olmütz and to Littau and Senitz, the return trip via Kostoletz and Mährisch-Trübau. The capitulation terms reached the train in Böhmisch-Trübau on the evening of 8 May. After making the

The new PZ 7, finished at the Ingolstadt BW, is seen on the way to the front in northern Moravia (April-May 1945). Photo: D. Baum/W. Sawodny collection

weapons unusable, the crew left the train on the morning of 9 May and tried to go westward, but were soon disarmed by the Czechs and became Russian prisoners.

PT 36 (formerly with the Replacement Battalion in Milowitz), stationed since the end of April in Petschek on the Böhmisch-Brod—Kolin line, was ordered to the Olmütz area. On the transfer trip it fell victim to the rebellion of Czech railroad men in eastern Bohemia. While negotiations went on with a railroad station master (station not known), it was parked on a dead-end line before the buffer and the way out blocked by a freight train. The crew left the train, but was taken prisoner later.

The line protection train "Moritz," assembled of captured Slovakian material at the Steyr works, was ready for action at the end of April and reached the Brünn region, which had been taken by the Russians shortly before. There it presumably secured the line leading there from the west (Trebitsch). In the last days of the war it still had to go through a fight with Russian tanks to protect two 8.8-cm anti-aircraft batteries. When the surrender became known, it set out toward the west. According to a crew member, the train was abandoned along the way after the weapons had been destroyed; the men tried to fight their way through to the Americans but ended up as Russian prisoners of war. This could be the armored train whose arrival at noon on 7 May is listed in the Iglau station book. It intended to go on toward Kolin, but the Czech station master stopped them with the false information that the line was partly in partisan hands. He also warned them not to go on to Tabor immediately, ostensibly with the remark that the line was occupied. It was clear: "From then on the train was captured."—This description, though, could also apply to PZ 27, of which it is known only that even before the general capitulation it was surrendered to insurgent Czech units south of Prague (Tabor was named, but this information is very indefinite).

The heavy scout train No. 205 was ready for action only at the beginning of May. On the 3rd of the month it was to go to Moravia, but found itself prevented from going farther by track explosions beyond Königgrätz and withdrew to Pardubitz. After the line from there to the east was also unusable, it tried to get through to Chudrim, but near Chrast the line was also broken, and it was attacked by Czech insurgents. When the armored train tried to return to Pardubitz on 5 May to escort several transport trains, this line had also been blocked, but it succeeded—either by disposing of the barricade or by taking the nearby Hermanmestez—Valy line reach the Kolin—Podebrad region. On 7 May the heavy scout train No. 205 escorted hospital trains—probably via Jung-Bunzlau and Böhmisch-Leipa—toward Saxony and guarded an ammunition train on the way back to Neuenburg. On the same day an armored train of unknown number took the line from Lissa through Alt-Bunzlau toward Melnik. It was stopped by a track explosion at Drisy. Although it disposed of this, it went back to Lissa afterward as night was falling. A heavy armored railcar sent out scouting on the morning of 8 May (an independently running heavy rail-going armored scout car?) was also stopped near Drisy by track explosions on both sides; the crew surrendered. The Czechs now strengthened the track blockage; among other things, two cars loaded with explosives were parked on the railroad bridge over the state road northeast of Alt-Bunzlau. The following German convoy—consisting of an armored train (that of the previous day) going ahead, a train with a load of tanks, Heavy Scout Train No. 205, an armored railcar, a Panhard scout car, a hospital train with 80 cars and a quarters train for crewmen—came to a stop. The attempt to remove the blocks under fire from strong Czech units who had taken up positions there failed. The demand to surrender, though, was not accepted; rather the convoy went back to Lissa. There a part of the crews left the armored trains and tried to march overland and fight their way to the American lines near Pisek. But even the ones who

Czech insurgents before the makeshift armored train that was stopped and partly destroyed at the tunnel of Nelahozeves (north of Kralup) on May 8, 1945. The picture shows that in this last phase A/A cars were also used by the Germans in such trains. Photo: Statni Ustredni Archiv, Prague

got there were turned over to the Soviets. The armored trains were turned over to the Czechs by the rest of the crews on the night of 8 May.

The members of the Armored Train Replacement Battalion in Milowitz and Neuenburg had already set out to the southwest when they got the news of the surrender on 8 May. They left some armored trains behind, which were taken possession of by the Czechs, including the heavy scout train No. 206 in Milowitz and PZ 82, which had been delivered in pieces and was still being fitted out, Workshop Train No. 2 in Neuenburg, and one light and one heavy armored rail scout car. They hoped to be able to reach the Americans southwest of Prague. Soon split into individual groups, they were generally caught and taken prisoner along the way. Even the few who reached the Moldau were turned over to the Russians by the Americans. In the end, none of the armored train crewmen in the Bohemian-Moravian region in the last months of the war were able to evade the fate of Russian or Czech imprisonment.

In closing, let us tell of one more event that has made its way into the Czech secondary literature about the war's end—not always reported correctly in every detail—as a particularly heroic deed. The portrayal here is based on the station book at Kralup and the accounts of German participants. On 8 May the Czechs learned that a German line protection train (number or name unknown; according to Czech accounts it was armed with A/A and machine guns, and also with a 15-cm gun of unknown type) had gone off from Raudnitz in the direction of Prague. According to German accounts, it was to pick up hospital trains there and take them to Saxony. To catch this train, the Czechs built a trap in the tunnel at Nelahozeves (north of Kralup). Ahead of the tunnel the line used by the line protection train was

mined; in the tunnel itself a locomotive was waiting on this track, pushing three cars loaded with rails and iron plates before it. The German line protection train rode onto the mines, which derailed the front cars. By the pushing of the—unmanned—locomotive with the heavily loaded cars, the train was completely blocked. At the cut leading to the tunnel, rebels were posted, including a whole series of liberated Russian prisoners, who opened fire from one side. After the attention of the train crew turned to them, a Panzerfaust from the other side put the 15-cm gun out of commission. In the ensuing battle, the German crew suffered considerable losses. Although another mine had been set off farther back, they were able to uncouple at least the rear half of the train and move out of the danger zone. They went back to Vranany. That part of the train was left there; the crew joined German troops who were struggling along the road to the west, but later got into the clutches of the Soviet troops coming in from Saxony. The survivors among those who stayed with the immobilized part of the train became prisoners of the Czechs.—In the Czech secondary literature, the active intervention of a heavily armored Czech "Stalin" armored train is described, which came up on the other track and is said to have fired on the crippled German line protection train. In the station diary of Kralup, as written by participants soon after the events, it is said that the improvised A/A "Stalin" armored train was sent out from Roztoky (a whole series of such makeshift armored trains had been made up, consisting of cars from German light A/A trains, which had fallen into Czech hands in and around Prague from 5 May on), but not a word is said of the participation of this train in the fight itself, and members of the German train could not remember such a train. For after all, a "Stalin" armored train could have made the German troops in Kralup surrender by aiming its guns on them in Kralup.

Captured German Armored Trains

The course of events led to many of Germany's war enemies coming into the possession of more or fewer intact German armored railroad vehicles: the British Empire, France, Yugoslavia, Poland, the Soviet Union, the USA, and Czechoslovakia. Both the USA, to whom a battle group of four armored trains (No. 65, 75, 83, and 350) and armored railcars (No. 21, 22, and maybe 37) had been turned over at Holthusen, Mecklenburg (they could scarcely have known that in the capture of Nürnberg on 20 April, two railcars—No. 20 and one "Littorina," No. 33 or 37?, were at the RAW there for repairs), and the British, to whom Armored Trains No. 4 and 78 plus PT 32 had fallen in southern Austria (the Command Train No. II fell into American or British hands in northern Germany between Grevesmühlen and Schönberg) had no interest in such weapons and—surely after inspecting them appropriately—either removed the armor, so they could be returned to normal railroad use (this was especially true of locomotives), or scrapped them. Not so the French, who set up PZ 32, captured by them in St. Berain on September 8, 1944, as a display piece and exhibited it in numerous French railroad stations in the first postwar years. In 1947 Rene Clement used it in his film "Bataille du Rail" (The Rail War). Which shows how a transport convoy intended for the invasion front was captured by the Resistance for the invasion front. In 1949, to be sure, this armored train was also scrapped.

Most of the German armored trains and railcars, though, remained in the East and were often reused there. The information on them is naturally very different from one country to another, and also full of gaps.

By far the most of the vehicles came into the possession of the Soviet Union. From reports by prisoners of war it is shown that in 1945 transports of German armored train material ran via both Warsaw and Budapest to Russia, and there were also sightings in railroad stations there, though always in a dismantled condition. This is not surprising, for the Soviets themselves had built a great number of armored trains during the war, so that there was no lack of them; moreover, the German units did not represent their conceptions in their composition and equipment. It was different with the armored locomotives. Here it is known that the Russians even armed a large number of captured Series 52 War Locomotives and used them to pull their own armored trains. This allows the conclusion that they also may have used usable or easily reparable German armored train locomotives that fell into their hands for this purpose, even though concrete data are lacking.

It is well known which German armored trains were lost in Polish or Czechoslovakian territory, but some of them could have fallen into the hands of Soviet units and thus been taken away as their captured material.

For both countries, information about their own armored trains after May 1945 is available, though not always complete or without contradictions.

In Poland there were hard fights with nationalistic Ukrainian forces, who fought for the independence of their country, in the southeastern section right after the republic was founded. They also

PZ 78, abandoned by its crew, fell into British hands on May 9, 1945, at the railroad station in Thalheim in western Styria. R.A.C. Tank Museum, Bovington

PZ 32, captured in St. Berain on September 8, 1944, was used by the French as a display piece in many French railroad stations after the war, here in Verdun in 1946. Archiv "La vie du rail," Paris

In 1947 Rene Clement used it in his film "La bataille du rail"; two years later it was scrapped. Archiv "La vie du rail," Paris

tried particularly to cripple the railroad traffic through attacks and raids. The Polish People's Army thus put a series of armored trains, for which suitable available material, preferably of German origin, was gathered, in service to fight against them. The Polish Army used Armored Railcar No. 16, captured south of Neustadt/Dosse on May 1, 1945, as the nucleus of a regular armored train, though without the tank-destroyer cars. Instead two other German armored-train cars were included. One of them was a two-turret artillery car of the type used for rearming older German trains. As its source, the armored trains No. 24 or 25, lost in Poland, come into question. Of the second car there is no information—since it was not preserved. The Polish Army maintained this armored train until 1974; then they put it in the railroad museum, first in Skarzisko Kamienna, now in Warsaw. There the railcar and artillery car can still be seen today as two of the very few German armored railroad vehicles that have been preserved. Four other armored trains were put into service by the Polish General Command for Railroad Securing (SOK) as of the autumn of 1945: No. 1 "Szeczin," No. 2 "Grom," No. 3 "Huragan," and No. 4 "Blyskawica."

The exact composition of these trains is known only in part, as No. 1 and 3 were also rearmed during the course of their existence. No information is available about Train No. 1. Armored Train No. 2 had a Series 57 armored locomotive plus one command and two infantry cars that corresponded to the rebuilt German type; their exact origin is unknown. Armored Train No. 3 in its second version consisted of one gun-A/A car of the BP 44 type with a "Wirbelwind" turret (very probably from PZ 77, lost in Pomerania), an A/A car of the rebuilt German type (without guns), and an infantry car of non-German origin. Armored Train No. 4 was made up of one car with a Russian BT-7 turret, such as were used on German line protection trains, one command car of BP 42 type, and the command car of the earlier German PZ 28 (which was driven out of Minsk on June 23, 1944, after being damaged and must have been left in Rembertow or Pruszkow) and control cars that, interestingly, were German light railroad anti-aircraft cars (without guns). The locomotives of the armored trains No. 3 and 4 were unarmored and of Polish origin. The armored trains of the SOK remained in service until the end of the 1940s; their further fate is not known.—It is also significant that early in 1947 the "Division" made up of these four armored trains

The former German PT 16 was used by the Poles as the central unit of an armored train of their own after World War II. Photo: S. Lauscher collection

It was equipped with two more German armored train cars, one of which—an artillery car of the rebuilt type, based on a Russian four-axle car chassis—is still on display today with the former PT 16 in the Warsaw Railroad Museum. Photo: S. Lauscher collection

Polish SOK Armored Train No. 3 "Huragan". In front of the unarmored Series Tw 12 (ex-kkStB 80) locomotive is a gun-A/A car of BP 44 type with a "Wirbelwind" turret. Photo: J. Magnuski collection

Polish SOK Armored Train No. 4 "Blyskawica." Behind the Type BP 44 command car is that from PZ 28. Photo: J. Magnuski collection

was assigned a single armored railcar, as had been built by Steyr for the German light scout trains (No. 301-304). Since none of the scout trains used only in the Balkans could have reached Poland, nor any from the manufacturer's factory occupied by the Americans, this vehicle is a further indication that the "command railcars" that were set up for the German armored train regimental staffs at the end of April 1944, and about which no other information is available, may have been these scout railcars used as individual vehicles (both regimental staffs saw service in the Polish region, and one of them was lost there).

The postwar Czechoslovakian armored trains were made up completely of captured German material. When the revolt broke out on May 5-6, 1945, several armed German trains—the great majority of them railroad anti-aircraft trains (armed with single or quad 2-cm Flak 38, sometimes also with 2-cm MG 151 in triple mounts)—fell into Czech hands in the Prague region, out of which a whole series of improvised "armored trains" were made up. Out of an A/A train captured at the Prague-Vrsovice railroad station on 5 May—completed with other added cars—the armored trains "Praha," "Moskwa," and "Vrsovice" were made up; from another A/A train taken at the freight station there on the same day—completed with transport protection cars—the armored trains "Orlik 1," "Zizka," and "Libuse." An A/A train captured on the Smichov—Jinonice line became the armored train "Smichov"; one captured between Hostivar and Uhrineves was named "Uhrineves." On the same day the three armored trains "Orlik 2," "Sokol," and "Stalin" (the last apparently renamed "Kralup" later) were made up in Roztoky of A/A trains captured there and in Kralup. "Sokol" was set afire in the battles around Prague on 7 May, but later re-equipped with German armored train cars (including a gun and A/A car of the standard BP 44 type—from an armored train with a number in the eighties). In all, 18 such improvised armored trains existed in the autumn of 1945, and along with those named above, the names of "Blanik," "Kladno," and "Libochorice" (the last probably named after their places of origin) are known.

At the capitulation, the following material fell into Czech hands around the last locality of the Armored Train Replacement Battalion: in Milowitz itself the heavy scout train No. 206, which was divided into the armored trains "Marshal Stalin" and "General Pavlik," various armored train cars with a Series 52 armored locomotive and condenser tender, which were used for the armored train "President Benes," and other cars that were held in reserve; in the outside site of Neuenburg one light scout car at the railroad station and one heavy one needing repairs in the workshop; in Lissa one new armored train, which was divided into the armored trains "President Masaryk" and "General Svoboda"; and at the railroad station in Vysocany (east of Prague) two factory-new heavy rail-going armored scout cars, which were obviously in transport, another one (left behind from the heavy scout train No. 205 after the tracks had been blown up?) turned up in Drisy (Lissa—Alt-Bunzlau line), one light rail-going scout car was discovered in Reichenberg on a reconnaissance run. Later parts of other German trains used in Czechoslovakia were added, such as Heavy Scout Train No. 205, out of which the Czech armored train "J. M. Hurban" was made. Another steam-powered armored train, "General Stefanik," was also set up, possibly of cars from the armored train (No. 81?) captured near Reichenberg.

In the summer of 1945, all the armored rail vehicles were united into one armored train battalion. This included in the 1st Company (in parentheses are the added reconnaissance vehicles, where it is noteworthy that the two Tatra railcars captured from the Germans in 1939, probably left at last with the Replacement Battalion, are still present) the steam-engine-drawn armored trains "President T. G. Masaryk" Panhard reconnaissance car), "General Stefanik" (Panhard reconnaissance car), "President Benes" (Tatra railcar) and, as a training train, "General Svoboda" (Tatra railcar); in the 2nd Company the motor-driven armored trains, made up of heavy rail-going armored scout cars "Marshal Stalin" (light armored scout car), "General Pavlik" (light armored scout car) and "J. M. Hurban" (Panhard scout car) as a training train; the Replacement Company had

Out of German light A/A trains large numbers of which fell into Czech hands in the last days of the war and after the surrender, a series of improvised armored trains was made up by them. Here is IOV "Smichov" with single and quad 2-cm A/A guns. Photo: Vojenski Historicky Archiv, Prague

The Czech IOV "Vrsovice" used railroad A/A cars with two gun mounts (triple MG 151 in concrete rings). Photo: Vojenski Historicky Archiv, Prague

The Czech IOV "Sokol" was later equipped with a captured gun and A/A car of BP 44 type. Photo: J. Magnuski collection

the improvised armored train "Orlik (1)" (heavy armored scout car) and a training train (its composition listed as one gun car, one A/A car with two 2-cm quads, three machine gun cars and an only partly armored locomotive) and three training vehicles of the Steyr type (light or heavy rail-going armored scout cars?). Also belonging to the battalion independently were an armored railcar of the "Littorina" type (ex-German No. 36), three heavy and one light rail-going armored scout cars, one Tatra armored railcar and a small passenger railcar. The improvised armored trains were later stripped, the A/A cars assigned to other uses. It is noted that the rolling stock still on hand would suffice to set up another steam-powered and a motorized armored train; but whether this increase was ever made is not known, but the existing armored trains were variously rearmed and armed anew (in April 1946 the Böhmisch-Leipa Car Factory delivered two BP 44 type gun cars, originally meant for PZ 82 but not yet finished by the war's end). The armored train battalion existed until 1954; then it was disbanded and the armored trains presumably scrapped.

In the regular Czech armored trains, German tank-destroyers cars with Panzer IV turrets were also used—here on the POV "President Masaryk". Photo: J. Magnuski collection

The armored 52 1965 with four-axle condenser tender from German PZ 81 or 82 is seen in Czech hands. Photo: H. Wenzel collection

Only a few cars have been preserved. The command car of the Czech armored train "President T. G. Masaryk" (undoubtedly of German provenance, but not corresponding to the standard BP 42/44 type), which after the Czechs did away with the armored train weapon was dug in at an airfield as an underground command post, is in the Military History Museum at Prague-Lesany (formerly in the Air Travel Museum at Prague-Kbely).

A command car of BP 44 type is rusting alone in a fairly neglected condition on the grounds of the Museum and Documentation Center in Pressburg-East. Two cars of the line protection train "Moritz,"

made up of captured Slovakian material, were obviously taken back to Slovakia after the German capitulation. One of them—a machine gun car—is now in the open-air display of the Museum of the Slovakian National Uprising in Banska Bystrica (Neusohl), one of the cars with a Skoda 35(t) mounted on it and surrounded by armor plate stands in front of the Railroad Repair Workshop in Zvolen (Altsohl). On the other hand, the armored train set up before the impressive background of the Zvolen Castle has nothing to do with original rolling stock. It was imitated in the seventies for use in a film.

Heavy Scout Train No. 206 was in Milowitz on May 8, 1945, and was captured by the Czechs there. Photo: Dr. Karlicky, Prague

Right center and lower right: The two ex-German command cars used by the Czech Army after 1945: at right center the one in the Air Travel Museum of Prague-Kbely (now the Military Historical Museum of Prague-Lesany), at lower right that of BP 44 type on the grounds of the Museum and Documentation Center (MDZ) in Bratislava-East. Photos: V. Francev and MDZ Bratislava

Above: The Czechs divided it into the two MOV "Marshal Stalin" and "General Pavlik". Here is one of the two arriving at the railroad station in Karlovy Vary (Karlsbad). The German lettering on the building is still legible. Photo: Vojensky Historicky Archiv, Prague

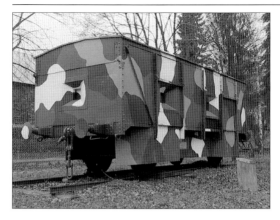

Two Slovakian armored train cars that returned to their homeland via the captured German line protection train "Moritz"..The MG car is now in the Museum of the Slovakian National Uprising in Banska Bystrica, the car with the LT Vz 35 or 35(t) turret before the Railroad Workshop in Zvolen. Photos: Museum of the Slovakian National Uprising, Banska Bystrica, and P. Milo, Zvolen

Similarly extensive was the array of German armored trains and railcars that fell into the hands of Tito's troops in northwestern Yugoslavia and southern Carinthia at the surrender: Armored Trains No. 23 and 73, Heavy Scout Trains No. 202-204, Light Scout Train No. 303, Railcars No. 30, 31, 34, 35, 38, and possibly 37, and a goodly number of line protection trains. Of PZ 73 it is known that it was used by the Yugoslavs for boundary guarding near Görz into the fifties; such data are lacking for the other units, but there is probably no doubt that most of them—if not all—were likewise used by the Yugoslavs after May 1945. In the Military Museum at Trieste are two armored railcars of the "Littorina" type. While one is undoubtedly of Italian provenance, the other bears German lettering. It must also—like a light rail-going armored scout car in the same museum—come from Yugoslav material. Thus they are evidence that this material may have found uses in the postwar conflict with Italy for Trieste and northwest Istria.

These few vehicles in the museums of Prague, Trieste, and Warsaw as well as in Slovakia (those in Alt- and Neusohl only conditionally, since they are originally Slovakian vehicles that were used only temporarily by the Wehrmacht) are the only remaining examples of the onetime German armored train weapon.

Above and right: The vehicles in the Military Museum in Trieste are in a somewhat neglected condition. Above is one of the "Littorina" armored railcars, at right the light rail-going armored scout car. Photos: N. Pignato collection

Afterword

The German Reich—although ranked among the first nations that recognized and used the advantages of the railroad as a means of military transport—moved only late into the development of rail-bound combat vehicles, namely only in 1899 with a test model. But only after the significance of the armored trains had been shown in the Boer War of 1899-1902, and after some practical experience could be gained with a makeshift solution in the Herero uprising in German Southwest Africa (1904), was the planning of their own armored train weapon promoted energetically, and although deletions had to be made from this originally very extensive program, Germany was—along with Russia—the only country that had such units on hand immediately at the outbreak of World War I.

The Germans went their own individual way from the beginning, in two senses:

First, they put much more emphasis—in a neat division from the railroad artillery—on the infantry component of the armored trains. Here the British example is tangible, although it was never followed there with the same results that can be observed in the German Reich through its whole developmental history of its armored trains. Both at the beginning of World War I (here only Austria-Hungary, other than the German Reich, followed the same tactics) as to some extent in World War II, as with the rail protection trains of the period between the wars, they were manned solely by infantry. Also, the artillery rearmament in both wars almost always remained relatively weak and usually had to make do with old, captured gun material. Only shortly before the end of World War II—at a point when this concept was already obsolete—was an armored train created in the BP 44 in which one can speak of equal shares, but in the light and heavy scout trains coming into service at about the same time (though their development goes back, to be sure, to 1943) the emphasis of the infantry components again emerged clearly. The justification of this particular path will be returned to later.

Second—surely influenced by the heavy emphasis of the infantry—the German trains always included fairly many cars and were therefore very long. This too was maintained over the entire time period. The armored trains of World War I contained twelve combat cars; the BP 44 at the end of World War II—like the light and heavy scout trains—still had ten or twelve. And this despite the fact that in the inclusive German requirements it was stressed over and over that an armored train should be as compact and short as possible for the sake of mobility and the size of the target for the enemy. As opposed to that, the Eastern countries (to which in this sense also the ally of World War I—Austria-Hungary—can be counted) always got along with two or three combat cars, while the Western countries—insofar as they had such units at all—inclined toward somewhat longer armored trains but usually stopped with five or six, very seldom exceeding that. So the German armored trains, compared with all the others, were always quite ponderous and offered the enemy a large target.

From the beginning through World War I, the rail protection trains of the between-wars period, into World War II, the German armored trains with their internally armored freight cars and weak armament were quite unlikely looking; the freight-train look was deliberately maintained over long periods of time for the sake of camouflage. Only with the utilization of captured Czech, Polish, and later Russian trains from 1940 on did the picture change, and with their own BP 42 design they even created an armored train in which the martial appearance concealed obvious weaknesses in armor and armament.

As far as one can tell from the meager information on their actions at the time, it appears that in World War I the German armored trains were assigned a broad spectrum of tasks: offensive as well as defensive and those of securing, in which the first-named apparently prevailed. This is somewhat unlike Austria-Hungary, where the armored trains were seen very primarily as defensive weapons. After disposing of several weaknesses, which became clear right after the war began, the German trains seem to have proved themselves very well in general terms, though they were robbed of their action possibilities by the solidification of the fronts in the positional war, so that their numbers were cut in half, and the remaining ones were used only in occasional cases of need.

This changed essentially with the end of the war. Not only for the Free Corps, which first supported the Baltic States' fight for freedom against the Soviets, but then, in view of their political leanings, were fought by their former allies, but also for the weak German forces that fought with their new and acquisitive Polish neighbors about the fixing of the eastern boundary, the armored trains were a valuable restrainer and an effective weapon, which were also used to a large extent by the enemies. But the armored trains became even more important for disputes within the German Reich, which developed, soon after the founding of the republic under Social Democrat leadership, between them and the extreme left, which strove for a soviet republic and dictatorship of the proletariat on the Russian model. To hold their own against the rebellious, even militantly agitating forces, the government had to make use of what remained of the regular army plus like-minded volunteer bands, although they were not at all well-wishing or even friendly to them, but rather dreamed of a return to the previous conditions. In the fighting that developed, armored trains very quickly proved to be a remarkably valuable aid on the side of the government troops. Often the mere appearance of these armed, armored and thus frightening units was enough to disperse the unorganized rebels, who usually had no goal-oriented leadership, and a few shots would break any initial resistance. Only when the other side got the idea of organizing in a strict paramilitary manner and proceeded with determination, as in the Munich soviet republic or the Red Army in the Ruhr region, did the inflexibility and thus the vulnerability of the armored trains become apparent. It is no wonder that the newly formed Reichswehr put great value on continuing to maintain armored trains, and that the Reich government tried by all means to gain the agreement of the Entente powers, but in vain, as they insisted at the beginning of 1921 on the complete disarming of these units.

It is not without a certain irony that the German Reichsbahn succeeded only a few weeks later, with the argument that in view of further unrest, insufficient securing of the railroad network could endanger the reparation transports along with the entire rail traffic, in persuading the Inter-Allied Control Commission to permit the maintenance of armored "rail protection trains". Of course they limited themselves to using them only for the security of rail traffic, but gradually they got around the rigorous regulations that the Commission had issued for their armament. Thus they were also compelled to keep them stored for the most part in garages before the eyes of the public. Only as the National Socialists, who had just come to power, arrested communists and other left wing or merely unpopular persons in connection with the burning of the Reichstag, and thus feared unrest, was the rail protection activated, and the available rail protection trains along with it. Their appearance aroused mistrustful reactions in other Western countries, but good-willed reactions among those in power.

The leadership of the hastily armed new German Wehrmacht, though, saw the armored trains as a subject outweighed by the favored and strongly promoted development of armored and air weapons and was not ready to invest in them. To be sure, they did not want to do away with them entirely, and thus they decided to take over seven of the existing rail protection trains with small rearming measures as armored trains. With these they went into World War II; in the first year, just a few more trains, which had been made up of material captured in the occupation of Czechoslovakia and Poland were put into service. Their action in the Polish and western campaigns was markedly offensive, with attempts made to use surprise attacks to capture railroad stations in the hinterlands, break through positions or take important bridges unharmed at the beginning of hostilities. The outcome of these actions was usually unsuccessful, and even in those that were assumed to be successful later, a closer look cannot deny questionable aspects. In the advance of PZ 3 to Konitz on September 1, 1939, the originally occupied railroad station could not be held; on the return trip the armored train came onto a meanwhile blown-up bridge, was thus immobilized on a railroad embankment and was exposed without protection to heavy enemy fire, which caused considerable damage. The crew even had to abandon the train slip off sidewards into the terrain. There they were able to hold out until the arrival of their own troops moving in from the border. — In the breakthrough of PZ 1 through the Peel position in Holland on May 10, 1940, the Maas bridge near Gennep was captured by other units. The armored train, followed by a transport train, was then able to pass through the fortified position in a quick move, since the rushed Netherlanders had no chance to close the barriers. Here too, the German forces broke through, drove them back and tried to wipe them out, but did not succeed. The armored train itself backed into the now-closed barrier in an attempt to open the way to the rear, was derailed and not only put out of action but also badly damaged. Here again it should be stressed that it was possible for the cut-off German forces—including the armored train crew—to hold out until they were relieved by advancing troops. It is also indubitable that their advance in both cases was eased, by confusion and diversion of the enemy, the quick breakthrough into the hinterland.

After this offensive use at the beginning of campaigns, the armored trains were used to reconnoiter the captured rail lines, to protect their repair and their subsequent securing, a largely unnecessary procedure, since acts of sabotage in the then-occupied countries were very rare.

Thus the experience to date scarcely encouraged the further expansion of the armored-train weapon. Despite the assumption that transport problems could be largely solved with motor vehicles, it was recognized in the planning stage of the Russian campaign at the end of 1940, looking ahead, that the railroad could also play an important role, and that in view of the vast areas to be captured, the securing of the rail network could take on a much greater significance than before. Thus the still-responsible In 10 developed two armored-train projects in December 1940, in which the main emphasis was placed on heightened flexibility and mobility. Aside from the fact that a considerable decrease in the number of cars was striven for (the SP 42 armored train was only supposed to include five combat cars), Diesel power, faster and constantly ready for action, and less noticeable by the enemy, was planned on; in fact, in the Armored Train 1941 it was meant for all the cars, so that they could operate not only in the united armored train but also individually. In addition, they wanted to create as easy uncoupling as possible for all the cars

from inside the train. The main weapons planned on were tanks carried on board and easily unloaded; they could fire from the train, but could also support the disembarked infantry or engineer shock troops on the ground to the side. The rest of the train was limited to the absolutely necessary infrastructure—radio equipment, transport possibilities for the shock troop, kitchen and medical facilities as well as, in some cases—anti-aircraft protection. These future-oriented projects would have created units best suited not to front service but rather to line and transport securing. Unfortunately, by the start of the Russian campaign only the immediate solution of the Armored Train 1941 could be achieved, which indeed included the carried and unloadable tanks, but provided only a very makeshift facility for the infantry on open cars, and with one exception, kept on using the steam locomotive for moving power.

Shortly before the eastern campaign began, the Chief of the Army General Staff saw that a central command for the armored trains should be created, but surprisingly, it was established not with the Chief of Transportation or the Commander of the Railroad Troops subordinate to him, but with the General of the Fast Troops. This must—although probably advisable for the fast buildup of the armored-train weapon—be regarded as a wrong decision in the light of the subsequent development of the fields of activity; the reasons for it are not known.

Shortly after the beginning of the campaign, the Germans in Russia—as also in the Balkans—were confronted with a completely new kind of warfare. The vast conquered areas could not be occupied entirely; the enemy forces enclosed by the fast advance of the motorized German troops now were only partially taken prisoner, but many soldiers hid in the huge impenetrable wooded and swampy districts of Russia or the roadless mountain regions of the Balkans and soon began a partisan war in the hinterlands, directed against the occupation forces and their long supply lines, but also with particular cruelty against their own countrymen who collaborated with the Germans. In view of the shortage of forces that grew ever more acute with the progress of the war, a lasting solution to this problem was inconceivable. The frequent attempts to master the partisans through sometimes large-scale encirclement operations failed because the enemy could either slip away in the unwatchable terrain thanks to their better knowledge of the region, or because—when they could be taken and wiped out—the areas thus gained could not be occupied permanently and were taken over by partisans again after a time. In the end the Germans had to make do with building up a veil of security—all too often inadequate—only along the transport lines and in the towns on them, so as to maintain supply traffic. The hope of being able to use mainly the roads for this purpose was an illusion, especially in Russia, in view of the terrible mud periods in the autumn and spring; in the end, the railroad proved to be the much more reliable and thus more important means of transportation. In protecting them against the constantly growing threat from the partisans, the armored trains, tested since the end of World War I in battle against irregular enemies, gained importance in a variety of tasks. They included securing runs, escorting important transports, supporting attacked posts, protecting important railroad facilities such as stations and bridges, securing of track repairs, finding and destroying partisan groups away from the rail lines, and participation in the larger anti-partisan operations by disembarked troops as well as combat vehicles, artillery support, blocking the rail lines against attempts to escape, and as central offices for intelligence operations. Irregular securing runs by armored trains at first had a thoroughly deterrent effect; the partisans, armed only with light weapons, did not feel confident to approach the tracks in the face of such patrols.

Soon, though—especially with the progress in mine technology—this changed, in fact it became almost a challenge to put an armored train out of action with explosions. The local railroad personnel, on whom the Germans were forced to depend, but who secretly collaborated more and more with the partisans and notified them of departures and destinations of the armored trains, was very helpful, so that the partisans were able to use appropriate countermeasures at the right times. Thus such explosions increased, not only putting the armored trains out of service temporarily, but also causing influential losses of valuable material and, all too often, of personnel.

The armored train designs made by In 10 should have been well suited to the requirements of partisan warfare. This was shown clearly later by the light scout trains that were based on similar viewpoints, while the heavy scout trains were delivered so late that their potential possibilities could no longer develop at all.

With the subordination of the armored trains to the fast troops, later the armored troops, though, these plans were not developed farther at first. In 6, now responsible, preferred to develop its own armored-train concept, the BP 42, which was then built in series. This tried to be ready for all imaginable action possibilities of an armored train—not only fighting partisans, but also combat use at the front—so the strong infantry crews of the earlier armored trains were kept; from the plans of In 10, two tank-carrier cars with unloadable tanks were also included. At the same time, though, every train received artillery armament of four guns, plus two 2-cm quads for anti-aircraft defense; but steam power for the locomotives was maintained. With the takeover of the Polish model of two howitzers as standard equipment besides the cannons that were better suited to direct fire as standard equipment, they also opted for their use as railroad batteries in the hinterlands as well as action in the front lines. In the BP 44 with its four howitzers (only the tank guns of the added tank-destroyer cars were planned on for direct fire), this trend was emphasized even more. Naturally, they were not able to reduce the number of cars to increase mobility under such conditions. So there arose very impressive looking monsters, but—as usual in such general solutions—they showed weaknesses in all kinds of action, resulting from the unavoidable compromises, and worse yet—this development of an "all-around" armored train took place at a point in time when the conditions would have urgently required a division into two types. For the partisan war, the heavy armament was unnecessary; the difficulty of keeping these trains in motion gave the enemy all too much time to either disappear or build mine traps, which for this elaborate design led to especially painful losses of material. The armored trains left this field increasingly to the more primitive but scarcely less effective line protection trains, and often stood inactive at railroad stations.

In front action, not only did the limited mobility, the long braking time and the time-consuming shifting from forward to reverse drive become obvious, but so did two faults in particular: the lack of an armor-piercing weapon and the insufficient armor. Thus the armored trains—the older ones in any case, which were later rebuilt according to the BP 42 plan—but also the BP 42 type were capable of facing only enemy infantry. In view of these conditions it is amazing how well the armored trains could perform in 1943—especially in the hard fighting in the southern sector of the eastern front, in which they were very involved. To be sure, the trains were damaged again and again—whether through partisan explosions, being hit by armor-piercing shells or bombs—but as long as the train could move or be hauled back out of the danger zone, it could always be restored. It is also significant that—despite Russian announcements of success, not a single German armored train was lost to partisan activity, and only two—and these under special conditions, namely PZ 10, enclosed and immobilized in Kowel, and Light Scout Train No. 302, by an airplane that crashed into and blew up a nearby ammunition train—were destroyed from the air, unlike all the Polish and Soviet armored trains that were destroyed by the German Luftwaffe. Here the advantage—perhaps the only one—of the multi-car trains is manifested: explosions and bomb damage always struck one, two or at most three cars. They could be uncoupled and taken away for repairs without completely costing the rest of the train its functioning ability. With a reduced number of cars it remained in action until they were repaired; sometimes provisionally armored cars were used as stopgaps. Even the loss of the armored locomotive was not crucial; they went on with an unarmored "black" locomotive, which was often "armored" temporarily with steel plates and wooden planks.

As 1944 began, naturally the losses increased greatly, especially because the Soviets systematically blocked the transit routes—roads and tracks—that led to the rear when they broke through. Armored trains that were thus cut off had scarcely a chance against the Russian tanks that stood in their way. Fortunately, most armored-train commanders were so sensible that in such a situation they did not get into such an unequal battle, but blew up and abandoned the train. The crew could often fight their way to their own lines without any great losses. Of the 39 German armored trains that were lost during the course of World War II, this was the case for no fewer than 14, and for another 13 of the 23 trains that fell victim to enemy warfare, the rail route to the rear was broken, so that they could not avoid destruction. About a third of all armored train losses thus occurred because there was no longer a chance to make a return trip.

Later (as of July 1944) the Soviets—very experienced in action and thus also in defending against such vehicles—set regular traps for the German armored trains. When they localized one of them, they tried to surround it or lure it forward, and not only blocked the track but set up a tank or antitank front along at least one side of it. This heavy fire not only destroyed the armored train, but also caused discouraging losses among the crew. The Germans tried to meet this threat by introducing tank destroyers with their armor-piercing 7.5-cm tank guns, but strengthening the armor was not possible, as with the exception of some captured cars, they retained the two-axle cars for the sake of easier overcoming of derailing, as extra weight set narrow limits in terms of axle pressure. Of course the armor was so weak that the Russian tank shells, made for much greater thicknesses, sometimes broke completely through the armor of a car, and—when they did not meet great resistance inside the car—could even fly out through the opposite wall without detonating and causing great damage. In spite of all that—measured by the cost in lives of troops had to suffer in comparison elsewhere on the fronts in the East—the losses in the armored trains remained comparatively light. The former members of these units agree almost unanimously that the commanding of them almost amounted to a form of life insurance.

Corresponding to the progress of the war and the movement of the eastern front to the west, the armored trains found themselves more and more, and finally exclusively, in combat against the regular Soviet army. Since they could be transferred easily and quickly, they appeared at focal points of the front from the start, such as borderlines between large units or even gaps in the front, which they tried to cover in mobile action. Here their effectiveness was still best. They could support weak German forces by bringing disembarking infantrymen into the defensive line and by artillery fire from the train; and the moral support was also not to be undervalued: the impressive appearance seemed to inspire courage. If the tracks remained intact for withdrawals, the armored train was often able to liberate surrounded troops in surprise counterattacks, bring back immobilized transport trains, or at least destroy them, and sometimes even to smash enemy forces. If it actually came to serious and massive attacks—especially carried on by armored troops—they were soon at lost posts. In view of the superior Soviet force that kept becoming more oppressive, this was naturally the case more and more often, and even for them, no serious resistance was possible. The wave of new armored trains set up shortly before the war ended can thus be seen only as a desperate measure. The mounting of heavy weapons, such as no longer driveable tanks, on railroad cars gave them, with their coal-fired locomotives at least a little of the mobility they had long since lost on the road or in the field through the glaring lack of fuel. They could not delay the final collapse.

All in all, World War II has shown that the armored train, in being limited to the tracks and thus in its possible action, were clearly inferior to the armored wheeled and tracked vehicles of the motorized units as means of front fighting, and even the building of a Diesel-powered, heavily armored and armed train by the Germans could not have changed that. As was recognized correctly by the German General Staff even before the war, the means expended on the building and maintenance of the armored trains had no real relation to the effect and success to be gained by them. With the downfall of the Third Reich, the unbroken history of more than forty years of unsuccessful wartime use of armored railroad trains in Germany came to an end.

The victory march of the motor vehicle had begun, sealing the fate of such units beyond hope. To be sure, they still found uses in a few colonial wars in the fifties where the railroad had an important opening-up function, but their days seemed to be numbered.

Of course, the Soviet Union kept a certain number of armored trains in service through the years, probably not so much for use against an external enemy as with thought of their effect against unrest in their own country. Nothing concrete has become known of their use in the former East Germany in 1953, Hungary in 1956 and Czechoslovakia in 1968, but it would be interesting to bring it to light—and maybe the opening of Eastern archives will let this happen. It is documented that such armored trains were stationed along the long-contested border with China on the Ussuri in eastern Siberia; since 1990, though, a whole series of them were disbanded there. And they are said to have played a role in the conflicts with and between the Caucasian republics.—In another conflict toward the end of the 20th century too, the war in the former Yugoslavia, they appeared again.—and even in greater numbers than, and in composition scarcely changed since, World War II. These are signs that they are still accorded a certain value under special conditions, and that they obviously were pronounced dead too soon.—It is still more unusual that the USA, a country that no longer did anything serious with armored railroad trains since the Civil War in the 19th century, in conjunction with its plans for making intercontinental rockets mobile by installing them on railroad cars, at least discussed the provision of armored and armed railroad cars to fight off anticipated attacks by militant enemies of war or nuclear weapons.

If rail traffic should gain significance in the future—not least for ecological reasons, but also with increasing fuel shortages—as has long since been discussed, and if demonstrations against unwanted transports (such as of radioactive materials) should turn more and more from pure demonstration to aggressive action such as blockades or even destructive attacks, then it cannot be dismissed out of hand that governments might think again of armored and armed railroad vehicles to protect rail-bound transportation, as they proved in the past to be especially suited to fighting such threats. So it might be conceivable that such vehicles—perhaps as advance railcars or cars placed in transport trains—could have a renaissance again. The Internet notice (2002): "Armored train in Wendland," still seems very exaggerated. It concerns only a Diesel locomotive that pulled an open car with a Water Cannon 9000 mounted on it for use against demonstrations in otherwise hard-to-reach areas along the line. And even if one can scarcely imagine that one will go beyond this here in Germany, in other countries that are less conscientious such considerations could certainly become concrete.

Decorations

Although the usual decorations of World War II (like the Iron Cross 1st and 2nd Classes, Assault Medal, Close Combat Badge, etc.) naturally also applied to the crews of armored trains, none of them could attain the most treasured decoration, the Knight's Cross. This indicates that armored train action was basically unspectacular and thus attracted no particular attention.

The next level down for an outstanding individual deed (thus the official requisite), not sufficient for the awarding of the Knight's Cross, being named in the Honors List of the German Army (Honors List Badge), was attained by only one member of an armored train:

* Lt. Fritz Gruber (PZ 71), decorated in March 1945 (presumably for bringing back part of the crew of Armored Train No. 71, abandoned in Romania in August 1944).

The German Cross in Gold, with which the "many extraordinary brave deeds, from which, though, the individual deeds do not suffice

for awarding the Knight's Cross" were recognized, was received by:

* Captain Helmut Vogler (Commander, PZ 7), on March 23, 1944,
* Captain Helmut Walter (Commander, PZ 26 and 1), on May 2, 1944,
* (Captain Walter also received, on the last day of the war, May 8, 1945, the Knight's Cross, but as a battalion commander in the 2nd Armored Division).
* Captain Ernst Seidel (Adjutant to the Commander of Armored Trains with the OB Southeast), on April 27, 1945.

The German Cross in Silver (awarded for particular achievement in the army administration as an added highest level above the War Service Cross 1st Class) was received by the Commander of Armored Trains with the Inspector-General of the Armored Troops:

* Colonel Egon von Olszewski, for building up and expanding the armored-train troops, though only at his departure from his office on April 4, 1945.

Appendix

To pp. 64-72:
A rail protection crew stands before the loco of the Insterburg train (later PZ 6 of the Wehrmacht). Photo: P. Malmassari collection

To pp. 84-92: The Armored Train Replacement Battalion rented the locomotive 040-k-518 that returned from France (the former Prussian G 8.1 Cöln 5182), with which the newly established second march company is being moved into the additionally built camp at Wesola. Photo: W. Sawodny collection

To p. 93: PZ 6 from East Prussia in its original composition. Photo: P. Malmassari collection

Above: to p. 94: In this photo the rail protection cars of PZ 6 have already been rebuilt, but the ex-Soviet armored railcar planned for use as a gun car has not yet been added. Photo: R. Prinzing/W. Sawodny collection

Upper left: to pp. 120 and 123: The rear half of PZ 26 with two added O-cars between the infantry and tank-carrier cars. *Upper right: to pp. 119 and 124:* PZ 27 at the start of the Russian campaign. The infantry car in front of the loco is uncoupled. *Below: to pp. 120 and 127:* The complete PZ 31 as built, seen in the spring of 1942 with two captured Russian cars. Photos (3): P. Malmassari collection

To pp. 121 and 134: PZ 51 was temporarily assigned a captured Type BP 35 car to replace its own rear gun car, which was out of action.

Upper left: to pp. 137 and 139: One of the rare photos of a BP 44 type armored train in the spring of 1945. *Upper right: to p. 159:* A line protection train using Latvian material, thus probably active in Courland. On the car in the foreground, with very angled steel armor plate, is a Soviet BT-7 tank without running gear. Further details of the train are not recognizable.

Above: to p. 157: The line protection train "Blücher" before being rebuilt in the winter of 1943-44. Along with the loco (38 3504), with only the cab armored, and G-cars with concrete-filled double walls, undriveable tanks were laded onto low-side cars at the ends of the train and surrounded by a (wooden?) cover. The one in front was a Panzer II.

Left: to p. 162: A line protection train somewhere in southern Europe. Of special interest is the octagonal concrete bunker with loopholes on all sides, in front of the Renault FT 17/18 tank. Photos (5): P. Malmassari collection

To pp. 165 and 197: The armored WR 360 C 14 at the Armored Train Replacement Battalion, along with a row of captured Soviet armored railcars of D 2 type. Since the loco was also assigned as a replacement to armored trains whose locos were out of action, it had—as the frame antenna shows—a radio set. In February 1945 it was the regular loco of PZ 83. Photo: P. Malmassari collection

To p. 195: The armored 55 042 of a line protection train, armored at the Roslawl field workshop, is shown in the central sector of the eastern front. Photo: H. Griebl collection

To p. 195: The fully armored locomotive (38 1940) of the line protection train "Michael." Photo: E. C. P. A., Paris

To p. 200: The armored loco of the armored train "Za Stalina," captured east of Wjasma in October 1941, at first pulled a (broad gauge) line protection train that consisted only of (internally armored) G-cars. Photo: P. Malmassari collection

To p. 161: The line protection train "Norwegen." On the stakeside car is a French Hotchkiss H 39/40 tank. On two other cars 2-cm A/A quads are mounted, on one even an 8.8-cm A/A gun. Photo: E. C. P. A., Paris

To p. 232: The low-side car carrying a Panzer III G, assigned to PZ 7 at the beginning of 1943. Photo: P. Malmassari collection

To p. 232: A Panzer III with the short 5-cm (Series E or F) tank gun (loaded on an SS car) was also assigned to PZ 27 already at the beginning of 1943.

To p. 238: A heavy 12-cm mortar was installed on the line protection train "Michael." Photo: E. C. P. A., Paris

To p. 246: The "Hetzer" 38(t) pursuit tank that was supposed to replace the 38(t) tank on the tank-carrier cars is seen here as a display piece. Photo: W. Sawodny collection

To p.15: Armored train (number unknown) at the western front. Note the Iron Cross at the front side, the wooden planks instead of sand bags as breastwork and the machine gun (French model?) on the observation post. Photo: P. Malmassari collection

To p. 15: Armored train No. IX at Tilsit in winter 1914-1915. The open cars are only covered with canvas. Photo: P. Malmassari collection

To p. 15: The same armored train in the area of Baranowitschi in autumn 1915. The cars now have fixed roofs and the observation stand is armored. Photo: P. Malmassari collection

To p. 15: The inscription reads "French armored train captured at Marle," but this is not true; it is the German PZ XI! Photo: P. Malmassari collection

To p. 15: Armored train of unknown number (but see the third picture from above on p 19!) in Lorraine. Photo: A. Przeczek collection

To p. 15: The same armored train split up in groups of cars in a railway station at the western front. Photo: P. Malmassari collection

To p. 25: Captured Russian broad gauge armored train near Segewold (northeast of Riga) in autumn 1917. The gun car was added by the Germans with a F.K.96 n.A. on a wheeled mounting in open air. It is likely that it was also used for the "railroad advance" in February 1918. Photo: P. Malmassari collection

Another captured Russian armored train during the "railroad advance" at Dobrusch (east of Gomel) in February 1918. Photo: P. Malmassari collection

But during this advance, in view of lack of armored material so called "patrol trains" were mostly sufficient, here on the line from Povorsk via Korosten to Kiew. Photo: A. Przeczek collection

To p 54: A total view (without locomotive) of postwar PZ IV. Photo: P. Malmassari collection

Bibliography

Unpublished Sources

Files of the following archives:
Federal Archives, Koblenz, with branches:
    Military Archives, Freiburg
    Military Intermediate Archives, Potsdam
Central Inquiry Center, Kornelimünster
Main State Archives, Munich—War Archives
Main State Archives, Stuttgart—Military Archives
Military History Research Office of the Bundeswehr, Freiburg, now Potsdam
Archives of the Bundeswehr Engineer School, Munich
German Wehrmacht Information Office (WASt), Berlin
Search Service of the German Red Cross, Munich
Railroad Museum, Nürnberg
Austrian Federal Archives—War Archives, Vienna
Historic Service of the French Army, Paris
Vojensky Historicky archive, Prague
Statni ustredni archive, Prague
Archives of Steyr-Daimler-Puch AG, Steyr
And many privately owned notes and materials

Published Sources

Adonyi-Naredi, F. von, Ungarns Armee im Zweiten Weltkrieg, Neckargemünd 1971.
Ahlfen v. & Niehoff, So kämpfte Breslau, Munich 1959.
Anonymous, Panzerzüge und Geschütze auf Eisenbahnwagen, in Schweizerische Zeitschrift für Artillerie und Genie, 1900, pp. 32-35.
Anonymous, Amerikanische Panzerzüge, in Zeitschrift des Vereins deutscher Ingenieure, Vol, 61 (1917), pp. 583-584.
Anonymous, Panzerzüge in der polnischen Armee, in Militär-Wochenblatt, Vol. 116 (1932), sp. 1581-1584.
Anonymous, Zuikunftsentwicklung des Panzerzugs, in Militär-Wochenblatt, Vol. 118 (1934), sp. 1266-1267.
Anonymous, Panzerzüge, in Militär-Wochenblatt, Vol. 122 (1937), sp. 1170-1172.
Anonymous, Der deutsche Reichsbahnschutz, in Lose Blätter, Beilage No. 9 zum Eisenbahnfachmann (1933), pp. 33-36.
Anonymous, Armored Railcars, in The Locomotive, 1936, pp. 152-154.
Anonymous, Pioniere "bauen" einen Panzerzug, in Vierteljahrshefte für Pioniere, Vol. 8 (1941).
Anonymous, Kowel, das Hohelied der Fronteisenbahner, in Reichsbahn, 1944, pp. 136-140
Anonymous, Eisenbahn-Panzerzug, in Waffenrevue, No. 20 (1976), pp. 3213-3238.
Anonymous, Die leichte Feldhaubitze 18/40, in Waffenrevue No. 70 (1988), pp. 3-20.
Anonymous, Die Festungswaffen des Gruson-Werks, in Waffenrevue, No. 81 (1991), pp. 115-144.

Anonymous, Bereithaltung von fahrbaren Festungen zur Unterdrückung etwaiger Unruhen, in Neue militärische Blätter (1907), p. 70.
Anonymous, Brennendes Mitteldeutschland, in Der Reiter gen Osten, Vol. 7 (1936), No. 7.
Anonymous, Das Schicksal der deutschen Stadt Argenau, in Der Reiter den Osten, Vol. 7 (1936), No. 1
Anonymous, Der Panzerzug, in Der Weltkrieg, Vol. 116, Reutlingen, no year.
Anonymous, Ein Eisenbahnpanzerzug beim Kampf um Konitz am 1. September, in Der Reiter gen Osten, Vol. 11 (1940), No. 8, pp. 3-4.
Anonymous, Panzerzüge und Panzerkraftwagen, in Illustrierte Geschichte des Weltkriegs 1914-16, Vol. 82, Stuttgart, no year.
Anonymous, Panzerzug V im Baltikum, in Der Reiter gen Osten, Vol. 8 (1937), No. 9.
Anonymous, Panzerzug 22 im Grenzschutz Ost, in Der Reiter gen Osten, Vol. 9 (1938), No, 3, p. 9.
Anonymous, Panzerzug im Einsatz, in Berliner Illustrierte Zeitung, Vol. 53 (1944), No. 2, p. 14.
Anonymous, Rollende Festung, in Die Wehrmacht, Vol. 7 (1943), No. 22, p. 6.
Anonymous, Die ersten deutschen Kampfpanzer, in Waffenrevue, No. 4 (1972), pp. 523-542.
Balfour, G., The Armoured Train, London 1981.
Balzert, R. & Rettinghaus, H., Die Bahnpolizei, Gross-Umstadt 1986.
Bauer, E., Der Panzerkrieg Vol. 1 & 2, Bonn 1965.
Bauer, Der Handstreich gegen die Eisenbahnbrücke von Dirschau über die Weichsel, in Pioniere, 1977, pp. 6-7.
Baur, H., Deutsche Eisenbahner im Weltkrieg 1914-1918, Stuttgart 1927.
Beckman, F. S. A. & Kurowski, F., Der Kampf um die Festung Holland, Herford 1981.
Behrends, H., Hensel, W. & Wiedau, G., Güterwagen-Archiv 1, Berlin 1989.
Below, V., Poslednije Bronepözda Sovietskoj Armii in Mir Orushija no. 2 (2004), pp. 14-19
Benoist-Mechin, J., Geschichte der deutschen Militärmacht, 7 vol., Oldenburg 1965-68.
Benussi, G., Treni armati, treni ospedale 1915-1945, Parma 1983.
Berlin, Waffenlehre, Berlin 1908.
Beumelburg, W, Flandern, Oldenburg 1939.
Bischoff, J., Die letzte Front, Berlin 1935.
Blümner, M., Panzerzüge in und nach dem Weltkrieg, in Heerestechnik, Vol. 21 (1925), pp. 21-24, 49-52.
Blümner, M., Aus den Geheimnissen der Technik der Kriegszeit, in Jost, W., Felger, H. (ed.), Was wir vom Weltkrieg nicht wissen, Leipzig 1938.
Bölcke, W. (ed..), Deutschlands Rüstung im Zweiten Weltkrieg, Frankfurt/Main 1969.

Boog, H., Förster, J., Klink, E., Müller, R.-D., Ueberschär, G.R., Der Angriff auf die Sowjetunion, Stuttgart 1983.
Bosch, H., Der Zweite Weltkrieg zwischen Rhein und Maas, Geldern 1971.
Brandis, von, Baltikumer, Berlin 1939.
Bruetting, G., Alaarm: Panzerzug, in Feldbreichte, Oct. 1941, p. 50.
Büchner, A., Eisenbahnpanzerzug im Kampf, in Der deutsche Soldat, Vol. 25 (1961), pp. 46-48.
Buchner, A., Der Polenfeldzug 1939, Leoni 1989.
Caiti, p., Artiglierie ferroviarie e treni blindati, Parma 1974.
Carell, P., Unternehmen Barbarossa, Frankfurt-Berlin 1963.
Carell, P., Verbrannte Erde, Frankfurt-Berlin 1966.
Carter, E. F., Railways in Wartime, London 1964.
Chamberlain, P. & Ellis, C., Pictorial History of Tanks of the World 1915-45, Harrisburg 1972.
Cooper, M., The Phantom War, London 1979.
Dahms, H. G., Geschichte des Zweiten Weltkriegs, Tübingen 1975.
Dauscher, K., Lokomotivführer und Heizer im Panzerkampf, in Reichsbahn, 1944, p. 30
Deutsche Bundesbahn (ed.), Eisenbahnen und Eisenbahner zwischen 1941 und 1945, Frankfurt 1973.
DiGiusto, S., I reparti Panzer nell' Operationszone Adriatisches Küstenland (OZAK) 1943-45, Mariano del Friuli 2002.
Dixon, C. A. & Heilbrunn, O., Partisanen, Frankfurt 1956.
Dost, O., Panzerzüge und ihre Verwendung, in Wehrfront, Vol. 4 (1937), pp. 19-21.
Dreetz, D., Gessner, K. & Sperling, H., Bewaffnete Kämpfe in Deutschland 1918-1923, Berlin 1988.
Drogovoz, I. G. Kreposti nakolesach, Minsk, 2002.
Ehrhart, K & Kopenhagen, W., Panzerzug-Neuauflage 75, in Armeerundschau (1976), pp. 64-68.
Englberger, F., Die rollende Festung, in Heer 1944, No. 9, p. 5.
Ferrenz, T., Armoured Trains, in Military Engineer, Vol. 23 (1932), p. 137, 469-472.
Fleischer, W., Deutsche Minen- und Granatwerfer, Waffenarsenal Vol. 150, Wölfersheim-Berstadt 1995.
Forschungsanstalt für Kriegs- und Heeresgeschichte/ Kriegsgeschichtliche Forschungs-anstalt des Heeres, ed., Darstellungen aus den Nachkriegskämpfen deutscher Truppen und Freikorps, 9 vol., Berlin 1936-1943.
Francev, V., Ceskoslovenske obrnene vlaky, in Zeleznice, Vol. 3/1994, pp. 23-26.
Freese, J., Schienenstrang nach Stalingrad, Munich 2003.
Fricke, G., "Fester Platz" Tarnopol 1944, Freiburg 1969.
Fürbringer, H., 9. SS-Panzer-Division "Hohenstaufen", Bayeux 1984.
Funck, H. H., Panzerzug im Einsatz. In Berliner Illustrierte Zeitung 1944, No. 2.
Gawrych, W. R., Panzer Triebwagen Nr. 16 (Armor Photo Gallery No. 7), Warsaw 2003.

Gayl, W. v., Ostpreussen unter fremden Flaggen, Königsberg 1940.
Gebhart, J. & Simovcek, J, Partisanen in der Tschechoslowakei 1941 bis 1945, Berlin 1989.
Giese, O., Fortificatorische Eisen-Constructionen, Leipzig 1866.
Gleiss, H., Breslauer Apokalypse, Vol. 1-6, Wedel 1987-87.
Glettenberg, Das "Regiment 62" greift an! In Der Reiter gen Osten, Vol. 5 (1934), No. 12, p. 8.
Glück, D., Erlebnisse waehrend der Polenkämpfe um Lissa und in Oberschlesien im Jahre 1919, in Grenzmärkische Heimatblätter, Vol. 14 (1938), pp. 93-99.
Görlitz, W., Der Zweite Weltkrieg 1939—1945, Stuttgart 1952.
Görlitz, W., Der deutsche Generalstab, Frankfurt/Main 1958.
Goltz, R. Graf von der, Als politischer General im Osten, Leipzig 1920.
Gordon, G. H., Soviet Partisan Warfare 1941-1944, dissertation, Univ. of Iowa 1972.
Gordon, H. J., Vom Kaiserheer zu den Freikorps, Frankfurt 1959.
Gornik, St., Die Front im Norden, in Der Reiter gen Osten, Vol. 8 (1937), No. 5, pp. 6-7.
Gosztony, P., Hitlers fremde Heere, Düsseldorf-Vienna 1976.
Gosztony, P, Die Rote Armee, Vienna 1980.
Gottwaldt, A. B., Deutsche Eisenbahnen im Zweiten Weltkrieg, Stuttgart 1983.
Gottwaldt, A. B., Deutsche Kriegslokomotiven 1939-1945, Stuttgart 1974.
Gottwaldt, A. B., Heeresfeldbahnen, Stuttgart 1986.
Griebl, H., CSD-Dampflokomotiven, Vol. 1 & 2, Vienna 1969.
Griebl, H. & Wenzel, H., Geschichte der deutschen Kriegslokomotiven, Vienna 1971.
Gschöpf, R., Mein Weg mit der 45. Infanterie-Division, Linz 1955.
Guderian, H., Erinnerungen eines Soldaten, Heidelberg 1951.
Habedank, G., Das Ende der Panzerzuggruppe "Kaukasus", in Die Wehrmacht, Vol. 6, (1942), No. 18.
Hackl, Panzerzug greift an, in Die Wehrmacht, Vol. 8 (1944), No. 2.
Hahn, F., Waffen und Geheimwaffen des deutschen Heeres 1933-1945, 2 vol., Koblenz 1986.
Hahn, K. E., Eisenbahner im Krieg und Frieden, Farnkfurt-Main 1954.
Halder, F., Kriegstagebuch, 3 vol, Stuttgart 1962-64.
Harrigan, A., The Armoured Train, in Commando, Vol. 14 (1963), pp. 18-21.
Haupt, W., Sieg ohne Lorbeer, Preetz 1965.
Haupt, W., Heeresgruppe Mitte, Dorheim 1968.
Haupt, W., Heeresgruppe Nord, Bad Nauheim 1966
Haupt, W., Kurland 1944-45, Friedberg 1979.
Hauptner, R. & Jung, P., Stahl und Eisen im Feuer (Oestereichische Militärgeschichte Sonderband 2003), Vienna 2003.
H.Dv.487, Führung und Gefecht der verbundenen Waffen, Berlin 1923.
H.Dv.300, Truppenführung, Berlin 1934.
Heiges, K., Der Bahnschutz ruft, Baruth 1937.
Heigl, F., Taschenbuch der Tanks (Teil I und Erg. Bd.), new ed., Munich 1970.
Hesse, E., Der sowjetische Partisanenkrieg 1941-45, Göttingen 1969.
Heubes, M.. (ed.), Ehrenbuch der Feldeisenbahner, Berlin 1931.
Hiltebrandt, Am Bahnhof sitzt der Bolschewik, in Der Adler, 1943, No. 9.
Hinze, R., Der Zusammenbruch der Heeresgruppe Mitte im Osten 1944, Stuttgart 1988.
Hinze, R., Das Ostfront-Drama 1944, Stuttgart 1988.
Hinze, R., Mit dem Mut der Verzweiflung, Meerbusch 1993.
Hinze, R., Rückzugskämpfe in der Ukraine, Meerbusch 1991.
Hnilicka, K., Das Ende auf dem Balkan 1944-45, Göttingen 1970.
Hollunder, G., Panzerzug VI, in Wehrfront, Vol. 4 (1937), pp. 78-79.
Holub, O., Ceskoslovenske tanky a tankiste, Prague 1980.
Hubatsch, W., Die deutsche Besetzung von Dänemark und Norwegen, Göttingen 1952.
Hülsen, B. von, Der Kampf um Oberschlesien, Stuttgart 1922.
Hülsenkamp, F., Zwanzig Jahre Bahnschutz, in Die Reichsbahn (1939), pp. 391-403.
Iwanow, W., Panzerzug 14-69 (Bibliothek Suhrkamp, Vol. 249), Frankfurt/Main 1970.
Jäger, J. J., Die wirtschaftliche Abhängigkeit des III. Reichs vom Ausland, Berlin 1969.
Jones, N. H., Hitler's Heralds, The Story of the Freikorps 1918-1923, London 1987.
Jurado, C. C., The German Freikorps 1918-1923, (Elite 76), Botley 2001.
Kannapin, N., Die deutsche Feldpostübersicht 1939-45, 3 vol., Osnabrück 1980-82.
Karl, J., Die Schreckensherrschaft in München, Munich 1919.
Kayser, O., Erlebnisse beim Grenzschutz in Lissa, in Grenzmärkische Heimatblätter, Vol. 18 (1942), pp. 89-93.
Kehrig, M., Stalingrad, Stuttgart 1974.
Keilig, W., Das deutsche Heer 1930-1945, 3 vol., Bad Nauheim 1956ff
Kemp, A., Trojan Trains 1940, in War Monthly, 1977, pp. 36-41.
Kerchnawe, H., Zur Geschichte der Panzerzüge, in Militärhistorische und -technische Mitteilungen, Vol. 60 (1929), pp. 336-339.
Kewisch, H., Festungen greifen an! In Die Panzertruppe, 1944, pp. 74-75.
Kiekheben-Schmidt, E., Unternehmen "Panzerzug" (Kriegsbücherei der deutschen Jugend, Vol;. 104), Berlin, no date.
Klietmann, K.-G., Panzerzüge, in Köhlers Heeres-Kalender 1942, pp. 65-69.
Klietmann, K.-G., Das Eisenbahn-Bataillon Bromberg 1919, in Feldgrau, Vol. II, 1963, pp. 140ff.
Kmet, L., Povstalecke pancierove vlaky, Banska Bystrica 1974.
Knipping, A., Eisenbahnen im ersten Weltkrieg, Freiburg 2004.
Knipping, A., Eisenbahn im Krieg, Munich 2005.
Knipping, A. & Schulz, R., Reichsbahn hinter der Ostfront, Stuttgart 2001.
Knipping, A. & Schulz, R., Eisenbahnen zwischen Ostfront und Atlantikwall, Stuttgart 2002.
Koch, Hj., Der deutsche Bürgerkrieg, Berlin 1978.
Kögl, O., Revolutionskämpfe im südbayerischen Raum, Rosenheim 1969.
König, A. R., Ironclads on Rails, dissertation, Univ. of Nebraska 1995.
König, A. R., Mars Gets New Chariots, New York, 2006.
Kolomiets, M., "Chunchuz"—pervij bronepoezd, in Model Konstruktor, 1994 No. 8, pp. 25-28.
Kolomiets, M., Bronepoezda Krasnoj Armii 1930-1941, Frontowaja Illustracija 2004, No. 3.
Kolomiets, M., Otoschestwennaja bronedrezinii I motobronewagoni, Frontowaja Illustracija 2005, No. 6.
Kolomiets, M., Bronepoezda dobrovol Tscheskoj Armii, in Mir Orushija 11 (14), 2005
Kolomiets, M., Legkie broneawtomobili Krasni Armii, Frontowaja Illustracija 2007, No. 2.
Kolomiets, M., Bronepoezda Krasnoj Armii ototschestwennoj vojna 1941-1945, Frontowaja Illustracija 2007 Part 1 No. 7, Part 2 No. 8.
Kolomiets, M., Bronja russkoj armii. Broneavtomibili I bronepoezda v mirovoj voijne, Moscow 2008.
Kopenhagen, W., Sowjetische Panzerzüge und Eisenbahngeschütze 1917-1945, Waffenarsenal p. 36, Wölfersheim-Berstadt 1995.
Kosar, F., Leichte Feldgeschütze, Munich 1971.
Kosar, F., Mittlere Feldgeschütze, Munich 1973.
Kosar, F., Panzerabwehrkanonen 1916-1977, Stuttgart 1978.
Kosar, F., Infanteriegeschütze und rückstossfreie Geschütze, Stuttgart 1978.
Krannhals, H. von, Der Warschauer Aufstand, Frankfurt/Main 1962.
Krawczak, T. & Odziemkowski, J., Polskie pociagi pancerne w wojnie 1939, Warsaw 1987.
Kreidler, E., Die Eisenbahnen im Machbereich der Achsenmächte während des Zweiten Weltkriegs, Göttingen 1975.
Kriebel, F. K., Der polnische Aufstand im Kreise Hohensalza und die Kämpfe um Argenau, in Grenzmärkische Heimatblätter, Vol. 10, Part 2, (1934), pp. 48-60.
Kriegsgeschichtliche Abteilung des Grossen Generalstabs, ed., Die Kämpfe der Deutschen Truppen in Südwestafrika, Vol. 1, Berlin 1906.
Kügelen, von, Die Aufgabe der Panzerzüge, in Münchener Neüste Nachrichten, Vol. 97, No. 87, March 29, 1944, p. 2.
Kühnrich, H., Der Partisanenkrieg, Berlin 1965.
Kützing, W., Panzerzug Hülsen, in Wehrfront, Vol. 4 (1937), p. 551.
Kurz, H. R., Die Triebwagen der Reichsbahn-Bauarten, Freiburg 1988.
Kurzman, D., Der Aufstand, Munich 1979.
Laar, C., Der Leberecht, in Die Wehrmacht, Vol. 8 (1944), No. 10-12.
Lang, E., Panzerzug gegen Panzerzug, in Alte Kameraden, Vol. 19, 1971, pp. 22-24.
Lankovits, J., Panzerzüge Österreichs und Ungarns, in Eisenbahn, 1986 No. 8, pp. 142-146, No. 9, pp. 164-167, No. 10, pp. 184-186.
Lasch, O., So fiel Königsberg, Stuttgart 1976.
Lasek, P. & Vanek, J., Obrnene drezina Tatra T-18, Prague 2002.
Lassmann, J. E., Der Eisenbahnkrieg, Berlin 1885.
Lauscher, S., Die Diesellokomotiven der Wehrmacht, Freiburg 1999.
Lebedinskja, O., Bronepoezd "Chunchuz", in Tank Master no. 2, 1994, pp. 14-17.
Lechner, "Fregatte" kämpft einen Bahnhof frei, in Die Woche, 1944 No. 28.
Le Tissier, T., Der Kampf um Berlin 1945, Frankfurt/Main 1991.
Le Tissier, T., Durchbruch an der Oder, Augsburg 1997.
Lindenblatt, H. Pommern 1945, Leer 1984.
Lith, H. van, "Panzerzug 1" verrast Peel-Raumstelling, in Legerkörier 30 (1980), pp. 6-8
Lorenz, E., Strecke bei Kilometer 86.9 gesprengt, in Die Wehrmacht, Vol. 7 (1943), No. 11.
Lucas, E., Märzrevolution 1920, 3 vol., Frankfurt/Main 1970-78.
Lüdersdorff, H., Die Maschinen des Weltkrieges, Munich 1916.
Lusar, R., Die deutschen Waffen und Geheimwaffen, Munich 1971.
Mabire, J., Die SS-Panzer-Division "Wiking", Preussisch-Oldendorf 1983.
Märcker, L. R. G., Vom Kaiserheer zur Reichswehr, Leipzig 1921.
Magnuski, J., Armata dywizyjna ZIS-3, Warsaw 1977.
Magnuski, J., Pociag pancerny "Danuta", Warsaw 1972.
Magnuski, J., Wozy bojowe LWP 1943-1983, Warsaw 1985.
Magnuski, J., Drezyna pancerna SOK, in Militaria, Vol. 1 No. 1, 1992, pp. 37-39.
Magnuski, J., Panzertriebwagen Nr. 16, in Militaria, Vol. 1 No. 3, 1992, pp. 32-35.
Magnuski, J., Pociag pancerny BP-43, in Nowa Technika Wojskowa 1994, No. 10, pp. 3-8.
Magnuski, J., Niemieckie pociagi pancerne BP-42/BP-44, in Nowa Technika Wojskoya 1995 No. 3, pp. 10-13 & No. 4, pp. 9-12.
Magnuski, J., Pancerne wagony motorowe, in Nowa Technika Wojskowa 1996 No. 9, pp. 14-18.
Magnuski, J., Pociag pancerny "Smialy" w trzech wojnach (Czolgi w boju 3, Warsaw 1996.
Malmassari, P., Deutsche Panzerzüge zwischen 1914 und 1945, in Modell-Fan 1988 No. 10, pp. 22-23.
Malmassari, P., Les trains blindees 1826—1989, Bayeux 1989.
Malmassari, P., Une experience militaire sous-estimee, Les trains blindes francais de la revolution industrielle a la colonization, Dissertation, Univ. de Montpellier, 1007.
Manstein, E. von, Verlorene Siege, Bonn 1955.
Mantüffel, H. von, Die 7. Panzer-Division im Zweiten Weltkrieg, Ürdingen 1965.
Marek, W., Zweimal 36 Schuss, in Der Adler 1942 No. 10, pp. 148-149.
Markovski, V., Poslednije bronepoezda Sovietskoi Armii, in Mir Orushija No. 9(12), 2005, pp. 42-51.
Mayer, F., Verwendung von Panzerzügen im Burenkrieg, in Jahrbücher für die Deutsche Armee und Marine, 1917, pp. 198-207.
Mayer, F., Verwendung und Bekämpfung von Panzerzügen im Burenkrieg 1899-1902, In Militärwissenschaftliche und -technische Mitteilungen, Vol. 60 (1929), pp. 794-800.
Meyers grosses Konversationslexikon Artikel: Panzerzüge in Vol. 15, 6th ed., 1908.
Mielke, O., Stosstrupp im Panzerzug (Spannende Geschichten, No. 96, Gütersloh, no Date.
Möller, M., ed., Der Eisenbahner, Charlottenburg & Magdeburg, no date.
Moll, G. & Wenzel, H., Die Baureihe 93, Freiburg 1979.
Müller, W., Die leichte und mittlere Flak 1906-1945, Friedberg 1990.
Müller, W., Die mittlere Flak bis 1945, Waffenarsenal S. 25, Friedberg 1992.
Müller-Hillebrandt, B., Das deutsche Heer 1939-1945, 3 vol., Frankfurt/Main 1959-60.
Mues, W., Der grosse Kessel, Erwitte—Lippstadt 1984.
Muther, A., Das Gerät der leichten Artillerie, 4 vol., Berlin 1925-1929.
Nehring. W. K., Die Geschichte der deutschen Panzerwaffe 1916-1945, Berlin 1969.
Neumann, J., Die 4. Panzer-Division, Bonn 1985.
Niepold, G., Mittlere Ostfront Juni 44, Herford 1985.
Oefele, Panzerautos und Panzerzüge (Die Mittel des Krieges Vol. 11), Leipzig 1915.
Oertzen, F. W. von, Die deutschen Freikorps 1918-1923, Munich 1936.
Oswald, W., Kraftfahrzüge und Panzer der Reichswehr, Wehrmacht und Bundeswehr, Stuttgart 1970.
Pauli, K., Rollende Festung, in Die Wehrmacht, Vol. 7 (1943), No. 22.
Pernavskij, G., ed., Belje bronepoezda v grazhdanskoj voine, Moscow 2007.
Pesendorfer, F., In Panzerzug in die Sowjetunion, in Die Wehrmacht, Vol. 5 (1941), No. 14, p. 19.
Pfeiffer, G. P., Die Elsasskämpfe, Camburg, no date.
Pickert, W., Vom Kubanbrückenkopf bis Sebastopol, Heidelberg 1955.
Piekalkiewicz, J., Die deutsche Reichsbahn im Zweiten Weltkrieg, Stuttgart 1979.
Piekalkiewicz, J., Krieg auf dem Balkan 1940-1945, Munich 1984.
Piekalkiewicz, J., Kampf um Warschau, Munich 2994.
Pirner, Eisenbahnpanzerzüge, in Der Kraftzug in Wirtschaft und Heer, Vol. 8 (1933), pp. 147-149 & 205-209.
Polster, Panzerzug und Panzerkraftwagen, in Allgemeiner

Anzeiger zum Militär-Wochenblatt No. 143 (1917), Sp. 3471-3475.

Pottgiesser, H., Die Deutsche Reichsbahn im Ostfeldzug, Neckargemünd 1960.

Pozeljujew, W. A., Bronevoszy schelesnich dorog, Moscow 1982.

Rabitsch, R., Panzerzug Lichtenauer, Basel 1936.

Rakow, W. A., Russische und sowjetische Dampflokomotiven, Berlin 1986.

Raschke, Kampf um Hopfengarten, in Der Reiter gen Osten, Vol. 6 (1935), No. 1.

Rauchensteiner, M., Der Krieg in Österreich 1945, Vienna 1984.

Rauchwetter, Aus der Luft vernichtet, in Die Wehrmacht Vol 7 (1943), No. 18.

Rebentisch, E., Zum Kaukasus und zu den Tauern, Boppard 1963.

Redelis, V., Partisanenkrieg, Heidelberg 1958.

Reetz, W., Die Grenzkämpfe gegen die Polen im Abschnitt Unruhstadt—Bomst im Februar 1919, in Grenzmärkische Heimatblätter, Vol, 11, Part 1 (1935), pp. 3-17.

Reichsarchiv/Forschungsanstalt für Kriegs- und Heeresgeschichte/Kriegsgeschichtliche Forschungsanstalt des Heeres, ed., Der Weltkrieg 1914—1918, 14 Vol., Berlin 1925-1944.

Reichsarchiv, ed., Der Weltkrieg 1914-1918, Das Feldeisenbahnwesen Vol. 1, Berlin 1928.

Reimer, M., Lokomotiven für die Ostfront, Munich 1999.

Reinecker, H., Stackelberg, K. G. von, Utermann, W., Panzer nach vorn, Berlin 1939.

Reinicke, A., Die 5. Jäger-Division, Friedberg, no date.

Remold, J., Die Befreiung Münchens von der Räteherrschaft 1919, in Deutsches Soldatenjahrbuch 1969, pp. 92-113.

Rijk, J. W. F. X. de, De overval op de Maasbruggen bij Venlo, in Spiegel Historiiael 3 (1968), pp. 265-266.

Roden, H., ed., Deutsche Soldaten, Leipzig 1935.

Röhr, G., Die Feldspurbahnen Südwestafrikas, Krefeld 1980.

Röll, von (ed.), Enzyklopädie des Eisenbahnwesens, Vol. 7, Panzerzüge, 2nd ed., Berlin & Vienna, 1912-1917.

Rohde, H., Das deutsche Wehrmachttransportwesen im II. Weltkrieg, Stuttgart 1971.

Romadin, S., Bronevaja gvardija revoluzii, in Model Konstruktor 1989, No. 11, pp. 19-23, 1990 No. 1, pp. 13-17, No. 3, pp. 21-25, No. 4, pp. 11-14.

Romadin, S., Sudba Zheleznajakowa, in Tank Master no. 4, 1998, pp. 17-22.

Rosenberg, Eisenbahnpanzerzug 22 im Grenzschutz, in Der Reiter gen Osten, Vol. 6 (1935), No. 6.

Salomon, E. von, ed., Das Buch vom deutschen Freikorpskämpfer, Berlin 1938.

Saucken, D. von, Die 4. Panzer-Division, Coburg 1968.

Sawodny, W., Deutsche Panzerzüge im Zweiten Weltkrieg, Waffenarsenal (Special Volume), Friedberg 1986, English version: Schiffer Military History vol. 17, 1989.

Sawodny, W., Panzerzüge im Einsatz, Waffenarsenal, S. 13, Friedberg 1989, English version: Schiffer Military History, 1990.

Sawodny, W., Les dinosaurs de la guerre, in La vie du rail No. 2314 (1991), pp. 27-30.

Sawodny, W., Die Panzerzüge Österreich-Ungarns und ihr Verbleib, in Eisenbahn 1992 No. 2, pp. 26-28, No. 3, pp. 44-46, No. 4, pp. 64-66, No. 6, pp. 105-108.

Sawodny, W., Panzerzüge an der Ostfront 1941-1944, Waffenarsenal Special Volume 28, Woelfersheim-Berstadt 2000, English version: Schiffer Military History, 2003.

Schamjakin, I., Der Streit um den Panzerzug, (Erzählerreihe Heft 262), Berlin 1982.

Scharf, H.-W., Eisenbahnen zwischen Oder und Weichsel, Freiburg 1981.

Scheibert, H., Einsatzversuch Stalingrad, Neckargemünd 1968.

Scheibert, H., Panzer zwischen Don und Donez, Friedberg 1979.

Schindler, H., Mosty und Dirschau 1939, Freiburg 1971.

Schleisner, S., Der Panzerzug, in Der Reiter gen Osten, Vol. 8 (1937), no. 12, pp. 4-8.

Schmider, K., Partisanenkrieg in Jugoslawien 1941-1944, Hamburg 2002.

Schmidt-Pauli, E., Geschichte der Freikorps 1919-1924, Stuttgart 1936.

Schmidt-Richberg, E., Das Ende auf den Balkan, Heidelberg 1955.

Schmitz, h. J., Der Kampf um Lissa, in Grenzmärkische Heimatblätter Vol. 13, Part 2 (1937), pp. 97-112.

Schmitz, H. J., Kampf um Rawitsch, in Grenzmärkische Heimatblätter Vol. 10 Part 1 (1934), pp. 4-25.

Schramm, P. E., ed., Kriegstagebuch des Oberkommandos der Wehrmacht, 4 vol., Frankfurt/Main 1961-1965.

Schröter, H., Die Eisenbahnen der ehemaligen deutschen Schutzgebiete Afrikas und Ihre Fahrzeuge, Frankfurt 1961.

Schubert, J., Stosstrupp—einmal anders, in Die Panzertruppe 1944, pp. 113-114.

Schulten, C. M., Duitsers vallen ons land binnen, in Legerkörier 30 (1980), pp. 3-4.

Schulze, H., Freikorps und Republik 1918-1920, Boppard 1969.

Schwabe, K., Der Krieg in Deutsch-Südwestafrika, Berlin 1907.

Selter, Über Panzerzüge unserer Feinde, in Organ für die Fortschritte des Eisenbahnwesens Vol 53 (1916), pp. 24-26.

Senger und Etterlin, F. M. von, Die deutschen Panzer 1926-1945, Munich 1969.

Senger und Etterlin, F. M. von, Kampfpanzer 1916-1966, Munich 1971.

Skaw'sh, V., Istorija bronepoezdov vojsk NKVD, in Lokotrans no. 2, 2003, pp. 13-19.

Später, H., ed., Die Einsaetze der Panzergrenadier-Division "Grossdeutschland", Friedberg 1986.

Spielberger, W. J., Der Panzerkampfwagen III und seine Abarten, Stuttgart 1984.

Spielberger, W. J., Der Panzerkampfwagen IV und seine Abarten, Stuttgart 1984.

Spielberger, W. J., Die Panzermakpfwagen 35(t) und 38(t) und ihre Abarten, Stuttgart 1980.

Stabsoffizier beim Kommandeur der Panzerzüge, ed., Panzerzüge Heft I (February 1944) Heft 2 (August 1944).

Stroop, J., Bericht ueber die Vernichtung des Warschauer Ghettos (facsimile), Neuwied 1960.

Sturm, R., Der Kampf um Lissa bei den Posener Grenzschutzkämpfen, in Grenzmärkische Heimatblätter, Vol. 17 (1941), pp. 3-7.

Telpuchowski, B. S., ed. A. Hillgruber & H. A. Jacobsen), Die sowjetische Geschichte des Grossen Vaterländischen Krieges 1941-1945, Frankfurt/Main 1961.

Teske, H., Die silbernen Spiegel, Heidelberg 1952.

Teske, H., Partisanen gegen die Eisenbahn, in Wehrwissenschaftliche Rundschau 3 (1953), pp. 468-475.

Teske, H., Über die deutsche Kampfführung gegen russische Partisanen, in Wehrwissenschaftliche Rundschau 14 (1964), pp. 662-673.

Tessin, G., Verbände und Truppen der deutschen Wehrmacht und Waffen-SS 1939-1945. 15 vol., Frankfurt am Main/Osnabrück 1965-1988.

Tessin, G., Deutsche Verbände und Truppen 1918-1939, Osnabrück 1974.

Tettenborn, H., Klweinkrieg nach rückwärts, in Der Reiter gen Osten, Vol. 7 (1936), No. 5-8.

Thalacker, Bericht über seine Tätigkeit am Bahnhof Amman an der Hedjastrecke Damaskus—Medina im allgemeinen und besonderen während der Rückzugs Der Hedjafront im Jahr 1918, in Beilage zum Nachrichtenblatt der Eisenbahntruppen No. 58 (1920)

Thiele, G., Im Schutze eines Panzerzugs, in Die Wehrmacht, Vol. 5 (1941), No. 26.

Thoms, R. & Pohanke, S., Handbuch zur Geschichte der deutschen Freikorps, Bad Soden 2001.

Thorwald, J., Es begann an der Weichsel, Stuttgart 1949.

Thorwald, J., Das Ende an der Elbe, Stuttgart 1950.

Tieke, W., Das Ende zwischen Oder und Elbe, Stuttgart 1995.

Tippelskirch, K. von, Geschichte des Zweiten Weltkriegs, Bonn 1951.

Trenkle, F. & Ellissen, H. J., Die deutschen Funknachrichtenanlagen, Vol. 1-3, Ulm 1989-91.

Troche, H., Die preussischen Normal-Güterzuglokomotiven der Gattungen G 3 und G 4, Freiburg 1992.

Trocja, H. & W., Der Panzertriebwagen "Kirowski", in Modell-Fan No. 4, 1994, pp. 53-55.

Trocja, H. & W. (No. II also J Ledwoch), Panzerzüge I und II, Warsaw 1995.

Urbanski, A., Über die Verwendungen von Panzerzügen im Feldkriege, in Mittheilungen über Gegenstände der Artillerie- und Genie-Wesens, Vol. XXXI (1900), pp. 402-412.

Velsen, S. von, Das Militäreisenbahnwesen, in Schwarte, M./, ed., Der grosse Krieg 1914-1918, Vol. 8 (1921), pp. 254-295.

Venner, D., Söldner ohne Sold, Vienna 1974.

Venohr, W., Aufstand für die Tschechoslowakei, Hamburg 1969.

Viertel, K., Ein Flakgeschütz zerschlägt zwei Panzerzüge, in Der Adler, 1943. No. 3.

Villanyi, G., Magyar pancelvonatok az elso vilaghaboru utan, in Haditechnika, 1994, No. 1, pp. 69-71, No. 2, pp. 48-52.

Vladis, Y., Motovagon vstupajet v boj, in Model Konstruktor, 1993, No. 8, pp. 28-29.

Völker, J., Die letzten Tage von Kolberg, Würzburg 1959.

Vogt, D., Der grosspolnische Aufstand 1918-1919, Marburg 1980.

Vopersal, W., Soldaten, Kämpfer, Kameraden, Vol, 3-5, Osnabrück 1985-1991.

Wagener, C., Heeresgruppe Süd, Bad Nauheim, no year.

Wagner, H., Panzerzüge, in Militärhistorische und –technische Mitteilungen, Vol, 60 (1929), pp. 30-40.

Wagner, H., Panzerzüge, in Militär-Wochenblatt, Vol,. ,113 (1929), Sp. 1126-1130.

Wagner, H., Schwere Panzerzüge, in Artilleristische Rundschau, Vol. 6, (1931), pp. 351-353.

Wagner, H., Gefechtswagen für neuzeitliche Panzerzüge, in Wehr und Waffen (1933), pp. 299-306 & 349-351.

Wagner, H., Zur Zukunftsentwicklung der Panzerzüge, in Deutsche Wehr, Vol. 8 (1935), pp. 156-158.

Waite, R. G. L., Vanguard of Nazism: The Free Corps Movement in Post War Germany, Harvard 1952.

Wegmann, G., ed., Das Oberkommando der Wehrmacht gibt bekannt…, 3 vol., Osnabrück, 1982.

Weidinger, O., SS-Division "Das Reich", Vol, 3-5, Osnabrück 1973-82.

Weidt, F., Düll mit Panzerzug, in Deutscher Soldatenkalender, 1960, pp. 50-52.

Weinman, W., Die 101. Jäger-Division in Dokumenten, Berichten und Bildern, Marbach 1966.

Wenker, A., Die entscheidenden Grenzschutzkämpfe um Bentschen im Januar 1919, In Grenzmärkische Heimatblätter, Vol, 11, Part 1 (1935), pp. 17-26.

Wenzel, H., Die Baureihe 57, Freiburg 1979.

Wenzel, H., Lokomotiven ziehen in den Krieg, Vol. 1-3, Vienna 1977-1980.

Westwood, J., Railways at War, London 1980.

Wetterau, Mit Sowjetpanzerzug gegen Sowjets, in Illustrierter Beobachter, 1942, No. 26.

Wetzel, "Fregatte" kämpft Bahnhof Ch. Frei, in Stuttgarter Illustrierte, 1944, No. 26.

Wiener, F., Gepanzert auf Schiene und Strasse, in Feldgrau. Vol. 10 (1962), pp./ 84f & 200.

Wittlich, E., Deutsche Eisenbahner im "Heiligen Land", in Wehrfront, Vol. 4 (1937), pp. 242ff.

Wittmaack, B., Im Osten, in Die Panzertruppe, 1942, pp. 188-189.

Wolff, T., Eisenbahn und Automobil auf dem Kriegsschauplatz, in Verkehrstechnische Woche, Vol. 10 (1916), pp. 129-135.

W. K., Die französischen Panzerwagen 1870-71, in Jahrbücher für die deutsche Armee und Marine, Vol. VI (1873), pp. 95-101.

Young, P., ed., Der grosse Atlas zum II. Weltkrieg, Cologne 1980.

Zanadil, R., Obrenena dresina Tatra T 18, Historie a plastikove modelar stavi No. 1, pp. 1-2

Zentner, C., Der Kriegsausbruch, Frankfurt—Berlin—Vienna 1979.

Ziel, R., Räder müssen rollen, Stuttgart 1974

Register of Armored Train Units of World War II

With action chronicles compiled from diary entries for several selected armored trains, and references to the publications of the Commander of the Railroad-Armored Trains with the Army High command, Chief, Army General Staff, recorded without listing the numbers of the armored trains in question, action reports naturally written in the style of that time (Panzerzug I: 1st Volume of February 1944: Panzerzug II: 2nd Volume of August 1944).

At the Commander:
+ = killed, * = became a prisoner of war

■ **Staff Officer of the Railroad Armored Trains with the General of the Fast Troops**
(Aug. 9, 1941—Jan. 24, 1942)
■ **Commander of the Railroad Armored Trains with the General of the Fast Troops**
(Jan. 25, 1942—March 31, 1943)
■ **Commander of the Railroad Armored Trains with the Commander of the Army or Chief of the Army General Staff** (April 1, 1943—Dec. 6, 1944)
■ **Commander of the Armored Trains with the Inspector-General of the Armored Troops**
(Dec. 7, 1944—March 31, 1945) (Field Post No. 39393)
Commander: Lt.Col.—Col. Egon von Olszewski
Staff Officer:
Lt.Col. Georg Dickhäuser (March 19—May 20, 1943)
Col. Friedrich Becker (May 20, 1943—Nov. 30, 1943)
Lt.Col.—Col. Hubertus Kewisch (from Dec. 1, 1943)
See pp.78-84

■ **Railroad Armored Train Regimental Staff No. 1:**
Commander of the Armored Trains with the H.Gr.F (as of March 23, 1945: E) with OB Southeast (Field Post No. 65672)
Established Feb. 1, 1944, withdrawn Oct. 14, 1944, again in office as of Nov. 15, 1944, remained until end of war
Commander: Col. Friedrich Becker
Command Train No. 1 (Cmdr. 1st Lt. Werner Freiherr Grote)
Workshop Train No. 1 (Cmdr. Lt. Ermert)
See pp. 82f, 172f, 300ff, 304f, 307

■ **Railroad Armored Train Regimental Staff No. 2:**
Commander of the Armored Trains with the H.Gr.A, as of Feb. 1945 with H.Gr. Weichsel (Field Post No. 29444)
Established for special purposes on May 11, 1944, active as staff with H.Gr. on Nov. 18, 1944, remained until end of war
Commander: Lt.Col. Hans Georg von Türckheim zu Altdorf
Command Train No. 72A (Cmdr. Capt. Gerhard Röming to Jan. 31, 1945
Command Train No. II (Cmdr. Lt. Georg Zartmann) as of Feb. 1, 1945
See pp. 82f, 172f, 198, 380, 394, 397, 400, 406

■ **Railroad Armored Train Regimental Staff No. 3:**
Commander of the Armored Trains with the H.Gr.Center, as of Jan. 27, 1945, H.Gr.North, as of May 1, 1945, to end of war H.Gr.Center
Established for special purposes on April 20, 1944, active as staff with the H.Gr. as of Oct. 16, 1944, disbanded on April 18, 1945, reestablished on May 1, 1945
Commander: Lt.Col. Dr. Gerhard Günther (+ March 21, 1945)
Major Ernst Naumann (as of May 1, 1945)
Command Train No. 72B (Cmdr. Lt. Wilhelm Sitzius, to Dec. 1944; Lt. Dietrich Lange Dec. 1944-Feb. 1945; 1st Lt. Günter Wydra Feb.-March 1945)
Command Train No. III (Cmdr. 1st Lt. Messer) as of May 1, 1945
Workshop Train No. 2 (Cmdr. ?) as of May 1, 1945
See pp. 82f, 172f, 273f, 380, 391, 395, 397, 406f

■ **Railroad Armored Train (Training) and Replacement Battalion,** established April 1, 1942, remained until end of the war
Commander:
Major Ernst Naumann (April 1, 1942—April 30, 1945)
Major Heinz Dieter Becker (as of May 1, 1945)
See pp. 84-92, 173f, 259, 279, 388, 406, 408

■ **Railroad Armored Train No. 1** (Field Post No. 07641)
Established on Sept. 7, 1939, ready for action shortly thereafter, received part of Armored Train No. 5 in autumn of 1940, rebuilt by K.St.N. 1169x Dec. 1942—Aug. 1943; lost on June 27, 1944, disbanded on July 14, 1944

Commanders: Lt. August Latton (Sept. 1939—Feb. 1940)
Capt. Fritz Mundus (March 1940—Oct. 1941)
Capt. Paul Grams (Nov. 1941—Jan. 1943)
1st Lt.—Capt. Helmut Walter (Jan. 1943—Feb. 1944)
1st Lt. Josef Kruells (Feb.—June 27 1944*)
Setup/rebuilding/cars: see 93f, 121f, 179, 181, 185, 202ff, 223
Equipment/arms/crew: see 93f, 225, 232, 236, 238, 256f, 259
Action: see 274f, 277f, 282ff, 285ff, 318, 320f, 323f, 331, 339, 341f, 367, 369f, 376ff, 380f, 382
Damage/loss: see 94, 179, 285, 342, 382f
Pictures/drawings: see 95f, 101, 129, 175, 178f, 186f, 202f, 205f, 222, 227, 239, 242, 285, 315, 320, 324, 330, 342, 368f, 376
Report: W. Böttner, Kampf mit sowjetischen Fallschirmspringern (Panzerzüge II)

■ **Railroad Armored Train No. 2** (Field Post No. 19835)
Established on Sept. 8, 1939, ready for action shortly thereafter. Rebuilt by K.St.N. 1169x, beginning in July 1944, disbanded on Nov. 2, 1944
Commanders:
1st Lt.—Capt. Albert Krumteich (Sept. 1939—June 1942)
1st Lt.—Capt. Georg Peters (July 1942—July 1944)
Setup/rebuilding/cars: see 93f, 122, 181, 185, 202ff, 223, 375, 380
Equipment/arms/crew: see 93f, 106, 225f, 233, 236, 238, 256f, 259
Action: see 274f, 277f, 318, 320f, 323, 325, 331f, 339, 341, 348, 367, 369ff, 376ff, 380ff
Damage/loss: see 370, 377
Pictures/drawings: see 96, 101, 184, 193, 215, 278, 316, 331, 340, 371, 376, 379
Reports: Uffz. Tomaszewski, Panzer gegen Banden (Panzerzüge I), Volldampf voraus (Panzerzüge I), Einmal ohne Panzerzug (Panzerzüge II).
K. H. Gläser, Vor zum Gegenstoss (Panzerzüge II), Wir holen euch raus (Panzerzüge II)

■ **Railroad Armored Train No. 3** (Field Post No. 03841)
Established on July 5, 1939, ready for action end of August 1939, rebuilt by K.St.N.1169x July 1943—July 1944, lost Oct. 10, 1944, disbanded Oct. 12, 1944

Commanders: 1st Lt. Erich Euen (Aug.—Sept. 1, 1939 +)
Lt./1st Lt. Rudolf Zettler (Sept. 1939—Nov. 1940)
Lt. Fritz Pohley (deputy) (Dec. 1940—March 1941)
1st Lt. Herbert Thieme (April—Nov. 1941)
1st Lt. Rudolf Opitz (March 1942—-March 1943)
1st Lt. Erhard Edom (April—Sept. 1943)
Lt./1st Lt. Werner Schade (May—Oct. 1944)
Setup/rebuilding/cars: see 93f, 122, 179, 181, 185, 202ff, 220, 223, 241
Equipment/arms/crew: see 93f, 122, 225, 229, 236, 238f, 249f, 255ff, 259
Action: see 274ff, 282, 287, 320f, 325, 332ff, 341f, 346ff, 367, 384f, 394, 402
Damage/loss: see 94, 179, 276f, 333f, 339, 348, 367, 385, 394
Pictures/drawings: see 97f, 102, 115, 128, 177f, 186f, 203f, 226, 241, 256, 274, 276f, 287, 320f, 325, 332ff, 385

■ **Railroad Armored Train No. 4** (Field Post No. 12663)
Established on August 11, 1939, rebuilt by K.St.N1169x Dec. 1943—Jan. 1945, remained until end of war
Commanders: Major Otto Heilmann (Aug.—Dec. 1939)
Major Heinrich Hönig (Jan.—May 1940)
Lt. Richard Wieczorek (deputy) (May—July 1940)
1st Lt. Werner Klose (Aug.—Nov. 1940)
1st Lt.—Capt. Friedrich Schlegel (Nov. 1940—Feb. 1943)
Capt. Heinz Dieter Becker (Feb. 1943—June 1943)
1st Lt. Kurt Rösch (June 1943—Dec. 1943)
1st Lt. Wilhelm Mauss (April 1944—May 1945)
Setup/rebuilding cars: see 93f, 122, 181, 185, 190, 202f, 205f, 223
Equipment/arms/crew: see 93f, 225, 236, 256f, 259
Action: see 274f, 277, 282f, 287, 305ff, 320, 322, 325, 330, 336, 338f, 348, 367, 369f
Damage/loss: see 308, 339, 369, 409
Pictures/drawings: see 98,103, 129, 177, 186, 204ff, 226, 256, 275, 282, 287, 307f, 316, 325, 330, 339, 347

■ **Railroad Armored Train No. 5** (Field Post No. 15107)
Established and ready for action at beginning of Sept. 1939, badly damaged on May 10, 1940, disbanded June 1940, remainder to Armored Train No. 1
Commanders: 1st Lt. Fritz Strauss (Sept. 1939—June 1940)
Setup/rebuilding/cars: see 93, 185, 202f, 205f

Equipment/arms/crew: see 93f, 225, 238, 256
Action: see 278, 282f
Damage/loss: see 94, 118, 283, 285
Pictures/drawings: see 99, 102, 187, 283

■ **Railroad Armored Instruction Train No. 5**
(Field Post No. 48073)
Established on Sept. 6, 1943, Armored Train 75 until March 1, 1944, action as of July 1944, on Aug. 25 1944 renamed Armored Instruction Train No. 5, lost on March 4, 1945, disbanded on March 27, 1945
Commanders: Capt. Erhard Edom (July 1944—March 1945)
Setup/rebuilding/cars: see 137
Equipment/arms/crew: see 230f
Action: see 173f, 388, 390, 397, 399, 402
Damage/loss: see 402

■ **Railroad Armored Train No. 6** (Field Post No. 09171)
Established on July 10, 1939, as repair train, ready for action end of August 1939, on Oct. 26 1939 Armored Train No. 6, rebuilt similarly to K.St.N.1169x May—Sept. 1942, lost on Oct. 1, 1944, disbanded on Oct. 12, 1944
Commanders: Major Ernst Linde (August 1939—June 1941)
1st Lt. Franz Kubrat (June 1941—April 1942)
Capt. Eberhard Mertins (April 1942—June 1943)
1st Lt. Josef Kruells (July 1943—Feb. 1944)
1st Lt.—Capt. Johann Wirtz (Feb.—Oct. 1, 1944 +)
Setup/rebuilding/cars: see 93f, 121f, 181, 185, 202f, 205ff, 220, 223
Equipment/arms/crew: see 93f, 225, 229, 236, 249, 256f, 259ff
Action: see 275ff, 282, 293, 296, 299ff, 303, 320ff, 331f
Damage/loss: see 94, 300, 303, 332
Pictures/drawings: see 99, 104, 187, 205f, 222, 226, 294, 322, 420f

■ **Railroad Armored Train No. 7** (Field Post No. 09454)
Established on August 1, 1939, ready for action end of August 1939, rebuilt by K.St.N.1169x March 1944—April 1945, remained until end of war
Commanders: 1st Lt. Gert Köhler (Aug. 1939—March 1942)
Lt. Fritz Wormit (deputy) (March—May 1942)
1st Lt. Helmut Vögler (May 1942—March 1944)
1st Lt. Dieter Baum (Oct. 1944—May 1945)
Setup/rebuilding/cars: see 93f, 122, 166, 179, 181, 185, 202f, 205f, 223, 320
Equipment/arms/crew: see 93f, 225, 229, 232, 236, 256f, 259
Action: see 275f, 278, 282f, 315, 320, 322, 325, 338f, 348ff, 357, 360, 406f
Damage/loss: 283, 350, 357, 360, 407
Pictures/drawings: see 100, 104, 129, 187, 242, 275, 349, 352, 407, 424

■ **Railroad Armored Train No. 9** (Field Post No. 38094)
(This number was to be given to a train made up in March 1940 of captured Czech material; it was changed in the setup phase to No. 25—see there)

■ **Railroad Armored Train No. 10** (Broad Gauge, Field Post No. 47390)
Established on Dec. 1, 1941, ready for action Feb. 1942, originally consisted of two combat trains, the second combat train became Armored Train No. 11 on July 31, 1943, converted to standard gauge and re-equipped July—Aug. 1942, badly damaged on March 21, 1944, disbanded on June 20, 1944
Commanders: Capt. Ernst Naumann(Dec. 1940—March 1942)
Capt. Paul Berger (April-May 1942)
Capt. Arno Dressler (June 1942—Jan. 1943)
1st Lt.—Capt. Gerhard Röming (Jan. 1943—April 1944)
Setup/rebuilding/cars: see 120f, 180, 189, 200, 216f, 247, 279, 337
Equipment/arms/crew: see 120f, 229, 253, 258f
Action: see 315, 328, 336, 338f, 348ff, 357, 361, 365
Damage/loss: see 237, 350, 365
Pictures/drawings: see 133, 135, 188, 218, 228, 236, 242, 335f, 338, 349f, 352, 361, 365

■ **Railroad Armored Train No. 11** (Field Post No. 57381)
Previously second combat train of Armored Train No. 10, independent Armored Train No. 11 on August 1, 1943, rebuilt by K.St.N1169x March—July 1944, lost on Jan. 13, 1945, disbanded on Jan. 27, 1945
Commanders: Lt. Horst Löfke or 1st Lt. Huiffner?(Aug. 1943)
Lt—1st Lt. Gerhard Röpke (Aug. 1943—Jan. 1944)
1st Lt. Rolf Lorscheidt (Jan. 1944—Jan. 12, 1945)
1st Lt. Heinrich Patzner (Jan. 13, 1945)
Setup/rebuilding/cars: see 122, 189, 216ff, 247

Equipment/arms/crew: see 120f, 229, 253, 258f
Action: see 197f, 355ff, 361f, 364f, 386f, 397
Damage/loss: see 355f, 365, 386f, 397
Pictures/drawings: see 129, 133f, 135, 188, 218, 263, 354, 361, 364, 387
Report: W. Geymann, *Wir sind schneller* (Panzerzüge II)

■ **Railroad Armored Train No. 21** (Field Post No. 08605)
Established on June 10, 1940, ready for action July 1940, lost on Oct. 30, 1944, disbanded on Nov. 16, 1944.
Commanders: 1st Lt. Arno Dressler (June 1940—May 1942)
1st Lt. Hans Bendl   (May 1942—Sept. 1943)
1st Lt. Wolfhart Schultze   (Sept. 1943—June 1944)
1st Lt. Gerhard Gorski   (June—Nov. 1944)
Setup/rebuilding/cars: see 105f, 122, 179, 185, 191, 198, 216ff, 223, 279
Equipment/arms/crew: see 105f, 227, 232, 236, 257, 259
Action: see 107, 287, 315, 318, 341f, 346, 348, 352, 354, 367, 369ff, 376ff, 380f, 382ff, 394
Damage/loss: see 348, 376, 382, 384, 394
Pictures/drawings: see 105, 107f, 114, 185, 193, 199, 217ff, 288, 342, 348, 368f, 383, 385

Action Chronicle of Armored Train No. 21
Diary notes for July 1940 to April 1941 plus—sometimes overlapping—May 25 1942 to Oct. 31 1944

1940
07/22	ready for action, stayed at first in Cracow (subordinate to AOK 18, as of 10/10/40 AOK 12. as of 12/15/40 AOK 17)
11/14-21	firing drill at Rembertow firing range

1941
03/31—04/04	transfer trip to France
As of 04/04	first station Blainville, later also Vitry and Langres, subordinate to XXVII. AK until 09/21, then XLV. AK (AOK 1), line securing runs in northern France
11/13	transfer to Dijon (Porte Neuve station) VIII. AK

1942
As of 02/26	Same station, subordinate to 337. Inf.Div. (XLV. AK), securing demarcation line to unoccupied part of France
06/25	trip to Paris
06/28—07/11	propaganda trip in two halves, one in central France, other on Channel coast and in Belgium
09/21—10/11	renewal of radio system and improvements in Paris (Clamant depot and Fort Ivry)
10/11	return to Dijon
10/25—11/07	transfer trip to Russia (10/31—11/02 Warsaw)
As of 11/07	subordinate to 286th Sec.Div (station Krupki), securing runs every night on Minsk—Smolensk line, especially in Borissow—Orscha region)
11/29	Combat on Smolensk—Dorogobusch line
12/01	Transfer to Durowo—Wladimirskoje to support withdrawal fighting and counterattack of Holste Group, participated in regaining of Nikitinka, afterward protected line from there to Wladimirskoje, as of 12/17 stationed at Igorjewskaja

1943
02/01-04	transfer trip to Kursk, arrived 02/03/43, two quarters cars burned in bomb attack in Brjansk
As of 02/04	withdrawal fighting in Kursk district (abandoned 02/08)
As of 02/08	covered Kursk—Lgow withdrawal line in Damerau Battle Group (4th Arm.Div.), withdrawal fighting 02/08 Ryschkowo, 02/09-11 Okolodok—Djakonowo, firing from Maslowo
02/11	took antitank shell in loco and car 4 in attack on Okolodok (1 dead, 3 wounded), then return for repairs

02/12-16	in Konotop
As of 02/17	repair and re-equipping (A/A quad) of train and buildup of quarters train in Darniza EAW
03/14	after finished, trip to station in Teterew for securing Korosten—Kiev line, also fighting with partisans
03/21	trip to Kiev
03/23	securing run from there to Kharkov
03/24	return trip to Popelnja
03/27	return to station in Teterew
04/14	transfer via Konotop to Sumy (subordinate to VII. AK), secured Belopolje—Basy—Boromlija line
05/24	transfer to Syrowatka because of artillery fire
05/30	two badly wounded in low-level air attack in Grebenikowa
June	transfer to Basy
07/28-29	securing run via Woroschba to Tetkino and then to Konotop, return to Basy, artillery and infantry action in Sumy—Solotnizki district, awaited attack on Basy railroad station canceled, but air attacks on 08/04-06
08/08	Psel bridge under heavy artillery fire
08/09	armored train goes to Smorodino (defensive fighting in 7th Arm.Div.), bridge guarding at Bakirowka, return to Boromlja must be gained in breakthrough fight (1 dead, 6 wounded)
08/10	return to Syrowatka, destruction of tracks
08/11	on return to Basy broken tracks must be repaired, low-level air attacks, farther back via Woroschba to Chutor Michailowski, bomb attack on 08/12
As of 08/12	securing lines from Chutor Michailowski to Unetscha and Nawlja
08/15-16	more bomb attacks
08/16	securing run to Sernowo
08/17	night run Swesa—Chutor—Sernowo, control car set afire by low-level planes
08/18	transfer to Snob
08/19-21	partisan action after track explosion, in combing woods 1 partisan killed, on own man wounded, train in lurking position
08/21-22	trip toward Brjansk, after return to Chutor air attack
08/23-24	securing runs
08/25	partisan hunt, over 4 kg explosives removed but pursuit of partisans fruitless, trip via Chutor to Nerussa, there transport train is bombed
08/26	men wounded in this bombardment taken to Seredina—Buda
08/27-30	securing runs
08/31	transfer back, quarters train in Newsorowo, combat train in Witemlja (securing Desna bridge)
09/02 50	explosions on Unetscha—Witemlja line, armored train removes five charges near Pogar
09/03	securing run
09/04	armored train is fired on, antitank guns fought down, two explosive charges removed, cover for explosive work in Witemlja, with anti-air defense
09/05	securing engineer units in destruction of Witemlja—Pogar—Newsorowo line, bomb attack on bridge (near Pogar?)
09/06-10	securing runs
09/11	return Newsorowo—Unetscha—Nowosylokow—Slynka
09/12	Slynka—Nowobelizkaja—Snowskaja
09/13-17	securing Snowskaja—Mena line
09/18-21	combat and quarters train in Gomel
09/21-24	stationed in Nowobelizkaja
09/25	new station in Wassiliewitschi
10/05	combed several partisan villages, one man wounded
10/06	trip to Retschiza

10/07	General picked up, hit mine on return trip (A/A car and car 2 tipped over, kitchen car derailed, 3 wounded)
10/08	transfer to Kalinkowitschi
10/14	securing run, cars 4 and 5 derailed by switch explosion in Kalinkowitschi
10/24	line securing, several charges removed
10/25-26	hit mine 3 km west of Ptitsch, car 5 derailed and damaged (1 wounded)
10/26-27	search troop before train defuses one mine
10/28	back to quarters train in Kalinkowitschi
11/06	securing run, at first to Wassiliewitschi, then back to Mikatschewitschi
11/06	fruitless partisan operation
11/09	securing run to Luniniec
11/14	to Schitkowitschi
11/16-17	to Korschewka
11/24	to Mikatschewitschi
12/10	repaired combat cars 2 and 3 and A/A car back from Dünaburg
12/20	fruitless partisan operation
12/21-22	trip to Luniniec and back
12/23	one dead in accident in Brinnewo
12/24	hit a mine on securing run 6 km west of Schitkowitschi, radio car (car 4) badly damaged (2 badly, 6 slightly wounded)

1944
01/13	3 wounded in bomb attack in Kopzewitschi
01/14	1 dead, 2 wounded in bomb attack in Ptitsch
01/30	fight 2 km west of Ptitsch, Lt. Gettwert killed by shell splinter, 1 wounded
02/05	1 wounded in action west of Ptitsch
02/15	16 men sent to Sec.Reg. Schitkowitschi, replaced by 7 men from Rembertow
02/22 6	more men sent off
03/14	front action near Korschewka
03/17-19	transfer from Korschewka to Drogitschin
03/24	from Drogitschin to Zabinka 03/24—04/10 partisan operations near Horodec
04/07	killed 3 partisans in combing wooded area, one machine gun captured (two of own men wounded)
04/09	mine detonated under A/A car 7
04/10	trip to Kobryn
04/19	partisan action near Turna, 4 partisans killed, 4 captured, shot by SD (one own man wounded)
04/27	between Kobryn and Antopol
04/30	4 partisans killed in combing Zosimy (one own man wounded)
05/07	large partisan operation on Brest-Litowsk—Baranowitschi line (train takes over line securing)
05/12-15	inspection by Lt.Col. Günther in Iwazewitschi and Beresa-Kartuska
05/21—06/15	partisan operation "Kormoran" with PZ 28 and 61 under Lt.Col. Günther, battle group to block Minsk—Orscha rail line between Smolewitschi and Krupki (stations 05/24 Borissow, 05/29 Prijamino)
06/07	large partisan operation (several PZ and infantry)
06/16	armored train transferred with Lt.Col. Günther's battle group from Portowitschi via Minsk to Kroleschisna (A/A car 7 hit a mine, slight damage), battle group disbanded
06/19	night line securing in Molodetschno region
06/20	armored train subordinated to Major Linke Battle Group (PZ 61, Minsk) (line securing Minsk—Molodetschno)
06/23	battle group (PZ 21, 28, 61) gathers in Minsk for departure toward Bobruisk, but train (as also PZ 28) hits a mine beyond Kola, cars 1-3 and loaded road vehicles (car, truck, Panhard scout car) badly, loco slightly damaged, back to Minsk for repairs

06/29	after provisional repairs (addition of makeshift-armored replacement cars) from Minsk to Lida to secure staff command train of Army Group Center
07/01	securing Lida—Baranowitschi line
07/04-05	defensive fighting in Molodetschno region
07/06	armored loco back after repairs, return from Lida to Wolkowysk
07/07	quarters train to Wirballen, then Wolomin (partisan attack there on 07/15, 10 attackers killed), 07/18 back to Wirballen, combat train via Mosty—Grodno to Wilna region.
07/08	fruitless attempt to break through Soviet ring to Wilna railroad station, loco and both tenders destroyed by Russian tanks, return trip, another fruitless attempt in evening, and artillery support of defense
07/09	Trip back to Kowno—Maurischkei, "black" loco (Series 52) replaces armored loco
07/19	return to Wirballen base
07/22	quarters train to Maurischkei
07/23	advance toward Kowno
07/25	low-level plane attack in Maurischkei (6 wounded), with PZ 3 via Kowno to Palemonas (artillery support of front)
07/27	from Palemonas to Kowno
07/29	return to Wirballen, at midday via Eydtkau to Tilsit
07/30	quarters train stationed in Weinoten, combat train makes reconnaissance run
08/01	combat train is to reconnoiter via Tauroggen to Widukle, but bridge northeast of Tauroggen is blown up
08/02	in Tauroggen
08/03-10	in Laugszargen
08/10	transfer via Memel to Moscheiken
08/12	stands ready in Ringen
08/13	artillery support and scout-troop operation
08/14	in Moscheiken
08/15-23	artillery support of front near Ringen, scouting troops toward Autz
08/24	supports attack of 4th Arm.Div. on Autz
08/26	at railroad station in Autz
08/30—09/08	armored train supports further attack attempts toward Bene with artillery
09/08-09	Return to quarters train in Weinoten, combat train overhauled there
09/13-14	back to front near Autz
10/02-04	several scattered Russians captured
10/08-10	Russian breakthrough near Schaulen to Baltic cuts train off in Courland
10/10	quarters train lost in capture of Weinoten and armored train remains enclosed in Moscheiken, infantry takes up position
10/14	Russian breakthrough to the Windau narrows action radius to before blown-up bridge, armored train is divided into cars set up in railroad station area
10/31	in new soviet attack, danger of surrounding of Moscheiken, village abandoned and move to north, armored train to be blown up but not all parts of it are (during combat around Moscheiken as of 10.16 14 dead, 11 wounded)

Reports: W. Schwarz, Panzerzug verhindert Durchbruch (08/09/1943) (Panzerzüge II)
H. Stock, Qürfeldein gegen Banditen (04/19/1944?) (Panzerzüge II)

■ **Railroad Armored Train No. 22** (Field post No. 30971)
Established on July 10, 1940, ready for action Aug. 1940, lost on Feb. 11, 1945, probably disbanded on Feb. 27, 1945
Commanders:
1st Lt/Capt. Paul Schuettke (July 1940—Aug. 1942)
1st Lt. Wolfhart Schultze (Sept. 1942—Mar. 1943)
1st Lt. Gerhard Riewendt (May 1943—Oct. 1944)
Capt. Philipp von Villiez (Oct. 1944—Feb. 1945)
Setup/rebuilding/cars: see 105f, 179, 198, 200f, 202f, 216ff, 223
Equipment/arms/crew: see 105f, 122, 227, 236, 252f, 57, 259, 261, 279
Action: see 107, 287f, 290, 393f, 399
Damage/loss: see 399
Pictures/drawings: see 105, 108f, 115, 199, 217ff, 236, 252, 288f

■ **Railroad Armored Train No. 23** (Field Post No. 36521)
Established on March 1, 1940, ready for action April 1940, disbanded on Oct. 2, 1940, re-established on June 19, 1941, ready for action July 1941, rebuilt by K.St.N1169x Oct. 1942—Aug. 1943, remained until end of war
Commanders:
? (March—Oct. 1940)
Capt.-Maj. Rudolf Jungke (June 1941—May 1945)
Setup/rebuilding/cars: see 105f, 118, 122, 179, 181, 185, 198, 202f, 215, 223, 280
Equipment/arms/crew: see 106, 225f, 251, 257ff
Action 107, 280, 287, 292f, 296, 299f, 302, 305, 307f
Damage/loss: see 106, 293, 307f, 415
Pictures/drawings: see 109f, 113, 116, 129, 175, 177f, 182, 184, 205, 216, 227, 237, 250, 280, 292, 294, 297, 300, 307

■ **Railroad Armored Train No. 24** (Field Post No. 37248)
Established on March 1, 1940, ready for action April 1940, disbanded on Oct. 2, 1940, re-established on June 19, 1941, ready for action July 1941, rebuilt to K.St.N.1169x March 1943—Jan. 1944, lost on Jan. 16, 1945, disbanded on Jan. 27, 1945
Commanders:
1st Lt. Friedrich Schlegel (March—October 1940)
Lt.—1st Lt.—Capt. Paul Budin (June 1941—July 1943)
Capt. Eberhard Mertins (August 1943—Jan. 1944)
1st Lt. Otto Pakheiser (Feb. 1944—Jan. 1945)
Setup/rebuilding/cars: see 105ff, 118, 121f, 179, 181, 185, 191, 198, 200, 213, 215, 223, 280, 410
Equipment/arms/crew: see 106, 225f, 257ff
Action: see 107, 280, 287, 290ff, 295, 311, 393f, 397, 398f
Damage/loss: see 106, 295, 399
Pictures/drawings: see 110f, 113, 116, 129, 182, 199, 214, 224, 280, 293

Action Chronicle of Armored Train No. 24
Diary notations for the period from March 06 to Sept. 20, 1940, plus Dec. 31, 1943 to Jan. 20, 1945, activity report Nov. 15 to Dec. 14 1941, combat report of Capt. Popp Armored Train Battle Group for Jan. 14-16 1945

1940		
03/06—04/05	PZ 24 set up in Rehagen-Klausdorf	
04/05	trip to Bremen (there until 04/08)	
04/08	trip from Bremen to Niebuell	
04/09	over Danish border, Tondern—Esbjerg—Ringköbing	
04/10	trip from Ringköbing to Holstebro	
04/11—05/27	stationed in Holstebro	
04/14	trip to Thyboroen—Stoppestedt isthmus	
04/16	trip to Oddesund	
04/24	trip to Vemb	
04/26	trip to Thisted	
05/27-28	trip from Holstebro via Hamburg to Menden	
05/29—06/04	in Menden	
06/04—15 to	Jülich RAW for improvements	
06/15—07-23	in Menden	
07/23	from Menden to Minden, loco repaired there	
07/24—26	from Minden to Allenstein, East Prussia	
07/27—08/06	in Allenstein	
08/06—09	from Allenstein to Sperenberg	
08/09—09/20	PZ 24 disbanded in Sperenberg	

The re-established PZ 24 was transferred to the military administrative region of Serbia at the end of July 1941; its first known station was Nisch, an activity report for 11/15—12/14/1941 is available:

1941	
11/15	return from Aleksinac in the morning
11/17	escorted passenger car of departing commander of 717th Inf.Div. (Gen. Hoffmann) to Belgrade
11/18-20	in Belgrade
11/21	to Nisch with new commander (Gen. Hinkhofer) of 717th Inf. Div.
11/22	day trip to Leskovac and back
11/22-26	daily night runs to Grdelica and back (without notable events)
11/26	road bridge and line blown up near Gramada railroad station (alarmed too late, partisans long since gone), PZ take part in line rebuilding, then advances to Svrljig (without events)
11/27	back to Nisch, loco to BW for exchange
11/30—12/01	night run to Leskovac and back
12/02	repair of burst heating
12/02-03	night run to Grdelica and back
12/03-04	night run to Leskovac and back
12/04	trips at first to Bela Palanka, then at night to Grdelica and back
12/05	line blown up south of Doljevac railroad station, PZ carries out rebuilding with Serbian workers, back to Nisch next morning
12/07—08	night run to Grdelica and back
12/09	inspection trip to Grdelica with Div. Cmdr. For look at new bridge securing measures, replacement armored loco (57 2043) arrives
12/10	1a of Div. taken to Belgrade in passenger car for conference
12/11—12	trip back to Nisch
12/13	installation of new loco
12/14	PZ to Pecenjevce, disembarked infantry is to search three villages east of there, PZ artillery can give fire support if needed, partisans flee on approach and cannot be caught, search fruitless

In this period 2668 km were covered (until then 12,792 km). No detailed data on further activities of PZ 24 in Balkans are available. In the spring of 1942 PZ 24 was transferred to Croatia, known station of Slavonski Brod, actions in entire north Croatian district. On 02/13/1943 PZ 24 was damaged in a collision during the partisan operation "Weiss" and at first went to the Marburg (Maribor) RAW, but then to the Munich-Neuaubing RAW for a complete rebuilding, which lasted until the end of 1943.

12/31/1943	departure from Neuaubing
1944	
01/03	arrival in Rembertow
01/05	armored loco (French 140 C 117) derailed at railroad station, set back on rails.
01/06	inspection (of Repl.Batt.?) by Colonel
01/08	shooting-in of guns
01/09	sharpshooting drill
01/10	acceptance run
01/12	washing out loco
01/18-22	work on train
01/24	carburetor damage on light generator
01/25	trip to Pasieki (toward Scharfenwiese)
01/26	rails loaded
01/28	inspection of loco, went well
01/29—02/02	trip from Rembertow to Innsbruck, towing device on car 8a damaged
02/03	repairs at Innsbruck RAW
02/04—06	trip from Innsbruck to La Rotta (Pisa—Florence line)
022/06	to Empoli
02/07	to Florence
02/08	trip to Fonglia(?), loco (to wash out) and car 8a (to reinforce buffers) to Florence EAW
02/11	from Florence to La Rotta, departure at night toward Viareggio
02/12	arrival at Torre del Lago (train located in pine woods)
02/13	added coal and water in Viareggio
02/14	four-engine bombers attack Pisa and Livorno
02/15	departure from Torre del Lago to Görz (arrival 5:02 PM)
02/18	loco and car 7 at Montesanto BW
02/19	examination by Gen. Kübler, departure to Cormons, alarm in evening, departure for S. Lucia
02/20	S. Lucia, to Piedicolle (German border) in evening
02/21	return trip to Cormons
02/23	alarm at night, to Mossa
02/24-25	in Mossa, men between 15 and 45 taken to Görz
02/25	departure to Florence
02/26	car 8a at Florence EAW
02/27-28	from Florence to Roccastrada (PZ is parked in tunnel there, line to the coast is totally bombed out and unusable)
03/01	loco to Siena for washing out
03/02-19	train in Roccastrada, must usually stay in tunnel because of air-raid danger, its own pumping station for taking on water is erected at Monte Amiata
03/91—06/20	diary keeper was in Rembertow for training. Meanwhile the train saw action in Umbria (Arezzo—Terni region); in May it was transferred back to Friaul
04/12	bomb attack in Alviano (2 dead, 6 wounded)

05/02	in partisan attack near Capolona (near Arezzo), 2 dead, 1 wounded
06/20	PZ in Gemona, trip to Spilimbergo
06/21	action run Spilimbergo to Gemona
06/22	transfer from Spilimbergo to Resiutta
06/24	via Carnia to Villa Santina, fired on partisans with mine thrower
06/25—07/01	in Resiutta
07/02	partisan action Tarvis—Assling—Piedicolle
07/03-05	in Piedicolle
07/06	from Piedicolle via Assling—Tarvis to Resiutta, on to Forgaria in evening
07/07	Forgaria, protected bridge building
07/08	to Spilimbergo
07/09	to Casarsa, then back to Forgaria
07/10	to Tarvis in afternoon, searched village, partisan woman captured, to Gemona, two gasoline tank cars burned out
07/11-12	securing runs Gemona—Forgaria
07/13	36 airplanes bomb Tagliamento bridge, train runs into buffer block in Pinzano, line blocked by bomb damage on both sides.
07/14-16	in tunnel between Pinzano and Forgaria
07/17	to Spilimbergo in evening, tracks blown up
07/18	via Udine to Cormons
07/19-20	train in Montesanto for repairs, loco in Udine
07/21	train finished, depart for Reich in evening
07/22	loco repaired in Villach
07/23	tender axle bearing examined in Munich
07/24	departure for France
07/30	arrival in Bourges, loco taken for washing out
08/03	loco back from depot
08/09-10	building a position (trench?)
08/12	car 2 derailed by broken rail
08/13	alarm readiness in evening
08/18-19	PZ, quarters train and 34 cars with airplane motors with loco 320 C 246 via Saincaize to Moulins
08/20	back to Saincaize
08/21	car 2 (hot axles) in Nevers for repairs
08/22	combat train to Bourges
08/24	to Reuilly, bridge blown up, via Vierzon back to Bourges at night
08/26	trip to Saincaize
08/27	back to Bourges
08/28	loco is washed out
08/29	from Bourges to Nevers
08/30	from Nevers to Moulins, blowup at night
08/31	via Paray-le-Monial to Montchanin
09/01	track blowup is repaired, PZ 32 met
09/02	from Montchanin with trains as escort via Chagny to Dijon, met PZ 22
09/03	PZ is to return to Paray-le-Monial, but 9 km before Montchanin tracks are bombed, back to Chagny
09/04	bomb attack, oil train burns, tracks repaired, departure for Dijon, fighter-bomber attack near Beaune, car 8a and control car lost (2 dead, 2 wounded)
09/05	escape toward Is-sur-Tille fails, back to Dijon-Porte Neuve
09/06	track toward Auxonne blocked by derailed train, 300-meter detour laid over a field, train reaches Auxonne
09/07	to Gray, cars 7 and 8 derailed, on to Vesoul in the evening
09/08	to Lure, took over securing there
09/09	fighter-bomber attacks all day
09/10-11	from Lure toward Belfort, line between tunnel and Belfort blocked by collision of trains, detour rails laid, in afternoon via Mühlhausen to Bantzenheim
09/12	to Haltingen
09/11-26	train is repaired and re-equipped (with tank-destroyer cars, etc.) in Haltingen BW
09/27-28	test run, two tender axles hot
09/29—10/09	at Offenburg BW
10/10	to Haltingen, quarters train still there, loco is washed out
10/15	loco finished, depart eastward in evening
10/20	loco to Gleiwitz RAW with boiler damage
10/22	after loco is repaired, to Cracow in evening
10/23	Cracow, briefing
10/24	via Sucha to Makow (new station)
10/26	trip to Chabowka
10/27	on to Rabka Zaryta, back to Makow
10.29	action run to Osielec
10/30	to Chabowka
10/31—11/01	in Makow
11/02	trip via Chabowka to Neu-Sandez
11/02	from Neu-Sandez to Zakopane
11/04	back to Makow
11/07	action near Osielec (three bridges blown up), to Jordanow with truck

11/08	in Makow
11/09	trip via Sucha to Kalwaria
11/10	on to Skawina, in Lencze in evening
11/11	to Makow and back to Lencze
11/13	to Kalwaria
11/14	to Stronie, loco 52 5720 for PZ 24 (besides armored French loco 140 C 117) in Sucha
11/15	back to Makow, to Radziszow in evening
11/16	Kalwaria 11/17-18 cars of combat train individually divided among Skawina, Radziszow, Lencze, Kalwaria, and Stryszow, quarters train still in Makow
11/25	quarters train to Stronie
11/26	quarters train to Stryszow, officers to Cracow to newly arrived commander of PZ at H.Gr. A (Lt.Col. von Türckheim)
11/27	back to Stryszow
11/28	quarters train transferred to Kalwaria
11/29	combat train assembled in Radziszow
12/01-02	loco 52 5720 to Bielitz for washing out
12/11-12	loco (French?) to Bielitz for washing out
12/17	preliminary order for transfer
12/18-19	combat and quarters trains hitched together in Kalwaria
12/23	departure from Kalwaria
12/24	in Skarzysko with broken pulling rod and hot axle on car 7, in new station of Tomaszow in evening
12/25-26	car 7 repaired at BW
12/26-30	trip to Litzmannstadt
12/30	PZ transferred to Jelen (placed in forest at "Anlage Mitte" headquarters prepared for but never visited by Hitler)
12/31	both locos go to take on water

1945	
01/01	shooting-in
01/03	loco to Tomaszow for washing out
01/10	to Opoczno
01/13	back to Jelen in evening
01/14	Popp PZ Battle Group (PZ 24 and 62) alarmed in morning, goes to Radom (defective armored loco of PZ 24 replaced by "black" one in Skarzysko Kamienna)
01/15	8:00 AM armored trains take firing positions near Jedlnia Letnisko, advanced observer with tanks on the Zwolen—Radom road, 10:45 AM order to Radom, midday back and forth on Radom—Jastrzab line, no enemy contact, to Skarzysko Kamienna to take on coal and water in evening, delay as railroad station is jammed with evacuation trains
01/16	3:15 AM departure toward Opoczno, line blocked by two collided freight trains in Wolka Piebanska, clearing work by assistance train would take until afternoon, meanwhile it becomes known that Soviets have already blocked railroad station at Nieklan with tanks and moved forward on line to north, armored trains are blown up around 7:45 AM, crews march off with 38(t) tanks to Ruski Brod, then Opoczno—Tomaszow, are dispersed in rolling air attack, collecting site is at supply trains in Pabianitz near Litzmanstadt

■ **Railroad Armored Train No. 25**
(F.P. No. 38094, second time 44707)
Established on March 1, 1940 (was at first to have been numbered 9), ready for action April 1940, disbanded on Oct. 2, 1940, re-established on Dec. 10, 1941, ready for action May 1942, rebuilt by K.St.N.1169x Sept.—Nov. 1944, lost on Jan. 13, 1945, disbanded on Jan. 27, 1945
Commanders:
1ˢᵗ Lt. Dörfer (March—Oct. 1940)
1st Lt.—Capt. Kurt Oslislo (Dec. 1941—Feb. 1943)
Capt. Friedrich Schlegel (Feb. 1943—July 1943)
1ˢᵗ Lt. Alfons Popp (July 1943—Feb. 1944)
1ˢᵗ Lt. Siegfried Ströh (deputy) (Feb. 1944—Aug. 1944)
1ˢᵗ Lt.-Capt. Friedrich Dietz (Sept. 1944—Jan. 1945)
Setup/rebuilding/cars: see 105f, 118, 120, 122, 179f, 182, 185, 198, 213, 215f, 223, 244, 247, 280, 410
Equipping/arms/crew: see 106f, 225f, 227, 257ff, 261
Action: see 107, 280, 286ff, 290, 315, 339, 341, 394, 397
Damage/loss: see 397
Pictures/drawings: see 112f, 117, 129, 214f, 227, 245, 286, 289, 291, 317, 339, 341

■ **Project Armored Train 1941**
(Realization as "Immediate Solution": PZ 26-31)
See p. 118f, 138, 180, 195, 244, 257, 320

■ **Project Armored Train SP 42**
See pp. 118, 138, 180, 195f, 197, 244

■ **Railroad Armored Train No. 26**
(broad gauge, F.P. No. 40046)
Established on June 1, 1941, ready for action on June 22, 1941, converted to standard gauge April 1942, rebuilt by K.St.N.1169x March 1943—February 1944, remained until end of war
Commanders:
Capt. Paul Berger (June 1941—March 1942)
Lt. Helmut Walter (at first deputy) (March 1942—June 1943)
1ˢᵗ Lt. Ludwig Steckmeier (June 1943—April 17, 1944+)
Capt. Richard Fischer (April 1944—May 1945)
Setup/rebuilding/cars: see 119f, 181, 190, 207, 220, 223, 244, 333, 343, 380
Equipment/arms/crew: see 119ff, 233, 257f, 260
Action: see 318, 320ff, 331ff, 342f, 375, 380, 382, 383ff, 386, 394, 406
Damage/loss: see 343, 380, 384, 406
Pictures/drawings: see 119, 123f, 129f, 179, 182, 190, 220, 222, 224, 233, 322, 343, 376, 379f, 383, 385, 421

■ **Railroad Armored Train No. 27**
(broad gauge, F.P. No. 40831)
Established on June 1, 1941, ready for action on June 22, 1941, lost all cars Jan. 2, 1942, new cars Jan.-Feb., converted to standard gauge April 1942, badly damaged on May 30, 1942, disbanded on same day, re-established on July 13, 1942 similarly to K.St.N.1169x, ready for action Nov. 1942, badly damaged March 21-24, 1944, disbanded on May 5, 1944, re-established April 1945, remained until end of war
Commanders:
1ˢᵗ Lt. Rudolf Opitz (June 1941—Nov. 1941)
Lt. Hermann Behrens (Nov. 1941—May 30, 1942+)
1ˢᵗ Lt.-Capt. Konrad Scholz (July 1942—May 1944)
1ˢᵗ Lt. Rudolf Dohms (April—May 1945)
Setup/rebuilding/cars: see 119f, 181, 189f, 207, 217, 220, 223, 244, 325, 333
Equipment/arms/crew: see 119f, 229, 232, 249, 253, 257f, 260f
Action: see 318, 320, 322f, 330, 332ff, 342, 346, 366, 369f, 376ff, 406
Damage/loss: see 120f, 190, 330, 334, 339, 342, 346, 377f, 381, 406
Pictures/drawings: see 119, 124, 129f, 189, 220, 332, 334, 342, 346, 421, 424
Report: G. Kretschmer, Panzerzug-Jagdkommando greift an (Panzerzüge II)

■ **Railroad Armored Train No. 28**
(broad gauge, F.P. No. 41360)
Established on June 1, 1941, ready for action on June 22, 1941, converted to standard gauge and rebuilt July-August 1942, re-equipped Jan.-May 1944, lost on June 29, 1944, disbanded on July 15, 1944
Commanders:
1ˢᵗ Lt. Eduard Seele (June 1941—Dec. 1941)
Lt.-1ˢᵗ Lt. Ludwig Erhard (Jan. 1942—May 2, 1944)
1ˢᵗ Lt. Dieter Frindte (May 2, 1944—July 1944)
Setup/rebuilding/cars: see 119f, 189, 200, 207, 220, 223, 244, 337, 410
Equipm,ent/arms/crew: see 119f, 229, 232, 257f, 260f
Action: see 320ff, 232f, 335ff, 339, 349ff, 352, 354ff, 357, 360, 378, 380f, 382f
Damage/lost: see 356, 382f, 410
Pictures/drawings: see 119, 125, 129, 131, 176, 188, 197, 200, 221, 228, 230, 245, 247, 323f, 335f, 338, 350, 352, 355, 378, 411
Reports: F. Elsner, Ein Panzerzug im Einsatz an der Ostfront (Panzerzüge I)
W. Böttner, Sowjetisches Skibataillon vernichtet (Panzerzüge I)

■ **Railroad Armored Train No. 29**
(broad gauge, F.P. No. 41856)
Established on June 1, 1941, ready for action on June 22, 1941, lost on Jan. 10, 1942, disbanded on Feb. 23, 1942
Commanders:
1ˢᵗ Lt. Rudolf Winterberg (June 1941—Sept. 1941)
Capt. Paul Okroy (Sept. 1941—Nov. 1941)
1ˢᵗ Lt. Rudolf Winterberg (Nov,. 1941—Feb. 1942)
Setup/rebuilding/cars: see 119, 197, 220, 244, 320
Equipment/arms/crew: see 119f, 257f, 260
Action: see 320f, 323f, 330
Damage/loss: see 120, 330
Pictures/drawings: see 119, 126, 131, 198, 323

■ **Railroad Armored Train No. 30**
(broad gauge, F.P. No. 42308)
Established on June 1, 1941, ready for action on June 22, 1941, converted to standard gauge summer 1942, rebuilt by K.St.N.1169x Nov. 1942—Feb. 1944, lost on March 21, 1945, disbanded on March 27, 1945
Commanders:
1ˢᵗ Lt.—Capt. Wilhelm Niemann (June 1941—Dec. 1942)
1ˢᵗ Lt. Kurt Hannes (Jan. 1943—Nov. 1943)
Capt. Albert Hollstein (Oct. 1943—March 1944)

1st Lt. Franz Molitor   (March 1944—March 1945)
Setup/rebuilding/cars: see 119ff, 181, 189, 200, 209, 220, 223, 244, 343
Equipment/arms/crew: 119ff, 229, 257, 260
Action: 320ff, 331, 343, 358ff, 390, 397, 401f, 404
Damage/loss: see 190, 320, 359, 404
Pictures/drawings: see 119, 126ff, 132, 181, 189, 207, 221f, 247, 322, 359f, 390f, 395

Action Chronicle of Armored Train No. 30
During the first period from the beginning of the Russian campaign to its withdrawal for rebuilding in December 1942, the train was only in the zone of the 18th Army (Army Group North), at first in Ljuban, the last months in Nowinka, and there are no detailed data. Diary notations exist from the finishing of the rebuilding in the Eberswalde RAW (January 1944) to the loss of the train on March 21, 1945.

1944

01/23	Combat and quarters trains set up (both in Eberswalde RAW)
01/25	Train inspected by Col. (von Olszewski?)
01/26-27	Trip from Eberswalde to Rembertow
02/03-04	shooting-in of the guns (did not work until second time)
02/08-10	surprising departure to action (planned in Luzk area), met PZ 60 (Rudolf) ahead of Lemberg, stationed together in Brzuchowice
02/12	Partisans blow up tracks 30 km apart, PZ 60 hurries there
02/15	departure for new action site, Nikolajew—Cherson line
02/21	arrival in Nikolajew, PZ 28 is there (in AW)
02/22	Stationed in Kupin (Kulbakino?), 30 km before Nikolajew, front 30-40 km away
02/24	Soviet Raja fighters attack town with guns (but not PZ)
02/26	trip from Kupin to Kopani and Pokrowskoje
02/27:	reception site for evacuation trains from Cherson in Kopani
02/28—03/07	in Kopani
03/08	departure for Nikolajew shortly after midnight
03/09	trip to Wodopoj and into action
03/10	village fired on
03/11	trip to action, tracks blown up beyond Lozkino, train is fired on by antitank weapons (1 dead), action in evening, PZ is rammed by ammunition train, control car pushed onto tank-carrier car
03/12	breakthrough in morning along with infantry to Jawkino, command car hit twice (car 5, 6, dead), return trip in afternoon (fogged in)
03/13	back to Wodopoj with 42 wounded on board
03/14	workshops in Nikolajew already abandoned, quarters train back across Bug bridge
03/15	transport train escorted to Lozkino, further to Marjunka, damaged armored loco back in Nikolajew for coal and water, combat train crosses Bug to join quarters train
03/17	first three cars to Odessa for repairs
03/18	bomb attack in Korkinskoje
03/19	action on Bug in evening, firing across river
03/20	PZ takes over air-raid protection of Dombrowa Verde railroad station, air raids all day
03/23	new commander and artillery officer, loco to Kolosowka for washing out, one wounded in air attack
03/25	PZ goes back to quarters train with "black" loco
03/26	PZ back to Dombrowa Verde, back to quarters train in evening, hit by bomb, little damage, no losses
03/27	trip back to Berezowka, subordinated to 6th Army
03/28-29	lines in Odessa jammed, to Jeremejewka
04/02	commander with motor car to accept order to Tiraspol
04/03	trip to Tiraspol intended, Russians already in Rasdelnaja, driven out, freight train coupled on at Rasdelnaja railroad station and taken back to Jeremejewka
04/04	back to Odessa with quarters train at night, to Karpowo with east riders in morning, task: hold railroad station until returning XLIV. Army Corps is through, scouting run to Jeremejewka, no enemy contact
04/06	four Russian tanks attack in advance to Jeremejewka, back to Karpowo, Russian tanks at noon four times at 300 m, gun car damaged, tanks draw back
04/07	unarmed "black" loco comes from Odessa at night, train separated, PZ infantry secures Karpowo with east riders
04/08	XLIV. Army Corps comes through at night, departure 4:00 AM with "black" loco

	toward Odessa, in Wygoda German troops in flight, infantry disembarked, artillery fires support, in Odessa in evening, air attack, important things unloaded to combat train and quarters train blown up
04/09	Departure toward Owidiopol to cross Dnjestr-Liman toward Akkerman, to Gross-Liebenthal, sergeant major fled with supplies
04/10	at Gross-Liebenthal, gets closer to train ferry only slowly because of many evacuation trains, artillery fire, commander back from Tiraspol, air attack (3 dead, several wounded)
04/11-12	slow forward motion toward ferry, steady air attacks but only little damage
04/13	PZ reaches ferry at 4:00 PM as last train, pier already under artillery fire
04/14	in Akkerman, return trip begins via Romania, Hungary, Vienna to Rembertow (arrival 6:05 AM)
May-July	train repaired and rebuilt (new armored loco, new gun turrets, added tank-destroyer cars
07/23	Rembertow is alarmed, as Russians have broken through near Lublin and are already 60 km ahead of Warsaw, infantry moves off, combat train's artillery remains manned, loaded
07/24	all kinds of ammunition loaded
07/25	departure from Rembertow in evening, 127 axles, bomb attack on Warsaw, Vistula bridge at midnight
07/26-29	trip to Neuenburg
07/30—08/24	further equipping of the train
08/25	inspection by Col. Von Olszewski
08/26	departure to General Government in morning
08/28	at first to Blonie, then back to Glowno
08/29	to Lawitsch in the evening
08/30	Kraft-durch-Freude trip
08/31	fruitless partisan action near Radziwillow
09/01-02	from Lawitsch to Opoczno
09/04	trip to action in Bialaczow
09/07	transfer from Opoczno to Petrikau
09/08-11	securing runs
09/15	transfer to Koluszki
09/16	securing run to Tomaszow
09/23	supply train to Slotwiny
09/24	securing trip to Baby and Petrikau
09/25	supply train to Petrikow
09/28-29	with Armored Instruction Train No. 5 and line protection train "Polko" to blocked line near Zyrardow, partisans caught, camp shot up in infantry action, great quantity of material captured
09/30	securing run to Skierniewice
10/01	in Zyrardow
10/02	in Tomaszow
10/03	back with supply train in Petrikau in evening
10/21	change position to Modlin for joint operation with Armored Instruction Train No. 5
10/22	arrival in Nasielsk, ca. 10 km behind the front, strong fire from both sides (artillery and throwers), to Modlin at noon
10/23	in Modlin, unload reinforcements (SS), front noise endless, no air activity
10/24	Modlin—Nasielsk and back, loco takes on water and coal, air attacks
10/26—11/02	front quiet
11/03	PZ comes under fire from heavy artillery
11/08	supply train in Baboczewo
11/13-14	PZ goes to supply train in Baboczewo
11/15-16	PZ with quarters train transfers to Treuburg (abandoned), Armored Instruction Train No. 5 (PZ 68) and Command Train 72B (Cmdr. of PZ at H.Gr.Center, Lt.Col. Dr. Günther) also there, departure to Allenbruch in evening
11/18	from Allenbruch to 3 km east of Reuß
11/19	train is completely camouflaged, lively air activity, A/A shoots down one fighter, loco to Treuburg for water and coal
11/20	infantry groups disembark and take up positions
11/26	relieved in position by Armored Instruction Train No. 5, departure to supplytrain in Allenbruch, inspected by Lt.Col. Dr. Günther (with PZ 72B in Kruglanken)
11/27	train supplied with ammunition
11/30	departure for Reuß (firing position)
12/01	Armored Instruction Train No. 5 relieved by PZ 76
12/02-09	PZ 30 and 76 ahead of Reuß, front quiet
12/10	two Russian planes, to supply train in Allenbruch in evening
12/11	with quarters train from Allendorf to Passdorf
12/12	bunker building, train supplied with ammunition
12/14	order to march at 2:00 AM, PT 19 and control

	car derailed, departure at 7:30 AM for Arnswald (near Goldap, along with PZ 76), lively air activity, bomb attack
12/15	low-level planes attack combat train
12/17	firing position near Urbansdorf, guns of front half of train home in (rear half in Benkheim)
12/18	entire train homed in along with PT 19 (145 rounds), few Russian planes
12/19	in firing position, 3:15 PM heavy fire from PZ 30 and 76 plus artillery position regiment in process of German attack
12/20	Arnswald railroad station in morning, air attack, to supply train in Passdorf in evening
12/21-22	supplied with ammunition

1945

01/04	fired 247 shells in morning (where?), to Passdorf in evening
01/05	depart to action
01/06	together with PZ 52 in Birkendorf (Angerapp—Goldap line)
01/07-08	take on water in Angerapp, coal in Angerburg
01/09	to supply train in Passdorf in morning
01/11-12	training and combat shooting in Lötzen in presence of Lt.Col. Dr. Günther
01/13	depart from Passdorf to Treuburg (with PZ 72B)
01/14	in firing position before Reuß
01/15	supplying (water and coal) in Treuburg
01/16	individual Russian planes
01/17	PT 19 fires at firing position
01/18	departure for Passdorf, air attack on the way, PZ Battle Group (PZ 72B and 30 under Lt.Col. Dr. Günther) is subordinated to 2nd Army
01/19	transfer (including supply train) via Rastenburg and Allenstein to Deutsch-Eylau
01/20	advance toward Soldau, camouflage in Alteiche, near Hartowitz 2:00 PM, 12 to 15 tanks, (including captured German ones), short exchange of fire, one tank hit, but also a direct hit to PT 19 (2 dead, 3 wounded), back in fog to Deutsch-Eylau, new advance to Alteiche, tanks there already, one hit
01/21	lively combat noise, own tanks disembark, 3:00 PM to Deutsch-Eylau, Russians have surrounded town on both sides
01/22	Eylau burns, wild shooting, women and children in PZ, breakthrough at 8:00 PM toward Riesenburg, short exchange of fire with enemy, blown-up track repaired, infantry secures on both sides
01/23	in Charlottenwerder in morning, abandoned, neither friend nor foe, on to Riesenburg, on the wrong side of a two-track line to Marienburg, therefore back, civilians leave train
01/24	in Riesenburg at night enemy tanks reported, advance, no tanks, in Marienburg 7:30 AM, A/A knocked out by hitting the bridge, heavy fire in evening, supply store emptied
01/25	Soviets advancing on Marienburg, heavy fighting, Stukas in action, heavy artillery fire on railroad station across the Nogat, at first wrong track and back again, then to Simonsdorf
01/26	securing runs between Marienburg and Dirschau
01/27	trip from Dirschau to Subkau and back
01/28	to Narkau early in the morning, train in Georgenthal, disembarked infantry and advanced observer in Kniebau
01/29	take on water and coal in Dirschau
01/31	warlike training run from Georgenthal to Schmentau and back
02/01	to Danzig and back
02/03	picked up infantry in Narkau in evening, trip to Laskowitz
02/04	shooting from firing position forward of Laskowitz toward Graudenz, back to Preussisch-Hagen
02/05	back in firing position, shooting from position near Gruppe, Russians fire on our batteries on the rail line in vain
02/06	to Laskowitz, take on water, escort 600 infantrymen to Osche, via Laskowitz to Wolfstal (Gr. Wollental?), coal and ammunition loaded
02/07	pumped water from lake, back in readiness position ahead of Laskowitz
02/08	shooting in vain because of fog, to Dirschau in evening
02/09	exchange locos, new brakes on cars, return trip

02/10	Ready in Preussisch-Hagen, heavy low-level plane attack in afternoon, loco destroyed, several wounded, pushed to Wahrlubien by PZ 72B, new loco, back in firing position at night
02/11	own troops depart, two bursts of fire for cover in planned shooting (99 rounds), back to Georgenthal, supply train also arrives
02/13	from Georgenthal toward Konitz in evening
02/14	firing position ahead of Rittel (ten shots), unsuccessful air attack, infantry disembarks and takes position
02/15	38 shots in direction of Konitz, several wounded among infantry, ammunition in Rittel at night, took on water in Heiderode
02/16	lively Russian air activity, own infantry comes back and takes new position, 17 rounds fired, back in evening, trip to Bonk at night
02/17	In Bonk with supply train, fill crew and ammunition, depart via Berent to new firing position near ? (name illegible, probably on line from Lippusch to Konitz)
02/18	train camouflaged, own and Russian planes, six shots, back in evening, coal and water taken on
02/19	back to firing position early (15 rounds), entire battle group leaves in evening (PZ 30, 52, 68 72B?)
02/20	Departure from Lippusch to Dirschau, bomb attack, to Georgenthal
02/21	Georgenthal, vigorous air activity, to Danzig in evening
02/22	ammunition, water and coal in Kahlbude
02/23	in Praust in morning, then departure for Preussisch-Stargard, firing position near Hochstueblau
02/24-25	firing position (21 and 5 rounds)
02/26	infantry disembarks early two rounds toward Dreidorf in evening (new firing position)
02/27	nine rounds fired, to Preussisch-Stargard in evening, loco washed out, OKH orders march back to Saxony
02/28	army holds back PZ regiment battle group despite OKH order, two rounds from firing position, but withdrawal at night
03/01	with supply train early in Hohenstein, water and coal, 9:45 AM trip continued, 9:00 PM in Lauenburg
03/02	from Lauenburg to Schlawe (about 4:30 PM), on the line to Stolpmünde, front half of train to Stolp for overhauling (new A/A installed), depart toward breakthrough site with PZ 72B, PZ 68 and 52 in front
03/03	PZ 68 and 52 near Neukrakow, PZ 30 and 72B near Schlawin, Russians blow up bridge over Grabow, infantry disembarks, only halfhearted measures to repair damage, in Schlawe at night (water and coal), bomb attack
03/04	front half of train comes back, PZ 72B now also before PZ 30
03/05	reconstruction train advances to blown-up bridge, PZ cover (PZ 30, 32 rounds), Russians active, reconstruction train is towed back, lasting break in the line, coal loaded at night in Karwitz, firing position scouted
03/06	direction of Stolpmünde, firing position (10 rounds), very much in a tight spot
03/07	to Stolpmünde at night to load ammunition, in morning battle group is near Strelin, then in Stolp, Russian advance unit at edge of city at 8:00 PM, firing position (8 rounds), leave at night toward Lauenburg
03/08	line totally jammed with refugee trains, provisions and coal in Hebrondamnitz, in Lauenburg in evening, no water, on toward Leba
03/09	firing position in Neuendorf (50 rounds), water loaded by bucket, fully ready for combat in evening (tank danger), to Lauenburg, make it through, Lauenburg is blown up, depart for Neustadt, roads jammed with vehicles
03/10	ammunition, water and coal in Neustadt, on to Gotenhafen
03/11	lively air and A/A activity in Gotenhafen
03/12	securing run toward Berent, fire from Russian artillery beyond Gross-Katz, back to Gotenhafen, get water
03/13	at old position as on previous day, artillery goes into position, heavy mutual fire,

	in Gotenhafen at night, water and coal, trip back to front line
03/14	strong enemy pressure and heavy fire (hit in air duct and communication cable), trip back without air to beyond Gross-Katz, damage repaired, ahead again in afternoon, heavy enemy fire, infantry disembarks, back to Gross-Katz in evening
03/15	water with hand pump, ahead again at 3:30 AM, infantry disembarks, Russian attack, under heavy fire, built mortar position, crew stays when train goes back in evening
03/16	ahead again at 3:00 AM, new Russian attack driven off, heavy fire, back to Gross-Katz, collision with PZ 68, it pushes two coal cars on the line at PZ 52
03/17	water and provisions, then ahead again, ceaseless enemy mortar fire, no relief (by PZ 68) because of collision
03/18	back to Gross-Katz at night, PZ 52 should relieve, does not come, forward early, calm before storm?
03/19	3:00 AM Russian again, 7:00 Russian drumfire, 7:30 breakthrough, line hit several times, must be repaired by engineers under fire, many planes (six kills observed)
03/20	go ahead to Gross-Katz athletic field, Russian attack, two T 34 on fire, two shot and immobilized, three antitank guns destroyed, bridge behind us blown up, no chance of going back any more
03/21	heavy Russian attack, last ammunition fired, toward 9:00 AM Russian infantry is at train, crew disembarks to other side and gathers in woods, fights its way through to Zoppot, one part reaches Hela peninsula and goes home by ship

Note: As of 02/14/1945 the shot totals presumably refer to a single gun (at which the diarist was).

■ Railroad Armored Train No. 31
(broad gauge, F.P.No. 42981)
Established on June 1, 1941, ready for action on June 22, 1941, converted to standard gauge summer 1942, rebuilt by K.St.N.1169x Nov. 1942—Oct. 1943, lost on Dec. 28, 1943, disbanded on March 4, 1944
Commanders:
Lt. Werner Dziembowski   (June 1941—July 1942)
1st Lt. Rudolf Schleiff   (July 1942—July 1943)
1st Lt. Erich Schubert   (July 1943—Jan. 1944)
Setup/rebuilding/cars: see 119ff, 181, 190, 220, 223, 244, 337
Equipment/arms/crew: see 119ff, 257f, 260
Action: see 318, 320, 322, 325f, 336, 357
Damage/loss: see 357
Pictures/drawings: see 119, 127ff, 132, 188, 221, 357, 421
Reports: 1st Lt. Schubert: Das Lergenfrühstueck (Panzerzüge I)
Hubert, Der schwarze Satan greift ein… (Panzerzüge I)

■ Railroad Armored Train No. 32 (Field Post No. 42981)
Established on April 17, 1944 (as successor to Armored Train No. 31, lost on December 30, 1943), lost on Sept. 8, 1944, disbanded on Oct. 11, 1944
Commander:
1st Lt. Theodor Wolters   (June-Sept. 1944*)
Setup/rebuilding/cars: see 137, 182, 201, 211, 246, 290
Equipment/arms/crew: see 137, 229, 236, 246
Action: see 290f
Damage/loss: see 291, 409
Pictures/drawings: see 142, 183, 201, 211, 230, 246, 291, 409f

■ Railroad Armored Train No. 51 (Field Post No. 37860)
Established on January 3, 1942 as line protection train "Stettin," renamed "A" on 10 May, renamed Armored Train No. 51 on June 16, 1942, ready for action August 1942, lost on Aug. 13, 1944, disbanded on Aug. 28, 1944
 Commanders:
Capt.-Maj. Fritz Elhaus   (March 1942—March 1943)
Capt. Paul Huhn (at first deputy)   (March 1943—May 1944)
1st Lt. Helmut Oppenhorst   (June—August 1944)
Setup/rebuilding/cars: see 121f, 164, 180, 195, 223
Equipment/arms/crew: see 121, 164, 227, 231, 236, 250, 260f
Action: see 332, 342f, 345, 373, 375, 380, 382, 383ff
Damage/Loss: see 134f, 176, 195, 225, 228, 262, 343, 345, 375, 422
Pictures/drawings: see 134f, 176, 195, 225, 228, 262, 343, 345, 375, 422
Reports:
E. Sujatta: U-Boot macht Gegenstoss (Panzerzüge II)
Same author: Panzerzug klärt auf (Panzerzüge II)

■ Railroad Armored Train No. 52 (Field Post No. unknown)
Reformed from line protection train "Blücher" on July 19, 1944, ready for action on Oct. 10, 1944, lost on March 21, 1945, disbanded on March 27, 1945
Commander:
1st Lt. Alfred Mirus   (Oct. 1944—March 1945)
Setup/rebuilding/cars: see 164, 181, 195, 223, 380
Equipment/arms/crew: see 164, 233, 261
Action: see 394f, 397, 401f, 404
Damage/lost: see 404
Pictures/drawings: see 164f, 394f

■ Railroad Armored Train of Type BP 42 (No. 61—72) and BP 44 (No. 73—84) (in general)
Setup/rebuilding/cars: see 136f, 151f, 180, 190f, 109ff, 224, 244
Equipment/arms/crew: see 136f, 229, 233, 236
Pictures/drawings: see 138, 139ff, 191ff, 209ff, 228ff, 233, 245, 252

Railroad Armored Train No. 60/Railroad Armored Train "R"
Put into service in the spring of 1943 as a training train for the Armored Train Replacement Battalion, went into service as Armored Train "R" in February 1944 (Field Post No. 59278), badly damaged on March 7, 1944, obviously not rebuilt
Commanders:
1st Lt. Rolf Henning   (Feb.—March 9, 1944*)
? (deputy)   (March—April 1944)
Setup/rebuilding/cars: see 137
Action: see 173, 361f, 364
Damage/loss: see 173, 362, 364f
Pictures/drawings: see 174

Railroad Armored Train No. 61 (Field Post No. 31453)
Established on Sept. 1, 1942, ready for action on Dec. 23, 1942, lost on June 27, 1944, disbanded on July 14, 1944
Commander:
Capt.-Major Wilhelm Linke (Sept. 1942—June 27, 1944*)
Setup/rebuilding/cars: see 375
Equipment/arms/crew: see 233
Action: see 342, 346f, 366f, 369f, 372f, 375, 378, 380f, 382
Damage/loss: see 382f
Pictures/drawings: see 233, 343, 347, 373, 379
Reports:
Anonymous, Panzerzug säubert die Bahnstrecke (Panzerzüge I)
Dr. Krausse, Die stählerne Faust (Panzerzüge I)
Corp. Gallinat, Vier Stunden eingeschlossen (Panzerzüge II)
C. Laar, Der Leberecht (Die Wehrmacht, Vol. 8)

Railroad Armored Train No. 62 (Field post No. 32164)
Established on Sept. 1, 1942, ready for action on Feb. 11, 1943, lost on Jan. 16, 1945, disbanded on Jan. 27, 1945
Commanders:
1st Lt. Frank Drexler (Feb.—Aug. 1943)
Capt. Ludwig-Ernst von Wedel (Aug. 1943—Jan. 1944)
1st Lt.-Capt. Alfons Popp (Feb. 1944—Jan. 1945)
Action: see 351f, 354ff, 357f, 366, 386f, 391, 393f, 397ff
Damage/loss: see 354f, 366, 393, 399
Pictures/drawings: see 231, 351, 355, 366
Report:
F. Waurich, Das tolle Wagnis (Panzerzüge II)

Railroad Armored Train No. 63 (Field Post No. 33374)
Established on Oct. 1, 1942, ready for action on May 1, 1943, lost on July 17, 1944, disbanded on Aug. 9, 1944
Commanders:
1st Lt.-Capt. Friedel Wesche (May 1943—March 1944)
Capt. Philipp von Villiez (April—August 1944)
Action: see 345, 365f, 373, 375, 382, 386
Damage/loss: see 373, 375, 386
Pictures/drawings: see 176, 258, 312, 315, 318f, 345f, 375, 386

Railroad Armored Train No. 64 (Field Post No. 34267)
Established on Oct. 1m 1942, ready for action on June 18, 1943, remained until end of war
Commander:
1st Lt.-Capt. Werner Sieg (April 1943—May 1945)
Action: see 296, 299ff, 304f, 309f, 318
Damage/loss: see 304, 309f
Pictures/drawings: see 296f, 309

Action Chronicle of Armored Train No. 64
According to diary entries for the entire time (the diary keeper belonged to the crew of a Panhard reconnaissance car that was often used away from the track)

1943	
05/02	PZ 64 is delivered by the Linke-Hofmann Works
05/08	train arrives at Replacement Battalion in Rembertow
06/18	PZ 64 departs for action
06/22	arrival in Ruma

06/26	transfer to Nova Gradiska
06/27-30	nightly securing runs; on such a securing run it hit a mine, both control cars destroyed, fight with partisans, rail line repaired
07/04	along with two infantry companies, searched terrain near Nova Kapela, village fired on with artillery
07/10	transferred back to Ruma
07/12	action after police had costly conflict with partisans, no enemy contact
07/17	coal transport train attacked near Voganj; PZ's Panhards fired on partisans
08/02-04	Panhard sent to Budanovci for harvest securing
08/07	Panhard posted at Mitrovica railroad station, line securing as armored railcar
08/09	Panhard goes to Vinkovci, village 35 km southwest of there attacked by strong partisan units, Croats had losses, no more enemy contact when Panhard arrived
08/11	fired on partisans at night near Martinci
08/29	freight train hit mine near Voganj, Panhard hit this train
08/31	prisoner exchange (22 German soldiers for 60 partisans)
09/02	PZ 6 and 64 to Indija, are to escort special train of King Boris of Bulgaria, PZ 64 called back in advance
09/11	trip to Kraljevci with repaired Panhard
09/18	PZ hit mine, slight damage
01/13	PZ goes to Semlin
10/14-17	action of disembarked units (infantry, tank, Panhards) with 1st Cossack Division in Petrovaradin—Beocin region (south of Neusatz)
10/21-28	action with 1st Cossack Division in Otok—Gunja region (line to Brcko)
11/17	PZ goes to Belgrade (visit Commander of the Armored Trains, Col. von Olszewski)
11/18	train inspected by Cmdr. of armored trains and officers of Army Group F
11/19	trip to Vinkovci
11/20	from Vinkovci to Deletovci, SF train hit mine near Kuzmin in evening, several cars derailed, PZ engineers free line,
11/25	PZ frees Deletovci—Slakovci line after attack
12/02	action near Batajnica
12/06-09	both Panhards with line protection train to Morovic (south of Sid) to get wood
12/10	PZ goes to Kukujevci
12/16	Col. Von Eschwege (RR Securing Staff, Croatia) inspects PZ, trip to Jankovci in evening
12/17	passenger train hit mine near Kukujevci, go there
12/21-23	action near Kukujevci
12/23	escorted express train to Vinkovci
1944	
10/01-25	at quarters train's radio station
01/26	service run to RR Securing Staff at Slav. Brod
01/29	PZ to Morovic to get wood
01/30	action near Alt-Pasua
01/12-14	PZ takes on securing runs to Sid
02/15	picked up Col. Becker (Cmdr. Of PZ with Army Group F) in Semlin
02/16	to Sid in afternoon
02/17-19	action near Morovic
02/23-28	securing runs in Sid area, shot 14 fleeing partisans near Kuzmin, captured 4
03/03	action near Budjanovci
03/06	Panhard secures near Voganj
03/07	action (one Panhard, one tank) near Radinci
03/18-19	PZ goes via Neusatz to Kiskunhalas, Hungarians let themselves be disarmed without resistance
03/29	return trip to Ruma
03/31	PZ to Semlin, inspected by a general
04/04-05	PZ in action near Mitrovica
04/09	PZ goes to Alt-Pasua
04/15	PZ goes to Kuzmin
04/19	PZ goes to Sid, fire on Morovic from Adasevci with artillery in evening
04/20	action near Morovic
05/18-19	action against partisan-occupied village near Kraljevci
05/19-21	action near Indija
05/22	all male inhabitants of Kuzmin taken to Mitrovica for service listing
05/25	Lt.General taken to Cortanovci
05/26	inspection by Col. von Eschwege
06/01	picked up Col. Neef in Mitrovica in evening
06/04	action near Besenovo
06/05	action near Vojka, removed mines under track near Voganj in evening
06/06	PZ makes securing run to Sid

06/07	one dead in mine explosion during removal
06/08	action near Martinci
06/09	tropical uniforms received
06/11-15	PZ in lurking position near Voganj
06/16	PZ goes from Ruma to Slav. Brod, then to Andrijevci, a little shooting on securing run at night
06/17	PZ to Strizivojna Vrpolje
06/18	from Andrijevci to Str. Vrpolje in morning, to Garcin and back in afternoon
06/19	PZ to Slav. Brod, to explosion site near Andrijevci at night
06/20-21	nightly securing runs, then PZ to Vinkovci
06/11	PZ to Strizivojna Vrpolje, later also quarters train (new station)
06/24	quarters train to Andrijevci
06/25	advanced observer site for PZ artillery built up in Djakovo
06/28	tanks and PZ infantry in readiness in Kondric
06/30	came under heavy partisan fire while advancing to Marja, one tank damaged, 14 dead (4 from PZ), back from Kondric to Djakovo in evening
07/01	advance of Panhard to Selce
07/04	moved back from Selce to Vrpolje to PZ, to Andrijevci on it
07/05	buried fallen men in Vinkovci, train transferred to Sid
07/07	reconnaissance near Morovic
07/08	trip to Adasevci, train camouflaged
07/09	trip to Kukujevci, to Bacinci in evening, securing village
07/11-14	trips to Kukujevci with artillery action from there
07/15	PZ to Ruma and back to Kukujevci
07/16-18	evening action in Kukujevci
07/19-21	with Panhard via Kukujevci to Kuzmin and back
07/24—08/06	PZ in action near Morovic
08/09	PZ goes to Voganj
08/10-12	action with tanks, Panhards and infantry near Radinci
08/12	PZ to Lacarak in evening
08/13	action with Panhard at Pavlovci
08/14	to Calma with Panhard
08/16	PZ goes to Klenak
08/19	inspection trip to Bosut, Calma and Mandelos with Reg. Cmdr.
08/23	action near Mandelos, one wounded
08/24	harvest protection in Mandelos, under partisan fire at night
08/25-31	action in Mandelos
09/01	low-level planes attack railroad station in Ruma, four gasoline and five ammunition cars burned out, 3 dead and 24 wounded in PZ
09/05	departed from Ruma to Vrpolje in evening, then blew up tracks
09/06	to new station Andrijevci in evening (until 09/09)
09/10-12	PZ in Mikanovci
09/13	to Vrpolje, drove off strong partisan attack there in afternoon
09/15	from Vrpolje to Garcin
09/19-21	ethnic German families from Kuzanica resettled to Ivankovo under protection of Panhard
09/22	PZ to Andrijevci
09/24	recovery with Panhard of radio equipment dropped for partisans in woods
09/25	joint action with PZ 6 (tanks and Panhards) near Kuzanica
09/26	PZ from Vrpolje to Ruma
09/27	action near Neu-Pasua
09/28-29	scout car action near Jazak
09/30	PZ action near Kukujevci
10/05	scouting trip (Panhard with infantry) to Platicevo
10/06	escorted Cmdr. of PZ with Army Group F from Ruma to Vinkovci
10/07	back to Ruma, picked up troops in Mitrovica in afternoon
10/08	Panhard action near Prhovo
10/09-12	Panhard action in Pecinci
10/13-14	back in Prhovo, then back to Ruma
10/15	low-level planes attack railroad station in Ruma
10/18-21	action near Sabac, with Panhard to find scattered men of 3rd Division
10/22	return to PZ, low-level planes attack, Panhard destroyed
10/23	quarters train transferred back to Jankovci, Indija—Ruma line blown up
10/24	signal boxes, leather factory and mill blown up in Ruma

10/25	PZ leaves Ruma, to Jankovci, then along with quarters train to Donja Vrba, air attack in Sid, one dead, one wounded
10/26-28	securing headquarters of Army Group F (OB Southeast)
10/29	PZ escorts command train of OB Southeast from Slav. Brod to Agram, strong partisan attack driven off along the way
11/05	PZ from Agram to Okucani
11/06	PZ meets quarters train in Andrijevci
11/07-11	PZ in Staro Topolje, on 11/09 partisan attack is driven off
11/11	PZ to Slav. Brod
11/12	PZ goes toward Esseg, quarters train stays in Andrijevci at first
11/14...	PZ in front action in Batina on Danube (based in Beli Manastir (11/14, one wounded, 11/15 one dead)
11/19	half of PZ derailed by fire (one wounded), rest goes back to Beli Manastir, cars put back on rails (one wounded each on 11/21 and 11/22)
11/23	damaged half of PZ taken to Fünfkirchen BW
11/26	action-ready part of PZ to Villany
11/27	Russians attack, artillery fire from PZ, then withdrawal
11/28—12/01	defensive position ahead of Fünfkirchen near Mecseksszabolcs (11/29 one dead, 11/30 one, 12/01 two wounded)
12/01	withdrawal to Szentloerencz (combat action there until 12/02)
12/03-04	action near Szigetvar
12/05	withdrawal via Darany to Barcs
12/07...	new action area Somogyszob (front action, firing position on Ötvös-Konyi, advanced observer in Beleg)
12/09	Lt. L. killed by shell splinter
1945	
02/05-08	PZ back to Gyekenyes to install new A/A gun
02/08-15	back in Ötvös-Konyi
02/16	transfer to Berzencze
02/17-26	securing runs on the Berzencze—Vizvar line
03/03-07	PZ in Nagykanisza
03/08	PZ to Ötvös-Konyi to support attack toward Nagybayom-Kaposvar
03/16-18	PZ in Beleg
03/20-25	PZ in Ötvös-Konyi
03/26	trip to Kutas, to Gyekenyes in afternoon
03/27-28	trip to Beleg, then back to Gyekenyes, quarters train transferred back to Zakany
03/29	PZ in new main combat line in Ötvös-Konyi, under artillery fire, return trip to Somogyszob
03/30	PZ covers withdrawal from Somogyszob, goes on to Gyekenyes
03/31	firing position near Gyekenyes. move across the Drau (bridge blown up afterward), Russians fire from Croatian shore
04/01	stationed at Drnje, trip via Koprovnica toward Varazdin in evening
04/02-06	PZ and quarters train in Ludbreg
04/07	both trains to Varazdin, PZ to go on to Lichtenwald
04/08	PZ hits mine on trip to Zapresic
04/09-11	PZ is repaired in Zapresic, quarters train comes afterward
04/12	trip via Brückel to Lichtenwald, via Steinbrück and Cilli toward Marburg in afternoon
04/13	quarters train is parked in Windisch-Feistritz, PZ goes on line to Pettau
04/14	track substructure too weak, back and via Marburg—Spielfeld to Mureck, firing position near Gosdorf
04/15	fired on by artillery in Gosdorf, back to Diepersdorf
04/20	stationed at railroad station in Gosdorf, advanced observer site Donnersdorf
04/24—05/03	stationed in Diepersdorf
05/04-06	stationed in Gosdorf
05/08	sent from Gosdorf to Spielfeld with PT 19 (15?), trip via Graz to Pernegg, there the commander disbands the unit at midnight

Report:
H. W. Müller, Alarm! Schienenstrang gesprengt! (Panzerzüge I)

■ **Railroad Armored Train No. 65** (Field Post No. 35917)
Established on Nov. 1, 1942, ready for action on July 9, 1943, remained at end of war
Commanders:

Capt. Heinz-Dieter Becker	(June 1943—March 1944)
Capt. Alfred Gergasevics	(April-Sept. 1944)
1st Lt. Karl Gnad	(Oct. 1944—May 1945)

Action: see 296, 299ff, 305, 400f, 405f
Damage/loss: see 302,. 406, 409
Pictures/drawings: see 237, 260, 296, 299f, 400f

Railroad Armored Train No. 66 (Field Post No. 36523)
Established on Nov. 1, 1942, ready for action on July 23, 1943,
lost on July 30, 1944, disbanded on Aug. 9, 1944
Commander:
Capt. Guido Pierstorff
(July 1943—July 1944)
Action: see 318, 367, 370, 375ff, 380f, 383f, 387f
Damage/loss: see 388
Pictures/drawings: see 258, 317, 319, 370, 381

Action Chronicle of Armored Train No. 66
According to diary entries for the time from Oct. 01, 1943 to
July 31, 1944 and paybook entries for the time from Aug. 23,
1943, to April 19, 1944.
Since August 17, 1943, PZ 66 was in action to secure the rail
line from Minsk to Orscha. Stationed at Tolotschin, since mid-
September 1943 Krupki.

1943
08/23	partisan action in Buschmin
08/24	partisan action in Wolosowo
08/25	partisan action in Jewlachi
08/27	partisan action in Mechkowo
09/02	partisan action in Nowoselki
09/14	partisan action in Losy
09/17-18	partisan action in Wolosowo
09/19	partisan action in Zarewsk
10/06	diary keeper comes to PZ, nice reception by Ivan (air attack)
10/08	inspection trip with members of WHW (winter assistance action)
10/23-26	partisan action against several villages with infantry and tanks, PZ artillery fires several times for support, wounded among population, mines and cattle captured, ammunition explosion in burning of village
11/01-02	partisan action in Filatowo
11/11-12	partisan action in Ljubischtsche, dead partisans, on return to train several suspicious civilians are caught
11/18	short action, PZ goes to Borissow
11/24-25	action run, PZ artillery fires on spotted airfield for partisan supplying
11/29	transfer to Mogilew
11/30—12/01	night alarm, trip to front action
12/07	Lt. M dies near Resta
12/15-18	front action, fog layers provide support
12/18	trip back to Borissow, stationed at Krupki
12/27	partisan action

1944
01/07	partisan action, tank hits mine
01/09	partisan action
01/10-12	partisan action, PZ makes securing run and goes into lurking position
01/14-16	partisan action
01/18-19	partisan action
01/24	partisan action
01/31	departure to action on front south of Mogilew
02/05	action in direction of main combat line
02/06	in Mogilew, took captured Russians along, air attack
02/08-10	action (at front?)
02/13	trip to Orscha
02/14-16	action trip from Orscha, then trip to Mogilew
02/18-19	action near S(chklow?)
02/19	back to Krupki
02/20	to Borissow for delousing, then back to Krupki
02/21	departure for front action near Stary Bychow
02/22	fruitless attack by bombers and fighters, in the way back heavy fire fight (mortar strikes), artillery action in evening, spotted by planes again on trip back, nearby bomb hit, wounded on loco and with A/A guns, immobile control car is blown up
02/23	advance to front, fired on by mortars and antitank guns, back and forward again, shot down an attacking airplane, firing artillery and A/A at full speed, again back and then forward, alarm at night, barred a breakthrough, tanks with infantry on them comb woods and hold position, lie under artillery fire
02/24	trip to front, fired on by artillery and mortars, cover withdrawal, tracks are blown up, more mortar fire, trip back to Stary Bychow
02/25	advance to cover explosion command, German artillery fire
02/26	in further cover of explosion command, sudden Russian attack (are also said to break

through to Stary Bychow with tanks and
antitank guns), PZ at foremost front with its
own tanks, Russians attack behind PZ, wants
to cut it off, PZ breaks through to Stary
Bychow (several wounded), own infantry
remaining in position at Lagodowa
railroad station is inspected, PZ goes
forward again after loading ammunition
and breaks through to ahead of railroad
station at Lagodowa, liberates own
infantry, back to original position before
railroad station.
02/27	Lagodowa railroad station set afire, PZ in sweeping Russian artillery and mortar fire, prisoners and deserters announce renewed Russian attacks
02/29	Soviet breakthrough, PZ moves forward and comes under heavy fire (hit by antitank gun), antitank gun is silenced, attack beaten off, support German infantry in counterattack, high Soviet losses (intercepted Russian radio message: "Cannot advance farther, as armored train is firing with all weapons"), doctor is shot in action outside the train
03/02	fire strike on train (one dead), air attack fought off
03/07	small fire strike
03/09	attack along with other units on Lagodowa railroad station, which is taken
03/10	Russians have railroad station again, PZ is fired on by artillery and sharpshooters, trip to Mogilew
03/12	to the front again
03/17	order to march in morning, trip via Krupki to Borissow
03/18	in Stolpce
03/21	front furlough train hits mine, many dead and wounded, immediate departure toward Brest-Litowsk, PZ gets only to Beresa-Kartuska, as tracks are blown up twice
03/22	PZ moves only slowly to Brest, to Chotyslaw (line to Kowel), readiness with 5th Jäger Division for attack to liberate encircled units, including PZ 27 near Zablocie
03/23	advance, fight, own infantry is supported (but also fired on by mistake), one Russian antitank gun silenced, PZ 27 meanwhile manned by Soviets can finally be won back after vigorous opposition, but is badly damaged
03/23-24	trip back to Brest-Litowsk
03/28	PZ 66 is assigned to VIII. Hungarian Army Corps for partisan fighting on the Brest-Litowsk—Baranowitschi line
04/05-13	partisan action in Kossow area
04/14-16	partisan action in Las
04/17-19	partisan action in Stolpy
05/08-11	in Baranowitschi
05/14	inspected by Lt.Col. Dr. Günther (PZ Reg. Cmdr. for special uses)
05/16	securing run to Brest-Litowsk
05/18	back to Baranowitschi
05/19	trip to Brest again

No diary entries referring to action until mid-July
07/02-03	partisan action, village set afire
07/06	mines removed in action
07/07	PZ to Byten, runway bombed
07/08	air attack on railroad station, low-level plane fire, two planes shot down, trip back to Beresa-Kartuska
07/11...	withdrawal before pursuing Russians
07/15	in Brest-Litowsk, air attack
07/17	trip to action in Tewle area
07/18	to the north, Russian tank spearhead advanced 20 km
07/19	Russian tank spearhead smashed by battle fighters, trip back to Zabinka
07/21	trip via Brest-Litowsk, Lukow, Siedlce to Platerow, low-level planes attack
07/22	breakthrough into enemy front line from Bug bridgehead at Fronolow, fire strike on enemy
07/23	unloaded tanks attack, taken under fire
07/24	radio message that Russians are ahead of Siedlce, train thus cut off, is to fight its way forward via Czeremcha and Bialystok
07/25	attack of Fronolow bridgehead (gains space but does not break through) several heavy air attacks (one wounded)
07/26	return through Platerow toward Mordy, Soviet tanks reported, when they turn up, they are German ("Panthers" of SS "Totenkopf" Division that broke through from Siedlce

07/27	action run toward Mordy and beyond, as line to Siedlce appears free, tanks lead, train follows, T 34 and "Stalin" tanks reported in evening, drop back
07/28	another advance westward from Mordy, threatened by Russian tanks, heavy antitank gun fires on train, train must back off
07/29	another attack ("Panthers" of SS "Totenkopf" Division make way from Mordy back to Siedlce, but PZ cannot follow, as tracks are broken, take on water, tracks damaged by artillery fire before and behind train
07/30	last attacks, ammunition used up, train is blown up about 4:50 PM, crew marches with tanks, Panhards and vehicles, some infantry on foot, to Sokolow and is sent on march from there to Replacement Battalion in Milowitz in freight cars

Reports:
E. Geselle, Fronteinsatz eines Panzerzugs (Panzerzüge I)
Fw. Treptow, Als vorgeschobener Beobachter eines Panzerzugs
in vorderster Linie (Panzerzüge I)
Fw. Lauterbach, Panzerzug gegen Banden (Panzerzüge I)
H. Brücker, Panzerzug im Bandeneinsatz (Panzerzüge II)

■ **Railroad Armored Train No. 67** (Field Post No. 57202)
Established May 15, 1943, to July 30, 1943, ready for action
on Sept. 22, 1943, lost on July 27, 1944, disbanded on Aug.
28, 1944
Commander:
1st Lt.-Capt. Hermann Hoppe   (Sept. 1943—Aug. 1944)
Setup/rebuilding/cars: see 190
Equipment/arms/crew: see 232
Action: see 370, 372f, 375, 378, 380, 382, 383f
Damage/loss: see 190, 372, 383f
Pictures/drawings: see 232, 248, 253, 370, 372, 379f
Reports:
K. Schmidt, Funker im Panzerzug (Panzerzüge I)
C. Wolff, Der "Zuckende Blitz" am Feind (Panzerzüge I)
R. Prudnikow, Im Panzerzug gegen den Feind (Panzerzüge II)
W. Hahn, Feuerüberfall (Panzerzüge II)
Lt. Henz, Panzerzug im Frühlingsreigen (Panzerzüge II)
W. Scharkus, Wir kommen (Panzerzüge II)
Fw. Felsch, Und die Flak schafft's doch (Panzerzüge II)

■ **Railroad Armored Train No. 68** (Field Post No. 9754)
Established on Aug. 1, 1943 (planned readiness for action as of
30 August), ready for action on Oct. 30, 1943, divided into two
parts in January 1945, Part I lost on March 28, 1945, Part II on
April 7, 1945, disbanded on April 18, 1945
Commanders:
1st Lt.-Capt. Hans-Joachim Wetz   (Oct. 1943—March 1945)
Part II: 1st Lt. Müller?/Capt. Scholz?   (Jan-April 1945)
Setup/rebuilding/cars: see 185, 190
Action: see 370f, 377f, 380f, 383f, 387f, 395, 397, 401f, 404
Damage/loss: see 190, 370, 378, 397, 402, 404
Pictures/drawings: see 184, 251, 253, 314, 370f, 378, 384
Reports:
J. Ehrhardt, Panzerzug befreit abgeschnittenes Bataillon
(Panzerzüge I)
E. Havenstein, Panzerzug befreit Pionier-Bataillon (Panzerzüge
II)
E. Nitschke, Panzerzug nach vorn (Panzerzüge II)

■ **Railroad Armored Train No. 69** (Field Post No. 58429)
Established on Aug. 20, 1943 (planned readiness on Sept. 30),
ready for action on Nov. 12, 1943, lost on March 22, 1944,
disbanded on April 15, 1944.
Commander:
1st Lt. Erhard Edom   (Sept. 1943—April 1944)
Setup/rebuilding/cars: see 190
Action: see 357, 361f, 364f
Damage/lost: see 190, 362, 364f
Pictures/drawings: see365

Action Chronicle of Armored Train No. 69
From diary notations for the period from Nov. 12 to Dec. 18,
1943, and action entries, including the combat report for March
04-22, 1944.

1943
11/12	PZ 69 departs from Rembertow to Radom
11/13	Jaroslaw—Przemysl
11/14	Lemberg—Tarnopol
11/15	in Schmerinka
11/16	in Winniza, from there to Kasatin and Berditschew (station)
11/18	trip toward Schitomir, before the city tracks are blown up, back to Berditschew
11/19-21	securing rebuilding of bridges over the Gnissa and Teterew
11/22	in Schitomir, infantry advances to Pitschanka
11/23	with tanks to Malaja Gorbaschy

11/25	Cavalry Regiment South goes back from Tschernichow to Mal. Gorbaschy
11/26	main front line is moved forward, infantry and tanks back to quarters train in Schitomir
11/27-29	VB in Mal. Gorbaschy, homing in the PZ's artillery
11/30	Russians take Sowkist, fire strike fired
12/02	barrage fire fired again
12/03-05	repeatedly fire aimed at Russians by advanced observer in Mal. Gorbaschy
12/06	Tschernichow taken again, artillery support back to quarters train in Schitomir
12/07	back to quarters train in Schitomir
12/11	trip to Kurnoje
12/12	trip to Andejew, back at noon
12/13	quarters train transferred from Schitomir to Berditschew
12/14	action toward Korosten to ahead of Fasowo
12/15	back to Schitomir, quarters train also there again, loco has broken axle
12/16	action trip
12/20	securing a provision transport to Uschomir
12/23	search of Marschlewskaja for partisans, then loco to be overhauled
12/25	to Berditschew
1944	
Early Jan.	fighting around Berditschew
Jan.	withdrawal fighting Berditschew—Schepetowka
Early Feb	presumably Schepetowka—Starokonstantinow—Gretschany
02/17	securing the Proskurow—Podwoloczyska line
03/04	securing from Podwoloczyska to north
03/05	reconnaissance to Wojtowzy railroad station, back to Wolotschisk
03/06	along with PZ 11 from Podwoloczyska to Wolotschisk, Russian tanks there, fight, securing bridge east of Podwoloczyska, enemy already reported west of there in afternoon, PZ 11 and 69—running diagonally side by side on two-track line and firing all guns at the enemy pushing from north toward the rail line—reach Maksymowka
03/07	Both PZ attack enemy-occupied Bogdanowka, but it cannot be held permanently, back to Maksymowka, on return to Tarnopol in evening PZ 69 meets enemy west of Maksymowka, enemy blocks line but PZ can break through, PZ 11 after it, scattered Infantry Battalion is picked up and taken to Tarnopol
03/08	PZ drives enemy out of Biala and secures line to it with disembarked infantry, PZ must go to Berezowica for water, since the facilities in Tarnopol are destroyed, enemy pushes into Tarnopol at night
03/09	advance to Tarnopol railroad station is broken off, as PZ comes under heavy antitank and tank fire, on return trip to Berezowica, enemy pushes forward from east near Petrykow, is driven back, own troops rescued, clearing track to Bucniow (enemy-free)
03/14	PZ to Tarnopol
03/15-16	PZ supports attack of 359th Infantry Division toward Borki Wk. with artillery, advance not possible because tracks are destroyed
03/17	PZ restores tracks from Tarnopol toward Zbaraz as far as main battle line for planned attack, which is not made
03/18	PZ ready in Borki Wk., tracks repaired to main battle line near Stupki
03/19	PZ back to Tarnopol, attack on Biala planned but not carried out, PZ back to Borki Wk. at night
03/21	Russian attack begins in morning, eight air attacks driven off, PZ fires on advancing enemy in Borki Wk. and covers retreat, hit puts one F.K. out of action, PZ fires on enemy in Dyczkow, hard fight with enemy pushing toward the line westward from Smykovce (tanks and infantry), car 7 is set afire by shots, on Gaje Wielki heights explosion under the armored loco, which falls into deep shell crater, cars 3 and 4 also derailed, train under enemy tank fire, crew disembarks and takes position on rail embankment, secures PZ, which takes serious hits in all cars, cars 2, 3, 5, and 6 burn out, but train can be saved from conquest by enemy, rear half of train is blown up, front to car 2 inclusive is pulled to Tarnopol by loco, recovery of derailed

	cars 3 and 4 by help train before daylight not possible
03/22	Rest of PZ can be secured by crew until evening, but then order to depart, the cars, burned out and almost completely destroyed by shots, and the loco are destroyed by explosion, crew back to quarters train in Tarnopol

■ Railroad Armored Train No. 70 (Field Post No. 00361)

Established on Sept. 16, 1943 (planned readiness on Oct. 30), ready for action on Dec. 8, 1943, lost on April 4, 1944, disbanded on June 21, 1944
Commander:
Capt. Werner Franke (Sept. 1943—April 1944)
Setup/rebuilding/cars: see 190
Action: see 357ff
Damage/loss: see 190, 358f
Pictures/drawings see 358

Railroad Armored Train No. 71 (Field Post No. 02843)

Established on Sept. 16, 1943 (planned readiness on Nov. 30), ready for action on Jan. 12, 1944, lost on Aug. 31 ,1944, disbanded on Sept. 13, 1944
Commander:
1st Lt.-Capt. Erich Schubert (Jan.-Aug. 1944*)
Setup/rebuilding/cars: see 190
Equipment/arms/crew see 232
Action: see 361f, 364f, 378, 391
Damage/loss: see 190, 362, 365, 378, 391
Pictures/drawings: see 232, 318, 362

■ Railroad Armored Train No. 72 (Field Post No. 01549)

Established on Nov. 23, 1943 (planned readiness on Dec. 30, 1943) ready for action on Feb. 15, 1944, divided into two Command Armored Trains No. 72A and 72B, but at first they remained under unified command
Commander:
Capt. Helmut Walter (Feb.-April 1944)
(He was transferred as Adjutant to Commander of Armored Trains with OKH; deputy Lt. Wilhelm Sitzius)
Pictures/drawings: see 381

■ Railroad Armored Train No. 72A

(Command train of Armored Train Regiment Staff No. 2—see there), as of February 1945 again combat train, lost on March 16, 1945, disbanded on March 25, 1945
Commander:
Capt. Gerhard Röming (May 1944—March 1945)
Setup/rebuilding/cars: see 172, 190
Equipment/arms/crew: see 190, 252
Action: see 172, 380f, 394, 397, 399ff, 402, 404
Damage/loss: see 190, 404
Pictures/drawings: see 173, 381
(see also Armored Train Regiment Staff No. 2)

■ Railroad Armored Train No. 72B

(Command train of Armored Train Regiment Staff No. 3—see there), lost on March 28, 1945, disbanded on April 18, 1945
Commanders:
Lt. Wilhelm Sitzius (March-Nov. 1944)
Lt. Dietrich Lange (deputy) (Dec. 1944—Feb. 1945*)
1st Lt. Günter Wydra (deputy) (Feb.-March 1945)
Setup/rebuilding/cars: see 172, 185
Equipment/arms/crew: see 252
Action: see 380, 391, 397, 401f, 404
Damage/lost: see 404
Pictures/drawings: see 172f, 184, 379, 381
(see also Armored Train Regiment Staff No. 3)

■ Railroad Armored Train No. 73 (Field Post No. 43159)

Established on Nov. 19, 1943 (planned readiness on Jan. 1, 1944), ready for service on June 17. 1944, remained until end of war
Commanders:
Capt. Hans Reiser (June-Oct. 1944)
Capt. Max Warda (Oct. 1944—May 1945)
Equipment/arms/crew: see 230, 233
Action: see 311
Damage/loss: see 311, 415
Pictures/drawings: see 311

■ Railroad Armored Train No. 74 (Field post No. 59251)

Established on March 20, 1944 (readiness planned for Feb. 1, 1944!), ready for action on July 15, 1944, lost on Feb. 28, 1944, disbanded on Aug. 9, 1944
Commander:
1st Lt. Dr. Hans Klaus Höcker (March-July 1944)
equipment/armament/crew: see 230f
action: see 388
damage/loss: see 388
pictures/drawings: see 388

■ Railroad Armored Train No. 75 (Field Post No. 12049)

Established on April 15, 1944 (readiness planned for March 1, 1944!), ready for action on July15, 1944, renamed Armored Instruction Train No. 5—see there, newly established on Oct. 23, 1944, ready for action on Dec. 31, 1944, remained until end of war
Commander:
1st Lt. Herbert Haschick (Oct. 1944—May 1945)
Action: see 305f, 404ff
Damage/loss: see 306, 406, 409

■ Railroad Armored Train No. 76 (Field Post No. 15585)

Established in May 1944 (readiness planned for April 1, 1944!), ready for action on Nov. 18, 1944, lost on April 15, 1945 (no official disbanding)
Commander:
Capt. Werner Franke (Nov. 1944—April 1945)
Equipment/arms/crew: see 233
Action: see 397, 401ff
Damage/loss: see 402
Pictures/drawings: see 395

■ Railroad Armored Train No. 77 (Field Post No. 01451)

Established end of May 1944 (readiness planned for May 1, 1944!), ready for action pn Jan. 19, 1945, lost on Feb. 26, 1945, disbanded on March 11, 1945
Commander:
Capt. Georg Peters (Jan.-Feb. 26, 1945+)
Action: see 399, 402
Damage/loss: see 399, 402, 410
Pictures/drawings: see 399f

■ Railroad Armored Train No. 78 (Field Post No. 27766)

Established in July 1944 (readiness planned for June 1, 1944!), ready for action on Feb. 6, 1945, remained until end of war
Commanders:
1st Lt. Johannes Crasselt (Feb.-March 27, 1945+)
Capt. Erhard Edom (April-May 1945)
Setup/rebuilding/cars: see 185
Action: see 309f
Damage/loss see 310, 409
Pictures/drawings: 184, 309f, 409

Action Chronicle of Armored Train No. 78

From diaries for the entire time

1945	
02/01	PZ 78 ready for action in Neuenburg
02/05	combat train departs toward Hungary
02/11	quarters train departs, meets combat train in Boehm.-Trübau
02/13	arrival in Hungary, enemy plane attack, goes on to Lake Balaton (Balaton-Szentgyorgy)
02/14	long aircraft alarm
02/17	"runway crow" drops bombs
02/19	action as mobile battery between Balaton-Szentgrörgi and B.-Bereny, shock troop to bridge in Balaton-Keresztur, Lt. fallen as advanced observer
02/20	in Balaton-Szentgyörgy
02/22	trip to Nagykanisza
02/23-24	alarm drill
02/25—03/23	no entries in either diary (probably no action or other notable events)
03/23	at railroad station in Nagykanisza
03/24	PZ in Balaton-Bereny
03/25	departure to Balaton-Szepeszd, action as mobile battery, position change to Dörgicse-Akali, heavy artillery fire and serious air attacks
03/26	withdrawal to Tapolca, two dead and two wounded in bomb attack
03/27	Cmdr. 1st Lt. Crasselt killed by bomb splinter south of Tapolca (Lt. Stallknecht takes command of train), to Balaton-Szentgyörgy
03/28	PZ reconoiters in direction of Zala-Szent Grot, then returns to Nagykanisza
03/29	action on line before Nagykanisza to the north
03/30	as mobile battery near Zala-Szent Mihaly
03/31	threat of encirclement, low-level plane attack, hit by its guns, PZ blows up track behind itself and goes back to Nagykanisza
04/01	Nagykanisza under artillery fire, trip back over the Mur to Kotoriba, line jammed, further movement only possible piece by piece
04/02-03	action as mobile battery in Mura Kiraly-Perlak area
04/03	moved out in evening, two railcars crushed between trains before Csaktornya, line is cleared by torchlight
04/04	trip over emergency bridge over the Drau to Varazdin
04/05	action near Csaktornya
04/06-08	securing of Drau bridge

04/09	again to Csaktornya, blowing up railroad station, action as rear guard in departure to Friedau
04/10	support of a counterattack near Friedau. Transport escort to Luttemberg under artillery fire
04/11	PZ passes through Radkersburg two hours before Russians take it, goes to Spielfeld
04/12	air attack near Mureck, firing position near Gosdorf
04/13	train is under artillery fire there
04/15	PZ 64 stuck through artillery fire on track
04/16	arrival of new commander, Capt. Edom
04/24-25	high point of fighting near Gosdorf—Mureck
05/04	position change
05/06	again action as mobile battery near Gosdorf; 10:00 PM beginning of departure to Spielfeld
05/07	trip through Graz to Leoben
05/08	in Leoben, surrender is announced
05/09	trip farther up Mur valley to Thalheim, combat train abandoned there, by truck over the Tauern to Trieben
05/10	march on foot over Enns bridge, surrender to Americans

■ **Railroad Armored Train No. 79** (Field Post No. 38902)
Established in August 1944 (readiness planned for July 1, 1944!), ready for action on Feb. 6, 1945, lost on March 27, 1945
Commander
1st Lt. Gustav Gelhaar   (Feb.-March 27, 1945+)
Equipment/arms/crew: see 231, 234, 238
Action: see 309
Damage/loss: see 309

■ **Railroad Armored Train No. 80** (Field Post No. 42448)
Established in Sept. 1944 (readiness planned for August 1, 1944!), ready for action March 1945, remained at end of war
Commander:
1st Lt. Gelbers?   (March-May 1945)
Setup/rebuilding/cars: see 180. 194, 404
Action: see 406f
Damage/loss: see 406

■ **Railroad Armored Train No. 81** (Field Post No. 33374)
Established on Sept. 26, 1944 (readiness planned for Sept. 1, 1944!), ready for action end of April 1945, remained at end of war
Commander:
1st Lt. Paul Obst   (April-May 1945)
Setup/rebuilding/cars: see 10, 404
Action: see 406
Damage/loss: see 407, 412

■ **Railroad Armored Train No. 82** Field Post No. 04579)
established presumably in October 1944 (readiness planned for Oct. 1, 1944!), was being delivered to the Armored Train Replacement Battalion when the war ended
see 180, 194, 404, 406, 408, 413

■ **Railroad Armored Train No. 83** (Field Post No. 11534)
The building of Armored Trains No. 83 and 84 was halted in February 1945, No. 83 received at the same time the line protection train previously running under the same number, which was now listed as an armored train, it remained until the end of the war
Commander:
Capt. Alfons Popp   (Feb.-May 1945)
Setup/rebuilding/cars: see 197
Action: see 400f, 405f
Damage/loss: see 406, 409
Pictures/drawings: see 423

Line protection trains (see there) listed as armored trains in February 1945 were:

■ **No. 350**   Commander: 1st Lt. Otto Pakheiser
                                           (April-May 1945)
■ **"Berlin"**   Commander: Lt. Wilhelm Sitzius
                                           (Feb.-April 1945)
■ **"Max"**   Commander: 1st Lt. Werner Schade
                                           (Feb.-May 1945)
■ **"Moritz"**   Commander: 1st Lt. Gerhard Gorski
                                           (Feb.-May 1945
■ **"Werner"** Commander: ?
                                           (Feb.-May 1945)

Action Chronicle of Armored Train No. 350
From diary notations for the time from Feb. 1—May 2 1945

1945
| 02/01 | from Milowitz to Berlin (to guard the building of line protection trains/armored trains by the Krupp-Druckenmüller firm, Berlin-Tempelhof) |

02/02	building of line protection train "Berlin"
02/05	line protection train "Werner" arrives
02/09	quarters train for "Berlin" arrives
02/12	"Berlin" leaves the factory and goes to Hoppegarten for final equipping on 02/13
02/14	line protection train 350 receives Panzer IV tanks
03/02	"Werner" leaves for Hoppegarten, quarters train goes there from Neukölln
03/03	quarters train for line protection train 350 arrives
03/04	Series 52 loco for line protection train 350 arrives
03/05	work on loco and G-cars for 350 begun
03/08	"Werner" is inspected at Hoppegarten
03/13	armor plate for PZ 65 delivered
03/23	ammunition for "Werner" and 350 arrives
04/01	line protection train 350 is transferred to Hoppegarten for final equipping
04/15	to Commander of PZ with Army Group Weichsel at Beenz
04/16	acceptance of PZ 350 by commander in Hoppegarten
04/17	trip to Freienwalde, briefing by the division
04/18	into action at Bralitz (on island until evening)
04/19	securing of Freienwalde in direction of Wriezen, off to Eberswalde, stationed at Britz
04/20	advance to Malchow, back to Eberswalde in evening
04/21-22	advance toward Niederfinow
04/22	to Templin in the evening
04/23	via Löwenberg to Beetz-Sommerfeld, PT 16 is assigned
04/24-26	in Beetz-Sommerfeld
04/27-29	in Radensleben
04/30	sent to Neu-Ruppin in afternoon
05/01	PT 16 derailed, after restoring it, on to Neustadt/Dosse, meets quarters train there, trip (without PT 16?) to Wittenberge, Soviet low-level planes
05.02	via Grabow—Ludwigslust to Neustadt-Glewe in the morning, meets PZ 65, 75 and 83 there via Ludwigslust toward Schwerin in afternoon, meets Americans (Intelligence Co of 8th U.S. Infantry Division) in Holthusen at 4:00 PM, surrenders to them, are taken on by them with trains to Hagenow-Land, leave the trains there.

■ **Railroad Armored Train No. 99** (Field Post No. 57605)
Established in April 1945 according to field post number list, no other information on this train could be found.

■ **Railroad Armored Trains: Heavy Scout Trains (No. 201-208) and Light Scout Trains (No. 301-304),** in general
Setup/rebuilding/cars: see 143, 146ff, 151f, 181
Equipment/arms/crews: see 143, 146ff, 234, 236, 240, 262
Pictures/drawings: see 143-150, 238

■ **Railroad Armored Train (Heavy Scout Train) No. 201** (F.P. No. 23865)
Established on Jan. 5, 1944 (readiness planned for Jan. 31, 1944!), ready for action on Nov. 11, 1944, lost on April 15, 1945 (no official disbanding)
Commander:
1st Lt. Helmut Schmitz-Reinthal   (Nov. 1944-April 1945)
Action: see 305f
Damage/loss: see 307
Pictures/drawings: see 306

■ **Railroad Armored Train (Heavy Scout Train) No. 202** (FP No. 58363)
Established on Jan. 10, 1944 (readiness planned for Feb. 28, 1944!), ready for action on Nov. 11, 1944, remained until end of war
Commander:
1st Lt. Gisbert Bartholme   (Nov. 1944—May 1945)
Action: see 305, 308
Damage/loss: see 308, 415
Pictures/drawings: see 306

■ **Railroad Armored Train (Heavy Scout Train) No. 203** (FP No. 13598)
Established on Feb. 21, 1944 (readiness planned for March 15, 1944!), ready for action on Jan. 18, 1945, remained until end of war
Commander:
1st Lt. Karl Herkenberg   (Jan.-May 1945)
Action: see 306, 308
Damage/loss: see 306, 308, 415

■ **Railroad Armored Train (Heavy Scout Train) No. 204** (FP No. 06495)
Established on March 23, 1944 (readiness planned for March 31, 1944!), ready for action on Feb. 6, 1945, remained until end of war
Commander:
1st Lt. Günther Diehl   (Feb.-May 1945)
Action: see 306ff
Damage/loss: see 308, 415

■ **Railroad Armored Train (Heavy Scout Train) No. 205** (FP No. 00683)
Established on April 4, 1944 (readiness planned for April 15, 1944!), ready for action at end of April 1945, remained until end of war
Commander:
1st Lt. Fritz Blohm   (April-May 1945)
Action: see 406f
Damage/loss: see 407f, 412

■ **Railroad Armored Train (Heavy Scout Train) No. 206** (FP No. 03410)
Established on April 17, 1944 (readiness planned for April 30, 1944!), was ready for action with the Armored Train Replacement Battalion in Milowitz when the war ended
Commander:
1st Lt. Hans Feuerlein   (May 1945)
Action: see 406, 408
Damage/loss: see 408, 412
Pictures/drawings: see 414

■ **Armored Trains (Heavy Scout Trains) No. 207 and 208**
Had not been finished when the war ended; the building of Armored Trains (Heavy Scout Trains) No. 209 and 210 had been canceled in January 1945.

■ **Railroad Armored Train (Light Scout Train) No. 301** (FP No. 07651)
Established on Sept. 16, 1943, ready for action on Feb. 29, 1944, lost on Nov. 20, 1944, disbanded on Jan. 26, 1945
Commander:
1st Lt. Fritz Blohm   (Feb.-Oct. 1944)
Action: see 300ff
Damage/loss: see 303
Pictures/drawings: see 301

■ **Railroad Armored Train (Light Scout Train) No. 302** (FP No. 04537)
Established on Sept. 16, 1944, ready for action on March 19, 1944, lost on Nov. 12, 1944, disbanded on Jan. 3, 1945
Commander:
Lt. Erwin Neumann   (March-Nov. 12, 1944+)
Action: see 301ff
Damage/loss: see 237, 303
Pictures/drawings: see 301

■ **Railroad Armored Train (Light Scout Car) No. 303** (FP No. 06423)
Established on Sept. 16, 1943, ready for action on June 14, 1944, remained until end of war
Commander
Lt.-1st Lt. Paul G. Römer   (June 1944—May 1945)
Action: see 301ff, 305, 307f
Damage/loss: see 303, 308, 415
Pictures/drawings: see 177, 301, 308

■ **Railroad Armored Train (Light Scout Train) No. 304** (FP No. 05308)
Established on Sept. 16, 1943, ready for action on April 22, 1944, lost on August 30, 1944, disbanded on Sept. 22, 1944
Commander:
Lt. Claus Herrmann   (April-Sept. 1944)
Action; see 301ff
Damage/loss: see 302

■ **Railroad Armored Railcar No. 15**
Established in August 1939, ready for action early September 1939, disbanded on Oct. 4, 1940, re-established on Nov. 21, 1941, ready for action May 1942, remained until end of war
Subordinate to:
Armored Train No. 6 or 7(?)	(Sept.-Oct. 1939
Independent unit	(May-June 1940)
Armored Train No. 25	(Dec. 1941—Sept. 1942)
Armored Train No. 24	(Oct. 1942—Feb. 1943)
Armored Train No. 6	(March-July 1943
Independent unit	(August 1943—March 1944)
Armored Train No. 65	(April-August 1944)
Armored Train No. 23	(Sept.-Nov. 1944)
Armored Train No. 65	(Nov. 1944—Jan. 1945)
Independent unit	(March-May 1945)
Commanders:
?	(Sept.-Oct. '939)
Lt. Paul Huhn	(May-June 1940)
Lt. Alfons Lademann	(Dec. 1941?—Sept. 1942)

Lt-1st Lt. Rolf Lorscheidt   (Oct. 1942—July 1943)
1st Lt. Helmut Oppenhorst   (Aug. 1942—March 1944)
?   (April 1944—May 1945)
Setup/rebuilding/cars: see 93, 118, 166, 181
Equipment/arms/crew: see 166, 240, 253, 256
Action: see 171, 286f, 293, 296, 300ff, 305, 310, 339, 341
Pictures/drawings: see 167f, 286, 297

■ Railroad Armored Railcar No. 16

Established on Jan. 27, 1944, ready for action in May 1944, remained until shortly before end of war
Subordinate to:
Armored Train No. 11   (June-1944-Jan. 1945)
(planned subordination to Armored Train No. 63 in July 1944 did not take place because train was lost.)
Armored Train No/ 65. 72A, 83 (?)   (Feb.-April 1945)
Armored Train No. 350   (April-May 1945)
Commanders:
Lt.-1st Lt. Heinrich Patzner   (to Jan. 12, 1945)
Lt. Georg Kliesing (deputy)   (Jan. 13-Feb. 1945)
1st Lt. Heinrich Patzner   (Feb.-May 1945)
Setup/rebuilding/cars: see 166, 180f, 197
Equipment/arms/crew: see 166, 171, 229, 233, 240, 262f
Action: see 169, 386f, 394, 397, 400, 405, 410
Damage/loss: see 397, 410
Pictures/drawings: see 167f, 180, 198, 386f, 410

■ Railroad Armored Gun Railcars, Soviet type NKWD D-2 (PT 17-23) in general

Setup/rebuilding/cars: see 169, 181
Equipment/arms/crews: see 169, 171, 220, 224, 233, 239, 240, 262f
Pictures/drawings: see 169

■ Railroad Armored Gun Railcar No. 17

Established on April 10, 1943, ready for action on Dec. 6, 1943, lost on June 27, 1944, disbanded on August 9, 1944
Subordinate to:
Armored Train No. 61   (Dec. 1943—June 1944)
Commanders:
1st Lt. Max Warda   (Dec. 1943—May 1944)
Lt. Robert Prinzing   (June 1944)
Action: see 373, 382
Damage/loss: see 382f
Pictures/drawings: see 373
Report:
C. Laar, Der Leberecht (Die Wehrmacht, Vol. 8)

■ Railroad Armored Gun Railcar No. 18

Established on Nov. 20, 1943, ready for action on July 14, 1944, lost on Jan. 16, 1945, no record of disbanding.
Subordinate to:
Armored Train No. 11   (July-Nov. 1944
Armored Train No. 25   (Nov. 1944—Jan. 1945)
Commander:
Lt. Hans-Hubert von Waldow   (July 1944—Jan. 1945)
Action: see 386f, 394, 397
Damage/loss: see 397

■ Railroad Armored Gun Railcar No. 19

Established on Nov. 20, 1943, ready for action on Aug. 30, 1944, remained until end of war
Subordinate to:
Armored Train No. 30   (August 1944—Jan. 1945)
Armored Train No. 64   (April-May 1945)
Commanders:
Lt. Borngräber   (Aug. 1944-Jan. 1945)
Lt. Robert Herlein   (March-May 1945)
Action: see 310, 391, 397, 401
Damage/loss: see 310, 402
Pictures/drawings: see 176, 391

■ Railroad Armored Gun Railcar No. 20

Established on Nov. 20, 1943, ready for action on Sept. 18, 1944, remained until end of war
Subordinate to:
Armored Train No. 62   (Sept.—Dec. 1944)
(then at Nürnberg RAW to repair damage)
Commander:
Lt. Karl Tomaselli   (Sept. 1944—May 1945)
Action: see 393
Damage/loss: see 393, 409

■ Railroad Armored Gun Railcar No. 21

Established on Jan. 27, 1944, ready for action on Oct. 10, 1944, remained until end of war
Subordinate to:
Armored Train No. 52   (Oct.—Dec. 1944)
Armored Train No. 65, 83 (?)   (Feb.—May 1945)
Commander:
Lt. H. Borries   (Oct. 1944—May 1945)
Action: see 394, 397, 400, 405f
Damage/loss: see 397, 406, 409

■ Railroad Armored Gun Railcar No. 22

Established on Jan. 27, 1944, ready for action on Oct. 26, 1944, remained until end of war
Subordinate to:
Armored Train No. 22   (Oct. 1944—Feb. 1945)
Armored Trains No. 65, 72A, 83(?)   (Feb.-May 1945)
Commander
Lt. Hans-Joachim Roddewig   (Oct. 1944—May 1945)
Action: see 393, 399f, 405f
Damage/loss: see 406, 409

■ Railroad Armored Gun Railcar No. 23

Established on Jan. 27, 1944, ready for action in Nov. 1944, lost on April 7, 1945
Subordinate to:
Armored Train No. 76   (Nov. 1944—Jan. 1945)
Armored Train No. 68/II   (Feb.-April 1945)
Commander:
1st Lt. Müller (?)   (Nov. 1944—April 1945)
Action: see 397, 401f
Damage/loss: see 402

■ Railroad Armored Railcar of Italian "Littorina" type (PT 30-38) in general

Setup/rebuilding/cars: see 171. 181, 224
Equipment/arms/crews: see 171, 233, 236, 240, 263
Pictures/drawings: see 171

■ Railroad Armored Railcar No. 30

Established on May 12, 1944, ready for action on June 17, 1944, remained until end of war
Subordinate to:
Armored Train (Light Scout Train) No. 303
                                        (June 1944—May 1945)
Action: see 301f, 305, 308
Damage/loss: see 308, 415
Pictures/drawings: see 308

■ Railroad Armored Railcar No. 31

Established on May 12, 1944, ready for action on June 17, 1944, remained until end of war
Subordinate to:
Armored Train (Light Scout Train) No. 303
                                        (June 1944-May 1945)
Action: see 301f, 305, 308
Damage/loss: see 308, 415
Pictures/drawings: see 308

■ Railroad Armored Railcar No. 32

Established on May 12, 1944, ready for action on July 12, 1944, remained until end of war
Subordinate to:
Originally intended for Armored Train (Light Scout Train) No. 302
Armored Train No. 64   (July—August 1944
Armored Train No. 65   (Sept.—Oct. 1944)
Action: see 301f, 305f, 308
Damage/loss: see 305, 308, 409

■ Railroad Armored Railcar No. 33

Established on May 12, 1944, ready for service on July 12, 1944, whereabouts unknown (may have been the railcar of this type that was in Nürnberg RAW for repairs in April 1945)
Subordinate to:
Originally intended for Armored Train (Light Scout Car) No. 302
Armored Train No. 64   (July—Nov. 1944)
Armored Train (Heavy Scout Train) No. 203?   (Feb. 1945)
Action: see 301f, 306
Damage/loss: see 409, 415

■ Railroad Armored Railcar No. 34

Established on August 21, 1944, ready for service on Nov. 11, 1944, damaged on delivery trip, effectively ready for action in February 1945, remained until end of war
Subordinate to:
Armored Train (Heavy Scout Train) No. 204 (Feb.-May 1945)
Action: see 305f, 308
Damage/loss: see 305, 308, 415

■ Railroad Armored Railcar No. 35

Established on August 21, 1944, ready for action on Nov. 11, 1944, remained until end of war
Subordinate to:
?   (Nov.—Dec. 1944)
Armored Train No. 23   (Jan.-May 1945)
Action: see 407
Damage/loss: see 407, 413

■ Railroad Armored Railcar No. 37

Established on August 21, 1944, ready for action in Feb. 1945, whereabouts unknown (surrendered either on May 2, 1945, in Holthusen with the Armored Train Battle Group Oder or was damaged in Nürnberg RAW in April, (see No. Railcar No. 33!)
Action: see 400, 405f
Damage/loss: see 406, 409

Railroad Armored Railcar No. 38

Established on August 21, 1944, ready for action on Nov. 11, 1944, remained until end of war
Subordinate to:
Independent unit
Commander:
1st Sgt. Herbert Ziehm
Action: see 305, 307f
Damage/loss: see 308, 415
Pictures/drawings: see 305

Railroad Tank-Destroyer Railcar No. 51

Established on March 15, 1945, was nearly finished when the war ended.
See 152, 169ff, 171, 181, 233, 263

■ Railroad Tank-Destroyer Railcars No. 52 to 55

Established on March 11, 1945, were under construction at Linke-Hoffmann in Breslau in January 1945, were not evacuated before the surrounding of Breslau
See 152, 169ff, 171, 180f, 233, 263, 404

Line Protection Trains

Listed by numbers, names (also commanders or stationing towns) and—if such are not known—units that built them:

No. 45 (ex-Ruebezahl): see 157, 163, 341, 378, 380, 385, 394, 397, 399
No. 83 (also 683): see 159, 165, 334f, 346f, 366, 369f, 372, 380, 385, 394, 400f, 405f, 409
No. 101: see 153, 162, 302, 339f
No. 102: see 159, 162, 302, 304
No. 104: see 162, 296, 299, 302, 304
No. 105: see 162, 296, 302, 304
No. 106: see 162, 302
No. 107: see 162, 302
No. 108: see 162, 302
No. 109: 162, 302
No. 202: see 162, 296, 302
No. 203: see 162, 302
No. 205: see 162, 302
No. 206: see 162, 296, 298f, 302, 306
No. 207: see 162, 302
No. 208: see 162, 296, 302
No. 209: see 162, 296, 302
No. 210: see 162, 296, 302
No. 214: see 162, 296, 302
No. 222: see 162, 302
No. 223: see 159
No. 312: see 159
No. 350 (ex-Zobten?): see 157, 163, 165f, 193f, 378, 385, 394, 397, 399, 405f, 409
No. 420: see 159
No. 601: see 159

List of used Abbreviations

Abt.	Battalion, unit
a.D.	out of service, retired
Adj.	adjutant
AHA	General Army Office
A.K.	Army Corps
AOK	Army High Command
Art.	Artillery
AW	repair shop
bad.	of Baden
bay.	Bavarian
Bbv.	Railroad Executive
BdE	Commander of the Replacement Army
Btl.	Battalion
Bz.	burning fuse
CFR	Romanian National Railways
Chef FEW	Chief of Field Railway Service
CSD	Czechoslovakian National Railways
C-Wagen	3rd-class passenger car
Div.	Division
DR	German Reich Railways
D-Wagen	4th-class passenger car
EAW	Railroad Repair Shop
EBD	Railroad Management
Eisb.	Railroad
Ers.	Replacement
F.H.	field howitzer
F.K.	field cannon
Flak	anti-aircraft gun (A/A)
Fla-MG	anti-aircraft machine gun
Fl.Wf.	flamethrower
Franz.	French
Fw.	Sergeant
Geb.K.	mountain cannon
Gen.	General
Gen.Insp.	Inspector-General
Gen.St.d.H.	Army General Staff
gl.	off-road capable
Gr.	grenade, shell
gr.	large
Gr.Gen.St.	Grand General Staff
Gr.Kdo.	Group Command
Gr.Wf.	mortar
G-Wagen	closed freight car
HDZ	Croatian State Railways
Hfw.	Master Sergeant
H.Gr.	Army Group
HKL	Main Combat Line
Hptm.	Captain
I.G.	infantry gun
IMKK	Inter-Allied Military Control Commission
In	Inspection
Inf.	Infantry
JDZ	Yugoslavian National Railways
K.A.N.	War Equipment Directive
Kav.	Cavalry
Kdo.	Command
Kdt.	Commander
kkStB	Austrian Imperial and Royal State Railways
Kl.	class
kl.	small
Komp	company
Korück	Commander of Backline Army Zone
K.St.N.	War Strength Directive
Kt.	cartridge
k.u.k.	Imperial and Royal
K-Wagen	chalk car with folding covers
KwK	tank gun
L	tracer bullet
l. or le.	light
Lin.komm.	Line Command or Commission
Lt	Lieutenant
LuP	overall length
Lw.Div.	Home Guard Division
Lw.Feld.K.	Luftwaffe Field Corps
Lw.K.	Home Guard Corps
m.	medium
Masch.K.	machine cannon
MAV	Hungarian State Railways
M.E.D.	Military Railway Administration
MG	machine gun
mot.	motorized
MPi	machine pistol
M.Wf.	mine thrower
n.A.	new type
OAW	Eastern Railroad Repair Shop
OB	supreme commander
Oberost	supreme commander in the East
Ob.d.H.	Army High Command
Offz.	officer
OFK	Chief Field Office
OHL	Supreme Army Command
OKH	Army High Command
OKW	Wehrmacht High Command
Olt.	First lieutenant
oe-u.	Austro-Hungarian
O-Wagen	open freight car
Pak	antitank gun
pfaelz.	Palatine
Pg-Wagen	baggage car for personnel or freight trains
Pi.	Army engineer
P.P.	Polish Armored Train (pociag pancerny)
preuss.	Prussian
PT	armored railcar
Pz	tank
PZ	armored train (official WWII: (Eisb.) Pz.zug)
Pz.Tr.	armored troop, tank troop
RAW	Reichsbahn Repair Shop
RBD	Reichsbahn Administration
Rev.K.	revolver cannon
Res.K.	Reserve Corps
Rgt.	Regiment
ROB	Reserve Officer Applicant
RVM	Reich Traffic Ministry
RW	Reichswehr, Armed Forces
R-Wagen	stakeside railroad car

Sd.Kfz.	special motor vehicle	stellv., stv.	Deputy, deputizing
Sich.	Securing, security	S-Wagen	flat railroad car
s.	heavy	Uffz.	Non-commissioned officer, NCO
S.	pointed shell	VB	advanced observer
saechs.	Saxon	Wg.	car, wagon
S.K.	rapid-fire cannon	Wkr.	Recruiting District
S.m.K.	pointed shell with core	wuert.	Wuerttemberg
Sp.	rail scout-car train	X-Wagen	work car
		z.b.V.	for special use

Note: for four-axle freight cars, the designation letter is doubled, for example, G-Wagen has two axles, GG-Wagen has four; for the meanings of the small letters added to railroad car markings, see the applicable literature (in the Bibliography), but bear the time order in mind, since these markings were often changed. The abbreviations for the names of railroad authorities can also be found in the literature.

List of Place Names

In the left column are the German names of numerous localities in other countries; in the right column are their names in their native language. The names of well-known large cities (Warsaw, Prague, etc.), districts (Prussia), rivers (Vistula), etc. are used in the text in the forms best known to the English-speaking world, while smaller localities are generally named in either their native or their German form. Many Slavic names can easily be recognized in their German spelling (w = v, l = y, -au = -ov, -itz = -ice, -itsch = icz, etc.).

Former Yugoslavia (Croatia, Macedonia, Serbia, Slovenia)

Agram	Zagreb
Assling	Jesenice
Betschkerek	Zrenjamin
Cilli	Celje
Czaktornya	Cakovec
Eichthal	Hrastnik
Esseg	Osijek
Friedau	Ormoz
Görz	Gorica (Italian Gorizia)
Gruebel	Grobelno
Heilenstein	Polzela Braslovce
Karlstadt	Karlovac
Kronau	Kranjska Gora
Laibach	Lubljana
Luttemberg	Ljutomer
Marburg an der Drau	Maribor
Mies	Mozirje?
Pettau	Ptuj
Piedicolle	Podbrdo
Pragerhof	Pragersko
Rain	Radece
Schoenstein-Warmbad	Sostanj-Topolscica
Semlin	Zemun
Steinbrück	Zidani Most
Stockhammer	Store
Uskueb	Sokpje
Unterdrauburg	Dravograd
Windisch-Feistritz	Slovenska Bistrica

Romania and Hungary

Fünfkirchen	Pecs
Galatz	Galati
Kronstadt	Brasov
Temeschburg	Timisoara

Slovakia and Czech Republic

Alt-Bunzlau	Stara Boleslav
Altsohl	Zvolen
Böhmisch-Brod	Cesky Brod
Böhmisch-Krumau	Cesky Krumlov
Böhmisch-Leipa	Ceska Lipa
Böhmisch-Trübau	Ceska Trebova
Bries	Brezno
Brünn	Brno
Deutsch-Brod	Havlickuv Brod
Deutschendorf	Poprad
Eger	Cheb

Freistadt is probably part of Karvina

Füllek	Filakovo
Friedland	Frydlant
Gross-Steffelsdorf	Rimavska Sobota
Hermanmestez	Hermanuv Mestec
Hohenfurth	Vissy Brod
Hohenmauth	Vysoke Myto
Iglau	Jihlava
Jung-Bunzlau	Mlada Boleslav
Karlsbad	Karlovy Vary
Kaschau	Kosice
Koeniggraetz	Hradec Kralove
Komotau	Chomutov
Lissa	Lysa
Littau	Litovel
Lisenz	Lucenec
Lundenburg	Breclav
Maehrisch-Ostrau	Ostrava
Maehrisch-Trübau	Moravska Trebova
Mueglitz	Mohelnice
Neuenburg	Nymburk
Neusohl	Banska Bystrica
Ober-Georgenthal	Horni Jiretin
Ober-Leutensdorf	Litvinov
Ober-Stuben	Horni Stubna
Oderberg	Bohumin
Olmütz	Olomouc
Petschek	Pecky
Pilgram	Pelhrimov
Pleisnitz	Plesivec
Pressburg	Bratislava

[page 440]

Priwitz	Prievidza
Raudnitz	Roudnice
Reichenberg	Liberec
Rosenberg	Ruzomberok
Rotenstein	Cervena Skala
Ruttek	Vrutky
Schwarzbach	Cervenka
Sillein	Zilina
Stefanau	Stepanov
Telgart	Svermovo
Tschirn	Strba

Poland

Allenstein	Olsztyn
Altdamm	Dabie
Angerburg	Wegorzewo
Argenau	Gniewkowo
Arnswald	Grabowo
Arnswalde	Choszczno
Augustwalde	Rebusz?
Bartenstein	Bartoszyce
Belgard	Bialogard
Bentschen	Zbaszyn
Berent	Koscierzyna
Bielitz	Bielsko-Biala
Birnbaum	Miedzychod
Bomst	Babimost
Breslau	Wroclaw
Bromberg	Bydgoszcz
Bublitz	Bobolice
Carlsruhe	Pokoj
Charlottenwerder	Falknowo?
Danzig	Gdansk
Deutsch-Eylau	Ilawa
Deutsch-Krone	Walcz
Dievenow	Dziwnow

Dirschau	Tezew	Neu-Krakow	Przystawy
Dölitz	Dolice	Neumark	Nowe Miasto
Drawehn	Drzewiany	Neu-Sandec	Nowy Sacz
Dreidorf	Kaliska?	Neustadt	Wejherowo
Elbing	Elblag	Neustettin	Szczecinek
Falkenburg	Zlocieniec	Oels	Olesnica
Gilgenburg	Dabrowno	Oppeln	Opole
Gleiwitz	Gliwice	Petrikau	Pjotrkow
Gosslershausen	Jablonowo Pomorskie	Pless	Pszczyna
Gotenhafen (Gdingen)	Gdynia	Poelitz	Police
Graudenz	Grudziadz	Posen	Poznan
Grodden	Grodziczno	Preussisch-Friedland	Debrzno
Grossgarten	Pozezdre?	Preussisch-Holland	Paslek
Gross-Katz	Orlowo?	Preussisch-Stargard	Starogard Gdanski
Gross-Neudorf	Nowa Wies Wielki	Prostken	Prostki
Gross-Schoenfeld	Gredziec?	Putzig	Puck
Heilsberg	Lidzbark Warminski	Pyritz	Pyryce
Hindenburg	Zabrze	Rastenburg	Ketrzyn
Hoch-Stueblau	Zblewo?	Ratibor	Raciborz
Hohensalza	Inowroclaw	Reimannswalde	Kowale, Oleckie?
Hopfengarten	Brzoza	Reuß	Cimochy
Horst	Niechorze	Riesenburg	Prabuty
Jorken	Jurkowo	Rosenberg	Olesno
Kandzrin	Kedzierzyn	Rosengarten	Radzieje?
Kankel	Kakolewo	Sarne	Sarnowa
Kempen	Kepno	Saybusch	Zywiec
Königsberg/Nm.	Chojna	Scharfenwiese	Ostroleka
Koenigshuette	Chorzow	Schneidemühl	Pila
Koerlin	Karlino	Schlawe	Slawno
Köslin	Koszalin	Schlawin	Slowino
Kolberg	Kolobrzeg	Schlobitten	Zlobity
Kolmar	Chodziez	Schlochau	Czluchow
Konitz	Chojnice	Schoenfeld	Skorka
Korschen	Korsze	Schwerin a.d.W.	Skwierzyna
Kostau	Siemianice	Schwiebus	Swiebodzin
Krenau	Chrzanow	Simonsdorf	Szymankowo
Kreuz	Krzyz	Soldau	Dzialdowo
Kreuzburg	Kluczbork	Sprottau	Szprotawa
Kruglanken	Kruklanki	Steinau	Scinawa
Küstrin	Kostrzyn	Stettin	Szczecin
Landsberg	Gorzow Slaski	Stolp	Slupsk
Lauban	Luban	Stolpmünde	Ustka
Lauenburg	Lebork	Stosnau	Golubki?
Lautenburg	Lidzbark	Strasburg	Brodnica
Lawitsch	Lowicz	Strebelow	Przewloki
Leobschuetz	Glubczyce	Sudauen	Suwalki
Liegnitz	Legnica	Tempelburg	Czaplinek
Liessau	Lisewo	Teschen	Cieszyn
Linde	Lipka	Thorn	Torun
Lissa	Lezno	Tichau	Tychy
Litzmannstadt	Lodz	Tirschtiegel	Trzciel
Loetzen	Gizycko	Treptow	Trzebiatow
Luben	Lubin	Treuburg	Olecko
Luschwitz	Wloszakowice	Tschenstochao	Czestochowa
Lyck	Elk	Unruhstadt	Kargowa
Märkisch-Friedland	Miroslawiec	Wildfurt	Pludry?
Malapane	Ozimek	Woldenberg	Dobiegniew
Marienburg	Malbork	Wollstein	Wolsztyn
Marienwalde	Bierzwnik?	Wreschen	Wrzesnia
Nakel	Naklo	Zichenau	Ciechanow
Netzwalde	Rynarzewo	Ziegenort	Trzebiez
Neuendorf	Nowa Wies	Zoppot	Sopot

Baltic States (Estonia, Latvia, Lithuania)

Apschuppen	Apsupe
Autz	Auce
Bixten	Biksti
Blieden	Blidene
Brotzen	Broceni
Doblen	Dobele
Dorpat	Tartu
Dubbeln	Dubulti
Dünaburg	Daugavpils
Elley	Eleja
Frauenburg	Saldus
Garrosen	Garoza
Hainasch	Ainazi
Jakobstadt	Jekavpils
Janischki	Joniskis
Janow	Jonava
Kemmern	Kemeri
Kiefernhalt	Priedaine
Kiejdany	Kedainiai
Koszedary	Kaisiadorys
Kowno	Kaunas
Kreuzburg	Krustpils
Krottingen	Kretinga
Kurschany	Kursenai
Lemsal	Limbazi
Libau	Liepaja
Memel	Klaipeda
Merecz	Merkine
Mitau	Jelgava
Modohn	Madona
Moscheiken*	Mazekiai
Olita	Alytus
Polangen	Palange
Ponewisch	Panevezys
Prekuln	Priekule
Radziwillischki	Radviliskis
Ramozki	Ieriki
Raseinen	Raseniai
Rosenow	Zilupe
Rositten	Rezekne
Schaulen	Siauliai
Schlampen	Slampe
Schrunden	Skrunda
Schwanenburg	Gulbene
Segewold	Sigulda
Stockmannshof	Plavinas
Szadow	Seduva
Tauroggen	Taurage
Telsche	Telsiai
Uexkuell	Ogre
Walk	Valga
Weinoden	Vainode
Wenden	Cesis
Wilna	Vilnius
Windau	Ventpils
Wirballen	Virbalis
Wolmar	Valmiera

* until 1918, Russian Murawjewo

Former USSR States

The German orthography often used in the text differs from the Russian, White Russian, Ukrainian, or other spellings, which often differ from each other (the onetime German Lemberg is Russian Lwow but Ukrainian Lwiw). The names of localities in White Russia and western Ukraine which belonged to Poland before 1939 are cited in the text in their Polish spelling and can easily be converted to Russian by taking into account the differences in the sibilants and that "h" is "g." Many German names would also be hard to convert to Russian. Names in the right column are those in present-day use.

Akkerman	Belgorod Dnjestrovskij
Angerapp	Ozersk
Czernowitz	Tschernovze
Eydtkau	Chernischevskaja
Fischhausen	Primorsk
Friedland	Pravdinsk
Gumbinnen	Gusev
Heiligenbeil	Mamonovo
Insterburg	Tschernjachovsk
Iskorost	Korosten
Jekaterinoslaw	Dnjepropetrovsk
Königsberg	Kaliningrad
Labiau	Polesk
Lemberg	Lvov
Leningrad	St. Petersburg/Petrograd
Pillau	Baltisk
Pleskau	Pskov
Postyschewo	Krasnoarmeijsk
Stalingrad	Zarizyn/Volgograd
Stalino (Jusowka)	Donezk
Stanislau	Stanislavov/Ivano-Frankovsk
Tapiau	Gwardeisk
Tilsit	Sovietsk
Wehlau	Znamensk

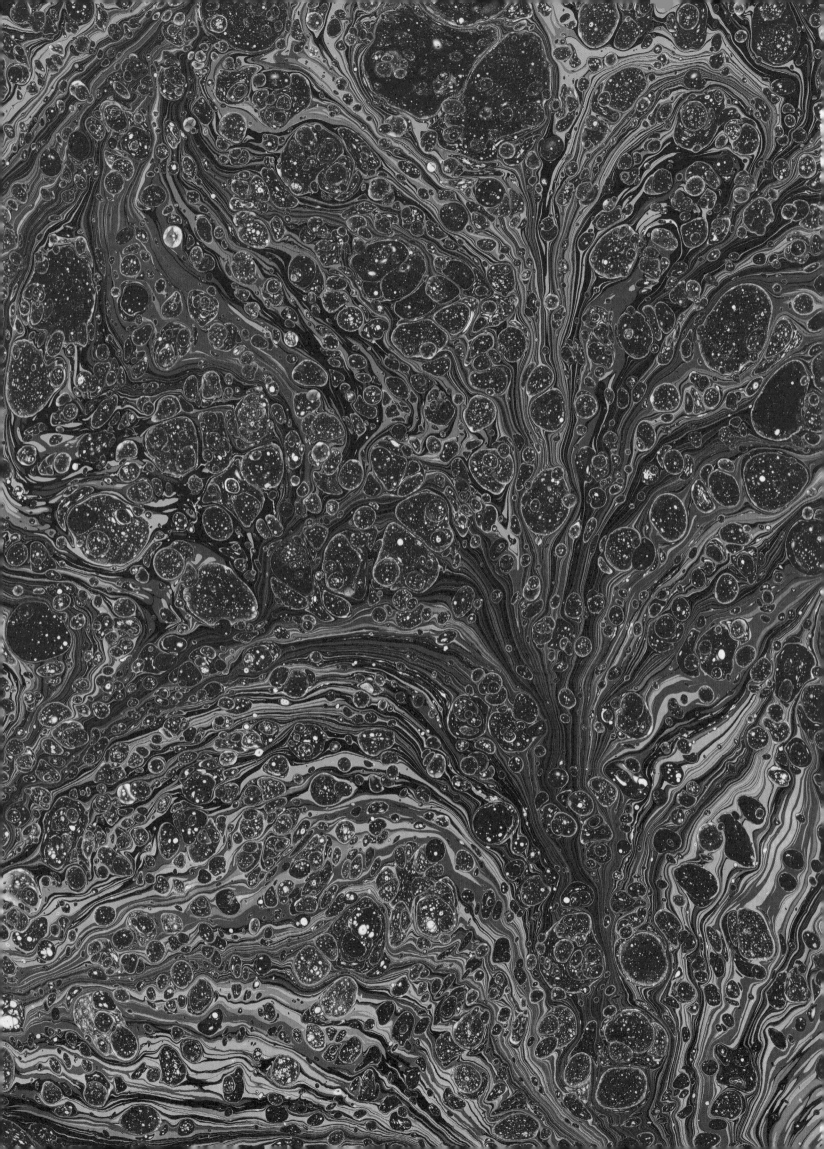